SVARTKONSTBÖCKER

A Compendium of the Swedish Black Art Book Tradition

FOLK NECROMANCY IN TRANSMISSION
VOLUME 4

SERIES EDITORS

Dr Alexander Cummins and *Jesse Hathaway Diaz*

OTHER TITLES IN THE SERIES

Cypriana: Old World, edited by Alexander Cummins, Jesse Hathaway Diaz, and Jennifer Zahrt

The Immaterial Book of Saint Cyprian, by José Leitão

A Book of the Magi, by Alexander Cummins

FORTHCOMING

The Way of the Living Ghost, by John Anderson

SVARTKONST-BOCKER

*A Compendium of the
Swedish Black Art Book Tradition*

DR. THOMAS K. JOHNSON

REVELORE PRESS
SEATTLE
MMXIX

Svartkonstböcker: A Compendium of the Swedish Black Art Book Tradition

© Copyright 2019 The Estate of Dr Thomas K. Johnson.

Fourth volume of the Folk Necromancy in Transmission series conceived and curated by Dr Alexander Cummins and Jesse Hathaway Diaz.

All rights reserved. No part of this publication may be reproduced or utilized in any form or by any means, electronic or mechanical, including photocopying, recording, or by any information storage and retrieval system, without permission in writing from the Publishers.

Book and cover design by Joseph Uccello.

ISBN 978-1-947544-22-2

Printed globally on demand through IngramSpark

First printed by Revelore Press in 2019

Revelore Press
220 2nd Ave S #91
Seattle, WA 98104
United States

www.revelore.press

Table of Contents

Foreword to this Edition, by Michael Tarplee 11
Preface to the PhD Thesis 12
Acknowledgements 16
Dedication 19

PART I
TIDEBAST OCH VÄNDELROT: MAGICAL REPRESENTATIONS
IN THE SWEDISH BLACK ART BOOK TRADITION

CHAPTER I. Introduction 23

POSING QUESTIONS 26
    Why? 26
    What? 27
    Where? 27
    When? 28
    Who? 29
    How? 30
PREVIOUS SCHOLARSHIP 31
    Examining Previous Studies 32
    Definitions: Charms, Spells, Rites and Recipes 33
    Theoretical and Morphological Classification 35
    Establishment of Age, Relation and Provenance 37
    Performance 38
    Charm Research in Scandinavia 39
COLLECTION AND PUBLICATION OF DATA 41
    Folklore Questionnaires 41
    Important Sources about Black Books: Questionnaire M100 42
BLACK ART BOOK RESEARCH 45
RECENT TRENDS 49

TABLE OF CONTENTS

CHAPTER II. *Folk Belief about Wise Ones* 59

| FOLK VOCABULARY DESCRIBING WISE ONES 60
| UNUSUAL APPEARANCE 62
| PATIENT VISITATION OR AT-HOME PRACTICE:
| LOCATIONS OF CONSULTATIONS 65
| CLERGY: MINISTER OR SORCERER? 66
| HÄXAN: THE MALEVOLENT WITCH 67
| FEAR OF THE WISE ONES 70
| OBTAINING MAGICAL POWER 72
| Obtaining Magical Power through Health Crisis 73
| Obtaining Magical Power through Ingesting Power Substances 73
| Obtaining Magical Power through Ritual 74
| *Ritual: Circumambulation and "Year-walking"* 75
| *Ritual: Timing* 75
| *Ritual: Personnel* 78
| Obtaining Magical Power through Objects and Fetishes 79
| *Objects* 79
| *Fetishes, Ancillary Spirits and Spertusar* 85
| Obtaining Magical Power through Inheritance or Apprenticeship ... 86
| *Circumstances of Birth* 86
| *"Picking things up" from Various Sources* 88
| *Apprenticeships in General* 88
| *Apprenticed to an Older Family Member* 90
| *Apprenticed to a Nature Spirit* 91
| *Apprenticed to the Devil* 92
| Taboo: Keeping Secrets 92
| SELF-PERCEPTION OF THE WISE ONES 95
| CONCLUSION 95

CHAPTER III. *Folk Belief about Black Art Books* 103

| INTRODUCTION: GENERAL BELIEFS 103
| *BLACK ART BOOKS*: Descriptions 103
| *BLACK ART BOOKS*: Written in Blood 105
| *BLACK ART BOOKS*: Owners 109
| *BLACK ART BOOKS*: Procurement 113
| *BLACK ART BOOKS*: Acquired from the Devil 114
| *BLACK ART BOOKS*: Requirement in Magical Performance 117
| *BLACK ART BOOKS*: Tracing Ownership, Tracing Power 119
| *BLACK ART BOOKS*: Removal from Circulation 120
| CONCLUSION 123

TABLE OF CONTENTS

CHAPTER IV. *The Data and Analysis* 127

ANALYSIS OF FORMAL CHARACTERISTIC 128
ANALYSIS OF FUNCTION (INTENT OR MOTIVATION) 130

THE MANUSCRIPTS 135

MS   1   (KULTURHISTORISKA MUSÉET I HÄRNÖSAND),
         "CÅNSTER ATT BRUKA, NEMBLIGEN…" 135
MS   2   (ESLÖVS MUSEUM 3329A), "NO. 1 RADEMIN" 137
MS   3   (ESLÖVS MUSEUM 3329B), "NO. 4 STORA KATEKIS" 140
MS   4   (ESLÖVS MUSEUM 3329C), "FÖR TANDVÄRK" 141
MS   5   (KUNGLIGA UNDERSÖKNINGEN 3335), "TROLLBOKEN" 142
MS   6   (KUNGLIGA UNDERSÖKNINGEN 11120), "SVARTKONSTBOK" ... 146
MS   7   (LUF A.285), "GLIMÅKRA SOCKEN, SKÅNE" 148
MS   8   (LUF A.795:26–31),
         "MAGISKA FORMLER OCH MAGISKA HANDLINGAR" 149
MS   9   (LUF ABC: C.W. VON SYDOW), "SVARTKONSTBOK FRÅN MO" ... 150
MS 10   (NORDISKA MUSÉET 33.823),
         "TJULA SOCKEN, SÖDERMANLAND" 152
MS 11   (NORDISKA MUSÉET 33.824),
         "ÅKERS SOCKEN, SÖDERMANLAND" 153
MS 12   (NORDISKA MUSÉET 40.034),
         "CYPRANIS KONSTER OCH LÄROR OCH DES INRÄT" 155
MS 13   (NORDISKA MUSÉET 41.652),
         "SVARTKONSTBOK, NORRA SKÅNE" 156
MS 14   (NORDISKA MUSÉET 41.674), "LÖNSBODA, 1674" 157
MS 15   (NORDISKA MUSÉET 63.180),
         "SAMLING AF UTOMORDENTLIGA…" 159
MS 16   (NORDISKA MUSÉET 63.711),
         "ÖSTRA GÖINGE, SKÅNE" 160
MS 17   (NORDISKA MUSÉET 271.600 15:1949), "KONSTBOK" 164
MS 18   (NORDISKA MUSÉET 271.601A), "SANKT PETRI NYCKEL" 166
MS 19   (NORDISKA MUSÉET 271.601B), "LÄKARBOK" 168
MS 20   (NORDISKA MUSÉET 271.601C), "UPPLYSA DE OKUNNIGA" ... 169
MS 21   (NORDISKA MUSÉET 271.602), "NEGROMÄNLISKA SAKER" 171
MS 22   (NORDISKA MUSÉET, UNNUMBERED),
         "GRYTS OCH GÅRINGE SKOGSBYGD" 173
MS 23   (NORDISKA MUSÉET, UNNUMBERED),
         "MÖNSTERÅS, SMÅLAND" 174
MS 24   (NORDISKA MUSÉET, UNNUMBERED),
         "OM FISKERI Å DES INEHÅL" 175

TABLE OF CONTENTS

MS 25 (NORDISKA MUSÉET, UNNUMBERED),
"ÅKERS SOCKEN, SÖDERMANLAND".. 177
MS 26 (IN PRIVATE OWNERSHIP),
"PER BJÖRNSSON, LUNNOM, SKÅNE" 179
MS 27 (FOLKMINNESFÖRENING I LUND),
"VARUTI JAG SKRIFVER VARJEHANDA, 1841" 181
MS 28 (PHILIPSTADS-BERGSLAGS LAGA, 1751),
"SIGNERI OCH VIDSKEPELSE"... 182
MS 29 (SKARA VETERINÄRBIBLIOTEK 1051),
"HELFWETESBREF, 1791"... 183
MS 30 (ULMA 984), "JUGAS OLOF JONSSON, 1873–74 DAL".................. 185
MS 31 (ULMA 36365), "SALOMONISKA MAGISKA KONSTER".................. 187
MS 32 (IN PRIVATE OWNERSHIP),
"SUPRIANIA, FRU ALSTADS SOCKEN" 190
MS 33 (IN PRIVATE OWNERSHIP),
"TROLL-MARKSENS SVARTKONSTBOK" 191
MS 34 (COLLECTIO LENGERTZIANA, SCANIA, LUB),
"ZIMPARTIER WETTENSKAP"... 193
MS 35 (LUF, UNNUMBERED), "C.O.SWAHNS SVARTKONSTBOK" 194

GENERAL CONCLUSIONS... 196

CHAPTER V. *Conclusion* 205

Organizational Principles of Black Art Books 208
Collectors' Generic Expections of the Black Art Book............................. 210
Scholars' Exaggeration of Illiteracy among the Lower Classes 212
Distribution and Provenance.. 213
Continental Evocation Meets an Ethnic Swedish Folk Belief 214
The Results of Statistical Analysis.. 215
Black Art Book Owners and their Claims to Power 216
New Light on Old Scholarship 217

PART TWO
THE MANUSCRIPTS: TRANSLATIONS

MS 1 (KULTURHISTORISKA MUSÉET I HÄRNÖSAND),
"CÅNSTER ATT BRUKA, NEMBLIGEN..." 223
MS 2 (ESLÖVS MUSEUM 3329A), "NO 1 RADEMIN" 238
MS 3 (ESLÖVS MUSEUM 3329B), "NO 4 STORA KATEKIS" 246
MS 4 (ESLÖVS MUSEUM 3329C), "FÖR TANDVÄRK" 259
MS 5 (KUNGLIGA UNDERSÖKNINGEN 3335), "TROLLBOKEN" 267
MS 6 (KUNGLIGA UNDERSÖKNINGEN 11120), "SVARTKONSTBOK" 274

TABLE OF CONTENTS

MS 7 (LUF A.285), "GLIMÅKRA SOCKEN, SKÅNE" 301
MS 8 (LUF A.795:26–31),
"MAGISKA FORMLER OCH MAGISKA HANDLINGAR" 305
MS 9 (LUF ABC: C.W. VON SYDOW), "SVARTKONSTBOK FRÅN MO" 308
MS 10 (NORDISKA MUSÉET 33.823),
"TJULA SOCKEN, SÖDERMANLAND" 347
MS 11 (NORDISKA MUSÉET 33.824),
"ÅKERS SOCKEN, SÖDERMANLAND" 357
MS 12 (NORDISKA MUSÉET 40.034),
"CYPRANIS KONSTER OCH LÄROR OCH DES INRÄT" 373
MS 13 (NORDISKA MUSÉET 41.652),
"SVARTKONSTBOK, NORRA SKÅNE" 399
MS 14 (NORDISKA MUSÉET 41.674), "LÖNSBODA, 1674" 405
MS 15 (NORDISKA MUSÉET 63.180),
"SAMLING AF UTOMORDENTLIGA..." 416
MS 16 (NORDISKA MUSÉET 63.711), "ÖSTRA GÖINGE, SKÅNE" 419
MS 17 (NORDISKA MUSÉET 271.600 15:1949), "KONSTBOK" 423
MS 18 (NORDISKA MUSÉET 271.601A), "SANKT PETRI NYCKEL" 426
MS 19 (NORDISKA MUSÉET 271.601B), "LÄKARBOK" 436
MS 20 (NORDISKA MUSÉET 271.601C), "UPPLYSA DE OKUNNIGA" 459
MS 21 (NORDISKA MUSÉET 271.602), "NEGROMÄNLISKA SAKER" 461
MS 22 (NORDISKA MUSÉET, UNNUMBERED),
"GRYTS OCH GÅRINGE SKOGSBYGD" 474
MS 23 (NORDISKA MUSÉET, UNNUMBERED),
"MÖNSTERÅS, SMÅLAND" 476
MS 24 (NORDISKA MUSÉET, UNNUMBERED),
"OM FISKERI Å DES INEHÅL" 495
MS 25 (NORDISKA MUSÉET, UNNUMBERED),
"ÅKERS SOCKEN, SÖDERMANLAND" 517
MS 26 (IN PRIVATE OWNERSHIP),
"PER BJÖRNSSON, LUNNOM, SKÅNE" 534
MS 27 (FOLKMINNESFÖRENING I LUND),
"VARUTI JAG SKRIFVER VARJEHANDA, 1841" 536
MS 28 (PHILIPSTADS-BERGSLAGS LAGA, 1751),
"SIGNERI OCH VIDSKEPELSE" 549
MS 29 (SKARA VETERINÄRBIBLIOTEK 1051),
"HELFWETESBREF, 1791" 553
MS 30 (ULMA 984), "JUGAS OLOF JONSSON, 1873–74 DAL" 553
MS 31 (ULMA 36365), "SALOMONISKA MAGISKA KONSTER" 560
MS 32 (IN PRIVATE OWNERSHIP),
"SUPRIANIA, FRU ALSTADS SOCKEN" 587
MS 33 (IN PRIVATE OWNERSHIP),
"TROLL-MARKSENS SVARTKONSTBOK" 591

TABLE OF CONTENTS

MS 34 (COLLECTIO LENGERTZIANA, SCANIA, LUB),
   "ZIMPARTIER WETTENSKAP" 595
MS 35 (LUF, UNNUMBERED), "C.O.SWAHNS SVARTKONSTBOK" 600

APPENDIX. *Toward a Swedish Botanical Pharmacopoeia*
Commonly Occurring Folk Names for Substances in Black Art Books 619

Bibliography 621
Index 636
About Folk Necromancy in Transmission ....

FOREWORD TO THIS EDITION

Michael Tarplee

Doctor Tom Johnson's journey to give voice to the voices of his ancestors began with a most fortuitous question. Tom was in a PhD program at UC Berkeley and was feeling uncertain as to which way to go with his dissertation. One of the women who was a part of his dissertation committee when he expressed his uncertainty asked him simply, if he could do whatever he wanted to do what would he wish to do most? He immediately answered without a thought that he would gather as many of the Black Art books that were still left in the libraries and farmsteads in Sweden and translate them for the preservation of his ancestral knowledge. He got a necessary grant to go to Sweden and gather the remaining Black Art Books. Which he did for many months in 1992 to 1993.

After coming back from Sweden, the pressures of everyday life, and lack of academic funding necessitated that he got a full-time job. So, he had to put finishing his dissertation off for around twenty years. However, a friend of ours finished her dissertation after an absence of 20 years. She encouraged Tom that it was still possible to finish his PhD. After talking about it and my encouragement he decided to apply to the University of Washington, which has one of the best Swedish departments in the world outside of Sweden.

Working at the University of Washington as a teacher's assistant, a teacher of Swedish and filling in for other teachers in classes in the Sagas, Old Norse, and the Mythology and Religion of the ancient Scandinavians while writing his dissertation was quite a challenge. He often had to translate archaic Swedish from hand written notes. He rose to the occasion, receiving praise from his academic superiors. I was given permission to sit at the table during the defense of his dissertation. All the leading Scandinavian scholars of this country at the table deferred to Tom as the expert in his field. The worst criticism was only that one examiner said she would have used a different modern word to translate a few archaic Swedish words. His dissertation was completed on February 22, 2010.

Dr. Johnson's first and until now only published work *Graveyard Wanderers, the Wise Ones and the Dead in Sweden* (Caduceus Books, 2012) is a compilation of the spells in his dissertation concerning the use of bones for spell casting and the gaining of magical power.

PREFACE TO THE PHD THESIS

I came to the study of folk magic and folk belief from a previous background in Old Norse Literature and cultural studies. Specifically, skaldic verse and its magical subtexts were of especial interest to me. The magically powerful *nið* verses were considered so emasculating and libelous that they required instant and mortal retribution to deflect. The composers of such magically potent verses were called *kraptaskáldar*, or power poets. In more recent times, folk belief and practice recognized a similar social role, and the practitioners were called wise ones (Sw. *klokfolk*) or sorcerers (Sw. *trollfolk*).

After the academic year 1988–89 and having compiled an exhaustive bibliography on folk magic and belief for a graduate seminar led by Professor Alan Dundes, then Chair of Folklore at University of California at Berkeley, my interest shifted from the archaic medieval material to the somewhat more recent beliefs and practices of the last four centuries in Sweden. This work took me to Sweden during the academic year 1992–93 for primary research in folklore archives and museum collections. During that time, I was in residence at the *Institut för folklivsforskning vid Stockholms universitet*, under the careful guidance of Barbro Klein and Åke Daun. Most days were spent in the archives of the Nordic Museum (*Nordiska muséet*), sorting through the file boxes that contained the manuscripts I was studying, those compendia of folk magical practice known as black art books (Sw. *svartkonstböcker*). I also traveled to Göteborg, to Uppsala, and to various district and county museums and folklore archives to retrieve more data and locate more examples of these manuscripts. The network of connections I established was extensive, and many works were generously made available to me that scholars have not had access to before or since.

The uncertainties in the software industry at the time, as well as other issues, prevented me from a swift and efficient publication of my results. However, I believe that the additional time spent with the material has only resulted in a more useful and more enjoyable work.

Titles of academic works must maintain a balance. On the one hand, it is poetically and bibliographically useful to have something that evokes the spirit of the subject, but also that provides enough of a description to furnish the researcher with a good idea of its contents. Recently, W. F. Ryan's encyclopedic treatment of Russian folk magic bore the title *The Bathhouse at Midnight: Magic in Russia*.[1] The bathhouse at midnight was the archetypical place and time that folk magical procedures took place. The subtitle, Magic in Russia, provides a more accurate idea of the actual subject of the study.

The title of this work, *Tidebast och Vändelrot: Magical Representations in the Swedish Black Art Book Tradition*, was, it turned out, appropriate on a number of levels. I had chosen the two magical herbs, *Tidebast* (*daphne mezereum*) and *Vändelrot* (*valeriana officinalis radix*), because of the frequency of their occurrence in the Swedish folk-magical pharmacopoeia. It has in Swedish a similar ring as the archetypical Shakespearean "eye of newt and toe of frog" that go into the witches' cauldron at the beginning of Act IV of Shakespeare's *Macbeth*. It was only after deciding on the propriety of that title that committee member and great friend Professor John Lindow reminded me of the migratory legend, known in Swedish variants as *Tibast sägen*, as recorded in Gunnar Granberg's monograph on the forest sprit known in Swedish as the *skogsrå*. For the exact tale, I refer the reader to Professor Lindow's excellent source for Swedish legendry, *Swedish Legends and Folktales*.[2] This legend or *sägen* belongs to the Reider Christensen's Migratory Legend Type Index between ML 6000–6005. In the tale, the two plants act as magical substances to free human or beast from the clutches of inimical nature spirits. Alternatively, the mere mention of their names serves as a kind of "Rumplestilskin" keyword, which acts as the physical herbs would in freeing the subject from the designs of the wood-spirit (Sw. *skogsrå*).

And finally, *Vändelrot*, or valerian root in English, is not only the source for a central nervous system depressant, from which is derived modern Valium. It is also that bitter herb which, when ground finely as a powder, goes by another folk name, "graveyard dust" (Sw. *kyrkogårdsmull*). Since cemeteries, their dirt and bones, figured so prominently in the procurement of magical power these wise ones wielded, what better way to invoke the entirety of the tradition than by also using this herbal ingredient together with its frequent and obvious pairing? The predominance of these two herbs in tinctures, incenses, plasters, and magical pouches bring immediately to mind a great deal of Swedish folk magic, belief and practice, and in a way that makes no distinction between the malevolent or the benevolent intent of the recipe, whether they are used to "heal" or to "hex."

My dissertation is primarily a study of a tradition, as it exists both in the realm of folk belief and in the realm of the written artifact. It provides an unprecedented number of complete and unedited archive records, both in Swedish and in English translation. It makes these records available to an international academic and popular readership. It also makes available in English translation thirty-five manuscripts, the largest corpus of Swedish black art books ever assembled in one study. An accompanying detailed apparatus assures that the translations can also be of use and interest to an international academic readership. By providing these exhaustive source materials, I have made conclusions that have not previously been possible. I draw attention to the points where oral narratives of folk belief about the books deviate from what is represented by the books themselves. Previous scholarship has used primarily archival narratives to generalize about these books and their owners, rather than examination of the manuscripts themselves. In returning to the manuscripts as primary source, I have been able to quantify the contents of these manuscripts both by procedural traits as well as by functional intent. This quantification, when compared with the unedited archival records I also include, allows us to contrast the belief with the artifact. This gives a more accurate and heterogeneous vision of the Swedish black art book tradition.

Chapter one provides definitions of an unfamiliar topic, and includes Swedish terminology as well as discussion of a culture that used language in ways that may also be foreign to many Swedes. I recount the work of previous scholars who have worked in the black art book tradition, and conclude with current trends in the study of the wise folk (Sw. *klokfolk*) who were the compilers and owners of these books. Chapter two is a study of the wise ones, using unedited archival materials, complete with translations. Previously, by reproducing only the one sentence found in larger archival excerpts which supported a thesis, a great deal of the context in which this lore was kept and passed was ignored. By understanding the folk belief about the compilers and owners of these black art books, beliefs about the books themselves can be more clearly discerned. Chapter three addresses folk belief about black art books, their generic expectations, and their preternatural qualities and origins. Chapter four is a description of the tools used to analyze both procedural traits and function or intention found in the contents of these books, followed by a description and discussion of each manuscript in turn. It provides paleographic descriptions, ownership and potential provenance, as well as whatever is known about the owners or compilers. It also provides for each manuscript a quantification of each procedural type and each function or motivation found in the manuscripts. It is by such quantification that we can begin to see a more accurate picture of the books, considered away from the sometimes contradictory oral narratives of folk belief. And finally, Chapter five considers the results of the foregoing, and their implications for further research and international comparison.

While I hope this volume will afford no small amount of pleasure in the reading, I also hope that the scholar will find in it a reliable source of Swedish folk narrative in both the original Swedish as well as in English translation, and that the translations of the manuscripts will serve in the future study of international traditions of charms, charming, and folk grimoires.

NOTES

1 W. F. Ryan, *The Bathhouse at Midnight: Magic in Russia*, Magic in History series, (University Park, PA: The Pennsylvania State University Press, 1999).
2 John Lindow, *Swedish Legends and Folktales* (Berkeley: University of California Press, 1978). No. 40, 111.

ACKNOWLEDGEMENTS

This work has been a long time in gestation, and therefore I have many to whom I must honor with gratitude for the thankless job of helping me on my academic odyssey. Because of the length of this project, there will doubtless be names that I will neglect to mention, or will only mention in reference to a professional organization. I can only beg their indulgence as I attempt to proffer thanks for aid given or services rendered.

Firstly, at the University of Washington in Seattle, it is to my very first contact with Old Norse literature and society, Professor Emerita Patricia Conroy, who opened a world of wonder in the love of the languages and linguistics of the Scandinavian area, that I owe a tremendous debt of gratitude. She was and continues to be an example of the scholar I can aspire to be. Professor Guntis Šmidchens, specialist in Baltic and Folklore studies, was truly heroic in his efforts to be of help in the completion of this project, and Ann-Charlotte Gavel Adams, specialist in Swedish literature, spared no effort in making sure that the translations were not only accurate, but that the English was also academically worthy. Professor Terje Leiren, Chair of the Department of Scandinavian Studies during the period of my residence, has always been a kind and cheerful authority to turn to when expectations of the university bureaucracy and my own limited understandings of it were at odds. Graduate Program Coordinator Debbie Mercer has been a real gem in learning about that bureaucracy on the fly, and sharing her insights without hesitation.

At the University of California, Berkeley, the late Professor Alan Dundes was truly a gentleman and a formidable scholar. His rigor in academics, and his breadth of knowledge were inspiring to behold, both in the seminar room and in the context of the Qualifying Examinations. Professor John Lindow, specialist in Old Norse and Folklore, continues to be a role model for me, in academics, the social graces and in a timeliness that I can only aspire to. Professor Carol J. Clover was a wonder not only in helping me to fashion a topic that would both sustain my interest for the lengthy time of composition, but also in instilling in me a love of writing, academic and otherwise. Professor Karin Sanders, specialist in Danish literature, was so helpful in working with me while at UC in the areas of modern Scandinavian literature, and post-modern literary theory.

For financial support during this project, I thank the Swedish Institute (Sw. *Svenska institutet*) for their award of a Fernström Travel Grant which enabled my trip to Sweden in 1992–93. My thanks go to both the Swedish Women's Educational Association (SWEA) of New Jersey for a stipend while completing the final stages of the project, and the Swedish Women's Educational Association (SWEA) of San Francisco for a stipend, followed by a chance to share the fruits of my research among an enthusiastic and rigorous academic audience in San Francisco. *Tack för senast!*

The role of University Graduate Programs to support their graduate students by awarding teaching assistantships is not only important, but it exhibits great confidence in the potential of the future academic scholar. For this, I thank the Department of Scandinavian Studies at the University of Washington, for the years while I pursued a Master of Arts degree, and more recently as I strove to finish the PhD. Thanks also go to the Department of Scandinavian at the University of California, Berkeley, where I performed my primary research, and learned how to participate effectively in a PhD Qualifying Examination.

In Sweden, I was honored to be shown great hospitality and a generosity with time and resources from a number of people and organizations. At *Nordiska muséet*, curator Birger Grape at *Folkminnessamlingen vid Nordiska muséet* was a tremendous help and was always a pleasant colleague during my many days in the archive rooms. At the *Institutet för folklivsforskning*, thanks go to Professor Barbro Klein who helped to orient me to the workings of the many and varied forms of Swedish research methodologies, and without whose help I'd not have accomplished half of what I did. Her welcoming reception, and openness to the area of my research was a source of inspiration during a very cold and very early Swedish winter. I also thank her for the opportunity she gave me to share the preliminary results of my research to the *Folkloristiska sällskap* in Stockholm. Åke Daun, the Chair at the time for the *Institutet*, was also generous and welcoming, and his familiarity not only with dialects, but with the functioning of every part of the Institute was always a help. Jonas Engman, then a student at the *Institutet*, but now a faculty member, showed a hospitality and a helpfulness that was always heartwarming. Thanks to you all.

At SOFI (previously, the *Uppsala landsmålsarkivet*), my thanks go to Maj Reinhammar, who made personnel and archival materials available both quickly and with a smile. And to her uncle, Carl-Martin Edsman, who has done so much work in the history and geographical distribution of black art books, my thanks to him for a morning spent "talking shop"—it was a pleasure and an honor.

At *Dialekt-, Ortnamns-, och Folkminnesarkivet* in Göteborg, my profoundest thanks go to Bodil Nildin-Wall and Jan-Inge Wall, who not only spent time and energy to orient me to the collections there, but also generously provided me with volumes that have subsequently enhanced this work and my own scholarship tremendously. Bodil has also helped at a distance, providing information that I had not previously had an opportunity to collect. She has been of immeasurable assistance and support in this project.

Thanks to all the personnel at the *Institutet för folklivsforskning* in Stockholm, at *Nordiska muséet* in Stockholm, at *Eslövs museum* in Eslöv, librarians at *Kungliga biblioteket* (KB) in Stockholm, *Lunds universitets bibliotek,* and the regional *Landsarkiv* in Göteborg and Lund. Thanks also to the kind and helpful staff at the various antiquarian bookshops (Sw. *antikvariat*) in Stockholm, who helped me find out of print sources to enable my further study.

Thanks also go to Professor Owen Davies, University of Hertfordshire, for a kind word at the right time, and for a collegiality that encouraged me on to this project's conclusion.

I must also proffer my thanks to Ruth Merriam of Louisville, KY, without whose technical assistance and incredible moral support, there would have been no graphics in the translations.*

And last, but certainly not least, my most profound gratitude goes to my life partner, Michael Tarplee, who has stood by me for the last two decades as I struggled to finish this life's work, and whose loyalty and understanding has never wavered. All my love to you.

*EDITORS' NOTE
The archival images have been restored in ritual fashion to high fidelity by Jesse Hathaway Diaz.

DEDICATION

*To my parents, Elmer and Brita Johnson, to my family,
and to my life partner and husband,
Michael Tarplee*

Part I

TIDEBAST OCH VÄNDELROT

Magical Representations in
the Swedish Black Art Book Tradition

CHAPTER I

✤

Introduction

THIS STUDY IS about Swedish black art books. They were and continue to be the notebooks in which the sometimes-rural, sometimes-metropolitan healer-magician-sorcerer recorded his or her spells, recipes, potions and rituals. As such, they contain a rich variety of material specific to the performance of magic, whether of magical medicine or of simple sorcery meant to affect the external environment.

Wise ones (Sw. *klokfolk*), those healer-magician-sorcerers were the composers, compilers and holders of these books, and often served a semi-professional function in Sweden, whether in the countryside or in the larger metropolitan areas. They served as healers, psychic advisers, counselors and were often a last resort when physical intervention no longer yielded a problem's resolution. They did this by means of spells, potions, incenses, plasters, rituals, spell-bags or other amulets, and spoken or written charms. With such a sizeable body of material to employ, these magical specialists often recorded their repertoire in hand-written books of varying sizes and thicknesses. These books became known as black art books (Sw. *svartkonstböcker*).

These black art books are often hand-bound volumes, though some make use of prebound books with blank pages, in which the healer-sorcerer might record his secrets. Some of these black art books are quite old, the earliest in the collection presented here dating from the end of the seventeenth century. The paper on which these entries are recorded is sometimes quite fragile, and even decaying. Reading the contents is often challenging and sometimes impossible. The collection described and translated here is one assembled from various folklore archives and museums across Sweden, which were assembled by folklorists and museum personnel mostly in the late nineteenth century. Some few entered the various collections, however, both before and after this period. This collection of translations represents a first effort to make this otherwise diffuse corpus available in English translation to an international readership.

The term black art book is a literal translation of the Swedish *svartkonstbok*, and as the term indicates, it is a book that ostensibly deals with the black art, or magic. Magic is a "traditional" fact, due both to the manner of its transmission and to the adherence to carefully conserved forms. In order for magic to be considered traditional, and therefore of interest to the folklorist, its procedures must be sufficiently similar over a period of time, typically handed down over generations, to warrant its inclusion in folklore studies. Even in cases in which procedural forms vary, the realm of shared metaphysical assumptions and associations that allow for magical efficacy, a sort of magical cultural matrix, is something that is handed on. This allows for the creation of new forms using a traditional magical "vocabulary." In the magical tradition, great attention is more often paid to the exactitude of adherence to previously established elements of performance, perhaps in the belief in a tried-and-true method which assures efficacy. This means that recording those elements in a way that can assure precise and accurate repetition is highly desirable. In cultures in which writing is one way to record those elements, we see in fact that the literate seek to write down those elements, the charms, rites and materials, to aid in remembering these details. These black art books are primary sources, personal collections or notebooks authored or redacted by practitioners. Often, notations in these more recent manuscripts match examples two to three hundred years older. Swedish black art books belong to the tradition exemplified by these primary sources and which exhibited this continuity of content and style.

The domain of folk magic in folklore studies has often been considered as only a branch of medicine or ethno-medicine, which sometimes results in labeling it as quackery (Sw. *kvacksalveri*).[1] This is an inadequate characterization primarily because the ideas of health and sickness, of luck and of being hexed, all exist in a common realm of ideas. Using a native vocabulary a person with sexual dysfunction may be diagnosed as being hexed, just as a rifle that doesn't fire is hexed. A child with the three-day fever (Sw. *tridjedags frossan*) is a victim of unseen forces just as is the mother with post-partum depression, or the defendant in a legal case in which he is being prosecuted. Magic and medicine have more indistinct borders in folklore studies. On the one hand, this is justifiable because native concepts and cultural matrix treat them similarly. Use of terminology to describe the subject such as "fraudulent pretenses designed to fool the credulous" has previously made a serious scholarly investigation of its traditions seem less respectable.[2] When the borders between magic and ethno-medicine are firmer, this has more to do with the intention of the practitioners than in the structural, procedural or medicinal virtues of a given treatment.

Magic has, as its ultimate aim, the happiness of the individual who seeks to use it. Whether the aim is medical, religious, cathartic or apotropaic (magically protective) is not a distinction that the tradition supports, so it does not do to categorize using such artificially imposed terminology. Because this aim, the happiness of the individual, is of such general interest, there can be said to exist two types of practitioners—the specialists or wise ones (Sw. *klokfolk*) and the common persons who are sometimes clients of such specialists, but who can also perform certain procedures on their own, as long as certain ritual pre-requisites are met. For this reason, there are some rituals that seem accessible to both the specialist and the common person. Invariably, the resulting difference is one of degree or duration due either to inherent skill, predilection or to the intention during its performance.

Magic has been a "hot" topic for at least a century and a half, as Industrial and Post-Industrial man sought to document man's egress from the "ignorance" of his past. A change in approach began at the turn of the twentieth century, with anthropologists such as Mauss and Hubert and those who came after them. This new social model of magic demonstrated the social role that magic plays in culture, and no longer focused on this evolutionary model, choosing instead to focus on how magic functions linguistically, sociologically and spiritually. This newer sociological model recognizes that even in the present, the root-doctor and the conjure-man still have vital roles to play in the societies that rely on them.[3] This means that the present study is poised at a scholarly juncture at which the field is growing self-conscious and therefore self-critical. This can have positive effects for a new evaluation of this traditional material.

By assembling narratives about the black art books and their owners, we can now ask to what extent might we see divergent narrative material presented in this study; that is, do we see common themes in *narratives about* black art books borne out by the contents of the books themselves? This study should not only answer these questions, but introduce new data that might be used in future studies of the black art book tradition, and of the wise folk themselves.

Posing Questions

Why?

THIS study will deal with these notebooks, their contents, their owners, and folk belief about all three, in Sweden between the seventeenth and the twentieth centuries. By analysis of the structure and contents of a broad selection of black art books, and of the cultural matrix of popular belief represented in archival excerpts, direct appeals to primary texts and archival narratives can either support or contradict previously unexamined and anecdotal statements about them. Expectations of their contents suggested by the folk narrative tradition can be verified or modified based upon an examination of actual examples.

While historically of great interest, and worthy of mention in most works dealing with folk magic, ethno-botany and ethno-medicine, scholarly editions of individual black art books have only occasionally seen print.[4] There has been no general treatment of the genre, nor an exclusive treatment of their contents that has been based on anything other than generalizations by the relatively few scholars who have had access to the disparate manuscript collections housed throughout Sweden, or to the few published examples. With no central repository, Swedish black art books have remained difficult to access even in Sweden, and no attempt has previously been made to produce English translations of any of them for an international scholarly audience. In many cases, previous Swedish editions favored heavily-edited versions of the manuscripts, commonly with omissions and a rearrangement of contents according to the editor's organizational principles and aesthetic sensibilities. Items were sometimes omitted as uninteresting if they seemed to demonstrate insufficient overtly occult or magical emphasis. There was also a tendency to favor what the editor considered the most typical examples upon which to characterize their contents. Many studies from the turn of the twentieth century focused upon individual manuscripts only, treating the most interesting contents one manuscript at a time. This not only made comparison of a larger body more difficult, but the editions thus produced presented an inaccurate picture of the books and those who collated and owned them. By presenting previously unpublished archival excerpts illustrating folk belief, and by presenting translations of a relatively large sampling of the books themselves along with historical and paleographical apparatuses, this study will not only provide previously unavailable material on which to base new generalizations, but will provide folklorists interested in the topic a larger and consolidated collection made available in a more internationally accessible translation.

In this Introduction, I will clarify the questions we seek to elucidate in this analysis. To do this, I will reevaluate definitions and previous scholarship, and will suggest what that previous work suggests for new, current scholarship, and how this study will address some of those suggestions.

What?

SWEDISH BLACK ART books are found in various circumstances. The items studied and translated here came from collections at the Nordic Museum's Folklore Archives (Sw. *Nordiska muséets folkminnessamling*), as well as the folklore archives in Göteborg, Lund and Uppsala.[5] While several reside in district museum collections, there are also those that only exist in transcriptions at these institutions, the originals having been returned to their owners. Exact provenance of each manuscript is given in Chapter Four of this work. These magical *grimoires*[6] or grammars, the black art books, are a definitive source for the procedure and belief matrix out of which magical ritual and charm arise. They record specific examples from the time of their writing that provide a glimpse into the consulting, counseling and medical procedures of a professional class of magical practitioner. With just under 2000 individual notations in thirty-five manuscripts, they provide a statistically significant body of material to compare with archived folk narratives in a reconstruction of the magic of the wise ones.

In Sweden, these compendia called "black art books" (Sw. pl. *svartkonstböcker*) are the more recent examples of the same type of ritual and ethnobotanical notebooks found in late Pharaonic and Hellenic literary culture. Many of the procedures we find in these Swedish texts are even for the same or similar ends as we find in their archaic Hellenic counterparts, displaying a surprising unity between the Greek magical papyri[7] and the Swedish black art books.[8] Not surprisingly, utterances of such power and danger should be hidden from common access, so some notebooks preserve them in a kind of secret code, substituting numbers for letters, or other ciphers, signs or symbols. In translating such texts, one has the double task of deciphering both this code and, as we shall see, an archaic style of handwriting that remains problematic even for native specialists.

Where?

THIS STUDY WILL examine materials found within Sweden, mostly to be found in the folklore archives or regional museums. Sometimes these manuscripts remained in private ownership, and were loaned for museum personnel to transcribe. In those cases, we have only a transcription available, a distinct disadvantage when the transcriber is sloppy,[9] is not interested in certain types of items,[10] or seeks to correct what he believes is a copyist's error. Sweden is geographical peculiarity, with the cultural influences found in its southernmost provinces owing much to continental Europe, and in the case of the black art book, especially to Germany. Sweden's northernmost provinces on the other hand are contiguous with Finland, a land between Scandinavian and Slavic cultural areas, and which shares certain aspects of both, but also retains its own cultural heritage. There is also the cultural influence of the non-Scandinavian Sámi, an ethnic and cultural group found all over the northernmost regions of Norway, Sweden, Finland and Russia. This creates an especially rich area of cultural confluence that could suggest much about the migration of ideas about magic, ideas which might be in evidence in the Swedish black art books originating in this area.

By limiting the scope of this study to Sweden, there is much that might have been said regarding the Swedish tradition's relationship with any of its neighbor countries either to the south or to the west or east that must, for now, be overlooked. But there is also an advantage in presenting a body of material which at the very least is geographically plottable. This smaller focus might suggest commonalities that would be overlooked in a more sweeping and inclusive study.

When?

THE BLACK ART books under examination here come from a period of about 275 years' duration. Using inexact methods of dating, most of these manuscripts are from the eighteenth (9) and nineteenth (17) centuries, and most were collected by folklorists between 1880 and 1910. Under normal circumstances, this might be considered too lengthy a period to yield unified data for analysis. The aim informing this study was to accumulate as many examples of black art books as were available during a period of residence at the Ethnological Institute at the University of Stockholm (Sw. *Institutet för folklivsforskning vid Stockholms universitet*) as a research fellow of the University of California, Berkeley during the academic year 1992–93. This residence allowed access to the Folklore Archives of the Nordic Museum, and made further research at the various folklore archives and regional museums in Sweden possible. The body of material uncovered during this period, though disparate in time, remained amazingly unified in content, and indicated much formal continuity. Because these manuscripts are handwritten, the publication dates that are a formal requirement of modern published books are not always in evidence, but we are fortunate that the black art book tradition supported annotations as to owners and years of composition or ownership, and provides a better idea of when the book was composed and the period of its utilization than a well-kept printed volume might have done. It is from such notations that we can identify our most recent manuscript to the year 1941, and to the city of Stockholm. Our earliest examples are not always so forthcoming owing to a concern with maintaining the anonymity of individual or family. Sometimes this resulted in such valuable pages being excised prior to donation or discovery. In those cases, generalizations have to be made from examples of writing styles, orthography, or the physical or chemical composition of the paper or ink. Happily, these rigorous efforts have usually already been made by archive, museum and library personnel much more qualified to make such evaluations, and it is from this previous scholarly work that we refer to the last decade of the seventeenth century as the time when our earliest example was being compiled. There are, no doubt, earlier examples of black art books that were kept by those able to write them out and to read them once written. Literary histories commonly point to the Swedish monastic manuscript, a so-called healer's book (Sw. *Läkarbok*), a book of medical remedies, written down by Peder Månsson, a monk at Vadstena priory, in 1522. In fact, Swedish collections contain much older examples of manuscripts with magical content according to scholars such as af Klintberg, Edsman and Peuckert.[11] It is not always clear, however, whether these older manuscripts are of the same genre as those under examination here, or were learnèd examples which served to inform the contents of the black art book at one point in history. Thus, it is useful to limit our investigation to those examples which have been previously collected and classified as black art books by museum and archive personnel.

Who?

IN THE INVESTIGATION of black art books, one cannot help but inquire about their authors, owners and editors. In this we have an especially rich narrative tradition that provides both common public opinion as well as the word of actual clients. In some cases, we will find that the public opinion which is often quoted as the final word about the identities and practices of black art book owners, does not accurately describe the contents of the books themselves. In other cases, we will find that public opinion has been rather kind to such individuals, as the contents of the books contain much more diabolical contents than an informant has described. For this reason, two chapters are included in this study that deal with public perception of the wise ones and of their books. The narrative excerpts recorded there provide varying pictures of the wise ones and their books. These will subsequently be compared with the contents of the books themselves to see if public opinion was actually informed by an acquaintance with the books, or merely represented a tradition about them with no actual personal knowledge.

In only nine of the cases examined here are we given any more than an author's or owner's name. In those nine cases, we have the work of collectors to establish the identity of the original owner or author, and in at least one case, the author was available to the collector to provide additional oral commentary, thus making the black art book even more accessible than others in the collection. Most of the examples, while mentioning names, give no hint as to the lives or the ongoing activities of the author or owner. This makes generalizations about specific individuals impossible. Keeping to the more concrete notations found in the black art books provides sufficient material upon which to base a concluding analysis.

Collectors, both professional and volunteer, have made further inquiry into this subject possible both by collecting field data in the form of personal narratives from which excerpts will be taken for this study, and by establishing the kinds of relationships with a general public that allowed these manuscripts to be donated or transcribed and subsequently housed in archives, museums or libraries.

How?

THIS STUDY WILL show the major areas of disparity and consonance between on the one hand the thirty-five manuscripts here translated, and on the other hand, two different traditions of narratives about these books and the people who kept and used them: folk legends about black books and scholarly interpretations by folklorists in the past. The first tradition is that represented by the tradition-bearers, those who told narratives in which expectations were established of what a black art book was, who its owners were, and the role that book played in both personal and professional metaphysics. The second tradition is that of folklorists, those who established scholarly expectations of the black art book as a genre, its contents, its authors and owners, and the magical world view they helped to inform.

The Introduction will present a summation of recent previous scholarship about both black books and their owners among the wise ones. Chapter Two will examine folk narratives that describe the wise ones, and establish expectations of their behavior, appearance, and psychic abilities. Chapter Three assembles archival excerpts that deal specifically with the black art books themselves along with narratives describing the relationship of book to owner, at least as they were understood by the tradition-bearers. Chapter Four will present the apparatus for an analysis according to formal traits of the items found in the manuscripts as well as according to the relative moral import of those items, from malevolent through ambivalent to benevolent aims. It will also present what we know about each manuscript in this study, paleographically, historically and statistically. Finally, in Chapter Five, conclusions will be presented about the accuracy of the characterizations of both black art book and owner that have been advanced in scholarship as well as in folk narrative. The second part of this study provides English translations of 35 manuscripts, the raw material analyzed here. Providing translations into English allows these texts to be used in future international studies of the charm tradition.

Since magical morality was seen on a spectrum from the very worst, the dangerous and powerful malevolent witch to the very best, compassionate and benevolent herbal healer or root doctor, and with every combination and admixture in between, discrete items in the black art books under consideration here are examined for a number of traits, and statistics are gathered regarding the type, frequency and magical intention which appear in these books. In this way, an image emerges as to just what sorts of activities most occupied the minds, even if not the professional practices, of the wise ones.

Morality is not the only matter that concerns us in this study. We are also interested in characterizations of the magical tradition that generated these compendia of spells, recipes and rituals.

Previous Scholarship

WITHIN the last century, magic has been viewed successively as imperfect science,[12] as transgressive religion,[13] or as anti-social or psychotic behavior[14] by scientific disciplines. Frazer, Linderholm and Eliade present models which can be combined into an understanding of a meaningful cultural matrix, one that acknowledges the role of magic as the satisfaction of the human desire to exert control on the environment and to ameliorate a sense of powerlessness in the face of the uncertainties of life. Since both psychology and sociology have more recently developed greater sophistication in understanding the role of the aberrant in social contexts, scholars such as Basilov have revised Eliade's understanding of the shamanic illness.[15] Magic is a cultural artifact, a phenomenon which exists on a continuum, and which includes a certain degree of each of the three, but none to exclusion or excess.[16] Ultimately, when attempting to describe and analyze magic in its own cultural milieu, none of these is sufficient to account for its presence or inescapable ubiquity, even in the face of ecclesiastical condemnation and horrific means of capital punishment.[17] Magic simply is. To restrict its domain as a strictly religious, strictly scientific or strictly psychological one is doing it a disservice as a cultural fact.[18] Its domain is essentially practical.

Examining Previous Studies

THE BLACK ART books that are the subject of this study belong to a genre of folk literature. They include written notations of oral (incantatory) charms, drawn symbols, accompanying or independent ritual descriptions, recipes for internal or external use, use of magical alphabets called Wittenberg Letters or magical figures (Sw. *Wittenbergska bokstäver* or *trollkaraktärer*), and items using some or all these elements. Different black art books include more of one and less of another suggesting that certain authors specialized in a particular manner of performance and less in another, a fact which is overlooked in previous scholarship. In a study of structural and functional elements of the contents of these books, a short survey of previous scholarship can help to place the role of this study among others in the larger field of folk belief and folk magic.

Not all previous scholarship on folk magic will necessarily concern us here in a consideration of the black art book. Because this study will examine structural elements contained in these books, studies which examine the structures of metrical charms and their accompanying rites are of interest. The work of previous scholars in describing the structure of oral charms and accompanying rituals will hopefully suggest other methods that can better describe them. Efforts to publish collections of charms beginning already in the eighteenth century resulted in a set of assumptions about morphological classification that have continued to be used into the twentieth.

Research on black art books as a distinct genre began most seriously in the mid-twentieth century and two scholars, German Will-Erich Peuckert and Swede Carl-Martin Edsman, and both stand out in the field. Both have pointed to classical antecedents that have only recently been treated by classicists and medieval paleographers. A short recapitulation of these authors' work is useful in understanding the distribution of books like these as a phenomenon which extends throughout Europe.

Wise folk (Sw. *klokfolk*) and the charming tradition (Sw. *trolleri, lövjeri, svartkonst*, etc.) of different nationalities and ethnicities have more recently become a popular field of academic inquiry, with the flourishing of specialized academic publications, regularly scheduled conferences and academic discussion email lists on these topics. Discussion of more recent academic resources on the subjects of folk magic and belief will provide further background against which to place this study.

And finally, a consideration of the manner in which the raw data was collected and assembled will conclude this survey of resources and scholarship, and pave the way for a consideration of primary texts in the form of excerpts from folklore archives and the black art book manuscripts themselves.

Definitions: Charms, Spells, Rites and Recipes

THE BLACK ART books examined in this study contain a range of magical genres, including metrical or incantatory charms which figure in the vast majority at 32.9% of the total items, ritual instructions, recipes for ingestion and for external application, as well as directions for assembling diverse power objects in the creation of a talismanic aid. Historically, nomenclature in magical studies has been fluid. For example, in studies of the folkloric genre of oral or incantatory charms, there exists a recurrent problem with terminology because in common English usage, the semantic field "charm" is too broad. It can include metrical or orally-performed formulæ, the ritual acts that accompany these formulæ and even materials somehow set aside for a magical purpose such as the small objects charged with hidden significance found on charm bracelets or in religious shrines (e.g., Sp. *milágros*). All of these can be combined with verbal formulæ to produce ritual.

Jonathan Trevor Roper writes:

> A more concise definition might simply be that charms are the verbal element of vernacular magic practice. Regardless of the definition we choose, it is clear that charms form some of the most interesting elements of both oral and literate traditional culture. And yet they have encountered surprisingly little scholarly attention, and charming, the process in which charms are enacted, has attracted even less. This is surprising when we consider how, in recent years, other more dramatic but less typical aspects of magical practice have taken scholarly centre-stage.[19]

Scholarship has sought to clarify terminology, making formal distinctions between "incantation," "charm," "spell," "rite," etc. Thomas Sebeok and Louis H. Orzack[20] distinguished between the terms "spell" and "charm"—two terms that by their relatively high frequency in daily vocabulary already carry too many associations to be suggestive of the genres they are meant to define. Sebeok and Orzack assign the term "charm" to those texts with a binary structure: "when...then," or "as...so." The first half of this binary structure is the epic introduction or "historiola," and serves to illustrate the prototypical event by which the power of the utterance is derived. On the other hand, Sebeok and Orzak assign the term "spell" to those with a singular structure.

The best example of the "charm" found in this collection combines the epic introduction like that of the Second Merseburg Charm citing the mythical event which serves as the historiola with a subsequent exorcismal formula, sending pain or injury "into that lake where no one rows, into that wood where no one goes, under log and rock, to harm no one."[21] Charms make use of Frazer's Law of Similarity in which the verbal recall of the desired result in the initial epic introduction produces the desired result of the exorcism of the second half.[22] An example here is from manuscript KU3335 from Lakbäck, in Rogsta Parish, Hälsingland, with the historiola ("As Jesus Christ did...") appearing after the exorcismal formula:

> 13. att Stä Blod.
> Blod mot blod Hud mot hud, kött mot kött Sen mot sen, Ben mot ben och Blod mot blod. Statt du onda blod, statt du goda blod. här skall du stå och intet rinna du skall wara så sen till att rinna, lika så som Jesum Christum när han bar sitt kors i Örtagården till att springa. Statt du blod här skall du stå och der skall du Stanna så säkert som den själ som e Helwettt står och Stannar.

> [13. To stop bleeding.
> Blood to blood, skin to skin, flesh to flesh sinew to sinew, bone to bone and blood to blood. Stand still, you bad blood, Stand still you good blood, here you shall stand and not run. You shall be so reluctant to run just as Jesus Christ when he carried his cross in the Garden of Gethsemane was to run. Stand still you blood, here you shall stand, and there you shall stop, as surely as the soul stands and stays in Hell.]

"Spells," on the other hand, do not require the mythical set-up of a historiola, and are thus singular rather than bipartite in structure. The following Swedish poetic formula from *Cånster att bruka* from Härnösand's Museum of Cultural History is just such an example of a "spell." Note that there is no event after which the goal is patterned, but rather a list of "power words" or "power concepts" which lend the spell its power.

> 23.
> At ingen häst sllår dig af, så skrik desa ord: «Astulis Astula Cosso forottis.»

> 23.
> [So that no horse will throw you, then yell these words: "Astulis Astula Cosso forottis."]

In this study, both of these types of oral recitation will be referred to simply as incantatory charms. They are magically operative, usually formulaic, utterances. These verbal formulæ sometimes resort to religious symbolism, either appealing to the order implied by that symbolism, or deliberately inverting or otherwise perverting it, in order to establish magical potency. Satisfaction in the adherence to orthodox ecclesiastical forms, or the shock and fear invoked by their inversion or desecration, could have been a factor in a consideration of a charm's efficacy, as was the numinous power held by the performer.

Studies dealing with charms have dealt mostly with their literary (æsthetic, historical or comparative), theoretical (sociological, religious or linguistic), or formal (morphological, functional) aspects. In the general scholarship of European magic, most attention has been paid to the world of the uttered charm, the verbal artifact, the text, rather than material components, accompanying ritual,[23] or the altered states of consciousness that Eriksson has posited obtain generally in the realm of folk sorcery in his work *Blodstämmare och handpåläggare: Folklig läkekonst och magi i Tornedalen och Lappland* (*Those Who Stop Bleeding and Those Who Lay on Hands: The Folk Healing Art and Magic in the Torneå valley and Lappland*).[24] Eriksson, a journalist for Swedish National Radio, conducted penetrating interviews of which six are presented in his published work, where he sought to discern those aspects of magical performance that are typically undescribed, such as the state of mind of the practitioner while working, or the reasons for various accompanying details, such as gesture or Bible verses. Concentration on text to the exclusion of the context or performance of magic had previously removed the study of charms from a holistic examination. Altered states are difficult to quantify, or sometimes even to discern in performance, and therefore are difficult to describe in a proper treatment of charms. It is only in manuscripts such as black art books that accompanying ritual steps are regularly recorded together with the oral charm.

Theoretical and Morphological Classification

THEORIES OF HOW magic was seen to work were isolated by Codrington,[25] Tylor,[26] and Frazer.[27] Frazer initially formulated these as two basic laws. The Law of Similarity dictates that like produces like, so that by imitating the desired result, that result will be produced homeopathically. The Law of Contagion states that two things once in contact will continue to affect each other even after their separation. An example of magic employing both the Laws of Similarity and Contagion can be found in Nordic Museum's unnumbered manuscript from Gryts and Gåringe Village in Södermanland (MS22), item number nine, in which one causes diarrhea in the target by taking some of their feces (Contagion), placing them in a goat's horn and putting it into a running river. As the water rushes past, so will their bowel movements run (Similarity). An example of the Law of Contagion might be the following, taken from the manuscript *Cånster att bruka* from Härnösand's Museum of Cultural History:

1.

Om du går efter en, såsom rider på en vägh, och du villt, att hans häst skal blifua halt, för att han skal intthet rida undan dig, så tag en spik och si till, att du sir hästens föttspår, som han hafuer tramppatt på vägen; tag spiken och stik där utti, så hallttar hästen. Spiken skall vara af en likkista.

1.

[If you're following after someone who is riding on a road, and you want to have his horse become lame, so that he won't ride past you, then take a nail and take care to see the horse's footprint, where he has stepped on the road; take the nail and pierce it, then the horse will become lame. The nail should be from a coffin.]

Here, the horse-shoe print and the horse-shoe that made it remain linked, so that the manipulation of one affects the other. These analytical principles continued to be used by scholars into the last quarter of the twentieth century to discuss charms and magic.[28] Beginning with Mauss and Hubert in the early years of the twentieth century, a socio-linguistic description of magic led to both sociological and linguistic studies of magic.

Af Klintberg discusses factors in the composition of charms in a 1978 article "Magisk diktteknik: tre exempel" (The Technique of Magical Poetics: Three Examples).[29] He isolates three primary approaches to the analysis of charm texts. The first is the importance of rhyme, rhythm and assonance in its composition, such that even misremembered formulæ still exhibit these characteristics in their continued performance. Another is the use of naming in the composition of charms, and the use of circumlocutions, synonyms or playfully altered nominal forms (Sw. *noa-namn*) to invoke the power of that which is being conjured. An example he cites is the use of "stinger," "short point/tack" (Sw. *sting, nubb*) used in place of the more literal "teeth" (Sw *tänder*) in speaking of snake bite. A third technique is the tool of rhetorical persuasion, in which the charm composer puts him- or herself on the same social level as the offending force, and can use that social equivalence in a rhetorical argument meant to exorcise it.

Structural studies were made, and excellent summaries of them appear both in Irmgard Hampp (1961)[30] and in Bengt af Klintberg's popular edition of 1965.[31] Both Hampp and af Klintberg see the major categories of charms as exhortational formulæ (Sw. *manande formler*, G. *Befehle*), comparison or simile formulæ (Sw. *liknelser*, G. *Vergleichssprüchen*), epic formulæ (Sw. *episka formler*, G. *Begegnungstypen*) in which a mythic precedent is narrated by which the following charm has efficacy, usually including a meeting of some kind (hence Hampp's categorical label) and finally formulæ employing secret words, magical diagrams and sigils and alphabetic sequences or *ephesia grammata* (Sw. *lönnformler*, G. *geheimnisvollen Zeichen und Formeln*). Tambiah (1968) favored a classification of charms according to function in ritual, and notes that current trends in scholarship make "rite" and "incantation" oftentimes inseparable.[32]

Establishment of Age, Relation and Provenance

MANY OF THE more thorough treatments of the charm collections deal heavily with the relative age of the text under consideration, its relationship to other texts in order to establish provenance or an *ur*-form, or they repeat Frazer's discussion of the sympathetic and contagious principles of magic and how they relate to the text under consideration. Studies have dealt predominantly with the imagery found in the charms, as much to ascertain interconnections and relative age as to perform aesthetic analyses.[33] The general results of these inquiries have been that basic forms of some charms previously thought to have been imported from the learned traditions of Middle Eastern magic are seen to be reflexes of charms found all over the Indo-European area, also appearing in the temporally and spatially distant Sanskrit Atharva-Veda, making age and provenance much more difficult to determine. This also makes the oversimplified concern with provenance which occupied scholars of the late nineteenth century about whether an item was Christian/learned or Native/heathen, a less interesting issue for European charms. Still other studies resulted in recognizing continuous charm traditions in texts like the Second Merseburg Charm, such as Reidar Th. Christiansen's 1914 study.[34]

The development of Type-Indices[35] has resulted in a classification based on both formal and thematic similarity found among charms. The most recent efforts along specifically *these* lines is by Jonathan Roper of the University of Sheffield, who advocates a classification of charms using the categories developed by the Dane Ferdinand Ohrt in his articles on *Segen* written for the *Handwörterbuch des deutschen Aberglaubens* (HdA).[36] Throughout this monumental cooperative effort, Ohrt not only identified charms by their historiolic type (e.g., *Longinussegen, Jordansegen, Drei-frauensegen*, etc.), but developed a vocabulary to discuss the other aspects of charm performance such as ritual "formulas" by which he meant non-verbal components of charm performance.[37]

It remains, however, that in a consideration of type or structure, scholars are working with concepts that the wise ones may not have considered. This dissertation finds that the wise ones did not think about formal characteristics or functional purpose as an organizational principle in these books. Examination of the manuscripts illustrates that organizing principles were not foremost in the copyist's mind as they recorded charms or rites of interest to them. Most often items are numbered in manuscripts. This seems only to have indicated the sequence in which the item was encountered rather than a system of organization based on formal or functional characteristics. This is supported by the occasional duplication of a charm under two different numbers in the same manuscript.

Performance

FROM A CONSIDERATION of the Charm-as-Text, scholarship is shifting to encompass the entirety of the performance in considering generic definitions. Ronald Grambo calls this constituent part "ritual descriptions" (Nw. *Rituelle beskrivelser*). He notes that these descriptions cannot themselves be considered charms.

> Rituelle beskrivelser danner en kategori for seg. De kan ikke oppfattes som formler i egentlig forstand. Det er oppskrifter på hvorledes en skal foreta visse rituelle handlinger...Slike ritualer må utføres korrekt, ellers virker de ikke. Kløver er lykkebringende. Her er velkjente magiske komponenter som motsols, tretallet, venstresiden.[38]

> [Descriptions of ritual constitute a category in itself. They cannot be perceived as charms in their truest sense. They are formulas upon which one carries out certain ritual actions ... Such rituals must be carried out correctly, otherwise they will not be effective. Clover brings luck. Here are the well-known magical components such as counterclockwise, threes, the left (sinister) side.]

With Grambo, Halpern and Foley, and Evans-Pritchard,[39] the performance context in which charming occurs attained a position of greater prominence. All three worked to include considerations of additional performative components, and not with the oral text alone. It is no longer adequate to consider the text of a charm in isolation from its context, the identity of its user, and its social efficacy. In comparisons with shamanism, of both a Siberian and a South American type, the ritual state of mind, the ecstatic trance, is also considered a part of the context. Eliade's discussion of "Archaic Techniques of Ecstasy"[40] affected subsequent scholars such as Michael Harner in his description of the Jivaro medicine men,[41] and Jörgen Eriksson in his work with the Sámi shaman [Sámi *noaijde*].[42] As a result, magic is no longer understood only as text, but also as context.

Mauss and Hubert maintained that magic was "a traditional fact"—acts not repeated cannot be magical. Evans-Pritchard[43] corroborated this view, although his study showed that within the cultures he observed there was usually at least one aspect of a magical act that was conservative in its transmission. This allowed for some variation from one performance to the next while still maintaining traditionality. For instance, among the Azande, it was the material constituent of the magic which remained constant, while the accompanying oral charm was often composed extemporaneously. With the Trobriand Islanders on the other hand, the oral formula was the conservative factor and the material considerations changed with each new performance. Evans-Pritchard's discussion has much to contribute to a formal discussion of verbal magic or charms. The primary point on which these two discussions agree is that efficacy requires the performance of certain acts which are credited by the culture as being magical. The traditional nature of these acts, the fact that they are "handed-down," is one factor in defining an act as magical, and age in transmission adds to the status they hold as magical acts. The archival narratives presented in this study describing the age and size of the black art books illustrate the veneration of age in a magical worldview.

Charms are often accompanied by certain ritualistic actions or gestures (accompanying rite, Grambo's *rituelle beskrivelser*, Ohrt's *Ritusanzeige*)[44] or by a manipulation of various materials (talismans, amulets, or other materials such as herbs, etc., called *pharmakoi* in recent Classical studies). Both action and *pharmakon* must, for our purposes, be considered an integral part of the charm, as it is often upon these factors that the efficacy of the entire ritual unit [text+rite+*pharmakoi*] is seen to rest in the manuscripts. To this list might possibly be added Eriksson's "altered" psychological or psychic state of the practitioner, one subject addressed in his studies among Sámi *noajde*.[45] His work is notable for its often penetrating interviews with Sámi healers from Tornedalen in Swedish Lappland. From these interviews, Eriksson maintains that the presence of a type of altered state of consciousness on the part of the *noajde* can be inferred.

Charm Research in Scandinavia

ONE CONCERN THAT arose from the efforts to publish critical editions of larger national collections of charms was establishing some principle of organization, and most relied on classification according to either structure or function. Morphological classification was and still is central to the structural approach. The interrelationships suggested by the similarities of certain charms to each other led collectors and editors to an interest in the implications these might have in establishing the age or provenance of a text. It was assumed that the older the text, the more interesting it is.[46] Ascertaining age became equivalent to establishing an *ur*-form. Attempts were made to isolate formal aspects, labeling what were seen to be recurring patterns, looking for unity in what had previously been considered a widely disparate phenomenon. Formal characteristics were compared and common mythic themes or structural traits were identified. Tracing the migration of a formal or thematic characteristic in a charm through the centuries from country to country led to a consideration of its "type" and its "homeland," an aspect of study that was important for emerging nationalist movements across Europe.

The last three centuries have seen great amounts of data collected, especially in Northern European and Slavic countries. Much of this data is represented in collections that begin to appear in published form from the middle of the nineteenth century, though the material presented in them was already being gathered as early as the late seventeenth. The first single manuscript collection of charms in Scandinavia seems to have been J. J. Törner's *Samling af Widskeppelser* [Collection of Superstitions], completed near the end of his life, in 1787. It remained in manuscript form, first in the holdings of Linköpings gymnasiebibliotek (The Library of Linköping's High School). Afterwards, it was transferred to Linköpings stiftsbibliotek (The Library of Linköping's Archbishopric), where hand copies were made and found their ways into collections in Uppsala and elsewhere. Törner's manuscripts are remarkable in the amount of data collected about informants, dates and places and other contextual commentary at a time when such data was not an established part of the folklore gathering process. The entire collection remained in manuscript form until Wikman's 1946 published edition, though a portion of that collection was published in 1789 at Uppsala, according to Rääf. Törner's research as represented in his manuscript was used first by L. F. Rääf in his *Svenska skrock och signerier* (Swedish Superstitions and Incantations, 1863) as well as by Gunnar Olof Hyltén-Cavallius in his published collection *Wärend och wirdarne* (Wärend and its inhabitants, 1864).[47] Rääf's collection consisted mostly of charms, ritual performance, and other forms of folk magic in Sweden, while Hyltén-Cavallius' work was a more well-rounded ethnography which makes use of some of the previous work by Törner. The first collection consisting exclusively of charms in Norway was published in 1901 by A. Chr. Bang.[48] This was followed first in Denmark by Ferdinand Ohrt's substantial volumes,[49] and thereafter in Sweden by Emanuel Linderholm's exhaustive collection.[50] These were in turn followed in Sweden by the Wikman's publications of Törner and Rääf. Swedish speaking Finland saw a treatment of the charm in the larger context of folk belief regarding the etiology of illness in Valter Forsblom's exhaustive treatment of 1927.[51]

In the collections by Forsblom from Swedish Finland and by Linderholm in Sweden, context was of only marginal interest, with the primary text in isolation deemed of greater importance. Finally, in 1965 a popular collection of Swedish charm texts employing Linderholm, Rääf, and material from folklore archives, as well as black art books was edited by Bengt af Klintberg and published. Because of its popularity it was subsequently to see several reprints. While some of af Klintberg's collection were from previously published black art books, the majority were taken from previously edited collections such as Linderholm, Forsblom and Tillhagen.[52]

Collection and Publication of Data

Folklore Questionnaires

NOT ONLY WAS it important to collect, catalog and analyze charm texts, but also of interest was a more thorough understanding of the cultural matrix from which they sprang. This was done by means of a concerted gathering effort, facilitated in part by questionnaires distributed and collected by national archives. Dan Ben-Amos summarizes in saying that the quest for a national identity and pride has been inextricably intertwined with folklore studies. Sweden had begun this with the institutionalization of folklore studies as a part of research into literary antiquities. Even as early as 1630, Gustavus Adolphus proclaimed the establishment of the Council on Antiquities (Sw. *Kungliga Gustav Adolfs Akademien*) and gave it its scope of activities. Military, nationalistic, economic and land interests were thought to be stimulated with greater interest in the literary legacy of ancient Scandinavia.[53]

Carl Wilhelm von Sydow writes in 1934 in the English journal Folklore that Mannhardt (1831–1880) "was the first to realize the importance of a systematic collection of folk tradition parish by parish, village by village, and he was the first to start magnificent collection work by sending out thousands of copies of printed questionnaires in Germany, Scandinavia and other countries."[54] However, we already see the phenomenon of folklore questionnaires with Jacob Grimm's Viennese circular from 1815, distributed to 400 individuals and receiving an astounding 360 responses.[55] Dundes speculates that Grimm first became acquainted with the idea of a distributed questionnaire when living in Paris in 1805, when the Academie Celtique was founded with the purpose of finding Celtic "survivals" [sic] in French folklore.[56] Hyltén-Cavallius's work *Wärend och wirdarne* also included some items collated from responses to questionnaires from the Romantic period to the middle nineteenth century, and Mannhardt's work makes use of the data subsequently assembled in Hyltén-Cavallius,[57] as well as data from other collectors from Scandinavia.

While the study of folklore was officially recognized as an area of Swedish academic inquiry with C. W. von Sydow's assumption of a newly created Chair in Folklore at Lund University in 1912, it had been a legitimate area of research and data gathering by volunteer ethnologists, school teachers and parish ministers for more than two hundred years. Charms, just one genre of folk narrative, were included in this effort according to Wikman at least as early as Törner in the years between 1690 and 1787.[58] Systematic organization and publication of the data collected with these first questionnaires began in Sweden with the establishment of the Nordic Museum (Sw. *Nordiska muséet*) and its folklore archive (Sw. *Folkminnesarkivet*) in 1873. Previously, folklore had been published occasionally, by interested authors and scholars.[59]

Regionally located national folklore archives were primarily responsible for creating, distributing and subsequently collecting the questionnaires and the data collected with them.[60] In addition to these larger national collecting efforts, local provincial museums and archives sent out their own shorter questionnaires. The data collected in these local efforts were often copied to one of the larger regional archives.[61]

Important Sources about Black Books: Questionnaire M100

WHAT WE KNOW of the wise ones and beliefs about them, for the most part, is extrapolated from the answers to questionnaires (Sw. *frågelistor*) that were distributed to volunteer ethnologists, who used these to elicit information about the wise ones and their books. To collect the charms that were ultimately published in larger collections, various archives and museums in Sweden developed these questionnaires to be used by collectors as a tool to elicit types of data that would be subsequently categorized for later retrieval. This was to be both an advantage and a disadvantage—an advantage in that a uniform format and phraseology was used to elicit data on discrete topics, but a disadvantage in that the wording of these questionnaires were often phrased as leading questions which provided examples of what were seen as common folk custom rather than asking open-ended questions to be answered with novel data. As has been discussed in Tangherlini,[62] not only are the collector's attitudes and speech patterns relevant in a consideration of elicited data, but the environment and activities around which collection occurs are too. By providing examples as these questionnaires did, we are left to question the extent to which those examples contaminated the type or amount of data collected for each topic. The questionnaire that was most frequently referred to in excerpts about black art books and folk magic is "Uppsala Archive for National Dialects Questionnaire M100: ABOUT WISE ONES (MAGICIANS AND WISE MEN)" (Sw. *Uppsala Landsmålsarkivets frågelista M100: OM KLOKA (TROLLKUNNIGA OCH VISMÄN)*) composed by Åke Campbell in 1935, and for which the first answers arrived in January of 1936.[63] While answers were in response to specific questionnaires, they were subsequently cataloged according to subject matter. Therefore, answers to several questionnaires might be cataloged together under the rubric of Wise Ones.

While a thorough catalog of all the pertinent questionnaires would be redundant in a study such as this, of particular import can be mentioned: M5: About Stealing Milk from Others' Cows; M7: Left Hand and Counterclockwise; M11: Evil Eye, Tongue and Disposition; M90: Magical Gestures, Signs, Numbers and Colors; M99: Illnesses of Domestic Animals; M101: Cupping and Bleeding; M103: Priests, Church-bell Ringers and other Church Employees; and M100: About Wise Ones (sorcerers and wizards).[64]

As Campbell states in the introduction to M100, other questionnaires also concerned the lore of the Wise Ones and dealt with smaller areas of inquiry. Questionnaire M100 is quite extensive, consisting of thirty lengthy groups of questions. Rather than reproduce the questionnaire in its entirety, I provide its introduction here:

> Denna frågelista avser de traditioner, som röra de kloka gubbar och gummor, som i äldre tid men på många håll ännu i våra dagar gjort sig kända som särskilt kunniga i att bota sjukdomar hos folk och fä (framförallt genom övernaturliga medel). Ofta ha de även rykte för att vara kunniga i spådom och andra hemliga konster, med förmåga att se i det fördolda, umgås med övernaturliga väsen etc. Märk att följande frågelistor beröra områden, som sammanhänga med de kloka och deras konster: M5: Frågor om tjuvmjölkning av andras kor; M7: Vänster hand och motsols; M11: Ont öga, ond tunga, hågsa; M90: Magiska gester, tecken, tal och färger; M99: Husdjurssjukdomar; M101: Koppning och åderlåtning.
>
> I denna frågelista avses framförallt skildringen av den klokes person, hans förmåga och egenheter, hans levnadsförhållanden o. dyl. enligt folkföreställningen. Vid skildringen härav kan det vara lämpligt att i ett sammanhang skildra allt vad man känner om en och samma kloka person i synnerhet om den kloke varit mycket namnkunnig, så att en rikare tradition kommit att utvecklas.
>
> [This questionnaire concerns those traditions, which touch upon wise men and women, who were famous as especially knowledgeable in healing people and animals (especially through supernatural means) in former times, and in many places even in our times. They often have the reputation of being knowledgeable about fortune-telling and other secret arts, with the ability to see into hidden matters, consort with supernatural beings, etc. Notice that the following questionnaires concern areas that are connected to the wise ones and their arts: M5: Questions about magically stealing the milk from others' cows; M7: Left hand and counterclockwise; M11: Evil eye, evil tongue, breath; M90: Magical gestures, signs, counting and colors; M99: Illnesses of house animals; M101: Cupping and Bleeding.
>
> This questionnaire concerns primarily the depiction of the wise one's person, his abilities and specialties, his living conditions and such, according to folk perceptions. At the descriptions of these, it can be useful to describe in one context everything that one knows about one and the same

wise person, especially if the wise one has been very renowned, so that a richer tradition has been developed.]

Questions deal with the origins of the wise one's power, typical professional trades with which the wise were involved, and with vocabulary used to indicate the person or the activity of the wise one. Questions concerning links with the diabolical or the divine presuppose the more metaphysical view of the wise ones' activities. They included enquiries about attitudes of the common folk towards the wise ones, about their appearance or modes of dress, living circumstances, and magical paraphernalia in which power was thought to reside. There were questions about the primary specialty of a wise one, whether prophecy, healing, cursing or protection. The questionnaires were commonly addressed to non-practitioners, and assumed that the informants were themselves not fluent in magical operations. Questions dealing with the circumstances surrounding, and manner of, reception of clients or patients, accompanying songs or music, portable paraphernalia such as knives or spirit boxes, spirit travels, "witch wars,"[65] recipes or prescriptions, and the geographical area from which he drew his clientele are all present, and seem to include some of the concerns from the previous questionnaires mentioned in Campbell's introduction.

The choice and phrasing of the questions largely shaped the informants' answers, and the extensive list of questions probably left little time or space for potential extemporaneous reminiscences by the informant, The questions seem ideally suited to the Swedish material, and indicate a comfortable familiarity with that tradition specifically. This was to be both helpful and problematical—if the questions seem aimed to elicit expected results, how can new data be gathered?

As an example of the data recorded about the questionnaires and their submissions, notations in the Uppsala archive are illustrative. According to a notation in the archive in Uppsala's SOFI, a total of 62 answers to questionnaire M100 were received. Out of these, there were few references to *svartkonstböcker*, and some specific statements that nothing was remembered about the wise ones' possession of a *svartkonstbok*. Out of those 62, 26 were discovered to be specifically in answer to the questionnaire, and there were 42 notations about *svartkonstböcker* in SOFI, including answers to M1, M16, M90 and M102, including some duplications. Clearly, data about black art books were gathered from responses to more than one Questionnaire.

Black Art Book Research

Most studies neglect a more thorough treatment of the provenance of these charms and rites, giving little more than a mention to the fact that many of them are recorded in "black art books." Oral elicitation in interviews or in archaic trial transcripts has only recently found popularity (Nildin-Wall & Wall, 1996; Wall, 1989; af Klintberg, 1980).[66] Studies which deal with the genre are few, but much information may be extrapolated from recent studies of classical charm texts such as the Greek Magical Papyri and the lead tablets mentioned in John G. Gager's *Curse Tablets and Binding Spells from the Ancient World*.[67] These recent studies discuss the textual tradition of magic, from collections of spells recorded on papyrus from the First Century BCE and into the Common Era. While these recent studies do not set out to prove a continuous tradition of magical manuscripts from this early period to the twentieth century, there is ample literature to make studies like this possible.

Carl-Martin Edsman, Professor of History of Religions at Uppsala University already reintroduced the study of charms, charming and folk grimoires in light of more recent scholarship in 1946.[68] He clarified a sociological understanding of magic: that magic will be found in a culture for as long as its population finds it meaningful, and that reinterpretation rather than preservation of an archaic understanding will often be necessary to maintain its practice, thus avoiding the concept of "pagan survivals" which had been problematic in previous scholarship.

Will-Erich Peuckert's study[69] of the migration of manuscripts and sometimes the lore they contained was the first major study of the genre of the type of book that would become known in Sweden as the black art book. Peuckert's study begins with a story about a neighbor boy, and a book on his shelf, "*ein wunderliches altersgraues Büchlein 'Albertus Magnus bewährte und approbirte sympathetische und natürliche egyptische Geheimnisse*'" [a curious little book, grey with age "Albertus Magnus's Tried and Tested Sympathetic and Natural Egyptian Secrets"] printed in Braband. In this article, Peuckert sets out to delineate the route by which the lore of this volume, the *Egyptische Geheimnisse*, found its way throughout Europe, and was even found in oral tradition in Scandinavia.

> Hat das Schwarzkünstler-Buch von uns gelernt, oder sind unsere Rezepte dieser wunderlichen Zauberschrift entsprungen? Das heißt, aus der naiven in die gelehrte Sprache übersetzt: sind die 'Egyptischen Geheimnisse' eine Sammlung alter volksgebundener Überlieferungen, oder sind sie als ehe-

mals oberschichtiges Gut "hinabgesunken"? Das aber legt die Frage nach dem Buche selbst nahe.⁷⁰

[Has the Black Magician's book learned from us, or do our recipes and prescriptions originate with these peculiar magical writings? That is, translated from a naïve to a more educated language: are the "Egyptian Secrets" a collection of older traditions from the folk, or are they a previously upper class treasure that has sunk down? This is the real issue when considering these books.]

It is clear that he argues the "gesunkenes Kulturgut" theory of folklore—that material from the learned and literate tradition found its way in a somewhat degenerated form among the lower classes, but that can be reconstructed by a comparative study of texts and oral tradition.

He also asks how we classify this genre.[71] To answer this, he cites Otto Brunner,[72] who identifies two main genres that went into the making of what he calls *"Hausväterlitteratur"*—the Economic in which the economy of the household is discussed and in which its order is described; and the Agrarian in which issues of crops, animal husbandry and matters of subsistence upon the land. Together, the Agrarian and the Economic combine to create a new genre of literature for the heads of households, or *Hausväterlitteratur*. Brunner sees the first and best prototype in Johannes Coler's *Œconomia ruralis et domestica* (1593/1603) which was found in Swedish translation as early as 1663. In it, not only was technical agrarian advice given, but also cooking recipes and veterinary medical advice. And the religious duties of the *pater familias* were strongly emphasized as well. These interests are perpetuated in the manuscripts examined here, which contain magic for healing ailing livestock or encouraging a good harvest.[73]

Peuckert then introduces a third type or genre, co-eval with the *Hausväterlitteratur*, and uses as an example Giovanni Baptista Porta's *Magia Naturalis*, which, in a printed edition of 1715 purports to be a "*Hauß- Kunst- und Wunder-Buch*." It explores the magic of nature, to be found in the doctrine of signatures in which the shape of an herb is suggestive of the organ it successfully treats. Peuckert enumerates a number of similarly titled works, all of which make use of "art- and wonder-" in their title, and showing a new emerging kind of literature that explores a magic that is not infernal, but natural, and thus within the province of the faithful. At first, these volumes consisted of needful things in the household, but gradually grew to include works that we will eventually see populating the black art books in northern Europe generally—To see if a woman is fertile or not; to see if a woman is a virgin; to assure that a woman will not have children by another man, etc. All of these still suggest that the *pater familias* must have sovereign rule over his household, and all who are in it.

The form of the magical text borrowed greatly from this *Hausväterlitteratur*, even including similar phraseology, as Peuckert illustrates with an item that begins with the same phrase, but when the latter provides an herbal cure, the former advises the use of a magical rite, "speak these words as you walk over the sore with the left foot: 'Acte Bande, zu brante bede.' +++3mal." ("Look out bindings, I pray you to burn." 3 times making the sign of the cross.)

In comparing a number of volumes of this type, he discerns connections, and concludes by an examination of manuscript-specific misspellings that some of the texts are the result of a collation of handwritten manuscripts. Once he has described the genre of the magical literature, he then traces its migration throughout Europe and into Scandinavia between the seventeenth and nineteenth centuries. He places texts of the Danish *Præst-Jenses Cyprianus* and the German *Egyptischen Geheimnisse* side by side and discerns in this way the similarities of wording between the two, and that one was a translation of the other.

His ultimate conclusion was that oral Swedish lore of the type found in the Sixth and Seventh Books of Moses (Sw. *Sjätte och sjunde Moseböcker*) participated in a pan-European culture of folk magic. Both of these cases suggested to him that the fact that texts such as Porta's *Magia Naturalis* or the German *Egyptischen Geheimnisse* found their way into geographically isolated areas indicates that Europe participated in a single magical world, one in which very similar texts could travel from Italy and France into Germany and Scandinavia and still make sense culturally and magically.

Edsman[74] continued in 1959 the preliminary work that Peuckert had begun in 1954 when he explored the literary (printed) sources for published Swedish literature of this type, which was to inform the contents of the black books. He delved more deeply into the Swedish tradition, and made distinctions where Peuckert had made none. He was interested in both the folk magical tradition as well as the learnèd magical tradition represented by printed grimoires. In the first of these two often-cited articles, he identifies published models for the hand-written black art books; the first gives a definition of the genre "Black art- or here more accurately a household-book, containing cures and recipes of both magical and non-magical types." In this article he limits his discussion to printed books available for purchase at bookshops, and neglects the handwritten corpus. This is due in part to the archival excerpts he uses to define the black art book—all of them discuss the book as being printed, and available for purchase. He includes no excerpt mentioning a book handwritten in blood, or other common motifs that are to be found in archives.

These books of Natural Magic however held not only domestic tips for the challenged farmer. For example, *Dr Johann Faustens Miracul- Kunst- und Wunder-Buch, oder di schwarze Rabe, auch der Dreifache Höllen Zwang genannt* [*Doctor Johannes Faust's Miracle and Magic Book, or The Black Raven, also called*

The Threefold Coercion of Hell]⁷⁵ contains a great deal of natural magic found in the *Hausväterlitteratur*, and yet this volume is a popular grimoire, a text instructing its reader in the art of Black Magic, or the conjuration of infernal spirits. As we will see below, at least two Swedish books borrow material from this book, at greater or lesser remove from the German original. Edsman calls this genre *Höllen Zwange Litterature*, or Literature of Infernal Conjurations, rather than *Hausväterlitteratur*.

Edsman's second work from 1962 provides a thorough treatment of the Type *The Sixth and Seventh Books of Moses* (Sw. *Sjätte och sjunde Moseböcker*), a representative of the household grimoire tradition found throughout Europe.⁷⁶ As with the previous article, Edsman deals exclusively with the published tradition of house-cure books, and while he mentions briefly that the Devil was necessary to effectively read the formulas in the books, he examines only possible printed proto-types and not the handwritten manuscripts themselves.

Carl-Herman Tillhagen, in *Folklig läkekonst*,⁷⁷ devotes little space to the black art book. He generalizes about beliefs about the black art book by using archival materials, and does not reproduce narratives about them for a greater context, nor does he provide excerpts from them. In short, Tillhagen treats the black art book as just one of a number of assorted paraphernalia that *all* wise ones owned.

More recently, Bengt af Klintberg addresses the black art book in a section of his Introduction to the oft-reprinted *Svenska trollformler* [*Swedish Magical Charms*].⁷⁸ Af Klintberg takes illiteracy as his point of departure, and the extreme respect it created in the illiterate toward the written word. He distinguishes between the handwritten "folk black art book" (Sw. *Folkliga svartkonstbok*) and the "published sources" (Sw. *Tryckta källor*) that, as Edsman claimed, gave rise to them. The rest of the section synthesizes the excerpts from archives, giving common traits of the black art book, just as we will attempt anew in Chapter Three using complete archival excerpts collected in context in the field.

Bodil Nildin-Wall devotes a chapter to the black art book in Nildin-Wall & Wall, *Det ropades i skymningen* [There Was a Yell at Twilight].⁷⁹ She begins her discussion with a preliminary definition, a definition in which she divides the genre into two main groups. There is the black art book (Sw. *svartkonstbok*) or book of sorcery (Sw. *trolldomsbok*), which is the handwritten collection of spells and advice with prayers and conjurations, with magical signs and combinations of letters, and with the help of which the owner is believed to be able to control supernatural powers and influence them according to his will. There is also the *Cyprianus*, also called the Book of Dr. Faustus (Sw. *Dr Fausts bok*) or Sixth and Seventh Books of Moses (Sw. *Sjätte och Sjunde Mosebok*), books which are attributed to well-known wizards, and the contents of which are aimed at establishing contact with powers or evil spirits, which the owner is able to force to do his will through the conjurations they contain. Books of this second sort, writes Nildin-Wall, contain among other things traces of older, pagan religions as well as Christian doctrine and ecclesiastical ritual, apocryphal and scientific works. Also included in these printed books are traces of folk belief. It is clear that the black art books that will be examined here contain both streams. The motivations or predilections of the owner/compiler in their collecting of spells, charms, rituals and recipes may also help to define the parameters of the genre.

Recent Trends

RECENTLY, there has been a flurry of interest in magic, charms and charming as indicated by publications, conferences, and email discussion lists. International conferences on charms, charmers and charming have been held, the first conference: "Charms and Charming in Northern Europe" held at the Warburg Institute, London, January 2003, and the second held recently in Prague, Czech Republic. One electronic news and discussion list administered from the UK is called "ACADEMIC MAGIC" which focuses on issues in folklore, ethnology, magical texts and practice, both ancient and modern.[80] Its membership spans the academic spectrum, from respected scholars at universities and colleges to students of all levels, as well as educated practitioners of magical ritual. It serves as a forum to announce Calls for Papers, advertise vacant academic positions and upcoming academic conferences, and as a forum where the merely curious can ask non-academic questions with impunity. *Societas Magica*, a group of scholars founded by Richard Kieckhefer at the University of Iowa, is a group of published or academically affiliated scholars with special interests in the field of magical studies, western magical traditions, and magical texts. It has particularly strong ties to the Pennsylvania State University Press, from which the series *Magic in History* is published. This is a series in which a large body of scholars who have specialized in a national or ethnic tradition, as an international community assembles to compare, contrast and discuss magic, ritual, folk belief and a host of related topics. *Societas Magica* also publishes the periodical *Magic, Ritual and Witchcraft*.[81] Its focus is more purely historical, with a strong emphasis on archaic magical texts, but with Ryan's work *The Bathhouse at Midnight: Magic in Russia* (1999),[82] ethnographic description is also represented.

There has been an increase in individuals who have worked with charms and charming, even if not the notebooks used to record them. International conferences have produced collections of papers, one of which, *Charms and Charming in Europe*,[83] is edited by Jonathan Roper of the University of Sheffield. This volume contains articles that deal with transmission of charms, the self-consciousness of the charmer, typologizing charms and studies of earlier folklorists and their methodologies in collection and analysis. For the English material, Owen Davies at the University of Hertfordshire has contributed heavily regarding both the cunning folk in England and folk grimoires found all over Europe.[84] His primary focus has been to present historiographies, in the first case of the phenomenon of cunning folk, the English term often used to translate the Swedish *klokfolk*. In his focus on legislation, he has discerned that many cunning men and women were unscrupulous, and sought to make easy money in a profession that was at the time difficult to identify or prosecute. In the second case, he assembles recent scholarship about western magical texts, and provides a historical-geographical account of their dissemination as well as the dissemination of ideas about them. Kathleen Stokker, also known for her studies of the black book minister in Norwegian legends, has recently published a more encompassing study called *Remedies and Rituals*.[85] This work focuses primarily on Norwegian and Norwegian-American material about folk healing, and briefly mentions the Norwegian *Cyprianus*, as well as the black book minister, a typical owner of black art books in Norwegian legends.

As interest in charms, charming and folk magic and belief grows, there will doubtless be an ever increasing number of new studies devoted to the topics. The present study makes traditional narratives and entire texts of black art books available in English translation to an international academic audience. Analysis of their contents shows that often, folk belief *about* the black art book was not consonant with the books themselves. It also shows that organizing principles of the books have often been misrepresented in earlier scholarly editions of them, which has led to typologies that do not represent the tradition itself. It provides a healthy corrective to an overemphasis on the metrical or oral charm, in relating rites, recipes and magical figures, letters and drawings which occur in the black art books and which can be used to see the oral charm as one area of specialization of the magical practitioner. Personal talents and traditional specialties also played a role in the selection of material for inclusion in these books. Finally, we are able to see from the texts themselves just what criteria the wise one used to include among a book's contents, including the functions that interested them the most, and the forms in which they were most proficient. We, in short, catch a glimpse of the minds that produced these books, and employed their contents for public service and often remuneration, and for good or ill.

NOTES

1 For examples of the use of kvaksalveri in the Danish material, see Birgitte Rørbye, *Kloge folk og skidtfolk: kvaksalveriets epoke i Danmark* (København: Politikens Forlag, 1976). For additional remarks concerning wise folk and the social and legal ramifications of their medical practices, see also Birgitte Rørbye, "Den illegale sygdomsbehandling som folkloristisk problem: Bidrag til en socio-kulturel oversigt for Danmark," in *Fataburen: Nordiska museets och Skansens årsbok* (1976), 203–20.

2 Owen Davies (2003) discusses in these terms the change in English attitudes brought with the Witchchraft Act of 1736 toward the practice of magical intervention such as that exercised by cunning folk.

3 James Haskins, *Voodoo & Hoodoo: The Craft as Revealed by Traditional Practitioners* (London: Scarborough House, 1990), 29; Yvonne P. Chireau, *Black Magic: Religion and the African American Conjuring Tradition* (Berkeley: University of California Press, 2003), 149; Favret-Saada, Jeanne, *Deadly Words: Witchcraft in the Bocage*, trans. Catherine Cullen, (Cambridge: Cambridge UP, 1980); Jörgen I. Eriksson, *Blodstämmare och handpåläggare: Folklig läkekonst och magi i Tornedalen och Lappland* (Stockholm: Gimle förlag, 1992). All of these works describe modern magical practice, and in Favret-Saada the author is also a participant observer. Each examines the needs that are satisfied by continued folk magical practices.

4 Anonymous, ed., *Svartkonstbok, [aka Fader Abrahams Svartkonstbok]* (Stockholm: E. Svenssons boktryckeri, 1877); P. G. Wistrand, ed., "En småländsk svartkonstbok," *Fataburen* (1906): 239–44; Olof Christoffersson, "Supriania, Fru Alstads Socken, Skytts Härad," *Folkminnen och Folktankar* (1915); Ossian Lindskoug, ed., *Lappmannen Jon Johanssons Signerier och Besvärjelser: Svartkonst från Lappland* (Malmö: Förlag Maiander, 1917); J. A Sandblom, ed., *Petter Johan Johannesson, 1841, varuti jag skrifver varjehanda* (Malmö: Förlag Maiander, 1917); Paul Heurgren, ed., *Salomoniska Magiska Konster: Utdrag ur en Westboprests Svartkonstböcker* (NL: G. Wendelholm förlag, 1986), which is a facsimile reprint of the original 1918 edition; Pehr Johnsson, ed., "En skånsk klok och hans svartkonstbok," *RIG: föreningens för svensk kulturhistoria tidskrift* 4 (1918): 208–12; Gottfrid Kallstenius, "En svartkonstbok," *Arkiv för norrländsk hembygdsforskning Härnösand: Härnösands-Postens Tryckeri Aktiebolag* 1&2 (1918); Jöran Sahlgren, "C. O. Svahns svartkonstbok," *Folkminnen och folktankar* 5 (1918): 169–205; Herman Geijer, "Troll-Marksens Svartkonstbok," *Fornvårdaren* (1923–24), I: 1–2, 59–69; N. Sjödahl, ed. "Jugas Olof Jonssons svartkonstbok med kommentarer," *Meddelanden från Dalarnes Forminnesförening* 9 (1924): 35–57; K. Robert, V. Wikman, ed., "Törners 'Svartkonstbok,'" in *Nordiskt Folkminne: Studier tillägnade C. W. von Sydow, 12/21/1928* (Stockholm: C. E. Fritzes Hovbokhan-

del 1928), 247–55; William Lengertz, ed., *En svartkonstbok från Kristianstads län: En nyfunnen handskrift i Perstorp, med en översikt over Naturläkare, kloka och undergörare i Skåne* (Malmö och Lund: Förlag Lengertz, 1937); K. Rob. V. Wikman, ed., *Johan J. Törners Samling af Widskeppelser*, Skrifter utgivna af Kungliga Gustav Adolfs Akademien 15, (Uppsala: Almqvist & Wiksells boktryckeri, 1946); Sven B. Ek, "Tre svartkonstböcker," Eslövs museums skriftserie 2, (Eslöv: Eslövs Nya Boktryckeri, 1964), 7–37; Lars Lundberg, ed. "En svartkonstbok," *Göingebladet* (Lund: Grahns tryckeri, 1989): 1:11–13; 2:28–31; 3:20–23.

5 Göteborg's VFF (West Swedish Folklore Society), IFFG (Institute for Folklore at Göteborg's university); LUF (Lund University's Folklore Society); and SOFI (Swedish Institute for Language and Folklore), ULMA (Uppsala Dialect Archive).

6 In the following, "grimoire" is a term widely accepted in the field for compendia of magical texts which provide instructions in the performance of magical ritual. For a very recent example of this English usage, see Owen Davies, *Grimoires: A History of Magic Books* (Oxford: Oxford UP, 2009), 1.

7 Christopher A. Faraone and Dirk Obbink, eds., *Magika Hiera: Ancient Greek Magic and Religion* (Oxford: Oxford UP, 1991); Hans Dieter Betz, ed., *The Greek Magical Papyri in Translation including the Demotic Spells. Volume One: Texts* (Chicago: Chicago UP, 1986).

8 Carl-Martin Edsman, "Svartkonstböcker i sägen och historia," *Saga och sed* (1959): 160–68.

9 *"Jag har anledning beklaga, att jag sällan ingående förhört mina gamla sagesmän angående deras förfäder, föräldrar, hem, uppväxtår, ekonomiska förhållanden, läsning och de övriga källor, ur vilka de hämtat sina traditioner. Ofta har de dock i sina berättelser nämnt, av vem de hört berättas det eller det i fråga om sägen, tro och sed..."* "I have reason to apologize that I seldom interviewed my old informants penetratingly regarding their predecessors, parents, home, the years in which they grew up, economic situations, education, and the other sources, from which they had received their traditions. Often, however, they name in their own narratives the person they heard tell this or that in regard to a tale, belief or custom." Carl-Martin Bergstrand, ed., *Gammalt från Kind: folkminnen från Kinds härad i Västergötland, Del III* (Göteborg: Akademiförlaget, 1961), 5.

10 See for example MS NM onumrerat, MS25, "Att bota en bössa som är skämd" [To fix a rifle that's hexed] from Åkers härad in Södermanland.

11 Bengt af Klintberg, *Svenska Trollformler* (Stockholm: Wahlström & Widstrand, 1965); Edsman, "Svartkonstböcker i sägen och historia"; Carl-Martin Edsman, "Sjätte och sjunde Mosebok," *Saga och sed* (1962): 63–102; and Will-Erich Peuckert "Die Ägyptischen Geheimnisse," *Arv* 10 (1954): 40–96.

12 Sir James George Frazer, *The Golden Bough: A Study in Magic and Religion*, 1 Vol., Abr. Ed., (New York: Macmillan, 1922).

13 Emanuel Linderholm, "Signelser och besvärjelser från medeltid och nytid," *Svenska landsmål och svenskt folkliv* 41 (1927, -29, -39): 1–478; George B. Vetter, "Words and Word Magic. The Psychology of Prayer and Profanity," *Magic and Religion: Their Psychological Nature, Origin and Function* (New York: Philosophical Library, 1958), 175–88.

14 Mircea Eliade, *Shamanism: Archaic Techniques of Ecstasy*, Bollingen Series LXXVI, trans. Willard Trask, (Princeton, NJ: Princeton UP, 1964).

15 "First of all, the ethnographic material does not support the 'biological' basis of the 'shamanic illness,'…It is more accurate to seek these factors in the particularities of the early forms of human culture." V. N. Basilov, "Chosen by the Spirits" in Marjorie Mandelstam Balzer, ed., *Shamanism: Soviet Studies of Traditional Religion in Siberia and Central Asia* (Armonk, NY: M. E. Sharpe, 1990). The Russian text *Izbranniki dukhov* (Moscow: Politizdat, 1984).

16 J. Neusner, E. S. Frerichs, and Paul V. McC. Flesher, eds., *Religion, Science and Magic: In Concert and in Conflict* (New York: Oxford UP, 1989).

17 Ryan, *The Bathhouse at Midnight*.

18 Willem de Blécourt, "The Witch, Her Victim, The Unwitcher and the Researcher: The Continued Existence of Traditional Witchcraft," in Bengt Ankarloo and Stuart Clark, eds., *Witchcraft and Magic in Europe: The Twentieth Century* (Philadelphia: The University of Pennsylvania Press, 1999), 141–219; Rørbye, "Den illegale sygdomsbehandling som folkloristisk problem."

19 Jonathan Roper, ed., *Charms and Charming in Europe* (New York: Palgrave MacMillan, 2004), 1.

20 Thomas Sebeok and Louis H. Orzack, "The Structure and Content of Cheremis Charms (Part 2)," *Anthropos: Internationale Zeitschrift für Völker- und Sprachenkunde* 48 (1953): 760–72.

21 "I den sjö där ingen ror, i den skog där ingen bor, under stockar och sten, ingen människa till men." This formula is found in this study in MSS 9:II,13; 11:15; 25:72; 31:118; 32:3; and 35:96.

22 In this case, the Second Merseburg Charm provides the pattern for the type, and is found in a number of manuscripts in this study. Two examples are in MS 5:13 and MS 9:For injuries or snakebite, I. Breaks, Sprains and Sprained Legs, 1. The historiola narrates a mythical moment when a supernatural being (Woden or Christ) heals a sprain in the horse upon which he rides. Then, in that same manner and by imitating that mythical precedent, the healer does likewise.

23 With the exception of Ralph Merrifield's excellent illustrated work, *The Archæology of Ritual and Magic* (New York: New Amsterdam Books, 1987).

24 Eriksson, *Blodstämmare och handpåläggare*.

25 R. H. Codrington, *The Melanesians* (Oxford: The Clarendon Press, 1891). Codrington was to formulate a "dynamistic" model which examined the

concept of mana, an impersonal but malleable force, in Micronesia.
26 Edward Tylor, *Primitive Culture* (New York: Appleton, 1871). Tylor posited that magic's potency could be found in the idea that all things had an indwelling conscious spirit with which one might rhetorically persuade and influence to one's advantage. This was eventually to be called the "animistic" model of magic.
27 Frazer, *The Golden Bough*. Frazer was heavily influenced by and made extensive use of Mannhardt's work in his theorizing. Mannhardt in turn made extensive use of the folklore gathering efforts in the Scandinavian countries during the late nineteenth century for his work. W. Mannhardt, *Antike Wald- und Feltkulte*, 2nd ed. by W. Heuschkel. Vol. 1: *Der Baumkultus der Germanen und ihrer Nachbarstämme: Mythologische Untersuchung* (1875; repr. Berlin: Borntræger, 1904).
28 e.g., af Klintberg, *Svenska Trollformler*, 126, n. 62.
29 Bengt af Klintberg, "Magisk diktteknik: tre exempel," in *Harens klagan: Studier i gammal och ny folklore* (Stockholm: P. A. Norstedt & söners förlag, 1978–82), 7–21.
30 Irmgard Hampp, *Beschwörung—Segen—Gebet: Untersuchungen zum Zauberspruch aus dem Bereich der Volksheilkunde*, Veröffenlichungen des Staatlichen Amtes für Denkmalpflege Stuttgart, Reihe C: Volkskunde, bd. 1. (Stuttgart: Silberburg-verlag, 1961).
31 af Klintberg, *Svenska trollformler*.
32 S. J. Tambiah, "The Magical Power of Words," *Man* 3 (1968): 171–208.
33 This is the primary emphasis in the Russian studies, and bibliographies can be found in: Yuriy M. Sokolov, *Russian Folklore*, trans. Catherine Ruth Smith, [Original: *Ruskii fol'klor*, 1938] (Detroit: Folklore Associates, 1971); A. M. Astakhova, "The Poetical Image and Elements of Philosophy in Russian Exorcisms," in *VII Mezhdunarodnyi kongress antropologicheskix i ètnograficheskix nauk*, Moskva, 3–10 avgusta, 1964. VII Congres International des Sciences Anthropologiques et Ethnologiques, Moscou, 3 aout—10 auot 1964, 6 (1969): 266–72; and Harold L. Klagstad, Jr., "Great Russian Charm Structure," *Indiana University Slavic and East European Series* 13 (1958): 135–44. An interesting study of symbolic logic in 2 Cheremis charms is in the first half of Thomas Sebeok's two part study: "The Structure and Content of Cheremis Charms, Part I," *Anthropos: Internationale Zeitschrift für Völker- und Sprachenkunde* 48 (1953): 369–88.
34 Reidar Th. Christiansen, "Die finnischen und nordischen Varianten des zweiten Merseburgerspruches: eine vergleichende Studie," *FF Communications* 18 (1914): 77–218; Tekla Dömötör's 1972 article performs a similar function for the "Bed of Rushes, Stone Pillow" formula. Tekla Dömötör, "A Type of Hungarian FaithHealing Charm and its Background," *Arv* 28 (1972): 21–35.
35 F. A. Hästesko, *Motivverzeichnis westfinnischer Zaubersprüche nebst*

Aufzählung der bis 1908 gesammelten Varianten, FF Communications 19 (Hamina: 1914); Christiansen, *Die finnischen und nordischen Varianten des zweiten Merseburgerspruches*.

36 Eduard Hoffmann-Krayer and Hanns Bächtold-Stäubli, and Gerhard Lüdtke eds. *Handwörterbuch des deutschen Aberglaubens* (Berlin and Leipzig: de Gruyter, 1927–42), most recently republished digitally on CD-ROM in 2006.

37 Ohrt begins to develop his typology in Ferdinand Ohrt, *Danmarks Trylleformler, I & II*. (Copenhagen: Gyldendalske Boghandel, 1917[I], 1921[II]). His œuvre on the topic of charms is extensive, regarding which see his entries in this volume's bibliography.

38 Ronald Grambo, *Norske trollformler og magiske ritualer* (Oslo-Bergen-Tromsø: Universitetsforlag, 1979), 13–14.

39 Grambo, *Norske trollformler og magiske ritualer*; Barbara Kerewsky Halpern and John Miles Foley, "The Power of the Word: Healing Charms as an Oral Genre," *Journal of American Folklore* 91 (1978): 903–24; E. E. Evans-Pritchard, "The Morphology and Function of Magic. A Comparative Study of Trobriand and Zande Rituals and Spells," *American Anthropologist* 31 (1929): 619–41.

40 Eliade, *Shamanism*.

41 Michael J. Harner, *The Jivaro: People of the Sacred Waterfalls* (Garden City, NY: Doubleday/Natural History Press, 1972).

42 Ericksson, *Blodstämmare och handpåläggare*.

43 Evans-Pritchard, "The Morphology and Function of Magic."

44 Ferdinand Ohrt, "Ritusanzeige" in "Segen," §3; Hoffmann-Krayer and Bächtold-Stäubli, *Handwörterbuch des deutschen Aberglaubens*.

45 Ericksson, *Blodstämmare och handpåläggare*.

46 This trend is exemplified by the following studies: W. Crecelius, "Alte Segensformeln," *Zeitschrift für deutsche Mythologie und Sittenkunde* 1 (1853): 277–80; Adelbart Kuhn, "Indische und germanische Segenssprüche," *Zeitschrift für vergleichende Sprachforschung* 13 (1864): 49–74, 113–57; V. F. Miller, "Assiriiskie zaklinaniia i russkie narodnye zagovory, ["Assyrian Incantations and Russian Popular Charms"], in *Russkaia mysl'* [Russian thought] 7 (1896); Kaarle Krohn, "Wo und wann entstanden die finnischen Zauberlieder?" *Finnisch-Ugrische Forschungen* 1 (1901): 52–72, 147–81; V. J. Mansikka, *Über russische Zauberformeln mit Berücksichtigung der Blut- und Verrenkungssegen*, Annales Academiæ Scientiarum Fennicæ. Series B, vol. 1, #3. (Helsinki: Finnish Literary Society, 1909); Christiansen, "Die Finnischen und Nordischen Varianten des zweiten Merseburgerspruches"; Lorenzo Bianchi, "Greichische Zaubervorschriften," *Hessische Blätter für Folkskunde* 13 (1914): 103–14; J. Schwietering, "Der erste Merseburger Spruch," *Zeitschrift für deutsches Altertum und deutsche Literatur* 55 (1914): 148–56; F. Ohrt, *Trylleord, fremmede og danske*, in the series *Danmarks folke-*

minder 25 (1922); F. Ohrt, *De danske besværgelser mod vrid og blod: tolkning og forhistorie*, in *Det Kongelige Danske Videnskabernes Selskab, Historisk-filologiske Meddelelser* VI, 3(1922); Hugo Hepding, "Beiträge zu magischen Formeln," *Hessische Blätter für Volkskunde* 23 (1924); C. J. S. Thompson, *The Mysteries and Secrets of Magic* (1927, Bodley Head ed.; repr. NY: The Olympia Press, 1972); F. Ohrt, "Fluchtafel und Wettersegen," *FF Communications* 86 (1929): 1–26; F. Ohrt, "Über Alter und Ursprung der Begegnungssegen," *Hessische Blätter für Volkskunde* 35 (1936): 49–58; F. Ohrt, *Die ältesten Segen über Christi Taufe und Christi Tod in religionsgeschichtlichem Lichte*, in *Det Kongelige Danske Videnskabernes Selskab, Historisk-filologiske Meddelelser* 25:1, (Copenhagen: Levin og Munksgaard, 1938); Carl-Martin Edsman, "Folklig sed med rot i heden tid," *Arv* 1&2 (1946): 145–76; Felix Genzmer, "Germanische Zaubersprüche," *Germanisch-Romanische Monatsschrift* (Heidelberg), N. F. 1, 32 (1950): 21–35; F. R. Schröder, "Balder und der zweite Merseburger Zauberspruch," *Germanisch-Romanische Monatsschrift* (Heidelberg) 34 (1953): 161–83; G. Dolphini, "Sulle formule magiche e le benedizione nella traditione germanica," *Reale Istituto Lombardo di Scienze e Lettere—Rendiconti*, Mailand 101 (1967): 23–62; Tekla Dömötör, "A Type of Hungarian Faith Healing Charm and its Background," *Arv* 28 (1972): 21–35; Olav Bø, "Trollformlar," *Kulturhistorisk leksikon for nordisk middelalder fra vikingtid til reformasjonstid*, vol. 28, (Oslo, 1974): 674–78; M. Kedem, "Russian Incantations: Magic Spells of the Atharvaveda," in *Slavica Hierosolymitana*, vol. 5–6, (Jerusalem: Hebrew University at the Magnes Press, 1981), 61–68; Ralph Merrifield, "Chapter 6: Written Spells and Charms," in *The Archæology of Ritual and Magic* (New York: New Amsterdam Books, 1987).

47 This period of time saw an especial interest in the collection and publication of national collections of "antiquities," as international folklore scholarship has shown. In England, one year after Rääf's collection was published, Thomas O. Cockayne published *Leechdoms, Wortcunning and Starcraft of Early England*, 3 vols., (London, 1864–66).

48 A. Chr. Bang, *Norske Hekseformularer og Magiske Opskrifter*, Norske videnskabsselskabets skrifter II (No. 1, 1901) Historisk-filosofisk klasse. Kistiania (Oslo: A. W. Brøggers Bogtrykkeri, 1901).

49 Ohrt, *Danmarks Trylleformler I & II*.

50 Linderholm, "Signelser och besvärjelser från medeltid och nytid." Linderholm uses Törner, Rääf, and other collections in the holdings at various folklore archives in his three-volume work.

51 Valter W. Forsblom, *Magisk folkmedisin*. Finlands Svenska Folkdiktning 7, Folktro och Trolldom, no. 5, (Helsingfors, 1927).

52 Carl-Herman Tillhagen, *Folklig läkekonst* (Stockholm: Nordiska museet, 1958).

53 Dan Ben-Amos, "Forward," in Reimund Kvideland and Henning Sehmsdorf, eds., *Nordic Folklore: Recent Studies* (Indiana University Press, 1989),

viii. The royal questionnaire is provided in its entirety in Oscar Almgren, "Om tillkomsten av 1630 års antikvarie-intitution," *Fornvännen* 26 (1931): 35–42.

54 Alan Dundes, ed., *International Folkloristics: Classic Contributions by the Founders of Folklore* (Lanham, MD: Rowman and Littlefield, 1999), 17.

55 Ibid., 3.

56 Ibid., 17.

57 For example, *Die Korndämonen* (Berlin, 1868), *Der Baumkultus der Germanen* (Berlin, 1875), *Antike Wald- und Feldkulte* (Berlin, 1877) and his posthumous *Mythologische Forschungen* (Straßburg, 1884).

58 Wikman here seems to recognize that the earlier material in the collection was from a generation before Törner was born, in the late 1690s. If indeed his collecting efforts began in the 1730s (making him at least twenty years old) then it is not inconceivable that some of his informants had been alive and active in the 1690s. Wikman, *Johan J. Törners Samling*, 12.

59 National collections of ballads (Sw. *folkvisor*) were, for example, already being published in 1814–16 by the Romanticists Afzelius and Geijer, followed quickly by Arwidsson's collection in 1834–42.

60 In Göteborg, IFGH (*Institutet för folklivsforskning vid Göteborgs Högskola*); and VFF: *Västsvenska Folkminnesföreningens arkiv*; in Uppsala, ULMA (*Uppsala Landsmålsarkivet*, which became SOFI or *Språk- och folkminnesinstitutet*, and is now reorganized as of 2006 as *Institutet för språk och folkminnen*); in Lund, LUF (*Lunds Universitets Folkminnesarkiv*, now housed in the University Library); in Stockholm, EU (*Europeiska Undersökningen vid Nordiska muséet*); Fm (*Folkminnesarkivet vid Nordiska muséet*—NM, now *Institutet för folklivsforskning vid Etnologi institutionen vid Stockholms universitet*). These regional archives have now been consolidated into one national organization together with the governmentally chartered body for the conservation of the Swedish language.

61 See Rolf Kjellström, *Nordiska frågelistor*, Nordiska museet. Kulturhistoriska undersökningen (Stockholm: Kulturhistoriska undersökningen, Nordiska museet, 1995); Charlotte Hagström; Lena Marander-Eklund, *Frågelistan som källa och metod* (Lund: Studentlitteratur, 2005); Bo G Nilsson; Dan Waldetoft; Christina Westergren. *Frågelist och berättarglädje: om frågelistor som forskningsmetod och folklig genre*. Nordiska museet, (Stockholm: Nordiska museets förl., 2003).

62 Timothy Tangherlini, *Interpreting Legend: Danish Storytellers and Their Repertoires*, Milman Parry Studies in Oral Tradition, (New York: Garland, 1994).

63 Bodil Nildin-Wall, chef för Folkminnesavdelningen, Institutet för språk och folkminnen, private correspondence, April 8, 2008.

64 Sw. M5: *Om tjuvmjölkning av andras kor;* M7: *Vänster hand och motsols;* M11: *Ont öga, ond tunga, hågsa;* M90: *Magiska gester, tecken, tal och färger;* M99: *Husdjurssjukdomar;* M101: *Koppning och åderlåtning;* M103: *Präst, Klockare*

och andra Kyrkotjänare; M100: Om kloka (trollkunniga och vismän).
65 The term "witch war" is typically taken to mean that kind of aggressive competition which includes harmful magic and is designed to malign the reputation of its victim/competitor. It seems to have had as its primary aim an increase in the winner's magical reputation.
66 Bodil Nildin-Wall and Jan-Inge Wall, *Det ropades i skymningen...: Vidskepelse och trolldomstro på Gotland*. Skrifer utgivna av Språk- och folkminnesinstitutet Dialekt-, ortnamns- och folkminnesarkivet i Göteborg 3, (Uppsala: Almqvist och Wiksell, 1996). Jan-Inge Wall, *Hon var en gång tagen under jorden...: Visionsdikt och sjukdomsbot i Gotländska trolldomsprocesser*. Skrifter utgivna genom Dialekt- och Folkminnesarkivet i Uppsala, Serie B: 19, (Uppsala: Almqvist & Wiksell, 1989); Bente Gullveig Alver, Bengt af Klintberg, Birgitte Rørbye, and Anna-Leena Siikala, eds., *Botare: En bok om etnomedicin i Norden* (Stockholm: LTs förlag, 1980).
67 John G. Gager, *Curse Tablets and Binding Spells from the Ancient World* (Oxford: Oxford UP, 1992). Betz, *Greek Magical Papyri*.
68 Edsman, "Folklig sed med rot i heden tid."
69 Peuckert, "Die egyptischen Geheimnisse."
70 Ibid., 42.
71 Ibid., 45.
72 "Adeliges Landleben und europäischer Geist," 1949 and "Die alteuropäischer Oekonomik: Zeitschrift für Nationalökonomie," 1950. Cited in Peuckert.
73 The examples of these are plentiful in the translated texts here examined.
74 Edsman, "Svartkonstböcker i sägen och historia."
75 (*G. Dr Johann Faustens Miracul- Kunst- und Wunder-Buch, oder di schwarze Rabe, auch der Dreifache Höllen Zwang genannt*) See http://www.magitech.com/faust/introfst.html and ff. Accessed most recently 9 July 2009.
76 Edsman, "Sjätte och sjunde Mosebok."
77 Tillhagen, *Folklig läkekonst*, 75–78.
78 af Klintberg, *Svenska Trollformler*, 21–27.
79 Nildin-Wall and Wall, *Det ropades i skymningen*.
80 This list-serv operates at < ACADEMIC-STUDY-MAGIC@JISCMAIL.AC.UK>
81 It also has an electronic distribution and discussion list, administered from the University of Maryland <http://brindedcow.umd.edu/socmag/>.
82 Ryan, *The Bathhouse at Midnight*.
83 Roper, *Charms and Charming in Europe*.
84 Owen Davies, *Cunning Folk: Popular Magic in English History* (London: Hambledon and London, 2003); also, *Grimoires: A History of Magic Books*.
85 Kathleen Stokker, *Remedies and Rituals: Folk Medicine in Norway and the New Land* (St. Paul, MN: Minnesota Historical Society Press, 2007).

CHAPTER II

Folk Belief about Wise Ones

IN ORDER TO provide a context for an analysis of the black art books, one must consider their compilers and owners, the wise ones. This chapter will examine some of their more common traits and associations. A consideration of common names to describe them provides native nomenclature to describe social categorization and historical associations. Characteristics of the wise ones, such as their unusual appearance, can show how one might be more predisposed to the magical arts due to an unusual appearance. A consideration of their lifestyle, whether itinerant or landed, may provide insight into how folk magic and medicine economically supported the wise ones. Folk belief about black book owners such as ministers and malevolent witches will be described. This will define how wise ones were perceived on a moral scale of pure malevolence to a more enlightened and benevolent self-interest. It will describe some of the beliefs commonly held about the clairsentient or psychic powers of the wise ones. It will examine the methods by which wise ones were believed to obtain their extraordinary healing or magical powers, as well as the methods by which such power was renewed or maintained. By appealing to archival descriptions of how wise ones became and remained powerful, traditional expectations of manuscript contents may be easier to discern. Examples of the wise ones' own beliefs regarding the care and tending of the magical power they possessed, such as secrecy or the accrual of spirit helpers, may also suggest probable black book contents. Finally, in providing examples of magical procedures we can begin to establish expectations of the types of content we might expect to see in the black art books themselves, and to see if these expectations are satisfied.[1]

Folk Vocabulary Describing Wise Ones

THE SPECIALIZED VOCABULARY used to refer to the wise ones and their sphere of activities gives some indication of just how they were perceived by their clientele, and a wealth of terms developed to refer to their unique social role. Tillhagen records some of these in his study, mainly as examples of the plethora of terminology available to describe these wise folk. Wise (Sw. *kloker*, a nom. masc. sg. adj.), from the Low German loanword "wise" (LG *klok*),[2] occurs often in the records and refers to the specialized knowledge of magic that these practitioners held, as does the Swedish *vis*, "wise." These produce the Swedish *kloker man* and *viskärring* (wise man and wise woman). Often, however, their magical or medical specialization gave rise to other, more specific appellations. Lead-woman (Sw. *blygumma*), melt-woman (Sw. *smältgumma*) or castwoman (Sw. *stöpgumma*) all refer to the practice of pouring molten lead into a pot of cold water to divine the cause of disease, and also refer to the practice of melting the lead prior to using it in divinatory activity. The prefix troll (Sw. *troll-*) in compounds referring to these practitioners: "trollman," "troll-hag," even "witch" (Sw. *trollkarl, trollkäring, trollpacka*) establishes a link with preternatural spirits such as the troll, and means the troll's art: magic. While the word *troll* referred originally to a malevolent nature spirit, its shift to refer to more generalized magical activities and phenomena was early. We see it used in Old Icelandic to refer to the werewolf as well as to nature spirits of either diminutive or titanic size.[3]

The method by which a wise person received a special ability might also be captured in the word used to refer to them. "Graveyard-wanderer" (Sw. *kyrkogårdsgångare*) refers to the common visitation of the wise folk to cemeteries to procure human skeletal remains or "graveyard dust" (Sw. *kyrkogårdsmull*) for use in magical rites, and to the practice of enlisting the aid of ancestral spirits. The following excerpt about Kristina i Prekebo, known locally as "Prekeborskan," and her errands in graveyards, is exemplary.

> En gång hade hon varit ända ner i Halmstad. Så var det en dräng, som skulle skjutsa hem henne med häst. Men det var den värsta resa han varit med om, berättade han, ty på alla kyrkogårdar de körde förbi om natten, skulle hon fram och tala vid de döda, samt hämta jord ifrån gravarna, som hon sedan använde som botemedel.

> [Once she had been all the way down to Halmstad. There was a farmhand who was to convey her home by horse. But it was the worst trip he'd ever

been on, he said, because at every cemetery they drove past that night she wanted to go and talk to the dead, as well as fetch some dirt from the graves that she could then use as medicine.]

> IFGH 1448, 1–3.
> Lars Johan Samuelsson.
> uppt. Elin Emannelsson, 1928
> Öxabäck, Västergötland

Some other lexical items are local dialect variants of terms that refer to healing or magic, of which only few etymologies are understood. The Swedish *mecklamentsgubbe* ("medicine-man") may come from a dialect word for intervention, *mekkla* ("to intervene"). Swedish *lövjerska* ("sorceress") descends ultimately from the Old Norse *lyf* ("healing material or medicine," "mixture of poisons," as well as "magic").[4] From dialect Swedish *kukkla*, "to use magic," is derived another term for sorceress (Sw. *kuckelgumma*).[5] The Swedish *putterkallar* may be a reference to pouring as in the examples above with pouring lead. Also, the obscure terms *kusmegubbe* or *kusmakäring*, from the substantive *kusma*, sometimes *kusla*,[6] means to work magic or heal using incantations.[7] The etymology of the dialect word *tete* or *tejte*, used to mean "magic" in ULMA 9735, is uncertain, but is suggestive of the Finnish word for shaman (F. *tietäjä*).

Terms for the "malevolent witch" (Sw. *häxa, häxkärring, trollpacka*) are recorded by Tillhagen.[8] He also notes that the names by which specific wise folk were known often had to do with their specialization, e.g., "Leg- or Bone-Lars" (Sw. *Ben-Lasse*), who was good at healing broken bones, or "Horse-Käri" (Sw. *Häste-Käri*) who was particularly known for her ability to cure horses. Common naming conventions included references to a connection with a place. This yielded such names as the "Woman from Prekebo" (Sw. *Prekebokärringen*), "Anders from Mandrake[9]-meadow" (Sw. *Anders i Alehagen*) and the "Old Man from Stenbäck," (Sw. *Stenbäckagubben*). In the same way, personal qualities, habits or ethnicities might be the distinction used in naming, such as with "Snuff-Lena" (Sw. *Snus-Lena*), who was probably given over to a fondness for snuff, or "Lapp-Stina," probably a woman of *Sámi* extraction. The belief was common that the Finns and Lapps were especially gifted in magic that was much more powerful than that of the Swedes, so the prefix Finn- or Lapp- often denoted a wise One, whether healer or sorcerer.

Timothy Tangherlini's study[10] documents the fluidity of terms used to refer to the magical practitioner, and that names at various points between the seventeenth and twentieth centuries described the reputation held by the wise one for being harmful or helpful. This produced a linguistic spectrum, with the "most harmful witch" (Da. *heks*, Sw. *häxa, trollpacka*) representing the most evil extreme which was concerned with harmful or malevolent witchcraft (*maleficia*), and the wise one (Da. *kloge folk*, Sw. *klokfolk*) at the most benevolent, especially in the areas of healing, identifying violators of person or property, or of restoring stolen goods. The Scandinavian term I translate as sorcerer (Sw. *trollkarl, trollkvinna*, Da. *troldmand, troldkvinde*) is used primarily to indicate ignorance on the narrator's part as to which end of the moral spectrum the subject occupied in the narrative. The powers of the *trollkarl* might stem from demonic pact as easily as from inherited or divinely bestowed gifts.

The activities of the wise ones were often referred to by using a euphemism, a common technique when an uninitiated public does not wish to attract the attention of the unseen forces at work. We have "he could do a little of this and a little of that" (Sw. "kunde både det ena och det andra") or a "good deal of little things" (Sw. "en del småsaker") or "a bit of the small and good" (Sw. "lite smått och gott").[11] Using deliberate understatement in euphemistic circumlocutions of magical powers became a linguistic *apotropoeisis* or protective averting. These understatements could have functioned as an indication of the immensity of the wise ones' perceived power.

Unusual Appearance

As MARCEL MAUSS writes: "We should point out here that all these individuals—the disabled and the ecstatic, the pedlars, hawkers, jugglers and neurotics—actually form kinds of social classes. They possess magical powers not through their individual peculiarities but as a consequence of society's attitude towards them and their kind."[12] Mauss and Hubert conclude that magicians are socially perceived as powerful by strong feelings elicited by an unusual appearance.[13] Tillhagen describes the role that unusual appearance of the wise ones had in bolstering the faith with which his clientele perceived them.[14] Elisabet Dillner of Uppsala wrote of Mor Lisa i Finshult (Lisa Katrina Svensdotter, 1815–1893) and her peculiar, almost frightening appearance due to an ocular disease that left her eye sockets almost empty. In efforts to elicit fear and thereby bolster her reputation as magically formidable, she stuffed tufts of wool or yarn in her eyesockets,[15] giving a frightful appearance. In this, it seems clear that the wise ones themselves knew of the fear with which they were perceived, and sought to enhance it by clothing, make-up or other deceptions. As in the excerpt below (ULMA 31150), narratives about Mor Lisa also mention the olfactory associations with visits to the health care provider of the time. The penetrating scent of aromatic salves and unguents lingered on a client's clothing well after returning home.

In one item from the Uppsala archive, styles of dress and unusual clothing can be the factor which elicits this strong predisposition:

Dessa kunniga brukade vanligen vara klädda på ett sätt så, att de i klädseln avveko från "vanligt folk," männen hade oftast långt hängande hår/dåtida pjatter/ – skägget var även annorlunda, oftast av s.k. "mefistotyp," de ville formodligen på detta sätt tydligt markera, att de tillhörde de "visas skrå." Kvinnorna, som utövade läkekonst och magi voro likaledes ovanligt klädda – det var något manligt, som vilade över deras klädsel, det hörde ej till ovanligheten, att de ståtade i mansbyxor, det långa håret hade de vanligen hängande, över pannan mot nacken sammanhållet med ett band, som var broderat i grälla färger, det broderade hade former av mystiska tecken och figurer. I sina sirliga – väl avmätta rörelser – väl enklast nämnt vid later, markerade de även sin upphöjda ställning – betydenhet." Det doftade också medikamenter lång väg om dem, ...

[These wise ones usually used to be dressed in a way such that as far as mode of clothing went, it was different from that of "regular folks," the men most often had long, hanging hair/that period's dread-locks—the beard was also different, most often of the so-called "Mephisto-type." Presumably, they wanted to mark clearly in this way that they belonged to the "fraternity of wise ones." The women who practiced medicine and magic were similarly unusually dressed—there was something masculine about their clothing. It was not unusual that they paraded in men's pants, the long hair they had usually hanging down over the forehead towards the neck, held together with a band that was embroidered in garish colors, with the embroideries having the forms of mystical signs and figures. In their ceremonious—even deliberate movements—quite simply, airs, they marked their elevated position—importance." They also smelled a long way off of medicines, ...]

> ULMA acc#31150, 1–4.
> E. J. Lindberg,
> 1/09/1968
> Ragunda, Jämtland

This excerpt is especially interesting for the detailed description of a "typical" wise woman. The similarity of the depictions of Mor Lisa i Finshult in Dillner's study, and Lindberg's description above of the style of dress and coiffure of his wise woman seem to indicate memorable encounters with real, and singular, individuals. The unusual appearance lent to an itinerant magician from Finnskogen, disfigured by a noticeable scar from trephination, also led the narrator to speculate the role his surgery had in his predisposition to the world of the unseen. It serves to connect an older idea of insanity and spirit possession with the surgery of modern medicine.

I min barndom (på 1890-talet) kom en gång en man vandrande. Han var från Finnskogen och påstod sig ha fått huvudskålen öppnad, och visade ärret efter trepaneringen. Vad orsaken var till denna operation minnes jag inte bestämt, men säkerligen sade han, efter vad jag vill minnas, att han varit vansinnig (besatt av onda andar?) och blev efter ingreppet bra. Om det var sant att hans hjärnskål blivit öppnad eller inte, eller om ärret härledde sig av annan orsak, kan jag naturligtvis inte säga.

Mannen hade en s.k. svartkonstbok som han förevisade, men jag som var liten vågade inte titta i den så att jag fick se hur den såg ut. Även de äldre tordes inte se i den farliga och märkvärdiga boken. Själv lät han förstå att han "kunde en hel del," och det okunniga folket trodde detta och hyste en vidskeplig fruktan för den underliga mannen, som troligen inte var normal, trots att huvudskålen blivit öppnad för att släppa ut de onda andarna som där regerade.

[In my childhood (in the 1890s), a man once came wandering by. He was from Finn forest and maintained that he had had his skull opened, and he showed the scar from the trephination. What the reason for the surgery was I don't recall for sure, but surely he said, according to what I remember, that he had been insane (afflicted by evil spirits?) and became better after the treatment. Whether it was true that his skull had been opened or not, or if the scar had its origin in some other cause, I can't really say, of course.

The man had a so-called black art book that he exhibited, but as I was so small, I didn't dare look in it so I didn't get to find out what it looked like. Even the adults didn't dare to look in the dangerous and extraordinary book. He let on about himself, that he "knew a fair amount," and the ignorant people believed that, and bore a superstitious fear of the strange man, who probably was not normal, in spite of having had his skull opened in order to let out the evil spirits who ruled there.]

VFF 2153, 1–3
G. Rodén
uppt. G. Rodén, 1942, 15/5
Munkfors, Ransäter sn., Värmland

The description of the itinerant wanderer disfigured by some kind of cranial surgery gives the audience a strong sense of his "otherness," and seems to bolster his reputation as one familiar with evil spirits and their disposition.

Patient Visitation or At-Home Practice: Locations of Consultations

IN 1958, CARL-HERMAN TILLHAGEN posited a continuity between the magic represented in the *seiðr* of the medieval sagas and the more modern wise folk. Many of the characteristic traits of *seiðr* such as the use of drums, scaffolding or high places, spirit songs and the like are not found in more recent descriptions of magical procedures. However, there are some traits that exhibit a consistency such as the common theme of the itinerancy of the traveling seeress and the wandering wise one.

Both the Old Norse sorcerer (ON *seiðmaðr, -kona*) and the more recent wise one might be summoned from his own home to make visits from farm to farm. Depending on the other means of economic support, travel might be one method with which the wise one advertised his services. In these cases, there was no "home office," and services were dependent upon the visitation of a traveling specialist. Early Scandinavian depictions of traveling diviners are found in the *Eiríks saga rauða* (Chapter 4), the earliest redaction of which we have from the early fourteenth century,[16] as well as *Örvar-Odds saga* (Chapter 2), a *fornaldarsaga* (legendary saga, generally assumed less reliable for historical purposes) dating to the mid-thirteenth century.[17] In both narratives, the female itinerant soothsayer (ON *völva*) is invited into the home to prophesy the fates of those attached to the farm. In *Eiríks saga*, Þórbjörg *litilvölva* is invited by the chieftain Þorkel of Herjólfsnes to perform *seiðr* to divine the end of a poor season. In *Örvar-Odds saga*, the prophecies uttered by the traveling seeress become the narrative vehicle by which the hero's fate is established, and was to be avoided for the inevitability it heralded. Odd tries to avert the fulfillment of his fate by preventing the *völva* from pronouncing her prophecy. He concludes his unsuccessful bid to rid himself of this imposition of fate by striking the seeress with a stick, an impulsive act that earned the ire of the seeress, in the same way as we will see below when we discuss the fear with which the common folk viewed the wise one.

Another case of the itinerant wise one is preserved in the narrative of Lars Persson provided below, in which the itinerant peddler Åberg, a notorious card shark, could demonstrate legerdemain and illusionism with decks of cards as well.

> Ja, Åberg var en märklig man. Kortleken kunde han behandla hur som helst. Han kastade ett kort hur som helst i luften, och då flög det och blev sittande på en vägg eller i taket eller var som helst. En gång brände han upp kortleken, och se'n bad han oss och hämta den ute vid leet (grinden). Han var egentligen lumpsamlare och gick omkring på ställena. Han söp så förskräckligt, och när han dog, slog det eld i halsen på'n.

[Well, Åberg was a peculiar man. He could handle a deck of playing cards like a wizard. He threw a card into the air just as you please, and then it flew and ended up stuck on a wall or in the ceiling or wherever. One time he burnt up the deck, and then he asked us to go and fetch it out by the garden gate. He was actually a rag collector and wandered around to places. He boozed it so terribly, and when he died, his throat caught fire! (Marginal note recorded by Lannestock, the interviewer: "This is a humorous double entendre recalling alcohol consumption and an association with the devil and the associated hellfire.")]

IFGH 923, 10–14
Lars Persson, f. 1843 i Bollebygd
uppt. G. Lannestock, 1927
Bollebygd, Västergötland

It is possible that the easily observable physiological irregularities they displayed made obtaining stable housing more difficult. Lack of stable housing led to an itinerant lifestyle, which in turn became a sort of poor-man's advertising campaign. It did not, however, seem to negatively impact the wise one's reputation as magically capable, as is illustrated below in the case of Anders i Alehagen (IFGH 3504).

Clergy: Minister or Sorcerer?

KATHLEEN STOKKER HAS examined Norwegian narratives which posit the learned clerical class as owners and users of black art books, and which tell of their alleged attendance at the legendary school of sorcery, the Wittenberg school, so named after the university at which Martin Luther posted his 95 theses,[18] but which in these narratives has been transformed into a kind of infernal training school for would-be sorcerers. These beliefs are found in the Swedish material as well.

Ministers of the State Lutheran Church held governmental and spiritual authority. With that authority and their higher level of education came social exclusion. Most often, the parish minister or priest was also from a different locale. He was an outsider, even while his ministrations required him to be intimately involved with his parishioners. This marginal status seems to have been explored in narratives dealing with the black book Minister. Here, the minister is both a benevolent shepherd of his flock and one skilled in those forbidden spiritual arts that his office and education made available to him.

The belief that the wise one was somehow able to discern unspoken motive or intent among bystanders is also reflected here in the minister, whose relationship with unseen forces gave him similar skill (ULMA 26903). Not only might one's thoughts no longer remain private to such a minister, but they might be the cause of public embarrassment from the pulpit, or worse, the denial of Holy Communion, a means to salvation. The following excerpt provides an example.

> Det var en präst på Millesvik, som skulle ha gått genom "Wittenbergsskolan." Han skrev, så inte vanligt folk kunde läsa det, han hade skrivit. Han såg mer än vanligt folk, för om han gav nattvarden, så kunde han se, om de var värdiga eller inte.
>
> [There was a priest at Millesvik, who was to have gone through the "Wittenberg School." He wrote in such a way, so that normal folk couldn't read whatever he had written. He saw more than normal folk, because when he gave out communion, then he could see if they were worthy or not.]
>
> IFGH 3751, 31–32
> Johan Aronsson, f. 1868 i Millesvik
> uppt. Ragnar Nilsson, 1936
> Millesvik, Värmland

Resistance is futile, at least as illustrated in the following excerpt. Should one dare to try to act contrary to the wishes of the minister, all one's efforts would come to naught, and all would be as it was before. An example, VFF 2153, tells that parishioners plowed a section of a field disputed by the local priest, only to find that the next day, the field was found untouched. The priest's power had caused the field to revert to its former, untouched state.

Häxan: The Malevolent Witch

THE HÄXA, OR malevolent witch, was an individual who engaged in magic for personal gain to others' disadvantage, and for the sheer pleasure of inflicting suffering. That there was ever any actual person who gleefully performed all the arbitrary evil behaviors listed in the archives is most unlikely. But the description of malevolence affected beliefs about those versed in magic, as did the belief in a contract with the Devil, two beliefs held about the wise one/sorcerer. Contracts with the devil did, evidently, exist, as proven in the manuscript from Skara Veterinärbibliotek included in this study. Ebbe Schön, head of *Nordiska museéts Folkminnessamling* in 1991, appeals in his book, *Häxor och Trolldom*, to old trial transcripts, archival entries, and other sources to delineate the scope of activity of the archetypical malevolent "witch."[19] While he begins his study with a discussion of wise ones, he quickly distinguishes between this primarily benevolent magician and folk healer and the purely malevolent *häxa* who, by means of a contract with the devil, could fly to her meetings at Blåkulla, the mountain top where witches were wont to celebrate their Sabbat in the devil's presence, and could steal both milk and *sanket*, that portion of the milk that was best used to make cheese and butter, from neighbors' cows, as well as inflict suffering of all sorts on both folk and livestock. The *häxa* was almost non-human in the scope of her abilities, and in the power she employed to destroy others' livelihood to her own benefit. The Swedish term *trollpacka* (troll-pack) gives a good example of the non-human realm in which the witch participated.

While the role of the wise one was benevolent in an obvious way, healing illness and counseling the unfortunate, there was also a recognition that the one who healed also had the capacity to hex. This is exemplified in the bystanders' fear of offending the visiting wise one. An interesting question is the degree to which an otherwise benevolent wise one was capable or interested in the occasional malevolent use of her powers. This study provides some data upon which to base a hypothesis. Was the archetypical malevolent witch a reality among those who specialized in the hidden knowledge of the wise ones? Some few of the characteristics of such a malevolent character is present in some of the archival excerpts, though whether there was anything to confirm suspicion of someone of such malevolence has not been adequately investigated.

As Schön shows, there were certain commonplaces in the Swedish narratives dealing with malevolent witchcraft: the blasting of another's crops to the advantage of one's own; the magical appropriation of cow's milk and its by-products away from another's cows and to one's own; and the magical removal of the ability of livestock to thrive, to result in a higher selling price at market of one's own; these are all common concerns of the malevolent witch. In the following excerpt, Spätta was reputed to revel in her ability to impress and frighten her clients, but this resulted in no economic advantage all the same.

> Spätta, dotter till en de kalla Fölongen, ho hette annars Sofia. Ho ble gift med Spätt-Erik. Ho kunne trolla. Ho hade fått svartkonstebok efter mor si, den skrämde ho dom mä. Ho kunne sätta två gafflar i bordet å mjölka, så kretura dö. Hur ho då trolla, så va dä inte annat än fattig ständigt.
>
> Ho hade e ko, som geck i grannens havre, å grannen sa, att om hon ite höll reda på koa, så skulle han slå ihjäl den. Slå du, sa Spätta, ja ska sätta på dej dä som ont ä. Trollkäring, skrek grannen åt henne.
>
> [Spätta, the daughter of one they call Fölongen ("The Foal"), was otherwise called Sofia. She got married to Spätt-Erik. She could do magic. She had gotten a black art book from her mother, she frightened them with it. She could put two forks in the table to milk, so that the cattle died. No matter how she did her magic, there wasn't anything other than constant poverty.

She had a cow that went into the neighbors oats, and the neighbor said that if she didn't have better control over her cow, then he would kill it. If you kill it, said Spätta, then I'll put a mighty curse on you (lit. I'll put on you that which is evil). Witch, screamed the neighbor at her.]

>IFGH 6151, 6
>Adolf Gabrielsson i Skälläter, f. 1873 i Järbo
>uppt. Ivan Markendahl, 1963
>Järbo, Dalsland

The excerpt above provides an actual example of stealing milk through magical means, and by a personality known to the family of the informant. In other excerpts, this was achieved through a knife stuck in the barn wall,[20] but here we have a variant in using two forks in the [kitchen] table. Inheritance was the means by which she obtained her black art book, and thereby her magical power. It isn't clear that her boasting of magical prowess was any real advantage in attracting a clientele, such as is described by Tangherlini. A reputation for exceptional magical powers did not evidently always result in economic or social advancement.

In speaking of how a cow had been hexed by a neighbor lady, Charlotta Andersson had the following to tell about the woman from Prekebo, and her help to reverse the hex. The neighbor lady was otherwise a nice person, says Charlotta, so it probably wasn't her fault—the exercise of maleficium might not be deliberate, but instead tied to an individual's luck and fate.

> När jag likväl var uppe hos "Prekebokäringen" nämnde jag om den besynnerliga turen vi fått. Då sa' hon, att vi ska bara inte låta den där käringen komma in i vår lagård, så ska det nog hjälpa. Det gjorde vi också, sedan bara käringen hölls från lagården. Djuren började trivas igen. Det besynnerliga var, att hon var en snäll gumma, så hon rådde väl inte för det.

> [Nevertheless, when I was up at the Prekebo woman's place, I told her about the peculiar luck we were having. Then she said, that we should just prevent that woman from coming into our barn, and that would probably help. And so we did, and thereafter only that old woman was kept from the barn. The animals began to thrive again. The peculiar thing was that she was a kind woman, so it probably wasn't her fault.]

>IFGH 3736, 13–15
>Lina Larsson, f. 1852, Hallaböka, Temsjö
>uppt. Arvid Göransson, 1936
>Torup, Halland

Fear of the Wise Ones

BOTH FEAR AND respect followed the wise ones. In the following excerpt the narrator attributes an ability to the wise one to see into the minds and intentions of those around him. The revelation of hidden matters otherwise kept to oneself could expose guilt or sin for all to see, and foul one's reputation.

Att spänningen vid dagen för kunnige-besöket var stor – särskilt bland oss ungdomar, som råkat snappa upp saken var ju en given sak. När så den kunnige anlände, kände man kalla kårar gå efter ryggen, väl oftast bottnande i, att man ej hade så särdeles rent samvete, vad småhyss beträffar, man hade ju av gamlingarna hört berättas, att dessa "visa" kunde se det som var gjort i det fördolda, till detta räknades nog även pojkstreck, etc. vilka om de nu blevo uppdagade, säkerligen komme att leda till smärtsamma efterräkningar i form av dåtida så vanliga "björkolja" = risbastu med björkris. Helst undvek man väl, att möta den "mäktige," nyfiken tog nog oftast överhand, man tog då risken – väl mest enbart för att få se vederbörande/oftast en man, mera sällan en kvinna, att man då visade en mycket överdriven hövlighet – av med huvudbonad och djupa bockningar var helt givet – även här med baktanke om, att på detta enda till buds stående sätt göra den mäktige vänligt inställd och således eliminera risken för den granskning hans "argusögon" som ohövlighet kunde ge upphov till.

[It was of course a given that the excitement surrounding the visit of the wise one was great—especially among us young ones, who had happened to get wind of it. When the wise one arrived, one felt cold shivers go along one's spine, most often because we didn't have an especially clear conscience regarding small mischief. One had heard from the elderly that these "wise" ones could see that which was done secretly, and that included boyish pranks, etc., which if they now were discovered, would surely lead to some painful results in the form which was so common at that time: "birch oil" = a birching with birch twigs. Preferably one would escape meeting the "powerful one," but most often curiosity won out, and one took the risk—solely to catch a glimpse of the person in question—most often a man, less often a woman. Then one displayed a very exaggerated politeness—off with the head-coverings, and deep bows were completely expected—even here with the thought that even such improvised measures make the powerful one more positively disposed and in this way eliminate the risk of scrutiny with his evil eye which impoliteness could give rise to.]

ULMA acc. #26903, Erik Jonas Lindberg,
Ragunda, Jämtland

submitted Jan. 9, 1968,
in answer to Questionnaire M100.

This narrative not only provides an example of the attitude of respect which was expected to be shown to the wise one, but also the justification for it—the wise one knew more than others, and would be able, by means of his evil eye (Sw. *argusöga*) to psychically intuit the presence of guilty thoughts or disrespect toward the wise one.

Magical retribution might also be expected for disrespect for other offences, as the next excerpt illustrates.

Stenbäcka gubbe va dæ många som sökte, han va vida känd. Dæ va en som hette Frans i Törnefalle, ha va arg på Stenbäcka gubbe. En gång då Frans kom från en markne i Undernäs, gick han in te gubben och slog honom riktigt och sen kasta han ut honom. – Men så mycke vet ja o kunde si, att Frans blev förgjord sen. Ja sjøεv æ riktit vittne på dæ. Dæ va så, att ja hölls o arbeta därnere strax ve Törnefalle. Frans gumma kom te mej o ba mej komma te dom o laga skor. "Hur æ dæ mæ Frans?" fråga ja. "Dæ æ dålit," sa gumma. "Då æ ja inte hågad på att gå dit," sa ja. Men gumma ba mej så dant, o då lova ja henne att komma. – Frans o hans gumma bodde i e lita låg stuga. Stuga hadde en låg vinn, o dæ fanns en stege från farsta upp te vinn. – Då ja kom dit, så fråga ja etter Frans. "Han ha krupe upp dit," sa gumma o peka upp te vinn. "Frans, æ du dær," ropa ja upp te'n, "ja æ hær o ska laga skor." Frans sa, att han va dåli o inte kunde gå ner. "Du æ tvungen o gå ner," sa ja, "annars går ja hem." Då kom Frans ner. "Frans," sa ja, "nu ska vi ha lika rolit som förr." "Dæ går inta," sa Frans. O så berätta han: "Ja gick in o slog Stenbäcka tr8llgubbe. Dæ va i fylla förståss. Ja misshandla honom o kasta ut en. O nu tror ja att han satt på mej dæ här."

– Frans såg så eländi ut. Han hadde plocka på sej en massa klär, o han va så lessen o bedrövad. – Efter en tid va han frisk igen, men dæ dær kom tebaks tidvis. En måne för varje år kom dæ. Annars va han så glad o pigg, men så i ett kom dæ. Sommartid kom dæ merendels.

[A lot of people sought out the man from Stenbäcka, he was widely known. There was one person who was named Frans in Törnefalle, and he was angry at the man from Stenbäcka. One time as Frans was coming home from the market in Undernäs, he went in to the old man, and beat him up, and then he threw him out. But this much I know and could see afterwards, that Frans had been cursed. I myself am an actual witness to it. It so happened that I was working down right next to Törnefalle. Frans's wife came to me and asked me to come to mend their shoes. "How are things with Frans?" I asked. "It's bad," the woman said. "Then I'm not inclined to go up there," I said. But the wife asked so insistently that I promised her I'd come. Frans and his wife lived in a low-roofed cottage, and the cottage had a low attic, and there was a ladder from the entryway up to the attic. When I got there, I asked for Frans. "He's crawled up there," the woman said and pointed up to the attic. "Frans, are you there?" I called up to him, "I'm here to fix shoes." Frans said that he was doing poorly and couldn't come down. "You have to come down," I said, "otherwise I'll go home." Then Frans came down. "Frans," I said, "now we'll have just as much fun as we've had before." "No, that won't do," said Frans. And so he explained: "I went in and hit the wizard from Stenbäcka. It was when I was drunk of course. I beat him up and threw him out. And now I believe that he has put this [condition] here on me."

—Frans looked miserable. He had put on a whole bunch of clothes, and he was sad and troubled.—After a while he became well again, but it came back occasionally. One month each year it came back. Otherwise he was so happy and active, but then all of a sudden it came. It came mostly in the summertime.]

> ULMA acc #10822, Emil Karlsson
> f. 1870 Davidstorp, Sågkvarnen
> Tiveds socken, Västergötland
> Hildegard Axelman
> 7/1937

This excerpt is a teaching tale, and offers an illustration of the consequences of being impolite to the wise one. It also provides a description of what a cursed state might look like, effectively defining the term "to hex" or literally "to put down" (Sw. *att sätta ner*) for younger generations not as fluent in the vocabulary of the supernatural. This cursed state might also be incurable, returning at regular intervals as a morbid reminder of both one's previous foolish impetuousness brought on by strong drink, as well as the considerable and unpredictable powers of the sorcerer when so rudely treated.

OBTAINING MAGICAL POWER

EXCEPT in cases where magical power was inherited as a predilection in a family line, it was obtained by some external means. These means could include the ingestion of certain rare or precious substances, performance of some ritual action at particularly magical times, procurement of some object or fetish which itself contained magical power and lent to its owner, or time spent in apprenticeship with another already fluent in the ways of sorcery. In some special circumstances, we have discrete narratives that describe one person obtaining power by more than one method, as for example in the narratives about Anders i Alehagen (fl. ~1854, Marks kommun,

FOLK BELIEF ABOUT WISE ONES

Västergötland), or by a simultaneous combination of more than one method at different times. Once obtained, maintenance of various taboos prevented the loss of magical power. In the following, these methods of obtaining and maintaining magical power will be examined with supporting archival material. By such an examination, the black art book can be recognized as one of the methods by which the wise ones obtained magical power.

OBTAINING MAGICAL POWER THROUGH HEALTH CRISIS

Social attribution of magical power to someone might also come about by various crises of health. Jan-Inge Wall describes the history of cases brought against Brita Biörns of Visby, Gotland. At her first interrogation in 1722 this folk healer explained that as a child she had taken to her bed, seriously ill, as her spirit traveled underground to learn healing secrets from the subterraneans. The hallucinatory experiences brought on by high fevers may have qualified as an initiatory illness or "Shamanic Illness" as described by M. Eliade among the Chukchee.[21] When Biörns' account was met with disbelief by the court authorities, she temporarily changed her story and said that she had been taught the healing arts by an old woman who had died many years previously. But, interestingly, at her second inquest in 1737–38, her account reverted to her first story, of being ill in bed for three days, during which time she visited the small folk underground where she was met with a human spirit ally who warned her not to eat there. Eating of the enchanted food would make her visit into a permanent tenancy.[22]

OBTAINING MAGICAL POWER THROUGH INGESTING POWER SUBSTANCES

Another method of gaining magical power has to do with the ingestion of a mixture of things which themselves are thought to be magical. Eating the slime of the legendary white snake (an interesting mix of slug and snake motifs), eating the boiled meat of that snake, or drinking of its broth were all considered sufficient to give the wise one the requisite power to heal or hex.

> Den vita ormen var sällsynt men lyckobringande för den som fick se honom förlänade åt denna vissa övernaturliga gåvor att bota sjukdomar. Fångades en sådan orm, kunde av dess kött inkokt på sakkunnigt sätt beredas droger med underbar verkan för botande av vissa sjukdomar.
>
> [The white snake was rare but auspicious, because the one who caught a glimpse of it was granted certain supernatural gifts to heal illnesses. If such a snake was caught, and its meat boiled in an expert manner, then from it

drugs with miraculous effects for the healing of certain illnesses could be prepared.]

> IFGH 3146,
> P. Johansson, 1933,
> Tarsled, Västergötland

Britta Lena Andersson (1824–1904), the famed *Kungsbackagumman* or Woman from Kungsbacka, a town in provincial Halland, was reputed to have caught and cooked the legendary white snake and drunk its broth.[23]

In the narratives about Anders i Alehagen, Anders was reputed to have gained his powers by a number of methods, one of which was eating berries over which a white snake had slithered.[24]

OBTAINING MAGICAL POWER THROUGH RITUAL

In addition to crises of illness or the ingestion of power substances, the performance of ritual was another. Ritual is the performance of action or verbal recitation along with the manipulation of substance in place and time to bring about change. It is not a mindlessly repeated action, but is meant to be somehow transcendent. In the performance of ritual, actions, words or power substances can all play a role, and are often weighted in their degree of importance to the success of the operation. One ritual procedure to obtain visions of future events consisted of creeping under a corpse-filled coffin, after which one became clairvoyant (EU 8643, Lars Wikstrand, Stenis, Mora sn., Dalarna, 08/1934).

Carl-Herman Tillhagen[25] writes that the wise ones' purview was not merely the treatment of illness, but that due to an intimate relationship with otherworldly powers, he could perform deeds that others could not. This relationship yielded an uncanny ability to perceive the order of things, the abilities that proceeded from this ability led to a perception of the wise one as not only a master of illnesses, but also master of the powers of evil that brought them about. This led to both faith in, and fear of, the wise one.[26]

A number of other magical prerequisites are mentioned below in ULMA 22662, from Otto Nord in Hultgården, Misterhult in 1954, such as performing the procedure on an empty stomach (Sw. *fastnes maje*), or the importance of silence in retaining the gift so obtained (*för kan di inte tie då kan di lätte va't*). Other pre-requisites are also mentioned, such as the performance of the procedure while naked.

¶ Ritual: Circumambulation and "Year-walking"

Sometimes performing a ritual at a particularly powerful time of the year is enough to obtain magical power, such as the deliberate circumambulation of church or home known as Walking the Year's Walk (Sw. *att gå årsgång*) and which consisted of the circumambulation of a building or area in a prescribed manner, after which divinatory or healing powers were bestowed. In the case of the common person, this power was transitory, while among the wise ones it was sufficient to obtain a lifetime of magical power.

The procedure of walking or running counterclockwise about the church or home in order to see portents in the windows afterwards was a common method of divination,[27] and was not exclusively a technique of the wise ones. Common folk typically used it in teaching narratives that warned of the dangers of seeking to know "too much." It was common that on some portentous day, someone with the requisite fortitude ran a prescribed number of times counterclockwise around the house or the church in order to know of future events. In the case below, walking once around the house was sufficient to determine who of the household would not live out the year. Metallurgist Gustaf Ericsson writes:

> 1. Julaftonen skall någon gå motsols kring stugan och då man gått ett hvarf skall man ställa sig och se in genom fönstret då allt folket sitter och äter qvällsvard. Synes då någon hufvudlös så är säkert att den dör inom årets lopp. För yttermera säkerhet så böra tre personer hemligen rådslå om och gå hvar sitt slag. Men få äro de som våga undersöka dylika förhållanden.[28]

> [1. On Christmas Eve, you go counterclockwise around the house, and when you've gone one circuit, you stand still and look in through the window when everybody is sitting and eating dinner. Then, if anyone appears headless, then it's certain that he'll die within the course of a year. To be even more certain, three people should secretly take counsel and each go his own way. But there are few who dare to experiment with such doings.]

The same procedure, with the substitution of the parish church for the residence, is often mentioned as one method to conjure the Devil in order to obtain lasting magical power.

¶ Ritual: Timing

The ritual of walking the years walk was usually performed at midnight on special holidays such as Christmas Eve, New Years Eve, or Maundy Thursday in Holy Week. Sometimes the vision of the future was only fleeting, and normal vision returned relatively quickly, but at other times, the effect on the seeker was more permanent, and endowed him or her with an ongoing gift to divine futures, illnesses and cures.

Sagesmannen 82-årige Otto Nord, Hultgården, Misterhult, f.d. lant- och skogsarbetare, förhörde jag mig hos angående årsgång nu strax före jul 1954. Genom att mitt förbiseende kom inte årsgången på tal vid föregående tillfälle, då jag intervjuade Nord. Om årsgången upplyste Nord klart och tydligt följande:

Messommersnatta å juɫnatta ä di bäste nättera te gå årsgång å ja ger ma ju hundan på, att Sven Mårtens mor i Stensjö hadde gått årsgång i sin ungdom för allt va ho kunne å säna (sedan) lärde bôrt te sônen, för han kunne mongt å môcke å dä va den djävelen, som säna fördärvede ma i mett ben, så ja få gå krycker te min siste da.

Dä går inte för vicken bɫadder (språksam person) som helst te gå årsgång, för kan di inte tie (tiga) då kan di lätte va't (låta det vara). Heɫe tia, di förberer sa, få di lôv å kunne hålle käft.

Å inte få di äte nô heller, för di ska va på fastnes maje (fastande mage).

Säna går di fram te körktrappen å dä ska va precis kɫocka tôɫv på natta. Di ska gå bakɫänges runt körka tri vârv.

Får di då se nô otäckt å bɫir rädde fö'ert (för det), då ä dä förköɫt (förkylt) för dom den gången å dei få vänte te juɫnatta, om dä ä messommersnatta, di går, elle tvärtom. Men dä kan också hände, di allri få lä'er'sa nô. Di få lôv å komme ihôj, att di ska gå ånsyɫs (motsols), anners få di vården si elle lä'er'sa nô.

Juɫnatta kan hände ska va nô bätter te gå årsgång för då har döinga juɫotte. Kɫocka tôɫv å få di si dä gönom fönstra, kan di få lä'er'sa môcke baɫa (bara) på dä.

[Narrator 82-year-old Otto Nord, Hultgården, Misterhult, previously a farm and lumber worker, whom I questioned regarding year's walk now immediately before Christmas 1954. Through my own oversight the topic of year's walk didn't come up during the previous opportunity when I interviewed Nord. Nord related the following about the year's walk clearly and plainly:

Midsummer night and Christmas night are the best nights to go year's walk, and I'd swear because of everything she could do and that she then taught to her son that Sven Mårten's mother in Stensjö had gone on year's walk in her youth. For he could do a great many things (many and much), and it was that devil who destroyed my leg, so that I had to go on crutches to my dying day.

It won't work for just any old talker to go year's walk, for if they can't remain silent, then they can just let it be. Completely keeping silent, they prepare themselves that way, just as long as they could manage to shut up.

And they can't eat anything either, because they have to be on an empty stomach.

Then they go up to the Church steps and it has to be exactly twelve o'clock at night. They have to walk backwards around the church three times.

If they then see something terrifying and become afraid of it, then it's over for them that time, and they have to wait until Christmas night, if it's midsummer night that they're doing it, or the other way around. But it can also happen, that they never get to learn anything. They should remember, if they should go counterclockwise, otherwise they neither see or learn anything.

Perhaps Christmas night is somewhat better to go year's walk, because that's when the dead hold Christmas vespers. At twelve o'clock and if they can see there through the window, they can learn so much just doing that.]

> ULMA acc. #22662, Gunnar Skogsmark,
> Otto Nord, 82, Hultgården, Misterhult
> intervjuad strax före jul, 1954, Stensborg,
> Oskarshamn
> inlämnad dec 28, 1954

Paul Heurgren tells that magical power may be obtained by picking the flower of a type of fern on Midsummer night when it blooms—but it must be plucked in silence and then put into an especially thick paper wrapping to prevent its escape.[29]

In the same way that plants were at their most potent at the time of Midsummer,[30] so it seems that certain days in the calendar brought with them amplified magical potential. Annually, any church holiday was a good candidate for the performance of ritual, and for those whose purposes could not wait for a day that came only once a year, there were also potent days of the week. As the black art books show, Thursdays seem to have been favored for both the performance of circumambulation to obtain powers, but also for rituals to make use of those powers. The most potent Thursday of them all, however, was Maundy Thursday, the day on which Christ celebrated the Last Supper, of which the ritual of taking Communion was a remembrance. On this day, Maundy Thursday (Sw. *skärtorsdag*), the powers of darkness obtain a temporary advantage against the powers of God, Church and Light. Witches' Sabbaths were commonly reputed to be held on this powerful day of the year, both to make use of its magical potential, as well as to mock the practices of good Christian men and women in a demonic perversion. Therefore, the feast held at the Witches Sabbath was a sort of Infernal Last Supper. In the black art books, Thursdays and Sundays, at twilight or at sunrise, were the preferred times to perform magical ritual, and as we might expect, repetition of a ritual over three Thursday nights in a row gave it increased power.[31] In IFGH 1133 given below, Kajsa is described as being used to walking the years walk each New Years Eve, perhaps indicating that the regular repetition of this ritual was what kept the magical power flowing through her veins.

¶ Ritual: Personnel

The rituals in which the wise ones obtained their preternatural powers were typically solitary. The power-seeker went alone in the dark to a fearful location, typically there to invoke the Devil or one of his minions to teach the hidden arts. But when magical power was to be gleaned from another human, then certain ritual preconditions applied to the personnel enacting that transfer. Gender requirements in teaching and passing lore suggest some kind of sexual element in the initiation to the magical arts. Age seems to have played a role, with an older practitioner passing learning or powers to a younger one.

In the following example, Karl's mother Kajsa not only performed the magical procedure annually to gain supernatural sight for herself, she also owned the black art book and was thus in league with the Evil One. It is interesting to note here, however, that she was able to pass on skills from both sources to her son. In this archival excerpt there is an artful emphasis on Kajsa's wild fearlessness as she first learns the black art for herself. Even though Karl learned the art primarily from his mother, the narrator must insert that Karl himself was no milquetoast, and was aggressive as well (Han var just inte så mörkrädd heller) in learning more of the art. In such an apprenticeship as illustrated by Karl and his mother Kajsa, other magical rules also applied, such as the manner in which the knowledge was imparted, such as from mother to son or father to daughter, male to female or female to male, as we see below in an anonymous narrative collected by Carl Martin Bergstrand from a woman born in Lena Parish in Västergötland in 1841. Since Kajsa's son isn't represented as himself going on "the walk," we must assume that it was because of his tutelage at his mother's hands that he received his power.

> I mitten av 1800-talet levde det i Ry en man som hette Karl. Han hade av sin mor Kajsa lärt sig mycket, ty hon var en gammal klok gumma, som hade svartkonstbok och brukade gå årsgången på nyårsnatten. Han var just inte så mörkrädd heller. En kväll kom pigan in och sade, att det stod något mystiskt ute vid knuten. Då tog Karl fram en bakgrissla med långt skaft. På den lade han lite svavel och tände på. Han såg själv ingenting, men pigan såg det, och efter hennes föreskrifter, stack han grisslan däråt. Då såg pigan hur spöket började höja sig mer och mer tills det nådde trädtopparna, där det försvann.

> [In the middle of the 1800s there lived a man in Ry whose name was Karl. He had learned a lot from his mother Kajsa, because she was an old wise woman

who had a black art book and used to go on the year's walk on New Year's night. He wasn't very easily terrified either. One evening the milkmaid came in and said that there was something mystical out by the corner. Then Karl took out a back-scratcher with a long shaft. He put a little sulphur on it and lit it. He saw nothing himself, but the milkmaid saw the thing, and according to her instructions, he stabbed at it. Then the milkmaid saw how the ghost began to rise higher and higher until it reached the tree-tops, where it disappeared.]

> IFGH 1133, 2
> Elin Emannelsson, 1927
> Veddige, Halland

In addition to the narrative above about Karl and his mother Kajsa (IFGH 1133), these comments by an anonymous informant stress the need to preserve not only the words of the various charms, but also their accompanying rites and especially that the lore be passed across the sexes.

> Mot ormbett ritade min mamma med en kniv runt om och läste. Hon ville lära min bror, men han ville inte lära sej det. Hon kunde inte lära mig, för kvinnfolk ska lära manfolk och tvärt om.
>
> [For snakebite, my mom drew a circle around it with a knife and recited. She wanted to teach my brother, but he didn't want to learn it. She couldn't teach me, because womenfolk should teach menfolk and vice versa.]

> en kvinna f. 1841
> Lena sn., Västergötland[32]

The restriction against passing lore between members of the same sex is by no means universal in the twentieth century, as is illustrated by Jörgen Eriksson's sampling of healing traditions passed among the Sámi between men or from an older practitioner to a younger.[33]

OBTAINING POWER THROUGH OBJECTS AND FETISHES

¶ Objects

While magical power was thought to reside in the wise one as the use of his or her bodily fluids such as saliva or urine in magical rituals indicate, it might just as easily be seen to reside in an object or possession of the wise one. The wise one remained powerful only for as long as the item in question remained in his or her possession. This object might be a stone or gem magically won, or a substance held close to the wise one. Natural objects such as stones or gems could yield specific powers, and, as we shall see, some black art books describe special procedures to obtain them. Sometimes the object was the black art book itself, and once access to its contents was removed, the power it evoked was also gone. It would seem that it might also be the interaction of objects that produced magical potency, as in the case of Anders i Alehagen, who was able to divine both situation and remedy by thumbing through his black art book with a magical ring (ULMA acc #9735, printed Bergstrand, 6).[34] This motif of book and ring was common enough to provide a second account, as Bergstrand collected the following narrative about Johan i Gillestorpet, also called "Fesen" or "Fesenhök," that describes how he made use of the black art book also using this secondary artifact, the magical ring.

> Drängen va' så eftersökt. Han hade ena bok, som han såg i å blädde. Å en ring hade han å gne' på boka, å så såg han i boka, å talte om hur dä va'. Far titta', men han såg inte att dä sto' varken tryckt eller skrivet i 'na. Far sa' att dä va' ena svartkonstbok.
>
> [The farmhand was so sought after. He had a book that he looked in and thumbed through. And he had a ring that he rubbed on the book, and then he looked in the book and spoke about how it was. Dad looked, but he didn't see that there was either printing or handwriting in it. Dad said that it was a black art book.]
>
>
> IFGH 2358, 25–28
> Gumman Osbäck, f. 1860 i Sandhem
> uppt. C. M. Bergstrand, 1931
> Sandhem, Västergötland
>

Here, a book seems to have been only powerful by use of the magical ring as a "key" of sorts. From this excerpt it seems to be the case that had Fesenhök neglected to rub the book with his ring, the book would not have produced the power to help his client.

The following excerpt describes a different object, a special cloth, that was used in magical procedures to diagnose or divine appropriate treatment.

> När det gällde att utröna vad sjukdom den eller den hade, tog han fram en duk, som finngubben förhjälpt honom till. Den var försedd med en massa kors och tecken, som liknade dem, man ser i den hebreiska bibeln. Sedan läste han ena bön, ibland flera, hjälpte inte den första bönen, försökte han med en annan. Då kom "en skugge" på duken, den stannade vid ett visst tecken. Av detta visste Nils, vilken sjukdom han hade att göra med och vilka

mediciner han skulle tillgripa. Men det var inte bara beträffande sjukdomar utan även i många andra fall han anlitade sin duk. Göta-Lina och Essungakäringen hade likadana dukar, påstås. När de gav sig till att läsa och muttra, kom en skogge på duken. Likaså hade Nils en särskild bok med sig hem ifrån Finland.

[When it was an issue to determine what illness this one or that one had, then he took forth a cloth that a Finn-fellow helped him obtain. It had on it a bunch of crosses and the types of signs one sees in the Hebrew Bible. Then he would read a prayer, sometimes several: if the first one didn't work, then he'd try another. Then there would come "a shadow" on the cloth, and it would stop at a certain sign. From this, Nils knew which illness he was dealing with, and which medications he should resort to. But it wasn't just for illnesses that he relied on his cloth, but also in many other cases. Göta-Lina and the old woman from Essungen had similar cloths, they say. When they began to recite and mutter, there came a shadow on the cloth. Also, Nils had a special book with him from his home in Finland.]

> ULMA acc #9735, Änkefru Lind,
> born in Hudene in 1880s or 90s
> Hudene socken, Västergötland
> Linnar Linnarsson
> intervjuad jul 4, 1936, Fåglavik

In the preceding excerpt, the primary magical tool is a cloth with magical signs on it which was owned by the wise one. Secondary support came in the form of conjurations or prayers. The entire narrative is meant to explain the use of a "special cloth" in magical diagnoses. Even so, the mention of the black art book, which Nils had taken with him from his distant home in Finland, was also required to provide the requisite expertise to use the cloth.

Sometimes power came from the literacy which gave the ability to read the black art book. Aid from religious agencies such as angels, devils or God was also commonly given as the source of the wise ones' power. One Fredrik obtained his special ability by reading the entire Bible from cover to cover, implying that his instruction came from a divine source (VFA 3570:38, male, b. 1844, Ullesjö, Västergötland).

Magical power could arise from a small constructed object, such as E. J. Lindberg relates in ULMA 26903. Here, the object consisted of two disks tightly joined to one another by a stick on their backs, on the front of which was carved two crosses, the one exactly positioned opposite the other. This small object was called a *dokada*. Another object, here called a magic box (Sw. *trollskrin*) is described by Tillhagen[35] and which was locked tight with nine clasps, but which were opened when employed to perform a healing. The construction of this box was a magical ritual in itself: it is to be made from nine different types of wood, grown by a stream that runs from south to north, and prepared during three Thursdays occurring during a waning moon by a person who was born between midnight and one o'clock. These two cases are interesting because the source of power was external to the practitioner himself. Without these objects and their proper preparation, one might assume that the wise one was no wiser than a common person.

> Anders i Alehagen var en trollgubbe. Hade det kommit bort något, gick de till honom. Då gick han bara ut om natten och visslade, så kom "den lee" fram och talte om, var det fanns. Barn fick aldrig vissla förr, då skulle Skam komma.
>
> Var det fästefolk, som giv varandra slut, kunde han sätta ner dem, så att de aldrig blev gifta. Då skulle man ha med sej en näsduk från den, han skulle sätta ner. Han kunde sätta ner en person t.ex. i en brännvinstunna för att han skulle fylla sej bra – bli en supare.
>
> [Anders i Alehagen was a sorcerer. If anything was lost, they went to him. Then he only had to go outside at night and whistle, then the devil would appear and would tell where it was. It used to be that children weren't allowed to whistle, because then the Devil would come.
>
> If there was a betrothed couple who were breaking off their engagement, he could "put them down" (curse them) so that neither would ever get married. In those cases, he needed a handkerchief from the one who was to be "put down." For example, he could curse someone in a liquor cask, so that he would get really drunk—become an alcoholic.]
>
>
> IFGH 3504, 7–8
> Lotta Henriksson, f. 1855 i Skölvene
> uppt. C. M. Bergstrand, 1934
> Skölvene, Västergötland
>

In this case, Anders obtained occult knowledge by magical ritual. In this case, he would go outside at night and whistle. This summoned the "Reaper" who, in this instance, we assume to be the Devil, as a statement follows that children were not allowed to whistle because of the danger of drawing attention from the Devil himself. The motif of the handkerchief recurs, but this time, it is a cloth obtained from the victim that provides the means of magical manipulation, rather than a possession of the wise one that allowed him to use his own powers. Anders i Alehagen required something that had shared close proximity with the patient, such as a handkerchief in order to perform the requisite magical healing.[36]

A common instrument imbued with numinous power was the magical knife (Sw. *botarkniv*). It could be the source of healing power, as in the following example:

> En man ifrån Myckelby socken hade överraskat en tjuv. Tjuven satte sig till våldsamt motstånd, och för att freda sig själv, måste mannen döda tjuven genom nedstickning med kniv. Denne nödvärnmördare blev sedan enligt många sägner mycket god att bota sjukdomar på människor samt djur. Det troddes att det var den kniv, varmed tjuven blev dräpt, som innehade en magisk förmåga vid sjukdomars botande.
>
> [A man from Myckelby parish had surprised a thief. The thief prepared himself for a violent opposition, and in order to save himself, the man had to kill the thief by stabbing him with a knife. This killer-in-self-defense became very good at healing sicknesses in people and animals, according to many stories. It was believed that it was the knife with which the thief had been killed which had a magical ability in the healing of sicknesses.]
>
> VFF 2139, Olof J. Larsson
> Ellös, Bohuslän (efter egna minnen)
> Morlanda, Myckleby sn., Bohuslän
> Olof J. Larsson
> 1942

Knives specifically were part and parcel of the sorcerer's tools of the trade.[37] This knife was typically called a healer's knife (Sw. *botarkniv*) or a sorcerer's knife (Sw. *trollgubbekniv*). Others also could use the knife, an implement of iron or steel, to obtain magical ends; for example a blade might reveal a witch in a whirlwind by stabbing the ground with it. The *botarkniv* was, however, expected among the wise ones. Among malevolent witches (Sw. *häxor*) these knives might be stuck into a table or wall to milk cows from another's farm.[38] Other materials which provided magical efficacy were items such as lead obtained from church windows (IFGH 5907: Jenny Nilsson, b. 1904, Ullared), as well as dirt or bones from a gravesite, as in the excerpt, told above about the well-known *Prekebokärringen* (IFGH 1448).

Sometimes the aid of functional objects was required in the performance of magic. Molten lead or wax was poured into a pail of cold water, and from the shapes that the wax or lead took when meeting the cold water would suggest the image of the thief, or the qualities of the steam given off would suggest the cause of the malady.[39] In this excerpt, it isn't clear whether the image is conjured by pouring (Sw. *stöpning*), or simply by clairvoyant scrying (divining by means of gazing into water, a crystal, etc.) into the surface of the water, but it suggests that she had power, and that this power may have had its source in the black art book.

> Prekeborska kunde läsa bort sjukdomar. Och hon kunde säga, vem som hade stulit. Det var en som for dit, och hon tog fram tjuvens bild i en vattenspann. De sa, hon hade svartkonstbok och läste i.
>
> [The woman from Prekebo could recite away illnesses. And she could say who it was who had stolen something. There was one person who went to her place, and she conjured forth the image of the thief in a pail of water. They said that she had a black art book that she read in.]
>
> IFGH 3637, s. 9
> Anna Helander, f. 1861
> uppt. Stina Christensson, 1935
> Kungsäter, Västergötland

The woman from Prekebo was a personality to whom many folk beliefs about the wise ones was attached, and the number and variation of methods attributed to her may demonstrate the range of beliefs rather than the methods actually employed by one person. The water-gazing or scrying was one method, while reading in the black art book was another.

Combinations of materials and ritual could also appear in the same narrative, and in the following, the water in the bowl seems to be infused with the numinous power of the magical knife with which the wise one stirred it. The involvement of the victim of misfortune in the procedure is remarkable, and may be a way for the wise one to account for an unsuccessful session if there was found to be insufficient belief on the part of the client.

> En allmän tro i fordna dagar var denna, att vissa kunniga personer ägde förmåga att göra en bössa förgjord, så att det skjutna icke dog, om och skottet träffade.
>
> Hos mången rådde den tro, att den som ägde svartkonstboken, eller varit i Wittenbergs lära i Tyskland, han ägde en kunskap och förmåga som ingen annan. Han kunde påföra andra sjukdomar och svårigheter av olika slag, i en vattenskål framkalla bilden av ens fiende eller av den man blivit förfördelad. Den kloke tog vatten i en skål, friskt källvatten, och under läsning av trollremsor rörde han omkring i vattnet med en täljkniv i vardera handen. Efter visst svängande med kniven i vattnet ombads nu den som kommit att söka råd och hjälp, att komma och se ned i vattenskålen. Hade han nu nog fast sinne och tro fick han se bilden av den, som t.ex. gjort honom ont, eller stulit, eller genom trolleri skadat hans kreatur.

[A common belief in older days was that certain wise persons had the ability to hex a shotgun, so that the game that was shot didn't die, if the shot hit its target.

With many the belief prevailed that the one who owned a black art book, or had studied at Wittenberg's school in Germany, had a knowledge and ability like no one else. He could put illnesses onto others and difficulties of different types; evoke the image of one's enemy or of the person by whom one had been injured. The wise man took water in a bowl, fresh spring water, and during the recitation of magic verses he stirred around in the water with a carving knife in each hand. After a certain turn of the knife in the water, then the one who had come to seek advice and help was invited to come and look down into the bowl of water. Now if he had firm conviction and belief, he would see an image of the one who, for example, had done evil to him, or stolen from him, or through witchcraft injured his livestock.]

>VFF 1465, ss 1, 10
>Johannes Andersson i Torsby
>Vitsands socken, Värmland

This excerpt relates a combination of factors in the magical investigation at hand. Water, which must be fresh, the recitation of verses, and the motion of knives in the water were all preparation for the client's own ability to divine by scrying, a process of gazing to obtain images that hinted at hidden truths. Perhaps by placing the onus on the client, with the precondition that he must have sufficient conviction and belief for the procedure to work, the wise one protected himself from accusations of charlatanry.

¶ Fetishes, Ancillary Spirits and Apertusar

The following excerpt dealing with Anders relates that the source of his greater magical power was to be found in the greater number of what the narrator guesses is ancillary spirits, though the narrative does not make this explicit. It is taken from Bergstrand's collection, and is identified only by the location of the informant and not by any defining features of that informant. It is presented in context, and includes a reference to the directional orientation of the client's home, presumably a reason for his magical vulnerability.

>Han låg och var full jämt. Han sa åt min far: "När du byggde ditt hus, ville du ha det till att ligga solrätt, men det är lite mer vridet åt vänster." (Sandhem)
>Den kloke drängen, honom var min svärfar hos. Bodde han inte i Dalum? Svärfar hade fått kreatur förtrollade. Den kloke drängen låg jämt. Han söp och var alltid full. "Jo, dä har du för att du hade ena fästemö å övergav

henne," sa han. "Å nu har ho var't ijämte Göta-Lena, å ho har förtrollat dina kreatur," sa han. "Å dä har ja inte lätt för å göra om. Men ja har en mer. Ho har elva, men ja har tolv," sa han. Det är nog troligt att han menade smådjävlar. "Så ja ska hjälpa dej," sa han. Och hans kreatur blev så granna, så rasande. (Sandhem).[40]

[He lay in bed and was always drunk. He said to my father: "When you built your house, you wanted to have it situated with the door facing south, but it is turned a little towards the left. (Informant from Sandhem)

The wise farmhand, my father-in-law was out to see him. Didn't he live in Dalum? Father-in-law had a hexed farm animal. The wise farmhand was always lying in bed. He drank and was always drunk. "Yeah, well, you have it because you had a fiancée and deserted her," he said. "And now she has been over to visit Göta-Lena, and she has hexed your animal," he said. "And that's not so easy for me to fix. But I have one more. She has eleven, but I have twelve," he said. It is probably the case that he meant demons in his service. "So I'll help you," he said. And his animal got so big, robust. (Informant from Sandhem)]

Professional competition for a dwindling clientele[41] is suggested when Anders boasts that he had "one more" than Göta-Lena, a wise woman in the neighboring district of Floby. It is interesting that Bergstrand, or his informant (whether amateur folklorist or primary informant) conjectures about just what Anders means when he declares his superiority in this way, and he assumes that the greater number refers to demons in his service. Anders may be referring to the imp (Sw. *spertus*) which is also a servant spirit, but with less association with the demonic.[42]

Examples such as the *trollskrin* with nine clasps and small wooden pegs with symbols carved on them, the *dokoda*, or the *gammkärn*[43] a wooden artifact in which joints were placed and chopped in mime, to be thereafter healed of pain: all of these could be understood as fetishes of one sort or another, each with its own resident magical power or spirit to be drawn on in the wise ones' work.

OBTAINING MAGICAL POWER THROUGH INHERITANCE OR APPRENTICESHIP

¶ Circumstances of Birth

Gunnar Skogsmark mentions some of the special circumstances of birth which led to the popular perception of an individual as a wise one: being born on Maundy Thursday, being born with the caul (Sw. *segerhuva*)—a piece of the amniotic sack covering the newborn's head, being "stamped" with a distinctive birthmark, etc. (ULMA 22662, given below). Emil Karlsson relates that a child born on a judicial judgment day (Sw. *förkastelsedag*) was to be counted as one of the wise.[44]

Inheritance within families was another method by which a wise one not only obtained supernatural power, but could also take on a pre-established clientele with little effort. An example of this appears in Otto Nord's excerpt below about Sven Mårten i Stensjö (ULMA 22662). This genetic inheritance made children of wise ones more likely to be consulted after the passing of the parent. In the following excerpt, Mårten had no need for advertising his services, since his mother's reputation was sufficient to engender popular confidence in the younger: "Like mother, like son."

> 8. Mårten i Stensjö, som ju hade sin trollkunnighet från födelsen började sin verksamhet som klok, så snart han var stor nog att fatta sina egna hemliga gåvor. Ingen särskild händelse var orsak till början av hans verksamhet eller någon anna prinns motor. Han behövde heller inte slå på stortrumma för sig, ty då folk ju visste, att hans moder var "klok," föll det sig bara naturligt att efter hennes död uppsöka och anlita sonen.
>
> Mårtens konster voro ju mer av godo än ondo, han hjälpte ju folk ur deras brygderier och betryck och högst sällan gjorde han "djävulskap." Det kunde han nog göra men då skulle någon ha sårat honom, som t.ex. då han hämnades oförrätten med den lilla flickan genom att "läsa döden" över en ko.
>
> [8. Martin of Stensjö, who had his ability to do magic from birth, began his activities as a wise one as soon as he was big enough to understand his own occult gifts. No particular event precipitated the beginning of his activity or any other ... He also didn't need to "beat the big drum for himself" (advertise), because since people just knew that his mother was "wise," it was only natural that after her death they would look up the son and rely on him.
>
> Martin's arts were more of the good than the evil, he helped people out of their stewing and oppression, and he extremely seldom engaged in "demonic magic." He could probably do it, but then someone would have injured him, as, for example, when he was wrongly taken vengeance upon by the little girl by "conjuring death" over a cow.]
>
> ULMA acc. #22662, Gunnar Skogsmark,
Döderhult, Småland
inlämnad okt 4, 1954

¶ "Picking things up" from Various Sources

The transmission of magical knowledge might be something as simple as learning a charm from a neighbor, or as complicated as magical rites. In a court case from 1751, presented in the manuscript "Signeri och Vidskepelse" provided in Part Two, Annika Mattsson claimed to have learned the art from another young woman of the same age as they both worked as shepherds in their youth. This may have been a common method to gain healing or magical knowledge according to the wise ones themselves. It seems to contradict the idea that sharing a formula results in the loss of its efficacy in the original owner's hands. Further questioning of Annika concerned only matters pertaining to her lore and practice to ascertain whether her techniques were religious or superstitious.

¶ Apprenticeships in General

In other cases, however, becoming a folk healer seems merely to have been much like learning a trade in which no specific magical procedures were prescribed. In such circumstances, knowledge was passed by observation of the more experienced. But even in such cases, there was usually reputed to be a moment at which the healer achieved a sort of magical or medical proficiency that followed him for the rest of his career. There were individuals of such renown that their supernatural power was attributed to more than one cause. For example, Britta Lena Andersson (1824–1904), the famed *Kungsbackagumman* was reputed to have more than one source of power. While she was reputed to have caught and cooked the legendary white snake and drunk its broth,[45] others told a more likely tale: that she learned in a lengthy apprenticeship with her maternal uncle.

> Det förefaller mest sannolikt, att hon under sin tid hos morbrodern erhöll de grunläggande kunskaperna i läkekonst och olika örters medicinska egenskaper. Han brukade hjälpa sina grannar och vänner vid olycks- och sjukdomsfall. Vid behandlingen fick den unga systerdottern assistera. Hon var läraktig och hade ett naturligt handlag att ta sig an de hjälpsökande.[46]

> [It seems most likely that during her time staying with her maternal uncle she obtained the foundational abilities in the healing art and the medical properties of different herbs. He used to help his neighbors and friends in cases of accident or illness. During the treatment the young niece was allowed to assist. She was teachable, and had a natural manner in dealing with those who sought help.]

Interestingly, Britta Lena was quite well known for her skin treatments and had actually obtained a patent for one of her more popular recipes. Other recipes have since been patented and marketed ascribing the recipe of the formula to the famous *Kungsbackagumman*. Other narratives stress a kind of mercantile arrangement whereby the apprentice actually learns the art after contracting with the teacher. It seems possible that entire lineages originated with this kind of instruction.

> Fru Snus (avliden) egentligen fru Holmgren, innehavare av en liten handel vid stationen, var enligt allmän utsago en av traktens förnämsta "trolleri kunnia." Hon botade ormbett, "stämmde blo," o dyl. och nyttjade i stor utsträckning häx för att få god tur. "Hon lärde ut konsten att skämma bössor."

> [Mrs. Snuff (deceased) actually Mrs. Holmgren, the owner of a little shop by the station, was according to popular rumor one of the foremost "magic experts" in the district. She healed snake-bite, stopped bleeding, and such, and used witchcraft to a great extent in order to procure good luck. "She taught the art of hexing shotguns."]

> —Gustaf Alén, f. i församlingen, 1860

> Fru Snus lärde upp skogvaktare Sjögren (avl), som i sin tur lärde Erland Bodin i Lugnet. Fru Snus var antagligen av finnblod.

> [Mrs. Snuff taught game-keeper Sjögren (deceased), who in turn taught Erland Bodin in Lugnet. Mrs. Snuff was presumably of Finn blood.]

> —Albertina Svärd, f. 1861
> IFGH 1020, 32–36
> uppt. Ingemar Lundgren, 1927
> Finnerödja, Västergötland

And finally, the following excerpt tells how the healer's apprentice often had to travel a dangerous and lengthy path to attend her lessons, establishing the value of the techniques which were only won at great danger to self and family members. Kristina i Prekebo, though known for her supernatural cures, is presented here as purely a folk healer, with no magic in evidence, nor even a black art book. The "requirement" of a wise one owning a black art book may have been an oral commonplace, rather than an observation by witnesses.

> De som hade svartkonstböcker skulle veta allt. Det var väl till att göra ont med. De sa, att de kunde sätta ner folk i sjukdomar. Här var ett par ute i Karl-

Gustav, som de kallte Lotta-Brudina och Flyxes-däka. De gick omkring och spådde folk i kaffe och kort.

De har talat om många som ha haft svartkonstbok. Det skyllte de Kristina i Prekebo för också. Jag var hos henne en gång, för jag hade ont i armen. Men jag såg då aldrig några trollkonster hos henne. Hon talte om för mej, var hon hade fått sin konst. Det var en käring i Burse, som hade lärt henne vad det nu var. Kristina hade gått till Burse, och det hade tagit många dar. Så visste hon inte, hur hon skulle komma hem igen – hon hade sin lille pojk med sej och bära på armen. Då lovade käringen i Burse henne, att hon skulle komma hem förr kvällen, bara hon inte vände sej om. Och det gick så bra. Men så när hon bara hade en liten bit igen, vände hon sej. Och sen blev det riktigt omöjligt för henne. Men hon kom väl hem till slut ändå.

[The ones who had black art books were supposed to know everything. It was probably to do evil with. They said, that they could hex people so they became sick. Around here, there was a couple out in Karl-Gustav that they called Lotta-Brudina and Flyxe's-däka. They wandered around and told people's fortunes in coffee and with cards.

They have spoken about many who have had a black art book. They accused Kristina in Prekebo of having one as well. I was at her place one time, because I had pain in my arm. But I never saw any magic with her then. She explained to me where she had first learned her art. It was an old woman in Burse who had taught her whatever was needed in the moment. Kristina had walked to Burse, and it took many days [to get there]. Then, she didn't know how she should get back home—she had her little boy with her and carried him in her arms. Then the old woman in Burse promised her that she would get home before evening, just as long as she didn't turn around. And it was going fine, but when she only had a little distance left, she turned around. Then it really got impossible for her. But even so she finally got home.]

IFGH 3637, 12–13
Anna Nilsson, f. 1854
uppt. Stina Christensson, 1935
Kungsäter, Västergötland

¶Apprenticed to an Older Family Member

Apprenticeships were of various types. Some were among members of the same family, and others not. Often, they could take the form of an older person teaching a younger person, a practice that suggests that the primary interest in passing lore from older to younger was the survival of the tradition to the next generation. Apprenticeships, whether magical or medical, might require all three conditions, of familial relationship, gender and age, in which a parent or older relative teaches the family trade to another generation, a mother to her son or a father to his daughter.

> Hur man kan få utväxter på spenar hos kor och hästar att försvinna. En kvinna, som jag känner, brukar ta bort utväxter på spenarna hos kor och hästar. Hon gör det med tillhjälp av örter, under det hon säger några ord. Hon har fått lära sig det av någon äldre. En yngre får inte röja någon sådan trollkonst för en äldre.

> [How you can get growths on the teats of cows and horses to disappear. A woman that I know used to take away growths on the teats of cows and horses. She does it with the assistance of herbs, while she says a few words. She learned that from someone older. A younger person can't reveal such magic to an older person.]

> ULMA 9194, 87, Tilda Rovainen f. Närkki, Ylitornio sn, Finland, 1870 Haapakylä, Övertorneå sn. Finland Stefan Tornéus 29/8 1935

¶Apprenticed to a Nature Spirit

Apprenticeships might even be of a preternatural sort, such as Anders i Alehagen's instruction by a mermaid. Anders i Alehagen was reputed to have obtained his power at least in the following case by means of instruction by a water sprite.

> En del sa', att han hade fått lära sin konst av havsfrua i Sämsjön. Han kunde ta fram bilden av en person i ett kärl med vatten och sticka ut ögat på honom. Det hade han gjort med en person här, men jag vill inte säga, vilken det var.
> Han kunde tala om för folk vad de hade för några sjukdomar. Hade de tandvärk, gav han dem några pinnar att pella tänderna med.
> Han var en lajer fyllegubbe.
> Göta Lena i Floby kunde ock trolla. Henne gick de till, när det hände dem något dåligt.

> [Some folks said that he had learned his art from the mermaid of Säms Lake. He could conjure forth the image of a person in a water pail and put out his eye. He did that to a person locally here, but I don't want to say who it was.

He could tell folks what diseases they suffered from. If they had a toothache, then he would give them some sharp sticks to poke holes in their teeth with.[47]

He was a sorry drunkard.

Göta-Lena in Floby could also do magic. People went to her when something bad happened to them.]

> IFGH 3504, 7–8
> Lotta Henriksson, f. 1855 i Skölvene
> uppt. C. M. Bergstrand, 1934
> Skölvene, Västergötland

¶Apprenticed to the Devil

An audience with the Devil was often the motivation of magical ritual—for it was the Devil himself who might become the tutor of the prospective wise one. In the narratives presented here, walking the year's walk was particularly popular as a means to conjure the Evil One, and among the manuscripts here translated is one "Hell's Letter" (Helvetes brev) which was left in the key hole of a parish church in order to procure the Devil's service as teacher and benefactor. For something that was so frightfully damning, it is surprising how many of these types of Hell's Letters are found. Tillhagen describes the phenomenon,[48] but such letters were also used in combination with other means, such as the circumambulation of the year's walk. Tillhagen writes that those who reputedly obtained their powers in this way were so feared that whatever clientele might have resulted from their notoriety was discouraged by the general fear of their demonic involvement.

TABOO: KEEPING SECRETS

THE PASSING OF lore and power across the sexes is not the only ritualistic prerequisite for the transmission of magical power. It would also seem that the power to keep silent was important to retain that power. Here we see repeated the requirement that the lore transmitted be kept secret, as we saw in the excerpt from Djurklou above.[49] As soon as a piece of lore such as a charm was learned by another, it was often thought to lose its efficacy for the original "owner."

> Om en klok bergsäkert kunde lita på en person och vara säker på att han kunde tiga, så hände det, att han lärde ut något av vad han kunde.

En karl skulle lära en kvinna, och en kvinna en karl (allm.). En som
skulle kunna lära sig trolla måste ha lätt för att lära. När en klok lärde ut en
besvärjelse, så läste han den bara en gång. Kunde den, som hörde på, inte
komma ihåg den, så dugde han inte att trolla.

[If a wise one's ability trust a person was rock-solid, and he was sure that he
could keep silent, then that was when he taught him some of what he could
do.

A man should teach a woman, and a woman a man (generally). A person
who would learn to do magic must have an easy time learning. When a wise
one taught a conjuration, then he recited it just that one time. If the person
who was listening couldn't remember it, then he wouldn't do as a sorcerer.]

> VFF 695, excerpted from
> Harbe, *Folkminnen från
> Edsberg härad I*, 205–6.
> Skagershult sn., Närke

From Lappmannen (sic) Jon Johansson's *Signerier och Besvärjelser*, Johansson
articulates the belief that with the revelation of his secret charms and rites he
will lose the ability to use the knowledge he has shared.

o med det samma jag sänder dessa stycken så upphör min makt d.v.s. jag äger
numera ej makt att ställa blod o dy. Det är ej humbug som nutidens mennis-
kor säger om s. k. kukkelgubbar ty sådan visdom i ord o läsning härstammar
ända från Kristi tid då Frälsaren gick här på jorden o ty han gav sina lärjungar
makt att bota all sorters sjukdomar göra de blinda seende uppväcka de döda
m. m. Ty vi äro även hans lärjungar Ty – den som tror men ej för den som inte
tror skall kunna göra under o tyvärr det fins ej många Troende...[50]

[and as soon as I send these passages, then my power will cease, which is
to say I will no longer have the power to staunch blood and such. It is not
humbug as modern people say about so called cunning men, for this sort of
wisdom in words and prayers descend all the way from Christ's times, when
the Savior walked here on earth, and because he gave his disciples power
to cure all sorts of illnesses, to make the blind see, to resurrect the dead,
etc. Because we are also his disciples. Because—he that believes and not for
those who do not believe, will be able to do wonders, and unfortunately there
aren't many Believers.]

Johansson tells his reader that with his revelation of the secrets of wonder
working, his own ability in these matters will cease. But, this excerpt is also
important to understand how the practitioner might have perceived himself.

While his clientele believed him to be in league with the Devil (a preconception it seems he did little to discourage), it seems that for the wise one, the tradition of healing and wonder-working he exercised was a continuation of the scriptural and apostolic belief in the powers of the spirit.[51] Johansson's comment cites the increasing lack of religious belief as the reason for the reduced efficacy of magical healing in these increasingly degenerate times, rather than an appeal to any scientific model which might call magical healing a mere superstition.

These excerpts reflect a number of folk beliefs regarding the transmission of magical power from one to another. Reinforcing that secrecy was important in the retaining of magical power, the narrator again stresses that a wise one should wait until the last possible moment, even should it be on one's deathbed, indicates a belief that once one passed along the secret lore, it was no longer of use to the original holder. Also, we discern a rather more sweeping description of the requirement for the transmission across the sexes. As Djurklou wrote in the nineteenth century,[52] and as we see in our archival excerpts, especially ULMA 22662 cited above, the importance of remaining silent regarding the procedures and oral formulæ was important if one hoped to retain the magic power one was given.

Eriksson also mentions secrecy in his modern study.[53] Eriksson's study consists primarily of case studies of practitioners of the healer's art in provincial Lappland, primarily among the ethnic Sámi in Tornedalen. Eriksson tries to place them in a context of historical Sámi shamanism which had become intermingled with the faith healing of the Laestadians, a pietist sect especially popular in northern Sweden and Finland. In the following , Eriksson's interest is in those whose specialty is the stopping of bleeding.

In this interview with healer Adolf Kelottijärvi, a folk healer then in his sixties from the Tornedal valley, Eriksson tries to illumine Adolf's methods of healing. In answer to a question about the modes of therapy for different illnesses, Adolf answers:

> Psoriasis tar lång tid, då behöver patienten besöka mig flera gånger. Eksem är lättare. I både fallen läser jag ord ur Bibeln för mitt inre samtidigt som jag stryker med handen så nära eksemet som möjligt. Fyra gånger drar jag med handen.
> Varför?
> Det är min hemlighet, svara Adolf snabbt, liksom vilka ord ur Bibeln jag använder.[54]

> [Psoriasis takes a long time, and then the patient has to visit me several times. Eczema is easier. In both cases, I recite words from the Bible inwardly, while at the same time I am stroking with my hand so close to the eczema as possible. I draw my hand four times.

Why?

That's my secret, Adolf answers quickly, just as which words from the Bible I use.]

Self-Perception of the Wise Ones

AS HAS ALREADY been related, a broken taboo of secrecy can lead to the loss of magical power, as in the example of Jon Johannesson. The wise one might also undergo a change of heart, such that his interest or belief in magic may wane through the years, such as in the case of Jugas Olof Jonsson. We are told that Jonsson collected charms as a schoolboy, during the years 1873–74 with which, according to N. Sjödahl, he would fuel a career as a wise sorcerer. Sjödahl goes on to tell, however,

> Någon trollgubbe blev Jugas Olof Jonsson dock icke, om detta nu berodde därpå, att han vid mognare år fann yrket mindre tilltalande, eller därpå, att han började förlora tron på trolldomen – i varje fall påstår han sig numera icke hysa någon tilltro till trolldomskonster. Sina uppteckningar bevarade han emellertid. (Sjödahl, 35)

> [Jugas Olof Jonsson did not, however, become a sorcerer, whether this now was dependent upon the fact that in more mature years he found the career less alluring, or upon the fact that he began to lose his belief in magic—in any case he maintains that he no longer puts any faith in the arts of magic. He kept his notes in the meantime.]

As in tales of the disappearance of wights and trolls from the Scandinavian landscape with the technical advance of the electric light bulb, a belief in magic was also fragile and was subject to similar causes for doubt. A youthful enthusiasm might easily wane with either the disillusionment brought on by worldly experience or by a number of failed magical experiments. There is also the effect of changing social attitudes toward the unseen and how it exercised social pressure on the practitioner to view his art as somehow archaic and ineffective.[55]

Conclusion

TILLHAGEN WRITES THAT the magical art was the province of all, without respect to a specialized role. This is supported by the narratives that show otherwise unextraordinary people engaging in extraordinary means to obtain magical power, wither transitory or lasting. It has, however, been demonstrated here that specialization was expected, and obtained by various means. Language seems to have borne this out. We know that the terminology used to describe the class of healers and magicians is primarily descriptive rather than pejorative, unlike the English-speaking tradition. The obvious exceptions are in cases where there is pure demonstrated malice which is exhibited in a charm or spell, when we see words that include references to ambivalent or malicious nature spirits such as trolls, or use of the negatively charged term witch (Sw. *häxa*, L. *malefica*).

Among other traits that were important to the folk perception of the wise one was his or her unusual appearance, difference in either fashion or due to remarkable physiological traits that invited speculation. This is a sociological fact that does not seem limited to the Scandinavian area, as Mauss and Hubert have remarked. Von Sydow has also discussed the appearance of the unusual in the perception of magical or numinous power.[56]

The specific techniques of the *seiðmaðr* or *seiðkona* in the early Scandinavian vernacular literature are not to be observed in the more modern tradition: the descriptions of *seiðr*, that peculiar form of Old Norse sorcery present in the Old Norse poetic and saga literature and which reputedly included the use of scaffolding, songs, dances and drums, do not find their way through the centuries into modern folk narrative and belief about folk magic. In an examination of the manuscripts of black art books here, we will see that reflexes of some archaic practices can be discerned in more modern narratives, such as when runes give way to magical letters and sigils or when pagan versified charms give way to charm verses descending from more general European prototypes. While we cannot draw specific parallels between the literary depictions of the practices involved in *seiðr* in Old Norse literature and the more recent cunning art of the wise ones of this study, some descriptions bear an obvious resemblance and deserve to be noted. The Old Norse swore oaths while standing astride a stone fixed deeply in the earth, an "earth-fast stone."[57] (Sw. *jordfaster sten*; cf. Herstein's wedding in *Hænsa-Þoris saga*). In the more recent magical tradition as represented in the black art books, spells are often uttered also while astride such specific stone. Such continuity of practice, however, cannot with certainty be called survivals, as the performance doubtless went through reinterpretation, but its presence in the manuscripts demonstrates that both exhibited areas of similar reverence, where some of the same objects held similar numinous qualities.

A description of where the wise ones were consulted has provided a small hint of a social and economic context. Excerpts are unclear about whether traveling wise ones were itinerant due to homelessness or to a preference to delivery services at clients' homes. Ambivalent attitudes toward morality among some wise ones support the idea that an unscrupulous reputation was used as a marketing technique for an individual's public practice, but it is also clear that even those who saw their practice within a context of religious faith may still have suffered from suspicion of diabolism. In a description of the black book Minister and the malevolent Witch, we discern the essential dualism upon which folk ideas of the magical universe are based, and the two main approaches available to those who wished to obtain extraordinary powers or riches by means of the black art books.

There were methods by which the wise ones obtained magical or healing powers, and these were shared among client and wise one alike. These methods included the performance of ritual, the procurement of magical objects or tools, establishing a relationship with nature spirits or infernal minions, or finally, by means of instruction across the sexes. Methods to retain these powers were believed to include secrecy, ritual repetition and sometimes ownership of a black art book.

General attitudes toward the wise ones were tinged with fear and respect, primarily due to a fear of discovery—unspoken thoughts or motives could not be hidden from one who dealt in the currency of the hidden on a daily basis. Some narratives serve to instruct the listener in the proper behavior towards wise ones. Improper behavior is cause for serious and lasting retribution. Competition for a limited potential clientele depended in some cases upon self-promotion, and the wise ones' boasting of powers superior to others was one method to accomplish this. Tillhagen writes that it was more common to consult wise ones in neighboring parishes than one's own.[58]

In trial transcripts, there are instances of how the wise ones perceived the manner of their empowerment: in one case, from a supernatural being, the fairies or elves under the earth, and in a second from a neighboring acquaintance of the same or similar economic class. In narratives about the wise ones, the source of their power was a river wight (Sw. *näcken*),[59] a relative with whom one spent time in apprenticeship, or, the most ubiquitous, the Devil himself. We have also seen that the wise ones sometimes doubted the efficacy of their powers, and abandoned their art if sufficient social pressure or economic necessity was strong enough. Frequent references to circumstances of birth as the origin of preternatural power, for example being born with the caul, or at a particular time or under peculiar circumstances, contrast with the wise one's self-perception of greater self-determinism, one which resulted in an ability to leave the practice behind. An itinerant lifestyle increased a potential client base and potential income from the seclusion of a sedentary domestic practice in which ones clientele remained fixed and static.

While the black art book might occasionally be obtained from a more neutral source such as a nature spirit such as the näcken in the case of Anders i Alehagen in IFGH 3504 (1934), in the narratives about the black book minister and the malevolent witch, an infernal source of the powers of the wise one and of the black art book is posited. The minister was able to tame this infernal power by means of an arsenal of ecclesiastical tools, and thus keep it manageable and under control. The witch, on the other hand, joined forces with that infernal source, and obtained power through an alliance with it. Both presuppose the dualism of the good of the church contrasted with the evil of hidden malevolence.

And finally, in our brief examination of the sources of magical powers in the wise one's toolkit, we have hopefully established an expectation of the contents of the black art books they kept. In the next chapter, we will examine folk belief about those books specifically, to further focus our attention on what we can expect to see in the black art books themselves.

NOTES

1. In the following archival excerpts in this work, parenthetical remarks from collectors are retained and are not inserted or excluded. They are used, however, to render an accurate translation of the original. Alternate character sets to reflect idiosyncrasies of dialect or vowel modification are reproduced here with no attempt to normalize. Misspellings are retained with no attempt to correct. Entire excerpts are produced as found in archival records, both for context and for accuracy. Occasionally, italics are used for emphasis. No conscious attempt has been made otherwise to edit them.
2. Elias Wessén and Lars Levander, eds., *Våra ord: deras utal och ursprung* (Nacka: Esselte Studium Herzogs, 1982), 215.
3. Ibid., 479. Richard Cleasby, Guðbrand Vigfusson, and Sir William A. Craigie, eds., *An Icelandic-English Dictionary* (1874; repr. Oxford: The Clarendon Press, 1982), 641.
4. Johan Ernst Rietz, *Svenskt Dialektlexikon: Ordbok öfver svenska allmogespråket I & II* (Lund: C. W. K. Gleerups Förlag, 1962), 418. See also Nildin-Wall and Wall's discussion of *lövjare / lövjerska* in *Det ropades i skymningen*, 21 ff.
5. Rietz, *Svenskt Dialektlexikon*, 362.
6. Ibid., 367a.
7. "kusla, v.n. 1 1) trolla, signa, hexa; 2) läsa bort sjukdomar genom trollord." ['kusla,' verb, noun. 1) to do magic, conjure, bewitch; 2) to recite away illness through charms] found in Östergötland, Småland and Blekinge.
8. Tillhagen, *Folklig läkekonst*, 47–48.
9. Frequently, the names of the domiciles in which these wise ones lived held ominous names, such as "Finn's or Sorcerer's Wood" (Sw. *Finnshult*) or "Mandrake Meadow" (Sw. *Alehagen*, from Sw. *alruna*) or "Aldermeadow" (Sw. *al*).

10 Timothy Tangherlini, "'How do you know she's a witch?': Witches, Cunning Folk, and Competition in Denmark," *Western Folklore* 59 (Summer/Fall 2000): 279–303.
11 Nordiska muséets Europeiska undersökningen 23375.
12 Marcel Mauss [with Henri Hubert], *A General Theory of Magic* (New York: W. W. Norton, 1972), 28.
13 Ibid., 32.
14 Tillhagen, *Folklig läkekonst*, 88–89. See also Tillhagen, "Die Zaubermacht des Ungewöhnlichen," *Schweizerisches Archiv für Volkskunde* 68 & 69 (1972–73): 666–75.
15 Elisabet Dillner, "Lisa of Finshult and her 'Smöjträ,'" in C.-H. Tillhagen, ed., *Papers on Folk-Medicine* (Stockholm: The Nordic Museum, 1961), 118.
16 Magnus Magnusson and Hermann Pálsson, eds. and trans., *The Vinland Sagas: The Norse Discovery of America* (New York: Viking Penguin, 1965), 38.
17 Hermann Pálsson, ed. and trans., *Seven Viking Romances* (New York: Viking Penguin, 1985), 20.
18 Kathleen Stokker, "To Catch a Thief: Binding and Loosing and the Black Book Minister," *Scandinavian Studies: Nordic Narrative Folklore* 61 (1989): 353–74.
19 Ebbe Schön, *Häxor och Trolldom* (Stockholm: Rabén och Sjögren, 1991).
20 Jan Wall, *Tjuvmjölkande väsen. II. Yngre nordisk tradition*. Studia Ethnologica Upsaliensia 5. Acta Universitatis Upsaliensis, (Uppsala: Carl Bloms Tryckeri, 1978).
21 Eliade, *Shamanism*, 253.
22 Wall, *Hon var en gång tagen under jorden*, 136–52; Bengt af Klintberg, "Hejnumkärringen," in Alver, af Klintberg, Rørbye, Siikala, eds.. *Botare: en bok om etnomedicin i Norden*, 35–42.
23 As told to Gustav Lannestock in 1927 by county judge Hjalmar Olsson of Vestergård, Fjärås. Published in Stig Tornehed, *Kungsbacka gumman*. Nordhallands Hembygdsförenings skriftserie III, (Kungsbacka: NHV-Tryck, 1965), 5.
24 Carl-Martin Bergstrand, *Trolldom och klokskap i Västergötland under 1800-talet* (Borås: H. Borgströms bokhandel, 1932), 6, 9.
25 Tillhagen, *Folklig läkekonst*, 63.
26 Ibid.
27 Gustaf Ericsson, Magdalena Hellquist, ed., *Folklivet i Åkers och Rekarne härader: 3. Tro, vantro, övertro*. Skrifter utgivna genom Dialekt- och folkminnesarkivet i Uppsala, Ser. B:18. (Uppsala: Dialekt- och folkminnesarkivet, 1992), 176.
28 Ibid., 128.
29 ULMA notation, from Heurgren, Djurskrock, 108.
30 Tillhagen, *Folklig läkekonst*, 52.

31 Axel Olrik, "Episke love i Gote-ættens oldsagn," *Danske studier* 4 (1907): 193–201.
32 Carl-Martin Bergstrand, *Gammalt från Kind: Folkminnen från Kinds härad i Västergötland. I–III* (Göteborg: Gumperts förlag, 1959–1961), 110.
33 Eriksson, *Blodstämmare och handpåläggare*, 45–46.
34 ULMA 9735, printed in Bergstrand, *Trolldom och klokskap i Västergötland under 1800-talet*, 6.
35 Tillhagen, *Folklig läkekonst*, 85.
36 Frazer, *The Golden Bough*, vol. 1.
37 Tillhagen mentions this fact as well (Tillhagen, *Folklig läkekonst*, 88).
38 One variant of this is found above in IFGH 6151, s. 6, Adolf Gabrielsson i Skälläter, f. 1873 i Järbo, uppt. Ivan Markendahl, 1963, Järbo, Dalsland in which forks are substituted for the more common knife. Another variant, this from Norway, is presented in Reimund Kvideland and Henning K. Sehmsdorf, eds. *Scandinavian Folk Belief and Legend* (Minneapolis: University of Minnesota Press, 1988), 171.
39 Tillhagen, *Folklig läkekonst*, 114.
40 Bergstrand, *Trolldom och klokskap i Västergötland under 1800-talet*, 6.
41 Tangherlini, "'How do you know she's a witch?,'" 280.
42 Wall, *Tjuvmjölkande väsen. II*.
43 Tillhagen, *Folklig läkekonst*, 84.
44 "1. Dæ fanns en kɫok gubbe ve Undenäs, Stenbäcke gubbe, hans klokskap va troligen medfödd. Kloka ska va födda en förkastelsedag, tror jag. Etter va ja hört, så ha inte de kɫokas barn velat ta emot lärdomen, eller också ville inte di gamla lära ut dæ." (ULMA acc #10822, Emil Karlsson, f. 1870 Davidstorp, Sågkvarnen, Tiveds socken, Västergötland, recorded by Hildegard Axelman, 7/1937).
45 As told to Gustav Lannestock in 1927 by county judge Hjalmar Olsson of Vestergård, Fjärås. Published in Tornehed, *Kungsbacka gumman*, 5.
46 Ibid.
47 As a reading of the manuscripts in the second part of this book will show, one method of treating tooth decay was to pierce the affected abscess or tooth to release the infected matter from it to allow it to clear somewhat and relieve the pain.
48 Tillhagen, *Folklig läkekonst*, 57.
49 Gabriel Djurklou, *Nerikes folkspråk och folklif. Anteckningar* (Örebro, 1860), 59–60.
50 Lindskoug, *Lappmannen Jon Johanssons Signerier och Besvärjelser*, 73–74.
51 Mark 16:20; Acts of the Apostles 2:19, 43.
52 Djurklou, *Nerikes folkspråk och folklif*, 59–60.
53 Ibid., 58.
54 Eriksson, *Blodstämmare och handpåläggare*, 58.

55 Frazer's theory that magic, religion and science all resided on a continuum might be seen illustrated here, though the reluctance to bypass religion, citing its decline rather than any posited loss of faith, might also argue against that.
56 C. W. von Sydow, "Det ovanligas betydelse i tro och sed," *Folkminnen och folktankar* XIII (1926): 23 ff; Tillhagen, "Die Zaubermacht des Ungewöhnlichen," 335–50.
57 Earthfast stone, (Sw. *jordfaster sten*) occurs in 11 of the 35 manuscripts translated here. Compare Herstein's wedding in Hænsa-Þoris saga in which oaths are sworn on such a stone during the wedding feast. Utterances made on such geographical features seem more "firm," just as the stone is firmly settled in the ground.
58 Tillhagen, *Folklig Läkekonst*, 47.
59 Noted above as IFGH 3504, received from Lotta Henriksson in 1934.

CHAPTER III

Folk Belief about Black Art Books

Introduction: General Beliefs

THE PREVIOUS CHAPTER was an exploration of the wise ones and of how they were commonly perceived by those people who encountered, patronized or recollected them. Against this background, we now turn our attention to the artifact of the black art book itself. This chapter will, again using exemplary archival excerpts,[1] examine folk belief about these books, their appearance, their powers, all with the goal of providing a holistic context to examine and analyze the actual contents of the books themselves. The beliefs that concern us most in this chapter concern the black art book and its appearance, (or at least its reputed appearance in the absence of proximate examples), the methods of its procurement, its requirement in the performance of magic, and tracing its succession of owners, and the methods used in its ultimate disposition.

Black Art Books: Descriptions

ECCLESIASTICAL BOOKS, BY virtue of their ubiquity, were the archetypical measure of volumes of all types, and the large family bibles and *Postillor*[2] were considered large not only due to their size and thickness, but because of the spiritual wealth they contained. Mentioning that the hymnal was of the old fashioned sort lends a kind of venerability that old spiritual books held to the description of the black art book. And just as tomes like the Bible and the

Collections of Sermons (Sw. *Postillor*) required specialized reading and comprehensive skills to derive benefit from them, so too did the black art book.

The popular perception of the black art book as being of great age is indicated in the following excerpt in which the volume was said to originate in Catholic Sweden. Although the informant, J. D. Nilsson, doesn't mention when the wise woman Hjulesa lived, the narrative was recorded in 1938, making the age of the book at least four hundred years old.

> Hjulesa skaffade även tillrätta tjuvgods men det måste vara före tre sammanringningar efter stålden å så måste tjuven ha det kvar.
>
> Hjulesa hade lärt konsten ur en svartkonstbok, som hon stulit för prästen. Prästerna hade inte gjort sig av med de böcker som var kvar sedan den tiden påven bestämde hur de skulle va.

> [Hjulesa also recovered stolen goods, but it had to be before three church bells had tolled[3] after the robbery, and the thief still had to have the goods.
>
> Hjulesa had learned the art out of a black art book, that she had stolen from a priest.[4] The priests hadn't done away with the books left from the time when the Pope decided how things should be.]

> IFGH 4226, 18–20
> J. D. Nilsson, Mjölnare
> uppt. Nils Sjöholm (otillförlitlig), 1938
> Agnetorp, Västergötland

Tales of encounters with the Devil himself, or with a water sprite, encounters which concluded with the ownership of a black art book, were of greater interest both in folk narrative and in folklore collection than tales of a printed book purchased at a local antiquarian bookseller. Studies such as Carl-Martin Edsman's 1959 study[5] show that often printed books also served the function of the black art book, as did handwritten manuscripts. Edsman points out that the titles of rustic folk collections were taken from learned publications of centuries previous, such as the published and well distributed *Magia Naturalis* of Giambattista della Porta and its partial remembrance in a handwritten book as "Maria Materialia."

Stokker also mentions the phenomenon of published black art books, specifically in Chicago. There, a small volume entitled *Oldtidens Sortebog* published by John Anderson in 1892, was a best-seller in the last decade of the nineteenth century.[6] A similar case was the publication of *The Sixth and Seventh Books of Moses* (Sw. *Sjätte och sjunde mosebok*) in Sweden, a translation from a German original, and which even today continues to be published throughout the West.[7] With published editions of black art books, folk belief in a metaphysical origin of them wanes.

Det berättas att det skall finnas tio Mose-Böcker. Sjette, sjunde och åttonde mose-böckerna handlade om sjukdomar, medicin och trolleri.

Under 1600 talet översattes dessa tre mose-böcker från Tyska till Svenska språket. Och den sålunda översatta boken kallades "Svartkonstboken." Men så togs den i beslag, och de exemplar som voro sålda indrogos. Ty, det ansågs icke rådligt att allmänheten fick läsa denna bok. Men en del här i Jämtland och Lapparna smugglade undan sina exemplar.

[It is told that there are Ten Books of Moses.[8] The Sixth, Seventh and Eighth Books of Moses had to do with illnesses, medicine and magic.

During the seventeenth century, these three Books of Moses were translated from the German to the Swedish language. And the resulting translated book was called "The Black Art Book." But then it was confiscated, and those copies which were sold were recalled, for it was viewed as inadvisable for the public to be permitted to read this book. But some, here in Jämtland and among the Lapps, hid their copies away.]

> As told by:
> Brita Eriksson, f. Österåsens by, Häggenås socken,
> Jämtland, 1824, d. 1915
> to Barnmorskan Jenny Lundgren, Näset, Häggenås, 1926
> Häggenås, Jämtland[9]

Interestingly, some narratives seek to cast doubt on their own veracity by throwing in a perfunctory statement disqualifying the status of the book in question. Whether indeed it was a question of disqualification, or a statement of disbelief in such supernatural or demonic phenomena is not immediately clear. It may indicate a belief that there was a difference between the handwritten notebook of home cures and remedies and the infernal volume with instruction in conjuration and magic.

Black Art Books: Written in Blood

THE DESCRIPTIONS OF the appearance of black art books were meant to give an air of age, and of the mystery of bygone eras. The occasional mention of characters in red ink may also be a reminiscence of the Demonic Pact, which was often sealed with a signature in blood. If a signature in blood was enough to confirm a pact with the devil, then perhaps an entire book written in blood-red letters was an even more frightening thing to ponder.

In any case, the presence of large red letters was observed. Later in this chapter, however, we will see that red letters did actually hold an association with blood, which was often believed to be a prerequisite to obtain such a book. The ominous red ink in which the black art books were printed or written also recalled the illuminated initial letters in the books of the Bible. Also of note are the various recipes in the manuscripts themselves to create special printing effects, such as white writing against a background of black paper, producing an eerie effect which inverted common expectations of "the book."[10] Clearly, the special effect of variously and unexpectedly colored printing in these books also lent an air of numinosity to the volume under examination. Wikman, in his article describing Törner's own collection of spells and charms, which contributed to his study *Samling af Widskepelse*,[11] reproduces a facsimile page created in one of Törner's manuscripts with a background of black upon which appear white letters, here a variation of a stenographic script that Wikman calls *takygrafi*, which would not only produce an interesting aesthetic effect, but would be unreadable by the casual browser.[12] The unreadability of the black art book by other members of the household is also a common motif.[13]

The tie between red ink and the blood ink of the demonic pact is made explicit in the following excerpt from stonemason Karl Andersson, collected in 1932.

> En gubbe i Risinge i Mörbylånga socken, Hasse (Johannes) hade svartkonstbok. Den såg ja när ja va där å jorde skor. Alla bokstäver i den va mä rött, å han sa att den va skriven mä blod. Men han va så rädd om den, så jag fick ej läsa i den. Hur han fått den vet jag inte, å hans gumma jorde väl av med den, han gifte sig när han var över 50 år.

> [A fellow in Risinge in Mörbylånga parish, Hasse (given name Johannes) had a black art book. I saw it when I was there and made shoes. All the letters in it were with red, and he said that it was written with blood. But he was so careful with it, that I didn't get to read in it. How he got it I don't know; and his wife probably got rid of it. He got married when he was over fifty years old.]

> ULMA 5390a., muraren Karl Andersson
> f. 1865 (?) i Kastlösa sn, Öland
> Bring, Mörbylånga sn., Öland
> Maja Ericsson, 1932

In this excerpt, Andersson tells us that his own informant, the actual owner of the black art book in question, has told him that the book was written in blood. It is also clear, though, that he has never himself had the opportunity to examine the book himself as the owner was so very careful with it. He must rely on the testimony of the owner for his information. This may be a case of increasing notoriety by introducing fantastic tales to an itinerant workman, in this case a shoe cobbler, knowing that by this means the tale would spread to advertise his access to occult knowledge. The secrecy surrounding the book served two purposes: the contents were never revealed and so remained under the power of the owner, and it provided a material narrative backdrop against which tales of the miraculous might seem more credible.

> Min mor tjänte på ett ställe i Karl-Gustav. Den bonden hade svartkonstbok. Mor såg boken en gång. Hon var uppe och städade och letade upp den. Där var både röda och svarta bokstäver, men hon kunde inte läsa ett ord i den. – Om bonden var borta, så visste han alltid, vad de tog sej för hemma. Och blev där någonting borta, kom det alltid tillbaka igen. Det skaffade han hem. Folk kom dit med det om nätterna.

> [My mother worked at a place in Karl-Gustav. The farmer had a black art book. Mother saw the book once. She was up and was cleaning and found it. There were both red and black letters, but she couldn't read a word in it.—If the farmer was away, even so he always knew what they were doing at home. And if anything went missing, it always came back again. He got it back home. People came back with it during the night.]

> IFGH 3637, 15
> Brita-Lena Andersdotter, f. 1857
> uppt. Stina Christensson, 1935
> Kungsäter, Västergötland

Red letters, this time mixed with the more commonplace black ones, are mentioned in the preceding excerpt. Since the source of the account is the informant's mother, it has, at least to the narrator, greater credibility than mere traditional expectation. It is also not clear whether the reason her mother was unable to read a word in the book was due to the threat of being found out by the farmer's occult ability to see over long distances, or that the book was written in a type of code of the type described by Wikman in the Törner material, or in the manuscripts in which a cipher is used to conceal words of power or critical ingredients.

The following excerpt is remarkable for its foiled expectations—all indications in the narrative lead one to believe that the narrator is describing a black art book.

> Hade en person ont i ögonen, brukade han att tvätta på dessa med smultronsaft som blandats med vatten vilket troddes bota detta.

"Figur'n" hade en stor bok med röda bokstäver i som han brukade att läsa i, och ur denna troddes det också att han hämtade sin vetenskap. Någon *egentlig* svartkonstbok var det dock inte.

[If a person had sore eyes, he used to wash them with wild-strawberry juice that was mixed with water, which was believed to cure it.
"The Figure" had a big book with red letters in it that he used to read, and it was believed that he got his knowledge from it. But it wasn't a *real* black art book.]

VFF 1391, 19
Maja-Lena Johansson, f. 1854 i Krokstad
uppt. Arnold Carlsson, 1926
Hede, Bohuslän

What purpose this last dismissive comment plays in the context of the narrative is matter for conjecture, but it is possible that the narrator has already begun to question the veracity of the tales she has been told about such books, as was becoming more commonplace with the passage of time in the last century.

Speaking of the wise woman Ulla på Linneskogen in Stafsinge, who had died forty years before, Charlotta Andersson had this to tell:

– En gång blev Ulla svårt sjuk och som hon kände sig nära döden blev Pastor Svensson i Vinberg hämtad. Han visste, att Ulla brukade trolldomsknep och ägde svartkonstbok, som var skriven med röda bokstäver. Han begärde, att hon skulle ta fram boken. Hon vägrade, men då prästen hotade med att överantvarda Ulla åt satan, fann hon för gott att plocka fram boken, vilken prästen genast kastade i elden. Ulla blev åter bra och fortsatte med sitt signeri.

[Once Ulla got really sick, and as she felt herself close to death, Pastor Svensson in Vinberg was sent for. He knew that Ulla used magic tricks and owned a black art book, which was written in red letters. He admonished her to take out the book. She hesitated, but when the minister threatened to deliver her over to Satan, she found it best to fetch the book which the minister threw immediately into the fire. Ulla got better again and continued with her conjuring.]

IFGH 3515, 21–22
Charlotta Andersson, f. 1857 i Stafsinge
uppt. Anders Ljung, 1928
Stafsinge, Halland

The mention of red letters in this excerpt seems almost a non-sequitur, since it is of little importance to the narrative, unless one posits that red letters were a hallmark of the genre, in which case it is proof that the volume was an actual black art book. One must assume that the removal and immediate destruction of the book were the cause of Ulla's improved health, until we hear that she promptly returned to her conjuring ways with no repercussions in either health or spiritual attitude. One thing the narrative accomplishes is the establishment of a connection between the black art book and an infernal source, and justifies the church's antipathy towards a book the use of which might be actual cause for damnation.

Black Art Books: Owners

THE POTENTIAL OF certain of these books to endanger the common folk is often a theme in the narratives. Warnings, couched so often in terms of a suspenseful and enjoyable narrative, seem to serve as teaching tales informing the common folk of the dangerous powers these books contained.[14]

> Han hade en svartkonstbok, som han hade fått från "dä som ont ä."[15] När han läste i den, kom Skam. Han fick med sej den boken i kistan. De tappa' mycket annat till honom i kistan.
>
> [He had a black art book that he had got from the Devil himself. Whenever he read in it, the Devil would come. They buried him with that book in his coffin. They dropped a lot of other things into the coffin with him.]
>
> IFGH 3504, 7–8
Lotta Henriksson, f. 1855 i Skölvene
uppt. C. M. Bergstrand, 1934
Skölvene, Västergötland

Unlike the cases in England described by Owen Davies,[16] black books were not found only in the hands of an educated middle-class entrepreneur whose primary interests included extorting ever-increasing payments for ever-dwindling results.[17] Rather the situation in Sweden, as we shall see from a consideration of the manuscripts themselves, seems to have been that the owners of these books had a strong predisposition toward healing both human and beast, and the occasional hexed shotgun. To be sure, there are some examples of the type of ecclesiastically derived and therefore learnèd angelic or demonic magic of the Renaissance that Tillhagen or Davies describe,[18] but judging from the tattered and torn state of most of these manuscripts, it appears that few were used purely as a cosmetic prop "to impress clients," as Davies describes about the English material. An impressive prop that was never used would not show the signs of wear and tear that would indicate frequent use.

Britta Lena Andersson, or Kungsbackakärringen, was, as we saw previously, most probably trained as an apprentice to a relative. Even so, she was not free from the folk belief that the wise ones typically owned and used the black art book gotten from the Devil in the exercise of their art, even when experiences of their medical treatments exhibited no sign of such infernal involvement. This anecdote tells how Britta Lena got her power from a black art book:

> Det fanns de som med bestämdhet hävdat, att hon stått i förbindelse med dunkla makter. Sådana kontakter tillskrev man gärna alla naturläkare och "kloka." I Dalsland visste man berätta, att "Kungsbackakäringa" hade en svartkonstbok, stor som en almanack och med röd skrift. När man skulle riva källaren på gården i Hambrö, var detta nära nog omöjligt, ty nattetid spökade det it ett. Man kunde höra hur Britta Lena flyttade sina buteljer och ordnade med smörjor och salvor.[19]

> [There were those who maintained with certainty that she was connected with dark powers. Such contacts were often attributed to all naturopaths and "wise ones." In Dalsland it was told that "Kungsbackakäringa" had a black art book as big as an almanac and with red writing. When they were going to tear down the cellar on the farm at Hambrö, it was next to impossible, because at night it was haunted. You could hear how Britta Lena was moving her bottles and organizing ointments and salves.]

In the following excerpt, the ability to read and the ability to work wonders seem contingent upon one another. If one was unable to read, and yet tried to read in the black art book, there was no telling the trouble one might get into. In one case, small devils flew out from its pages to wreak havoc, and here, the implication is that magic would still work, but not at all as the would-be magician planned.

> "Svartkonstrebok" kunde ingen ha, som inte kunde trolla. Det var ingen annan, som kunde läsa rätt i den. Om en inte kunde läsa, så "läste en fast sä."

> [No one who couldn't do magic could have the "black art book." There was no other who could read it correctly. If one couldn't read, then he would be magically "stuck to the spot."]

IFGH 3751, 31–32
Johan Aronsson, f. 1868 i Millesvik

uppt. Ragnar Nilsson, 1936
Millesvik, Värmland

And sometimes, mention of the black art book seems nonessential to the flow of the narrative. In the following narrative, the black book minister does not resort to finding some magical remedy for uncompliant neighbors. Rather, the mere mention of it at the beginning of the narrative serves to let the listener know that the tale concerns not just a common member of the clergy, but one who owns an black art book, and has that magical resource at his disposal.

> De säger, att prästerna har svartkonstböcker nu. Det berättas om en präst, som hade en svartkonstbok. Han lag i tvist med grannarna om en åkerteg. Grannarna ville plöja opp tegen, men det ville inte prästen. En dag gick de o plöjde, utan att prästen gav löfte till det. På morron efteråt, låg tegen likadan, som innan den plöjdes.

> [They say, that the priests have black art books now. There is a story about a priest who had a black art book. He got into an argument with the neighbors about a strip of field. The neighbors wanted to plow up the strip, but the priest did not. One day they went and plowed, without the priest giving permission for it. On the next morning, the strip of land lay just as it had before it was plowed.]

VFF 2153, 10
Anna Katrina Mårtensson, f. 1845
uppt. Hulda Hammarbäck, 1927
Västerlanda, Bohuslän

Another example follows, in which this idea becomes so commonplace that one expects to find a black art book at a parsonage. As the Minister was a representative of the church, his was the only authority that was not only assured to adequately control a black art book in his ownership, but also to keep the dangers of the black art book at bay.

> *I alla prästgårdar sa de att det skulle finnas en svartkonstbok.* Det var en präst i Gällstad som skickade i väg drängen till Dalstorp med svartkonstboken, men prästen sa: "Du får inte öppna den, för då är du olycklig." Men när drängen kommit en bit på väg, så kunde han inte hålla sig utan öppnade boken, och då kom han inte ur flädren, för där vimlade av smådjur, och han måste stanna, tills prästen kom.

[*In all the parsonages they said that you could find a black art book.* There was a priest in Gällstad who sent away his farm hand to Dalstorp with the black art book, but the priest said: "You may not open it, or you will become unlucky." But when the boy had come a bit along the road, he couldn't keep himself from opening the book, and then he couldn't get away from all the fluttering, because there was a swarm of small creatures, and he had to stop until the priest came.]

>IFGH 2058, 3
>fru Anna Olson, Bomstorp, f. 1877 i
>   Månstad
>uppt. Viola Gustafsson, 1930
>Månstad, Västergötland

The ability of certain types of books to endanger the common folk is reinforced in narratives like this, though this one substitutes small beasts (Sw. *smådjur*) instead of the more common small demons (Sw. *smådjävlar*), a subtler change in Swedish than in the English translation. In this example, it is noteworthy that merely opening the volume is dangerous to those without the training to control it. The recitation of its contents seems almost incidental, reenforcing a view of the black art book as a source of power in itself, a sort of fetish. The black book's status as a repository or resource containing hidden spiritual truths affecting the physical plane become secondary in a consideration of the inherent power it exuded or represented.

Det var en präst i Holmedal som hade svartkonstbok. Men det var inte mer än han som fick läsa i den. Pigan hade sett prästen läsa i den boken en gång. Hon såg att det var stora röda bokstäver i den. Det var farligt för den som inte kunde läsa i boken. Han kunde läsa fast sig så att han inte kom loss. Mattes i Glansnäs hade svartkonstbok. Det var därför han kunde trolla så bra.

[There was a priest in Holmedal who had a black art book. But no one could read in it except him. The maid had seen the priest reading in the book once. She saw that there were large red letters in it. It was dangerous for anyone who was unable to read in the book. He might read a charm that would get him stuck, so that he couldn't come loose. Mattes in Glansnäs had a black art book. That's why he could do magic so well.]

>IFGH 3619, 1–2
>J. Holmberg, f. 1867 i Holmedal,
>   Björkviken
>uppt. Ragnar Nilsson, 1935
>Holmedal, Värmland

This narrative presents a number of interesting points in a consideration of folk belief about the black art book. Ownership by a priest or minister of the state church is by now a theme that has been remarked upon by a number of scholars,[20] a theme illustrating the power of literacy just as much as the respect held for the governmental authority that was the local religious establishment. In this narrative, therefore, we have the forbidden volume, in which no one might read but the priest himself. However, it was possible for others of the household to observe the priest reading in it. It was during those rare times that any knowledge about the black art book and its contents could be gleaned. The casual mention of another black art book owner and his magical proficiency at the end of this excerpt serves to place the rest of the narrative in context. Others also held black art books, the mere ownership of which provided its owner with magical abilities.

Black Art Books: Procurement

THE BLACK ART book was one of the items that served as a source of the magical power of the wise one. Access to its contents itself provided magical power. Ownership of black art books was often believed to be the result of pacts with spirits or the Devil. However, in examining the manuscripts themselves it often seems more likely that they were a compilation of collected bits of folk magic and medicine learned from neighbors, traveling craftsmen or family members. This does not mean that some of the contents do not imply a certain intimacy with the darker forces; rather that the actual provenance of the books was far more prosaic than their contents might have indicated.

The manner in which such a book was said to have been obtained was one way to establish notoriety among potential clients, and credibility of its contents. A supernatural origin suggested supernatural contents yielding supernatural abilities. As Tangherlini has discussed, a certain notoriety was an advantage in the establishment of a more numerous clientele.

Still other methods of obtaining preternatural power relied on being well-read, with the legendary black art book high on one's reading list. According to Emil Tiberg's account below elicited by Thomas Larsson, the black art book and compacts with the devil were commonly associated with each other. By pledging one's soul to the Devil, one gained the privilege of obtaining this reference book in which the secrets of healing and magic were recorded.

After establishing the contract with the Devil, the postulant received his black art book for the rest of his life. The benefactor was not always the Devil, however. In one account describing how the legendary wise man from Västergötland, Anders i Alehagen, got his book, a proposed sexual encounter with a nature spirit is the catalyst that provides the book which will endow him with his magical power. In fact, we are told that he received not only the book itself, but also the power to use it, as the underlining in the original emphasizes.

> Anders i Alehagen / Alboga socken / var en gång ute på kräftfiske. Han hade rott ut till en liten holme i Sämsjön. Fram på natten vart han sömnig, och ljumt och gott väder, som det var, lade han sig att sova ute på holmen. Som han låg där kom sjöjungfrun upp och ville bekanta sig med honom, men han ville inte ge sig i kast med henne.
> - Men här ska du få en bok att läsa i, sa hon då.
> Anders tog emot boken, och med den fick han även <u>makta</u>, så efter den dagen kunde han både det ena och det andra.

> [Anders in Alehagen / Alboga parish / was once out fishing for crayfish. He had rowed out to a little islet in Lake Säm. Along towards evening he got sleepy, and since the weather was as nice and warm as it was, he lay down to sleep out there on the islet. While he lay there, a water sprite came up, and wanted to "get acquainted" with him, but he didn't want to grapple with her.
> —But here's a book you can have to read in, she said then.
> Anders accepted the book, and with it he got <u>the power</u>[21] as well, so after that day he could do both some of this and some of that.]

ULMA acc #9735, Änkefru Lind,
born in Hudene in 1880s or 90s
Hudene socken, Västergötland
Linnar Linnarsson
intervjuad jul 4, 1936, Fåglavik

Black Art Books: Acquired from the Devil

THE MAGICAL POWER of the wise ones was passed in different ways, writes Thomas Larsson, in introducing a narrative told him by Emil Tiberg. One way, he says, is to forswear oneself to the Evil One. This could happen by:

> tre torsdaskvälla i ra sprang naken ansjurs umkring stuva å svor å åkalla faan, för han rejerar jo£a (jord) å frälsarn hemmel, å imat att de l8va sä te skråån då, su feck di lära sä en heler hoper k8nster än å um di sum va försv8rna te skråån velle ha jälp å n mä n8t, su va dä bara te viss£a på n, su kåm han å jälpte dum män su feck di uj va beredda på att han kåm å hämta dum en vesser da, sum va bestämt dum imälla. Di kunne uj l8va sä te dän onne jenum te springa ansjurs umkring ena körka tre torstasnätter i ra, su kåm han te dum dän trejje torstasnatta å jo£a upp kuntrakt mä dum, å dä kuntraktet skrevs

mä bεo, sum han toj ifrå vänstre lellefingern på dum, å likadant kunne di uj skaffa sä na svartk8nstbok ute skråån på så sätt, sum di lärde sä k8nstera i.

[running naked three Thursday evenings in a row counterclockwise around the house, swearing and invoking the Devil, because he rules the Earth, and the Savior Heaven, and when they had promised themselves to the Devil then they got to learn a whole load of skills, and if someone who was sworn to the Devil wanted any help with something, then it was only to whistle for him, and he'd come and help them. But they also had to be prepared for him to come and fetch them on a specified day that was agreed upon between them. They could also pledge themselves to the Devil by running counterclockwise around a church three Thursday nights in a row. Then he would come to them on the third Thursday night, and make up a contract with them, and that contract was written in blood, that he took from their left little finger. And in the same way, they could procure for themselves a black art book from the Devil, so that in that way they could learn the arts it held.]

> ULMA acc #9128, Emil Tiberg
> b. 1871 Baltakassn.
> Thomas Larsson
> 1936, Agnetorp, Västergötland

This account is interesting as it changes the focus of the purpose of the procedure from obtaining a fleeting glance into occult matters to a reliable method to conjure forth the Devil, from whom one might presumably obtain the legendary black art book, or at least miraculous powers that would provide ease and comfort from a hard life working the soil. In addition to the black art book, which itself often contained methods for discovering hidden treasure, the demonic pact was to obtain wealth and power from the start.

Aid from supernatural agencies such as angels, devils or God was also commonly given as the source of the wise ones' power. The black art book was sometimes the container of these demonic spirits, and one had only to open its cover to release an overwhelming host of winged demons.

Dä va många f8r di påsto hade svartkonstböcker. Te å mä Pär Brahe hade ena, sa di, å um han hade fått levet lite te, så sulle han ha tatt småjävla te hjälp å anlakt en väj över Vättern å tatt hela Umbärj et fölle (fyllnad), män han bεe dömder te dön å feck kössa jongfrua. Han feck kεiva upp för ena trapp, å n8r han trampa på ett vesst trappstej, kåm dä två saker å kεöppte å huvut på n, å hanses huve dä sa va förvarat i Visingsö körka, å hanses svartkonstabok dän tok di å förvara i h8vrätten i Jönköping, män nu sa ho finnes i Ståckh8εm. Inna Pär Brahe do, su spådde han, att barnt, sum hustrua hanses jeck mä, sulle je tecken n8εä föddes, för att han bεe döater (blev döder), å te tecken su grät dä bεo då. En i Baltak, sum hette Adel Hammarroth å sum bεe su gammel su han feck mj8εkatänner (mjölktänder) på nutt, sum sulle hatt mä sä ka änna ifrå Danmark.

[In olden times, there were many who were reputed to own black art books. Even Per Brahe had one, they said, and if he had lived a little longer, then he would have enlisted the help of demons to build a road over Lake Vättern, and would have taken all of Omsberg as a result, but he was condemned to death, and "kissed the maiden." He had to climb up a staircase, and when he had come to a certain stair, then there came two short-swords and chopped off his head. His head is said to be preserved in Visingsö church, but his black art book they took and kept at the high court in Jönköping, but now it is said to be in Stockholm. Before Per Brahe died, he prophesied that the child his wife was carrying would give a sign when it was born that he was dead, and as a sign it would cry tears of blood. Someone in Baltak named Adel Hammarroth who was so old that he started to get his milk-teeth over again, was reputed to have (such a book) with him all the way from Denmark.]

ULMA acc #9128, Emil Tiberg
b. 1871 Baltakassn.
Thomas Larsson
1936, Agnetorp, Västergötland

Per Brahe (1520–1590), a nephew of King Gustav Vasa, was the first Count after the introduction of the title under the rule of Johan III. He held lands on the island of Visingsö in Lake Vättern in south central Sweden. His mention here along with an aged noble, Adel Hammarroth, in a narrative collected in 1936 is remarkable for its separation from the events it purports to relate by four hundred years, even if Brahe remains a folk personality along the shores of Lake Vättern. This excerpt also points to the folk perception that the idea of the existence of black art books was of considerable age. With Brahe's reputation in folk narrative, crediting him with ownership of a black art book may have introduced the idea that such political power and wealth were not the result of mundane or merely political circumstances, but only came about by the intervention of supernatural means. This narrative also illustrates the use of servant-demons to build impressively engineered structures.

Power over such ancillary spirits could be the result of contractual pacts with the Devil. At first glance, it seems strange that contracts with the Devil were made to procure supernatural power in benevolent healing. When one considers the oft-occurring ambiguity in distinguishing between the benevolent wise one and the malevolent witch, it is perhaps not so surprising. The themes of demonic pacts, attendance at the "Wittenberg School" and the black art book seem especially linked in the archival excerpts gathered here.

Black Art Books: Requirement in Magical Performances

THE REPUTATION OF the black art book was well known, even if its actual nature as a book of recipes and magical healing procedures was misunderstood. Curiously, however, folk narratives do not mention the more mundane aspect of the books as how-to books in magic and medicine. Rather, they often focus on the misuse or unauthorized use of them by the folk, as we have previously seen in the case of the inadvertant release of many small demons by opening the book in spite of directions discouraging this. In the following tale, Lina Larsson tells of Röe-Lasse and his dependence upon the book in order to find a procedure for divining how many piglets a sow was carrying. At the end of this narrative, Lasse returns to tell them that there'll be no piglets—the sow wasn't even pregnant. Whether Röe-Lasse used a procedure found in his book, or used the book itself as a divination tool is not clear from the excerpt.

> Röe-Lasse hade svartkonstbok. En vinter var han i Baggås och hugg staver. Vi hade en sugga, som skulle grisa en tid efter, och så frågade vi Röe-Lasse, huru många grisar han trodde suggan hade. "Det ska' ja si sen' ja fått vatt hemma o sett i min svartkonstbok."

> [Red-Lasse had a black art book. One winter he was in Baggås and chopped lumber. We had a sow that was to have piglets sometime later, and so we asked Red-Lasse, how many piglets he thought the sow had. "I'll find out after I've been home and looked in my black art book."]

>> IFGH 3736, 13–15
>> Lina Larsson, f. 1852, Hallaböka, Temsjö
>> uppt. Arvid Göransson, 1936
>> Torup, Halland

In one of the manuscripts under consideration in this study, the illusion of flying snakes is presented. Another presents a method by which guests' heads transform into those of animals. Both illusions might well have been seen to originate from powers obtained from the book. The book was also credited with being occupied with small demons, usually winged, that flew forth when an unwary innocent had the bad judgment to crack its cover.

The black art book was not just a sourcebook for the spells and rites. It also served as a type of fetish, a magical prop, from which magical power exuded independently of an ability to read in it. This made it useable as an amuletic power source as well. Mere ownership, regardless of the literacy of the owner, guaranteed the owner preternatural powers. In the following excerpt it is almost credited with its own volition, in its ability to "do" evil.

Så fanns det nåt de kallades svartkonstboka, och hon kunde visa fram allt möjligt hundigt, och vad som ske skulle. det kan jag inte beskriva, varifrån de fick den, men hon var inte bra, hon gjorde ont. I denna socknen (Örby) vet jag inte om nån sån fanns, men hemma i Öxnevalla fanns det en.

[Then there was something they called a black art book, and it could reveal all possible unacceptable things, and also what would happen in the future. I can't tell you where they got it from, but it wasn't good, it did evil. In this parish (Örby) I don't know if there were any of them, but back home in Öxnevalla there was one.]

IFGH 3374:126, 31
mor Britta Larsson, f. 1849 i Hyltnäs,
Öxnevalla
Örby Ålderdomshem
uppt. Viola Gustafsson, 1934
Öxnevalla, Västergötland

In the following, the black art book takes its place alongside nature spirits, supernaturally occuring illness and healing, and occult knowledge, providing a context within which the book can be understood as a repository of hidden knowledge.

Dä va' på ett ställe här (Sörbyn), som di hade tomtegôbber i stal. Disse hade rö tôppmösser på sej. Hôspen där hade e brun mar, å den skälte di om. Men va dä inte tyst om kväl ble dä inte bra. Te slut tog di alldeles överhanna, så att han feck rive ner stal å flötte'n dit han nu står. Dä va' en möra som den ene mara va' sjuk. Tomtegôbbera hade gjort ve' a. När ho' kom utteför staldöra, stöp ho'. Men hôspen ställde sej på knä på mara å tog å sej mössa, senna läste han nöa böner, men va' dä va' vet ja' inte, men han hade svartkônstrebok. Mara ble bra.

[It was at a place hereabouts (Sörbyn), where they had farm spirits in the stable. These had red caps on them. The farmer there had a brown mare, and they were arguing about it, but if it wasn't quiet at night, then it wasn't good. Finally, they took things into their hands, so that they tore down the stable and moved it there, where it is now. It was one morning that the one mare was sick. The farm spirits had done it to her. When she came out of the stable door, she tripped. But the farmer got on his knees on the mare, and took off his cap, and then he recited some prayers, but what that was I don't know, but he had a black art book. The mare got better.]

> IFGH 959, 5
> Bernt Hagman, f. 1858 i Borgvik
> uppt. Ragnar Nilsson, 1927
> Borgvik, Värmland

This excerpt refers to the black art book as the implied source for the requisite prayers to recite to heal the mare. The structure of the tale doesn't seem to require it, until he tells of his ignorance in the matter of just what prayer the farmer uttered to heal the mare. To account for the part of the tale which he was unable to furnish, he appeals to the secrets contained in the black art book, saying that whatever it was, it came from that book. Appearing at first as an afterthought, this mention serves a function in the narrative, providing the means by which a common farmer could become a magically potent healer.

Black Art Books: Tracing Ownership, Tracing Power

SINCE OWNERSHIP OF the black art book often denoted in itself supernatural abilities, it would be interesting to trace the lineage or path by which a copy of such a book reached a particular wise one. In some cases, ownership was a matter of public record, and some members of the community were able to recite a chronological list of owners, as if tracing some kind of magical lineage.

> Elfström var en av smederna, som kom från Tyskland. Han hade svartboken. Den sålde han sedan till en smed, som hette Jan Varg. Efter honom fick August Bjässe den. Han bodde i Närsen. Petter Johannes och Klingas Erik är de sista som haft den. Sedan vet jag inte vart den tagit vägen. (En som heter Klings Eriker lär bo nu i Nås, säga flera personer i Säfsnäs.)

> [Elfström was one of the smiths who came from Germany. He had a black book. He sold it then to a smith who was called Jan Varg. After him, then August Bjässe got it. He lived in Närsen. Petter Johannes and Klinga's Erik were the last who owned it. After that, I don't know where it went off to. (Someone who is called Kling's Eriker is reputed to live now in Nås, so say several people in Säfsnäs).]

> IFGH 982, 6
> Karl Tysk, f. 1857 i Säfsnäs
> uppt. John Granlund, 1927
> Säfsnäs (Tyfors), Dalarne

How old a black art book was thought to be is sometimes mentioned in archival excerpts. Whether a black art book was thought to be a remnant from the pre-reformation period, or from only a century earlier, it appears that a book with a long and venerable history and which had passed through the hands of several notorious and powerful local wise ones, would bring with it the potential for similar power to its current owner. In at least one case, this led to a consideration in its purchase price.

> Det var en som hette Åberg, som hade en svartkonstbok. I den kunde han läsa hur han skulle göra vid alla möjliga tillfällen. Se'n fick jag hans svartkonstbok och hade den länge, så jag hjälpte många. Men den kom bort, alla ville ha den, jag hade säkert fått tio kronor för den.

> [There was a person named Åberg who had a black art book. In it he could read how he should deal with all possible situations. Then I got his black art book, and I had it for a long time, and I helped a lot of people. But it got lost—everyone wanted it—surely I could have gotten ten crowns for it.]

> IFGH 923, 10–14
> Lars Persson, f. 1843 i Bollebygd
> uppt. G. Lannestock, 1927
> Bollebygd, Västergötland

In the immediately preceding, Lars Persson is describing his own experiences with a black art book, one that he actually owned, but with its loss all his magical power he once had to aid people left him as well. Finally, he concludes his reminiscence with a comment about how much he might have sold the volume for if he had still owned it. In his reduction of the artifact to a financial asset in spite of his helping many with it, he seems to recognize its utility regardless of its magical content.

Black Art Books: Removal from Circulation

FOR BOOKS WITH an ostensibly supernatural origin, it is interesting to examine the very physical ways they were disposed of, once their owners no longer had need of them.

> Der var för länge sedan vid midten af 1800 talet en "klok gumma" i norra Halland hon kallades "Prekebo-käringen," som kunde bota alla sjukdomar i benbrott o kunde mycket annat o folk for långa vägar för att söka henne hon hade "svartkonstbok" den var stor som en gammaldags psalmbok, men den

blef tagen ifrån henne o är nu "uppspikad i ett muséum i Göteborg" "för att ingen skall kunna använda den o ställa till mycke ont."

[A long time ago, in the middle of the eighteen hundreds, there was a "wise woman" in northern Halland—she was called the Old Woman from Prekebo, and she could heal all illnesses in broken bones and knew a lot more, and people traveled a long way to seek her out. She had a "black art book." It was as big as an old-fashioned hymnal,[22] but it was taken away from her and is now "nailed up in a museum in Gothenburg" "so no one will be able to use it to cause great evil."]

IFGH 3651:126, 10–15
Hulda Ericsson, 1935
Stafsinge, Halland

The black art book's disposition—nailed up in a museum in Gothenburg where it was safely kept away from the general population—seems to indicate a belief that though *Prekeborskan* was best known for her healing and good works, the book itself was a liability to any but those few specialists who could navigate its dangers unscathed. To remove the potential danger of the volume falling into the wrong hands, it was not only kept away from general view in a museum, but it was also *nailed* to avoid any chance that it might fall open by accident. It is amusing that it is in just a museum, presumably in some storage vault, that the volume is nailed—perhaps this is a commentary on the accessibility of such institutions in the mind of the narrator. Perhaps the gathering efforts of folklorists had influenced the tradition, those who taught that black art books should be given over to museums because of their importance to recording tradition. The fact that they were portrayed as nailed, however, seems to give a sense that without constraint, they still represented a threat.

In the Heptameron attributed to the fifteenth century magus Henry Cornelius Agrippa (1486–1535), a procedure is described in which a book contained within its pages invocatory sigils. After conjuring each spirit whose sigil appeared in the book, merely opening the book was sufficient to conjure that spirit.[23] It is tempting to think that Agrippa's magical world-view contributed to the perception that a desire for safety made nailing such a book shut necessary. It might also provide insight into the power of the grimoire, and its ability to release upon an unsuspecting viewer a throng of winged demons.

Its removal from popular circulation seems to have the effect of making space and time safe once more for the average person, now free from the threat of great evil. In the following excerpt, "Kaptén" Elin i Lönnemåla (fl. Ronneby, Småland, 1650–79[24]) is credited with owning a black art book, though the only data we have about her is from trial transcripts from Ronneby in the mid-seventeenth century. Once again, removal to a museum removes immediate danger, making the book an historical artifact rather than a source of magical power currently in use.

> Det var en kvinna oppåt trakten av Vänersborg här som hade svartkonstbok. Hon kallades "kapten Ælí." En del säger att en präst fått boken, en del att den kommit på museum, en del att den fastspikats på hennes likkistegavel. De ha allt talat om att sådana som hade svartkonstböcker och sysslade med trolldom saknade skugga. En gammal Trollhättebo som kallades fiskar-Olle, talade om sådant.

> [There was a woman up around the area of Vänersborg here who had a black art book. She was called "Captain Elin." Some folks say that a priest got the book, some that it went to a museum, and some that it was nailed firmly at the head of her coffin. Everyone said that those who had a black art book, and were involved in magic, didn't have a shadow. An old resident of Trollhättan named fisher-Olle talked about such things.]

> IFGH 3451, 38–39
> John Ekström, f. 1877 i Gärdhems sn.
> uppt. Maja Ericsson, 1934
> Gärdhem, Västergötland

Finally, returning again to IFGH 3504, it is told of Anders i Alehagen that:

> Han hade en svartkonstbok, som han hade fått från "dä som ont ä." När han läste i den, kom Skam. Han fick med sej den boken i kistan. De tappa' mycket annat till honom i kistan.

> [He had a black art book, that he had gotten from "he who is Evil itself." When he read in it, then the Devil came. He had that book with him in his coffin. They threw a lot else into his coffin.]

> IFGH 3504, 7–8
> Lotta Henriksson, f. 1855 i Skölvene
> uppt. C. M. Bergstrand, 1934
> Skölvene, Västergötland

In these last two excerpts, it is clear that burial with the owner was thought of as one way to remove the threat from the common good. Only the most fearless would attempt subsequently to violate the grave to obtain the secrets held by the dead.

Conclusion

IN A CONSIDERATION of the narratives above, we can discern that the provenance of the black art book is believed to be demonic, and that it is given as a result of summoning the Devil, often in unusual and ritualized ways in order to make a pact with him. A variation on this theme appears in the narratives about Anders i Alehagen, in one of which the book comes from an established pact with Old Shame, and in the other as a gift from a mermaid after a presumed intimate encounter. In those narratives above that deal with tracing the ownership and therefore the lineage of a volume, we find that these books can be inherited, stolen, bought and sold, but in order to make effective use of them, some supernatural event or natural talent must predispose the owner to its effective use. Ingestion of unusual substances, supernatural encounter, demonic pact, or the agreement to inherit and thus take on the weight of a continued demonic pact as we have seen have all preceded at one time or other the exercise of the arts contained in the black art book.

NOTES

1 A total of 62 answers were received to Questionnaire M100. In the archives, 42 notations were about svartkonstböcker, but which included answers to M1, M16, M90 and M102, including some duplications. While some of these might be formally characterized as legends (Sw. *sägen*), more often there was a short mention of black art books as a parenthetical comment, or even to remark that nothing was remembered regarding the black art book. The excerpts appearing in this chapter were chosen for their exemplary nature of those found in various archives, the total number of which was not recorded for this study.
2 *Postillor* were a genre of collected sermons, considered edifying reading and therefore commonly found.
3 The method to call parishioners to church was by means of ringing the church bell in the nearby bell tower (*sammanringning*), so presumably this meant that it had to be before three weeks after the robbery had elapsed, one *ringning* for each Sunday morning assembly.
4 In Swedish, there is ambiguity regarding the word *präst*—there was no shift in usage between the pre-Reformation "priest" and the post-Reformation "minister" or "pastor." Both are referred to as *präst*.
5 Edsman, "Svartkonstböcker i sägen och historia," 163.
6 Stokker, *Remedies and Rituals*, 100.

7 For Swedish examples, see: Gwen de l'Holm, trans. *Den Svarta Bibelm: Sjätte & Sjunde Mosebok samt Moses Besvärjelser (Översättning från gammal Hebreiska)* (Stockholm: G. Wendelholm förlag, 1986). For English examples, one can see available in both bookstores and on-line the following: *The Sixth and Seventh Books of Moses, The Mystery of Mysteries, Moses' Magical Spirit-Art, Rare Old Mosaic Books of the Talmud and Kabala, Containing Copies of Original Seals and Talismans, Translated from the German Original, Word for Word, according To The Old Ancient Writings and Famous Manuscripts of the Hebrews* (Arlington, TX: Dorene Publishing, n.d.); *The 6th and 7th Books of Moses, or Moses' Magical Spirit Art, known as the Wonderful Arts of the Old Wise Hebrews, taken from the Mosaic books of the Cabala and the Talmud for the Good of Mankind* (New Lewis de Claremont Edition, n.d.); Henri Gamache, ed., *The Mystery of the Long Lost 8th, 9th, and 10th Books of Moses, together with the legend that was of Moses and 44 keys to universal power* (Bronx, NY: Original Publications, 1983).
8 In the Swedish translation of the Bible, the first five books of the Bible, Genesis, Exodus, Leviticus, Numbers and Deuteronomy are called The First-, The Second-, The Third-, The Fourth-, and The Fifth- Books of Moses. That there were would be additional lost books of Moses with hidden lore in them is a folk tradition common throughout the West.
9 As published in W. Liungman 550, 8–9.
10 See in this collection MS 1 *Cånster att bruka nembligen*, from the Museum for Cultural History in Härnösand, item number 96, for an example.
11 Wikman, *Johan J. Törners Samling*.
12 Wikman, "Törners 'Svartkonstbok.'"
13 Examples include: IFGH 3651, 10–15, Hulda Ericsson, 1935, Stafsinge, Halland; IFGH 5907, 9–10, tre berättare, recorded by Hugo Spendrup, 1956, Ullared, Västergötland; IFGH 3751, 31–32, Johan Aronsson, f. 1868 i Millesvik, recorded by Ragnar Nilsson, Millesvik, Värmland; and IFGH 3107, 9, Klara Johansson, f. 1848 i Murum, recorded by Carl-Martin Bergstrand 1933 in Murum, Västergötland.
14 For one example of the legend type 3020 Inexperienced Use of the Black Book, see Brita Eriksson, f. Österåsens by, Häggenås parish, Jämtland, f. 1824, d. 1915, recorded by Jenny Lundgren, barnmorskan, at Näset, Häggenäs, 1926. Printed in W. Liungman, 550, 8–9.
15 Compare this with the account found in ULMA 9735 in which the Black Art Book was bestowed upon Anders by the mermaid mentioned in the following paragraph.
16 Davies, *Cunning Folk*.
17 Ibid., 138.
18 Tillhagen, *Folklig läkekonst*, 14; Davies, *Cunning Folk*, 143.
19 Tornehed, *Kungsbacka gumman*, 26.

20 af Klintberg, *Svenska trollformler*, 22; Lindow, *Swedish Legends and Folktales*, 47; Reidar Christiansen, ed., Pat Shaw Iversen, trans. *Folktales of Norway* (Chicago: University of Chicago Press, 1964), xxv, 19, 28, 32. See also, R. Christiansen, *The Migratory Legends: A Proposed List of Types with a Systematic Catalogue of the Norwegian Variants* (Helsinki: FFC 175, 1958), Index numbers 3000–3025; Kathleen Stokker, "Between Sin and Salvation: The Human Condition in Legends of the Black Book Minister," *Scandinavian Studies* 67 (1995): 91–108.; Kathleen Stokker, "'The Would-Be Ghost': Why Be He a Ghost? Lutheran Views of Confession and Salvation in Legends of the Black Book Minister," ARV: *Scandinavian Yearbook of Folklore* 47 (1991): 143–52; Stokker, "To Catch a Thief."

21 Underlined in the archival excerpt.

22 Sw. *psalmbok* is descriptive of both a hymnal used to accompany singing in the church, but also a book of the lyrics which was often owned by any confirmed member of the church.

23 Stephen Skinner, ed. *The Fourth Book of Occult Philosophy* (Berwick, ME: Ibis, 2005), 44–45. "Which book being so written, and well bound, is to be adorned, garnished, and kept secure, with Registers and Seals, lest it should happen after the consecration to open in some place not intented [*sic*], and indanger [*sic*] the operator."

24 af Klintberg, *Svenska trollformler*, 127–28.

CHAPTER IV

✦

The Data & Analysis

THE DATA USED in this study come from a collection of thirty-five manuscripts in holdings throughout Sweden. The largest sampling in the collection resides in the Folklore Archive (Sw. *Folkminnessamling*) associated with the Nordic Museum at the time of research, but now annexed to the Department of Ethnology at Stockholm's University. Among the written or typewritten materials in the archive are file-boxes and one entire file-box there is devoted to the manuscripts of black art books. Other manuscripts came from various local museum collections or archives. Various National Archives (Sw. *landsarkiv*) and local district museums (Sw. *länsmuseum*) were extremely helpful in furnishing copies of the manuscripts in their holdings. The collection included here is the largest sampling gathered in a single study of these manuscripts, and includes 35 manuscripts from various locations throughout Sweden. These manuscripts are found in English translation in Part Two of this book.

In the previous two chapters, common expectations of both wise one and black art books were established using archival materials from which to extrapolate trends. The goal of this chapter is to discover whether the contents of these black art books satisfy the expectations established in the previous two chapters. By using the manuscripts themselves, rather than narratives about them given by those who had, in all likelihood, never seen an example of one, it is the aim here to provide data independently of the musings of either tradition-bearer or folklorist. Trends will be isolated, and where appropriate, examples from the translations in Part Two will be provided, so that those trends might be better exemplified.

In order to categorize and analyze the items in these manuscripts, metrics were gathered for both their structure and their intent.

Analysis of Formal Characteristics

THE CHARACTERISTICS OF the various items in the manuscripts were classified in the following way:

S-1 Total number of purely verbal charms (Sw. *trollformler*, Gm. *Zaubersprüche*)
S-2 Total number of purely stipulated ritual actions (Sw. *riter*, Gm. *Ritusanzeige*)
S-3 Total number of ingested recipes
S-4 Total number of applied recipes (plasters, soaks, ointments, etc.)
S-5 Total number of burned recipes (incenses, Sw. *rökelser*)
S-6 Total of verbal charms combined with accompanying ritual action
S-7 Total of verbal charms combined with accompanying recipes
S-8 Total number of written formulæ including *Ephesia Grammata*, drawn figures, and unintelligible markings similar to letters (Sw. *Wittenbergska bokstäfver*, or *trollkaraktärer*)
S-9 Items of lore, such as the importance of an animal, animal part, or substance in the performance of magic.

These categories adequately describe the items found in these manuscripts, and additionally provide insight into the preferred mode of operation of the original holders of these books. For example, one user may have favored the assembly of recipes, preferring to cook in the kitchen to provide the *materia magica*, while another with perhaps a stronger voice may have favored spoken charms in the written collection. As we shall observe, the data can be used to characterize the preferred *modus operandi* of the compiler.

It may also be useful to consider material shared from one manuscript to another, or the frequency of specifically written formulæ, to glimpse into a shared tradition that perhaps spanned social or economic classes, with the land-owner just as capable in the execution of the items as the rural, secluded wise one, tending their verdant pharmacopœia in back of the cottage. Writing was a necessary skill in the perpetuation of these magical notebooks, and while many could read enough to learn the Augsburg Confession from memory, fewer had the requisite active skills to write, and thus produce the type of manuscript under study here. The current study will not compare item by item the contents of these books, but this might be an interesting topic for a future study using these manuscripts, in order to ascertain their interconnections, and perhaps even borrowings or indebtedness to a particular *ur*-form.

Another interesting result of analyzing the manuscripts from a formal perspective is to see to what extent the accompanying actions of charms are recorded in them. The more recent published collections of the Swedish Charm corpus (Linderholm 1917–1940, af Klintberg 1965) have included solely the orally recited charms, which as we will see in this corpus is not the most commonly represented form.

Perhaps some generalizations might be made based on the metrics thus gathered to identify in what sorts of procedures, whether recitation, prescribed ritual, ingested, applied or burned recipes, individual practitioners saw their efficacy to be most in evidence. In a collection of mostly recited charms, the power of the word[1] could be foremost in the mind of the practitioner and be perceived to lend the procedure its efficacy. In wordless ritual procedures[2] one might say that recited charms for the practitioner are only secondarily important to a consideration of magical substance and its manipulation in ritual. The written word, exemplified in the Wittenberg Letters (Sw. *Wittenbergska bokstäfver*) or magical characters (Sw. *trollkaraktärer*),[3] *Ephesia grammata* [Ephesian letters] or linguistic formulæ in these manuscripts, might be indicative of an imputation of greater power to the written over the spoken word, lending literacy prestige in the acquisition of magical power.

And finally, it may be possible, based on the types of items most in evidence in a particular manuscript, to make some kind of generalization about the predisposition of the owner toward a more naturalistic or a more metaphysical view of the world and of how his art functioned. The predominance of recipes for ingestion, or for soaks and plasters might indicate a growing degree of comfort with an emerging health profession much as we know it today, based on observations in the natural universe. Those manuscripts with a majority of spoken charms, ritual actions, or the application of obviously non-medical substances (such as a bat's heart) for the supposed psychic power they possessed to affect the individual might indicate a previous stratum, in which the house cure was based not so much in the natural universe, but in a magical universe where causes of disease were more likely to be found in troll-shot than in contagion.

As we will see, each manuscript has a different distribution of each of these groups, and now with this study we can begin not only to look at the distribution in the manuscript genre as a whole, but to look closely at each book's individual tendency to include more of one type and less of another.

Analysis of Function (Intent or Motivation)

TO MEASURE THE intention of the various items in the manuscripts, one must assign specific workings to a function or intent. The following headings represent the types of intent I was able to isolate, and is the basis of this part of my analysis. Below this list I will discuss the types of magical, or medical workings included under each rubric.

I-1 Healing human beings, including protection from physical and psychic threat
I-2 Healing animals, including from physical and psychic threat
I-3 Healing inanimate objects, such as shotguns and ammunition from physical or psychic threat
I-4 Hunting luck, including procedures to improve aim or transfix game
I-5 Personal advantage not necessarily to the disadvantage to someone else
I-6 Manipulation of others, whether living or dead
I-7 Overt harm to others or their possessions or livestock

Since this tabular summary of the intentions of magical procedures and charms is general, here follows an enumeration of the subheadings found under each of these broad categories.

I-1 Healing humans involves a broad category of concerns that include workings that are not necessarily tied to the immediate safety of the human, but also of his closest and most immediate surroundings. The concerns most immediate to the safety and well-being of the individual include workings to benefit the eyes and their sight, the ears and hearing, the skin and hair, either the ache or decay of teeth, bleeding sores, burns, warts, skin parasites (also called vermin in the texts), rickets, jaundice, malaria, constipation, colic, broken bones and sprains, painful conditions, general illness, complications of pregnancy and difficulties with the reproductive organs or renal systems, alcoholism and mental distress, also called anxiety and insanity in the texts. In addition to this list of physiological ailments, we can include ailments of the immediate milieu, such as hexed butter, cooking, distilling and brewing, harvesting, and control over domestic fire, such as putting the fire to bed (Sw. *eldbön*).[4] A more metaphysical component of the healing procedure attempted to treat spirit possession by exorcism, and to protect the individual from physical harm from snakes, scorpions, shooting, stinging, poisons and injury. It sought to remedy hexed conditions, prevent psychic attack or harm from the realm of spirits, protect from the envy of humans or the shot of the invisible trolls or spirits who aimed to inflict misery wherever they went. Magically extinguishing wildfire and protection of one's own personal property were also considered under this general rubric.

One thing that appears to be common through all of the considerations under I-1 is the fundamental benevolence, the altruism of seeing benefit to the client. This general sentiment carries on into headings I-2, I-3, and I-4.

I-2 Healing animals here includes not just remedying the physical ills of livestock, but also protecting them from both unseen enemies as well as predators such as wolves, bears, bobcats and other wild animals. Under this rubric, the cow whose milk is being appropriated by means of a milk-stealing *puke*[5] or milk-hare is under the onslaught of malevolent witchcraft, and needs to be protected. Similarly, bees kept in an apiary need protection from losing their way back to the hive, or from an envious bee farmer.

I-3 Healing inanimate objects is perhaps the hardest for the modern reader to understanding in terms of the word "healing." In actual fact, the term used in Swedish is *bota*, "to heal," but we are not used to thinking in terms that something not living would be in need of specifically medical intervention. It might help to understand the term as "remedy" or "fix" in addition to the more common medical definition implied today. Under this rubric, we find charms and procedures to remedy a shotgun that either misfires, doesn't fire at all, or misses its mark too often. The ammunition, the shot or bullets used in the shotgun can also be treated to imbue them with extraordinary capability to hit their target. Fishnets and game traps also can, by magical means, increase their effectiveness, and can also be the targets of malevolent magic which removes their ability to perform their function.

I-4 Even if one's hunting paraphernalia has not been the target of malevolent magic, one might still tip the scales in one's favor by performing certain procedures to improve one's hunting luck. The occasional lucky substance smeared on the shot-gun barrel, or the requisite rite to settle one's nerves before shooting are typical of this group. Also included are magical procedures to cause the target to remain transfixed for long enough, or to approach close enough, that a successful hunt is assured.

As we have seen, in headings I-1 through I-4, we can discern altruistic intention, seeking to either protect from harm or bless with good fortune. The headings which follow are a bit more ethically ambiguous. In these last three categories of intent, we proceed from a concern with personal advantage that initially does not encroach into others' conditions or concerns, through an overt manipulation of others through curtailing their freedom of choice or of nature, and on into causing actual harm to others, either in vengeance or for personal gain or enjoyment.

I-5 I have arbitrarily dubbed this category "Personal Advantage." This category is still primarily disinterested in overt manipulation of others, seeking rather to focus primarily on procedures that will bestow luck, wealth, strength and other advantageous traits to the client or worker. Under this heading, we find charms or procedures for physical strength, especially in contests. Working for improved memory and understanding, such that these increased faculties might be used in novel and ingenious ways to attract wealth and recognition are included here. Divinatory procedures to identify thieves, or future fiancées, or to discover the sexual experience of a potential love interest or even to discover the location of hidden or buried treasure are all found under this category. Procedures to assure winning the lottery, or at playing cards or other gambling accompany others to attract wealth from whatever source is most expeditious. Spells to unlock locks or loosen fetters may have come from a time when treasuries were kept under lock and key, and the unfortunate who was discovered while trying to appropriate it would have use of spells to facilitate his escape from custody. Becoming invisible could have a wealth of uses, not least in order to enter the site of a robbery unseen. Along with invisibility, there is a family of procedures by which the operator can procure a stone, often called a raven, snake or toad stone, which bestows upon the bearer this invisibility, though it might also provide general luck, divinatory powers, or wealth when held in the mouth or elsewhere on one's person.

Also included under this rubric are procedures to afford protection from sword injury, presumably coming from a time when battle was a common method of conflict resolution. Invincibility to the blade, as well as to romantic infatuation assured that one might not become the victim of another's malevolent efforts to cause one misfortune or loss of self-control. The elimination of fear, the ability to buy inexpensively and sell to a substantial profit, obtaining a fine voice (which commands attention and respect) and the creation of a divining rod to discover hidden treasure are also listed here, as are procedures to approach that treasure safely, without threat from the dragon that guarded it. And finally, those procedures which bestow the individual with the requisite mystical power that defines him or her as a sorcerer, capable of shape-changing, and of conjuring a familiar spirit (Sw. *spertus*), harvest spirit (Sw. *tomte*, Sk-Da. *goanisse*) or a demon (e.g., *Marbuel*) to do one's bidding rounds out those procedures and charms performed to influence one's own circumstances for the better.

I-6   In the manipulation of others, there is a tacit implication that this manipulation is to ameliorate the negative perceptions of others after one has rightly earned them. A common procedure is for luck in court cases, either exercising control of potential witnesses to prevent a negative testimony against one, or of the judge to prevent a negative verdict. This kind of procedure is current even today in the working of North American root doctors, and "Court Case" candles can be purchased at metaphysical shops across the US. Causing others to like one, perhaps in spite of previous mistreatment, is also common, as is its extreme form, causing women to do what you will, from lifting their skirts to allowing one to have one's way with them. Charms to prevent dogs from barking are useful when facilitating a robbery, or when coming home to a sleeping spouse after a night at the pub carousing. Sleep spells are sometimes used to provide relief from insomnia, but can also be used to facilitate illicit acts while another sleeps. Causing hallucinations in another, sometimes called illusions, are a pretentious display of magical know-how. The ability to transfix thieves so that they might be identified with their ill-gotten gain, as well as other forms of compelling certain behavior, appears here as well. And finally, the ultimate manipulation, the conjuration of the dead, binding spirits and necromancy are included under this rubric.

I-7   Lastly, we have the working of overt harm on another, whether in vengeance or to one's own advantage. Here, we include taking advantage of others, cursing another's shotgun, cursing another's hunting, cursing another to blindness, cursing another with diarrhea, cursing others' relationships in sowing discord, leading to divorce or a break, cursing another's livestock in order to steal strength, milk, crops, well-water, etc. The creation of the troll-hare (Sw. *puke*), a diminutive spirit that travels to another's farm to steal the best milk (Sw. *sanket*) from the cows, is included here. Causing fiddle strings to suddenly break is not unusual, and one wonders whether breaking another's strings might afford oneself the opportunity to play for remuneration. General hexing is found in this category, with no mention of motive, as it is in the appropriation of personal strength. Finally, there is one occurrence of a spell for psychic infanticide in a case where the child's mother died in childbirth. Since infanticide was a punishable offence,[6] its performance by magical means difficult to detect would be useful in dealing with a domestic situation in which there was none to care for the surviving child.

In one manuscript only, there were some non-magical procedures in the art and science of smith-craft that were related, and that display an acquaintance with metallurgy. Since these are not magical or involved with ethno-medicine, being rather more involved with the exercise of a trade, I have not listed them among these categories.

One obvious use of these categories is to characterize the typical interests of the owners of these books, the cunning or wise folk themselves. Tim Tangherlini[7] takes issue with Johanssen's oversimplification[8] of the wise ones into two main camps: the benevolent and the malevolent. In many cases, writes Tangherlini, the distinction was made in terms of the narrative, and that without additional data regarding the practice of any individual wise one, the function of their practice on that moral scale was nebulous. Indeed, Tangherlini is correct when he doubts the veracity of a division of magic users into two simple categories, the benevolent and malevolent. As the analysis of the contents of these manuscripts will demonstrate, most cunning folk included charms, spells and rites for a full spectrum of intentions, making even the more benevolent healers suspect in a consideration of potentially malevolent witchcraft. Tangherlini convinces us that the reputation of a cunning man or woman might be enhanced by narratives told about them by their clientele, but now it can be stated for the record that the books themselves also present similar evidence. This analysis shows that black art books contain items that span the moral and ethical spectrum, and some books favor more of one sort, and another more of the other. We may also find that the narratives upon which the reputation of a given cunning man or woman are based are contradicted when examining the evidence from the magic books they compiled.

In this discussion, it might be useful to introduce a third category to Tangherlini's analysis of folk narrative and popular belief. On the one side of the spectrum exists the healer, the wise one (Sw. *klokfolk*), whose work consisted of the altruistic activities of bettering the health and environment of his or her client. At the other end of the spectrum exists the purely malevolent witch (Sw. *häxa*, *trollpacka*), that individual who exclusively seeks personal advantage to the detriment of neighbors and competitors, and in worst cases, inflicts harm or death in vengeance, envy or simple glee. I would argue for an intermediary term to use for those whose repertoire contained elements of both, the sorcerer (Sw. *trollgubbe*, *trollkärring*), who perhaps understood sufficiently well the mechanisms at work behind both styles of working. With this knowledge, they were able to employ or counteract them. As we will see, this third category seems implicit in narratives of reputation, with suspicion going hand in hand with reliance. Since we have no evidence that the contents of these books were typically common knowledge, we might assume that the practitioners themselves led their clientele to certain conclusions regarding their spheres of activity.

Another interesting conclusion from such an analysis is that, in the absence of biographical data regarding the owners, we begin to see what kinds of concerns preoccupied specific magic users based on the items they chose to include in their books. This could be complicated by what may have been a cunning man's preconceived notion of what kinds of items *should* be included in such a collection, and we must assume that not every item in a black art book was actually employed by the compiler, or at least not with regularity.

THE MANUSCRIPTS

FOLLOWING is a description of each of the manuscripts being considered in this study. It includes whatever is known of their histories and cataloging, where they are currently housed, anything we know of their one-time owners, and a breakdown of percentages for each formal category, and each category of function, motive or intent. Then, at the end of each consideration of individual manuscripts I will discuss them using metrics gleaned to make conclusions regarding the compiler. This will end in a summation, using the totals for formal and functional analyses in a spreadsheet for a higher level discussion of formal and motivational trends in these manuscripts. The numeric analysis might seem odd in that the total number of items in each category might surpass the total number of items in the manuscript. This is deliberate—categorization sometimes required that one item be recorded under more than one category.

MS 1

KULTURHISTORISKA MUSÉET I HÄRNÖSAND
"CÅNSTER ATT BRUKA, NEMBLIGEN:"
THE MUSEUM OF CULTURAL HISTORY IN HÄRNÖSAND
"ARTS TO EMPLOY, NAMELY:"

¶ An inscription inside the front cover reads: "Svartkonster af And P.." [Black arts of Anders P...]. This manuscript was left to the Wester Norrlands Läns Muséisällskap by D. J. Pontén, on March 17, 1882. An edition of this manuscript appears in Gottfrid Kallstenius, "En svartkonstbok."[9]

Since its donation to Wester Norrlands Läns Muséisällskapet, it has been held by the Kulturhistoriska muséet in Härnösand, and in April of 1917, Gottfrid Kallstenius presented an edition of the text in the periodical *Arkiv för norrländsk hembygdsforskning,* with much useful apparatus, with notations solicited from pharmacist J. Lindgren in Lund, and professor O. von Friesen in Uppsala.

The manuscript consists of 4 larger leaves, with 12 smaller leaves interposed, all in a binding of heavy construction paper. On the first of the smaller leaves, recto, in the outer margin appears the word "Coppia," leading us to believe that this was in turn a copy of an older manuscript. Indeed, Kallstenius concurs with this. He uses orthographic norms as well as penmanship to establish an age for the manuscript of hardly older than the last quarter of the eighteenth century, however the use of some particular word forms indicates that the original from which it was copied was substantially older. He makes no guess as to just how old.

Kallstenius notes with the zeal of the dialectologist that the language in the manuscript doesn't exhibit typical Norrlandic tendencies, and much of the terminology for animals, plants and pharmaceutical wares show ties with Danish or German, so he posits a south Swedish original. Some herbs do not occur beyond the northern borders of Västergötland and Småland, also implying a south Swedish origin. He conjectures that the use of some Latin names for genus and species suggests that the writer may have been learned to a degree. After presenting some of the more peculiar orthographical features, he presents the text with an extensive apparatus.

This manuscript contains a total of 97 items.

S-1 6	I-1 15
S-2 60	I-2 9
S-3 10	I-3 1
S-4 9	I-4 13
S-5 1	I-5 26
S-6 1	I-6 22
S-7 0	I-7 3
S-8 5	
S-9 5	

DISCUSSION

MS 1 is notable for the preponderance of wordless ritual contained in it. Second in frequency are recipes for both ingestion and application. Third are oral charms, written charms and collections of lore regarding the magical properties of various substances. One recipe for incense and one rite accompanied by an oral recitation completes the description of its contents. While 61.8% of the contents were devoted to wordless procedures, the remaining 38.1% consisted mostly of recipes. Five items were specifically formulæ to be written on paper or parchment and carried on one's person, and this suggests that writing, while not a primary means of spell-casting, was at least on a par with oral charms.

As for an analysis of motive or aim, the very first item in the manuscript is a procedure to make a horse lame so that one might win a horse race. Taking a nail taken from a coffin, one locates a hoof print made by the competing horse and hammers the nail into it. From examples such as these, one is tempted to conclude that personal advantage is sufficient reason for malevolent magic. The largest category of intent consists of workings for personal advantage, and the second largest includes manipulation of judges, witnesses, enemies, and women. Also in evidence are rites to gain physical strength. Altruistic healing is third in a reckoning of the contents of this manuscript. The smallest category, containing only one item (#3), is the healing of inanimate objects, in this case a shotgun.

This manuscript, believed to be from the late 1700s in southern Sweden, is less a healer's book than a notebook of techniques through which one might obtain advantage, with little attention to the ethical considerations of the means. The emphasis on procedural details, with a noticeably small selection using oral charms, may indicate an individual who was more a product of a learned atmosphere, and the inclusion of written spells would seem to bear this out. The vocabulary and spelling idiosyncrasies indicate a south Swedish origin, but the volume was discovered in Western Norrland, in Härnösand. This may indicate that the owner was well traveled, or that the volume was at one point sold to someone from a distant place. In MS1, we have a volume that is less preoccupied with ethical or moral constraints in the performance of magic, though the presence of helpful magic indicates that these types of procedures were a part of his repertoire as well.

MS 2

ESLÖV #1 [EM 3329 A]
"NO 1 RADEMIN: DÄTT ÄR ÖFNING I VETTSKAPP OK KONSTER"
[NUMBER 1 RADEMIN: THAT IS THE PRACTICE OF KNOWLEDGE/
SCIENCE AND (MAGICAL) ARTS]
"DENNA BOEK TILLHÖR MIG B.I.AHLSTRÖM"
[THIS BOOK BELONGS TO ME, B. I. AHLSTRÖM]

¶ The three Eslöv manuscripts are treated in Sven B. Ek, "Tre svartkonstböcker."[10] This article is a commentary on the manuscripts, and no transcription or published edition of the books has been made.

The following three manuscripts came to Eslövs muséet from J. Sallius,[11] who had himself received them from woodcarver Bertil Lilja, inherited from his father N. E. Lilja, who was the executor of the estate of the books' original owner, Bengt Ahlström of Eslöv. Ahlström was born in Reslöv in 1827, where he trained in his early years as a carpenter. From Reslöv, he moved to Nöbbelöv and thence to Eslöv, where he bought a little house on Pärlgatan between the old Folkets Park and Tvättedammen in 1883. He lived there until his death in 1919. He died utterly destitute at 92 years of age.

We are told by Sallius that Ahlström was a talented carpenter, and with his move to Eslöv he split his time between woodwork and healing. He soon went over entirely to healing, and was known locally as "The Professor." He is described as a pleasant and talkative man. During his lifetime, he managed to procure quite an extensive library. Word began to spread that he was able to heal both people and animals. It was said that his door was always open, no matter the hour. He was also reputed to be able to retrieve stolen goods. He had many bottles containing different medicines, and in his small garden he cultivated medicinal herbs. The following narrative from an elderly native of Eslöv is presented by Sallius in his foreword to Ek's commentary:

> The poor always went to professor Ahlström. The real doctors were too expensive for anyone to be able to afford going to them. Professor Ahlström was a talented man who could cure all sorts of sickness. You could have a pain wherever, and he could get rid of the evil. He was inexpensive and knowledgeable. I was at his house one time, when I had gotten an ache. He had me keep my leg in a tub with water, and then he poured in some common salt into it. And it helped. My husband had a boil and he took that away too. I don't know if he cured scurvy (the English Sickness). I never heard about that, but I'm sure he could do that as well. There were always terribly many people at his place. He didn't just heal people, but animals as well, for example pigs that had bone sickness. The farmers often came with a heifer or a horse for him. Then they tied the animal outside, and after a while the professor himself came outside and began to put a plaster on the animal.

This first in the collection of three volumes consists of 15 bound leaves, with 29 pages of written material. It has a sewn binding, and measures 18.5×11 CM, and is coverless. The first page gives a conscious title, i.e., it is labeled "*N° 1 Rademin dätt är öfning i vettskap ok konster*" [*#1 Rademin, that is exercises in science and arts*] but one assumes that with the numbering of the volume, it was the writer's intent to have more than one. The three volumes from Eslöv are each numbered, and each labeled as to the compiler, B. I. Ahlström, and the second of the three, labeled N° 4, is dated April 13, 1865, which places all three around the middle of the nineteenth century when Ahlström was 38 years old. Of the three Eslöv manuscripts, this first is the hardest to make out. Problematic readings, or where text runs off the page are indicated in the translation by brackets [like this]. Also, Swedish for which no English equivalent was found in any lexicon were included in brackets as well.

There was no numeration of items in this first manuscript, but numeration was inserted in the translation. This manuscript contains a total of 53 items.

S-1	14	I-1	18
S-2	12	I-2	5
S-3	8	I-3	1
S-4	4	I-4	2
S-5	1	I-5	10
S-6	8	I-6	6
S-7	0	I-7	8
S-8	9		
S-9	0		

DISCUSSION

MS 2 exhibits traits that we might be more apt to expect in this form of literature, with the largest formal category in oral charms. Healing is also the largest motivational category, also something that we might be more apt to expect, especially given the narratives about Ahlström and his abilities in healing. However, the relatively large numbers of procedures for personal advantage, often to the disadvantage of another is interesting for the contrast it provides. With Ahlström's large clientele, these less altruistic procedures may not have been common knowledge, and thus his reputation as one of the wise ones (Sw. *kloka*) would have been untarnished. We might be able to take this manuscript as an example of the broad spectrum of intentions represented in the cunning-folk's repertoire, and the contrast between popular reputation and actual areas of activity.

Also of interest is the paragraph near the beginning of the manuscript entitled "Foreword" and which is obviously copied from some printed text, the purpose of which is not clear. It may serve as a reminder of a "reputable source" in case of questioning either by authorities or the dissatisfied client, or it might be the source for Ahlström's popular reputation as an unofficial "Professor." In any case, the difference in tone between this single paragraph and the rest of the contents of this manuscript indicate different sources, the "Foreword" copied from another printed book, while the rest of the items representing Ahlström's actual collecting efforts.

MS 3

ESLÖV #2 [EM 3329 B]
"N° 4 STORA KATEKIS"
"NUMBER 4 THE GREAT CATECHISM"
"TILL HÖRIG B. AHLSTRÖM, ESLÖF. DEN 13DE APRIL. 65"
[BELONGING TO B. AHLSTRÖM, ESLÖV, APRIL 13TH, 1865]

¶This volume measures 21×17.5 CM, and the writing is larger than in the previous manuscript as a result of the larger pages. The volume consists of 30 pages (15 leaves sewn binding), containing a total of 57 items. At least three different hands are represented in this volume, and they are interspersed but with regular numeration. Might this mean that this manuscript was shared among an entire family or over generations? Numeration begins with item number two, yet there are no pages missing between the title page and this first page.

S-1	0	I-1	38
S-2	10	I-2	5
S-3	21	I-3	0
S-4	13	I-4	0
S-5	5	I-5	5
S-6	6	I-6	1
S-7	0	I-7	1
S-8	7		
S-9	0		

DISCUSSION

For Ahlström, this volume rectifies the imbalance found in Eslöv #1, and contains primarily healing procedures and recipes. Ingested recipes are by far the most numerous, with applied recipes and rituals evenly divided as the second most numerous. It appears from an examination of these first two that Ahlström kept charms and procedures of similar form and intent in discrete manuscripts. It was probably from the type of procedures and recipes/prescriptions provided in this volume that Ahlström gained his reputation as a healer and "Professor."

MS 4

ESLÖV #3 [EM 3329 C]
"FÖR TANDVÄRK"
"FOR TOOTHACHE"
"B. I. AHLSTRÖM, ESLÖV"

¶This volume also measures 21×17.5 CM, and the writing is approximately the same size as volume 2: Stora Katekis. The volume consists of 15 pages (sewn binding), with a total of 42 items according to Sven Ek, though I count only 41, and it includes a rather substantial section on the conjuration of the demon Marbuel. Also of interest is a conjuration of a "goanisse" or farm spirit to attend upon one's agricultural livelihood.

According to Sven Ek, the General Conjuration to Marbuel agrees substantially word for word with *Particular-Citation des Gross-Fürsten Marbuelis* in a seventeenth-century book *Dr. Johann Faustens Miracul- Kunst- und Wunder-Buch oder die schwarze Rabe auch der Dreifache Höllen Zwang genannt*.[12]

Items are not numbered in the original, but are numbered in this translation for ease of reference.

S-1	18	I-1	6
S-2	10	I-2	3
S-3	5	I-3	1
S-4	1	I-4	1
S-5	1	I-5	17
S-6	6	I-6	2
S-7	0	I-7	8
S-8	9		
S-9	0		

DISCUSSION

This third manuscript of Ahlström's departs from the general ethno-medicine of MS 3, and the unsophisticated procedures to obtain advantage at others' expense that characterizes MS 2. This item is interesting for the very lengthy conjuration to the Demon Marbuel, an Arch-Duke in the demonic hierarchy, which has obviously been copied either directly from a printed source, or from another copy descending from that printed source. As Ek points out, the handwritten copy agrees well with the printed version of 1846, though the original printed copy appeared in German, requiring either Ahlström or his predecessor to have translated it.

Another item of note is that there is a procedure to obtain what is termed a good gnome (Sw. *goanisse*). This name is interesting as it uses the typical Danish and Skånian name for this spirit of barn and farm (Da. *nisse*), usually called in Swedish a *tomte*. The tomte has a venerable history in Swedish folk belief, and we have literary references to the *tomptegudhi* as early as the mid-fourteenth century in the *Revelationes* of Saint Birgitta of Vadstena (6:28). It is a nature or land spirit whose role is to oversee the productivity and well-being of a farm. It is tied to Scandinavia's pagan past, but in this manuscript, it is coupled with appeals to Satan to procure the favor of such a spirit. This syncretism is noteworthy, in its mixture of two domains, the learnèd ecclesiastical domain and the realm of folk belief.

Appeals to the demonic are more common in this manuscript. Invocations to these demonic powers include one to Beelzebub (#13) to "stop" a man, two to Satan in numbers 14 and 17 for a farm wight and to poke out a thief's eye respectively, and two to Leviathan in 16 and 22 for transfixing a thief and charming a shotgun respectively. Items numbered 27 through 41 consist of the conjuration to Marbuel. These appeals to the demonic include no procedures of healing or altruism, but represent manipulative or destructive intentions exclusively.

With this accumulated data, we can re-characterize the magical practice of "Professor" Bengt Ahlström as heterogeneous, including both benevolent procedures and recipes for healing, as well as more manipulative and malevolent procedures that the client never saw in a typical consultation with him. Ahlström is characterized in the narratives that describe him as a good old soul, a capable healer, a gregarious sort and very approachable, and yet the decidedly manipulative and malevolent items in his repertoire would indicate that he was much more the sorcerer, and that public opinion was based on only fragmentary evidence, or clever concealment.

MS5

KU[13] 3335 LAKBÄCK, ROGSTA SOCKEN, HÄLSINGLAND
"TROLLBOKEN"
PRIVAT ÄGO: J. ARBORÉN
KU 3335, FROM LAKBÄCK VILLAGE, IN ROGSTA PARISH, HÄLSINGLAND
"MAGIC BOOK"
IN THE PRIVATE OWNERSHIP OF J. ARBORÉN

¶This manuscript was lent to the Royal Library by J. Arborén, who retained ownership. The following description of the circumstances under which the manuscript was created is included in the collection's file box.

THE MANUSCRIPTS

Erik Johan Arborén, J. A.' s father, who was a fisherman, farmer and a sometime businessman in the fishing community of Lakbäck, copied this "magic book" as a 17-year-old in the year that is on the title page, 1881. The book itself is secondary, only used to write down original texts. The book itself is substantially older than the version we see here.

J. A. explains that his father when he, as a cunning man, knew "Pusten," a squatter in Västanbäck, Rogsta parish, was in Hudiksvall one day, his father went to Pusten's wife, and got to borrow his black book and copied as much as he had time to during the same day, before Pusten came home. He was compelled to bring back the original. This is the copy borrowed from A.

—Carl Olof Cederlund, Statens sjöhistoriska museum, Oct. 23, 1970.

This black art book, given the title "Trollbok" in the manuscript, was loaned to the Royal Research Collection (Sw. *Kungliga Undersökningen*) in October of 1970. The format stood at 16×20 CM, had a brownish green cloth binding with brown leather spine and corners. It included partly printed pages, and partly some pages that were sewn in. On the inside cover is pasted a sort of glossy paper, white with raised gold print. Erik Johan Andersson, Rogsta, Westanbäck is listed as the owner, August 15, 1881.

On the facing surface is print, and thereafter follow 18 numbered pages, the last two of which are blank. On page 11 appears a gilded oval pasted in, on which is printed in English PATENT SILK; FINISHED VELVET, and a seal with St. Göran and the dragon. Thereafter is sewn in a section from circa 1789. On page 24, the signature Johan Gustav Åström 1830, March 25th appears. On the final dustcover appear the names for successive owners of the book: Gustafv Åström in 1819 and again March 31st, 1823, and finally Jonas Magnus Åström in 1850. Presumably the recording of the generations of owners was one way of establishing the authenticity and magical efficacy of the volume. With age comes authority.

Though there is no numeration of the items in the original, I have labeled page number and item number for ease of reference. The translation is otherwise after the original. This manuscript includes a total of 40 items.

S-1	14	I-1	15
S-2	7	I-2	9
S-3	7	I-3	0
S-4	2	I-4	1
S-5	0	I-5	4
S-6	11	I-6	3
S-7	0	I-7	4
S-8	5		
S-9	5		

DISCUSSION

This manuscript begins with an enigmatic passage within an ornamented oval, in which is the inscription: "My oath is broken. This Economy or Maria Christina Naturalia belongs to..." One can only imagine what was meant by a broken oath. The writer could perhaps have been bemoaning his broken baptismal or confirmation vows. If there had been some kind of oath to preserve the secrecy of the contents, making any recording of them in writing a breach of some oath, this might be the oath referred to here. The two titles "Economia" and "Maria Christina Naturalia" are also interesting for their appearance in this genre, and seem to be patterned after such titles as Porta's *Magia Naturalis*. Appearing just within the front cover, these phrases capture the spiritual and the scientific implications of its contents. By a broken oath, one's salvation was threatened, and by means of godless Science godlike wonders may be imitated or wrought.

The very first item of the book concerns the fashioning of an iron/steel blade for use in works of healing. As we have seen previously, the healers' knife (Sw. *botarkniv*), was part and parcel of the paraphernalia of the cunning person, and the manner of its assembly was important to its eventual efficacy in magical and healing procedures. With it, the village sorcerer could locate and bind the source of an illness, could consecrate brandy for scrying purposes, could sanctify space within which a magical operation could take place, and focus his or her will at the location of a sore or wound. There were many taboos regarding the use of the *botarkniv*, one of which was that it not have been used in slaughter.

The construction of the *botarkniv* required that the tang extend through the length of the handle, which was to be of black or dark wood. The blade was to be of ferrous metal, and the wooden handle was often to have a certain number of brass nails in specific places as ornamentation. The connection between practitioner and the *botarkniv* was so strong that should another come and try to carry it off, it became both heavy and slippery, making it difficult to hold onto.[14]

The sorcerer could scry in liquor of various sorts as long as it was previously consecrated by him with the knife held in his left hand, stirring the liquor counterclockwise. In a manuscript from the beginning of the 1500s found in the Library of Linköping's Cathedral, even a priest is instructed to use a sorcerer's knife to trace the sign of the cross, while he recites a prayer for healing over a sick person.[15] There are other more malevolent cases in which the sorcerer's knife was used in the execution of magic (*see* MS 27).

In one item, collected by Jon Johansson in 1919 from the cunning man Erik Törnlund of Indal parish, Medelpad,[16] we see the magical method of stabbing the healer's knife (Sw. *botarkniv*) into a footprint to cast a curse:

Hugga kniven i ett spår

"Jag stampar kniven i fäla och där skall du stupa under en hälla i helvetets eld skall du ligga

och där skall du kvida
och där skall du jämras
och där skall du plågas."

Stabbing a knife in a track

"I heave the knife in the footprint and there shall you stumble under a stone. In the fire of hell you shall lie

And there you shall wail,
And there you shall moan and whine
And there you shall be tormented."

Af Klintberg's comments:

"Denna form av magisk förgöring bygger på den kontagiösa magiens princip att allt som tillhört eller haft beröring med den åsyftade personen kan användas. I ett tillägg till formeln meddelar Jon Johansson att man riter ett kors och hugger i spåret med en kniv, som är tvåeggad."

[This form of magical cursing builds on the principle of contagious magic, that everything that has belonged to or has been touched by the intended target can be used. In a supplemental paragraph to the charm, Jon Johansson relates that one traces a cross and stabs in the track with a knife that is double-edged.][17]

Interestingly, however, the content of the book seems generally not to have been occupied with anything more than the healing of people and livestock. Spoken charms are the most plentiful, which is surprising in a volume that purports to provide the secrets in Nature that produce wonders. Rather, one might expect to see a preponderance of ingested or applied recipes, much like the more modern apothecary, and of which we have an example in "Professor" Ahlström's second manuscript (MS 3).

While healing is its primary subject, manipulative and malevolent concerns still make an appearance. Included here are methods to transfix thieves and to cause pain in another. Presumably these intentions were deemed warranted in the execution of justice, since the volume is otherwise concerned with altruistic aims.

MS 6

KU 11120 SVARTKONSTBOK
SLIMMINGE SOCKEN, VEMMENHÖGS HÄRAD, SKÅNE, 1853
KU11120 BLACK ART BOOK
SLIMMINGE PARISH, VEMMENHÖGS JURISDICTION, SKÅNE, 1853

¶ The entire surviving manuscript is published by Lars Lundberg, ed.[18] The volume was discovered among handwritten manuscripts at an antique store in Skallstorp, in Vemmenhögs county by antiquarian Lars Lundberg. It currently rests in the Lund *landsarkiv* in the Lars Lundberg collections. The first of its 80 pages was torn off, possibly to disguise the identity of its original owner. Also, some damage in the upper right corner makes reading a photocopy impossible, so I will refer to the Lundberg transcription where questions arise. The book itself is on 85 handwritten pages, with numeration beginning at 13 and continuing up to 144, after which items appear in an "appendix" (Sw. *tillökning*) and begin numeration over again, through 9, when numeration becomes irregular. The size of the manuscript is 16×20 CM and it is dated March 31, 1853.

As for the content of various parts of the manuscript, numbers 1–144 deal with typical folk magic and healing techniques and recipes. While the blacksmith has occupied a central space in folk magic and lore, and the creation of alloys could be seen as a type of alchemy, the appendix deals wholly with the more prosaic aspects of metallurgy, and will not be translated here. However a listing of the major sections will appear in the appendix, and might be the subject of study of a later scholar with a more rigorous background in chemistry and metallurgy.

This manuscript contains a total of 132 items, with an appendix of 18 items that deal specifically with smith-craft and metallic alloys.

S-1 5	I-1 33
S-2 49	I-2 13
S-3 22	I-3 4
S-4 23	I-4 3
S-5 4	I-5 45
S-6 16	I-6 28
S-7 0	I-7 5
S-8 7	
S-9 0	

DISCUSSION

At 132 items, this is one of the larger manuscripts in the collection, surpassed only by MS 9 from Västnorrland county at 174 and MS 24 from Skirö and Virserum parishes in Småland at 231. It contains comparatively few exclusively oral charms, though procedures, with or without oral components, and recipes comprise the majority of items. Relatively little is contained that deals with hunting, trapping or fishing, but this is not surprising if we consider that this book may have originally belonged to a blacksmith. Personal advantage and manipulation of others was of slightly greater concern than the healing of humans and livestock, and overtly malevolent spells (46, 67, 79, 84 and 85) occupy a spectrum from vengeance to malicious bewitching of animals and shotguns. The volume is encyclopedic in its scope, and does not appear to be organized after any recognizable pattern. The consistency of handwriting makes it clear that it is the work of a single collector, though whether it was the work of many years or a transcription made over a short period is difficult to tell.

The largest form represented in the manuscript is ritual performance. Oral charms and incenses comprise the smallest categories, and ingested and applied recipes are roughly evenly divided. Rituals with an oral component are represented. Written charms are more plentiful than either oral charms or incense recipes. The blacksmith's attention to proper procedure and proportion might explain the preponderance of ritual items, and the paucity of oral charms. Some of the items in this book presume an audience; the production of "wonders" or stage-type illusions; the appearance of star-like flashes when shooting at night, or the illusion that all present seem to have the heads of calves. Apart from the sheer entertainment value of such displays, there was doubtless the boost that such performances might give to one's reputation. In a consumer economy, where the wise one worked essentially for hire (whether for cash or barter), the importance of reputation gained through public display would serve a marketing function, and solicit an ever greater circle of potential clients.

The concern for the wellbeing of human and livestock is documented in numerous rituals and recipes for general illness and for bewitchment. It might be that this was the sphere of influence for which most clients sought assistance. Once again, as with the Ahlström manuscripts, the full extent of the cunning man's repertoire is kept hidden, with only those items used publicly which were of use to the general community.

The two items which seek to work malicious witchcraft on livestock both concern horses, with one seeking to cause lameness, while the other to cause a horse to be uncontrollable. In other manuscripts, this kind of magical manipulation of horses is quite obviously to control the outcome of horse races or other competitions to the favor of the actor. The extent to which this gambling was frowned upon is the degree to which such procedures can be said to be demonic.

MS 7

MANUSCRIPT LUF[19]. A. 285
SVARTKONSTBOK FRÅN GLIMÅKRA SOCKEN, ÖSTRA GÖINGE HÄRAD, SKÅNE
BLACK ART BOOK FROM GLIMÅKRA PARISH, ÖSTRA GÖINGE JURISDICTION, SKÅNE

¶The following informative paragraph accompanies the manuscript in the file box. "The book in question which has been somewhat more detailed than what is produced below, belonged to an 80-year old man, who died this past year in the vicinity of Broby, and was called 'Skägelen' ('little beard'). His father, who dwelt in Simonstorp, Glimåkra parish, was a so-called 'wise one' who owned the book in question, which exists in a manuscript from the 1700s."

According to af Klintberg, this item was originally transcribed by hand by Eva Wigström in the 1870s, and then a typed transcription was undertaken by C. W. von Sydow. It contains a total of 26 items.

S-1 11	I-1 9
S-2 3	I-2 0
S-3 1	I-3 4
S-4 5	I-4 1
S-5 3	I-5 6
S-6 0	I-6 3
S-7 0	I-7 4
S-8 6	
S-9 0	

DISCUSSION

Skägelen's father was the first owner of this book, and it presumably passed from father to son after the father's passing. Skägelen himself passed on in the 1870s, at which time the transcription was made by Wigström. It is unclear from the notes in the file box whether material was omitted, or if some items were merely simplified from a "more detailed" original.

The largest group of items in this manuscript is oral charms, at 42.3%. At 19.2% and 23.0% are substances externally applied and the creation of written spells (such as the reduction charm of numbers 18 and 19) respectively. The applied recipes are not of the type of medicinal soaks or plasters, but rather the binding of magically potent items in such a way that they make contact with the skin, presumably transferring their inherent numinous power to the bearer.

Thirteen of the items represent healing magic. There is an equal distribution of items to heal and hex shotguns. One spell for divorce (#24) is a reminder of the manipulative type of love magic that has been in continuous use since the second century BCE.[20]

This manuscript is clearly not indebted to a more naturalistic approach to healing, but rather the manipulation of magically potent substances or the knowledge of incantatory or written spells to affect the client.

MS 8

LUF. A. 795:26–31
MAGISKA FORMLER OCH MAGISKA HANDLINGAR
DIVERSA ANTECKNINGAR
MAGICAL SPELLS AND MAGICAL PROCEDURES
DIVERSE NOTES

¶This is only a fragmentary manuscript, and it is only available in transcription from LUF in Lund. This transcription contains a total of 17 items.

S-1	4	I-1	11
S-2	5	I-2	0
S-3	0	I-3	1
S-4	1	I-4	0
S-5	0	I-5	2
S-6	3	I-6	1
S-7	0	I-7	2
S-8	2		
S-9	0		

DISCUSSION

Two items invoke the power of the devil, while the remaining charms draw on images of Christ or the Trinity. The two with demonic imagery are both to control thieves, with one invoking the return of the thief with his booty, and the other putting his eye out in vengeance. The remaining charms are primarily for healing, with a small number devoted to either personal advantage or harm.

The manipulation of a girl by "Teeth and tongue, mouth and bonedust" presents some interesting problems for interpretation. Taking the nail and graveyard dust "in all the names" could be in the names of all the demons, or of all the angels, of God, Jesus and Mary, or of the occupant of the grave and his predecessors, so the interpretation makes a difference in the perceived source of the spell's power.

Because this manuscript is incomplete, some of the readings have been reconstructed, but its general tone appealing to angelic or demonic powers is unobstructed.

MS 9

LUF, MSS A, B, C, COLLECTION C. W. VON SYDOW
SVARTKONSTBOK FROM MO, RÅDOM, VÄSTNORRLANDS
LÄN, LAPPLAND
BLACK ART BOOK FROM MO, RÅDOM, VÄSTNORRLANDS
COUNTY, LAPPLAND

¶This manuscript is assigned the title *Signerier och Besvärjelser,* or Spells and Conjurations. This collection of spells and old folk belief, recorded in Lappland, was originally in the collection of the folklorist C. W. von Sydow in Lund. The first recording was carried out by the Sámi Jon Johansson, from Mo, Rådom, Västnorrlandslän prior to 1915. The first manuscript that was submitted was written without any order and on loose papers, and was therefore hard to navigate. Jon Johansson was asked to organize his collected items into a book with his spells, which he kindly did. The first manuscript is noted below by the letter B. The items in the later ordered book are designated with the letter A. This collection, A alongside B was ready in 1916. Jon Johansson promised still another volume.

This third volume arrived in 1917 and is designated with the letter C. When it arrived, the printing of A and B was already underway, which meant that some of the charms didn't make it into their proper place, but were relegated to a special appendix. For the most part, manuscripts A and B contain spells of a more unspecified type and little malevolent material. The C collection however has a great deal of the latter, and is interesting for the analysis of the entire corpus presented in the manuscript. The chapter on cures for example is for the most part conveyed in B.

The title of the collection *Signerier och Besvärjelser* was chosen by Jon Johansson himself. In the printed copy, we are assured that nothing has been altered save for a few spelling mistakes. All the dialect forms have been retained. As Jon Johansson wrote to C. W. von Sydow:

... in this way I've assembled these over a decade from widely disparate locales within Norrland through great cost and effort. It happened that I paid 10 kr. just for one item, and in addition by sending these to you, I have surrendered my power, that is to say I no longer have the power to stop bleeding and such. It isn't "humbug" as modern folk say about so called "*kukkelgubbar*" [magicians] because such wisdom in words and spells finds its origins all the way back to Christ's time when the Savior walked here on Earth and because he gave his disciples power to heal all sorts of sicknesses, make the blind see, resurrect the dead, etc. Because we are also his disciples, because he who believes, but not for those who don't believe shall be able to do wonders, and unfortunately, there aren't many believers...

This book is singular in that it is a collection made by an actual practitioner of the cunning arts, and represents *not only* his own repertoire, but a collection of lore from a relatively large geographical area. In this one book, we have not just the verbal formulæ that we find in other collections of this type, but we have beliefs informing them, as well as examples of their employment.

This published work of three discrete manuscripts contains a total of 174 items.

S-1	46	I-1	132
S-2	33	I-2	13
S-3	1	I-3	0
S-4	7	I-4	0
S-5	0	I-5	13
S-6	77	I-6	0
S-7	6	I-7	15
S-8	1		
S-9	4		

DISCUSSION

The data that immediately impressed the reader is that oral charms, rites with no oral component and combinations of these comprise the largest formal category, with appeals to recipes, written formulæ and informing lore comparatively small. Rites and accompanying oral components is the largest category, and might imply that both were required in a common definition of magical efficacy. The small representation of ingested or applied recipes could suggest that, at least for Johansson, efficacy was primarily found in the oral component, and only secondarily in the performative component.

As regards the concern or motivation of a manuscript item, this collection can really be broken down into three main concerns: healing, spells for personal advantage and, especially in C, purely malevolent magic. This latter intention includes the typical malevolent witchery of magically stealing milk, as well as works of vengeance, death or other physical harm. In two items, we have spells to break fiddle strings. Also in this last manuscript, in addition to divination, invisibility spells and procedures aimed at wish fulfillment, we have two procedures for shape-shifting, and three to become a sorcerer which are notable for their contracts with the dead rather than with any demonic power. There is clearly a primary concern with the health of human and beast, but still a tacit assumption that in order to heal, one must know how to hex. This ambiguity or ambivalence toward what we might categorize as malevolence introduces a world view that is clearly different from that expressed in the modern medical Hippocratic oath. It leads us back to our question as to the existence of a purely benevolent healing tradition.

The texts in these published manuscripts are remarkable for their assumptions about the spirit world, and the way in which healing works. Powerful words and powerful rituals are favored over the folk remedy for a cold or flu that characterizes other books. The preoccupation with investigating hidden knowledge by means of arrangement with unseen spirits presents a world view similar to the Sámi in which the natural world is still overseen by a world of spirits, and by their intercession, we gain knowledge of that natural world for the purpose of affecting it.

MS 10

NORDISKA MUSÉET #33.823 SVARTKONSTBOK
TJULA SOCKEN, SÖDERMANLAND
*NORDIC MUSEUM #33.823 BLACK ART BOOK
FROM TJULA PARISH, SÖDERMANLAND PROVINCE*

¶This manuscript consists of 16 leaves, 10.5×15.5 CM. It has a sewn binding and no firm covers, either front or back. The last page is little more than scribbles. This manuscript contains a total of 59 items.

S-1 7	I-1 11
S-2 28	I-2 5
S-3 5	I-3 6
S-4 2	I-4 1
S-5 0	I-5 27
S-6 9	I-6 11
S-7 0	I-7 1
S-8 0	
S-9 8	

DISCUSSION

Ritual actions predominate in this manuscript, with a majority (47.5%) unaccompanied by an oral component, and ritual actions with an accompanying oral component only at a third of that total (15.3%). An inventory of animals and animal parts and their uses in various magical endeavors (S-9) comprises 13.6% of the total number of items. The preponderance of procedural items seems to indicate that the procedure itself, rather than the inclusion of words of power, are the source of the item's efficacy, though a listing of the magico-medical pharmacopœia provides another model of correspondence.

The largest motivational category are of the items dealing with personal gain, with workings for physical strength and protection, discovery and obtaining treasure without incurring personal injury and divination comprising the majority. Unlocking locks, invisibility spells, and luck, both in gambling and generally, round out the category. The single malevolent spell is afflicting one's enemy with diarrhea.

Ingested recipes and those applied externally are relatively few (11.7%), but their presence speaks for an association of healing with other more nefarious aims, at least in the mind of the compiler. This manuscript presents both malevolent and benevolent materials, mostly relying on procedures rather than oral recitations or recipes.

MS 11

NORDISKA MUSÉET MS# 33.824
ÅKERS SOCKEN, SÖDERMANLAND
NORDIC MUSEUM #33.824
ÅKERS PARISH, SÖDERMANLAND PROVINCE

¶According to a short notation in the back of this manuscript, it was found in 1886 in Åkers parish, Södermanland by metalworker Gustaf Ericsson. Its dimensions are 11×17 CM. It has no front cover, is glue bound, and it looks like a portion torn out of a larger volume. The back is of card stock.

There is a list of what looks to be owners on page 3, beginning with the name Erik Länmark in Spånga, with the date in Roman numerals of 1838. Thereafter are listed Carl Lager from Länna Works, then an Amanda Josefina from Åkers parish.

This manuscript was written with a great deal of cipher, mostly with a system that substitutes numbers for letters. In the case of the letters å, ä and ö, we have the numbers for a and o with the requisite markings above. All code was realized in this manuscript by Gustaf Ericsson, and in my translation, both [brackets] and *asterisks* indicate use of code.

This manuscript contains a total of 98 items.

S-1	15	I-1	30
S-2	47	I-2	0
S-3	4	I-3	11
S-4	1	I-4	9
S-5	0	I-5	19
S-6	16	I-6	16
S-7	0	I-7	15
S-8	23		
S-9	1		

DISCUSSION

This manuscript shows a majority of the items to be procedural (48.0%) and the second most common to be either oral charms or procedures that integrated an oral component (31.6%). In this manuscript there is a comparatively large number of written spells, and out of the total of 27, seven consist of recognizable letters. The remaining 20 are composed of Wittemburg letters or other letter-like figures.

As already noted, a numerical code was employed periodically in this text. Code was often used here to indicate the magical core or power source of the spell. This was in some places the use of words of power, such as the name of the Trinity, and in others, the use of forbidden substances such as blood or human bones. Whether this was to safeguard the power of the spell, or to protect the manuscript owner from legal prosecution for either illegal or irreligious activities is unclear, but probably both came into consideration.

The motivational analysis of the items is notable in that roughly half of the items are for altruistic aims such as healing, protection, or luck in hunting, and the other half for less altruistic aims, such as personal advantage (e.g., divination procedures, procuring a charmed "raven stone"), manipulation of people or animals (e.g., causing women to do one's will, influencing a magistrate in a court of law, preventing dogs from barking) and what is a surprising number of malicious procedures (e.g., working vengeance, cursing another's shotgun) with one to cause fiddle strings to break.

The majority of spoken charms deal with matters of health and healing, though one spoken charm for hexing is curious for its invocation of harm by the power of the resurrection "your shotgun will bleed and nevermore kill, as truly as Christ is risen from the dead." Charms for protection from swords, poisons and injury may perhaps originate in a time when dueling, and deception were common ways of conflict resolution. Swords particularly recall a time when swordfights were perhaps more common than they were in the nineteenth century. Swords were also not commonly held by lower classes, and this might indicate an origin among a privileged class.

MS 12

NM 40.034
"CYPRANIS[21] KONSTER OCH LÄROR OCH DES INRÄT"
ONSBY SOCKEN, SKÅNE, 1809.
"THE ARTS AND DOCTRINES OF CYPRIAN, AND THEIR EMPLOYMENT"
ONSBY PARISH, SKÅNE PROVINCE, 1809.

¶This manuscript has a leather case (Sw. *fodral*) in which the book fits perfectly. The covers are leather over wood with a center tie, with the dimensions 10×16.5 CM, and consisting of 60 leaves. The first page includes the title *Cypranis konster och Läror och des inrät* or "The Arts and Teachings of St. Cyprian and its equipment." Nils Jönsson , 1809, is labeled as its original owner, and then it was inherited by Anna Larsdotter, n.d., and [illegible] Pehrsdotter, 1857. This manuscript exists in both an original and a cleaner transcription from the turn of the twentieth century.

The language of this manuscript is heavily flavored by Germanisms, with verbs and helping verbs occurring at the end of subordinate clauses, which may be expected in a parish in Skåne, but also might indicate translation of a continental original.

This manuscript contains a total of 30 items.

S-1	10	I-1	11
S-2	8	I-2	9
S-3	3	I-3	0
S-4	2	I-4	0
S-5	1	I-5	9
S-6	8	I-6	0
S-7	0	I-7	2
S-8	2		
S-9	0		

DISCUSSION

Analyzing this manuscript formally, 60.0% of the items involved some oral component, while 16.7% were either ingested or externally applied recipes. Only two consist purely of a written component.

As regards motivations, 66.7% deal with healing, 30.0% with personal advantage (e.g., discovery of treasure, wealth, psychic power and various sorts of divination—3 with divining rod, 1 with eye secretions from a horse). A single item appears afflicting a milk-thief with diarrhea, and another for transfixing a thief. The entire manuscript appears to revolve around a single long ecclesiastical evocation which is presumably the vehicle of efficacy for all the constituent magical procedures.

MS 13

NM 41.652 SVARTKONSTBOK
FRÅN NORRA SKÅNE
*NORDIC MUSEUM 41.652 BLACK ART BOOK
FROM NORTHERN SKÅNE PROVINCE*

¶The description of this manuscript in the file box at the *Folkminnessamling* stated that this manuscript consisted of 12 leaves with writing, and 2 unwritten leaves, together with a transcription of the entire book on 3 pieces of 4°-quire totaling 12 pages. When I examined this manuscript, the original was missing from the collection, and the only text I was able to examine was the transcription, however photographs of some pages from this original have appeared in Bengt af Klintberg's book *Svenska trollformler*,[22] so as of the early to mid-1960s the original still resided with the *Folkminnessamling* in Stockholm. According to the description at the *Folkminnessamling*, it was received by *Nordiska muséet* on September 26, 1881. It contains a total of one item, a lengthy ritual of exorcism.

S-1 1	I-1 1
S-2 0	I-2 0
S-3 0	I-3 0
S-4 0	I-4 0
S-5 0	I-5 0
S-6 0	I-6 0
S-7 0	I-7 0
S-8 0	
S-9 0	

DISCUSSION

This manuscript appears to be a handwritten copy of a liturgical text, though inconsistencies of spelling and grammar make it likely that it was at least at a generation removed from the original. The figures in the manuscript are drawn crosses, with text in both the longer vertical as well as in the shorter horizontal pieces. The manuscript is an exorcism of demonic influence from an individual, and calls upon both supernal and infernal powers in its recitation. Since its form is liturgical, and consists of verbal exhortations, it is technically categorized as a verbal charm, although its length would make recitation from memory unlikely. It does require some ritual performance, as the exorcist is to procure human bones from the cemetery and soak them in water, which is then used to wash the client. Apart from this initial direction, the form is exclusively verbal. As it has the intention of protecting an individual from demonic influence, I have categorized it as a work of healing. There are other items in other manuscripts that take a similar view of spiritual health and healing.

Exhortations are presented as those made by St. Cyprian, and call upon the powers of all those biblical and ecclesiastical personages to drive out the four primary Princes of Hell and their minions. There is nothing in the manuscript to suggest that anything other than benevolence is intended, but the form of the ritual implies that an ordained churchman should perform it. Its performance by someone else might be considered an appropriation of the church liturgy by someone not trained in its performance, making it more magical than religious.[23]

MS 14

NM 41.674 LÖNSBODA 1674
PER PERSSON "NERINGEN" (1759–1834)
NORDIC MUSEUM 41.674 FROM LÖNSBODA VILLAGE, 1674
PER PERSSON, CALLED "NERINGEN" (1759–1834)

¶Black Art Book NM 41.674 from Lönsboda in Osby parish in present-day Osby Kommun in Northeast Skåne was a gift from Carl Persson in Lönsboda, given October 13, 1881 to P. G. Wistrand. According to Edith Svensson (10/11/1909–?), the great granddaughter of Per Persson "Neringen," the following is what she related on a visit to the *Fornminnessamling* on August 12, 1983. "Per Persson was born in Strömhult on June 3, 1812. When his father became sick, the farm was sold with the exception of Holmatorpet, which became Per's home. He lived in a cottage in Frostentorp until the time of his death on Nov. 15, 1893. He is said to have inherited the book from his maternal grandfather, Per Persson "Neringen" who lived 1759–1834. He was my maternal grandmother's father. Edith Svensson." Mrs. Edith Svensson was born on October 11, 1909 in Tyresö.

If "Neringen" was indeed the author of this text, then we might be able to date it no earlier than the late eighteenth or early nineteenth century. On page 2 of the manuscript, we have recorded the date August 2, 1674, though this manuscript may well be a copy of an older original. The manuscript measures 10.5×16.5 CM, has a twine-sewn binding, though no front or back cover. It contains 32 pages, though only 28 pages contain writing. There are 15.5 leaves, as one page is cut in half with what looks to have been a sharp edge. While the pages are in good repair, the extremely sketchy hand makes deciphering it a challenge. The original contains no pagination or numeration of items, but for ease of reference I have used pagination in this translation.

This manuscript contains a total of 11 items.

S-1	2	I-1	2
S-2	4	I-2	0
S-3	0	I-3	0
S-4	0	I-4	0
S-5	0	I-5	9
S-6	3	I-6	0
S-7	0	I-7	0
S-8	2		
S-9	2		

DISCUSSION

The context of the larger work is a copied work explaining the correct procedure to obtain a divining rod with which to locate buried treasure. Part of the procedure is to assure that said treasure may be obtained without awakening the wrath of the dragon that guards over it. There is also a procedure to assure that the treasure stays hidden in the earth until such time as the diviner can return to fetch it. Also included are letter names of the Greek alphabet, as well as an alleged Syrian alphabet. These may have been included as a key to write in a "secret" alphabet, though nothing is written in either in this manuscript.

Also included are exhortations to a host of nature spirits by the powers of Christendom, that they might work no evil upon the operator. The list of spirits is rather exhaustive, and includes trolls of various types, sorcerers, serpents, forest spirits, water sprites, elves, house and farm spirits, earth spirits as well as malicious spirits or poisonous ghosts. The operator seeks to "quell, bind and exorcise" these spirits by the ecclesiastical powers of the events of the Passion, by saints and evangelists, and by the four elements. The juxtaposition of the locally and elementally defined nature spirits with the Christian imagery of the Church makes this manuscript interesting.

MS 15

NM 63.180
"SAMLING AF UTOMORDENTLIGA MENNISKORS STÖRSTA
HEMLIGHETER I FORNTIDEN."
URSHULTS SOCKEN, SMÅLAND PROVINCE.
NORDIC MUSEUM 63.180
COLLECTION OF EXTRAORDINARY PEOPLE'S GREATEST SECRETS OF
ANCIENT TIMES. FROM URSHULT PARISH, SMÅLAND PROVINCE

¶ This item is a thick volume, at one time bound in leather, but decaying bindings led at least one cataloger from *Nordiska muséet* to assign part of it to a different accession number, in spite of similarities in both paper composition and penmanship. After my work at the *Folkminnessamling* in Stockholm, this error was corrected. It was received into *Nordiska muséets* holdings on January 2, 1895. Since the text of this volume represents published works, a definitive edition has never been carried out, and this is why my fragment of a photocopy includes only its table of contents (with source attributions) and one page that is clearly copied from the German edition of the *Clavicula Salomonis*, thus making it quite certain that it was hand copied from already published sources. In comparison with an English edition of the *Clavicula* produced in 1888 by S. Liddell MacGregor Mathers, the portions from the Key match with respect to both text and drawings. Providing its table of contents here will, however, provide some context for the types of items which this compiler sought in his creation of what for him was the definitive black art book.

This manuscript is leather bound, and its quires were originally sewn into the leather, though as these threads have decayed, they are all separated from the leather binding. There are 13 quires, 404 leaves, 788 pages of which 9 are blank—two additional unnumbered leaves found separately in the file box should accompany this manuscript which provide a table of contents. All totaled, there are four pages of contents, thereafter the text begins on page 1, in a hand that is extremely easily read. In the first quire, 3 pages are torn out. In the second quire, the "*Veneris lilla bok att Besvärja onda andar på guddomligt sätt*" ur den latinske Johannes Dee öfversatt af Leopold F*** ["The Little Book of Venus to Conjure Evil Spirits in a Righteous Way," translated from the Latin of John Dee by Leopold F***] includes traced ink figures covering penciled originals. This leads one to believe that the penciled originals were tracings of the original published graphics. It is clearly a handwritten copy of a printed book. This manuscript contains a total of 22 chapters, considered as items for this analysis.

S-1	4	I-1	0
S-2	3	I-2	0
S-3	0	I-3	0
S-4	0	I-4	0
S-5	0	I-5	21
S-6	10	I-6	0
S-7	0	I-7	1
S-8	1		
S-9	4		

DISCUSSION

This thick manuscript presents handwritten copies of published texts of ceremonial magic of the same genre as the *Clavicula Salomonis* or the *Lesser Key of Solomon* and the *Grimoireum Verum* or *True Grimoire*. Source texts are given in the text.

Formally, the rituals and sigils are accompanied by lengthy evocations. Talismanic diagrams make heavy use of Hebrew characters, as well as goetic sigils.[24] The aims of the workings in this manuscript are to discover hidden treasure, or to discover hidden knowledge in divination. The choices of texts are interesting for the light they shed on what this practitioner thought most representative of the magical arts, though the workings described are of a sort and complexity that a typical cunning man or woman would not have the means, economic or otherwise, to perform them.

MS 16

NORDISKA MUSÉET #63.711
SVARTKONSTBOK FRÅN ÖSTRA GÖINGE HÄRAD, SKÅNE
NORDIC MUSEUM 63.711
BLACK ART BOOK FROM EAST GÖINGE JURISDICTION, SKÅNE PROVINCE

¶This manuscript has the dimensions 12.5×19 CM, while pages are 16.5×10 CM. Thirty-seven leaves are with writing, making a total of 59 pages with writing. Among the blank pages there are dried flowers and plants. On the last page is written *omkr. 4 år sedan Östra Göinge gräns mot Småland, köpt af en klok gubbe. Lunden fått.* [approximately 4 years ago on East Göinge's border with Småland, bought from a cunning man. Received from Lunden.] Pagination begins with page 1. The binding is sewn, and the cover is card-stock covered by wallpaper that has been glued onto it. This manuscript was added to *Nordiska muséets* holdings 2/16/1893. It exists also in a typed transcription made by Bo Thullberg. There is a note with the manuscript that says: "Gumman Osbäck's father and Johan in Gillestorpet (a.k.a. Fesenhök)."

This manuscript contains a total of 24 items.

S-1 0	I-1 23
S-2 2	I-2 0
S-3 7	I-3 0
S-4 16	I-4 0
S-5 0	I-5 1
S-6 0	I-6 0
S-7 0	I-7 0
S-8 0	
S-9 0	

DISCUSSION

Carl-Martin Bergstrand in his *Trolldom och klokskap i Västergötland* has written a chapter on Johan i Gillestorpet, also known by the name Fesenhök.[25] From an assumed single informant from Sandhem, Bergstrand relates the following:

"Johan i Gillestorpet var lite trolsk. De kallade honom Fesen eller Fesenhök. Far var god vän med honom. Vi hade två kor hemma, och den ena slutade mjölka. 'Ja ska gå te Fesenhök,' sa far, men det ville inte mor. Hon tyckte det var orätt.

"Det kom en gårdbo in till oss en kväll, och det var just den, som far misstänkte hade förtrollat kon. 'Ja begriper inte va ja ska göra,' sa mor, 'för den ena koa mjölkar inte.' 'Ho ä la sjuker,' sa han. 'Nä, koa äter och dricker, så sjuker ä ho inte,' sa mor; 'men ja ä gla att den andra mjölkar,' sa hon.

"Men dagen efter mjölkade inte den heller. När mor kom in, grät hon. 'Vill du inte än att ja ska gå te Fesenhök?' sa far. 'Ja, ja bryr mej inte om'et,' sa mor. Han gick efter Fesenhök. Och far had lagat hem brännvin och bjudde honom, för han var kär i brännvin. Så, när de hade suttit en stund, sa Fesenhök: 'Nu ska vi gå ut å se på kora.' Och när han hade sett på dem, sa han: 'Di ä förgjorda. Dä ä en som har tatt mjölka för dej, men dä ska inte dröja länge, innan han kommer, och då vill han låna något, men du får inte låna honom något, för då går det om intet.'

"Och en liten stund efteråt, så kom den samme gårdbon, som far hade misstro till, och han såg lite förlägen ut, 'Ja har vart tvungen att gå efter Johan, för mina kor ä inte bra,' sa far. 'Mina ä inte bra, di heller,' sa karn. Han ville låna ena drätt, och det var då något, som han inte behövde. Och han fick inte låna.

När han var gången, sa Johan: 'Ser du, att ja kunde ställa hit honom!' Sen frågade han mor: 'Vill du ha igen mjölken, som han har tatt ifrå dej?' 'Nej, det ville mor inte, bara ja får den mjölka, som ja ska ha härefter.' 'Ja, dä ska du få, men dä får inte tas för häftigt. Den ena koa ska börja mjölka i morron, men den andra dröjer dä mä några dar.' Och så gick det."

[Johan in Gillestorpet was a little magical. They called him "Fesen" or "Fesenhök." Dad was good friends with him. We had two cows at home, and the one stopped milking. "I'll go to Fesenhök," dad said, but mom didn't want him to. She thought it wasn't right.

A neighbor farmer came to us one evening, and it was just the one that dad suspected of bewitching the cows. "I don't know what I'm going to do," said mom, "since the one cow doesn't milk." "She's probably sick," he said. "Nope, the cow eats and drinks, so she isn't sick," mom said; "but I'm happy that the other one is milking," she said.

But the next day, the other one wasn't milking either. When mom came in, she was crying. "Do you still not want me to go to Fesenhök?" said dad. "Yes, I won't worry myself about it," said mom. He went to fetch Fesenhök. And dad had prepared some liquor back at home and offered it to him, because he sure liked his liquor. So, when they had sat for a while, Fesenhök said: "Now we'll go out and have a look at the cows." And when he had taken a look at them, he said: "They're hexed. There is someone who has taken the milk from you, but it won't be long before he'll come, and then he'll want to borrow something, but don't you lend him anything, or otherwise it'll all be for naught.

And a little while later, then the same farmer that dad had suspected came by, and he looked a bit perplexed. "I needed to go fetch Johan, because my cows aren't well," said dad. "Mine aren't very good either," said the man. He wanted to borrow a linen tablecloth, and that was something that he certainly didn't need. And he wasn't allowed to borrow it.

When he had left, then Johan said: "You see, I could force him to come here!" Then he asked mom: "Do you want the milk back that he has taken from you?" No, mom didn't want that, "just that I get the milk that I should get from here on." "Yes, you'll get that, but you shouldn't take it too vigorously. The one cow will begin to milk again tomorrow, but the other one will take take a few days." And that's just what happened.]

According to the Nordic Museum's notation, it is unclear whether this manuscript belonged to Fesenhök himself, or to Gumman Osbäck's father, who was either a friend, contemporary or associate of Fesenhök. If the contents can say anything about it, it is notable that there is no spell to fix milk-bewitched cows, nor to transfix or compel a thief, which occasionally appear in some of the manuscripts, while the passage above about Fesenhök tells of both abilities. The matter is further confused as Bergstrand admits that in his collecting, he regularly neglected to inquire about the circumstances of his informant, with the result that here we haven't any ability to estimate the age of the informant, or his or her father, and therefore the years of Fesenhök's activity in the area of Sandhem.[26] Most of Bergstrand's collecting was between the years of 1925–1935, and he mentions that his best informants are those born before 1860. If his informant in Sandhem was born in, say, 1855 (making him or her at least 70 years old at the time of collection), this would have made the memory from childhood sometime during the 1860s. The notation on the last page "approximately four years ago..." has no date from which to estimate, and tells us nothing about the age of the manuscript, but its accession date into the Nordic Museum's collection in 1893 implies that the latest possible date for this manuscript is 1889.

In this manuscript, there is one spell for personal advantage, for memory. The majority of the remaining recipes are topical soaks or ingested recipes for healing humans. Only two magical procedures are recorded, and presumably the efficacy of the healing came from knowledge of substances rather than from charming ability. Given the rather lengthy narrative about Fesenhök, and this manuscript which may represent the book he used to record his knowledge, we have two very different pictures of the cunning man and his art: a specialist in the natural remedies of folk medicine represented in the manuscript, and the psychically powerful sorcerer who is able to manipulate others at a distance. One item in the manuscript, a procedure for jaundice, provides an example of non-linear cause and effect, hanging a bladder filled with the patient's urine in the flue of the hearth to encourage the resolution of the condition. The rest are clearly recommended substances for healing various conditions, with little or no reliance on the presence or absence of psychic ability in the manuscript's owner. The discrepancy between the perception of the cunning man, and the content of a book from the circle of his influence is illustrative of the disconnect between the client/patient and the cunningfolk.

MS 17

NM 271.600 15:1949
"KONSTBOK"
NORDIC MUSEUM 271.600 15: 1949
"BOOK OF ART"

¶This manuscript is written on cardstock, and has a sewn binding, with one torn page. Measurements are 9×11 CM. One leaf is torn in half, producing 5.5 leaves. The manuscript was added to the Nordiska muséets holdings in 1949.

The first page is rather artfully done, with "KONST-BOK" ["Book of Art"] written in white, with the surrounding area blacked out. The numeration of items is doubled, i.e., there is numeration beginning at 19, and then renumbered to be 41, and it is clear after examination that the book represents a partial collection, and includes incomplete items. Whether the renumbering represents the work of a later owner is unclear. This manuscript contains a total of 29 items. This manuscript also includes a recording of a tune in musical or tabular notation.

S-1 0	I-1 4
S-2 14	I-2 3
S-3 7	I-3 0
S-4 1	I-4 1
S-5 0	I-5 8
S-6 0	I-6 3
S-7 0	I-7 5
S-8 3	
S-9 0	

DISCUSSION

In his 2003 study, Owen Davies mentions the magical grimoire as stock-in-trade of the practitioner of popular magic in England. He characterizes the role of the book in the practice of the British cunning folk as he writes:

> ...literacy meant power. It comes as no surprise, then, to find that cunning-folk made a great show of the fact that they possessed and used books and manuscripts. Not just any books, however, but ones that would impress. Size mattered, as did the appearance of antiquity...[27]

However, the diminutive volume here considered would bespeak the opposite. The tiny hand-manufactured collection might have easily been hidden in a breast pocket, and was probably a memory-aid, to facilitate or prompt when an item was no longer fully remembered. Apart from its artfully produced cover, it seems that the volume was not meant to be seen by any other than the owner, and it was certainly not of a type or size that would impress a client who was familiar with the family bibles, psalm books or collections of sermons that were typically found in rural farmhouses.

Interestingly, in one manuscript (MS 6, KU11120:47) we are given the procedure to produce the artistic effect of white print on a black background. In J. J. Törner's black art book manuscript, preserved at Linköpings Diocese Library at the time of Wikman's publication, K. Rob. V. Wikman reproduces a page upon which Törner has white stenography on a black background, and the first transcribed page (plate 4) tells us:

> Svartkonsteboken skulle vara en liten bok inuti svart med vita bokstäver full av allehanda övernaturliga, obegripliga hemligheter vilka allenast utaf de studerade kunde fås genom kompakt med den onde...[28]

> [The black art book should be a little book with a black interior with white letters filled with all sorts of supernatural, incomprehensible secrets which could only be obtained by the well trained through a pact with the Devil...]

Presumably, at the time of Törner's collecting in the years around 1743, this was a common enough expectation that it warranted mention in this notebook. In this small manuscript from the collection of *Nordiska museét*, however, it is only the cover that satisfies this expectation. The rest of the small volume is written with dark ink meant to be easily read.

The high frequency of rites with no spoken element also seems to indicate less comfort with the recited word, and were it not for the troll-letters and astrological symbols on its first page, as well as three other spells requiring written components, we might even assume that there was a disinterest in the written component generally. Oral charms are completely lacking.

In a discussion of intentions, it is noteworthy that the majority of the items are found in categories I-5 through I-7, on the decidedly less altruistic end of the spectrum. There may be a correlation between the silence of the procedures and the more harmful intentions to which they appeal.

The final item in the manuscript is mysterious, though it may represent a tabular recording of a melody, with the variations in pitch indicated by upward or downward strokes of the pen, resembling the neumatic notation of medieval plainchant. The role of music in the performance of magic is something that appears in folktale, but isn't often mentioned in personal narrative. Learning to play the fiddle from the "man of the rapids" (Sw. *forskarl*) or the water sprite (Sw. *näck*) was a common motif.[29] The belief that fiddlers (Sw. *spelmän*) could cause party-goers to dance themselves to death is also elsewhere documented.[30] Perhaps a melody learned at the feet of the nixie might be recorded here, in a book devoted to the dark arts as well.

MS 18

NM 271.601-A SANKT PETRI NYCKEL
NORDIC MUSEUM 271.601-A THE KEY OF SAINT PETER

¶This manuscript measuring 10.5×16.5 CM, and consisting of 16 leaves, for a total of 30 handwritten pages, is obviously an accounting book from this century. The binding is with staples. The writing style is modern, even where some of the orthography is not standard. Numeration occurs consistently through 23, and then continues with 28, though no pages appear to be torn out, yielding a total of 83 items. The first items in this book are regularly dated to October of 1939. This item along with the other items listed under NM 271.601 were a gift of Elsa Halmdahl of Stockholm in 1941. The earlier manuscripts (1920–29) originated in Hälsingland, where Ms. Halmdahl studied under numerous cunning practitioners, while the later (1939–40) were probably penned in Stockholm.

S-1	34	I-1	45
S-2	12	I-2	7
S-3	4	I-3	1
S-4	7	I-4	0
S-5	0	I-5	10
S-6	19	I-6	6
S-7	0	I-7	8
S-8	4		
S-9	2		

DISCUSSION

It is interesting to note that the three manuscripts from Elsa Halmdahl all bear titles. This first manuscript, entitled "Sankt Petri Nyckel" or The Key of Saint Peter recalls both the well-known volume of ceremonial magic, the *Little Key of Solomon* or *Clavicula Salomonis*, as well as the long-time association of keys with Saint Peter. Drawing on Matthew 16:17–19 in which Christ calls the apostle Peter the "rock" upon which he will build his church, the ensuing passage about keys to the kingdom of heaven and binding and loosing in heaven and earth has not only been invoked in Christian magical ritual, but also as a biblical apologia for the primacy of the apostolic papacy. In this manuscript, the first full item invokes the charge "whatever you bind on earth shall be bound in heaven, and whatever you loose on earth shall be loosed in heaven" (verse 19), a verse historically used to justify thaumaturgy or the working of magic as acceptable behavior for Christians.

Elsa Halmdahl has collected a body of charms and rites, primarily from one Olof (Olle) Åberg of Gåltjärn (d. 9/10/1932) during the period between 1920–1929, though this first volume contains other attributions and is from a later date 1939–40, just one year before Ms. Halmdahl would donate these volumes to the Nordic Museum in 1941. In the second volume, entitled *Läkarbok* [Healers' book], this is the first name listed among those whose reputations were known to Ms. Halmdahl as magically capable healers. Among Ms. Halmdahl's informants for this first volume however are a K.Å., P.S., Pelle, Signe E., Selma H., G.D., P.S.Å., R.M.Eriksson, Efr. Z., Sköndahl-Watersson, and an anonymous Gypsy woman. Items are dated from 1939 into 1940. The careful attention to attributions leads one to think that perhaps Ms. Halmdahl perceived the power in these charms to be found in their age or perhaps their intact transmission. Careful attention to exact transcription is also remarkable.

The spoken charm is favored in this volume, whether accompanied by ritual actions or not. Rites unaccompanied by an oral component are the next largest category, while written charms and pieces of lore are the smallest categories. This may indicate that Elsa found oral recitation to be a favored form of magic. As we look through all three of these volumes, we find emphasis on the power of the spoken prayer, even when it is recently composed (e.g., numbers 80a and 80b).

63.9% of the items are devoted to altruistic aims, with healing painful conditions and workings to provide psychic protection from demonic forces in the majority. Interestingly, seven from that number are devoted to the health of livestock, in spite of the fact that the collector was living in an urban area during the time this first manuscript was written.

With the preponderance of devotional prayers in this book, it is interesting to note that even here we have 12.0% devoted to workings for personal advantage, and 9.6% to destructive workings. Compelling, hexing and causing fiddle strings to break all make an appearance, in spite of the pious nature of the other items. This is interesting for the case it makes that even among those who kept an outward appearance of the benevolent healer, there was still an expectation to see some malevolent items in such a collection.

MS 19

NM 271.601-B LÄKARBOK
NORDIC MUSEUM 271.601-B HEALERS' BOOK

¶This manuscript measures 10×16.5 CM and consists of 50 handwritten pages (25 leaves, sewn binding in a black leather cover). It is an accounting book from this century. There is writing on both the front and back inside covers. Three pages are cut out of the first quire, 8 from the second, 7 from the third, 8 from the fourth, 3 from the fifth and 8 from the sixth. The numeration of items is consecutive until 47, after which 55, 59 skips to 66, 91 to 103 and 110 to 113. The writing style is modern, even where some of the orthography is not standard. This manuscript contains a total of 119 items.

The manuscript has the following title on the first page:

Book of Healing
Dedicated to Elsa by Olof, years 1920–1929
All this I have learned to help those who are in need. Olle said.

S-1	59	I-1	56
S-2	19	I-2	9
S-3	8	I-3	2
S-4	1	I-4	1
S-5	2	I-5	29
S-6	26	I-6	1
S-7	0	I-7	14
S-8	2		
S-9	22		

DISCUSSION

This manuscript is earlier than the *Sankt Petri Nyckel* by a decade or two, and Elsa's primary informant to judge by her carefully made attributions is her teacher, Olle. There are other attributions occasionally, including S. Jansson of Ljustorp, S. Pr., Alma in Uppsala, Selma, Norla S. J. Sångberg, Adolf Lundblad in Härnösand (1935), "Fjällpälle," and lore heard over the radio (#26). Also, it seems as if Ms. Halmdahl was the recipient of posthumous instruction from Olle in visions and dreams (#56). She has consciously titled this first volume in her series "Book of Healing" (Sw. *Läkarbok*), perhaps to differentiate it from the subsequent volumes she would produce.

Once again, the largest formal category are those that contain some verbal component, with charms and rites with an oral component comprise 71.4% of the items in this volume. A total of 9.2% is devoted to ingested, burned or applied recipes, perhaps indicating a degree of discomfort with the prescription of medicinal materials or the methods of their decoction. With only two devoted to written spells, clearly the spoken word (perhaps with its implied breath) is the vehicle for the efficacy of her procedures. 18.0% are explanations of the uses of plants or substances, and do not describe a charm or rite.

At 56.3%, the largest motivational category is healing, though here we include under that rubric the healing of psychic ailments and protection from hostile spirits. Nine items are for the healing of livestock, again remarkable for the urban setting in which these were recorded. A full 11.8% are devoted to the business of non-specific hexing. And among the personal advantages for which one might work, such as winning the lottery or obtaining wealth, Ms. Halmdahl also includes the procurement of psychic power.

MS 20

NM 271.601-C "UPPLYSA DE OKUNNIGA"
NORDIC MUSEUM 271.601-C "TO ILLUMINE THE IGNORANT"

¶This manuscript, with embossed title "Ordbok" on the cover, measures 11.5×34.5 CM, and is an accounting ledger with a stapled binding. Originally, it consisted of 21 leaves, only two of which were retrievable at the time of examination. This portion of the manuscript contains 5 items.

The title assigned by *Nordiska muséet* to this volume comes from the first line of the written manuscript: "To enlighten the ignorant is to accumulate merits."

S-1	0	I-1	3
S-2	0	I-2	0
S-3	3	I-3	0
S-4	0	I-4	0
S-5	0	I-5	2
S-6	2	I-6	0
S-7	0	I-7	0
S-8	0		
S-9	1		

DISCUSSION

The first three items in this oddly shaped volume are devoted to simple herbal house cures, such as a tea to tonify the kidneys made from dandelion root, or carrot juice or black coffee to strengthen the eyes. The first item (carrot juice) has an accompanying charm to be recited over it, while the other recipes for ingestion are simple recipes. The last two items are interesting because they appear to be hypnotism, both a trance induction as well as retrieval. There is no additional information about the inclusion of these items, and we might posit that Ms. Halmdahl used this technique when treating someone for pain management or to curtail an addiction for a client. The title of this third volume "To enlighten the ignorant" seems to appeal to a world view informed by John 1:5–9, in which Christ is referred to as "the Light that enlightens every man." If the magical content were not so clearly recorded, we might be tempted to think that Ms. Halmdahl was evangelical in her religious beliefs. Her repeated appeals to Mary, however, seem anchored in a form of Roman Catholicism, and her understanding of psychic power is very mystical.

This third manuscript rounds out a period of training lasting from the early 1920s in Hälsingland and on into the early 1940s in Stockholm—about two decades of material collected from various sources and locations, with a rudimentary form of attribution that is less useful in an identification of her informants but rather more in establishing her need to cite authoritative sources. In places, she provides the teachings of her teacher as if she is transcribing a session with him, as when she relates Olle's teaching about his personal healers' knife (Sw. *botarkniv*) (19:25) or the method of the effective transmission of charms (19:38b).

The material proceeds from the recited charm, often recorded in forms that we recognize from much older manuscripts in the tradition, and then concludes with the more scientific, psychological practice of hypnosis. These three manuscripts show a development in Ms. Halmdahl's apprenticeship to one of the wise ones. What ultimately caused her decision to donate the entire body of her collections to the Nordic Museum is a mystery that we can only guess at. It may have been that she was left without a magical heir, or that she felt the time for charms and charming had passed, like belief in the legendary waning of nature spirits, with the increasingly widespread use of the electric light-bulb.

MS 21

NORDISKA MUSÉET #271.602
"NEGROMÄNLISKA SAKER"
NORDIC MUSEUM 271.602
"MATTERS OF NEGROMANCY"

¶ The provenance of this manuscript is unknown. It contains 24 leaves, 20 cm w×17 cm h and has a sewn binding. There is a chance that this manuscript was originally entitled "Negromäntiska saker" or "Necromantic matters" but with an uncrossed "t," which makes better sense in the context. In one transcription, the title was given with a "t" instead of an "l," and a second reader has gone and scratched out the cross, turning the letter back to an "l," presumably to correct an inaccurate editorial alteration.

On the title page of the manuscript, the following text is provided:

Negromänliska Saker – författade i Trycket af Upgifvaren år 1315 Öfversatte från Ebreiska, Grekiska och Latin på Götiskan – 1410 – och sist på Svenska utskrifvit.

[Negromänlish Matters—authored in print by the author in the year 1315 Translated from Hebrew, Greek and Latin in Gothic—1410—and lastly written out in Swedish.]

This manuscript is the second of the two in the collection here that contains a conjuration to the arch-demon Marbuel. As Sven B. Ek has remarked in his commentary on manuscript EM 3329-C from Eslöv Museum, the standard conjuration of this demon appears in *Particular-Citation des Gross-Fürsten Marbuelis* in a 17th century book *Dr. Johann Faustens Miracul- Kunst- und Wunder-Buch oder die schwarze Rabe auch der Dreifache Höllen Zwang genannt*.[31] This manuscript seems to make sense of problematic readings in Ahlström's manuscript.

This manuscript contains twenty-six discrete items.

S-1	2	I-1	4
S-2	9	I-2	3
S-3	0	I-3	3
S-4	0	I-4	1
S-5	1	I-5	11
S-6	9	I-6	3
S-7	0	I-7	2
S-8	6		
S-9	2		

DISCUSSION

69.2% of the items in this volume are either rites or rites accompanied by an oral component. With only two purely verbal charms, it may be the compiler saw efficacy primarily in the action of rites. Six items are written spells, either *ephesia grammata*—words meant to be pronounced but here appearing in written form—or a list of letters that are called "words" but are probably not meant to be pronounced orally. Also in this volume are written out two codes for secret writing. The first is a "Romani" or Gypsy alphabet, and the second is a Runic alphabet that illustrates a certain familiarity with actual runic characters. When the Pater Noster is written out backwards (#10), the first line is written out in Runes. For this reason, we may assume that the compiler was confident that the casual reader would be unfamiliar enough with runic characters that they would be put off from deciphering it.

The largest motivational category is for workings to procure personal advantage, such as discovery of hidden treasure, divination and obtaining psychic powers. The largest item is an evocation of the archdemon Marbuel, who is presumably able to confer upon the operant the desired mystic powers. This evocation displays the belief that all magical powers ultimately derive from a demonic rather than a divine source, and are sought only at great peril to the immortal soul.

Regarding the title, *Negromänliska saker* may be a reference to "black" art, or be a misspelling for "necro-," a reference to necromancy, the discovery of hidden knowledge by appeal to departed spirits. The compiler was unable to spell either option satisfactorily, and we are left to wonder at his or her intention. If only for the appearance of the demonic arch-Duke Marbuel, we are tempted to see it as containing operations of the Black Art. While in the larger tradition, power was obtained from the slime of a white snake, or a trip under the mound with the subterraneans, in this book the source of power is the magical evocation by infernal orison.

Apart from healing physical ailments in the human patient, animals and shotguns were also recipients of the healing attention of the wise one. Psychic protection of the individual and the protection of his goods from theft are also reckoned in this category.

MS 22

NM ONUMRERAT GRYTS OCH GÅRINGE SKOGSBYGD,
SÖDERMANLAND
"1. ATT LÄSA MOT VÄRK – 10. ATT FÖRGÖRA EN FIOL"
*NORDIC MUSEUM UNNUMBERED, GRYTS AND GÅRINGE WOODLAND,
SÖDERMANLAND PROVINCE
"1. TO RECITE AGAINST PAIN—10. TO HEX A FIDDLE"*

¶This manuscript consists of 2 leaves (4 pages) representing the transcribed contents of a book from Södermanland made by metalworker Gustaf Ericsson. The original stayed with its original owner. It consists of 10 items.

S-1	1	I-1	3
S-2	3	I-2	0
S-3	0	I-3	0
S-4	0	I-4	0
S-5	0	I-5	0
S-6	5	I-6	5
S-7	0	I-7	2
S-8	1		
S-9	0		

DISCUSSION

This little book is one of the smaller volumes in the collection under consideration here. The largest formal category is rites with oral components or accompanying charms. One item is a charm with no stipulated accompanying action, and three are rites with no oral components. There is one that involves an exorcism of the *mara* written in one's own blood, with the concluding invocation of the Trinity written in common ink.

Bleeding, painful conditions and psychic protection are the more altruistic intentions, while manipulation of people's volition and the hexing of another are of a more malevolent type, in this manuscript a majority. The final rite to hex a fiddle is curious because it prevents the instrument from sounding while it does not break the fiddle strings, as we have seen in previous manuscripts.

The principle of efficacy is in the majority of the items the invocation of the Trinity, and even items of a more malevolent intent make use of this standard rubric invoking the Father, Son and Holy Ghost.

MS 23

NORDISKA MUSÉET, UNNUMBERED MANUSCRIPT[32]
FRÅN MÖNSTERÅS, SMÅLAND
*NORDIC MUSEUM, UNNUMBERED MANUSCRIPT
FROM MÖNSTERÅS TOWNSHIP*

¶In *Nordiska muséets* holdings, this manuscript is among the few lacking an accession number in the file box. The museum has provided a place of provenance as Mönsterås. Mönsterås is the name of both a town and an administrative district (kommun) in the county of Kalmarslän in Småland. The manuscript's dimensions are 10.5×16.5 CM. It has a sewn binding which includes 54 sewn leaves. The front cover is missing, and the back is wood covered with paper. It was added to *Nordiska muséets* holdings 10/26/1907 by P. G. Wistrand. There are 20 leaves in the first half of the quire while only 8 are in its second half. Clearly, about 8 pages are removed or missing. The description left by Gustaf Ericsson on September 27, 1882 in the file box at the *Fornminnessamling* notes that the manuscript was found in Strängnäs, but it was uncertain if it might in fact have been originally from Selaön or Länna.[33] The manuscript is written in at least three different hands, and is also available in typed transcription made by Bo Thullberg. Ownership of the manuscript is indicated on page 49: "Denna bok ha tillhört Capten Waduman men tillhör nu för tillfället Johan Snack Kirawitz upå Mönsterås, den 20 maj, 1854." [This book has belonged to Captain Waduman, but now happens to belong to Johan Snack Kirawitz up on Mönster ridge, May 20, 1854.]

This manuscript contains 67 discrete items.

S-1 0	I-1 14
S-2 48	I-2 5
S-3 9	I-3 11
S-4 9	I-4 26
S-5 0	I-5 5
S-6 0	I-6 3
S-7 0	I-7 3
S-8 0	
S-9 2	

DISCUSSION

This manuscript contains primarily rituals which are unaccompanied by oral recitations (71.6%), and an equal number of ingested and applied recipes

(26.9%). As the title it was given at the Nordic Museum would imply, the primary concern of the rites in this manuscript have to do with hunting, marksmanship, magical care of shotguns and ammunition (55.2%). At 28.3%, healing humans and livestock is the second largest category, and the less altruistic end of the spectrum represents 9.0% of the items in this manuscript.

With hunting concerns in a position of prominence, we might assume that the compiler supported himself by hunting, or had a clientele which consisted primarily of hunters. With only five items dealing with the health of livestock, and 27 dealing with the care and maintenance of shotguns and traps and an additional four devoted to methods to exercise control over game, it is clear that the potential clients of such services were not wealthy enough to own livestock, or to perhaps have a farm large enough to support them. It is interesting, however, to note that cures for eyes, bleeding, painful conditions, skin eruptions, eyes and teeth were within the purview of this manuscript in addition to concerns for hunting, so the two spheres of concern were tied together in the mind of the compiler in some way.

The paucity of oral charms in this collection is worthy of note, since it is one of the few manuscripts that display this characteristic.

MS 24

NM ONUMRERAT, "OM FISKERI Å DES INEHÅL"
SKIRÖ AND VIRSERUMS SOCKNAR, SMÅLAND.
NORDIC MUSEUM UNNUMBERED, "REGARDING FISHING AND ITS EQUIPAGE"
SKIRÖ AND VIRSERUM PARISHES, SMÅLAND PROVINCE.

¶Only excerpts of this manuscript were printed by P. G. Wistrand.[34] A partial transcription was made at the Nordic Museum in 1938 by an unknown transcriber.

This item is labeled "A fragment of a black art book from Skirö parish, Småland, received by Nordiska muséet 5/31/1910." It consists of 19 separated leaves in very fragile condition. There are 38 pages with writing, though a number of them have sufficiently decayed that it is difficult to translate. Its age and condition make it very difficult to read. Its size varies between 15.5–16×19.5 CM. Although the partial published version lists the first item as "om fiskeri å des inehål" [about fishing and its equipment] which in the translation presented here occurs on page 15 of the manuscript, the first page in the collection upon personal examination was "*at piga eÿ blir med barn...*" [So that a maiden will not conceive...]. This may well be due to subsequent examination by scholars who were not careful to retain the original order of pages. The total number of items is 230. It is doubtful that this manuscript will survive much longer in the conditions in which it was kept at the *Folkminnessamling* in Stockholm in the early 1990s. To judge from gothic-style handwriting and rag-paper age, I would judge this to be from the late seventeenth to the early eighteenth century, while Wistrand writes in his edition that it is from the late eighteenth century.

Work with this manuscript has been problematical. Wistrand, in his attempt to publish a clean transcription in 1906, bemoans: "Unfortunately the manuscript is so ragged, that it, regardless of its frequently unreadable handwriting and text which is difficult to interpret, cannot be provided in its entirety."[35] This will mean that in a translation of this manuscript, there will still remain lacunæ and misreadings. I believe I have been successful in recovering more of the original content than Wistrand found possible in 1906.

This translation is the first attempt working with the entire manuscript, with the help of the material first published in 1906 by Wistrand. Because the loose pages are no longer bound together, but are still obviously of the same paper stock and contain the same handwriting, the order of items will vary from Wistrand's, but some of his sleuth work will help in the interpretation of an older gothic penmanship presented on decaying paper. Because it has no pagination, I will arbitrarily associate page numbers with the copy I retain. Items in the original manuscript were not numbered but were separated by lines. Here, I will number each item for ease of reference. In this manuscript there are 231 discrete items.

S-1 3	I-1 140
S-2 44	I-2 13
S-3 84	I-3 2
S-4 81	I-4 27
S-5 5	I-5 10
S-6 7	I-6 7
S-7 0	I-7 11
S-8 0	
S-9 3	

DISCUSSION

This manuscript is the largest collection represented among these manuscripts, with 231 items, divided in the manuscript by lines that separate one item from the next. The largest formal category are recipes, for ingestion (36.4%) and for external application (35.1%). Rituals unaccompanied by an oral component comprise the third largest category (19.0%). Three verbal charms, five incense recipes, seven rituals with an oral component and three passages explaining the use of an element of the pharmacopœia make up the rest of the items.

In spite of the assignment of the title "About fishing and its equipment," the primary motivational category is healing humans (60.6%), and the book is a catalog of physical ailments and their various treatments. Hunting and fishing luck is the second largest category (12.6%), and magic of a slightly less benevolent bent is roughly evenly divided, with ten items devoted to personal advantage (money, luck, unlocking locks, memory), 7 to manipulation of others (having women perform at the behests of the client), and 11 to hexing or destruction (total: 12.1%).

An especially interesting item is to magically cause the death of an infant whose mother has died in childbirth. Infanticide, while not the horrific moral dilemma it is today, was still a punishable offence, and it can be imagined that a child left motherless might be seen as a liability rather than the cause for rejoicing that another helping hand on the farm could bring. Thirty-one items are devoted to issues of the reproductive organs or pregnancy. General illness (17.7%), bleeding (6.0%), complaints of the skin and hair (7.8%) and painful conditions (9.5%) were the target of the largest number of procedures under the rubric of healing. A total of nine items were devoted to hexing.

Generally, the medical approach of ingested or applied recipes seemed privileged, while rituals and charms, while still quite numerous, constituted a smaller category. The absence of written formulæ may imply that prepared medicines and ritual actions brought greater efficacy to the item. Also, even with a clear predominance of healing spells, there remained a number of overtly malevolent magic items.

MS 25

NORDISKA MUSÉET, ONUMRERAT
ÅKERS SN., ÅKERS HÄRAD, SÖDERMANLAND
"ATT BOTA EN BÖSSA SOM ÄR SKÄMD."
NORDIC MUSEUM, UNNUMBERED
ÅKERS PARISH, ÅKERS JURISDICTIONAL DISTRICT,
SÖDERMANLAND PROVINCE
"TO FIX A SHOTGUN THAT IS HEXED."

¶In information provided to Gustaf Ericsson, and which he provides on the last page of the transcription,

> å mig har varit årtalet 1819 men titelbladet är förkommen. Är skrifvet med bättre stil såsom af den tidens klokarna eller välbestäld fjerdingsman – Är tiu ö:- m:- No 73 original fullt lik mm sedermera sammandragit hufvudmenin-

gar – Har varit praktiß utöfning innom Åkers härad i Södermanland och förvaras ännu med omsorg innom en viss familj, afvskrifen af Gust. Ericsson Söderm: Fornminnesförening ombud in ...

[given to me in 1819, but the title page is lost. It is written in with better penmanship such as that used by the period's cunning folk or well-placed parish constable—Up through No. 73 the items are exactly as in the original, but many thereafter are summarized by Ericsson with main sentences. It represents the practice of one in Åkers District in Södermanland, and is still carefully kept within a certain family, copied by Gustav Ericsson, Södermanlands Antiquities Collection's representative.]

This handwritten transcription was made in a small notebook with sewn binding, and both sides of the paper were written on. This manuscript contains 98 discrete items.

S-1 9	I-1 22
S-2 44	I-2 5
S-3 3	I-3 18
S-4 0	I-4 11
S-5 1	I-5 15
S-6 15	I-6 8
S-7 0	I-7 4
S-8 5	
S-9 15	

DISCUSSION

Formally, the vast majority of the items in this manuscript are rites unaccompanied by any verbal recitation, at 44.9% of the items. A considerably smaller percentage employed a recited component, with charms and accompanying rites at 15.3%, and oral charms alone at 9.2%. Both recipes for ingestion and for incenses are comparatively few, with 4.1% and 5.1% respectively. 15.3% were lore about the use of different *materia magica*.

Once again, healing is the largest motivational category, and 45.9% of the items are divided between healing of humans, livestock or shotguns. The largest number of items concerned with the health and well-being of humans is devoted to psychic protection, that is, the protection from magical attack. 11.2% of the items are concerned with personal advantage, including the discovery of treasure, divination, winning at gambling and invisibility. The remainder of the items, at 12.2% of the manuscript, is less benevolent, with 8.2%

to manipulate the volition of others (control of magistrates, of women, and sleep spells), and 4.1% devoted to hexing either persons or shotguns.

Because of the preponderance of wordless ritual intended to heal, one is tempted to view this manuscript as the product of one with the altruistic intention to provide aid, whether in healthcare or psychological well-being, but the inescapable presence of morally or ethically nebulous items reinforces the emerging view that a good Black Art Book is a well-rounded Black Art Book.

MS 26

PER BJÖRNSSON
LUNNOM, BROBY, SKÅNE, 1690
PER BJÖRNSSON
LUNNOM TOWN, BROBY PARISH, SKÅNE PROVINCE, 1690

¶According to Pehr Johnsson,[36] Per Björnsson was a cunning man during the end of the seventeenth century in Lunnom, Broby parish, and was discussed in Cavallin's *Herdeminnen*.[37] The manuscript was discovered by Cavallin after Pastor A. Helgesson from Stehag mentioned the trial records of the exorcist Per Björnsson, along with a much damaged black art book he owned. These items were kept at *Lunds landsarkiv* among other documents included in the *Acta cleri* there. Helgesson wrote an excerpt of the trial transcript which he made available to Johnsson and which provides some biographical material about Björnsson. As far as is known, Björnsson was an older man and a free farmer in the village of Lunnom in Broby parish in Skåne during the late seventeenth and early eighteenth centuries.

The trial records begin with the complaint registered by Pastor Christian Jacob Noviomagus on March 7, 1689 against Per Björnsson. In this same complaint, he names various people who had been recited over, in order to help those who had become "crossed in water and wind." Dean Erman, the recipient of the complaint, ordered Björnsson to come down to Mellby to be examined by him. Björnsson demured, saying that "if Mr. Christian or anyone else wanted him for something, then they certainly knew where he had his home," and that it was quite out of the question for him to make such a long journey. On May 28, 1690, the Östra Göinge County Court declared that Björnsson, "in superstition and conjuring had used unusual prayer forms which he recited over sick people," and that he was to be sentenced to fourteen days' imprisonment on bread and water.

This manuscript is of 20 pages in octavo, though the final four pages bear no writing. The book is also torn through the middle, which makes it a little difficult to actually interpret in places. In this translation of the manuscript, elipses included in brackets in the translation represent obviously lost text, while sometimes the text, even when it appears, doesn't flow as one would expect. This might as easily be a result of Per Björnsson as it is of the carelessness of a modern transcriber.

The reader should note the extreme similarities between this manuscript and "Cypranis konster och läror och des inrät," from neighboring Onsby parish (NM 40.034, MS 12). The similarities could be attributable to a mutual familiarity with a common tradition, or a friendship between two cunning folk. This manuscript contains one lengthy item that may have been divided into manageable length in actual practice.

S-1	1	I-1	1
S-2	0	I-2	0
S-3	0	I-3	0
S-4	0	I-4	0
S-5	0	I-5	0
S-6	0	I-6	0
S-7	0	I-7	0
S-8	0		
S-9	0		

DISCUSSION

As we see from Björnsson's Black Art Book, the "unusual prayer forms" mentioned in his trial record from Östra Göinge County took the form of a single lengthy liturgical orison for the purpose of exorcising demonic influence from the body and mind of the client. Because of the excessive length of the single orison, one wonders whether the item was in practice divided up into less lengthy portions suitable for recitation from memory, or tailored to a specific condition. It remains, however, that with the entire conjuration contained in this manuscript, it would have been possible for Björnsson to recite the entire thing over a single client.

While the orison has the declared intent to cast out demons from the patient, it appears from the charges leveled at Björnsson in Östra Göinge that he appropriated the orison to recite over patients in order to treat physical illnesses or injuries as well. In form, the lengthy orison is probably copied, for the most part accurately, from an older liturgical text. The inclusion of the Greek liturgy "Kyrie Eleison" from the Tridentine Roman Mass, the only non-Swedish passage in this manuscript, may indicate that this has its origins in either a country with continued ties to the Roman Church such as Lithuania, or can be dated to the pre-Reformation period in Scandinavia.

The other issue requiring resolution is the appearance of the name St. Cyprian, who was neither St. Cyprian of Carthage (d. 258 CE) nor St. Cyprian, bishop of Toulon (d. 546 CE), two respected saints of the Roman Church. Rather, this is the legendary St. Cyprian of Tyre, who allegedly lived (and was martyred) during the reign of the Emperor Diocletian (fl. 284–305 CE) who was called St. Cyprian the Magician, so called because prior to his conversion to the Christian faith, he was a practicing magician. The appeal to this St. Cyprian causes one to doubt that the orison of this manuscript was a legitimate liturgical text of the Roman Church, but rather a composition of a later writer familiar with this legendary (and unattested) saint.

MS 27

PETTER JOHAN JOHANESSON, 1841
VARUTI JAG SKRIFVER VARJEHANDA
PETTER JOHAN JOHANESSON, 1841
IN WHICH I WRITE A BIT OF EVERYTHING

¶This manuscript was published by Förlag Maiander in 1917. According to the publisher, "Petter Johan Johanessons black art book is here published according to the transcript of the original that J. A. Sandblom, a teacher in Hultsjö, placed at the *Folkminnesförening* [Folklore Society] in Lund in the year 1916. This is the third in a series of black art books being issued from that organization."

As with the publication of the black art book from Skytts county, the manuscript has been dealt with most carefully. Nothing has either been changed or added to. The authors' spelling and comments are retained overall; only in a couple of cases has the all too naturally occurring expression been replaced by more common usage, inside parentheses.

The edition is produced here with a scientific aim, and all of the material found in it is useful for researchers, due to how hard it is to get."[38]

This text has sixty-nine items, both numbered and unnumbered. Dialect is strongly in evidence, and standard orthographic norms are not followed. Often reading aloud is the only way to discern meaning, as the manuscript follows colloquial pronunciation rather than *rikssvenska*. Punctuation is wholly lacking, and this has been inserted occasionally in the English translation to aid the reader. Even so, the language is vague enough that a definitive translation is often not possible.

S-1	2	I-1	24
S-2	32	I-2	17
S-3	8	I-3	1
S-4	7	I-4	1
S-5	1	I-5	5

S-6 14   I-6 6
S-7 2   I-7 15
S-8 1
S-9 6

DISCUSSION

The largest formal category in this manuscript is the rite unaccompanied by any verbal component at 46.4%. Charms alone, or rituals with an accompanying charm constitute 23.2% of the items here, and recipes requiring that a charm be recited over them constituted 2.9% (# 18, 19). A single item (#42) to cause someone to visit under secrecy of night required a written component, in this case writing the Pater Noster backwards in a circle—presumably the writing was to be in the shape of a circle rather than that the operation be performed within a magic circle such as is found in ceremonial grimoires such as the *Clavicula Salomonis*.

As we have grown to expect, the largest motivational category (59.4%) is devoted to healing with 46.4% directed towards livestock. Unexpectedly, the second largest category is harmful witchcraft, including hexing livestock, blighting crops, hexing people, shotguns and wells, and creating a trollhare to magically steal milk, representing 21.7% of the contents. Operations promoting personal advantage, one in the form of invisibility and four in some form of divination, represent 7.2%. Manipulation of the volition of others (8.7%) primarily takes the form of causing women to perform one's behests, or causing others to show affection.

MS 28

"SIGNERI OCH VIDSKEPELSE" – 1751
FILIPSTADS BERGSLAGS HÄRAD, NU: FERNEBO HÄRAD,
VÄRMLAND
"CONJURING AND SUPERSTITION"—1751
FILIPSTADS BERGSLAGS JURISDICTION, NOW: FERNEBO
JURISDICTION, VÄRMLAND PROVINCE

¶This manuscript is an excerpt from the court records, recording the proceedings held at Philipstads-Bergslags Laga Winter Court in Philipstad in the year 1751. It provides the transcripts of the trial of Annika Mattsdotter, 1/24–1/26/1751. A guilty verdict in the case was rendered 4/16/1751, and Mattsdotter was sentenced to twentyfive silver *riksdaler* or eight days imprisonment on bread and water. Two witnesses called to testify against her were fined five silver *riksdaler* each, for having consulted her for healing. Apart from the interrogation of the accused and of witnesses, this transcript presents 5 discrete charms revealed during the course of interrogation.[39]

S-1	5	I-1	5
S-2	0	I-2	0
S-3	0	I-3	0
S-4	0	I-4	0
S-5	0	I-5	0
S-6	0	I-6	0
S-7	0	I-7	0
S-8	0		
S-9	0		

DISCUSSION

While this transcript is not technically a *svartkonstbok*, it provides the legal and social context of popular perception of the wise folk. In this case, Annika Mattsdotter was accused of healing by means of supernatural ability and by means of her recitation of charms over the patient. She is eventually found guilty as charged, but not before she surrenders to the court recorder some of her repertoire of charms.

All five charms recorded in the trial transcripts are recited charms, and all five have as their intent the healing of human patients. It is ironic that the accused is one of the few whose repertoire does not include overly malevolent content, and yet she is being charged with providing healing under false pretense, i.e., she was not a doctor. It seems from just this record that the reputation of the accused as either primarily benevolent or primarily malevolent was inconsequential in a consideration of whether or not she would be accused and brought to trial. Malevolent witchcraft was not the only exercise of the magical art that was fraught with danger for the innocent healer.

MS 29

MS SV 1051
SKARA VETERINÄRBIBLIOTEK
MANUSCRIPT S V:BIBLIOTEK 1051
SKARA'S VETERINARY LIBRARY

¶ This *Helfwetesbref* [Letter to Hell] was found in an almanac for the year 1791 which was in the ownership of cleric Clas Bjerkander. It consists of two pages folio of 8.5×16 CM. It comprises a letter in the form of a contract, as well as the directions regarding its ritual handling, and is here considered as one item.

S-1	0	I-1	0
S-2	1	I-2	0
S-3	0	I-3	0
S-4	0	I-4	0
S-5	0	I-5	1
S-6	0	I-6	0
S-7	0	I-7	0
S-8	1		
S-9	0		

DISCUSSION

While this item is clearly not a handbook of the cunning man or woman, it does provide a procedure whereby such a one is able to procure preternatural powers. Since other manuscripts have described similar evocations of demonic powers to this end, this single written page belongs rightly among the more lengthy manuals that describe similar operations.

It is clear from the specificity of the conditions to be met in exchange for the writer's soul that this is patterned after what the writer believed to be legal and binding language. In exchange for the writer's soul, he or she would receive success in winning the Stockholm lottery, be loved by those of high or low birth, receive the favors of women and to have luck in all endeavors. This may be an example of a method to obtain the special powers that cunning folk possessed. It contains directions for its disposition, in that it is to be written entirely in blood, and must be placed in an open grave. It is clear from this that the dead were viewed as uniquely qualified to address either side of the moral scale, both the infernal and the supernal realms. They also seemed to have powerful abilities exceeding those of ordinary mortals, for example the power to divine the future, or to exercise power over unruly spirits or demons.

MS 30

ULMA 984,[40] JUGAS OLOF JONSSON, 1873–74 DAL
NÅS SOCKEN, VÄSTRA DALARNA
*ULMA 984, JUGAS OLOF JONSSON, 1873–74 DAL
NÅS PARISH, WESTERN DALARNA PROVINCE*

¶The manuscript itself is housed at the *Språk- och folkminnesinstitutet* (SOFI, previously ULMA or *Uppsala Landsmålsarkivet*) in Uppsala.[41] This was where I was able to examine the original and obtain an official copy of it. Later, I obtained a copy of the 1924 published edition by N. Sjödahl, interesting for its divergence from the original.

This manuscript appears in two quires contained in a heavy construction paper outer folder with the dimensions 11.5×8.5 CM. The first 6 folio leaves consist of high grade, low rag content heavy paper and are folded but unsewn; and the second 5 folio leaves are a finer grade glossy paper and are sewn together, all for a total of 37 written pages. Each page is filled with writing, and there are 52 items in this small volume, though Sjödahl's edition has only 37 numbered items. Sjödahl edited the manuscript in such a way as to group items with the same or similar intentions together, a tendency not present in the original. The pages are now numbered, though by a different hand, probably an archivist.

The published edition is complicated by a rearrangement of the order of the items in the manuscript, but which I have restored here, and by the insertion of parenthetical remarks that the original did not contain. For this translation, I have opted to go back to the original for the order and content, and only use the apparatus in the published edition for explanatory footnotes when needed. The original contains no punctuation, so all insertions are my own. The original also had no numeration of items. The published edition had numeration, but followed neither the order nor the grouping of the original. I have inserted numeration for ease of reference, and follow the original order. The numeration of this translation and that of the Sjödahl edition will therefore not match.

From the introduction of the published version:

> Jugas Olof Jonsson was born in Nås parish in Western Dalarna on the 26th of March 1859 and is still living in his birth parish.[42] As a schoolboy, he collected and recorded charms (*trollformler*) and other things, which a knowledgeable sorcerer should be acquainted with, because he hoped that with time he would become a famous one. Even so, Jugas Jonsson didn't become a sorcerer, if this now depended upon the fact that in more mature years, he found the career less attractive, or upon the fact that he had begun to lose his

belief in magic—in any case, he maintains that he no longer has any belief in the arts of magic.[43] In the meantime he saved his notes. Even if these could have partially been copied from some printed black book, he has maintained that he mainly received the material orally, which is also reinforced by the large number of dialect forms preserved in his notes. The black book that is produced here, which is now being published, was written from the years 1873 and 1874, and consists of a little handwritten volume in approximate folio format of 35 pages.

During the summer of 1916, the present editor visited for a time in Nås to research the Nås dialect (nåsmålet), and visited during that time with Jugas Olof Jonsson. Our conversation came to touch upon old superstition. Jugas Olof Jonsson took forth his black book and displayed it, which the editor promised to transcribe and publish. The book was transcribed also, with the exception of a few (about 2) pages where notes either were unreadable or also didn't have anything to do with magic. This transcription is now found at the Dialect archive in Uppsala. In the original Jugas Olof Jonsson has made some changes and as a rule, to make certain dialect forms comply with the corresponding standard Swedish forms or the other way around. This edition takes into account these changes, and when so, notes are made...

The publisher uses the chance here in his own way and on behalf of all those who have interest in the culture of older times, to forward his thanks to Jugas Olof Jonsson for an account of our people's cultural history that he left through his Black Book. It comprises a valuable contribution to the sources we already have for the customs and practices of the Swedish People, their belief and their mode of thinking during the past time and forward to our days.[44]

This published manuscript contains 52 discrete items.

S-1 14	I-1 15
S-2 17	I-2 17
S-3 11	I-3 0
S-4 4	I-4 2
S-5 1	I-5 8
S-6 6	I-6 4
S-7 0	I-7 6
S-8 0	
S-9 3	

DISCUSSION

Formally, oral charms and rites with an oral component comprise the majority (38.5%) of the items in this manuscript. Rites with no oral component were the second most plentiful at 32.7%. Ingested, externally applied and burnt recipes were third at 30.8%. Three items catalog a number of materials which can be used to effect a single magical end, and describe the manner of their application.

Healing was the largest motivational category, comprising 61.5% of the items in this manuscript, and items to treat livestock outnumbered those for humans by only two. Workings for personal advantage (15.4%) include rituals to procure strength, money, the ability to unlock locks, divination and invisibility. Lastly, malevolent magic comprises 11.5% of this manuscript, and includes three items to break up marriages.

Once again, the preponderance of healing procedures does not preclude the presence of overtly malevolent magic. The preference of items that stress the power of the spoken word is only slightly more in evidence than rituals that are unaccompanied by any recitation. Jonsson was only 56 when he had come to the conclusion that he no longer believed in the magical power that these spells and rituals meant to exercise, and one wonders if part of the motivation for sharing it was to obtain greater notoriety as a cunning man in the region, having had his own secrets put to print, with all the prestige that this would involve. His claim to no longer believe in magic is one way that he can surrender these secrets to Sjödal: otherwise, he would be surrendering all his perceived power in the revelation of what would more normally be considered secret.[45] The apparatus provided by Sjödal based on Jonsson's commentary is helpful in providing additional clues as to how many of these items were used, though it seldom provides any clue as to the context in which they were used.

MS 31

ULMA 36365
"SALOMONISKA MAGISKA KONSTER"
NOTTEBÄCK-GRANHULT SN., SMÅLAND
ULMA 36365
"SOLOMONIC MAGICAL ARTS"
NOTTEBÄCK-GRANHULT PARISH, SMÅLAND PROVINCE

¶Heurgren's edition[46] is based on transcriptions of a "black book" and a "red book" transcribed by Gabriel Djurklou in the holdings of the Örebro läns museum. Items from Djurklou's transcription also appear in P. G. Wistrand's article of 1897.[47]

Nils Arvid Bringéus (1967)[48] has looked the most thoroughly into the provenance and serial ownership of ULMA 36365, called in this collection "Salomoniska magiska konster." At the time of Bringéus' 1967 article, only the first volume, in black ink, had been found and catalogued in Lund University's Library, which had bought it at book auction in 1924. A notice by Bringéus in 1991[49] refers back to a "red book" (i.e., a volume written in red ink) belonging to the family of Småland clergyman S. P. Gaslander, and the contents of which were published together with the contents of the "black book" by Paul Heurgren in 1918. Heurgren's sources at that time were not the manuscripts themselves, but rather later copies made by Gabriel Djurklou. The whereabouts of the "red book" were unknown in 1967, but Bringéus eventually found it as well, this time in the archives of the Lund Museum of Cultural History, to which it was donated by a private individual in 1953. The "red book" is of the same origin as the "black book," and confirms Bringéus' earlier conclusions about ownership of the two volumes. Like its black counterpart, the "red book" primarily contains magic cures for human and animal diseases, along with many "love tricks." Bringéus (1967) says that after a comparison of, specifically, MS 31, MS ULMA 36365 with the following three printed sources, a positive identification of source could be made, comparing it first with *Den sluga och förståndiga gubben, som lärer de oförfarna både i städerna och på landet, at igenom hwarjehanda hus-curer, hela och bota mångfaldiga sjukdomar, så wäl hos människor, som fånad; jämte mycket annat, som kan tjäna til förmon och nytta i åtskilliga hushålls-stycken* (1755),[50] and second, with its source, Hildebrand's *Wolffgangi Hildebrandi Magia Naturalis Libri Quatuor. Thet är: Fyra besynnerlige böcker aff undersamme konster, författade vthi åtskillige Naturalium rerum Secretis. Allom ährebare och lofflige konsters kärhafwandom til märceligh nytta, sampt synnerligh lust och wälbehagh, nu nyligen förswänskat och aff trycket vthgången hoos Henrich Keyser, åhr 1650*, and finally of the translation undertaken by Erichus Schroderus, of the German work *Magia Naturalis: Das ist Kunst vnd Wunderbuch / Darinnen begriffen wunderbahre Secreta, Geheimnüsse / vnd Kunststücke / wie man nemlich mit dem gantzen Menschlichen Cörper / Zahmen vnd wilden Thieren / Vogeln / Fischen / Vnzieffern vnd Insecten / allerley Gewächsen / Pflantzungen vnd sonsten fast vnerhörte wunderbarliche Sachen verrichten / Auch etliche Wunderschrifften künstlich bereiten / zu Schimpff / Kurtzweil / löblicher vnd lustiger Vbung / vnd zu Nutz gebrauchen / vnd damit die Zeit vertreiben kan: Beneben erzehlung vieler wunderlichen Dingen / so hin vnd wieder in der Welt gefunden werden. Allen Kunstbegierigen und Liebhabern solcher geheimbten Künsten / zu sonderlichen Gefallen aus vieler alter vnd newer Ertzte / berühmbter vnd bewehrter Naturkündiger Bücher vnd eigner Erfahrung colligirt ... Durch Wolfgangum Hildebrandum Gebesens. Tyrigetam* (Darmstadt, 1610).[51]

This leather bound item is in 8° (octavo) format, with a red-brown cardboard cover. There are 100 numbered pages, of which 92 are written on in ink. It comes from Sten Palmgren, son of the late Pastor Ludvig Palmgren in Nottebäck-Granhults parish (1844–1915). Previously it was owned by the Pastor in Burseryd, Petrus Gaslander (1680–1758), and then by his son, Johannes (1718–1793), making the period of compilation sometime between 1700 and 1750. The Palmgrens came by this volume through family connections rather than as a purchase. The "black book" was purchased at auction in 1924, while the "red book" came as a gift into the holdings of the *Kulturhistoriska föreningen* in Lund in 1953.

On the first page of this manuscript is a black and white representation of two outstretched hands, above a skull and crossbones, above a line of alchemical symbols of uncertain meaning. On the third is printed what looks to be a template for an astrological chart, circular with 12 areas corresponding to the twelve houses and twelve signs. The sixth page bears the title "*Salamoniska Magiska Konster*" with some additional alchemical symbols, much smaller, beneath. The first page of text is actually the eighth page of the volume, and begins the pagination that follows throughout. In the original, the items are not numbered, but in this translation I will use numeration for ease of future reference.

Heurgren's edition of 1918 is based on Djurklou's transcription of both volumes, and irregularities in wording or in sequence can be attributed to Djurklou, as Bringéus as aptly demonstrated. The translation that appears here is of the "black book," and will use the number and content of the original rather than Heurgren's edited text.

The manuscript contains 126 discrete items.

S-1 6	I-1 39
S-2 47	I-2 17
S-3 15	I-3 5
S-4 9	I-4 12
S-5 0	I-5 27
S-6 30	I-6 20
S-7 0	I-7 7
S-8 18	
S-9 8	

DISCUSSION

Silent rites predominate in this manuscript at 37.3%, while recited charms alone or with a rite are the second most numerous at 28.6%. Written charms and *trollkaraktärer* are more common in this manuscript than in others, at

14.3%, and the smallest formal category is recipes for either ingestion or external application, at 7.1%.

As we have come to expect among these manuscripts, the largest motivational category is healing at 48.4%. Other than strictly conditions of physiological illness, this manuscript includes cures for hex, a hexed distillery, spells to protect goods, possessions and crops, and to eradicate vermin. Rituals to establish personal advantage, including a pleasing voice, physical strength, magical power, luck and money were the second most numerous at 21.4%. Manipulative spells comprised 15.9% of the items and finally, at 5.6%, we have procedures to produce overt harm, including works of vengeance, cursing (humans, livestock, crops and shotguns).

Item #40 in this collection is essentially a death curse, and makes use of imitative magic—as the shotgun is fired, in just such a way so the individual is shot wherever he may be. With the types of malevolent workings present in this manuscript, especially the blighting of crops (#112) and of livestock (#98) one can clearly discern the pattern of the malevolent witch, in spite of the numerically predominant workings for healing of human, livestock and livelihood.

In 1991, Nils-Arvid Bringéus discovered the companion volume which was published together with this volume by Heurgren in 1918.[52] It is now kept at the University Library at Lund, as was located too late to include in this study.

MS 32

SUPRIANIA
FRU ALSTADS SOCKEN, SKYTTS HÄRAD, 1858
CYPRIANIA
FRU ALSTADS PARISH, SKYTTS JURISDICTIONAL DISTRICT, 1858

¶The original of this manuscript[53] was found among family papers in a farmstead. It is in octavo format, bound in variegated cardboard. The name of an assumed second owner of the volume is crossed out, and Christoffersson does not record it in his edition, but under the name is given the year 1858.

This manuscript contains 17 discrete items.

S-1 12	I-1 16
S-2 0	I-2 0
S-3 0	I-3 0
S-4 0	I-4 0
S-5 0	I-5 0
S-6 5	I-6 1

```
S-7 ............ 0      I-7 ............ 0
S-8 ............ 2
S-9 ............ 0
```

DISCUSSION

Oral charms or rites with charms figure in 100% of the 17 items in this manuscript, though 11.8% also include a written or drawn component (#5, 12). Once again, the largest motivational category is the healing of humans, at 94.1%. The inclusion of one conjuration to the dead (#5) for the vague purpose of obtaining three words is noteworthy. Necromancy, the divination by means of the conjuration of the shades of the dead, is an underrepresented type among these manuscripts. The remaining items seek to heal bleeding, toothache, painful conditions or skin conditions, all of which are commonly occurring in this genre.

MS 33

TROLL-MARKSENS SVARTKONSTBOK
THE WIZARD-MARKS'S BLACK ART BOOK

¶This manuscript appears in print in Herman Geijer, "Troll-Marksens Svartkonstbok. *Fornvårdaren* 1923–24, I:1–2, 59–69. According to Geijer, the original author and editor of this manuscript was Gotthard Wilhelm Marks von Würtenberg (1758–1822), who was known locally as "Troll-Marksen" or "the Magical Marks." Troll-Marksen was active in Resele, Ångermanland. He died at Storholmsjön, Föllinge parish, Jämtland in 1822.

This manuscript was a gift to a private owner (who retained ownership) from Carolina Olsson of Näset, Aspås parish in Jämtland, the great-granddaughter of the original compiler of this volume. The black art book itself is bound in a brown leather notebook of 10×15 CM, with pockets on the upper and lower edges bound in parchment. On the side of the book that faces the pages there are pockets with writing paper and on the side of the cover is stamped or embossed "G:W:M:V:W:ÅHR 1775." The first leaf preserved in the book contained on the verso the notation "the 29th of March, Gothardt traveled to Norway." The text begins on the the verso of the second leaf, and occupies 10 full pages. Four leaves in the back of the book remain empty. Leaves are torn out. The entire book is written in the same hand, and some pencil notations are written over in ink, also in the same hand. There are some spelling corrections, leading one to believe that as orthography became more standardized (or as the writer became better acquainted with it), there was an attempt at modernization. There are a total of 23 items in the manuscript, some of which are written in code or cypher: numbers 1, 2, 7, 12 and 13. Of these, numbers 12 and 13 are additional methods for the maladies represented in numbers 1 and 2. The items containing code do not exhibit consistency in the types of words reserved for such treatment. In other manuscripts, words of power, or power substances were regularly put into code, but here it is as likely to find a title as it is a random set of phrases in code. Numeration of the items stops after item number 14. Numbers 15–23 are in an older orthography, indicating that perhaps they were copied from a still older book.

S-1 0	I-1 17
S-2 7	I-2 6
S-3 6	I-3 0
S-4 10	I-4 0
S-5 0	I-5 0
S-6 0	I-6 0
S-7 0	I-7 0
S-8 1	
S-9 0	

DISCUSSION

Formally, the most prevalent form is the applied recipe, specifically plasters and soaks, at 43.5%. There are equivalent numbers of silent ritual and ingested recipes, while the entire manuscript is free of any oral component. One item (#1) makes use of the written word, specifically the name of Beelsebub, one of the four Princes of Hell, into which nails are hammered to treat toothache.

All of the items in this manuscript deal with healing, and there are no morally, ethically or spiritually questionable motives represented. In spite of the altruistic intentions of all of the items in this manuscript, the contents of five items are kept secret, as they are recorded in cipher. The items in cipher include two items treating nosebleed, two for toothache, and one for an exhausted horse (presumably useful when betting in racing contests). The cipher here does not function as it has elsewhere, in which words or substances of power were disguised to preserve the integrity of magical secrecy.

MS 34

ZIMPARTIER WETTENSKAP
PERSTORP, NORRA ÅSBO HÄRAD, KRISTIANSTADS LÄN, SKÅNE
SYMPATHETIC SCIENCE
PERSTORP VILLAGE, NORTHERN ÅSBO JURISDICTION,
KRISTIANSTADS COUNTY, SKÅNE PROVINCE

¶This manuscript was discovered in an attic in Perstorp, Norra Åsbo Härad in the county of Kristianstadslän, Skåne in 1936. The first page in the manuscript is torn, and is presumably where the owner's name was written. It is of 24 pages in a small octavo quire. On the last page is found the date "7 marts åhret 1829." This manuscript is held (as of Spring, 1937) in the Lengertz collections in Skåne [Collectio Lengertziana: Scania]. This manuscript contains 15 discrete items.

S-1	0	I-1	8
S-2	5	I-2	7
S-3	5	I-3	0
S-4	3	I-4	0
S-5	2	I-5	0
S-6	0	I-6	0
S-7	0	I-7	0
S-8	3		
S-9	1		

DISCUSSION

In this manuscript, there are 33.3% each of silent rituals and ingested recipes. Smaller in number are applied recipes (20.0%) and incenses (13.3%). 20.0% make use of written letters, both ingested and externally bound. One item describes the use and magical effects of a wolf's tooth on a horse.

The entire contents of this manuscript are altruistic, that is, they are primarily for the healing of human and livestock. Two items (#10, 11) are to repair an ability to distill strong spirits when the still is suspected of being hexed in some fashion. Since the repair of paraphernalia is considered to be an act of healing (such as that of shotguns), these two items are categorized with care and protection of the human and his belongings. One item (#14) is for the restoration of the ability to churn butter, when the churn is hexed.

With no items devoted to personal advantage, manipulation or malevolent magic, this compiler might have seen these as morally reprehensible.

The inclusion of a chapter heading "Rc 9th Chapter" between numbers 11 and 12 is curious, and leads one to believe that the primary source for these items was a previously published book rather than a traditionally transmitted corpus of charms.

MS 35

C. O. SWAHNS SVARTKONSTBOK
THE BLACK ART BOOK OF C. O. SWAHN

¶This manuscript was, as of 1918, in the private ownership of commercial councilor Carl Sahlin in Stockholm.[54] Sahlin bought it at an anonymous book auction, and lent it to the Folklore Society in Lund for eventual publication. The manuscript, according to Sahlgren, is from the early- to mid-nineteenth century (1830s), judging from penmanship. The latter part of the manuscript in pencil is younger than the previous portion in ink. Aside from those newer formulæ (numbers 58–101), the entire manuscript is written in ink, and the watermark is J A S. The manuscript is a single quire in a small quarto without jacket, and consists of 34 leaves.

The volume contains a total of 102 items, though only the first 57 are numbered in the original. Sahlgren has chosen to continue numeration in brackets and continues to 102. Sahlgren makes use of dialectology to try to determine the manuscript's origin. After nineteen discrete points of dialect usage, he determines that there is only one area of Sweden that could have possibly produced such a document, the northern part of Kalmarslän county in North Eastern Småland, and most probably Tveta parish in Aspelands län county, an area that is well represented in the Swedish dialect archives.

On the last page occurs in a third handwriting "De Laveretabla Konststycken af C. P. Carlström" [The Venerable Artwork of C. P. Carlström] and in a fourth "Författad af C. O. Svahn 1:ste Troll Professor" [Authored by C. O. Svahn]. Sahlgren posits that "laveretabla" may be a spelling error for an intended "veritabla" or "true." He also notes that on the top of page 4 in the same fourth handwriting appears "C. O. Swans" and in the same handwriting a page later the initials "C. O. S." However, it is clear from Sahlgren's concluding remarks that he has no idea who either Carlström or Svahn are, and that anyone with information regarding their identities, home environs, year of death and occupation should contact him or the editors of the periodical.

S-1 6	I-1 20
S-2 53	I-2 8
S-3 8	I-3 15
S-4 7	I-4 23

S-5 3	I-5 13
S-6 13	I-6 9
S-7 0	I-7 15
S-8 9	
S-9 4	

In the manuscript translation here, items 58–102 are numbered in accordance with Sahlgren's edition, but though in his edition those numbers appear in brackets, they will not be here. Sahlgren's apparatus has often provided Latin names for the herbs mentioned, and they will appear in the fully translated text, rather than attempt a popular name with a reference to the Latin in a footnote.

DISCUSSION

Though we have no clue as to the identity of C. O. Svahn, his title as "*1:ste Troll Professor*" [First Professor of Magic] is reminiscent of Bengt Ahlström, the compiler of the manuscripts from Eslöv (MSS 2, 3 and 4). In narratives about some owners of Black Art Books, especially owners of the ministerial class,[55] it was related that they studied theology (and imply training in magic) at the mythical Wittemburg, once the location where Martin Luther promulgated his 95 theses, but which became in folk consciousness a seat of learning not only for theologians but, it seems, for budding sorcerers.

The largest formal categories in this manuscript are rites (64.7%), both without (52.0%) and with (12.7%) a recited verbal component. 17.6% of the items are comprised of recipes, including ingested, externally applied and burnt. A surprisingly large 08.8% make use of both *ephesia grammata* and unpronounceable letter strings written or carved onto various ingested materials. The uses of a maiden's menstrual flow (#5), the "evil" parts of the human body (fingernails, head-lice and earwax, #15), squirrel ears (#17) and various herbal properties (#102) all present lore about the powers of various substances in the performance of magic.

The motivational distribution in this manuscript is more even than in previous examples, with 27.5% of the items devoted to the healing of humans and livestock, 14.7% displaying malevolent intent, including the blighting of crops and hexing another's shotgun, and 21.6% devoted to ethically nebulous but socially harmless intentions for personal advantage, such as the power of invisibility, divination, and manipulating the volition of individuals. A relatively large number of items (22.5%), second only to the healing of humans and livestock, are devoted to the bestowal of hunting luck and accurate marksmanship.

It can be surmised from the preponderance of hunting magic in this volume that the compiler was intimately acquainted with hunting as a primary means of survival, and even item #36 is concerned that there be plenty of food, transforming a regular stove pot into a cauldron of plenty by writing on it *ephesia grammata* prior to the lighting of the stove. Cursing another's shotgun or his hunting presumably leaves more game intact for the one who is casting such a curse, and could be categorized together with personal advantage, though the negative impact on another is what is being evaluated in the assignment of this item to a malevolent intent.

It remains that in spite of a majority of items devoted to healing and protection (#26 is a spell to slake a wildfire), there are still items which are unequivocally malevolent in intent. #8 and #22 are both to wreak vengeance, and #93 is to blight a crop, both typical of the kind of malevolent witchcraft with which some were accused during the period of witchcraft hysteria during the sixteenth and seventeenth centuries.

GENERAL CONCLUSIONS

IN considering the data examined here, it is possible to characterize different manuscripts according to the preponderance of one formal type as opposed to another, and this allows us to glimpse in which forms a particular cunning man or woman felt most at home, or felt the most magically potent. While the most obvious division is between the spoken charm and the silent rite, recipes and magical figures also provide us with data to gauge the degree to which the written medium was privileged in the performance of magic, or the degree to which the concept of the prescription had permeated the culture and generic expectations of the compiler.

With some exceptions for which we can only establish an *ante quem non*, this body of material spans the period of 1690 to 1941, and therefore provides a unique historical perspective into the practices employed by cunning folk over two and a half centuries. Indeed, we see very little change over the course of that period in either structure or intention, but rather a continued concern with issues of illness, adequate food, desire for economic security, and the slight advantage that some of these procedures allegedly provide, and which provided the client with a degree of self-confidence that would otherwise be lacking. The added confidence generated by psychological reinforcement the procedures in these books produced provided a competitive edge in the business of survival.

We can observe that certain formal types were also wholly lacking in some manuscripts, and this also provides information as to the folk belief that informs the employment of these charms and rituals. Attitudes toward the written word, toward the recited word can be extrapolated from their presence or absence in individual manuscripts. In fact, the dearth of written charms in some books may have indicated a general discomfort with the process of writing, while the more passive reading skills had been suitably mastered. Manuscripts that contain mostly recipes or rites with very few oral charms may have indicated a person whose comfort in performance of a more oral repertoire was not adequate to include too many of these. Recipes assembled from the Swedish ethno-pharmacopœia also provide information about attitudes toward both learned medicine as well as folk healing, with some items copied from published sources and others representing recipes handed down traditionally.

The frequent occurrence of rituals without any accompanying recited charm reveals a wealth of the tradition not heretofore explored in print, and at 32.4% of the total number of items in these manuscripts, is the largest formal category represented. Combined, rituals with accompanying oral recitations and oral charms represent 33.3%, making the total percentage of items with some ritual, non-verbal element of 65.7%. Oral charms with no accompanying ritual represent a mere 15.9% of the assembled corpus.

Ingested recipes (13.5%) and externally applied recipes (11.5%) sometimes appeal to folk cures that have found some justification in modern medicine, while others seem to be actually harmful, such as the ingestion of heavy metals such as mercury, or the use of sulfur. The number of items with incense recipes was so small (1.6%) as to be insignificant, but their presence may indicate a formal borrowing from the liturgical use of incense, or an older practice such as the *recels* present in the Anglo-Saxon charms.

Reliance upon written or drawn figures is present in 6.6% of the items here, and certainly depends upon the written medium for its perpetuation.

With the composition of recipes, there are comparatively few that have an accompanying charm (0.4%), though in the Halmdahl manuscripts (MSS 18, 19 and 20) mention is made to an unspoken requirement that prayers be recited over the materials being prepared.

As a result of the functional analysis executed here, we can also say that the *purely* altruistic healer was relatively rare, and that most practitioners of folk magic and healing were also familiar with, if not practitioners of, malevolent magic. Only 31% of the 35 manuscripts examined here (11 manuscripts, or less than 1/3) contained no overtly malevolent witchcraft, leaving the majority (69%) to contain at least one example. Twenty-one manuscripts (60%) contained two or more items intended specifically to harm. Even in cases where the book owner enjoyed a good reputation (the Ahlström manuscripts: MSS 2, 3 and 4), either as a sociable person or as a capable healer, there were items that would have condemned him or her were they to have been made common knowledge. Even in the case where the intent of the book owner, in this case Per Björnsson, was altruistic, the unorthodox contents were sufficient to condemn him or her (MS 26).

Having said this, it remains that the motivation represented by the majority of items in these manuscripts (40.3%) is for the healing of human illness, injury, or for their physical and psychological safety and for the security of their belongings. Clearly, whatever other goals these wise folk pursued, the utility and marketability of healing and protection was paramount both for themselves and in catering to the clientele they served.

Worthy of note is that the pursuit of preternatural advantage in luck, money and love (18.3%) surpassed even that of luck in hunting, trapping and fishing (6.9%). Psychic control over others (8.6%), and overtly malevolent witchcraft (7.4%) was also a more popular goal of workings than success in providing food for the table. The expectation that the majority of these cunning folk would only participate in innocently altruistic ends is clearly foiled by the data assembled here, and we can assert with confidence that whatever the reputation of the healer in question, those with at least some knowledge of *maleficium* were still probably in the majority.

As af Klintberg relates in the Introduction of his 1965 edition *Svenska trollformler*:

> Allmogen har betraktat den som ägde en svartkonstbok med en respekt, som ofta slagit över i fruktan. Från sina uppteckningsfärder i Skåne berättar Eva Wigström att hon mötte folk som inte vågade vara ensamma med henne, än mindre svara på tilltal, därför att det sipprat ut att hon läst och skrivit av svartkonstböcker. I folktron har den fått egenskaper som är rent otroliga.[56]

> [The population has viewed the one who owned a black art book with a respect which often has given way to fear. From her research field work in Skåne, Eva Wigström tells that she met with people who did not dare to be alone with her, much less answer her enquiries, because it had gotten out that she had read and written from black art books. In folk belief it had been attributed with qualities that were completely unbelievable.]

After glimpsing just what kinds of materials are represented in these books, it is small wonder that a pious rural populace feared the power of the devils conjured in some of these books, and that it was entirely possible that some of them knew just enough to inform others of their content. For those who were less fearful, but rather more concerned with issues of orthodoxy in either State or free churches, discussing these books and their contents could have been viewed as a more current form of heresy, or indulging in the work of the devil, who as everyone knew was alive and well in the Swedish countryside.

While the majority of healing charms included a perfunctory invocation of the Holy Trinity, there were also those charms that specifically forbade the inclusion of the final "Amen" to assure efficacy (MS 9C:39). Even those procedures invoking infernal powers could only work through the supremacy of the supernal.

Charms, rites and tools to find buried treasure were more likely to make reference to mythical beasts such as dragons (Sw. *drake, drakar*) than they were to refer to demons. A good question to ask is whether the compiler actually believed in the existence of this kind of animal, or they included the lore about it merely because it traditionally accompanied traditions in the discovery of treasure. In one manuscript, (Ms 25:60), the dragon acts in much the same way the magical mandrake plant (*mandragora officinalis*) does when dug out of the earth. Just as it is recommended to have a dog pull the mandrake from the ground for the danger of hearing its cries, similarly a dog is a required assistant to lure the attention of the dragon while the operant is busy excavating the treasure chest. Yet another (25:59) claims that the insubstantial dragon will fly through the simulacrum of the individual which is prepared in advance. That the dragon seems to be ephemeral here may indicate a belief that may have been more likely in the spiritual rather than the physical reality of it.

Physical strength such as that required in contests or in races was also an advantage, and running from an enemy may have made swift running a much soughtafter skill. Divination about lotteries, luck in gambling, and spells for economic wellbeing are all present, and perhaps indicate a greater reliance on a currency-driven rather than a subsistence economy. The *comparative* paucity of items specifically for luck and skill in the hunt seems to bear this out.

Finally, in consideration of the raw data represented by these manuscripts, we can create a more accurate and well-rounded picture of the practice of cunning folk during this period in Swedish history. We can thereafter begin to see the individuals who made up the specialized class of cunning folk, rather than merely the phenomenon which displayed certain often-explored characteristics. In the exploration of this body of manuscripts, we definitely begin to discern a more complex picture of the cunning folk, one which can inform a more accurate picture of magical healing and practice and the individuals who engaged in them.

NOTES

1 See, for example, Louise Hagberg, "Ordets makt," *Fataburen: Nordiska Muséets och Skansens Årbok* (1932): 75–88.
2 Ohrt, "Ritusanzeige," in "Segen," §3; Hoffmann-Krayer and Bächtold-Stäubli, *Handwörterbuch des deutschen Aberglaubens*.
3 For more on these characters, see af Klintberg, *Svenska Trollformler*, 56.
4 This term is perhaps best defined in af Klintberg, *Svenska Trollformler*, 131: "Den lästes om aftonen, samtidigt som askan rakades över glöden i eldstaden och hade till uppgift att hålla elden levande till följande morgon." [It was recited in the evening, as the ashes were raked over the glowing coals in the fireplace, and had as its purpose to keep the fire burning until the following morning.]
5 See Jan-Inge Wall, *Mjölktjuvande väsen i yngre nordisk tradition*, Studia ethnologica Uppsaliensia, 3 and 5, (Lund: Carl Bloms boktryckeri, 1977–78), for a thorough treatment of this belief complex.
6 Johannes Andenaes, "Deterrence and Specific Offenses," *The University of Chicago Law Review* 38.3 (Spring, 1971): 539.
7 Tangherlini, "'How do you know she's a witch?,'" 296.
8 Jens Christian V. Johanssen, "Faith, Superstition and Witchcraft in Reformation Scandinavia," in Ole Peter Grell, ed. *The Scandinavian Reformation: From Evangelical Movement to Institutionalisation of Reform* (Cambridge: Cambridge UP, 1995), 179–211, here 196.
9 Kallstenius, "En svartkonstbok."
10 Ek, "Tre svartkonstböcker."
11 J. Sallius. Förord, 5–6, in Ek, "Tre svartkonstböcker."
12 *Dr. Johann Faustens Miracul- Kunst- und Wunder-Buch oder die schwarze Rabe auch der Dreifache Höllen Zwang genannt*. I. Scheible, ed. *Das Kloster* 2 (Stuttgart, 1846). [*Dr. Jon. Faust's Miracle-, Art-, and Wonderbook or the Black Raven, also called the Threefold Conjuration of Hell*. I, Scheible, ed. *Das Kloster* 2 (Stuttgart, 1846).]
13 KU refers to *Kungliga Undersökningen* or the Royal Investigation or Inquiry. For simplicity, the initials KU will be retained for this collection.
14 Tillhagen, *Folklig läkekonst*, 88.
15 Ibid., 104.
16 af Klintberg, *Svenska Trollformler*, 88, no. 62. Af Klintberg cites this as "NM Mskpt 4, s 673"
17 af Klintberg, *Svenska Trollformler*, 126.
18 Lundberg, "En svartkonstbok."
19 LUF is, like KU, a common abbreviation for the Folklore Society at Lund University (*Lunds universitets folkloreförening*). As with KU, the initials LUF will be used for brevity and ease.

20 Betz, *Greek Magical Papyri*, 217.
21 Cypranis is an obvious misspelling of "Cyprianis," named after St. Cyprian, who was a magician in the Christian tradition, and after whom the genre of black art books are named in Denmark, *cyprianer*.
22 af Klintberg, *Svenska Trollformler*.
23 The discussion of the contrasting elements of magic and religion has often included references to the difference between private versus public performance of their respective rites.
24 Goëtic theurgy was the demonologist's answer to the invocation of angels—its magic sought to conjure and bind infernal spirits to the magician's will. The sigil of the spirit was its "signature," with which it was bound to a pact to obey the magician in all things.
25 Bergstrand, "'Fesen' i Sandhem," *Trolldom och klokskap i Västergötland under 1800-talet*, 17–18.
26 "*Jag har anledning beklaga, att jag sällan ingående förhört mina gamla sagesmän angående förfäder, föräldrar, hem, uppväxtår, ekonomiska förhållanden, läsning och de övriga källor, ur vilka de hämtat sina traditioner. Ofta har de dock i sina berättelser nämnt, av vem de hört berättas det eller det i fråga om sägen, tro och sed.*" Bergstrand, *Gammalt från Kind*, 5. [I have reason to apologize, that I seldom entered into an interview with my elderly informants regarding ancestry, parentage, home, years growing up, economic conditions, education and the other sources from which they had gotten their traditions. Even so, in their narratives they've often given the name of whom they had heard this or that told with regard to story, belief and custom.]
27 Davies, *Cunning Folk*, 119.
28 Wikman, "Törners 'Svartkonstbok.'"
29 "*En blodsdroppe i lön för spelkonsten*" IFGH 1484:1. Ragnar Nilsson 1928, according to homeowner Erik Gustav Andersson, b. 1842, Tösse parish. Published in Bengt af Klintberg, *Svenska folksägner* (Stockholm: Norstedts & Söner, 1972, 1986), 102, #54.
30 "*De dansande kunde inte sluta*" ULMA 4780:2–3. Karin Fransson 1932, according to the Andersson brothers, Bjälösa, Vreta Klosters parish. Published in af Klintberg, *Svenska folksägner*, 102, #55.
31 Especial Evocation of the Main Prince Marbuelis in a 17th Century Book, *Dr. Johann Faustens Miraculous, Art and Miracle Book or the Black Raven*, also the so-called *Three-fold Evocation of Hell*. I.
32 NB: *This manuscript could be NM 33.822, since that MS was not included in the file box at the time of examination, but was listed among its contents. According to the description of the missing manuscript in the file box, both began with an item entitled "Att hafva lycka till at skiuta"[To have good luck in shooting].*
33 "Funnen i Strängnäs, men ovisst om icke hon kan vara endera från Selaön eller Länna. Smeden Gustaf Ericsson vid Eriksberg i Södermanland

27/9/1882."
34 Wistrand, "En småländsk svartkonstbok."
35 *Tyvärr är manuskriptet så trasigt, att det, oafsedt den många gånger oläsliga handstilen och svårtydda texten, ej i sin helhet kan återgifvas.*
36 This manuscript appears in Johnsson, "En skånsk klok och hans svartkonstbok."
37 Cavallin writing in *Lunds stifts herdeminnen* [Memories of the Pastorate of the Diocese of Lund], n.d., ongoing.
38 (Malmö: Upplagd och till trycket befordrad af Förlag Maiander, 1917). From the publishers in an afterward, 41–42.
39 Another selection of trial transcripts exist in Wall, *Hon var en gång tagen under jorden*. There, the transcripts include oral charms from the repertoire of Brita Biörns recorded over a period of time between 1722 and 1738, and record oral variants. The Matsson trial for which these transcripts are previously unpublished occurred 13 years later.
40 ULMA or *Uppsala Landsmåls Arkivet* underwent a name change and was called SOFI, only to find after a governmental reorganization, its new name had become *Svenska institutet för språk och folkminnen*. Their website continues to be found under the search term SOFI.
41 A printed edition of this manuscript is given in Sjödahl, "Jugas Olof Jonssons svartkonstbok med kommentarer."
42 This makes Jonsson 65 at the time of publication, though 56 at the time of collection.
43 Perhaps this is why he was willing to share not only his black book, but also the instructions in its use, with an "outsider." If he no longer believed he was surrendering his power through such sharing, then there was nothing to prevent it.
44 Sjödahl, "Jugas Olof Jonssons svartkonstbok med kommentarer." This passage appears in the introduction.
45 Regarding secrecy in the cunning art, see Tillhagen, *Folklig läkekonst*, 52. "*Att direkt fråga en klok om hans verksamhet var i regel icke lönt. Den kloke var mycket noga med att bevara sina hemligheter och att inte låta någon presumtiv botare se i sina kort. Under inga förhållanden lärde han ut något om sin konst (med de undantag, som nedan skall anföras), ty hans tro var, att han därigenom förlorade sin egen kraft, i all synnerhet om han lärde någon som var äldre än han själv.*" [To question a cunning man directly about his work was pointless as a rule. The cunning man was very careful with keeping his secrets, and in not allowing some presumptuous healer 'see his cards.' Under no conditions would he teach anything about his art (with those exceptions which will be related below), because his belief was that he would lose his own power in doing so, especially if he taught someone who was older than himself.]
46 This item is published in Heurgren, *Salomoniska Magiska Konster*, which is

a facsimile reprint of the original 1918 edition.

47 Per Gustaf Wistrand, "Signelser från Småland, antecknade under några på Nordiska museets bekostnad företagna resor 1879 och 1880," (Meddelanden från Nordiska museet, 1897), 15–50.

48 Nils-Arvid Bringéus, "Västboprästens svartkonstböcker," *Svenska landsmål och svenskt folkliv* (1967), 13–27.

49 Nils-Arvid Bringéus, "»Röda boken« påträffad." *Svenska landsmål och svenskt folkliv* (1991): 89–91.

50 *The cunning and wise fellow, who learns the fearless both in the city and in the country, through which he might learn every type of domestic cure, to heal and fix manifold sicknesses, both of people as well as livestock; as well as many other things, which can serve to be of use in diverse matters of the household.*

51 *Book Four of Wolfgang Hildebrand's Natural Magic. That is: Four Peculiar books of wonderful arts, authored from diverse Secret Matters of Nature. All honorable and permissible arts of desire for miraculous use, as well as particular desire and well-being, now newly translated into Swedish and from the press of Henrich Keyser, year 1650.*

52 Bringéus, "»Röda boken« påträffad."

53 This manuscript appeared in print in Olof Christoffersson, "Supriania, Fru Alstads Socken, Skytts Härad," *Folkminnen och Folktankar* (1915).

54 A published version of this manuscript appears in Sahlgren, "C. O. Svahns svartkonstbok."

55 See K. Rob. V. Wikström two works dealing with Rev. J. J. Törner's *Samling af Vidskeppelser* [*Collection of Superstitions*] for one example that lent some of these narratives credibility.

56 af Klintberg, *Svenska Trollformler*, 26, citing E. Wigström, *Folkdiktning* II, 1881.

CHAPTER V

✣

Conclusion

PERHAPS THE MOST joyous task in putting this volume together was assembling the raw data, unedited excerpts from folklore archives throughout Sweden, as well as gathering black art books from museums, archives and libraries. By providing them here in their unedited original form, an image emerges of a more informal, conversational exchange, occurring within the matrix of tradition. Complete excerpts can be inconvenient to navigate to find the one statement that illustrates the point under discussion, and may seem to include too much material not specifically germane to the topic. However, seeing how these items appear in an original and spontaneous discussion, or in an excerpt that includes much more than just a mention of black art books, serves well to remind the reader and the folklorist that tradition is larger than any one area of it under immediate examination, and that folklore occurs within a context.

Providing unedited manuscripts and excerpts also keeps the scholar honest—no longer can that one gem which occurs amidst so much extraneous verbiage be extracted out of context to support a pre-established thesis. While we are indebted to the work of folklorists and field collectors of the past, it behooves us to consider the context in which they presented their collecting efforts. Avoiding the pitfalls of selective recording, we perceive the richness of the traditional process, the *art* involved in handing over lore to a new receiver, in a context which is both natural and more complex than any academic thesis can imply.

By appealing not only to folk narratives that describe folk belief about the black art book, but also to the black art books themselves, we find that some of the generalizations of previous scholarship have presented a mistaken characterization about those books. Were we to rely exclusively on the archival narratives, we would indeed see the source for scholarly summaries over the last century and a half. However, with a corpus of 35 manuscripts containing 1,961 notations, the basis upon which to build a more accurate picture of the archetypical black art book is much clearer and more accurate—we no longer make our assessments based on second-hand evidence. The books themselves tell their own tale. In legends about the black art book, it is typically represented as a printed volume, often with red letters imitating blood. As represented among the actual examples, handwritten manuscripts were the rule rather than the exception. Even when a volume was clearly using a printed original as a source, the handwritten word was the tacit assumption of the owners and compilers of these books. The more fabulous elements of the legends about black art books were that they were written in blood, that they were bestowed under contract with The Devil, that merely opening them let loose a small army of small demons flying forth from the pages.[1] However, the majority of black art book notations had to do with healing both human and livestock, with the occasional element of *maleficium*, perhaps to instruct the benevolent wise one in the workings of the malevolent workings of the witch in order to counteract them, or to employ in case of malevolent attack.

Another issue in considering the characteristics and contents of the black art book is the collecting tastes of the collector. In cases in which a black art book original was loaned to a collector for transcription and later inclusion in folklore archives, it is clear in at least one instance that the collector's expectations played a role in which items he chose to copy. In Gustaf Eriksson's transcription of Nordiska muséets manuscript from Åkers parish in Åkers county in Södermanland (MS 25), items 91–93 were summarized with a short "general superstition about livestock" and items 95–96 were omitted with "not worth writing down." Unfortunately, the scholarship of that period has left us with incomplete or altered materials, since the original was subsequently returned to its original owner. We have no real idea of the number of black art book manuscripts that actually existed that were not submitted to the scrutiny of collector or museum. This is why the current collection is both as large as it is, being the largest single assemblage of such black art books under a single cover, but also as small as it is, as we have no real idea of the number of manuscripts in existence. With new manuscripts being discovered even as late as the 1970s, we may yet see a growth in the number of manuscripts available for study.

In collections by Wistrand, Linderholm and af Klintberg, the majority of the items appearing in them were of strictly oral or narrative charms.[2] As we have seen, however, 66% of the contents of the black art books in this study are comprised of ritual notations which don't see analysis in works dealing with primarily oral charms. By reproducing entire manuscripts, rather than selecting for structural or functional characteristics, we perceive a more varied repertoire of the folk healer/sorcerer, and can even begin to discern the genres in which he felt most at home. Some manuscripts favor the spoken text of the narrative charm, while others focus on the chemist's art, or the herbalist's kitchen. An assumption that each wise one was a master of all genres of folk magic and healing is now suspect, and each manuscript can be examined to discern a specialization or proclivity of the compiler or owner.

These excerpts are presented in English translation. While as a Scandinavianist my first interest is to examine works in their original language, it has to be conceded that the Scandinavian languages are not yet the languages of global scholarship. As long as the original texts have existed only in the Scandinavian languages and only been gathered with great difficulty, whole bodies of charm research and textual study have remained excluded from international consideration. With a newly emerging enthusiasm for charms, charming, charmers and their metaphysical world views, the utility of a work that presents a large collection of black art books in an internationally accessible translation is of significant importance. Scandinavianists are uniquely qualified to provide idiomatically faithful translations of previously specialized terms and procedures, recipes and rites.

Because of the novelty of this translating endeavor, there have been numerous occasions when magical idiom presented challenges in translation. Just as there is specialized vocabulary in Swedish for cursing, hexing, oppressing, drawing, transfixing, healing, etc., the corresponding vocabulary in English folk magic is equally specialized. This leads to awkward translations, in which one specialized term is translated with another specialized term, and the reader is left no closer to understanding either. In some cases, one is forced to resort to circumlocution, even if there is a perfectly fine English equivalent, but one which is uncommon enough to be foreign to a majority of English readers. This is why the discussion of terminology in Chapter Two was especially important, exploring equivalents for practitioners, practices, ingredients and procedures of the wise one.

Terms such as "putting down" (Sw. *sätta ner*) or "heal" (Sw. *bota*) are terms that in this context no longer translate literally, as we learn new vocabulary to understand the magical mindset of the wise. Botanical ingredients present special problems. As they occur in our texts many are imported from German as calques, words created from translations of constituent parts [e.g., Sw. *dyfvelsträck*=G. *Teufelsdreck* (*Ferula asafœtida* or simply devil's dung)] or as loanwords in which the foreign term is borrowed and (often unsuccessful) efforts are made to retain its original pronunciation [e.g., Sw. *libberstukk* or *libbsticka*=G. *Liebesstöckel* (*Legusticum Levisticum* or common lovage)]. Dialect-specific plant names, while technically all still Swedish, are often confusing, and vary from parish to parish. Names are also re-used in different locales to identify different plants. It has been helpful when a previous editor has had the service of a qualified medical, botanical or dialect expert to aid in the identification of just which herbal or material component is meant. More often, the only recourse is to dialect dictionaries that may or may not record local variations or include Latin botanical names.

Organizational Principles of Black Art Books

AFTER EXAMINING A substantial number of manuscripts, it is possible to state that the primary organizational principle of the material in the black art books is temporal: items are recorded in the order they are encountered and copied. Only a few are wholly devoted to conjuration and exorcism of angelic or infernal spirits. Organization in those cases is purely according to the order of the elements performed in a previously existing ritual. Occasionally, two or three techniques for the same aim are recorded in a sequence, and the result is a small subsection with the first item named, and the subsequent items labeled "The Same." In such cases, however, it doesn't appear that the book has been completely recopied, in order to pay attention to the placement of all charms or rituals for a single aim under a single rubric. Rather, it seems that the organization is temporal, and relies on the personal collecting history of the wise one.

It is worthwhile noting that among the compilers, no attempt was made to distinguish moral, material or technical motivation of any of the contents of the black art book. In one way, this serves to confound the casual browser— a magical spell of questionable or ambivalent moral intent is much harder to locate in a book filled with items which are not grouped together by their intent. Numeration of the items in these books is ubiquitous and seems to be a trait that is a requirement of the genre for their author-compilers. Books separated in time and space still seem to exhibit a common tendency to present items accompanied with numbers. When a table of contents is lacking, associating a number with a particularly well used procedure might have been one way to reliably locate an item among a hundred others not as often employed.

The lack of generic organizing principles might indicate that each book represented an "open canon," allowing for the continuous collection of items throughout the wise one's lifetime. In this case, the lower numbers indicate items encountered earlier in life. This continual encounter with new material may indicate that the tradition was a shared one. A wise one might obtain a new spell, recipe or ritual from another, thus expanding their own collection, and establishing ties and links in the distribution of that lore. If indeed the lore was shared, and potentially shareable with others in the same occupation, then we no longer have isolated, solitary practitioners using material handed down in one single volume. Rather, we have a shared magical culture which allowed cross-fertilization by means of shared lore and shared techniques.

We also have at least three manuscripts in which more than one handwriting style is present: MS2 which has three handstyles, MS23, also with three and MS35, with two distinct hands in evidence. This may be the result of the changing penmanship of an individual at different periods of his life. It might also indicate more than one owner, each of whom added to the canon.

There is a very important difference between the folklorist's collecting and the wise one's recording: it is a difference in motivation. While the folklorist maintains a certain distance from the subject of his study, the wise one gathers lore that will be of utility in his magical and healing work. We might say that a black art book that is compiled and then published by a "nonbeliever" is perhaps less a genuine artifact than a compilation submitted by someone whose original endeavor was to increase his magical repertoire, and only secondarily and much later to provide the academic with raw data. In the case of ULMA 984, Jugas Olaf Jonsson's lore was collected and recorded, and his black art book created, during a period in his youth when his belief in magic was still intact. His collecting efforts were motivated by personal goals, increased magical power, greater healing expertise, etc. Jon Johansson, the wise one from Norrland whose collection was eventually published as von Sydow's *Signerier och besvärjelser*, believed in the efficacy of the charms he was collecting, and believed in their power to effect change. He participated in the assumptions that made magic not only possible, but a worthy spiritual vocation in apostolic tradition. It was only upon submission to von Sydow that Johansson admits, with some wistfulness, that now that he has shared these spells with von Sydow, they have lost any further potency for him, as he has broken the covenant of secrecy that assured their continued power in his hands, the hands of a wise one. *Signerier och besvärjelser* takes its place among the manuscripts translated here for just this reason. It is a collection by one who was himself a wise one, and so Johansson's collecting participated in the otherwise traditional sharing of charms and rituals.

While it can be argued that Jon Johansson's *Signerier och besvärjelser* is not a true black art book because Johansson was sometimes gathering material for remuneration, material that was intended by von Sydow to see publication, it is Johansson's stated belief in the power of the lore, and in the tradition to which it belongs, that gives his collection credibility as an example of the genre. This same thing occurs in the case of Jugas Olaf Jonsson's black art book, when in 1916 he states to his informant N. Sjödahl that he had originally collected the lore contained in his black art book when he was a youngster, in hopes of becoming a famous sorcerer. He tells Sjödahl that he has no further need of the book, and that he no longer believes in magic. In both cases, the material would be useful in the performance of folk magic, and the collecting efforts took place when the respective collectors believed in the efficacy of the materials they collected. The fact that they later underwent some change of heart or mind that allowed them to subsequently share it suggests a type of conversion experience, which resulted in two discrete individuals, separated by time, each with his varying beliefs about magic and the lore of the black art book.

While not all black art books were submitted to scholars for eventual publication and analysis, having only been discovered after their original owners had passed away, there is a way in which wise ones, in collecting the items in their black art books, were actually folklorists of a type. Certainly, their black art books were field notebooks, and they were an open canon. As new techniques, better or different rhymes, or materials from especially notorious or talented sorcerers were discovered, these were added to the collection (e.g., Jon Johansson's *Signerier och Besvärjelser*). A genre that ignores structural or functional characteristics as organizational principles can do this easily, adding new items as they are encountered. In this case, the black art book is the field notebook of the wise one, who in this instance plays the role of the amateur folklorist, collecting lore from any and all sources, recording them with numeration potentially for easy retrieval. Rather than collecting folklore for eventual submission, archiving and academic analysis, the wise one's efforts resulted in an increased repertoire of charms, recipes and rituals with which to help a local clientele. In rural locales, this might entail going to discuss the "tools of the trade" with another practitioner down the lane or in the next parish. In metropolitan centers, any source was fair game: Elsa Halmdahl in Stockholm gathered items from neighbors as well as from radio broadcasts, and Kungsbackagumman, Britta Lena Andersson, in suburban Halland actually treated members of the medical profession in Göteborg, thus engaging in a mutual exchange of medical knowledge of both folk remedy and established allopathic medicine.

Collectors' Generic Expectations of the Black Art Book

WHAT THEN DEFINES the genre of the black art book? At least one very important factor, as we have seen in these last two examples, is the attitude of the collector, compiler or owner. The two examples of Jon Johansson and Jugas Olof Jonsson provide a stark contrast to the published chapbook black art book. One example of such a book was published in Stockholm in 1877, and bought at that time easily for a mere 25 öre.[3] The attitude of the collector, if in fact a collector he was, is that of a disbeliever. He unapologetically scoffs at the material he presents as primitive superstition. He boasts of gaining the trust of the wise one, fader Abraham, who owned the volume, in spite of his own persisting disbelief. The items in this book were collected by someone who never had confidence in their magical efficacy in the first place, and never sought to utilize any of the techniques it contained. While the title of the work is Svartkonstboken, it is the work, potentially fictional, of a satirist, who mocks in his parenthetical remarks the traditional magical culture that produced such volumes.

-- Jag har förlorat en klocka, sade jag, hur skall jag få den tillbaka?

Gubben gaf mig ett swar; det återfinnes i N:o 5 af den här medföljande "Swartkonstboken." Jag, liksom hwarje förståndig med mig, kunde ej finna den der föreskriften annat än löjlig. Jag kunde ej afhålla mig från ett skratt.

Gubben gaf mig en wred blick. – För den som inte tror, hjelper ingenting, sade han med dof stämma. Ugglan fladdrade med wingarne till bifall.

Jag misstog mig ej. Jag hade framför mig ej en kall charlatan, utan en person, hwilken så länge sysselsatt sig med mystiska beswärjelser, att han sjelf trodde derpå.

-- Jag tror wisst, sade jag, fastän jag tyckte, att sättet war lite konstigt. Men hör, fader Abraham, will ni göra mig en riktig glädje: will ni låta mig se "Swartkonstboken".

-- Swartekollaboka; den har jag ej!

-- Jo, det har ni!

-- Ingen menniska får se den mer än jag!

-- Men om...

Dock jag will ej upprepa detta och flera andra följande samtal. Ware det nog sagdt, att jag lyckades innästla mig i gubbens förtroende. Ja, jag misstänker, att han hoppades i mig finna sin efterträdare.

[I have lost a watch, I said; how shall I get it back?

The old man gave me an answer; it is found as number 5 in the accompanying "black art book." I, as each intelligent person with me, couldn't find the instructions anything other than ridiculous. I couldn't keep myself from a chuckle.

The old man gave me a wrathful glance.—For those who don't believe, nothing will help, he said under his breath. The owl flapped its wings in accord.

I didn't make a mistake. I had before me no cold charlatan, rather a person who had dealt so long with mystic conjurations that he himself believed in them.

—I believe truly, said I, although I thought that the manner was a bit strange. But listen, Father Abraham, would you do me a great gladness: would you let me see the "Black art book?"

—Black art book? I don't have one!

—On the contrary, you do!

—No person may see it other than me!
—But if...

I really don't want to repeat this and many other subsequent conversations. It would be enough to say that I succeeded in gaining the trust of the old gent. Yes, I suspect that he hoped that in me, he had found his successor.][4]

The material gathered in the published volume however is clearly drawn from the same cultural matrix as that which produced other, handwritten volumes, but the intention that lay behind its compilation and eventual publication did not participate in that same cultural matrix. We have no confidence that the narrative describing its procurement is even true. So, while the title and contents all point to potential identification with the folkloric genre of the black art book, the motivation that lay behind its collection and publication were not of the appropriate cultural matrix. We find the narrator untrustworthy. However, after the purchase of a small chapbook, the lore it contained could have easily re-entered the practitioner's realm, blurring the edges between these two attitudes.

The motivation underlying compiling the contents of a black art book is not the only generic expectation that has emerged in this study. Some of the expectations are especially clear in contrast with material from the tradition itself. Narratives from the archives repeatedly set the expectation that the black art book is either a printed book, i.e., a typeset and "official" looking volume similar to a hymnal or bible. They also describe a book that is handwritten in blood, presumably of the owner, blood which was also used to sign and ratify the demonic pact by which the book was obtained in the first place. What we find among the actual black art books is a different story. The black art books we find in museum and archive are all handwritten manuscripts. Even in cases where it is clear that the compiler is copying verbatim from printed volumes, e.g., MS 15 (NM 63.180, *Samling af Utomordentliga menniskors största hemligheter...*), a handwritten manuscript remains a generic expectation, and in at least this case, printed texts are carefully copied by hand into a thick but diminutive leather-bound book, presumably purchased for the purpose.

In Wikman's study of Törner's eighteenth century black book, not only is Törner's volume a hand-manufactured artifact, but special attention is paid to produce white, illegible characters (a modified shorthand, Sw. *takygrafi*) on black pages, also a generic expectation that appears in the narrative tradition.

The Exaggeration of Illiteracy among the Lower Classes

IF INDEED THE black art book was expected to be handwritten by those who compiled it and wrote it out, then there is a secondary expectation that those same compilers were literate. Not only must they have the passive ability to read, but they must have mastered the skill to write, and well enough to be able to decipher later what they had written. As Egil Johansson writes in his historical review of the Swedish Government's various attempts to foster a reading and writing population "Literacy Campaigns in Sweden," there was already in 1700 a concerted campaign to teach reading (this time in Gothic characters) so that a general population could read their Bible and the Augsburg Confession. The second major campaign was with the institution of public schooling in the mid-nineteenth century, and was an attempt to teach both reading and writing, using the Latin alphabet. Johansson provides quotations from educated foreign visitors of the past in which they marvel at the literacy of the Swedish peasantry, saying that "you seldom meet one above ten or twelve who cannot read, and the most of them write their own language;...".[5] Clearly, assumptions of an illiterate peasantry in seventeenth century Sweden are vastly exaggerated, and already under the reign of Karl XI in 1686, it was assumed that at least the heads of households were able both to read and write. This makes the rarity of literacy against which the black art book was previously seen less accurate,[6] and an inability to read one is more likely the result of codes (Sw. *skiffer*) or magical characters (Sw. *trollkaraktärer*), which we now see were part and parcel of the Swedish black art book tradition. Older manuscripts are written in the older Gothic script, which one would expect after Johansson's historical overview.

Scandinavia, Sweden especially, as we now see, has a rich history of promoting literacy among primarily rural populations.[7] Even as we read of Martin Luther's encounters with Satan in his chamber at the University at Wittenberg, a newly literate but perhaps naïve public became enamored of the possibility that through this demon's intervention, there was the possibility of obtaining hidden treasure, of exerting power over social and legal situations, of obtaining luck in hunting, fishing and economic pursuits. Most popular among free thinkers and those lured by solitude, such heretical ideas held less threat to them than for those whose daily bread relied on proper local social standing. Reputation, then as now, often translates into economic terms.

Distribution and Provenance

PERHAPS THE SINGLE most popular trend in older scholarship on Swedish black art books has been to attempt to identify their distribution and provenance. Certain general statements are borne out by an examination of the corpus represented here. For example, the majority of the manuscripts currently held in museums, archives and libraries are of southern Swedish provenance. This is not surprising, as literacy campaigns in Denmark and Skåne preceded Swedish ones, so more of that population had access to the tools of their construction. Additionally, even those black art books that eventually found their way to more northerly parallels contained references to flora that did not flourish that far north in the country, but rather represented a southern Swedish environment. And finally, grammatical forms suggest an acquaintance with Danish generally, and in certain manuscripts German, again pointing to a southern Swedish origin for these manuscripts.

A more recent trend to mention the longer history of folk grimoires, a history stretching back to Hellenic and Pharaonic texts, is also gaining popularity since the work of scholars such as Faraone and Obbink, and is mentioned in the recent work of Stokker and Davies regarding the Norwegian and the general European material, respectively.

Peuckert and Edsman have remained the benchmark against which any new studies can be evaluated which purport to investigate the geographical dissemination and distribution of specific titles and texts, as well as of the published works that contributed to the handwritten genre. The tradition of handwritten black art books owes much to a continental and printed tradition of what is variously called *Hausväterlitteratur* by Peuckert, or *Cyprianus Höllen Zwange*.[8] Nowhere is this more clearly seen as in the magical conjurations of the Prince in the Demonic Hierarchy, Marbuel, which appears in two of the manuscripts examined here.[9]

It remains that the previous work by Peuckert and Edsman has been borne out repeatedly, and continues to be the benchmark in newer scholarship such as that by Nildin-Wall & Wall, and Davies.

Continental Evocation Meets an Ethnic Scandinavian Folk Belief

THE SYNCRETISM OF one system of magical evocation which was rooted in a southern continental renaissance magical model together with the Swedish folk belief in nature spirits is an interesting point to examine. We first saw this syncretism in a narrative describing how Anders i Alehagen received his black art book from a lake nymph (Sw. *sjörå*). This theme returns in MS4 (Eslövs museum 3329 C), in which Ahlström records an evocation to lure a good farm wight (So. Sw. & Da. *goanisse*) to one's farm.

A number of factors contribute to the noteworthiness of this last item. Firstly, the book occurs in the Swedish area, yet the Swedish name for this type of spirit (Sw. *tomte*) is substituted with one much more common in the Danish area (Da. *nisse*). *Tomtar*, according to folk belief, really don't participate in the religious life of the Swedish peasant. One doesn't go to church with offerings to the *tomte*. Rather, it is a very geographically local nature spirit that, if satisfied with its treatment by the farm-dwellers, can bring wealth and success. If dissatisfied, however, it brings financial difficulties, illness and disease, and bad crops. The milk doesn't churn properly, and the cows don't produce as they should. Keeping these spirits satisfied is a relatively easy task—keep their domain clean, and their food uncontaminated, and they will exhibit their satisfaction in granting good fortune.

In Ahlström's manuscript, however, to see this wight being "created" or "lured" (the text is not clear on this count, and uses both terms) specifically by demonic powers is a marriage of two previously distinct domains: one of religious diabolism and the other of folk belief. The rarity of this combination of domains makes it clearer that this was an uneasy marriage, and the domain of the *sjörå* and *tomtegubbe* was perhaps distinct from the realm of ecclesiastical evocation, blessing and demon conjuration.

The Results of Statistical Analysis

THE CONCLUSIONS FORMULATED in the previous chapter provide the statistics for some general theories for the future of research in Swedish black art books. Each manuscript is characterized by a majority of items that exhibit certain formal characteristics favored by the compiler. From this, we can deduce that each compiler, and therefore each practitioner, had a method of operation they found especially suitable to their skills and temperament. A preponderance of incantations in one book contrasts with a greater number of recipes for plasters and tinctures in another, leading the folklorist to recognize that each practitioner was not master of the entire repertoire, but rather of only those techniques in which they felt especially empowered. This is an important conclusion, since it removes from consideration any idea of an ideal black art book, a volume with examples representing the entirety of the tradition. Rather, each book is quite different from another, and when all available manuscripts are considered together, what emerges is a picture of a community of specialized practitioners rather than some idealized homogeneous tradition.

Ten of our 35 manuscripts contain no overt *maleficium*, though a demonic pact for worldly gain might qualify. Perhaps the demonic source of power meant an eventual and inevitable misuse of it. Even those black art books primarily focused on fixing the broken, righting the wrong, or promoting well-being were composed with the assumption that one might not adequately protect against *maleficium* unless one were familiar with its methods. There seems to be a requirement that even a benevolent wise one had to know the workings of *maleficium* in order to heal its effects, or counter it with a counter attack of greater degree. However, the mere presence of *maleficium* in a black art book is not enough to condemn an otherwise benevolent wise one—sometimes this sort of reference is left for posterity, long after the researcher is able to explain the significance of it. It cannot be assumed to have been a part of an active repertoire.

That black art books were all healing books (Sw. *läkeböcker*) is clearly not the case, and the entire notion of healing as a suitable translation for the Swedish term "*att bota*" may represent a mistranslation *in this context*. Perhaps a better translation for this term might be "uncrossed" in the vocabulary of modern English hoodoo.

The idea that all wise ones were merely misunderstood healers and had no interest whatsoever in either magic or in powers obtained through supernatural or infernal means is clearly in error. The lines were never that distinct, though individual wise ones may have presented that image to a skittish public. According to our texts, healing was in greatest demand, but the satisfaction of revenge or the hope for sudden wealth obtained by harmless means were merely other states of mind that required their own attention and treatment, treatment that the wise one was prepared to provide.

Black Art Book Owners, and Their Claims to Power

RECORDING OWNERSHIP EVEN in a book that had every page filled with procedures, recipes, charms and rites was considered important enough that some of the books considered here have a single page devoted to a list of previous owners, sometimes even recording the dates of ownership. To posit whether it was the ownership of the book, or the access to its contents that bestowed preternatural power upon the wise one is difficult. It was both, as archival narratives explain. Both played a necessary role in lore about black art books, their ownership and role in folk magic.

At least in three examples, MS 18, MS 19, MS 20 (NM 271.601A, B and C), Elsa Halmdahl took especial care to record her sources. This was by no means a universal practice, and in an earlier period would have clearly implicated others in one's own practice of the black art. But by 1939, the year Elsa's first volume of folk and faith healing was compiled, her interest was to preserve sources where possible. Perhaps by retaining attributions, the confidence which comes from an independent source is preserved. Making up one's own spells, recipes or rituals is a recent phenomenon, and relies on a studied knowledge of the entirety of the tradition from which to select elements. It also posits a source of knowledge and power independent of the preserved and time-tested charms held in the black art books.

A secondary result of preserving source attributions is that, as mentioned above, the black art book begins more and more to resemble a folklorist's field notebook. The careful preservation of utterance, recipe and ritual, along with a named source, a date, time and place of collection, these all make their appearance in Elsa's archival record. We must compare favorably, as we did earlier, the role of the wise one with that of the folklore collector, as the work of one informs the work of the other.

Elsa's primary informant was her first and primary teacher, Olaf Åberg in Hälsingland, but others' names were also recorded, from neighbors to the occasional radio broadcast by well-known folklorists of the day. In the first pages of one of her books, Elsa has gone to the trouble to record the names of all the known wise ones of which she was made aware, presumably by Olaf. It was her master's intimate knowledge of the subject that allowed him to state with certainty what others might only conjecture. And, with the devotion with which she wrote of him, master is not too strong a word to use for their magical apprenticeship. It is clear that she felt she owed him a tremendous debt for teaching her the art. Once again, her writing shows a distinct lack of organizing principles. Her notebooks contain writing at all angles on the pages, as she struggled to immediately record a teaching or a new bit of lore, before the opportunity passed her by.

Based on the new texts made available in this study, researchers in the field now have more information about the sources, as well as the recorded owners and compilers, upon which to base new significant findings. As in Chapter Four, there have been some scholars who attempted historical and ethnographical research to place these volumes in a cultural and personal context, and now there are further possibilities with the additional material assembled in this study.

New Light on Old Scholarship

RESEARCH IN CHARMING has entered a new era. No longer are we focused only on comparative and historical analyses of texts. We are entering a time when a holistic approach to the practice of charms, charming, ritual, magic, "healing," and alternative spirituality can yield new models of how humans sought, by special, magical behaviors, to control their environments to promote health, wealth, well-being and security in an uncertain world filled with demons, sprites, darkness and solitude. It was by means of this black art, the art of magic, that such positive circumstances might be brought about.

The insignificant change we see in both structure and function or intention through four centuries of manuscripts is remarkable—a continuity of concerns has kept the wise ones' repertoire stable, practically static, preserving archaisms that might have otherwise been abandoned in favor of novelty as new life concerns became predominant.

With the attention the Second Merseburg Charm has received over centuries, a trend in charm research was established that focused on the orally recited charm and its provenance. Collections, while doing their best to preserve ritual actions in parenthetical comments, still concentrated on the uttered charm, the oral form, and its relationship to other metrical charms over a larger geographical area, and its ultimate descent from some ideal *ur*-form.

In our analysis of the black art books, a new picture emerges. Rather than a tradition characterized primarily by oral forms or uttered charms, we have a tradition that contains many more genres. More plentiful are the rituals, the recipes for plaster and tincture, the small scraps of paper or parchment with magical characters written in the blood of small animals, and also parts of those small animals carried hidden on one's person. Already in 1979, Ronald Grambo produced a volume that was a of a similar type to Bengt af Klintberg's 1965 *Svenska trollformler*. However, Grambo's title seemed to better reflect the variety of the authentic tradition, Norwegian Charms and Magical Rituals, (No. *Norske trollformler og magiske ritualer*).[10] His volume included more than the oral charms, but also rituals and recipes as well.

The case of Jon Johansson illustrates to us that the black art was seen as in no way demonic, but rather as a survival and persistence of practice in response to Christ's exhortation to his apostles to go out and perform miracles in His name. In any analysis that claims to take motivation into consideration, this blurring of the edges between the diabolical and the divine puts perhaps greater emphasis on whether the end result is meant to help or hex, and for whose benefit.

Previous scholarship to identify routes of transmission and provenance have yielded much fruit, but with an entirely new current of work in the classical Hellenic and Pharaonic corpus, there is now more academic work and new access to texts that can be explored in establishing a unified western magical paradigm. Performative theory, first introduced with Hubert and Mauss at the turn of the twentieth century, and continued with Trevor-Roper, Sebeok, Tambiah, and others, uses sociological and linguistic theory to inform analyses of magical language and action.

With the availability of additional texts, both black art books and narratives about them, we are better equipped to explore the Swedish folk magical tradition and its place, both in pre-Industrial rural and post-Industrial metropolitan Swedish society. The interesting divergence between the folk's expectations of the black art book, and the books themselves have already shown here that the understanding of academics who rely primarily on folk narrative about the wise ones have been led astray as to the wise ones' actual sphere of activity and influence, and even as to expectations of what an actual black art book may be.

In an examination of individual black art books, we discern the predilection of the wise one, and their preferred mode of operation. Were they skilled speakers, perhaps the oral charm might find favor. Were they artistically inclined, then an emphasis on *trollkaraktärer* might predominate in that volume. If they had the chemist's inclination, then recipes such as plasters, ingested recipes or incenses might find favor. This new data can yield a more personal picture of the wise one as an individual, and not merely a representative of a homogeneous class of specialists.

That magic exists is demonstrated in many cultures including Scandinavian culture. In the future, the question can be broached of how it exists, in what domain its efficacy lies, and why it continues to find practitioners in a world of the electric light bulb.[11]

NOTES

1 Tillhagen, *Folklig läkekonst*, 75–78.
2 Wistrand, "Signelser från Småland"; Linderholm, "Nordisk magi: studier i nordisk religions- och kyrkohistoria"; af Klintberg, *Svenska Trollformler*.
3 A copy exists in the Royal Library (*Kungliga biblioteket*) in Stockholm, and has recently been digitized for electronic retrieval at http://www.kb.se/OT/Svartkonstboken.htm and which was accessed for this study in June, 2009.
4 Anonymous, ed., *Svartkonstbok [Fader Abrahams Svartkonstbok]*, 8–9.
5 Egil Johansson, "Literacy Campaigns in Sweden," *Interchange* 19.3/4, (Fall-Winter, 1988): 135–62, 138.
6 af Klintberg, *Svenska Trollformler*, 21–22, "*För att förstå den skräckblandade vördnad den svenska bondebefolkningen hyst inför begreppet svartkonstbok, måste man göra klart för sig den reaktion det skrivna ordet i sig måste ha väckt bland människor som till en inte obetydlig del var analfabeter.*" "To understand the awed respect in which the Swedish rural population held the concept of the black art book, one needs to be clear about the reaction the written word in itself must have awakened among people who to a substantial degree were illiterate."
7 Johansson, "Literacy Campaigns," 135.
8 Davies, *Grimoires: A History of Magic Books*, 123, no. 124.
9 In this collection, MS 4:EM3329-C, B. I Ahlström (~1865), and MS 21:NM 271.602 Negromänliska saker (no date).
10 Grambo, *Norske trollformler og magiske ritualer*.
11 Gunnar Granberg, *Skogsrået i yngre nordisk folktradition*. Skrifter utgivna av Gustav Adolfs Akademien for Folklivsforskning 3 (1935): 168. "*Dessutom finnes ett flertal andra förklaringar, i det att råets utdöende säges bero på de elektriska anläggningarna...*" ["In addition, there are several other explanations upon which the dying out of the forest sprite depend, including the introduction of electricity..."

Part II

MANUSCRIPT TRANSLATIONS

ms 1

CÅNSTER ATT BRUKA, NEMBLIGEN:
"SVARTKONSTER AF AND P…"

ARTS[1] TO USE, NAMELY:

1.

If you're following after someone who is riding on a road, and you want to have his horse become lame, so that he won't overcome you, then take a nail and check to see the horse's footprint, where he has stepped on the road; take the nail and pierce it, then the horse will become lame. The nail should be from a coffin.

§ 2.

So that you will never lose no [sic] court case, then take the tongue of an otter and put it in your right shoe under your bare foot, when you go to court.

To hit [§ 3.] with a shotgun whatever you want.

Take a cuckoo and take the first feather that sits in the wing, and chop up the cuckoo while the heart is warm, and stick the feather into the heart and put it together in a linen cloth. Put *Rosmarinus officinalis*[2] into the cloth with the heart and hang it on a kettle hook over a stove for 9 24-hour days. Then take it down and tie it on your right arm, which is covered with it.

---

1 Here, "arts" is to be understood as "Black-" or "Magical Arts."
2 The original reads *väyrott*, which either could be a misspelling of *väyrak* or *virak*, Germ. *Weihrauch*, or could refer to *Weirauchwurz, Rosmarinus officinalis*. Since *virak* is the imported tree resin *Olibanum*, and the reference is to a root, I have opted for the latter.

4.
To shoot and hit the mark.
Take bat's blood and apply it to the bullet or the shotgun.

5.
Ditto
A spell for shotguns, when it doesn't fire: "God the Father, God's Son, Holy Spirit, help me for whom this shotgun doesn't shoot, for whom it doesn't go loose, for whom it doesn't produce fire for the shot powder, in the name of the Father and of the Son and of the Holy Spirit! I, Martin, swear today that everything that has happened during this day has been done since Christ's birth, that to my body neither cut nor arrows or slashing and shooting, as long as my God's mother[3] is nursing their second son, in the name of God the Father and of the Son and of God the Holy Ghost. Amen. Proven.

6.
To hex a shotgun.
I conjure speak to you, I conjure you, shotgun and shot, it[4] is mine and the bullet is mine. The heart an abomination. When I see this shotgun before me, stand still like a stick, this I say to you, fire to the shotgun, in the name of the Father and of the Son and of the Holy Ghost.

7.
To speak to a shotgun, so that it doesn't go off too loosely.
Take a knife with three crosses, which is made on a Friday morning before the sun comes up, and hold the knife in a sheath, and then he looks into the shotgun, and turns the knife about in the sheath, so that the handle is formost, and say these words: "*Astine Marina destete.*"

8.
Good for hunting.
Dig sharp what is called in German *Vegerik* or *Vägbredh*[5] on Saint Jöran's day.[6] Carry it on you: it is good for protection from arrows and shootings.

---

3 The Virgin Mary. This is an interesting reference to her "second son," Jakob/James.
4 Grammatical gender indicates this "it" refers to "the shot."
5 German *Wegerich*, *Wegbreit* is the English plantain or waybread.
6 Sk:t Görans dag, the Feast of St. George, April 23.

9.
So that you hit the mark when you shoot.

Take a hoopoe[7] bird and take the heart out of it and the tongue and carry it with you.

10.

So that no wolf can do you any harm, say "Cristus est nattus, lapus est capttus intt nina Dnus."[8]

11.
Good for hunting.

Take the blood out of your right hand and make a powder from it and mix it with the shotgun powder.

12.
To shoot whatever you want.

Take the heart and the liver of a bat, put it under the lead when you shoot bullets or shot, then you'll hit whatever you see.

13.
So a dog won't bark.

Take a wheatear,[9] that lives among the stones, and lay it on the shoulder,[10] then no dog will bark.

14.

He who takes the eyes of a hoopoe bird makes a person agreeable to strangers.[11] If one carries them about the throat over the chest to a trial, then all enemies with become good again.

15.
Of ravens.

Among his virtues are wonderful things: when one boils a raven's egg, which you then put back into the nest, and they then go to lie on it again, then they'll fetch a stone, with which he will touch the egg. Then it will immediately

---

7 Sw. *videhåppe*, from Gm. *Wiedehopf*, mod. Sw. *härfågel*, L. *Upupa epos*.

8 Clearly this must have been "*Christus est natus, Lupus est captus, in Nomine Domini.*" or "Christ is born, the Wolf is captured, in the Name of the Lord."

9 Sw. *stenskvätta*, Eng. wheatear, [*Oenanthe oenanthe*], a small white-rumped northern bird related to the stonechat and whinchat.

10 Whether of the enchanter or of the dog is not clear from the text.

11 So. Sw. dial. *främmat*, either visitor or stranger, depending upon context. Not clear which here.

become raw again. If one takes this stone and then puts a laurel leaf under it and then has it set in a ring, and the goldsmith shall make an oath, that he will say nothing about it if he doesn't want to die; and that ring is good if one is bound in iron chains or some other imprisonment: if one touches it with this ring, then he is free again. Whoever has this stone in his mouth, he can understand the language of birds.

16.
So that everyone will be fond of you.

Take a stone that is found in a swallow's nest and carry it with you

17.
Take the root of an *Artemisia vulgaris* plant and carry it on you, then no one is able to slander you.

18.
How one obtains a swallow-stone.

Take a swallow chick out of the nest and stab out its eye, and tie it in a silk thread around its throat and put him back into the nest. On the third day, go back there again, then you will get three stones, one white and one black and one red. When one has the white stone in one's mouth, then he'll neither hunger nor thirst; if the black stone is in his mouth, then all women will be crazy about him; and if he has the red stone in his mouth and he kisses a virgin, then she'll fall in love with him over all others. The one who has the red stone with him cannot be harmed by anything.

19.
To melt a steel binding between your hands.

Take the root of the wolfberry, *Atropa belladonna*, and tie it under your right arm.

20.
If someone has done you ill, to know who did it.

Buy some oregano spice (*Origanum vulgare*) at the pharmacy, tie it under the right arm and go to bed to sleep, then you'll see the one who has done you wrong.

21.
So that the ladyfolk will lift up their skirts.

Take the blood of a young hare and smear it on the candle there where they're inside.

22.

To get the strength of 3 men.

Take the root of *Artemisia vulgaris* and saffron and spread it all over your arms.

23.

So that no horse will throw you, then yell these words: "Astulis Astula Cosso forottis."

24.

~~Take a tongue of a young swallow, that hasn't been out of the nest yet, and put it under your tongue when you kiss a virgin so that your tongue goes into her mouth, then she'll not let go of you until she's had her way with you.~~

25.

Another: take an otter's tongue with arsenic and carry it with you, then you will have favor with highborn men and others.

26.

To give to a horse to eat, so that no other horse can outrun him, Eber-root[12] dug up on Bartholomew's day[13] is good. If you eat it yourself, then no other will be able to outrun you.

27.

Tie a raven's tongue on the middle finger, as he lies and sleeps, then he will reveal all his secrets to you.

28.

Artemisia root, carry it around your neck, then no poisonous creature can harm you.

29.

The one who puts the powder of that root over their door, no harm will befall that house.

30.

The one who carries a hoopoe bird's tongue on themselves, will have no harm befall him, and all his enemies will like him.

---

12 Acc. to J. Lindgren, Lund, this is *Radix Carlinæ*, or the root of *Carlina vulgaris*. Acc. to Schübeler: *Viridarium norvegicum*, this is *Artemisia abrotanum*, from the L.Gm. *Eberoth*.

13 Bartolomeus dag, Feast of St. Bartholomew, August 24.

31.

The one who wants to ride out, should hang *Verbena officinalis* around the horse's neck, then he won't become tired.

32.
To make oneself invisible.

Go before Saint Jakob's day[14] to an anthill and pour warm water on it, then they'll all run out, and look into it and go a little bit away, and then return and seek in it, then you'll find a stone that has three colors; you should have that with you.

33.

Take an egg between 11 and 12 o'clock and put it in an anthill, and when you go back again, then you'll find a stone: you should take that with you.

34.
~~To get a virgin to lift her skirts.~~

~~Take bat's blood and put it into a linen cloth, and when you are sitting with her, then light it on fire, then it'll work.~~

35.
To get the strength of 9 men.

Take a heart of a wolf, 2 of a fox and 3 of a dog and sew them in place on the left side.[15]

36.
To know where money is.

Write these words on virgin paper:[16] D. + . + . 8 . X . 3: d d U: W. 6. X. V. Z.

37.

Take an old hen and clean it well and boil it together with oxmeat in a new pot. When it is cooked, take a new wooden plate and put it together with the oxmeat on it and bury it all deep in the earth at a fork in the road, and put another plate over it, so it is quite tight, so that no earth will come between, and let it sit for 9 days – it should be arranged so that it will be a Monday when it will be dug up again – then there will have been three spirits with it that ate it up: the first having replaced it with a table cloth, the second with a mirror

---

14   Sk:t Jakobi dag, Feast of St. James, July 25.
15   This formula is vague on the specifics. Right side of a coat? On the right side of one's body, into the skin. The latter would require a great deal of strength already.
16   Cf. *jungfru pergament* with *jungfru papper*. Virgin parchment and virgin paper, that is, parchment or paper that has not been used before.

and the third with a dice-piece. The table cloth when one spreads it on the table, means that one will have food enough; in the mirror one can see what is happening in the whole world; the dice-piece one can throw as much as one wants and never lose. One of these three things you should leave behind.

38.
To make yourself invisible.

Shoot a raven on Maundy Thursday and take the tongue and tie it to the right arm.

39.
If one is captured, to get free.

If one is in a stock or in irons, then they'll loosen and not harm one. Have these words on you: allb. +. Fellea +. ieyiga +:nex +. FanstiG + gennt + Sebortt + G + S + ff + ScHutAueG.

40.
So that no one will outrun you.

Take quickroot[17] and tie it under your right toe.

41.
So that a horse can't throw you, then yell these words in his ear: "Alius as aba ara via capel."[18]

42.
So that no one can defeat you when you argue your case, and so that they will all escape.

So that if one is preparing to go to court, then one won't lose.

When the sun goes into the sign of Taurus, then seek a viper, that is a snake, and take the skin off it and burn it to a powder and carry it around your throat. It has virtue. It should be taken during the first 5 days when the sun is in the sign of Taurus: all of this should be done. If one has that powder, then when one argues, then no one can defeat him. And if it lies in a house where no one knows about it other than he, then no one can remain inside it. Third, when one has to go to court, put it into your shoes, so that it lies under your bare feet, then one won't lose.

---

17 Sw. *siälkerrott*, uncertain. May be *Triticum repens*.

18 Some of this incantation is obviously Latin. Perhaps its original could have been "Alius est ab ara via capela" or "The other is from the high place, by way of the chapel." Such are the mysteries of misremembered Latin.

43.

If you drink *Rute* water each morning on an empty stomach, then your eyes will become so clear that you will be able to see the stars in heaven during the daytime.

44.
To release a lock.

Notice when the frog is out. Grab hold of it and put it in a glass and put a stone on it. Then there'll come a spirit and he will have an herb and hold it before the glass. With this it will burst asunder. If one holds it in front of a lock, then it will release and open.

45.
To make a couple become enemies.

Take an egg and boil it hard and write both of their names on it and cut the egg right in two and give the one half to a dog and the other to a cat.

46.

~~Take hare's blood and apply it to a haystraw and put it in a virgin's bed, then she won't give up until you go to bed with her.~~

47.

Tie a rabbit's foot to your right arm, then no dog will bark at you.

48.

So that you get what you ask for, then carry these words with you: + Los + pastor + a v B 1 C.

49.

So that you are liked by everyone, then carry these words with you: pnu Sanilo Pro C Sanctus: Pro.

50.
So that no one is your enemy.

Have these words with you: M. G. C. B. y. Jn nomino Pattris: et Fyly. x et. Spiritus amenque eta gramatam. p.[19]

---

[19] Kallstenius has "Jn nomino Patteis: et Syly. x et. Spiritus amenque eta gramatam. p." Being versed in the letter forms, the S in "Syly" is more likely an "F" and clearly makes better sense. So then, this is clearly Jn nomine Patris et Filii, et Spiritus Sancti [Sk:ti Spiritus], amenque (and amen). Following that is either a partial Tetragrammaton, the four-letter name of God found in grimoires dating to the early (continental) Renaissance and later; or "äta grammatam," "eat the letter," referring to ingesting the paper with the inscription, a common magical procedure. The

51.

If a wife runs away from her the husband, then take her right shoe and put it in smoldering coals. As long as the shoe smolders, then she'll have no peace until she comes back to him again.

52.

Take a needle with which a corpse was sewn into a burial shroud, and stick into the underside of the table where you are sitting and playing cards, then you'll win.

53.

Carry a "*gåldevedh*"[20] as it is called in German, put it in your right shoe, then you'll win at cards.

54.

If you want the strength of 9 men, then carry on your left side a wolf's heart or a fox's heart or a dog's heart.[21]

55.

Take ~~the heart~~ a thrush, that is a small edible bird, and put it under one's head, then he'll tell you what he knows; or put it underneath you.

56.

Take a pea and put it on a frog. Stick out its left eye, and put the pea in its place. Bury it and then the pea itself will grow, and the peas that grow on that plant, if you take one of them and put it under your tongue, then you're invisible, as long as it remains there.

57.

When someone has stolen something from you or from another, then on Christmas night between 11:30 and 12:30 make yourself a hammer, and on Easter night between 11:30 and 12:30 smith yourself a nail; paint an eye and put the nail on it and hit it with the hammer, then you'll put out his eye.

58.

So that you'll have good memory.
Take a hoopoe bird's tongue and carry it on you around your neck.

---

final 'p' is perhaps "probatum" or 'proven'.
20 German *Goldweide, Salix alba v. vitellina.*
21 See also previous, #35.

59.

Take grapevines on which grapes are growing, and burn it to ashes and make from that a soap and wash your head with it, then your hair will grow.

60.

Take a young swallow, roast it in honey and eat it up, then you can understand whatever you want.

61.

A saining for pestilence
"A fiend I have received, it has bitten me this wound;
    and that one disappeared,
    when he received the first nail,
    with which they bound our Lord Christ on the cross.
In the name of the Father and of the Son and of the 'oly Ghost. Amen."

62.

So that a woman daren't or can't take hold of the dish after food, then take a green basil and put it secretly under the dish, then it will happen.

63.

To get luxuriant hair, and is also good for the head.
Take the larger "*carbör*"[22] roots, they usually have large leaves; wash them clean, grind them in a mortar and soak them in soap/lye. Wash your head often with this. Let it dry on its own, then you will become wonderfully perceptive. This soap will also give you good memory.

64.

When you can't sleep near your wife, then take ringflower,[23] soak them well, mix it with honey and drink of it.

65.

If one is hexed by an evil woman, take a dead person's tooth and cense yourself with it,[24] then you will surely be helped.

---

22 No note in Rietz, and German and Swedish searches bore no fruit. However, butterwort, the folk name of the *genus Pinguicula*, may be suggested by the last half, "beurre" or butter. They are the family of carnivorous plants, and Linneaeus wrote that the leaves could be used to cover wounds in cattle to prevent infection.

23 *Calendula officinalis*.

24 Presumably one would have ground it or shaved it before putting on coals.

66.

So that no more wine will ensnare one, then take a piece of eel and put it into the wine or liquor. Then give him the same to drink, then he won't suffer from that any more for all the days of his life.

67.

So that one will sleep for three days.

Take a hare's gall,[25] administer in wine, then he'll fall asleep immediately, and when you wish that he shall awaken, then pour some vinegar in his mouth, then he'll wake up again. Or take sow's milk and apply, he will have the sting of a corpse. Or take the gall of an eel, mix it in the drink, then he'll sleep for 36 hours; pour rosewater in his mouth, then he'll be awake again.

68.

So that no one can sleep, then carry a bat secretly on your person. The second way: Whoever carries a bat's or a raven's heart on himself, he won't get sleepy, until he puts it away again.

69.

So that one will never be frightened.

Take the water from human blood[26] and distill it; anoint your face with it, then it will happen.

70.

The sign that a person who is sick will recover.

Take a piece of bread and stroke the patient's forehead with it and then throw it to a dog; if he eats it, then the patient will recover, if he doesn't, then there is something to fear.

71.

So that the snake will lose its venom.

Take a hazel staff that is one year old, and write a circle around it,[27] then it must die, and all snakes must flee from you, as long as you have the staff.

---

25 In this item, the forms "gala," "gallan" appear to refer to the same anatomical part. If umlaut was present, it could mean the reproductive organ of the male of the species, and in dialect, this is the sort of variation we expect.

26 Plasma?

27 This "it" presumably refers to the snake rather than the hazel sapling.

72.
To see a chamber full of snakes.

Beat a snake to death and put it in a new pot and with new wax onto the fire. Cook it until it is dried inside. Then make from that a candle and light it in a chamber, then it will appear to be full of snakes.

73.
To drive away scorpions.

Take lapwing feathers, light them on fire, and let them fall where you go visiting. Make there at the same place a furrow.

74.
To find out if there is poison in the food at mealtime, take a pitcher of ore or tin and put it on the table. If there is poison in it, the pitcher will change colors, the more the poison, the more the colors.

75.
To find out if your wife is with boy child or girl child, then pick some ivy by the roots and put it on her head secretly. If she names a boychild first, then it will be a boy.

76.
If you spread salt on warts and it dissolves, then it is a boy.

77.
To walk and not tire.

Take greyhouse[28] or ironwort[29] dug up during the 8 days prior to St. Bartholomew's day,[30] and take it for 8 days before you intend to depart, then you'll not tire.

78.
Carry a walking stick of aspen, and the leaf in the shoe, then you will not tire.

79.
So that a horse will not work himself loose.

Smear his muzzle or the bridle with pig's feces, then he'll stand still.

---

28 *Artemisia vulgaris.*
29 *Verbena officinalis.*
30 Sk:t Bartolomei dag, the Feast of St. Bartholomew, August 24.

79.[31]
So that a horse won't miserably fall down and act as if he were dead.

A snake tongue kneaded into virgin wax and placed in the left ear of the horse will cause him to throw himself down to earth, but when this is removed again, then the horse will [not] only wake up, but will be better than before.

80.
So that frogs and milkhares[32] won't suck out the milk from the cows.

Take wagongrease and put it in a pot, then all will flee from there.

81.
To drive away flies.

Hang glow-worms up in the house, they are said to glow in the dark, then no fly can remain inside there.

82.
Camphor is good to ward off lice, and also for evil magic; you should carry it with you.

83.
To trap wild fowl.

Take wheat or grain and put it in blood in wine dregs and the juice of *Conium maculatum* and throw it out for them.

84.
So that hens will lay a lot.

Give them to eat small crushed hare droppings mixed together with wet feed, then they'll lay. If you give them 2 or 3 doses, then they'll lay themselves to death.

85.
So chickens will get as many colors as you want.

Take the eggs and paint them with the colors you want and apply cottonseed oil and let them dry. Then put them under the hen.

---

31 This misnumeration is preserved from the manuscript. Kallstenius revises the numeration for clarity. Instead, I will use the numeration 79.a., and 79.b. to distinguish these two in any analysis of these texts.

32 Sw. *tåsor* is an unattested dialect word. Rietz is silent. According to Wall in his "Tjuvmjölkande väsen" the form mjölktusse is attested in Värmland, Perhaps tåsa is a variant of tusse.

86.
To pluck a hen without water.

Give a hen some pigeon droppings to eat in food, then the hen's feathers will fall loose as if it were dead.

87.
When you cut off the outermost edge of a rooster's tongue, then he won't crow during the night.

88.
Take old lard and wild mint (well-fermented) put it into a pan, stir it together well in a pot, then put it in a cloth and tie it with eel bait then you'll catch a lot of fish.

89.
To catch eels with eel bait.

Take hemp, when it begins to ripen and cut up with its tops and put it into the bait. All eels love that.

90.
To get a lot of fish.

Boil rye in water and put it in a place that is clean in the lake. Drag the net, and you will get a lot of fish.

91.
To get fish with hook.

Put the hook bait in nestle leaves over night, and fish with that.

92.
To fertilize the field without dung.

Take the seed grain and put it in dung to soak in it, then sow it, then it will grow as well as for those who fertilize.

93.
So that a Baltic herring will turn itself over on the grill.

Take a goose quill and fill it with mercury; stick it then in the herring, then it will turn itself over when needed.

94.
To mend a broken glass.

Take eggwhite, whisk it well and mix it with slaked lime; glue the glass with it.

95.

Write a passage with vinegar or piss and let it dry. When you want to read it, then spread ground coal on it.

96.

A way of writing that can be read at night.

Take rotten wood and grind it finely, so that it will fit into the pen, mix it with eggwhite and write.

What is useful from birds and animals.

From ravens:
    dogs:
    cats:
    wolves:
    hares: blood
    small edible birds:
    bats: the heart and the liver, the blood.
    hoopoe bird, Upupa: the heart and the tongue, the eyes.
    otter: the tongue.

From cuckoos: the first wing feather, and the heart.
    Plantago lanceolata:
    rose petals and sweet marjoram:
    wheatear:

ms 2

ESLÖV #1 [EM 3329 A]
"N° 1 RADEMIN: DÄTT ÄR ÖFNING I VETTSKAPP OK KONSTER"
DENNA BOEK TILLHÖR MIG B.I.AHLSTRÖM

NUMBER 1 RADEMIN
THAT IS THE PRACTICE OF
SCIENCE AND ARTS
THIS BOOK BELONGS
TO ME, B. I. AHLSTRÖM
J. H. FORSKÄLL
B AHLSTRÖM

1. <u>toothache</u>
Take a carved wooden pin and write these words with the edge of your knife and then work it in the middle, and then in the middle and you put [...] all the *styan* and *fly* that you can, and let it lie on the frog and burn them up and then he should spit three times after them Padden · at : H. ∴ J W : N : B : L : O : Z

Forward
This dissertation, containing teachings of inorganic healing methods, it to be viewed as the second part of my textbook in Pharmacology when it is left into the hands of studious youths. I would like to take this opportunity to publicly forward my thanks to Herr Professor and receiver of commendations the Friherre Berzelius [*Jelässman efsa y*] Lund Oskar's Day 1837.

2. If there is something stolen from you, then write on a paper this name and these words

Pax sax max

and then the suspect's name, then the thief will flee when you use his name, but this is to be done on a Thursday morning before the sun comes up.

3. to take away the even temperament and strength from a horse
Take a piece of bread under your little finger on the right hand. Dry the horse's teeth then throw away the crust "Strength and fortitude, stay in this piece of bread, as you, writer, who sit in hell and know right but do wrong. In three names...

4. So no one will hex you –
Ccarbeon faber melas si[33]

5. Another
I recite for you, *fidfi* and for God's tablecloth T and for our lord Christ X x sake Flee away, injurious poison.
N : F: S : H : A : A : (In the name of the Father and the Son and the Holy Ghost, amen.)

6. To stop bleeding
NN: I stop your bleeding as the Lord Jesus Christ stopped the water in the River Jordan. The water was dammed, the Blood was stanched, through three names God the Father, Son's and the Holy Ghost's.----

7. Red Coral 2 s, Asafetida 32, olibanum 3, Mastic 2, Spanish Fly, Calfhead or Dog's Calf, yellow sulfur, Musk, [fläs] incense, Saint John's Bread, Amber 29, Myrrh, sharp glass, Paradise seed (Aframomum melegueta), Aloe succotrina, Sassafras, Flyrön 39, garlic 39, [*Dendaslag*], [*Belfleder*], [*Bäs..*] ---

8. A method to treat *Frossan* (fevers and chills)
To be taken internally: The first day "K," the second day "K : A," the third day "K : A : L"

$$\begin{array}{c}
:K:A:L:A:M:A:R:I:S:\\
:K:A:L:A:M:A:R:I:\\
:K:A:L:A:M:A:R:\\
:K:A:L:A:M:A:\\
:K:A:L:A:M:\\
:K:A:L:A:\\
:K:A:L:\\
:K:A:\\
:K:
\end{array}$$

---

33 Ek has "Czerbeon faber melarsi."

9. To stop bleeding.
There was in a sunny [slå...] that Jesus came ... Marie. The Devil he promised Jesus to turn away from you.

10. To take the fire from a shot (To make a shotgun not fire)
Hold yourself around your cock and say "I order you, doctor Faust, as the Blackest Powerful Sorcerer, and you, General Lyksenborg, as the grimmest among all generals and discoverer of gunpowder's improvement, in the name of the *Säl...*: X : X, to dull the powder for NN: then you can name them by name.

11. Take mercury and put it into the pot. Remove all the peas now from the pot.

12. For dry ache.
For N:N: I exhort everything by the sun, moon and stars, all the glowing planets to immediately turn away and leave this Christian brother and be to him as bound as Christ was to his holy cross. In the name of God the Father and the Son and the Holy Ghost, amen. This note is written for whomever needs it, and yourself having kept oath.

13. tooth ache
Take a needle, pick at the tooth till it bleeds. Write: : Bonva : Bello : Billeora ---

14. When women think themselves walking in water.
Take red [*kejllande pastiar?*] and mercury. knead it into a dough, and let them go over it, then she will be [*tiråt*].

15. To show one's fiancée.
Go to a grave or take a human bone. Drop three drops of King's water on it. Begin so that one may speak with the one under there, which you wish to be able to see, or their fiancé, or fiancée, and a determined time when you want, but don't laugh or talk. Don't be afraid.

16. On evocations.
If you old overlord of hell, who here lie on this treasure, and reveal to me by god and people, and give to know, so I swear you and exhort you immediately that you leave here and take your place until that day there, where I shall show you with my created finger.[34] Release that treasure that you have lain upon so long, so that you now immediately turn away from and do not harm me more than a mouse can harm an earthfast stone in Jesus Holy name. : + : + : + | Our Lord Christ said to his disciples. Barii Peace be with you, the same strong

---

[34] Created finger is a shortened version of the phrase "This finger of God's Creation," and is common in magical formulæ.

peace I wish over me and also the servants name N. N. and I forbid all types of Troll and Sorcerers, and calves white [*kustar*] and all kinds of poisonous dragons and evil spirits, I extinguish, bind and exorcise them by the power of God the Father and the Strength of God the Son, and by the [unreadable text under a dividing line] holy Spirit's wisdom that it will immediately turn away from this [...] you are now, and no longer injure this one than a mouse can injure an earthfast stone, with these holy words and this holy exorcism shall these Christ's servants be freed and free from all evil, in the name of God the Father and of the Son and of the Holy Ghost, amen.

17. Exorcism
Jesus Christ Virgin Mary they went on a road. There they met Elf women and Elf men, Mermaids and Forest men, and subterranean trolls, and above the surface of the earth and everything that in the water and in the air, and as this wind goes, you all shall go home, said the Lord Jesus. You shall not go to N. N. [*vänke och vonda ok blåna ok laba*] their blood-robbing strength, power and courage; you shall not do that, said the Lord Jesus, for myself and my name shall bind you and hold you here with my ten fingers and twelve of God's angels, you shall not do NN any more harm than I can do to an earthfast stone. 3 times.

18. To win at gambling.
Take a tose egg with you.

19. If you want to creep through a piece of [*Ryomde*] counterclockwise. Artefys – Mefisto – Sidim – Alles Galli – yntro – nama – nama – nam:
creep slowly.

20. So that a girl won't stray
Take blood of a bat and a little ink and write her name in your left hand in the Devil's name and as long as you live she will stay yours, not to get married to anyone else amen.

21. To show the way
Hence you shall go, and hence shall you two, and not there where you are. Come away for the farm is burnt, and the moose [*laban*?] was still on the chase, : a : a : a.[35] The man is hanged

22. Buy [*töke*] seeds and give them internally to a woman, then she will be willing to do your desires.

---

35 "a:a:a" is an abbreviation of "amen, amen, amen."

23. If one is "fearful." Take internally a quart of red wine and 2 shillings worth of saffron, mix it together a little and half is drunk during the new moon, and half during the waning moon, then you'll lose the fetus.

24. Give a woman 10 or 15 drops of opium then she'll fall asleep and you can lie with her and she will have just as much of her own movement as if she were awake.

25. A Plaster that will heal all sheep. *Barkåda*, wax, white chalk and pigs lard, equal amounts of each. Cook it all together in a stone pot until it becomes a kind of gruel for the [...]

26. So that no one will hex your horse
Give him garlic and St. Johns Bread. Cense him with [*Säfvenbom*] then he will never be hexed.

27. For toothache
Take camphor, alum, salt, equal amounts of each, grind it all together and put it in a linen cloth and put it next to the tooth, it helps.

28. For enemies
Buy at the Apothecary *mana* – it looks like grey sugar. Grind it and put it in liquor [*svän...*]

29. For toothache
Buy [*lin kom sante*] soak it in liquor and hold it in your mouth a half hour. It helps.

30. Ditto for toothache
Write on the edge of a piece of paper the following words, and put the paper together like a five-pointed-cross (pentagram) and tie it around the neck for three 24-hour days.
    Throw it on the fire then, and burn it up and say: Here I throw all my toothache. – The words are these:
    BAGEM SATEGEN RENOGEN REPIEMNAR PIANON. It will help immediately.

31. When the livestock are loose-(stomached?)
Quick fry herring [well short] on the fire. Salt it. Helps. put it cold in Tibast = 25; virak = 25; kristilaa = 24; garlic = 23.

32. If you want someone to scratch the skin on his face.
Then take a candle that is dipped on Candlemas (February 1) and light it, and

drop three drops in each corner of the house. Put some water in the middle of the floor. Before you put water there, drop wax in the shape of two crosses under where you will put the water, and then recite afterwards the following words: Ex pentus per filus Eplisyenmiat Ex pietus pellam. 4 and 5 the water and sing the psalm then for dominis deus felalis 3 bon filies tibi vik losto pro catom.

33. When a house is burning, walk three times counterclockwise around it and say: "Stop, you fire, in your coals, just as Jesus Christ the living God's son stood bound on the tree of the holy cross, with his holy blood shed for the good of all, I warn you fire that you not go further by the Power of the Father and by the Might of the Son and by the wisdom of the Holy Ghost, that you stop in your coals as was said, in the names of God the Father and of the Son and of the Holy Ghost. I nom patris et filius son natus, a / a / a / (Amen, amen, amen).

34. To fix a shotgun, then shoot a shot and say three times "I shall have her."

35. To hex a shotgun. Take a sewing needle that has sewn on a corpse, and stick it into the muzzle three times and pull on the lock and iron at once.

36. To take snake or injury
I conjure you by the holy trinity's power that you keep your poison that the holy Virgin Mary kept her virginity – this is said three times.

37. To ease pain
Your pain shall disappear away as a dead person that is in the earth lies in the name of the F and S and the H Gh, three times.

38. To train livestock,
Which will surely help: when you come home with the animal, then you should put your garter along the door threshold and the other garter is put in back of it, and then you make three circles on the ground and then lead the animal in over them. When you do this, you should be silent. When you have bound it, then you pull on its ear and say three times:

> [*Hit skall du gå*
> *och hit du trå*
> *där du är kommen ifrå;*
> *För gården är bränd*
> *och mannen är hängd;*
> *och qvinan är död i barnasäng*]

> Hence you shall go,
> and hence you shall be led
> from the place you came from;
> For the farm is burned
> and the man is hanged
> and the woman is dead in childbirth.

Where you harness it, then the bonds will take.

39. To shift the sight
Take the heart of a swallow, cat feces, take it in the sunlight and put it under your left arm, then none can see you.

40. GA BET CAN : carry these words with you then all will wish you well.

41. Take the eggs from a swallow's nest and cook them, and then put them back in the nest again. 3 days afterwards then you will find a stone on the bottom. Take it and keep it [...] then he'll go up again (?)

42. If you want to have a girl love you dearly.
Take a hair from her and buy a new sewing needle, pay whatever it costs. Take the hair and thread it in the needle and sew three times through your clothes that you had on you when you went to Holy Communion. Go then to an aspen tree and break a branch off and stick the needle into it on the side of the branch, and put the branch in a river in the bottom so that the water flows through the hair, and as long as the sewing needle and the hair are there, and when you take it up again, then it's finished.

43. So that enemies will not harm you.
I exhort you and conjure you all weapons and defense such as point and edge, shotguns, arrows and other weapons, that you will no more come to injure me or my body than Satan has aimed at Christ, than the battles of Caneller against Josän (?), Goliath against David, the Lion against Samson, but all my enemies will flee from me like God flees from sin, and avoids it. Through F, S HG name, 3 times.

44. Let this sit at the right side [*sic*].

45. If you wish to win at cards, take iron that has sat in a covered box. Have a ring made from it and engrave these letters on it – n e p s o 1 l masit – put it on the little finger, then you'll win.

46. If you want to race with someone then tie these letters under your right arm: (b t j g o)

47. So that no one will hex you.[36]
C b erbeon faver melarsi

48. An exorcism to recite over malt and salt.
Give it to your animals during summer time, then no bear or wolf will touch them –

The bear lies on the hillside,
Drag it over the neck,
the wolf also went against God's wrath –
Maria's wrath can turn
The Queen's pillow can be in the middle of the hill, bridge, path.
Our Lord went faithfully up and
Recite the name of the bear and wolves between heaven and earth,
I conjure them; amen/amen 3.

49. When you want to call forth wild game, and shoot it, then take the bread and wine when you go to Holy Communion, and put it on a tree and shoot to the target = take three branches off of the same type of tree that the Elements sat upon, and put earth for each branch you take, then you say: the dove will drive them forth for me a couple of animals of whatever type you want between this and that time.

50. If you want to hex the powder, then say these words 3 times; kea fannen, and put yourself between the powder and the fire three times.

51. If you want to tend to the shotgun so that it will kill –
Then take graveyard dirt and put it in the shotgun three times through. Then load it at the first availability, this should be on a Thursday evening when the sun has gone down. When you have done this, then carry the shotgun back and put the muzzle towards the floor and the stock upwards towards wood, and go there in the morning. Take the shotgun and shoot some kind of gamebird. Take the heart out of it, and put the powder in the shotgun, then the heart and shoot it towards a [...] then your shotgun will kill.

52. If you want to hex a hunter
Then take his ammunition where it has been and put into it a paper and write his name on it and bore a tree, and put it in by sunset. I saw you hexed, so

---

36 Cf. Item 4, this MS.

surely you shall shake, as the Red Sea stood still to travel through. Through three names P F S a/a/a. (Patris Filii, Spiritus Sancti).

53. You take something that you believe has belonged to the thief. Go a Thursday morning. Take it fasting to the churchyard bury it under a gravestone or [...] Say: I conjure you, you spirit of the dead one's body, that you will drive the damned thief that stole from me N. N. so that he confesses; this publicly or carries it back again or Pain and Suffering for him until I shall order you in the name of F: S: the H: Gh: amen.

MS 3

ESLÖV #2 [EM 3329 B]
"N° 4 STORA KATEKIS"
TILL HÖRIG B. AHLSTRÖM, ESLÖF. DEN 13DE APRIL. 65
STORA KATEKIS

N° 4
BELONGING TO B. AHLSTRÖM
ESLÖF, APRIL 13TH, 1865
GREAT CATECHISM

N° 2
For the healing and curing of all wounds and all occurrances of sickness, this following recipe is taken internally in these three points: For throwing up and colic: To a pot of liquor or a quart of good beer put: Camphor 1 fifth, Calamus root 9 fifths, strong pepper 1 fifth, white ginger 1 fifth. When all of this has been ground in a bottle, take a shot when you feel colic or morning sickness (*moderpassionen*). It is very good for pregnant women and doesn't injure the one lying under their heart (the fœtus).

N° 3
Stings and club-foot
To a quart of beer or a pot of liquor, put Oil of Turpentine 2 measures, gentian root 1 measure. This bottle is shaken each time one shall take a drink, before it is poured into the glass. You take a drink each evening. It is also good with this mix to prepare for scabies and itching. It is poured hastily onto the body and clothes, scabies disappear, if not apply more.

N° 4
For one who has kidney stones (?)
Then take one measure oleum emperis, 3 measures Oleum Turpentinum, mix this together, take 12 or at the most 16 drops at a time on an empty stomach. This helps. It cures, and will surely relieve the kidney stones of both men and women. But if they wamt to be sure about the stones, then they should use it for a long time – 1 to 2 years each morning – these drops also drive out all fistulas, blood worms and stomach worms, as well as all cold pains – A mature person take in now and again against colds and stomach upsets 35 drops at a time; a child is given less at a time, and is put preferably in liquor. These drops prevent hard stomach in children, infants are given it preferably in milk or pate a 3 month old 8 drops, a 6 month old 12 drops at a time a couple times a day, and so the proportion for older with a cold. A mature person takes 30 to 70 drops at a time, with all the three written points, and eat a little sandwich each time you have a drink. For the one who always takes in on a regular basis, in that one no sickness can thrive.

N° 5
Aspen bark boiled in fresh water for 2–3 hours until there is only a little motion, take it then with sweet milk and a little of each type, and boil together, a tea cup of this is drunk during the entire waning phase of the moon, 3–4 or 5 waning moons in a row. Then the worm is driven out of the stomach. It is an unpleasant drink, but there isn't anything in all the world that is the equivalent and which will overcome bone worms.

N° 6
To cure peculiarities in the head.
For peculiarities on the head like boils and other things that rise up, such as deformities all the time it is in the inheritance from the parents.[37]
Take a piece of fatty meat that is from the back of a pig. Fill it completely with oats. Fasten it to the oven flue when it is burning in the baking oven. Take the fat from lowest on all four sides now in the chimney, and take from beer and yeast when it stands and is made the best soot base, and impurity from the smoked brick. Take the fat from the food kettle when it begins to cook and throw it on the fire and take it up quickly again. Prepare all this together to a salve and this is applied to the head but should be washed off before 9 24-hour days go by and is kept. Then into that salve for 6 weeks, and if it blisters up again, then start again and let it sit for 9 24-hour days before it is washed off and used with this warning that the first time you apply it is in the waxing moon, and the second in the waning.

---

37 Although this title is only partially readable, the reference to the inheritance after the parents is obviously a reference to genetic inheritance!

N° 7

So that a mother can with one method cure her children from troubles of all kinds. When man and woman have "the way of their flesh" together, and the woman then dries off her "secret parts," the moisture and the slime that falls from her, this she should take when it is released from the mouth. Wash then this lip in a little running water that is taken with the stream and spit into the river before you take it. And just as the outside a little can get in and a little of the inside can get out, just so shall you smear them over their entire bodies, each joint and limb, and give them internally from this water in the new and waning moons, but be careful that no one puts their hands on or touches this salve, or any person drinks from it or not either that any mouse comes too near to it, for then it won't help at all.

N° 8

In another way to without fail help for all people's deformities which each must do for him[38]self. When the parents are not living, go away to a churchyard. In the summer time when there is a lot of dew, and the graves are open. Take a corpse's bone and put it to the side of the churchyard, but the bone is borrowed for your limbs that you are suffering injury in; go to the churchyard early in the new and waning moon. Dip this bone in the dew, and stroke it upon your injuries, it will surely help. For a type of pain it is taken from a ·q· to a ·M·. Then put the bone back in the same place when one is finished using it, and put earth over it and say as you throw the earth "Let now my weakness which this bone now owns rot with you in the earth."

N° 9

For Headache –
Take ¼-pot; strong Swedish liquor: 1 fifth; fresh white ginger 1 shilling. Mix them together. Each evening pour your Eustachian tubes full of it, is also given on a dried mushroom and is held alternately close to and far away from the nose. Also snorted strongly up into the head now and then. This must be done each evening for three or four months. It will drive away ringing in the ears. And headache and deafness which has persisted for many years, which is why it carries with it a [örsla] against when the pain disappears. But use it without fail, for when this pain comes again, then it will soon disappear away, and this with all certainty.

N° 10

For the white erysipelas. take a ¼ pot, Strong Swedish liquor and as much finely ground alum as a small hen's egg. And put it in it. Smear this on healthy

---

[38] This begins new handwriting, which continues half-way through item 12, and then returns to this less legible hand.

[*tag*] 3 to 4 times each day, it will drive away the white swelling and the white erysipelas.

N° 11

For blood sickness for people or livestock, as well as lost energy. Take tormentilla root, grind it to a fine powder with just as much finely ground hard coal. This is mixed together and is taken internally in beer. It will stop lost energy and blood sickness in both humans and animals within 24 hours after taking of the powder, you must not take liquor, because then it will take away all the good. This tormentilla root is flicked with a knife on the gums and put on painful teeth in the mouth. It takes away from the teeth the swelling, pain and knots, takes out pus and tooth blisters.

N° 12

For large stools and constipation, the following contents are taken internally, for also many pains or for constipation. The powder is –
Cream of Tartar 5 grams; *Gina lappa* 10 grams; Rhubarb 30 grams. This is mixed together and taken internally all at once in beer, and if it doesn't provide an opening when going to the bathroom within 6 hours, then it is taken again similarly, but as soon as it provides an opening, then don't take any more that time, but then the following day take the following powder internally: *Imperiales stomakalis* 1 measure; *gjalappe* 1 measure; [*Pulfvis Sena*] Mustard powder ½ measure, Rhubarb powder 1 fifth. Mixed together and taken internally in beer three times a day as long as it lasts, and as much as a hazelnut in the morning on an empty stomach, 10 o'clock a.m., 5 o'clock p.m., and during this dosing, it is forbidden to eat ham or milk, or drink liquor, but cabbage and porridge, meat, butter and drink are good to open the constipation, it is best for this to use as much so that it helps, 4 or 5 [...], more if it is needed.

[HERE NUMERATION ENDS IN THE MANUSCRIPT]

N° 13

Against dry pain
Djaltea, 4 shillings; bayberry salve 4 shillings; stick oil 2 shillings; Petri oil 2 measures; juniper oil 2 measures. This is mixed together in a glass jar and is warmed up against the fire in a tin or silver spoon each time it will be used and it will help.

N° 14

For the one who cannot sleep. Take from the church some baptismal water after three girls to one boy and for one girl after three boys, and give it internally three times. Then that person will certainly be better from it.

N° 15
Against the white fire.
Take water with the current from a river that runs towards the north and take coal from a place where the house is burned and no one knows the entrance to or the exit from.[39] The water is prepared on a Sunday morning before the sun comes up, and is taken silently. Put the coal in it. Wash the white fire with it in new and waning moons, then it will disappear soon, it is also good for a bowl -----

N° 16
For the moment of marriage to be protected on the wedding day: take 5 sewing needles and bend them at angles so that they can't be used, and put three in the bride's clothes, and 2 in the bridegroom's, on just the day that they are to be married before the sun comes up. Put the points upwards in the air. If anyone has done something evil with sorcery, then the needles will break, but they cannot harm any other body in the least. Also cense yourselves with the Golden Incense in the morning before they get dressed and when they are going to bed then take both their shoes off them and put them under the head the first night. It will mean they will have good cooperation and faithfulness as well as love in the marriage. The book of Tobias, Chapter 6, verse 22, good.

N° 17 [N° 25 in manuscript]
A Golden Incense for all ill luck for people and animals, it is good for everything. [list appears in manuscript written sideways, here for ease it appears in the normal manner.]

    Red Coral
    Asafetida
    Olibanum
    Gum Mastic
    Spanish Fly
    Calf's head or Hen's cap
    yellow Sulfur
    Musk
    Flus incense
    Saint John's Bread
    Amber
    Myrrh
    Spisglas (a type of powdered glass?)
    Paradise seeds (*aframomum melegueta*)
    Aloe succotrina

---

39 The manuscript returns to the first handwriting style.

Sassafras
Flyrön (mountain ash – red berries)
garlic
denderslag
Belfleder berries

Another incense:
red coral
gjeltlak
pulvid
hellekos tree
asafetida
"bald head"
flyrön
flus incense
black cumin
myrrh
Gum mastic
Johannes Bread (plantain?)
Belfleder berry
Musk stone
Olibanum
Amber
St. Johannes grass
Paradise seeds
Tidebast (*Daphne mezereum*)
aloe
white coral
grey sulfur

Another:
Spanish fly, grey sulfur, musk, sassafras, pointy glass, *tentrafflus*

N° 18
NB. Before you take it, also cut nine types of wood on the same Wednesday at noon. Stand at night in this way, turn counterclockwise, that is against the sun, and cut away from you and against the sun, but the top off and hang it from you. Thread each one and cut and keep the same branch on this; cut all nine branches now and remain silent when you cut them but [*hy*] and [*hay*] may not be used for that. When you come home with the branches, then cut a little of all the branches and mix it into n=25 which is finely ground and is put into water that has stood for the evening, put it on the tile oven so it will get a little warm by morning, which will be Thursday morning. While you have

an empty stomach, you put some of all the 9 branches that you have into the water, then you will see strange things, so that as many types of sorcery[40] that have spoiled it can be seen.

N° 19
To cure sunburn, take a pad of butter and stroke it on it. It will help soon.

N° 20
To transfix a thief on the spot.
You borrow a bone from the churchyard at a certain time. Then you go around the place three times counterclockwise and say: Stand still, like that in which this body lies; So still shall you stand, until I come. Then bury this bone again in its place. When you begin to walk, when you've made it through the place, write then these words on the top of the bone: I . N . R . I.

N° 21
To stop a wildfire.
Write these words and throw it over the fire, then it will go out:

N° 22
> Black anelisa
> Musk
> *Denderslag*
> white coral
> Gum mastic
> [*gade-*]stone
> purified salt-petre
> [*alva-*] cotton

N° 23
At the black Apothecary in Copenhagen, take 9 types, grind fine, and then a teaspoon is taken and is put on a glowing coal in a clay pot and the one who will be censed is well shut in, so that the smoke can get everywhere.

---

40 'Laperi' or "lapperi" should not be understood ethnically here. It was a generic term for sorcery of any type, and was a synonym for "trolleri."

N° 24
To stop a toothache.
Write these following words or 9 letters on an unused paper:
A . M . B . R . A . M . B . On. Then take an old nail, sharpen it fine, and tear the tooth so that it bleeds and stick each time one of the letters, from the first to the last at the end. Then the pain will stop. Then the paper and put it in a place where neither people nor animals can get to it. The nail should be bloody when you stick the letters.

N° 25
So that no one will hex you.
Write these three names on an unused paper and keep it with you.
Barbas | Faber | Messitap –

N° 26
To stop bleeding in people and animals.
Write these following words on an unused paper, and let the blood run on it:
Belata, Belta, Mia, Belta

N° 27
A way to cure livestock from being hexed.
Mark all your livestock in the ear, and give them internally of their own blood, and cense them with the Golden Incense and close your doors and portals while you do this. Then go to the churchyard and take a handful of soil in God's name for healing and protection against all evil. And put two buttons in exchange. Put the dirt down at all the thresholds in your house, in portals and openings, and throughways. As well as inner doors. Put it down so that it won't get swept out, and if the house is built onto, then take the same dirt and put it down in the new house again. Then no devil will have power to go in through your doors, to harm either people or livestock. If any animal dies during this time, then bury it alive in your farm when you see that there is no hope for recovery. Bury it down in your farm and say: Here shall my misfortune die, under earth. Turn the head so that it faces the port hole, or a cross. Then it will return to it and all 4 legs in the air.

N° 28
For beer and distilling.
When this goes all wrong when you have been a guest somewhere, then sit next to the mash tub and S – HIT and you say: You Devil, you take yours but my beer and Liquor's blessing, that God has loaned to me and granted, keeps me and my house-goods, as well as the requirements of its people and livestock. [I am ...] next to the mash tub until you have brewed the brew, and even more as well, and put it into the tub.

N° 29
On lending.
Lend nothing from the room of your house. Look out for those who don't greet, who borrow and carry home on Thursdays. With these words that are written here. If one whispers quietly these words, then they will have the same power alone, if you believe them – food and drink that you give away, taste it first before you leave, away from you all that you leave, and be borne home. Then throw a little on the floor the floor [sic] but you and your people taste it.

N° 30
To cure pain.
Then say these words: I say to you free from hot N:N:, I say to you, free from cold N:N:, I say to you, free from impatience N:N:, In the name of the Father and of the Son and of the Holy Ghost. a: a: a:

the second time in the name of the Lord Zebaot, the third time | amen in the name of Jesus Christ of Nazareth.

The first time you recite these words, then you say amen and then you write a 5-pointed cross (pentagram) with a silver coin where the pain is – the second time you say a a a in the name of the Lord Sebat, and then you write the second four-cornered figure; the third time :a:a:a: in the name of Jesus Christ of Nazareth, and then you write the third sign, namely the net-cross. NB. You begin up where the pain is, and write downwards whether it is the arm or the leg.

N° 31
To know if it is the correct thief that has stolen.
Say this: Our Lady went toward land and had three weapons on her hand, the first for pain, the second for hunger then I write his name In The Names as the one who has stolen from N:N: These words should be read three times but you write a cross on [sollet] and put the scissors in a cross, and name whom you will, and their name three times. And when you name the one who has stolen from you, you walk around the [sollet], otherwise it isn't proven and keep for certain period of time.

N° 32
For bugs take unsalted cucumbers and smear them on the stall.

N° 33
To know hidden things that will happen.
Take a fat 4-leg[41] in the first quarter of the moon, burn it to a powder on a clear coal-fire that doesn't smoke. When you want to know something that will happen, then take a blue wool scarf and tie the powder to your head when you go to bed, then you will know through dreams what will happen; ditto, put this powder in water and wash yourself with it, then your enemies will become afraid of you; the third, keep this powder with you, then every man will be polite and attentive; the fourth, if you become injured, then spread it in the wound, then it will heal in three days; 5 if you want to win in court, then spread a little in your left shoe, then you and your word will be affirmed, even if you are seeking unjustly.

N° 34
Another way to get the judge to change the matter in your favor, take a piece of wood and then put a red shirt on, then he cannot overturn the matter for you but 9 for 9.

N° 35
To win at gambling.
Take a black mole that has 3 feet. Keep him until midsummer's eve when the sun has gone down. Then kill it with a coin, little or large, and you should keep that coin with you when you gamble: But you should burn up the mole to a powder and you should have that with you and you should put it in your left shoe under your feet.

N° 36
For deformity
Go early to the churchyard and borrow a corpse bone and soak it in the dew and stroke with it for healing and for your limbs. It will certainly help with injuries. It is done in the new and waning moons to help women. Then the bone is put back at the same place and earth is thrown onto it and say: Let my weakness now rot away with you in the earth as this bone does.

N° 37
To know who will be your wife.
Take 9 flowers on midsummer eve night, one of each type, and put under your head, it will be told in your dreams, acquaintance or not. When you prepare all the flowers, you should go silently from home and silently back, but don't

---

41 Sven Ek devotes a paragraph in his study of these Eslöv manuscripts to the identity of this "fat 4-legged" and posits that it may be a type of poisonous lizard, what in Skåne was called "firenbene" and in Öland "fyrfotingar."

make a joke of it, but rather be serious and don't think of the one you want to have.

N° 38
To cure stroke.⁴²
Take 9 pione stones, ditto mergnass-powder, ditto rhinoceros horn or claw in a human skull. This is all ground to a powder. For a newborn child 1 Pion stone and one of the above powders, a little on a knife point. For a larger person 10–16 years, to the first powder one pione stone, ditto the second and the third 5 pione stones. For a middle-aged the first 3 pione stones, the second 5 stones, the third 7 stones, as well as a good knife's measure of powder, but 2 knife-measures when the sickness persists the second morning after, and the third morning, and it is taken in Swallow Water that is bought at the Apothecary.

N° 39
To cure stroke take 3 measures of *Sickendenum*; ½ measure burned hartshorn powder; 9 measures of [*qvinika*] stones. Mix it together with 2 measures dragons blood, the heart of a mole. Everything is dried and ground to a powder. Then it is divided into three equal parts, and then is made also a third part of 9 powders which is taken internally each morning on an empty stomach. Three days afterward the vein is opened on the little finger on the right hand and on the left ankle, as well, and then two spoonfulls of blood is taken internally. Nine days the veins in the forehead are opened and you take internally three spoonfulls while the blood is warm.

N° 40
For an old cough. Can candy 12 shillings, licorice 4 shillings, fig 3 shillings, [ålans]root 3, [*isop*] 3. This is put in a new clay pot under cover in a hot new milkpitcher. Cook until it is reduced by half, and drink also quickly during three evenings with the same ingredients.

N° 41
When peeing blood. Take six or eight crayfish, boil them living, pour 18 measures of wine-vinegar, crush them well through a cloth, warm it up and drink it.

N° 42
To protect your livestock.
Then give them of the fat, of the blood and piss in a young growing tree. The fox takes this lung and foot, cream and gives it first, then the fox will take them.

---

42 Stroke here does not mean a cerebral vascular incident. Rather, it is a folk name for a generic complaint.

N° 43
The 23 April then the 9 following is given for 9 weeks following until there is a good egg of food quality and for 2 eggs the second day, neither food nor drink until one hour after sunset.

N° 44
To quickly heal a wound, then take fresh honey and put it on the wound and let it lie for 1 ½ hours, and then change it in the same order; then it is ready in 6 hours.

N° 45
For burns. Put the wound in warm water then it will heal quickly, in a 24 hour day.

N° 46
For the evil bite.[43]
Take beech ashes and make a sharp pile from it, and hold the fingers there for an hour as hot as you can tolerate and a while out, and back a while again. Then there will be a blister; tap it loose, as nicely as one can, and quickly as you can. As long as there is a glowing coal, it works. Then you can heal it with a plaster. Then it will be good.

N° 47
For horses, take *Salmeack* for a shilling and licorice for 4 shillings and a quart of water. It is dissolved and is drunk warm in the evening and then at bedtime.

N° 48
For the heaves in horses.
Asafetida 4 shillings, licorice 6 shillings, and a quart of beervinegar and this is dissolved in a bottle of warm water. The dose is a quarter in the morning and fasting three hours thereafter.

N° 49
For chest-sickness.
To a pot of water add for 2 shillings *salmeack*, for 4 shillings licorice powder. The water is boiled and then the things will dissolve in it.

N° 50
A means to treat scrofula.
The 23 of April, St. George, then it begins. The 22nd hour, before sunset, then eat your dinner that consists of three eggs. Then fast the whole of the 23rd

---

43 *"Onda bettet"* or "evil or painful bite" is another folkname for a general malady.

of April until one hour after sunset. Then this is continued for 9 weeks in this way: that every other day you fast. This is a means of treating all kinds of scrofula that exists. It helps assuredly if it is done correctly. *Probatum*.

N° 51
To cure for stroke
Take peas so that they sprout, and put them aside. Take a human skull from whom the stroke seems to be from. Then the mother will pee three drops each morning into it, and give internally to the child on an empty stomach, and silently for 9 mornings in a row, and if you forget, then you need to start over again, and if you haven't a skull, then she can pee into her right hand and give it to her child.

N° 52
To cure for stroke
The mother takes her child and carries it to where male pigs are being slaughtered. Then the butcher takes the child and puts it on the animal, and lets the child lie there until the animal is dead, and the child shall have three drops of blood. This should happen silently.

N° 53
For all types of deformity of a child.
Give them a drink that stands and ferments, and apply them with the same. Helps.

N° 54
For horses
Take a greensnake stinger and fold it up in a paper. Put it in the horse's harness forward toward the mouth, backward still. The neighbor-lady said to the side.

N° 55
To waken love, take a hair and sew [a pattern of a diamond with interior lines crossed].

N° 56
For toothache
Seek out 9 hidden pins, and pick at the tooth until it bleeds. Then put the pins down under the roots of a tree, preferably aspen, then the toothache will disappear, the pain, everything.

N° 57
Chloroform and Olive Oil 15 grams

ms 4

ESLÖV #3 [EM 3329 C]
"FÖR TANDVÄRK" (FOR TOOTHACHE)
B. I. AHLSTRÖM, ESLÖV

*   *   *   *

1. For toothache.
A swallow is taken, take 9 pins out of the side and thread is taken a measure for each. Pin the God of Noah, the God of Isaac, the God of Abraham, in the name of God the Father and of the Son and of the Holy Ghost a. 3 times.

2. For [sål] cows: *enförnallis* for 12 shillings, divide up into 9 parts that are put into flour dough. 3 parts to each cow, one part each morning for three mornings in a row one hour before the cow [soi]

3. Burn in incense some black dragon 2 shillings, red snake 2 shillings, white snake powder 2 shillings. Flying dragon 2 shillings, *Daphne mezereum* 2 shillings, *flyrön* 2 shillings when the mash is well raised, [siökes an sus siine ni äs A de asia] for 6 shillings. Bear gall 6 shillings.

4. For roots.
Take a half a quart sweet milk and finely sifted barley flour. Cook them into a porridge and when the gruel is ready, the pot is taken off.

5. Take a mustard grinder and put a glowing coal in the opening in all the names of all the devils, and say: just as this grinder goes around with a coal in the Devil's name, so too this person will neither have peace nor rest until he dies. N: N: In a [baret] that he has stolen, in the name of F: and S: and the Holy Ghost. In nom. Patris: ett: filius: Speritus Sannitus a 3.

6. If you want to drive the thief to return, then write these words
Leppa: Lejitur: Segitur: Bleqitur: and throw it at them, and say like this: I, N: N: conjure you, by the living God, as well as his mother Mary, that you return

that which was stolen :N:N come back again :in: nom ien: Patris: ett Filius: ett Sannitus: Speritus: amen: 3

7. Another:
M: h: p: c: b: g: p: n: a: t: p: g: Z: b: P: a: a:

8. To stop bleeding.
As truly as our Lord Christ was born on Christmas night, and all the streams and rivers at that time became still, and were stopped, just as truly the blood shall also be stopped on N: N: a [te m...] run, and this in the name of the Father and of the Son and of the Holy Ghost amen. :a: 3 times.

9. For toothache:
:M:a hr: U B E R

10. To write away a toothache, write on four pieces of bread

R A G A M
W A G A M
O M G A M
F I N G A M

3 pieces give to a dog. The fourth eat up yourself. If it is a man, give it to a female dog. If a woman, to a male dog. But no more than the sick one should be in the room.

11. To silence gunpowder.
As truly as Jesus Christ stopped the man who wanted to destroy the virgin Mary with fire, in that way I stop the powder for you N: N. who are carrying the shotgun. I. F. S. and. the. H. Gh. a. 3 times.

12. To unhex yourself and your shotgun.
Go on a Sunday morning on an empty stomach and silently to a place where there is an earthfast stone, close to a fruit-bearing tree. So that you can shoot in a hole, bore a hole in the fruit tree. When you are going to shoot, say: Here I put myself with thigh and leg on this earthfast stone, so that I will cure myself and my shotgun again. Now shoot. And now I shoot off myself and my shotgun, and upon that one who hexed me, I send back in 18,000 Devils' names, and shoot the shotgun and then put a rowen twig into the hole.

13. To stop a man. Diabolus. Beelsebubb. Brother Russ. rib right. Be now with me, these three overlords, when I conjure and destroy both body and soul in the Devil's name: a 3

14. To create for yourself a "goanisse" or farm wight, write your name with your own blood in Satan's name on a contract for a certain time and put it under your own head and sleep on it for three nights. Then take the contract and go in Satan's name and bury it at the left corner of your house, but when you do it you should go silently and on an empty stomach. Then he will draw everything to you, whatever you wish, in the evening. When the contract is done, it is burned and buried.

15. To stop a nosebleed.
Take a piece of good paper. Throw counterclockwise around you, and each time around then say: Elustriks | Eturals | 3 times.

16. If someone has stolen from you and you know at which place, then take two pounds of nails and put there two pieces of paper on which are written the name: Satan=Lefviatan on the first, and the suspect's name on the second. The pieces of paper are now put on the nails that were mentioned before, stuck through on a cork, and let them sit for three days. Then the one who has stolen will have no peace for Lefviatan.

17. To poke out the eye of someone who has stolen.
Take a spike and hammer it into an oak post and put a hammer that is red-hot and hit three times on the head of the spike, and say each time you strike "I strike you in Satan's name you thief, so that your eye will go from you, and Satan will get that eyeball." Then go three steps backwards but don't look back. This should happen three Sundays in a row before the sun comes up.

18. To punish an enemy.
Take your shirt off before the sun comes up, and write your enemy's name on the back with Storax water mixed together with *Lapis Infinalis*, and then take 2 canes and with each rap of the canes he will feel it, but speak quietly while you strike.

19. To make girls fond of you.
Take the blood of a bat in a handkerchief and put before her eyes, then she'll love you so much that you [...]

20. The art of winning at gambling.
Buy magnet water at the Apothecary, and wash your hands in it and say "I shall and I want to win at gaming as far as [*buel*] is found.

21. The art of driving out rats and mice|
1 pound Bergamot, 2 pounds red sandalwood, ditto [*lifverame*]. Mixed together and put out for them, then they will flee.

22. Take an apple on a Sunday morning before the sun comes up, and carve the name |Lefviatan| and spit out that portion, then your shotgun will always shoot sure.

23. For a man who is hexed.
Go on a Sunday morning before the sun comes up, fasting and silently to a fruit bearing tree. Split it towards the south and north. Creep through three times. Begin with the feet and go counterclockwise around and be completely naked. Then put your clothes on, and take three cords by their ends and put them between the two parts of the split so that it is closed together.

24. To know if people and livestock are hexed.
Take 3 stones, one on the road to the church, one on a cross (at a cross roads?) and one from home. Put them in a mill, and the one that breaks is the one you should heat up on coals.

25. 1 Quart Red Wine well corked, and if you go to an anthill on a Maundy Thursday morning before the sun comes up, you can take it on Good Friday morning before the sun comes up.[44]

26. Understanding horses.
Say into a horse's ear: "Hold firm and your bit and suffering, as Christ also suffered on his holy cross, go faithfully and suffer, in Jesus' name" 3 times.

27. General Conversation with Marbuel
           #   #a
I conjure you Marbuel, by God, the ruler of everything, that you reveal to me all the princes of the world's foundation, and for the sake of Jesus the highest winner of victory that you send all the chieftain spirits as many as are here and are also away from the earth, that they prepare themselves in this moment and let themselves be seen before my human sight, that for me and no other, so that I may speak with you and give instructions to each after his purpose according to his shape. I absolve and herewith loose them from all other assignments during that same time NB NB. I conjure you, Marbuel, by the great and holy name Ejhevut + Aola Z Aoly° Z Tolland Z Jehovat + Adonaj Z Etthanadoj Z The God of the heavens Z Ja! by Jesus Christ + and his holy word lives. I make you Marbüel? [sic] so that you fulfill my wishes. Hear Jehovat + The Heavens' Z The Firmaments' Z Planets' Z and Earth's Lord. I, a son of earth, sanctified by God and [...] do conjure you that you do my will that I shall instruct you. Amen.

---

44 Although there is no "purpose" of this procedure, we know from other manuscripts that it is for increasing one's strength.

MANUSCRIPT TRANSLATIONS

28. The Main Citation to Marbuel.
                 #   #a

I call upon you, spirit Marbuel, by the Host of Jesus Christ or the consecrated host + Sehelam Z Jehovat + For mehasile Z Seheboruch Z אל׳ה Adonaj Z Pra uni Sehoa Z he created Z O! Aola Z Sehaffokanelan Z by יהוה Jehovat + Padasehoja Z These shall be my friends and stand by me Sela Z אל ה Adonaj Z the daso hamari Z Beroris יהוה Jehovat + Maffis Pordi Z I call upon you spirit Marbuel by Palkeneijon Z hipnite Z Aola Z Elohim + Keremisihe Z Jehovah + I conjure you Marbuel? Who lies in wait until the day that flees in the morning on the earth, and by him who washed his disciples feet, that you also show me all obedience. I cease not, but conjure you anew Marbuel? you who lie in wait, in the name of the Highest of All, by Dajtum Z Polamus Z Aeom Z who fly over the air Z and by the the rulers of air, and the highest spirit Rectaoria, listen. Adonaj Z O יהוה Jehova + The God of Gods + O! Malfus Z Per deiami sicke Z Imese eteminisick??

29. The further Citation of Marbuel
                 #   #a

O Jesus + now is the time to help me + O! Suemes Hland Z O! Imanuel + The Truth + Alhimasus Cuma Z O! Jehvat יהוה N stamigbu + Ansej Z Press + Japhet The Son of the Sun? Help me Z Hisehahoj Ahes miej Z O! Felsehaehand Z Potmes eiat Z O! Adonaj Z O! Jehovat + O Aola ZZ Sela Z O! Oles Z O! Hisehahos Z You who dwell with Devina. O! kyrie blessed you kyrie and you Salonaegiamo Z Medesholt Morlea Z Bryase! יהוה Elohim + O! kyrie + Paudeschod יהוה Jehovat + He who shortens the devil's Z No Aanda Marbuel, hurry without confusion and fuss to this summoning. I yell, call and conjure you by all these names, that now in this instant you come to this place – kamia Z Hisehachos, Pracoll Z do not forsake me but stand by me! Aglam אלך Adonaj Z Oyifisco אלהים Jehovat Bis Mira + You who force the Devil with only your word! Month to month blessed Jesus who forces the spirits! O! kyrie + O! kyrie + O! kyrie Eliyson + Jehovah + Amen.

30. Still further Citation of Marbuel
                 #   #a

O! Jehovah + Zag gottnemun Z Yana Z Gaens Zamach Z Masurama Z Kelÿ Z Nesemel Z Zaamechon Cater habet Arta. Saman Zusaton Pataphararare Schal Met Machaÿ O! Schiman Prada miseh, O! Marbulis Schehortia sehelam Vott medha Selaprae priseha Hasedaj oija her Deia M Mischui Messe amen.

31. You come alone this time.
When the spirit comes now without confusion or loud noise, then you speak the following words like this: O! Agland + Jesus is before me and at my side + Morsalen Z quandum Sola + O! Jehovah + Dorsat + I am the one, whom Christ

preserves + Soland + and through whom Jesus works. Here is Jesus with me + Amen.

32. The Spirit is bound in the following way
                    #   #a
God the Father binds you Z+ Jesus keeps you Z God Z the Z Holy Z Ghost Z binds and hold you Z the Prince of Peace Michael binds you O! Annael Z binds this spirit through your peace ± O! rest.

33. The Dismissal of the Spirit
                  #   #a
O! Melias Gudi orat + Jesus + Be Blessed + I wish to always bear your holy cross + O! Marbuel, be dismissed + go back to the realm of the devils and spirits + Jesus be with me, Amen.

34. Another dismissal that is the best.
O! Jesus Christ + Has won victory + Zasunabula + Soi + Merarora + Sileubram + Amen.

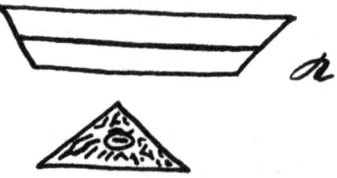

Gott Helmoj Adonaj I seriot Jafarnat Alpha + Omega --------------------------

35. When one has summoned the spirit and not received a sign of its arrival, then you say: I summon you M. but such a being giving no little sign, I will see or hear some convincing speech: otherwise I must believe that it is finished or concluded. Name.

 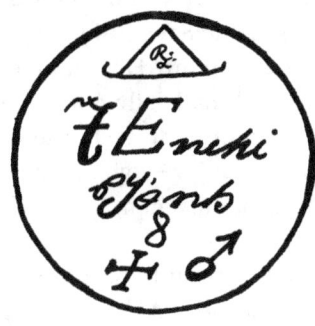

36. Christ Jesus, The Light, the Truth, the Love, the way of Day and Life become flesh. Glory be to God in the Highest. Hallejuja. The seed of woman shall trample the head of the serpent. Thou death, where is thy sting, thou Hell, where is thy Victory?

Tetragrammaton. The Triune Adonai Agla Jehovah! Holy Father Holy Son Holy Ghost + + + In the beginning was the Word, and the Word was with God and the Word was God. Three are they who witness in heaven + The Spirit, the Word and the Holy Ghost and the three are one.
Psalm of David 109.

37. Jesus, God and Mary's Son Hallejeluja [sic]

38. Marbuel's Citation
      #   #a
I summon you O! Marbuel before me immediately. Troren Z Lasunabula Z and by Jesus Christ + victory over the power of the moon and by the strength of the Sun Z M come, come before my circle; this instant in beautiful human shape. Marbuel 3 a, a, a.

39. Marbuel's General Citation
       #   #a

I conjure you by the almighty God the Creater and Ruler over the heavens and the earth and of the water and in the air, over fire and Hell and outside of Hell. Yea, I conjure you by the word that was from the beginning with God. That is Jesus, the Savior of the whole world and hero Z by him who in his victorious descent into Hell subdued you, Marbuel, who trod you Marbuel under his feet, and made all your might to a mere small domain, here remain during your suffering to be humble and to do our will – by his suffering blood and death I conjure you that you in this instant present yourself before this my circle. amen. amen.

40. If you want to have a woman, take three sewing needles and 3 buttons, 3 brushes and put them over you in the bed, and one button in the eye of the needle and brush over them.

41.

MS 5

KU 3335
LAKBÄCK, ROGSTA SOCKEN, HÄLSINGLAND
PRIVATE OWNERSHIP: J. ARBORÉN

Though there is no numeration of the items in the original, I have labeled page number and item number for ease of reference. Otherwise, the translation is as the original.

* * *

MY OATH IS BROKEN
THIS EKONOMIA
OR
MARIA CHRISTINA NATURALIA
BELONGS TO
ERIK JOHAN ANDERSSON
ROGSTA WESTANBÄCK
THE 15TH OF AUGUST, 1881.

[ON THE DUST PAGE:]

1. For a knife with nine kinds of steel[45]
Make yourself a knife of 9 kinds of steel in the sign of the zodiac that is the 13th day of the month of November.[46] And slaughter a rooster on Good Friday and let the blood remain on it. Then buy dragon's blood[47] at the Apothecary and anoint the knife with it, and whatever you wish to keep, then draw a cross on it.[48]

---

45 In the folklore of steel and iron, something made of 9 different types is especially magically potent. Examples of types include: Sky or meteoric iron, iron found in a rock, iron found that had killed a man, iron from a broken blade, etc.

46 This would be under the influence of the astrological sign of Scorpio, the scorpion, with planetary ruler Mars at the time this manuscript would have been written. Mars governs all things Martial, and hence a blade of 9 types of steel would most properly be undertaken in this period.

47 A red tree-gum that burns heavily but sweetly.

48 Presumably on the knife.

[PAGE 1.]

2. Take from a churchbell on a Sunday morning between the second ringing and the third ringing and mix with it 7 earth [*myger*] at an earthfast stone.

3. Hanish oil. Anoint under the left shoe-heel and step into a fox's footprint. Recite: "Now I take [inserted between the lines: 3 pieces from the northern road or direction] you who are in a foreign country and I take you into my country, and you will come and remain immovable. The Virgin Mary gave me a wrapping that I tie about you, just like She bound the soul-killer all on the Final Day, so that you won't get away from me until I will transfix[49] you.

4. You come here in the world and teach me to play in the name of the Father and of the Son and of the Holy Ghost, and three parts I have left for you at an earthfast stone, and the fourth you'll have in my heart's blood, and that I have in a bottle, with which you can bind and bandage your body.

3 silver coins, 3 calf bones, 3 pieces of bread.

4. French heaven drop 3 on a black woolen cone.

[PAGE 2.]

5. For a horse whose strength has been stolen.
There was a man who went out along the road; then he met a horse. Why are you crying, my horse? Why should I not cry, I who have lost my power and my fortitude, both blood and strength? And you shall go back into the lake where no one was, in the mountain where no one dwells, there is an earthfast stone where no man shall go. Your conscience will burn, and in Hell you will be forced, in the name of the Father and of the Son and of the Holy Ghost.

Draw a ☆ and bore a hole, and recite three times, and twist the bit of bread three times counterclockwise, pour liquor in the middle of the corner [*sic*].

6. To make men follow you.
Take a silk thread and thread a needle and stick it into a living snake, and fasten that thread on a man.

[PAGE 3.]

7. For stolen power in cows.
There was a man who went out on a road. Then he met a cow. What are you crying about, my cow? Why shouldn't I cry, who is bereft of power, and bereft

---

[49] Perhaps an error, and "release" was meant?

of blood, and bereft of milk? Don't cry, my cow, I shall fix you up. I work now against all the evil in God's name, and not for any ill-doing. Now I take back everything all together, lack of power, lack of blood, and lack of milk. Now I send everything evil from here, to a boat that is on a lakeshore, in which there is an iron vein, there I drive the evil, and they will dwell in a mountain in which stands an earthfast stone, and there you'll be buried until Doomsday.

8. To stop bleeding
I stop this blood like Jesus Christ our Savior stopped Noah's flood in three names, Father, Son and Holy Spirit, Amen.

[PAGE 4.]

9. For colic with horses.
Säfverbom 6, fenugreek 6, antimony powder 6, *Lifsensdroppar* 24, strong pepper 6, a used sanitary napkin from a woman as payment, and soaked in liquor ½ a quart. Jeppe rode out over a mountain, he rode so he fell into the path, and intestinal blockage and colic from here.

10. A horse cure.
Säfverbom 6, fenugreek 6, antimony powder 6, Red Horse-powder 6, Dragon's blood 6, Asafetida 6, Garlic 6, Aloe 6. Brain's Testament 6, three parts measure for 1 quart of water, boiled down to a ½ quart, a half quart liquor, tried with a [virgin?], which is given internally and then it will be seen in his eyes if he becomes wet in the eyes.

[PAGE 5.]

11. A Cow Cure.
Brain's testament 3, Asafetida 3, St. John's bread 3, *kolokris* 3, gray Cattlepowder 3, White Cattlepowder 3, Milk powder 3, True Beaver musk (Castor) 12 *öre*'s worth, Ambergris 3, Valerian root 3, Angelica root 3, *fundelrot* 3, *Säfverbom* 3, fenugreek 3, soaked in liquor and give to the cow a ½ measure.

12. For pain in people and in animals
The Virgin Mary she went to the Churchyard. She soothed pain, she healed wounds. There they died, in my name, and in your name, and in the name of all Three Persons, of the Father and of the Son and of the Holy Ghost, and you shall go to Hell. and make the sign of the cross with a knife in liquor for each time you recite.

[PAGE 6.]

13. To stop bleeding.
Blood to blood, skin to skin, flesh to flesh sinew to sinew, bone to bone and blood to blood. Stand still, you bad blood, Stand still you good blood, here you shall stand and not run. You shall be so reluctant to run just as Jesus Christ when he carried his cross in the Garden of Gethsemane was to run. Stand still you blood, here you shall stand, and there you shall stop, as surely as the soul stands and stays in Hell.

14. When you are going to stop bleeding and you are not present with the patient, if it is a man or a woman, then you will know exactly where the wound is, and put your left ring finger on yourself [at that place] and begin in the names of God the Father and of the Son and of the Holy Ghost. And name the name if it is a man or a woman, and recite three times.

[PAGE 7.]

15. For sprain.
When you work for a sprain, then recite three times and draw with the knife down over the hair.
Jesus rode out on a heath, then his ass became lame. When he came to the road, he himself got down and worked for the sprain. This his ass, back in joint. In the joint and in position, now it will be as it was before. All three Persons at one time. Amen.

16. For sprain again.
I rode on a horse out over a field, then I broke off a horse's leg. I healed it. The sprain in joint and in position, then it became as it was before.

17. A simple way to stop bleeding.
Draw a cross with a knife over the ring and middle finger of the left hand. Each time you recite, and recite three times: Here I draw the Savior's cross, in the three names, God Father, Son and Holy Ghost.

Recite this three times and draw with the knife down over the hair.

[PAGE 8.]

18. For snakebite
The snake bit and then we bandaged, then came the Virgin Mary with her bandages and was going to bandage about his head, and soon bound it, it happened in three names, God the Father, Son and Holy Ghost.

19. For snakebite.

The snake bit and there we bandaged, then the Virgin Mary (Jesus' mother) comes with her bandages, and bandaged about his head, and soon. All three Persons at once. Amen.

20. For a cow, a fistful of salt and recited three times and draw the knife towards it, and recited three times at the bite, and stroke with the knife down over the bite.

21. To work for sharp things, nails or angles, you should work for nails and angles, then make in a quart of weak beer and use nine grains of sand that you take from a churchyard and tie a bag, and put it in an anthill from the

[PAGE 9.]

one Thursday evening to the other Thursday evening. You'll use 9 grains of sand from these.

22. To transfix thieves.
When one enshrouds a corpse, then speak to the one who sews so that you will obtain a needle and thread, but it must be the same thread that they have sewn with, and no other thread. And when you get hold of a grass snake, then take him living and unharmed, and put him in front of your possessions upon an earthfast stone until he dries up, and take his head off him, and stick the needle through and let it remain there on the thread, and thread it through that which you want to keep.

[PAGE 10.]

23. A doubly-good cure for three-day's *fråssa*.
Grind 12 *öre*'s worth of Paradise seeds and divide it in four parts that are taken internally in Liquor on the day one catches the chill, you understand.

24. To restore stolen goods.
Get yourself an English needle and talk to the one who is enshrouding a corpse and get a needle with five quarters thread that has been sewn, and keep this needle and thread and take off three pine cone scales and take them apart and cut them up finely. Take off the seed pods from the seeds that are on it. From three springs in the same stream a little from the knife's measure 9 grains of salt, 3 drops of blood out of the left ring finger, 3 pinches of flour, and recite the Our Father, and the Lord's Benediction. "As truly as you are a thief in the world, just as truly you will come back over mountains and valleys." and draw such a figure ♡ in wood. 7 button-holes and blow through them away without seeing where they go.

[PAGE 11.]

25. [Inside an oval]
If we had good flour, then we would make dough balls, and you understand. Faust. Here I conjure you in the three names. F. S. H.Gho. Amen. Erik Johan, N° 7 in Rogsta, 1881.

[PAGE 12.]

26. To dull pain.
Jesus he walked into the churchyard. There he sought the means, and there he healed wounds and dulled pain and you will fall asleep and the pain will dull, and this in the name of the Triune God, amen.

27. For sprain
Jesus rode through a pathway. Where he rode, his horse got a sprain, and then he recited out of the roadway and into the joint, from the outer part and into the inner part, and that, in the name of God the Father, Son and Holy Ghost, ammen.[sic]

28. To staunch blood flow
Jesus went over a bridge, and there he twisted his shoes, he stopped water, he stopped bleeding and you shall stop just as the woman stood in Hell, who boiled stink on a Saturday, and if the twelve men who sit in court and know right but judge wrong sit in Hell, but you shall stand and this in the name of the Holy Trinity, ammen.

29. For snakebite
The Virgin Mary went forth on a road. There she got to see the naughty snake. Mary takes her small keys,

[PAGE 13.]

and will strike the naughty snake. The snake ran and disappeared. In the name of the Holy Trinity.

30. To cause pain to a person.
Take blood from the person you want, and put it into the air three times counterclockwise. Then pass it three times through the outhouse cleaning brush. Put it then in the air or go to the northern direction, and say these special words: "As truly as you bore your cross, just as truly you will have un-healable pain."

31. Another (to cause pain to a person)
You take blood on a piece of paper from the person and heat the scrap in front of the fire. Then you blaspheme it three times and then you go to the northern corner and say these words: "As truly as you have borne your cross, just as truly will you have an uncureable ache, or become insane, as truly as three devils jump up to aid, just as truly shall my soul burn in Hell.

32. If you want to put a person to sleep
Take hare musk and give to him in wine, then he'll fall asleep immediately. If you want to wake him up, vinegar in his mouth then he'll awaken.

[PAGE 14.]

33. Another (to put a person to sleep)
Take [*gallan*] out of an eel and put it in a drink. Then he'll sleep until you put rose-water in his mouth.

34. Something fun to know if you are fighting.
If you get a ear-clap, then have a linen cloth in your hand and wipe with it at that place that you got hit, and wipe three times under the left foot from the toes to the heel, and say these words: "..."[50]

Genuine Castor [*Bäfvergäll*] – 12, valerian – 2, heart-strengthening drops – 3, fuldelberries – 3, asafetida – 3, and soak all together in liquor and have a dropper bottle ready.

35. To transfix thieves. Take a woolen yarn in a needle that has been threaded counterclockwise, go to a corpse and thread through the left hand, and go three times around the grave counterclockwise and put the needle and the thread in the grave.

[PAGE 15.]

36. Certain means against the Rose.
Mix together pig-dung and lard. And pulverized slate that is strained fine – and mix with vinegar until it ... prepare a piece of paper that is applied.

37. German Hunter remains, plantain in that way.
Fakut, Fa. kut, Fak. ut, amen
Then it is recited over the fallen game. Christ was born, Christ was betrayed, Christ was found, Christ was crucified and bound. This I recount to you for atonement so that God will help me.

---

50 The text is missing in the manuscript.

38. For stolen strength with horses.
The beginning is like before, "o weep not you, my horse. I give to you back that which you have lost..... But there we drive all evil demons you are as Christian people, so everything evil from here in the name of the Father and Son and the Holy Ghost. Everything evil away from here and the same one who has done evil will die in it, so that the devil will take both body and soul.

[PAGE 16.]

39. Means to heal toothache
Take a splinter out of a threshold that is situated towards the north and south, and take this splinter and gouge the painful tooth so that it bleeds. Then take this splinter and put it in a crossroad that is oriented from north to south and east to west. Then put some threads there three times and with reverence say these words: The one who has this toothache, he will suffer as much as our Lord Christ suffered on his Cross.

40. Another way.
I went out on my way, and I met Jesus Christ. He asked me what I was lacking. I got pain in my teeth. Take water in the mouth, spit out into the fire's coals, then you'll be healthy and sound for all your lifetime. And the pain will not stay in the Lord's name. But it will stay in Satan's name.

41. Printed material follows, as well as a page of good dates for bleeding. The manuscript is not clear whether these are previously printed or something that was transcribed from another source.

KU 11120 SVARTKONSTBOK
SLIMMINGE SOCKEN, VEMMENHÖGS HÄRAD, SKÅNE, 1853

*   *   *

No. 13
So that a person will receive tremendous strength.
Take good clear red wine in a quart bottle, cork it and tie over it a bladder and then with a piece of leather. Then go to an anthill on the evening of Maundy Thursday and bury it deeply down into the hill, and let it stay there a year, and

the day of Good Friday morning, before the sun comes up, take the bottle out and drink up the wine, then you will certainly have received wonderful and unbelievable strength.

No. 14.
So that a horse won't soon tire out.
Hang some of the large wolf's teeth under the neck of the horse, then we won't become tired.

No. 15.
To stop bleeding in people and animals.
Take a knob that sits on the foot of a spinning stool or foot stool, anoint it with the blood of the sick one, and then put the knob back in its place again.

No. 16.
To stop bleeding in women.
Take 2 pounds broom straw and 2 pounds of German Salvia. Dry and grind it to a fine powder, fine as a hair. Then a pot of water, put the herbs into it, and boil it in a covered pot until it reduces by half. This she should drink in 1 or 2 days.

No. 17.
So that one who must walk a great deal doesn't tire.
Take garlic, cottonseed oil, and lard. Make from this a salve and apply to the footsoles.

No. 18.
For gunpowder that neither lights nor shoots.
Take a pound of fine powder, let it dissolve in spirits of alcohol. When it is well dry again, then mix one measure each of borax, salalmoniac and *Galmeja*, but make sure that these parts are well pulverized before it is mixed.

No. 19.
To shoot at night so that it appears like stars.
Put dried peas into melted ham drippings. Let them sit, roll them into fine gunpowder, put them then in the shotgun, shoot them out then, and it will appear quite wonderful.

No. 20
If a woman has bewitched you so that you have to run after her.
ut on a pair of new shoes, and run or dance until your feet become sweaty. Take your right shoe off, pour beer or white wine in it and drink it up, then you will be done with her.

No. 21.
If a man has lost his virility.
Just piss through a wedding ring.

No. 22.
If a shotgun is bewitched for you.
Take moss from a human skull. Put it between the gunpowder and the shot. Then shoot off the shotgun.

No. 23.
To preserve yourself from sorceries.
You take a nut with a hole in it and fill it with mercury. Then you take the beautiful rose that is at the end of peacock feathers and put it in the hole. Then stop up the hole with virgin wax. Then sew the nut into Carmosin-red silk or taffeta, and carry it on a red silk thread around your neck, over your chest. It helps also for those who are troubled by anxiety.

No. 24.
To shoot accurately and true.
Cut yourself in your right hand. Take the blood and mix it with a little gunpowder, then you will shoot accurately as long as it lasts. Or take the liver and heart of a bat, and mix it in with the lead when you load the shot, then you will hit without fail.

No. 25.
So that a dog won't bark at you.
Take a heart of a dog and a tooth of a dog, stick the tooth through the heart and hold it in your left hand, then the dog will not dare to howl or bark.

No. 26.
To light a candle, so that people will have heads of calves.
Take calf's blood and a little sulfur and make of these a candle. Put it in a lantern, then everyone who is in the room will appear to have calf heads. But no other candle in the room should be lit.

No. 27.
If some evil befalls you, and you want to know who has aimed it at you.
Take the herb that in Latin is called Oeucium. Tie it under your right arm, go to bed, and then in your sleep you'll see who is responsible.

No. 28.
So that womenfolk will lift up both their skirt and underslip.
Take hare's blood and anoint a candle. Light it; then it will happen. Or if you

take bat's blood and anoint a linen cloth and let it dry. Light it on fire afterwards, that will also work.

No. 29.
To incline a girl to come and love you.
Take a few hairs from her head, and then a piece of unused lead. Make a hole in it. Put the hairs through the hole. Put it into a new clay pot and cook it over a slow fire, then she'll come and will want to love you. Or take the tongue of a swallow chick that hasn't yet left its nest. Put it under your tongue, then kiss the girl that you want to have love you, and fix it so that your breath slips into her mouth.

No. 30.
To get one to sleep for a long time.
Take the head of a bat and put it under their head.

No. 31.
To make yourself invisible.
Saint Jacob's Day (July 25) before the sun comes up, then go to a large, old anthill. Thoroughly soak it in water all over, so the ants will flee. The water should be warm. Look carefully in the anthill and you will find a stone with three colors. Put it under your tongue.

No. 32.
To become clear in your eyes.
Drink each morning a spoonful of *Rute*-water, then you won't have gunk in your eyes.

No. 33.
So that a lock will open by itself for you.
When frogs are mating, then take one frog and put it into a drinking glass. Cover it well with a flat stone. Put it next to where frogs come and mate, then they will attempt to get the trapped on free. When finally there is no other help for it, one frog will go away and will fetch an herb or grass, which she will hold before the glass. When it breaks, be careful to get that grass, because with it you can unlock whatever lock you want to, without a key.

No. 34.
To get a girl to love you.
Write these words found below on your left hand on a Sunday or Thursday morning before the sun comes up, and with that hand, touch the head of the one you wish to love, then you can believe that she will be fond of you.

No. 35.
To get someone to tell you all they know in their sleep.
Take a hawk's heart, tie it on the foot of the sleeping one, then she'll tell you everything you ask about.

No. 36.
To get someone to say what they know while their sleeping.
Take the heart of a thrush or a birch-starling. This is put under the head of the sleeping one, then she'll say everything she knows.

No. 37.
If your wife is unfaithful to you and runs away.
then take her right shoe and put it into an unused clay pot and put it over a fire and cook it, then she won't have any peace or rest until she comes back to you.

No. 38.
To find out where money is buried.
Write the following letters on virgin parchment. Lay it at night under your head, then you will dream of the place.

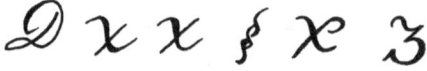

No. 39.
To always win at gambling.
Take a needle with which a corpse has been sewn in a shroud, and stick it under the table where you're sitting and gaming, then you can never lose. Or carry with you the herb that in German is called Godsveis in your right shoe. Or carry with you an owl's heart, then you won't lose, rather you'll win.

No. 40.
So that no poisonous animal will be able to harm you.
Carry with you the herb that is called Dittany.

No. 41.
To become invisible.
Take one of the large and poisonous frogs and stick its left eye out. Then take a pea and put it in place of the eye. Bury the frog in the earth, so that the eye-socket in which the pea now sits stays above ground. There will grow from there a pea vine. Take one of them and put it under your tongue, then you are invisible.

No. 42.
To know if a wife is pregnant with a boy- or a girlchild.
Stretch out your hand and say like this: *Utbenam mudio maskulium oatafenum allune paret*. And at the same time, stroke her hand downwards with your middle finger. If she brings her hand up again, then it's a girl. Otherwise it's a boy.

No. 43.
Cure for kidney- or bladder stones, or difficulty in urinating.
Take some turnips, grind them to a pulp, press out the juice through a linen cloth, sweeten with sugar, and one spoonful each hour taken internally.

No. 44.
Cure for those who can't hold their urine (incontinence).
Take a little fish that is found inside a pike (fish). Burn it to a powder, and from this powder taken internally two times on an empty stomach. a. p. b. (*aproberat*)

No. 45.
For sicknesses of livestock
Take mushrooms that are growing on a linden tree, and put them into a trough or some other pail, so that the livestock will come and drink over them. If any of them should sicken, then burn the previously named mushrooms to a powder and give it to them in water.

No. 46.
To hex a shotgun.
When you hear the shot, then take from under your left foot and cut up a piece of turf around your foot. Turn the turf upside down and put it back in the hole again. Then go your way.

No. 47.
To write white letters, so that the paper is black and the writing is white.
Take first a raw egg-yolk and whip it in water so that it gets so thin that it can flow through a pen. Write or draw on paper. Let it dry, and cover it with ink or

India ink, and let it dry out again. Then take a knife and scrape out the letters, then the egg-yolk will come off, and the writing is white.

No. 49.
To make fire-shining snakes
Take camphor and put it in liquor and apply it to the edges of the parchment. Let them dry. Then set them on fire, and release them at night or in the evening in very windy weather, then they'll fly and will appear terrible.

No. 50.
So that no shot from a shotgun will hit you.
Take a snake's head, burn it to a powder. Put it into a clean cloth on your head, or if you put that powder into some water, then you are free from being shot, and your enemies love you.

No. 51.
To preserve a shotgun, so that no one can bewitch it.
Cut on the side of the cut-hole that faces you a five-pointed cross (pentagram). Bore a hole right in the middle of the newly carved star approximately an inch deep. Pour into it mercury and put the heart of a bat in it. Plug the hole with *flyrön*[51] that you gather on a Sunday morning before the sun comes up.

No. 52.
To incline one to sleep for three 24-hour days.
Take hare gall. Give to him in wine, but if you pour vinegar in his mouth, then he'll awaken immediately. To incline one to sleep for 36 hours, then anoint him with sow's milk on his pulse points.

No. 53.
A candle to show buried money.
Take virgin wax and sulfur, make of it a candle with [*hårpix*]-oil, and a wick that a virgin maiden has spun remaining silent on a Sunday morning before the sun comes up. Illuminate with this, and when you come to where the money is, then it will go out.

No. 54.
A candle that shows headless people.
Take yellow sulfur and grind it completely, and pour it into a lamp with the oil. Put out all the other candles in the room, light the lamp and sit in the midst of the people, then you will see a miracle.

---

51 Swedish *flyrön*, or *flygrön*, is rowan, or mountain ash, but specifically one that is growing as a less mature side growth from the base or a trunk of another, more established, tree.

No. 55.
So that a woman in sleep will say everything she knows and whatever you want to ask her.
Take the tongue of a frog[52] and put it on her heart.

No. 56.
To find out in your sleep what will happen to you.
Take the rancid blood of an ass, hart-tallow and storax in equal parts. Mix it and cense your room with it when you intend to go to sleep.

No. 57.
To find out if a maiden or farm-maid is a virgin or not.
Take hare's gall or also the head of a stallion and put it into the drinking bucket. Let her drink. If she's not a virgin, then she will pee immediately where she stands.

No. 58.
So that a maiden will love.
If you are aware of where she pees, then have ready an old chopped-off horseshoe nail. Stick it immediately into the earth where she has peed while it is still warm.

No. 59.
To open a letter so no one will know.
Take an eggshell. Wash it clean and grind it to a powder and sift it through a fine sieve. Mix it with glue water. Make from this a dough and form a clump. Knead it on the side that seal sits on on a glass, so that it will become slippery and flat. Then wet the envelope you want to open. Put the glass with the mixture on it and press, so that you will have the same seal. Let it dry then. See, then you can open the letter, and then seal with your sigil.

No. 60.
To see the thief in your sleep.
Dig up a human bone. Put it under your head pillow when you sleep. Then you will see the thief.

No. 61.
To get the thief to bring back what he has stolen.
So, if you know in which room the stolen goods were, then cut off a shaving from it, and write on it in this way: *miruga Ring Snälla* 𝓏𝓏𝓵 . This shaving should be carried silently to the woods to a pine tree and put under the pine

---

52 Sw. *fröda*, Rana temporariens.

root. The characters written on the shaving should be written in the blood taken from a rooster's comb, and then you recite: *Barlike, tå Barlike yng. Pöö de pudra Borike peng peng troa parolla Eatina gatta sorvis pecalis est. Doctor Faus amarij. Barta ut fiedasie full melljer de peng. Lamat Doctor Fau et leitor in de skola Coriatas feurunt Doctor Malkus Depre Septoris Doctor Faus amarij* Thief, stop![53]

No. 62.
A way to cure all livestock which are bewitched.
Take some of their droppings while they are warm and put them in a raven. Hang in the chimney in the smoke. Let it hang there 24 hours, then they'll be well immediately.

No. 63.
To be loved of great lords.
Carry with you a testicle of a rooster, as well as the left claw. But if you want to be loved by everyone, then hang a young magpie heart on your chest.

No. 64.
To wake yourself up from sleeping.
Take as many bayberries as the hours you wish to sleep, put them into a clean cloth and tie them over your crown. Then go to bed and sleep.

No. 65.
To discover secrets in your sleep.
Write these letters in your right hand:
then let it dry. Put your hand under your cheek when you go to sleep.

No. 66.
To drive away thirst.
Take a capon (castrated rooster) that has been a capon for four years, and in his liver is found a clear stone. Put this same stone under your tongue then you won't get thirsty. But then you will be invincible to your enemies.

No. 67.
To make a horse lame.
Take three pieces of old horse-shoe nails, and a nail from a coffin that you have found at the churchyard. Hammer them in the middle of the foot print where the horse has walked, then the horse will be lame until the nails are taken away.

---

[53] All but the last two words of this incantation is composed obviously of a bastardized Latin, mixed in periodically with obvious Swedish words. In time, a suitable reconstruction could be made.

No. 68.
So that you never get sleepy.
If you carry a heart of a raven or a bat on you, then you won't get sleepy until you take them off again.

No. 69.
So that one may get the "ant stone" (the stone from an anthill).
Procure for the ants a rooster's body, then they'll flee and then you can find the ant-stone.

No. 70.
To make a candle that won't go out.
Dip the wick into whetting oil and pour the wax or tallow over it. Then when it is lit, it won't go out, even if you want to throw it into the water in the lake.

No. 71.
To dig up money that is buried.
Take from the communion wine and drip it around where you are standing. When you do that, then throw behind you a knife into the hole again, and then read section 1 from no. 61 as you drip the wine. NB. You may do this if you want, but I pray God to preserve me from using the blessed materials in such a way.

No. 72.
To get a sorceress to fart in church.
Take a wolf's intestine, stand then on a Good Friday in the weapon house, and blow through the intestine. Then the sorceress will roar loudly through the air in church.

No. 73.
To triumph over one's enemies (in court).
Take the heart of a mole and the herb *Selladonia* and tie it inside your clothes, then you can go to court and you will win.

No. 74.
If someone robbed your house.
Then write these words on a piece of cheese and give to the suspect to eat. The one who is guilty will immediately begin to drool out of his mouth: Sator Arepo Tenet Opera rotas: If you want to write these words in such a way that are presented below, it can be recited in several ways. If you read now each line down, then say the first line Sator, the second arepo, the Third Tenet, the fourth opera and the fifth rotas.

S	A	T	O	R
A	R	E	P	O
T	E	N	E	T
O	P	E	R	A
R	O	T	A	S

Recite now from right to left and begin on the lowest line, where it says Sator – arepo – Tenet – Opera and rotas. Be careful that these words are well spelled. But you can also write on a piece of cheese to a suspected thief, after you've written on it Pax Sax max and when he eats the cheese then he'll begin to drool out of his mouth.

No. 75.
To discover buried goods.
Take Merien incense and Hårpex oil and unused wax. Then let a maiden spin a wick before sunrise for a candle. Then dip it. Light and put it in a lantern. When you come to where there are buried goods, then the candle will go out. NB. You should also know that you can often be led astray, because if you come over earth with a lot of iron ore in it, then it will give the same sign that the candle will go out.

No. 76.
To find out who stole stolen goods.
Write these letters written below, and put it under your right side when you sleep. Then you'll dream of the thief.

No. 77.
Another way to know the thief.
Write these letters and put them under the threshold of the door.

No. 78.
To make yourself invisible.
Take a white rooster and put it in a crossroads between two boxes. Let it lie there for three days, and when you dig him up he will be gone; but in stead there will be a Ring, a Stone and a Dice. When you have the dice with you, you'll win at gambling. When you have the ring with you, you are invisible. When you have the stone with you, you will not be penniless.

No. 79.
To get a horse so feisty that no one can steer it.
Give him as much as a pea's size of the so-called *Tolfmannakraft* (Strength of Twelve Men, an herb). But if you want the horse to be more even-tempered, then just spread a little over the meal.

No. 80.
To incline a horse to eat well.
By the following species and mix them in the oats and give to the horse 3 to 4 mornings in a row before he is watered, and ride him slowly so that he stays warm: [*Säfvenbom*], antimony powder, fenugreek, Asafetida, two *öre*'s worth of each.

No. 81.
For scabies on horses.
Buy for 4 *öre* good potash and grind, put it in 1 quart of water and let it sit for 24 hours. Wash the horse with it, and cover the horse with a blanket.

No. 82.
To transfix thieves when they're about to steal.
Take a human skull at the churchyard and borrow it for a certain period of time, and when that time has passed, then bring it back again. This skull is borrowed in the name of the Holy Trinity, and say at the same time what use you will make of it. With this skull go three times around your property, and each time recite the Our Father. When you now come to the place you started, say: As still as this corpse lies, that's as still as you will remain, you thief, who invites himself in to steal, remain here inside this place that I have walked in

a circle around until I myself come to you and give you permission to go. Then bury the skull and recite the Our Father.

No. 83.
When you want to see a will o the wisp.
Take a silver coin and throw it towards the Ghost and say three times: "You may burn in the devil's name, for I have given you coins that you yourself have as long as I want." Then go immediately and take the treasure, remaining silent, until you come home to your house, then you can ask it to go in the Devil's name.

No. 84.
Against those who are enemies without cause.
When you see enemies, then say: I see over you[54] and I see under you, and bind you with the bonds that our Lord Jesus Christ bound all the devils of Hell, and there you shall eat your own flesh and drink your own blood, and let me remain in peace. I N F O S O T H A [In the name of the Father and of the Son and of the Holy Ghost] Jesus Christ X X X be with and over me.

No. 85.
To triumph over one's enemies.
Go silently and wash your hands in the dew in the early morning and say like this: I see you, and you don't see me, all the hate and envy that you bear towards me, I push away from me and to you. In the name of the Father and of the Son and of the Holy Ghost. Amen.

No. 86.
A way to cure falling sickness (epilepsy).
Take the skull of man who is hanging in a gallows, and prepare it to a powder. Give to the patient ½ fifth at a time each day until they find themselves well again. This is given in Lille *Comvalls*-water (a text?). Have then a dining-room-root around the neck, so that it hangs below the chest for 40 weeks.

No. 87.
A way to cure [*frossan*] (feverish shaking or seizures?)
Take a grey stone as big as a goose egg. Put in in the fire so that it gets hot, put it then into a pot of good beer. Then let the patient drink the beer right up, then one will see a wonderful thing.

No. 88.
To transfix wild (animals).

---

54 Cf. English, "to overlook" meaning "to hex."

First, shoot yourself a raven, and take the heart out of him. Put a hole in it large enough so you can see through it. When you see some game, then only look through the heart, then it will stand still as soon as you catch a glimpse of it, which is tested.

No. 89.
To put down a wildfire.
Say like this: Saint Peter and our Lord wandered on a road. Saint Peter spread out his blue cloak. Our Lord Jesus lit a fire on it, and when the fire was over, then the cloak was burned. O! You Good Son of God that stopped that fire: Stop this wildfire as well, in the holy name of God the Father and of the Son and of the Holy Ghost. Amen. Ride or walk around the fire three times and each time recite the Our Father.

No. 90.
A sure cure for wind colic.
Take a spoonful of powdered sulfur in water completely fasting. This is suggested by a Doctor Kjelke.

No. 91.
If the seeds go a little bad.
Take for 3 spoons of sulfur, 3 spoons of salt, 3 spoons of sewing needles; put them in the center of the field, then no one has ability to take the power from the growth. Bury the same outside the seed barn.

No. 92.
For domestic animals that aren't thriving.
Take from nine different kinds of fruit-bearing trees, and cut a shaving from all the door thresholds, and cense the animals for nine days. Then take the yellow from hen's droppings and a little human feces, mix it in pitch and anoint hooves and cloven hooves. Then to give them internally: take 15 spoonfuls of water going against the stream, and 13 with the stream and give them 2 Thursday mornings and one Friday morning. Then take a rooster-chick and bury it alive in that place with the feet up in the air.

No. 93.
A cure for toothache.
Take Vitriol and birch [laka] and grind it together. Then take a broken off birch branch and prick the tooth that aches so that it bleeds. Then take the blood and saliva and mix it into the ground mixture into a dough ball. The patient throws the branch into the fire, and the dough ball is tied up into a cloth. If the pain is in the right side then hang the cloth on the left, but if the pain in on the left, then hang it on the right. *Probatum est.*

No. 94.
For dry ache and gout.
Take goat's blood[55] and black currant leaves, a little of each type, put into clean water and drink as much as a quart in the morning and evening, but not when you've just eaten. Note that the goat's blood should remain moist from evening to morning and vice versa.

No. 95.
For gout and dry ache in another way.
Take three parts marrow fat and one part juniper oil, mix together and apply to the aching limb.

No. 96.
For the same sickness in another way.
Take fresh blood 4 teaspoons, which are boiled for 15 minutes in water, half a quart in a tea kettle, two coffee cups are to be drunk in the evening, but liquor is forbidden.

No. 97.
To cure sheep sicknesses.
Take a thimble-full [*glasgalla*] and crush it fine and mix in into a spoonful of flour and this is given to each sheep. Then take a quart of vinegar and a quart of [*Rös*] oil. Mix together and give to each sheep a spoonful to wash the flour down with. Don't allow them any water that day.

No. 98.
A means of curing the rose (erysipelas).[56]
Take French liquor and venetian soap and make a salve from it and apply to the rose-like place with it.

No. 99.
For pain.
Take ground mustard and put it between two fine cloths and tie over where the ache is, then there will be a blister. Cut a hole in it and then heal the wound with Basil salve.

No. 100.
When people and livestock are sick.
Take the following ingredients and cense them with it. Begin at the nose and then at the middle and then at the end.

---

55 plant or animal?
56 Ros is erysipelas, a streptococcal cellulitis that causes the skin to be red.

Castor, Asafetida, Mastrix, Olibanum, Sulfur, Amber, Black Cumin, Red Coral, *Flyrön* and 9 types of fruit-bearing trees, all of this is put into an oaken pail and is used to cense them.

No. 101.
For scabies on sheep.
Crush gunpowder and old fat and apply it. NB: all the wool should be clipped off.

No. 102.
A recipe/prescription to buy for horses.
Asafetida, fenugreek, bayberries, [*Forbium*], yellow sulfur, grey sulfur and verdigris, 2 *öre* of each for 12 horses. Boiled in a drink and is given to each horse, one glass full. *Probatum est.*

No. 103.
So that a horse will become fat and put on weight in 14 days.
At 4 o'clock in the morning it is given drink, and two hours after that he should be given two hand-fulls of ground peas, then again at 12 o'clock and the same at 2 o'clock and at 4 o'clock in the afternoon he is given drink again, and at 8 o'clock in the evening he is given 2 hand-fulls of peas and continue with that for 14 days, then he will soon get fat.

No. 104.
To get a good memory.
Take 2 spoons of wine, three spoons of cottonseed oil, 4 of the same of Rutewater, and 4 of the same of winterflower water. With good, strong manure. Mix it together and bathe for a whole year once each week, then you will retain in your memory all that you hear and read.

No. 105.
To get long hair.
Boil hops roots in water and wash yourself with it, then you will quickly get very beautiful and long hair, and no worms will come out of it.

No. 106.
For lice.
Spread "*Desman*" on the clothes, then the lice will turn away, this works also for cloth. Another, Camphor in the clothes is also good both against lice and against sorcery. Or sew a corpse bone into the clothing.

No. 107.
So that bees won't sting you.
Take three or four [spetsört]⁵⁷ leaves in your mouth, then you'll be sure not, and will go amongst them without danger.

No. 108.
To recite when one goes out in the morning.
I go out today with the power and strength of Jesus, all who will meet me today shall fall at my feet. All of them who would stand against me will go with me. All who want to hate me, God will set them with bindings around their hands, chains around the feet and fetters about the roots of their tongues.

No. 109.
To recite in the morning.
I, NN, rise up today, and go towards mine enemies, all those who want to be against me, they shall fall down in mind and bravery. The Jews fell against Jesus, and they must now fall to his feet, when in the Garden he sweated blood, I put my foot on the black earth with my hair and weight, I give myself into the Lord's control.

No. 110.
Go to a water spring that runs from east or north, and place yourself over it as you recite these words and turn yourself towards the east: I look to the east and see three burning villages and 3 mixed skies, I see Saint Peter and I see Saint Paul and I see Saint Nickolaus and I see the Virgin Mary. She is the enemy, who has the seed of peace in her womb. She can still the wrath between NN and me, and NN will be to me so protective, and faithful and pleasant, as the Virgin Mary was to her blessed son where he was on the cross. NN's mind shall so melt before as snow before the Sun and Fire before water.

No. 111.
If you want to triumph over someone at court.
Then say: I look over you, NN, with 6 eyes. The two are mine, the 2 are yours, the two are the Devil's in Hell. You, NN, will be silent before me in the Devil's name, and I shall speak before you in the Devil's name.

No. 112.
To get the riches girl to love you.
Take a Hazelnut and put it in a box that has been prepared with many small holes bored in both the top and the bottom. Put the box in an anthill and let it sit for 24 hours. Then take it from there, and then you'll find two bones, the

---

57 This could be a type of rosemary (pointy herb leaves) or some other.

one looking like a Hay Hook, and the other looking like a pitchfork. If you want the girl to come to you, if it is evening or nighttime, go out under the bare sky, and carry the bone three times towards you in the air from where the girl lives, and name her both by her Christian name and her last name each time quietly with these words *Lami Poli Koli*, then she won't have any peace until she comes to where you arrange. If you want to do some monkeyshines with her, then take the other bone shaped like a pitchfork and push it three times away from you in the air towards the place she lives and say her name three times each time, and these words: *Go back, Go back, I have nothing to say to you*. Then she'll turn around.

No. 113.
About love, in another way.
Take a bat, stab it in the heart with a awl under the left wing, then there will come out three drops of blood. Let them drop on a clean handkerchief, but don't allow it to be washed. Dry the girl in the face with the handkerchief, and within a half hour she will become fond.

No. 114.
Ditto in another way.
Take a snake and take its stinger from it. Let it dry really hard. Take it then in your mouth and kiss a girl, she may be never so rich or beautiful, as long as you kiss her hand or her mouth then she will become fond of you.

No. 115.
Ditto in another way.
Take notice when a rooster mates with a hen, and when you think the mating is happening, then sneak up quickly and takes [sic] out one of the long feathers in the males rump. With this feather you stroke three times on a woman's dress, but silently of course, and in a half an hour thereafter she will be fond.

No. 116.
If you want to know whether a farmgirl is a virgin or not.
Take the dust from the pizzle of a stallion and put it into a drinking vessel and give a girl to drink. If she is not a virgin, then she will pee immediately. But if you want to see which girls in a group are virgins or not, then take a dead bat and put it into a garbage pail and put it at the threshold of the door, and let the girls walk over it, all of those who now are not virgins will immediately pee.

No. 117.
To win at the lottery.
You go to the churchyard and borrow a human skull with these words: *I ask you my brother in Christendom or sister if you are, that here rest these bones, in the*

name of the Holy Trinity, G F O S O T H A (in the name of God the Father and of the Son and of the Holy Ghost), that I may borrow your head for three nights, which I shall bring back at the same time and place. And I order you my brother or sister in Christendom, that upon the third night to come and tell me what numbers will come up in the Royal Number Lottery (such and such a date, such and such a position). Then, take the skull and put it under the head piece of your bed and the third night the dead one will come and will want his or her head back. Then you say to the corpse: *Tell me first the numbers that I order you, then you shall have your head brought back.* Then he will say all five numbers, and then you have to have a piece of board on top of the blanket and a piece of chalk, and as quickly as the corpse says the numbers then write them up. But no light can be lit, and then the dead one will leave, and after that you take back the head to its place again.

No. 118.
To make yourself invisible.
Go to a tree in which a raven has built a nest, climb up the tree and take a raven chick and kill it and tie a thread around its feet and hang it onto a branch. Then get down from the tree and watch. When the raven comes back and sees its chick hanging, he will yell and scream and will want to have the chick loose, for she kind of is shy to have her chick hanging up to its shame. When she now sees no other way, she will fly away and will be away for 24 hours, and when she comes back again, she will have a stone that she stuffs into the beak of the chick so that no one will see it. Put a sheet under and around the tree, for since the chick can't hold the stone in its beak, it will fall down. Take the stone and hold it in your mouth, then you are invisible.

No. 119.
To see a thief in a water bucket.
Fill a water bucket full of water, especially running water. Then put three strong jackknives very firmly in a triangle under the bottom of the bucket. Then take a toad, tie a long thread about all four legs and fasten the thread to all three of the knives. Then take a bat and put 4:- crowns worth of mercury in it. Put it in the water. It will sink to the bottom. Then put a fork in the left wing and into the bottom of the bucket and then put two hay-straws in a cross over the edge of the bucket. Then light a candle; but no more than one candle should be lit. Then drop three drops of grease on each side of the cross; but all of this should be done while keeping silent. Then you will see precisely the same thief who has robbed [you].

No. 120.
To conjure forth a thief.
First, in the waning moon, whether summer or winter, you take a snake skin,

then take the heart out of a porcupine, which is hacked to pieces together with basilisk[58]-gall, and fill the snake skin with it. Spread a little Cartinel-seeds and mercury in it. Sew the hole together, even the end. Bury it in the earth and leave it for 3 nights under a linden tree. Remove it again and hang it up, and in this way it will be borne back.

No. 121.
To conjure forth a dead person from the earth.
If you was to do some trickery[59] with a corpse, then you take a little earth from the churchyard from a grave. Tie it into a little piece of cloth with a long thread attached. Then go into the air over the place where the dead one's corpse lies. Bore a hole and tie a knot down on the corpse's chest. Haul up the knot very slowly, then the corpse will rise. Do it several times, raising and lowering the corpse again.

But if you want to conjure either a dead mother or father or whatever relative you choose even if they've lain in the earth for twenty years, then you go out in the evening out the door and take a bit of chalk and write the dead one's baptismal and common name over the door, as well as over all the doors that enter the house. Then put a jack-knife between the names over each door and then the Latin with Hebrew: Comotote Prili Sali. Two hours thereafter the dead one will come and place themselves inside the door of the house. But no one should speak to them. And when the dead one has stayed a little while, then you go out and take the jack-knife out and strike out the Latin and Hebrew. Then you go inside and cast [spräng]-seeds and mercury all over the dead one, remaining silent. Then the dead one will depart.

No. 122.
If the cows are milking blood.
If the cow milks blood or is otherwise sick, then buy the following from the Apothecary: Asafetida, Castoreum, [säfvenbom], lovage, [flyrön], onions, garlic, sulfur, "Hell's Blisters and [spräng]-seeds for 1:- sek each. Then take a little of each and cense the cow under the belly, but put a cover over it so the smoke can get in close to the body. When this is done, take a little of each and bury it under the cattle-shed threshold, and give the cow a tarred[60] herring and a half a fistful of salt. A half and hour afterwards give it some water and some fodder. A half an hour after that, milk the cow, and there will be only blood, and that you should throw on the threshold. Then chop with an axe 3 crosses in the blood and let the axe remain stuck in the last cross. A half an hour after

---

58 The Basilisk is a mythical creature, said most often to be in the shape of a snake. What might be referred to here then is ormgalla, *anguis fragilis*.
59 Sw. *apespel*, monkeyshines, high-jinx, tomfoolery, trickery.
60 Sw. *tjärad*, tarred, with pitch from a tree, some way of preserving herring?

that, milk it again, and it isn't quite so full of blood, then chop three crosses as before. But a half hour after that if you milk it, it will be pure milk.

No. 123.
To get strength.
Take a little of each of the following: Asafetida, Castor, [Säfvenbom], [Flyrön], lovage, Roof-leek, Water-leek, garlic, mercury, sulfur, Hell's Blisters, [Spräng]-seeds, a snake's stinger,[61] a piece of human bone. This you should carry under your chin. It provides not only strength, but gives luck in gambling and keeps away contagious diseases and lice.

NB. You should always have garlic in your pocket in case you run into someone who wants to try your strength, then take a little garlic in your mouth and chew. Then breathe and then another bit in the mouth. If he is not so strong, then he will immediately lose his strength and you will be stronger than he.

NB. If you sew in a bat's heart in your sweater-sleeve, then you will be strong to fight.

NB. If you are out traveling, then you can get together with those who want to have a race with you. Then you should always have a bit of Asafetida on you and apply a bit to the nostrils of the horse, then you will drive the race, and the others will not be able to pass you, because when they come up even with your horses, then they get a whiff of the odor of Asafetida. This takes the strength away from the other horses, just as garlic makes it so the one can strangle the strength of the other.

NB. Put a bat's heart with it is still living into a tool of whatever sort, and cover it with a plug, then anything you wish to do with that tool will be successful. I have tried this myself. I put it into a writing pen which I never used except in certain writing efforts.

No. 124.
To be sure in shooting as well as whatever.
Ask a woman who has a daughter who has not had her period before,[62] if you can have a piece of her undershirt that there is blood on. Put it under the altarcloth in the church and let it lie for three High Holidays.[63] Then take it and carry it on your body, then it is assured to you that no bullet will harm you.

No. 125.
To have luck in hunting wild game.
You take a living snake and put it over the ammunition in the shotgun and

---

61 Could be ormgall[a], in which case *Anguis fragilis*
62 I.e., from context this is her first menses.
63 Sw. Högtidsdagar, High Holidays, i.e., not just three Sundays.

then shoot the shot off in the air. If you want to hex a shotgun, you take it in your hand and glare into the muzzle with crossed eyes, and turn your back to the other whose shotgun it is, and spit three times quietly. To make a hexed shotgun good again, you always have a dead bat on you with which you trace three times around the muzzle, then it will shoot sure again.

No. 126.
To get an entire room filled with snakes.
Take a snake stinger and light a candle and put it away in a corner and place yourself in front of the candle so that it doesn't shine too brightly in the room. Then hold the snake stinger and singe it well – the longer you singe it, the more snakes will be seen there, and so that they creep on the walls and in people's clothing. But as soon as [you] take the stinger from the candle, you won't see anything.

No. 127.
To get an entire room filled with snakes in another way.
You take a living snake and put it into a pot, and pour oil and whale oil on it, and cover it well with a cover. Cook it long enough so that all the flesh is cooked off in the whale oil, and the backbone of the snake is left. In a clean lamp with a clean wick, use this oil to light it, and the room will appear to be filled with snakes. Or melt a little tallow and cook a living snake in it. Fill the lamp with the tallow and the same will happen, but you can't have another light lit.

No. 128.
To heal rabies
Burn as much juniper so that you can get a quarter measure's full of the ashes into a tin can. Then take a pitcher of strong beer, mix the ashes in it, pour it into two seltzer bottles. Cork them well and bury them in the earth for 24 hours. Then drink one or two glasses a day, then you will be healthy in 14 day's time, as long as no other strong drink is consumed during this time.

No. 129.
For Gout and Pain.
During the summer, take a pound full of earthworms. Put them in a white bottle. Hang it on a wall towards the sun, and an hour afterwards it will just be oil. Strain it into another bottle. Then take a pound of ants, pour a quart of liquor on them, and a half a quart [förtårar] as well as 4:- crowns of soap balsam. Hang it also in a white bottle in the sun, then there will also be an oil. Mix these oils together and apply to the limbs which have pain. Warm it two times a day, then you'll be healthy in 4 or 5 weeks.

No. 130.
A method against toothache.
Cut 9 pieces off of an old broom, and make them pointed in one end. Then take a bit of old rancid meat that is fatty. When the teeth hurt the worst, prick with the pieces from the broom so that it begins to bleed. Stick the broom pieces into the piece of meat and go silently to a fruit-bearing tree. But you may not ever return to that tree.

No. 131.
A method against all sickness.
Take 12 handfulls of white oats and wash them well and clean so that the slime comes off. Then take 6 kettles of fresh water and a handful of fresh chicory roots, [*nitrialmoniæ*] 6 measures, and red sandalwood 1 measure. Cook it all together in a covered pot until it is reduced to half, but you have to stir it often so that it retains its red clarity. When it is reduced, you take it off and strain it several times through a fine cloth. Mix it then with fine powdered sugar, so that it will be mildly sweet. Pour it into seltzer bottles, bury them in the earth for 24 hours. Then drink one or two glasses per day, then it will keep off sickness and helps for all sicknesses, and that, with God's help, in all certainty, and you will reach a ripe old age.

No. 132.
A treatment against jaundice.
Take a large carrot, hollow it out and pee into it so it is full. Then hang it in the chimney and smoke it for three days. Then drink of the piss, and eat up the root. Do this several times, and then you will be free of your jaundice.

No. 133.
A treatment against deafness.
Put a Spanish Fly in back of your ear, and keep it there for 8 days with warm footbaths from boiled hay stalks. Then stick a hole in the ears,[64] and put lead rings in them. Dip a little piece of black sheep's wool in almond- and scorpion oil, and put a little camphor with some hay seeds into the wool and put into each ear, then you will get your hearing again.

No. 134.
A treatment against water sickness.
Take a water snake or a green snake that keeps itself in the water. Tie a long twine about its tail and hang it up in a tree with the head lowermost. Then put a large water dish under the head with a quart of water in it, but fix it so that

---

64 Not clear from context whether this is a hole through the actual eardrum, or a hole in the ear lobes into which can be fit two lead rings.

the green snake or snake isn't hanging too high away from the dish. When it has hung there for two hours and vomited and writhed, then he'll be so weak that he will spit up a stone into the dish, and that stone will soak up all the water that is in the dish. Take that stone and put it on the sick one's stomach, then that stone will soak up all the unhealthy water from the sick one, and the sick one will be free and healthy from the water sickness.

No. 135.
A toadstone that is useful for the eyes and pain in the body, as well as for stomach cramps, as well as having that property that it will give notice if poison is in food or drink.
Take a toad and put it in a bird cage. Go up and down with the cage, and hang it in a window where the sun shines and hang a piece of red scarlet cloth over the cage. Let the cage hang with the toad until it grows faint from the heat. Then put a bowl or dish under the cage, and when the toad becomes so weakened from dryness inwardly, it will spit up a stone that will then fall into the dish. Then take that and save it. Now, whenever anyone becomes ill, then let the sick one hold the stone under his arm for 4 hours, then he will be free of his illness, whatever sickness it was. If you have the stone set into a gold ring for your finger, then it will immediately notify if there is poison in the room, in food or drink, because then it will sweat and grow moist immediately. The closer it comes to the poison, the wetter is becomes until finally it will drip. A prince in Paris saved himself with such a stone.

No. 136.
To know what my wife or any other does outside my presence.
When you want to travel away, you clip a little from a dog's ear and a cat, and a pig, and if there are several doors to enter your house, then take the fourth ear of a hare. Fasten one ear over each door with a horse shoe that has been in use on a stallion. Write then a cross with red chalk inside over the door, and when you leave, leave backwards. When you leave, don't look back, and in this way you will promptly be able to ask what has happened while you have been away. But it should happen during the waning moon. When you come home, if it your wife, then greet her and say: *I haven't been gone long, my best friend.* Then you will be answered: *I have had much uneasiness while you were away.*, but you don't answer that, but rather remain silent. Then you go out and take down from the doors all that you have put there before, and hide them for another time. And in this way you can do it as often as you want. Notice when you come home, you walk in backwards.

No. 137.
If children cry too much during the night or otherwise have been attacked by a stream sprite [*kommit för bäckaskarn*].[65]
Take three English sewing needles, 3 ends of sulfur matches and three coarse salt grains. Put them into a cloth and take a stick of tinder or touchwood. Light it on fire and hold against the other. Take it three times around the sick one silently. Then go immediately to a stream, turn yourself around and throw it over your left shoulder into the stream with these words: *Play now with this, and play no longer with NN.* Then go home silently.

No. 138.
In another way.
If one finds themselves uneasy of mind, and they know how they became so, then scrape a shaving from all the metals that are in the house. Gold, silver, copper, brass, ore, tin, lead, iron, and steel, a shaving of each of the thresholds, a bit of saliva and spoons, of bowls, dishes, from the whisp, from the broom. Then let the sick go himself to the place, and when he arrives there, then he says as he spreads out all these shavings into the stream: *Play now with this in the Devil's name, and let me have peace in the name of God the Holy Trinity.* And then they will be well.

No. 139.
To stop wildfire.
Write the following letters on a shaving and cast it into the fire:

When the shaving is thrown into the fire, you run three times around the fire and say: *As truly as the Lord lives and has created Heaven and Earth, so also this wild fire will stop and stand still. In the name of God the Father and of the Son and of the Holy Ghost, amen.*

No. 140.
So that no one will speak against you at judgement or court.
If you want no one to speak against you at judgement or in court, then take the tongue of a viper and put it under your right foot while you hear 9 mass-

---

65 Sw. *bäckaskarn*. Bäck is the stream, so this is a water spirit of a lesser rank than the *näck*?

es. Thereafter carry it with you and these four words: *Galatt atte Homig ar att amen, and you, Jesus Christ, do have mercy upon me, my soul and my body, from the Devil and all the force and power of my enemies, amen.*

No. 141.
To stop bleeding in people and livestock, just if one knows the name of the person, or if its livestock, to know the type and the color.
Recite this verse: *Our Lord Jesus Christ's blood, that stopped Noah's flood. He stops the bleeding of NN in three Holy names, God the Father and God the Son and God the Holy Ghost, the blood will flow just as much as I will spin on the sabbath, in three Holy names. God the Father and the Son and the Holy Ghost.* Now recite the Our Father. This prayer is recited 3 times and each time is followed by the Our Father.

No. 142.
To win at gambling.
Take a toad's eye and tie it on you, then you will win as much as you want to bet.

No. 143.
If thieves stole from you or from someone else.
Go a Thursday evening to a running stream or river, that runs from north to south, and take a coin in your hand and throw it in the water and say: I conjure you water from the north and earth from the north and Belsebub of Hell with all your company, that you now take this coin, which is now given in order that you allow that person to never have peace or rest until he has brought back that which he has stolen from NN, who is a Godly person. In nomina Patris Filius Et Spiritus Sancte Amen.

No. 144.
If a thief stole from you or someone else.
Take three glowing coals and put them in a [*handkvarn*] (hand-mill; mortar?), and grind three times over and around counterclockwise, and say: *Just as I drag this mill around counterclockwise, so too do I drag the thief back who has stolen from NN. justly as the traitor Judas who sold his master our dear Savior Jesus Christ for 30 pieces of silver, and he justly bore the same money back again, so shall you, damned person and thief who took goods from NN and has robbed them; with shame and timidity return them back again, or this curse will be and will attack you as is written in King David's Psalm 109.* This is done in the morning before the sun comes up, on an empty stomach.

ADDITION

No 1.
If you want steel very soft and weak so that you can engrave in it like lead.
No 2.
To work Gold ore.
No 3.
To alloy Iron with Tin.
No 4.
If you want to alloy silver, copper, iron ore or brass with tin.
No 5.
To "tinify" raw iron.
No 6.
The art of making spurs with tin.
No 7.
Plating fine things with tin, and on things that are rusty, which you are unable to clean up with a file.
No 8.
Button-makers plate their iron button with tin in such a way...
No 9.
Corset makes plant with brass like the brass buttons in the same way.

No 1.
Black [Fernissa] for wagons and other such iron works.
No 2.
Fernis against rust for iron, steel and copper.
No 3.
Fernissa for thread, iron thread, ...
No 4.
To prepare your own linseedoil fernissa...

To write white letters on black paper.

To write something that can only be read over a fire.

To smith clockbells.
Tamback, made of copper and brass.
About Tin.

THE END

MS 7

MANUSCRIPT LUF. A. 285
BLACK ART BOOK FROM GLIMÅKRA PARISH, SKÅNE

1. To silence a shotgun.
Come, devil and all the evil spirits that are in the abyss and keep stone and fire from the gunpowder in the evil one's own name.

2. To release the gunpowder to burn.
Jesus Christ has ordained that all shall burn on the last day, just as truly shall the gunpowder burn in this shotgun. Spiritus silo santo on klare.

3. To be able to shoot whatever one wants.
Shoot a raven, take his heart and burn it to ashes; mix it in the gunpowder, in this way you can enjoin to shoot whatever you desire and no one shall be able to "spoil" (hex) your shotgun.

4. When the shotgun is "spoiled" (hexed).
Take a viper's head and put it in the barrel, then no one can do anything to it,

Or:
Take apart the shotgun and take black crow chicks, take the one kidney from one, as well as a little asafetida[66] and a little bit of graveyard dirt and polish the iron on the day with the Sun goes in Sp P J h. Thereafter no one is able to hex the shotgun.

6. To silence gunpowder.
Say: Out of your shotgun it will never go to hiss, the Evil One himself he shall stand in the abyss. And I order you upon all these powers that you shall silence both fire and powder so that nothing goes out.

7. To stop bleeding.
Jesus Christ stood on the green earth and bandaged his five wounds. Thus do I bind the wound on you N. N. in the Father's and the Son's and the Holy Ghost's name. Amen.

---

66 A particularly malodorous substance used in demonic conjurations.

8. Another way:
I order that the blood on you, N. N. stops as the water in the Red Sea stopped. In God the father's, God's Son's and God's Holy Ghost's name. Amen.

Or:
It happened in a blessed moment that Jesus came out of Mary's embrace. He freed us from the eternal death, and suffered with his dear bloody wounds, so assuredly as this is true, so stanch this blood in the name of the Father, the Son and the Holy Ghost.

9. To win at card-games
Take a "*tocka*-eye" and bind it on you, then you will win as much as you want to bet.

Or:
10. Take a hazelnut and have it on you, then you'll always win.

Or:
11. I order you, Bälsebub, that you keep yourself to my right hand, so that no one may take the winnings from me except what I bet, and they who bet everything against me may belong to me, in the Father's, the Son's and The Holy Ghost's name. (A prayer that is read three times if it is going to have any effect.)

12. <u>To anæsthetize snakes</u>. (pacify, calm)
You cursed snake, who broke Adam's command in Paradise, here you shall meet me! Bl.! Take in this way a year-old hazel staff and write a circle on the ground and put the staff in the middle of the circle. Then, at the ringing of the church bells the snake is there. And then you take the staff and stab it with it. It is a sure method.

13. <u>For boils or abscesses</u>.
Take the remains of a [sålata], and rub with them vigorously, then they will disappear quickly.

14. <u>Against wrath/rage</u>.
I look over you and I see under you N. N. and over you all with the bindings that Jesus Christ bound all the evil spirits of the abyss. And they shall eat your body and drink your blood and let me be in peace in Spritus silo sankte Amen. Recite this three times when there is danger.

15. <u>To anæsthetize a toothache</u>:
This ache will turn away and stand still as a testimony in the abyss. They know

right and wrong. On these words you shall have no power over N. N. in the name of the Father, of the Son and the Holy Ghost.

16. For "*kåller*" (cholera?)
to write on a paper and have the sick one ingest:

    abra cybbra   cola bry

    abra cybb   cola br

    abra cyb   cola b

    abra cy   cola

    abra c   col

    abra   co

    abr   c

    ab

    a

17. For "*fråssa*"

    Bylmankii

    Bylmanki

    Bylmank

    Bylman

    Bylma

    Bylm

    Byl

    By

    B.

18. To put the fire to bed.
Run three times, backwards around the fire and write the following letters on an oak chip/shaving and throw it through the fire: A. B. O. M. I 2 2. D. 1 2 s d s s 1 B A.T. P.E. B.S. E.R. T.A. N. When the shaving is thrown, say the following words: as truly as the Lord lives and has created heaven and earth, so shall this fire stay in the name of the Father, of the Son, and of the Holy Ghost's name. Amen.

19. To restore stolen goods:
Write these words on a piece of cheese: In Belsebub's name and that one you now believe, give them to eat. If he is guilty, then he can't eat it up, but rather remains and asks with his mouth like a raging snake. These are:

D e e a j v a x t a s m a.

20. To make oneself strong.
Take a bottle of wine and cork it very well and put it in an anthill on a Maundy Thursday morning. Let it stay until Good Friday night after that, and drink it up.

21. To bring hostility between man and woman.
Write over the door these words: a.x.e.o.b.

22. Carry a heart of a bird with a feather-crest on one, then you will wrestle well.

23. Take the blood of a skate, then you'll win that woman you like.

Or:

24. Take a tongue of a swallow and place it under your tongue and when you kiss a girl then she will not jilt you.

MS 8

LUF A.795:26–31
MAGISKA FORMLER OCH MAGISKA HANDLINGAR
DIVERSA ANTECKNINGAR
*MAGICAL INCANTATIONS AND MAGICAL PROCEDURES
DIVERSE NOTATIONS*

PAGE 1.

Nr. 38 Another method:
If you are a male then to a mare's skeleton; if you are a woman, then to a stallion's skeleton, and knock a tooth out of the head, either one of the foremost or known teeth, but it should be from a real head of a [*Raken*]. On the same side top or bottom as that that you yourself have pain in. That tooth that you shall use, bind it with a thread when you come home or sew it into a cloth on it. The thread that that (sic) the tooth --- the sewing needle is out --- so that it hangs down --- and tested m --- you want to carry the tooth, hang it around the throat --- as long as it hangs ---.

Nr. 39 Another method:
--- prepare with it the --- bleeds hit --- or a tree that ---

PAGE 2.

Think about coming close, then you will hardly ever again get a tooth ache in your lifetime. Is tested by many.

Nr. 10 Another method
Mix together equal parts of each, namely one or a bunch of white tartar oil and and one or a bunch of white amber oil. When you or someone else need help, then take some new, virgin cotton. Drop into it three drops of the previously named oil, and put it outside that tooth you have pain in, then the pain will go away before a short time, and you shall hardly get it any more. It is tested and --- few would be that you know --- then use the same ---. --- then take three live coals in the devil's --- es of white around --- and recite in the devil's --- Devils, that --- there would come to the one --- my stolen goods --- es it neither --- peace until he ---

PAGE 3.

Nr. 21 Take afterwards the blood of a [*pcke*] and spread it around your eyes, then you will see at night just as you do in the daytime.

Nr. 22 Take the blood of a magpie and then come in to a girl. Then she will say to you whether she is a virgin, and everything that she has done, bad or good.

Nr. 23 So that witches won't have power over you, write these figures on a piece of paper on a Sunday morning.[67]
Need Prayer
Our Lord Jesus Christ be with you, Jesus Christ is the true blessedness, Jesus Christ lament me. Jesus Christ loosens the bonds of Death. Jesus Christ is a present sign. Jesus show me the right way to all virtues, in your holy name I walk all my paths. Jesus Christ teach me, and teach me all good. Jesus Christ takes from me all suffering and trouble. Jesus Christ (faith-)healing eyes watch over me and before me and be on all sides, that they and all my enemies may see you for me when they see me. Jesus Christ the Nazarene and the King of the Jews be mindful of me and hear me. Jesus Christ, son of the living God, who was crucified --- bless me and help me and lead me in your --- and blessedness God may blame me. Jesus Christ keep me and turn from me all evil in the name of God --- and of the Son and of the Holy Spirit. That which is Holy shall shine over me in heaven, when God, he shall come with his judgment. Ammen (sic).

V. So that no one shall curse you.
Carry these words with you, Rabrox Sabox Welarf

PAGE 12.

V. To stanch blood.
Jesus stood on the green earth
And bound his five wounds, that
I bind as well this wound on N.N.
That it shall not fester or swell.
Nor to run, rather to stand still
In r6+ Father and Son and the Holy Spirit's name. Amen.
Untried and sure.

V. Another
I stanch your blood as the Lord Christ stanched the water in the River Jordan.

---

67 There are figures missing in the manuscript at this point.

The water was dammed and the blood was stanched, in the name of the Father and the Son and of the Holy Spirit, hand ons and ... mice...(?)

To bind a snake.
Cut a hazel staff on a Sunday morning, and write a ... around the snake and say: "Lie, you snake, into Jesus the Nazarene. I exhort you by the honor of God's majesty, that you not go outside of this circle, in the name of the father and of the Son and of the Holy Spirit, Amen.

To conjure out a snake.
Take a hazel staff, and scribe a circle, and put the staff in the circle, and say then "Here you shall meet me, in this hour in the Father's name" and say "in the same time, and in this circle you will remain lying." When you have killed it and walk away from it, then say "Now I walk away from here in the name of God."

To Blunt a blade.
"You shall not bite into skin or bone, more than a mouse can on an earthfast stone, the edge of K. K." and stroke the edge away from you with the three fingers.

To "lower" or suppress a girl.
Take a nail from a grave and some dirt. Take it in all the names, put it into where a girl has peed while it is still warm, and say thereupon "Teeth and Tongue, Mouth and Bonedust."

PAGE 8

And short life, and strengthen the power and will and all that is within them, and that is on them and always in the name of God the father and of the Son and of the Holy Spirit. I.H.S.X.X.X. our Lord Jesus he said to his disciples peace be with you. The same holy and strong peace illuminate and wish now and forever over this person of God N: N: and forbid all witchcraft and all evil spirits and mischief that never after this day shall any injure this person of God N: N:, in any way more than a mouse can injure an earthfast stone, and by these powerful words of God and holy exhortations that are now recited shall this person of God N.N. have good wholeness in his body and body, inside and outside, joy and wholeness and peace Tide and Time outside and in, in all the days of my life, in the name of God the father, and of the Son and of the Holy Spirit, Amen. I.H.S.X.X.X.

PAGE 9.

N. 32. <u>If your shotgun is hexed</u>.
Get up on a Sunday morning before the sun comes up. Go out into the woods silently. Take there 9 types of fruit-bearing trees, but you must know where the trees stand, so that you don't have to look for them, namely, rowan, pear, oak, beech, juniper, hawthorn. Lay these on an earthfast stone and light a fire there. Put the shotgun and all your hunting supplies through the fire, and walk yourself through it.

N. 33. <u>For thievery</u>.
Take a mustard mill and put a glowing coal in the eye in the names of all Devils, and say: "Just as this mill glows around with a glowing coal."

MS 9

SVARTKONSTBOK FROM MO, RÅDOM, VÄSTNORRLANDS LÄN, LAPPLAND
LUF, MSS A, B, C, COLLECTION C. W. VON SYDOW

MANUSCRIPT A

I. To staunch blood.
Joshua 3:16

1. The Artery
Stay, stay, stand blood on the man [the woman]. In this way did Noah's flood when Jesus Christ stood before it. As surely shall your blood stay as the Red Sea stood for all the true, in the the three holy persons' name: God the father's the Son's and the Holy Spirit's name stay, stay, stay blood for the man [the woman].
– A. Larsson, Graninge.

2. N. N.[68] the blood stays, the blood stills as Christ stopped the River Jordan in the Father's Son's and the Holy Spirit's names.

3. N. N. stop and stay the person's [animal's] blood as Christ stopped the water of the River Jordan. Our Lord stopped the person's [animal's] blood in the

---

68 N.N. is always the baptismal name or Christian Name.

name of the Father and of the Son and of the Holy Spirit.
– P. Höglund, 73 years, Holm, Medelpad.

4. I stop your red blood N. N. with God's power and help. As Christ, when he stretched his staff over the River Jordan and said: Stay, river, Stay river, so say I: Stay blood, stay blood, stay blood in the name of the Father and of the Son and of the Holy Spirit.
– Lars Henriksson, Vestby, Hellgum.

5. Blood shall stay in N. N. like the water stayed in the River Jordan, when the children of Israel went over it in the name of the father and of the son and of the holy spirit.
– Hulda Holm, 23 years, Näset, Ragunda.

6. N. N. The red blood, that ran, shall stop in the stem in the name of the father and of the son and of the holy spirit.

7. N. N. Stay and stop the person's [animal's] blood; stay at rest in the three holy names of the father and of the son and of the Holy Spirit. Recite three times the "Our Father" and "Benediction" three times.[69]
– Erik Gärdin, 80 years, Järkvittsle, Indalsliden.

II. Bleeding from the Nose and Wounds

8. Halt, blood and stay artery, Suffer to run as a woman spins on a Saturday. Halt blood and stay artery in the three names of God Father Son and Holy Spirit.
– Edvard Svedberg, 60 years, Bodasåg, Lidensboda.

9. N. N. I stop your blood, stay in the stem/trunk in the name of God the Father and of the Son and of the Holy Spirit.

10. N. N. Stay artery and stop blood as Christ stopped the river. The Blood will run no more. Jesus shall force it to be soon, through three names of God the Father, of the Son and of the Holy Spirit.
– P. Höglund.

---

[69] The "Fader vår" is the Lord's Prayer, and the Benediction "The Lord bless you and keep you, the lord make his face to shine upon you and be gracious unto you, the Lord lift up his countenance upon you and give you peace. Amen."

Pulse artery

11. N. N. Stay blood, stay blood, stay blood in the holy name of God the father, son and holy spirit.

12. N. N. Blood shall stay in the holy name of God the father the son and the holy spirit.

13. Just as when Jesus stopped his bleeding, so too do I stop my bleeding in the name of God the father and of the son and of the Holy Spirit. (when one has chopped or cut oneself.)

14. With three names I stay your bleeding N. N. as Noah stopped the flood with three names: God the father the son and the holy Spirit.

15. N. N. stay blood, and stop blood, just as Christ when we stopped the pain and bleeding in the Garden, in the name of God the Father, of the Son and of the Holy Spirit.
– Lappkvinnan Margareta Nordström, 67 years, Graninge.

16. Johannes went down to the beach and struck with his staff into the ocean, and the water stood still in the name of God the Father and of the Son and of the Holy Spirit. "Our Father" three times and "The Benediction" three times.
– during the time that you recite these you should point to the north star with your index finger.
– E. Gärdin.

17. You chop (with an axe) on the north side into the root of a standing healthy tree and recite: I saw a Satan who sat in Hell, who smeared his shoe with blood. 1 name. 2 names. 3 names. God the Father, the Son and the Holy Spirit. – then the bleeding will stop.
[Two years ago I met a 50 year old reindeer Saami – P. G. Larsson – in Skyttmon, Jämtland. He taught himself in this way to staunch blood from a Finn. When one read this conjuration, one should think about the one who has injured themself.]

18. Take that object whatever it might be with which you have chopped [cut, torn] yourself with, and wrap it about as you bind the injured limb, and the blood will cease to flow.

19. When you stop bleeding, you should have your right thumb between your teeth – if it's for a married man – and the right index finger, if it for an unmarried man. For a married woman it's the left thumb, which is held between the teeth, and for an unmarried woman it is the left index finger. The finger is held between the teeth as one recites.

To take away Pain

Both for inner and outer pain. One recites in water or liquor and washes the place where the pain is, or takes it internally when it deals with inner pain.

I. Pain in general

1. Your pain, N. N., shall stop in the holy names of God the Father, the Son and the Holy Spirit.

2. N. N. Petrus and Johannes went forth on their way, and there sat a man by the road and begged. Silver and gold have I not, but your pain I stop between two sharp rocks, where no one rows and no one dwells, in the name of God the Father, and the Son and the Holy Spirit.
– E. Gärdin

3. N. N. I stop your *rensel*[70] of whatever type it may be. Stop, you rensel, stay you rensel, stay you rensel just as it stops in hell on Sunday morning in the name of God the Father, and the Son and the Holy Spirit.
[To be recited either in water or liquor and anointed or drunk. One can also recite it at the painful place when one spits three times and smears it over.]

4. The Virgin Mary went forth on her way, then she met her son Jesus. Where are you headed? asked Jesus. I'm going to the farmers farm to break bones and blood. You shall immediately go back in the three holy names: God the Father, the Son and the Holy Spirit
[recite this three times over the painful place; spit three times and smear it over, then the pain will cease soon. This is a sure thing. Guaranteed. Observe: This is only for those who believe, but not for the unbeliever.] . – E. Gärdin.

5. N. N. The Virgin Mary went to the cemetery to stop *rensel*, smarting pain and ache. The Ache shall go numb, man and woman shall fall asleep in the three holy names of God the Father, the Son and the Holy Spirit.
[One recites this three times over water and anoint the painful limb three times.] P. Höglund.

6. Jesus went out on the road, he saw a woman. Where are you headed? – To a village to gather bones and blood. – You shall go into a lake and there smash

---

[70] *Rensel* is a folk name for a painful malady, but a direct translation has not yet been found.

up bones under a root, where all trolls live, where fires burn and tar runs, in the three names of God the Father, the Son and the Holy Spirit.
– Edv. Svedberg.

7. Stand still and say as Noah's ark. Just as God placed Noah's ark on Mount Ararat, in that way I bind you: Stand still and stay with God's power in the name of God the Father and the Son and the Holy Spirit.
[Ante Molander here in Mo he knows a lot of useful things, as for example to heal confusion and ache; for when he works for "rensel" he recites just this conjuration, where the ache is, and before the sun comes up the pain is gone, even as harsh as it was.

There are people who are born with the caul (wisdom's cap) on their head. These people are called those with the sixth sense. Ante Molander here in Mo – 77 years old – had such a cap when he was born.] – Lundquist, 89 years, Flodmoran, Bispgården.

8. N. N. For ache and for sprain in marrow and in limb and stop and stay you pain and smarting in the name of God the Father and the Son and the Holy Spirit. [To be recited over lard three times over three evenings. The lard salve is put where no one sleeps.] – Lappkvinnan M. Nordström.

II. For Stomach ache

9. I want, through Jesus Christ and the Holy Spirit's power, that you NN may be freed and finished with your ache and your pains that hit you in your stomach and are in your entire body. In the name of God the Father and of the Son and of the Holy Spirit.

10. You take a knife, the tang of which goes through the handle, and put it counterclockwise into coffee, water or best into liquor while one counts: If you stick one, I'll stick two; If you stick three, then I'll stick four; If you stick five, then I'll stick six; If you stick seven, then I'll stick eight; if you stick nine, then I'll stick ten.
[This recipe has been tried by me and others, and has shown itself to be of infallible effect for stich and pain.]

III. Untreatable sickness

11. I, NN, order you in the blood of Jesus Christ, God's Son and in the name [power] of the Holy Spirit, that you, NN, may become healthy, as long as you live. Our Father and Benediction three times.

[This should preferably be recited over liquor. It should be recited while looking the sick person straight in the eyes of one who has an untreatable sickness.] – Anna Sefasson, 39 years, Vestanede, Bispgården.

IV. For toothache

12. As surely as Moses stopped the water in the Red Sea, just as surely I stop you toothache for you, NN. In the name of God the Father and of the Son and of the Holy Ghost.
– Per Isaksson, Holmstrand.

13. I stop your toothache from one and to nine under the sun, underground, and under nine earthfast-stones, in the names of God the Father and of the Son and of the Holy Ghost.

14. I stop your toothache for you, NN, from one and till nine and ninety. In the names of God the Father and of the Son and of the Holy Ghost.
[Recited over liquor that is taken three times in the mouth, after which one spits it out into the burning fire.]

15. Recite over liquor three times and move your knife three times counterclockwise in the three names. One takes the liquor in a common food-spoon and keeps it in the mouth on the side with the ache for five minutes, and then spits it out into fire; the second time three minutes and the third time as long as one wants. Each time you spit out the liquor into burning fire, and the last bit of liquor is thrown into the burning hearth fire.
[This recipe is from Tupp-Jätte (Lapp-Jätte) in Långsele, who taught it to my mother-in-law fifty years ago.]

16. In the Triune name of the Father, of the Son and of the Holy Ghost I pray you, that you will take away the toothache from NN. – You prick the aching tooth with a nail until blood comes onto the nail, whereupon you recite the above prayer and hammer the nail into a growing tree.

17. You take a common nail, pick at the aching tooth, strike the nail into a tree or into a gatepost or door, and the one who takes that nail, gets the toothache so terribly, that he either commits suicide or becomes crazy.

18. One takes a stick and picks at the aching tooth, so that blood gets on the stick; then you go and bit the stick on the north side of the trunk of a growing tree, then the toothache will disappear into the tree trunk. But if anyone comes and chops down that tree, then he'll get the toothache.

For injuries and snakebite

I. Breaks, Sprains and sprained legs/bones

1. NN, Jesus rode over a bridge; the foot got stuck in the root of a fir tree. Then Jesus himself got down and put joint to joint and bone to bone, sinew to sinew, flesh to flesh, veins to veins and skin to skin, in the name of God the Father and of the Son and of the Holy Ghost.
[Recited over lard and is used in combination with the treatment.]

2. Jesus rode out over a borderland with a white horse. Then the horse got a dislocation. Then Jesus got down and put the joint back in, that all as it was before, through three names: God the Father and the Son and the Holy Ghost. – Edvard Svedberg.

3. Jesus and Saint Peter rode over a wet mossy bog. Then the horse misstepped. Then Saint Peter got down and worked to stop ache and for sprain and for turned shoulder. – As soon as there is pain, then it will be okay again in the Trinity's name: God the Father, Son and Holy Ghost.
[This spell is used for back-ache. It is recited three times into water, and after which one anoints the horse with it.] – P. Höglund.

II. For Snakebite

4. Jesus went out on the road, and he saw the snake slithering and the wound disappeared, through three names: God Father, Son and Holy Ghost.
– Edvard Svedberg.

5. NN The Virgin Mary went forth on her way, she met the snake. Then she took a binding and bound the snake. She bound his liver, she bound his lungs, she bound his poison within its tongue, in the name of God the Father, the Son and the Holy Ghost.

6. NN., The snake bit, what did he bite into? The Virgin Mary bound that snake with the name of Jesus Christ. The Virgin Mary bound both head and tale in the name of God the Father, the Son and the Holy Ghost.
[Recite three times into the wound, and stroke over it, then there will be no danger. Or also you can recite it over liquor and wash the wound with it, then the poison will disappear.]

7. There lay a snake in by a root, he intended to make illness; but there is found healing in the name of the Trinity: God the Father, Son and Holy Ghost.

III. To recite for Glass

8. There stood two maidens at a weighing scale. – and if you don't want to go this way, then you go that way! So say I NN, in the name of God the Father, of the Son and of the Holy Ghost.

This is recited over a liter of water mixed with a few drops of liquor and a few cottonseeds that is taken internally. Then one should wash oneself as is necessary for the treatment.
– A. Molander

IV. When cattle have swallowed something sharp

9. NN, I measure needles, I measure steel, I measure glass, and I measure everything that can cause injury to cattle's life, in the name of God the Father, the Son and the Holy Ghost.
– Margareta Nordström

For Numerous Complaints

I. Pimples or blemishes – chronic blemishes and grey cataracts

1. NN. Jesus stepped onto Christ's table; and began to measure, and measured truly, he measured pain, he measured blemishes, he measured everything in the name of the Trinity, of the Father and the Son and the Holy Ghost.
– P. Höglund.

2. [Measuring] NN., The three mothers of God, who sat at Christ's table and measured, they measured truly, they stopped "*rann*," they stopped pain in the holy names of God the Father, the Son and the Holy Ghost.
[For measuring one can recite in the eye three times, or also in granulated sugar, since it has the same effect.]

3. NN., I measure blemishes, I measure truly, as ran over the eye, in the name of God the Father and of the Son and of the Holy Ghost.

4. NN., Jesus Christ himself measured; he measured stings, he measured straw, he measured everything in the name of God the Father and of the Son and of the Holy Ghost.

5. NN., Jesus and his sones they measured stings, they measured straw, they measured everything and I, in the name of the Trinity, of God the Father and of the Son and of the Holy Ghost, measure the mote out of your eye.

6. NN., I measure of axe, I measure of husk, I measure of sand, I measure of bark and I measure of the mote which is in your eye, in the name of God the Father, the Son and the Holy Ghost.

7. NN., Jesus Christ, who knows and can do everything, he takes from your eye both motes and sand. It happens with powerful words in the name of God the Father of the Son and of the Holy Ghost.
[One can recite in the eye where the cataract is, and also three times. One pulverizes granulated sugar into the finest powder, but then you should have a tea-spoon and pour the sugar into the eye three evenings in a row. One can recite from a 6 to 8, well all the way to a ten league distance and it will have the same effect.]

8. I measure it away, I measure away sand, I measure away blemishes, which ran under the "brisk." In the name of God the Father, of the Son and of the Holy Ghost.

9. NN., Jesus went over a muddy patch, there he meets a man who had seven pimples and seventy. He himself bandaged, he himself bound, Jesus himself, who triumphed over all wounds from the wind and the water and from all black in the name of God the Father, the Son and of the Holy Ghost.
[To be recited three times in the aching eye; spit there three times, stroke it with a knife with a tang that goes all the way through the handle, three times from the bottom up of the eye. Then the ache will stop and the cataract will disappear from the eye within three 24-hour days.]

II. For growths, nodular bumps, and goiter

10. On the last Thursday in the month, before the sun goes down, you count counterclockwise, either in water or with your index finger around the growth of whatever type it may be. One moves one's finger around the growth nine times and counts from twenty to one, nine times. If it is done in water, you count as related above and anoint it [with water].

11. One counts from twenty to one, three times, each Thursday with the pointing finger counterclockwise around the growth, three Thursdays in a row, when the sun is still up.

III. For rickets

12. NN., Jesus went forth on his way, he met a crying child.
- Why are you crying?
- I have rickets: I have head rickets, neck rickets, chest rickets, back rickets,

stomach rickets, joint rickets, bone rickets, cross rickets, wall-bound rickets.
- I heal you in my name, in the name of the Trinity, the Father, Son and Holy Ghost.
Recite: Madness – Pain – Depression – Our Father and Benediction three times in water, and anointed according to treatment.
[Recited three times into water or liquor and used to anoint after the treatment.] – E. Gärdin.

13. You make a hole through the earth in a high mound of dirt or such on a Thursday night; afterwards, you take the child and take him through the hole three times counterclockwise – then the child will be liberated from rickets.

IV. For epilepsy

14. When the afflicted has an attack, all the clothing is cut all the way from the neck down to the feet – as well as the shoes – and everything is thrown into the fire, so that the sick person is completely naked. This cures epilepsy.
[This case is told in its entirety in Västergötland.]

V. Children's rash

15. You look into the child's eyes and recite the Benediction over the child three times [completely silent, and to oneself].
[Regarding rashes on small children I have learned from Lars Henriksson, Vestby in Hellgum, how one should pray away them, and he has learned this from his father. – If a child had a rash and was also sick, then you should look at the child and recite the Benediction over it three times completely silently to oneself, then it should be healthy, however sick it was. And I have also tried this three times with the result that each child I treated became well, "for" said Lars Henriksson, "this is gotten from the Gospel of Matthew, when Christ blessed the little children."

VI. Staunching

16. In Jesus' name the water will go in its proper path as usual.
[If the staunching should be healed, then one shall take a board or piece of one with a hole where a branch has been. Then one takes a wedding ring and a house or cellar key and then pours water through these holes into a coffee cup, while one recites the spell. This experiment one does three times and then is given to the sick one to drink. It will surely help.]

VII. Mental disorders

17. You recite into water and liquor – as is prescribed in the treatment – the spells for depression, madness, enchantment, pain, the Our Father and Benediction and anoint with it the one who has been wrenched, three times and give him as many drinks of water.

To Recite Over Animals

I. To transfix Predators

1. Go up on the mountain in the area and yell: "As far as this sound is heard, then for that distance shall all wolf- and bear-skins turn away, through the name of the Trinity. God the Father, Son and Holy Ghost.
– Edvard Svedberg.

2. Jesus spoke to the bride in this way: Lock up those bindings, which have the keys of the whole world, and lock the teeth of all wolves, from bear claws and eagle talons and all injurious animals, which are found out in the woods, in my name, the Father, the Son and the Holy Ghost. [Recited into the feed]
– Edvard Svedberg.

3. [For envy] I bind away all those who have envy with these words: Stand as stand, and cliff as cliff in the name of God the Father, and of the Son and of the Holy Ghost.
[As one recites this, one strokes from the snout of the animal and down the back all the way to the rump. This one does three times. Then you will protect the animal from all envious folks and every evil.]

4. God's hand, which can protect everything, may he protect you from the jealous hand, from the predator's hand, from bear claws and wolves' teeth; here you will go and never more return, in the name of God the Father, and the Son and the Holy Ghost.
[One recites this for each cow into the cattle feed and gives each and every one one at a time. One strokes from the snout and down over the whole back. Then one goes three times counterclockwise around the herd, then the animals won't go out of the demonstrated area (the grazing area) all summer and are protected both for predators and evil people.] – Erik Persson, 67 years, Bispgården.

II. To recite for wasps

5. Wasp, wasp, with a sting, you are like Satan; sting into log and rock, but not into flesh and bone; sting in the meadow, but not in the stomach; sting in Hell. – spit three times.
[When one sees a wasp or hornet's nest, then one goes there and recites over the thousands of swarming and buzzing wasps this conjuration.] – A. Laurén, Graninge, from J. A. H. Sving, 45 years, Hassela. He learned the conjuration from his parents.

6. I bind you with a binding like Christ bound the Jews in the Garden, so that your stinger will never more injure me, in the name of God the Father, and of the Son, and of the Holy Ghost.
[This is recited to transfix the wasps in their nest; then go counterclockwise and recite the entire conjuration until one comes back to the place one started from. This you do three separate times.]

III. To transfix a snake

7. Lie still, you steed of hell, while the Virgin Mary wraps her child in the name of God the Father and of the Son and of the Holy Ghost.
[Recite with devotion three times.] – A. Laurén.

IV. To get the cattle home at a certain time

8. You shall go to the woods and have fat sides and plump "*jur*"[71] and the milk will run as the stars in the heavens burn and the wind blows and the river flows and at [6, etc.] o'clock you will go home in hoof in hoof, and trot in trot, and foot in foot. On my land, there you will graze and stay there where i live, in the three names of God the Father and the Son and the Holy Ghost.
[Recite over the cattle feed and give to the animals in the door the first day they go out for summer grazing.] – Edvard Svedberg.

9. You gave me a piece of property – the enemy took it, but I say in your name that they [it] will come home at [6, etc.] o'clock in the name of the Trinity, God the Father, Son and Holy Ghost.
[Recite over the cattle feed three times and give to the animals for the first time before they have tasted green food. When you've given the animals three times, save some food for next year in a place where no one sleeps. I have done this many times and at no time has it failed me.] – P. G. Edström, 45 years, Nordsjö, Långsele.

---

71 Sw. *djur*? animal.

V. When the cattle just want to run home in the mornings

10. You gave me a piece of property – the enemy took it but I say to you in the name of the Trinity, that you go hence and graze until [6 etc.] o'clock in the name of God the Father, of the Son and of the Holy Ghost.
[One follows the animals to the woods, as far as one wants, and gives to each animal from the cattle feed one time while one recites this conjuration. Then they won't run home in the mornings, but will stay out in the woods until the evening, till that time you have worked to have them home.] – P. G. Edström.

11. The farmer is dead and the farm burned and here you shall go and here you shall dwell again. Three names: God the Father, Son and Holy Ghost.
[To be recited over the cattle feed.]

VI. To fix the cattle at whatever place you wish

12. One selects the place where you wish to put the animal and leads it three times counterclockwise around it. Then, you take under the left back foot something that has stuck there under the foot, and that same thing you put into the selected place. Then you take from that same place – not on the outer border but rather a bit down; if it, for example, is a stone that is the chosen place, under that – something – for example a little chaff or the like. Then, you take a little chaff or some such under the cottage corner and then back under the animal's left back foot and put it on the place you've marked out. Finally, you lead the animal for a second time three times counterclockwise around it.

At the chosen place you have a little salt prepared in advance, and when everything is prepared in the proper order and method, then you let the animal eat up everything all together, and thereafter the animal won't leave that place all summer long.
– Hanna Eriksson, 87 years, Vike, Holm.

VII. For milk

13. The Virgin Mary went to her blessed son, Jesus:
- Stand up, my Son, and heal my animal.
- I shall stand up, healing they shall have; give them salt and July's malt (liquor); milk and butter shall run as stars in the heavens burn. In the three names: God the Father, Son and Holy Ghost.
[Recite over the cattle feed and give to the animals.]

To Send Back, Envy, Depression

[Depression or sendings have the same meaning as the word sorcery or – as one says, enchanted.]

I. Enchantment and Depression[72]

1. I liberate and protect you, NN., and save you from all evil, whatever has happened through malevolent witches and sorcerers.
But not a single drop of blood or a hair be touched or injured on you, any more than you can take a piece of an earthfast stone in the ocean's deep; in the name of the Trinity: God the Father, Son and Holy Ghost.
[Recite in liquor.] – Edvard Svedberg.

2. I give to you, NN. power, I give you fortitude, I give you flesh, I give you blood in the name of God the Father, Son and Holy Ghost.
[Recite in liquor and give to the one who is depressed to take internally three times.] – Gärdin.

3. If there is taken from you, NN., power and fortitude, flesh and blood, then I shall give to you power and fortitude, flesh and blood. I shall save you from all evil, from all human malice, envy, sorcery and every invisible means and result and everything evil, in the three holy names: God the Father, Son and Holy Ghost.
[One recites in liquor for depression and confusion and gives it to the one who is depressed. – Enchanted.] – Torparen P. Höglund, Holm.

4. Are you, NN., bereft of power? Are you robbed of fortitude? Are you drained of blood? God give you your power again; God give you your fortitude again; God give you your flesh again; God give you your blood again – in the name of God the Father, and of the Son and of the Holy Ghost.
[For people. To be recited over liquor.] – Gärdin.

5. Jesus Christ, whose body and blood you receive, preserve you unto eternal life.
[This is recited three times into the eye for depression.] – A. Molander.

6. There went three maidens on a road: The one took an axe, the second took sand, and the third took whatever she wanted – in the name of God the Father, and of the Son and of the Holy Ghost.

---

72 "Modstulen" is literally "robbed of fortitude." but can be loosely translated as depressed when speaking of humans. In animals, it is generally translated as "skittish" though cowardly is along this same vein. Thus, being robbed of fortitude covers both human and animal realms.

7. NN., is the cow bereft of power, are you robbed of fortitude, are you robbed of marrow, are you robbed of milk, are you drained of blood? But I shall give you power and fortitude, flesh and blood, you shall milk, as the envy would be released before three sunsets, in the name of God the Father, and of the Son and of the Holy Ghost.
[Recite over cattle feed.]

8. Jesus and Saint Peter went forth on their way, he met a horse.
- What sickness do you have?
- I am bereft of power, robbed of fortitude, robbed of marrow and drained of blood.
- I heal you in my name, in the name of the Trinity, Father, Son and Holy Ghost.
[Recite over bread or salt. Recited three times in salt and give to the horse to eat of it, then he'll be good again before the evening.] – Gärdin.

9. The Virgin Mary went down the road and cried; then she met Jesus:
- Why are you crying?
- My cow is bereft of fortitude even to his liver and lung, to his teeth and his tongue; can you heal her? - Oh yes, with malt and with salt and valerian root shall your cow be healed, in the name of God the Father and of the Son and of the Holy Ghost.
[Recite over cattle feed, salt and valerian three times, when the cow has been robbed of its fortitude.] – Gärdin.

10. Jesus went forth on his way; there stood a cow at a fence and cried.
- Why are you crying?
- They have taken my power, fortitude, milk, skin and blood from me.
- Your power shall be as a bear's power; your fortitude shall be as a bear's fortitude; your skin shall be as slippery ice and your milk shall be as a honey cake, in the three names: God the Father, Son and Holy Ghost.
[Recite over cattle feed and salt.] – P. Höglund.

11. Jesus went over a muddy patch. There he met a cow crying.
- Why are you crying, blessed cow?
- I have lost my flesh and my blood, my power and my blood.
- You shall have again your power and your blood, your flesh and your blood, you blessed cow, in the name of God the Father and of the Son and of the Holy Ghost.
[Recite over cattle feed.]

12. Jesus traveled over a heath. There he met a person, a Satanically abominable (hideous) person, who had been in my farm and taken the fortitude of my cattle.

- In my and the Son's name, and through the name of the Holy Ghost I put you over the road; over mountain and valley you shall go. Where no Christian person will see nor cattle be. There burns a lake with brimstone. With malt and with salt you shall get your power, in the blood of God's Son you shall get your fortitude, through three names: God the Father and the Son and the Holy Ghost.

II. Sending Back

13. I cast depression, I cast envy, I cast Fan (Satan); I cast evil people to that mountain where no one dwells, to that lake where no one rows, under a stone, where no man is to my detriment, in the name of God the Father, and of the Son and of the Holy Ghost.
[Recite over liquor.]

14. Your evil mouth I shall bind, so that you will not injure me, for before the tree shall sink and the grey stone move, in the three holy names: God the Father, Son and Holy Ghost.
[For either man or beast.] – P. Höglund.

15. Jesus went forth on his way. Then he met Satan.
- Where are you heading? - I'm heading to the farmers farm and will suck both people and livestock crazy.
- You shall go back to him, to the one who sent you, and there you shall gobble up and there you shall slurp up in his house, in his dwelling, and his liver, and in his lung [in his tooth and in his tongue], for you'll not get any more from me than I can get from an earthfast stone, which is in the ocean's deep, in the three holy names: God the Father, Son and Holy Ghost.
[Recite into cattle feed and salt.] – P. Höglund.

16. There came a raven and flew from a foreign land. he flew over the sea to a foreign shore; he stole fortitude and blood out of my horse. From Hell are you come, and to Hell you shall return, in the three holy names: God the Father, Son and Holy Ghost.
[Recite into salt three times and give to the horse to eat.] – P. Höglund.

17. [If a horse has been enchanted by a person] You, who have enchanted and destroyed my horse and destroyed my possessions, I send it back as a howling storm over the highest tree tops in the name of God the Father, and of the Son and of the Holy Ghost.
[Recite three times.]

III. To drive out the effects of the Evil One

18. Mare, Mare, you are surely in here, so I will drive you out with iron and with steel, seven prayers in Our Father's and the Virgin Mary's names, in the name of the Trinity, of the Father and of the Son and of the Holy Ghost. The "Our Father" and "Benediction" three times.
[When one recites, one takes a knife, the tang of which extends through the handle, and whip it counterclockwise in liquor, while reciting. Give it to the sick one, who is plagued with evil spirits and devils or is destroyed by evil people. It helps.] – Mårten Mårtensson, 77 years old, known by the name Lapp-Mårten, Bergsbyn, Berg in Jämtland. He learned spells for depression from his mother-in-law, Lapp-Maria, who died now 27 years ago.

IV. For Trollshot

19. The Virgin Mary went on her way. Why are you sitting here? Out with the ingot (bullet) and in with the healing, cow-shot, filth-shot, that I can deny with the name of the Father alone: In the name of God the Father and of the Son and of the Holy Ghost.
[When an animal has gotten troll-shot and falls and remains lying on the road, then open its mouth and recite the above three times, then the animal will be healthy again.]

V. For envy

20. You jealous spirit, you cunning of Satan, you shall sit in Hell's Gallows, but here and here you have nothing to do. If you were stronger than the river and hotter than fire, so you shall creep and walk for us as fallen trees and immovable stones in fire over the highest tree tops for your words.
[For envy, one recites over liquor for people and over salt for animals. For horses, recite over salt. – Recite this three times over liquor or coffee, then no envy will bite hold.]

Confusion, evil sendings, spirit fires

I. Confusion. Craziness.
[For all such complaints one should always recite three prayers, so for example, for pain, one – recites – for pain, confusion/madness, Our Father, the Benediction, depression, sendings etc., for there is no good way to know from what direction the malady comes: One might have had a run-in with the invisible ones – wights – or for the spirits of evil in the dark spaces through evil people or so-called sendings, etc. In such difficult cases as harsh pain, etc., or confusion from which one cannot be free, then one is forced to work for pain

according to the treatment and wash oneself over the entire body for three evenings, because that will help.]

1. NN., Jesus and Saint Peter went forth on the road, they met a man who had seven problems and seventy. But Jesus triumphed over them all, both in wind and in water, in the three holy names: God the Father, Son and Holy Ghost. [Used in combination with the treatment.] – Erik Gärdin.

2. Take water, that runs to the north, and put three straight pins in it; cut then three pieces of silver – food-spoons – ditto three pieces of brass. Massage after that, and begin the massage in the middle and smear in a cross over the chest and out along the legs! Then, go to a crossroad; step back counterclockwise three steps and throw over your left shoulder! Then go home without looking back, then one will be free from his suffering. – E. Svedberg.

3. One takes glowing red coals [best the coals be in a container] from the fire, goes out, before one goes to bed, throw them over the left shoulder towards the church and says: - There you have yours, and I will regain mine, so now we are finished with each other.

4. When one works to stop insanity, one should take hairs from all over the body of the person you're working for, and put a little bit of the nail from the left big-toe, and the same from the left hand, and thereafter put all of this in a coffee cup with liquor. Then go, when the sun has set, to a road – preferably a highway – throw it over your left shoulder and say:
- Too quickly you came here, and too late you left from here.
[To be recited for one who is crazy, that is, has had a run in with the subterraneans.] – A. Molander

5. One takes from the sick one nails from all the toes in the left foot and hand, a little hair from all over the body, a little brass, copper and silver and put all this in a silver goblet full of liquor. Go then to a crossroad after sunset and throw it over your left shoulder. Then you go home without answering or greeting if one meets anyone. Then that one who has been crazy will soon be liberated from his suffering.

6. One takes a little nail and hair from the one who has been affected, a little brass and copper and put it into a rag. Go to a crossroad, throw it over your left shoulder and say:
- Here, this you may play with, and leave in peace flesh and blood. This you should do after sundown. If one meets anyone, you should neither answer nor talk, until you come inside, for otherwise it will go ill.

[This spell is for one who has had a run-in with the invisibles and got some problem with a limb.]

7. If one has met with something "wrong" at a certain place, then you should after sundown go there and throw a one crown coin over the left shoulder, then one will be free from the evil.

8. Crazy or nervous animals: One takes a straw from under the left back foot of the animal and recites:
- A thousand times a thousand bites. What do you have to do for a thousand bites?
Then give the animal that straw in his fodder, then it'll be back to normal.
– A. Molander. [Ephesians 6:12]

II. Evil Sendings and Wight Fires

9. Have you, NN., fallen into the hands of Spells and Spirit bites from one to eighteen? I conjure it toward that lake where there is a boat with iron oars. And on the other side of the lake there sits an old hag with the bite in her mouth, in a hole with a dwelling in it, and smash it to pieces in the three holy names: God the Father, Son and Holy Ghost.
[Enchanted. – to be used in conjunction with treatment. – recite three times in the water and wash three evenings. Besides this, recite for depression, craziness, the Our Father, and the Benediction three times.] – E. Gärdin.

10. Saint Peter went on a road. Then he met a man.
- Where are you going?
- To a farm [where no one dwells]
- In logs and in stones, that's where you'll live, but not in the person's marrow, flesh, bones and blood in the name of God the Father and of the Son and of the Holy Ghost.
[Recite in liquor – also for confusion and depression.] – E. Gärdin.

11. A man went and headed for the woods. There he met two "*kväser*" [? Blemish? Hoarseness?]
- Where are you going, to his or her house?
- I am going to the farmer's house and break the table and brewing.
- You shall immediately go to a mountain where no one dwells, to a lake where no one rows, under a stone, where there is no danger to men, in the name of God the Father and of the Son and of the Holy Ghost.
[Recite in liquor.] – E. Gärdin.
[These two bits, 10 and 11, are for those who have become targets for sendings from evil people, who have evil powers of the spirits of air among their imple-

ments and emissaries to disturb and destroy their peers. These people are called sorcerers and malefic witches.]

12. If one has gone really mad, then he'll sweat as if he were lying in a fire; then one has gotten in the way of wights – that's "wight-fire."
If one has been crazy or confused in this way, then you should recite over water for confusion, ache, [*rensel*], loss of fortitude, the Our Father and Benediction three times. Then you take six hollow straws and blow through them three times. Then you take a knife that is red-hot or sickle and cut a cross ☩. Then you can wash the place where the suffering is.

But one may not go out thereafter; and in the morning, you should throw out that water nicely. If one doesn't do that, then one can get back the same pain and irritation.

If this doesn't help, then you have to undertake anointing in accordance with the treatment.

MANUSCRIPT C

Shape-shifting – Becoming Invisible

I. Bear- and Wolf-skins

1. To clothe oneself in animal shape, a thing that our forefathers among both the lapps and the swedes understood, is an undertaking that few are able to succeed in, as it often leads to the one who is involved in it, loses his mind and becomes more or less crazy.
To acquire the ability to take on the shape of an animal – bear- or wolf-shape – one must procure a belt with magical power. This belt, which is made of human skin, is taken a Thursday night – preferably towards Christmas, Pentecost or some other of the greater holidays – between twelve and one, from a corpse one digs up in the cemetery. And it should preferably be a man's corpse. But the belt is taken from around the corpse's waist and three or four thumbs wide. In order to flay it off, one uses a knife. The one who owns this belt undamaged, can whenever he wishes take the shape of a bear or a wolf.

But to transform yourself, do the following: One creeps with the head first through the belt three times; the first time one creeps through it one gets the head of the animal; the second is half animal and the third time the transformation is complete.

When one wants to return to human shape again, one creeps with the feet first through the belt, three times as before.

It was about thirty-five years ago, when in my travels I came to a village in Ramsele, Västra Vimmelvattnet, where they told me about a man who had such a belt.

It was a few years before my arrival that they hired the Lapp Anders Fjällmark as a horse grazer, whose job it was to take care of the horses for several villages, as a horse grazer hired in common. When the autumn came and Fjällmark brought the horses back and was going to receive his remuneration, there was a stingy, rich farmer, who didn't want to pay according to the agreement.

Fjällmark became very angry over this, and said that since the farmer didn't want to pay willingly, then both wolf and bear would devastate his cattle and horses. The farmer only laughed at his threats and said that if the Lapp didn't leave off, he would throw him out.

The Lapp left. But then when he came to the woods, he took his belt-ring and transformed himself into a bear, went and teared up the farmer's horses, so that he became completely drained of such animals. Then, he took a wolf shape and tore to death all the cows, sheep, goats and hens, so that there were no animals left of the farmer's livestock.

As the last comment, Fjällmark set loose lice and vermin on the greedy farmer and this ailment he suffered from all the days of his life.

Another time, this same Fjällmark was in Jämtland, in Hammardals parish, where he lived one summer with his family.

On one occasion he was in the woods and was helping some farmers with the wood harvesting. When the people one night during this slept in a hay-barn, one of the girls awoke when Fjällmark went out. And since she was lying close to the barn wall and could peek out through the cracks, she decided to see what it was that Fjällmark had to do outside.

Then she saw how he took forth something out of the folds of his sweater and crept through – it was the remarkable skin-ring. Then she saw how Fjällmark step by step was transformed into a bear. The girl naturally became completely outside herself with dread and could neither move nor call out to anyone. In a while, the bear returned and took again its correct shape.

When day came, she described for the farmer what she had seen. He wanted in the beginning to put hardly any belief in her words, but asked her not to reveal to anyone what she had seen.

The farmer began to spy on Fjällmark and when he had fallen asleep one time, he managed to steal the ring-belt from him. Then when he had it in his hands, he threw it in the fire to destroy it; but in the same moment as it was surrounded by flames, it hurled itself back; the second time it was thrown back as before, but the third time it stayed there and was burned to ashes. During that time, Fjällmark agonized greatly in his sleep, broke out in a cold sweat, and threw himself back and forth.

But after that time, it was the end of Fjällmark's ability to transform himself into a bear or a wolf.

Another method to procure for yourself such a ring-belt I heard from an old Lapp, Paulus August Nilsson, Nora Parish.

He had heard from his parents, that if one wanted to procure for oneself such a belt, one should go to a place where the corpse of a suicide or also another corpse was buried, and then between twelve and one on a Thursday or some larger feast day night take from the left arm's sinew down to the hand and spin threads of the sinew and from this make a rope in the form of a ring, so that one could creep through it. This was for the one who wanted to have the ability to transform oneself into a bear or a wolf.

II. To make oneself invisible

2. One takes [buys] a human bone on a Thursday night between twelve and one.
On it, one scrapes with a knife, so that it becomes as flour. One takes this flour and strews it on the head as one says:
- With this I disguise myself in an invisible way as a spirit, that at one time was united with this bone, and I leave my soul in pledge [as security]. Bornus Bister under the Devil's sigil in the name of God the Father and of the Son and of the Holy Ghost.

When one wants to once again become visible, heave the knife into a tree, or a wall in the house.

3. One borrows a bowl made from a cranium on a Thursday night at the Churchyard and leaves a one crown coin on the grave.
In the skull bowl one takes graveyard dust and puts it in a hollow tree or under a rocky outcropping north of the church. On that, one plants a pea in the dirt in the skull bowl. When the pea has grown and borne fruit, one take a mirror in front of oneself and stuffs the peas one after another into your mouth, until one comes to that pea that gives to you the power of invisibility.

In the same moment one gets that pea in your mouth, your own image will disappear from the mirror and with that pea you can make yourself invisible whenever you please.

Envy – Sendings

I. Envy

1. When one has envious persons in one's surroundings and can't get any peace from them, then it's a sign that one feels peculiar and strange in one's mind and that one has a feeling of anxiety about oneself. For us up here in Lappland, it has expression among other things in procedures.

I know a person who, when he had slaughtered a reindeer or shot a wolf or some such, didn't have luck whether it was with meat, skin or otherwise, but that rats and other vermin destroyed it for him.

Another example I have from my childhood:
There was once when I was nine or ten years old, when my father came home with an unusually beautiful wolfskin.

In the meantime, there was a person who, though rich, had that sickness of being envious, and he had the chance to see the wolf-skin and thought that it was a beautiful skin, even he.

When we would make an evening of it and go to bed, pappa took a large piece of wood and put it on the fire, as one always does in the Lapp tents so that the fire would keep up all night. And just when pappa put the log there, it was as if an invisible hand had slung the beautiful wolf-skin into the fire and before anyone had the chance to fetch it out, it was destroyed.

It was the power of the thought of our envious neighbor, who right in front of all our eyes had thrown the pelt into the fire.

Another time we were in the middle of cooking meat, and as we were five people, it was a right big and heavy cauldron that hung over the fire. Just as mamma was lifting the cauldron from the hook – in Lapp tents the cooking pots hang over the fire by a hook in an iron cable – it was as if the cauldron came to life. It hopped up and down and was shaken and swung in the air.

Then my parents understood that it was someone who had their thoughts aimed towards us, and that we would soon have visits from some distant travelers. It showed itself also to be correct, for within one hour my maternal uncle arrived who was completely starved and dead tired from a long journey.

2. But to avoid envy and thought magnetism – or whatever I should call it – hypnotism with other words, there is no better means that I know than to recite in coffee, or preferably into liquor, the exorcism:

You envious spirit [or thought] etc.,[73] – thought and spirit are namely the same thing according to spell-work – then the envious one will have no power over one.

II. Sendings

3. In Selånger, Sättna, Indal, Lidan, Holm and other parishes in Medelpad, there are different terror-waking people, who practice their dark, devilish deeds yet to the day that is today.

---

[73] This conjuration seems incomplete, though understanding the process as one of naming as establishing the identity of the malicious spirit, may be sufficient to establish control over it.

Although it is a era of enlightenment, I will maintain that Medelpad is no better today than it was under Karl the 9th's or Karl the 10th's reign – or, in other words: it isn't any better now than five or seven hundred years ago, that time when witch-power was in its highest flowering.

Have a look here at what is going on in the time of grace in the beginning of the 20th century. A while ago, H. H. in Holm had poached moose whenever he wanted. But then a farmer there thought that this was going too far, especially so since he discovered both the poacher and the moose and registered the criminal. The result of this was that the poacher had to do six months at "The White Dove" as the Sundsvall royal prison is called.

When he got out of there, he went with thoughts of revenge to the farmer who had given him up, and said:

- Now I have served from mine, but now you have yours left!

Therefore, he went to the churchyard and took a coffin nail, drew his enemy's picture on a fir tree and drove in the nail into the chest of the picture.

Some time afterwards the farmer began to pine away and then it wasn't long before he died. When H. H. heard that, he uttered once under the influence of intoxication:

- I thought that bastard would kick the bucket in three years, but that devil lived on for five.

In a village a quarter Swedish mile from here, belonging to Lidens parish, there was a farm that was completely poorly disposed to get everything evil. It began to knock during the nights, tables and chairs began to move and out in the corners were large, spotted worms that crept here and there.

This had happened the previous summer.

The oldest daughter began to be depressed and grey in her countenance, even though she was twenty-two years old. And no improvement came, even though P. Höglund traveled there. Höglund said to me, that they didn't carry out correctly that which he had ordained.

Thereafter I was there and treated her, but I don't know if she ever got better, since I haven't been back to farm since.

They said that it was envious people, who destroyed them through envy, since the girl had had several fiancés and was pretty to look at and had parents who were well off. But the envious people succeeded in splitting her and her fiancés apart.

To succeed in their [the envious ones'] intent, they had sought the help of a sorcerer, who got hold of graveyard dirt; and when she had a fiancé and became engaged, then at parties, balls and in social gatherings they would throw graveyard dirt between her and her fiancé. This she had seen with her own eyes and she had even found dirt that had stuck to her clothes. And this had not gone on for more than around eight days before the fiancé broke off the engagement.

Now it was last autumn a nineteen-year-old girl in the same village sent an invitation to this girl and wanted to settle her issue with her before she died. She described then terrible experiences from the departed with whom she had been in contact, and she said that the spirits were no longer friendly towards her and her helpers, since they had disturbed their peace. But the spirits didn't have any power to harm them since they paid everything for their upkeep, these two.

Further, she said that she had followed with the sorcerer many nights and even another, a sorceress, to the graveyard in Lidens parish. But now, on her deathbed, she wanted to settle her account with the girl, since she had been one of those who had fetched the dead's dirt and thrown it on her and her fiancé. She even said that she settled her account with her sorcerous leader, but what happened between them no one living ever got to know. And eight days afterwards, she was dead. Although this girl was a malicious witch, she "fell asleep" died even so in faith with her savior Jesus Christ.

But woe to the evil sorcerer and the evil sorceress and to their devilish spells, since it is not for amusement that it is written:

» Vengeance is mine, I shall repay! «

Thieves – "Bjäran"[74] – Stealing of Fortitude – Stealing of Milk

I. To show a thief in a glass of liquor, to Protect one's property

1. It works like this, that you go to the cemetery and get a hold of a skeleton that is not destroyed by the teeth of time. From this you take the long finger (middle finger) of the left hand and leave a 1-crown piece in payment for it, while you say:
- Thou dead, this I borrow from you, so that you will help me, when I call upon you, to show who the thief is, and to have the stolen goods returned.

If you want still another wish, you can state it, since you have three wishes but no more.

This experiment you should do alone on a Thursday night between twelve and one o'clock.

---

[74] Rietz has this to say: "litet troll med tre ben; ett slags underbart väsende, som säges uppkomma genom att sammanknyta 9 slags olika tråd, hvarpå sedan drypes 3 bloddroppar ur venstra lillfingret, hvarefter nystanet får lif. Haran är sin husbonde en trogen tjenare genom att draga till gårds mjölk från andras kor o.s.v. Enligt folktron på Gotland framkallas dett troll genom att på en korsväg antända en eld af 9 slags ved. Detta troll anses till besvärjarens tjenst mjölka andras kor, hvarefter det under homspringandet tjärnar mjölken till smör i sin mage. Bäran: bärande; af bära, v.a. portare."

Now if someone is robbed and you want to show him who the thief is, then you move the finger of the dead counterclockwise three times around a glass with liquor. Then the thief will become visible, so that anyone can see him. If you want to have the stolen goods returned, order the spirit of the finger to restore the stolen goods.

I heard winter last year at one place, that it was during a wedding that one of the guests made off with a gold watch. And because there was a cunning man among the wedding guests who knew the art of showing the thief and getting stolen goods returned, the one who was robbed wanted to get the watch back again. This the sorcerer promised; and in an hour's time one of the neighbors came running as if for his life with the watch in his hand and returned it to the owner.

Then the thief said that he, when he had come home with the stolen watch and gone to bed, was surrounded by a group of spirits who ordered him to return the stolen goods; if he didn't want to obey, they would take him with them to eternity. From this the thief become so frightened that he didn't even have time to put on more than a pair of pants before he headed off to return the watch.

The owner of the watch said, though, that if he had known that it was he who was the thief, then for all the world he wouldn't have wanted to show all the people there that this was the case.

This finger of a dead man is a singularly good amulet of protection. For if one day and night carries it on oneself, then there is no one who can injure or shoot down the bearer of it. If a bullet comes towards the body, then it will rebound back and fall down without doing anyone harm.

It's the spirit of the bone who receives the bullet.

If you want to protect your possessions, for example those things that are under the open sky, and you own such an amulet, then you go three times counterclockwise around them. If there comes a thief then, and grasps something, he will remain standing and won't be able to move out of the spot until the owner returns. To release the thief, you say:
- Thanks shall you have, you who have stood here and guarded my possessions.

Then the thief will be released from his enchantment. But if the owner is angry and carries out abuse, then he will expect other after-effects which can destroy him for is whole life.

II. To force a thief to go back with the stolen goods

2. Run, run, you good Sir Devil! I promise you that if you can help me with the stolen goods, I will follow you down into darkness. Run, run, run!
– J. A. Åberg
[If one has been robbed, then recite the above silently to oneself and even if the thief is 10 Swedish miles away, then he will be forced to run for his life and bring back the stolen goods. – An example of this: It happened in the beginning of December, 1916, that a villager came to Åberg and wanted him to get a leather shirt back that he had thought had been stolen from him. Åberg asked him then: "Do you want the thief to walk or to run?"

"Run," said the villager.

Åberg recited this conjuration silently with the result that he, who had lost the leather coat had to run with all his strength 1 ¼ miles to the woods where he had been during the day and felled timber; there he found his leather shirt.]

3. Home to me with your stolen goods you shall go and wend your way to me, and a great burden of conscience you shall have, and Satan shall take you, if you don't return to me that which I shall have, in the name of God the Father and of the Son and of the Holy Ghost.
[If one has been robbed or otherwise are missing something, or with violence have been robbed of anything, then one should with meditation and inner power recite this three times in liquor and consume it. And just as certainly as one has lost a possession, just as certainly will the thief be forced to return again with the stolen goods, or otherwise he will be so strongly affected that if he doesn't return it, he will become crazy or will die. When one recites such a conjuration, the power lies in the confidence inside the person, so that one actually feels inside of oneself that one will regain one's stolen goods. But it won't work to do it for those who don't believe. If he recites the above a thousand times and drinks up all the liquor.] – Jonas Norberg, Indal.

4. I order you spirit, you devil of Lucifer, wherever you may be with the stolen goods, that you shall within (day, hour) return the stolen things to me NN., otherwise you will fall head first the lowermost in Hell's most red room, in the name of the Trinity, God the Father, Son and Holy Ghost.
[Recite three times in liquor, that one drinks before going to bed.

During my travels this winter, I came to a place where I read in a book and in the book there was a pad of paper on which was written this conjuration. And after that the words attached themselves in my mind. In truth, powerful words!]

III. Stealing Fortitude

5. Since you, N.N., are a devil towards me N.N., who am a poor (rich: title) man, and have comported yourself with lying charges/imputations, then you shall in the Evil One's name suffer double of the others, in the name of God the Father, Son and Holy Ghost.
[Recite three times.]
– Lappman Erik Törnlund, 77 years, Indal.

6. Jesus went forth down the road, then he met the Virgin Mary.
– Where are you going?
– I am going to the farmer's farm and steal the fortitude of my enemies, through three names, God the Father, Son and Holy Ghost.
[Recite three times in liquor and spit into it three times. Give it to your enemy to drink, then he'll become depressed.]
– Lappman Erik Törnlund, 77 years, Indal.

7. If you, N.N., are my enemy, then I will show you to the lowest step to the burning lake. And there you shall wail and there you shall suffer, in the name of God the Father and of the Son and of the Holy Ghost.
[Recite three times in liquor.]
– Margareta Nordström

8. I order you, N.N., in the blood of Jesus Christ God's Son, in the name of God the Father and the Holy Ghost, that you may be sick as long as you live.
[Recite over an enemy three times, while you look him straight in the eye.]

9. If you, for example, may not ride with a farmer who is alone in the sled and he won't even let you ride for payment, then you should do this, that you come in front of the horse on the same road and the farmer will be riding on. When you have succeeded in this, you take nine zig-zagging steps over the road before the horse gets there. Now when the farmer gets there, then the horse won't have the strength to run any longer before he tires and finally stops completely. It won't help, however the farmer drives or how good the horse he has.
– Jonas Norberg, Indal.

IV. Take away Milk

10. To take away milk from cows, you should get a little milk – approximately a coffee cup full – from the cows in question.
This milk you take with you a Thursday night after sunset and go to a manure heap, where you throw it under the left knee joint out into the manure heap.

This is done three times during which one says:
- *Tvi, tvi, tvi,* N.N. (the farmer's name) your cows will never again milk, for your milk will disappear and become as nothing. Tvi, tvi, tvi.

Spit three times, then the milk will disappear for the farmer.
– Jonas Norberg, Indal.

V. "Bjäran" [Milk Hare]

11. At the house of a farmer in Nordsjö, Långsele, there is found the "*bjäran*" or the "Puken." When I was there a while ago, I heard from a righteous, forty-year-old faithful and deeply religious name, that he had seen it with his own eyes.

The one who can make a milkhare, must probably be a cold blooded and not have any thoughts about where he'll end up after this life. For that one who makes the milkhare, has sold himself to the power of the Devil.

But to make a milkhare, do the following:

One takes nine differently colored threads of woolen yarn and go with them to a crossroad on a Thursday night between twelve and one o'clock. Here, one makes a fire from nine different kinds of wood and wind counter-clockwise around the fire a ball of the woolen yarn threads.

When the ball is ready, one drops three drops of blood out of the left ring finger with the following words:
- If you will run for me here on earth, then I shall burn for you in Hell.

Then one takes and whips the milkhare with a birch twig and says:
- Money you will draw, butter you will draw (or whatever one wants the milkhare to draw).

Everything that one desires one can get the Milkhare to draw, and the Milkhare follows generation after generation.

To Curse – Become a Sorcerer – Amulets

I. Stab the knife into a footprint

There are different ways (incantations) to stab the knife into a footprint.
It depends upon if one wishes pain or other sufferings.
One stabs the knife into the footprint and says:

1. I heave the knife into the footprint and there you shall fall and there you shall lie and there shall you bleed to death.

2. I heave the knife into the footprint, and there you shall fall under an outcropping of stone. In the fires of hell you shall lie and there shall you wail and there shall you moan and there shall you be afflicted.

3. I heave the knife into the footprint and there shall you fall, under a rock in hell shall you lie until judgment day.

4. Under a rock in Hell shall you lie until you return (something, that you wish returned) in the name of God the Father and of the Son and of the Holy Ghost.

5. The Farmer went on his way, then he met a man.
- Where are you going, my man?
- I'm going to the farmer's farm to stab into a footprint.
- Stab in the hand, in the head, in the foot, in the body! Stab with a two-edged knife, stab into the footprint, in the name of God the Father and of the Son and of the Holy Ghost.
[One draws a cross and stabs in the footstep with a knife that is two-edged. One stabs in the head, hand, foot, etc. means that "I stab in the head, etc., for pain, "*rensel*," broken bones, and blood" or whatever suffering one wants to stab for.]
[1. – 5. – Erik Törnlund.]

II. For those greedy for vengeance

6. If one feels that there are some evil people who have thoughts of vengeance towards your person, then one should bite oneself in the left arm muscle and hit with the right fist under the left armpit, and recite:
- I order you, Devil of Lucifer, that you turn away from me in the name of the Trinity, God the Father, Son and Holy Ghost.

The one who is thinking ill towards you, will receive the distributed bumps, wherefrom will proceed so that it will become stronger the worse one bites and hits. – Jonas Norberg.
[I tried out this experiment a long time ago. It was a time I became so strange from I don't know what, but I had immediately clearly before me, that there was some canal, that had a horn to the side of me. I did according to this conjuration, and within 15–20 minutes I was back to normal again.

The day after I was going to go to Ante Molander with some errand and there was a person staying there renting, in the bed, and they were bad-off. Then I asked Molander, what had come upon the person in question. Molander said then that in the evening hours of the previous day he was inside and spoke about that he probably should pay me for a certain thing. One, two, three, in the meantime it was as if he got a slap from an invisible hand so that he fell off his chair and down on the floor.

Then I understood what time it was.

But Ante Molander had a great ability to put him to rights, for he believed completely and firmly, that he had sometime during the day met up with some devilry.]

III. To make violin strings break

7. One recites the following conjuration while a fiddler plays:
- As truly as David's harp sounds, so shall your strings break, in the name of God the Father and of the Son and of the Holy Ghost.

IV. To become a Sorcerer

8. If one wants to be a true sorcerer without needing to sell oneself to the Devil, then one should go to to the church yard's confines a Thursday night between two and four o'clock.
Here's what one says:
- Inhabitants of the kingdom death! This payment I borrow from you, so that you sometime might describe for me how I shall proceed to find out that that I wish to know.

Then one goes up to the church-bell, scrapes a little ore from it and keeps it in a bottle.

If one then wants to find out about something, whatever it may be, then one goes to the churchyard enclosure on a Thursday night and says:
- Inhabitants of the kingdom of death! Step forth here, and tell to me how I should restore this. This coin I have borrowed from you, shall be paid back to you on that day that I enter with you into eternity.

Then one may know that which one possibly and impossibly wants to know from the spirits, and each time one wants to find out about something, then one goes to the churchyard and repeats in the same way.
– J. A. Åberg, Karlsmyran

9. If one wants to know about the sciences of the invisibles' wisdom – namely about the families of Wights and Lucifer's, then one goes to a grave on a Thursday night between twelve and one o'clock.

Here one takes a little dead-dirt, opens the left ring finger, so that three drops of blood fall down on the dead-dirt and then throw the earth on yourself as the priest does when he casts the dirt on a corpse.

When one has done so, one has sold oneself into the power of the invisibles, and then you can learn from them everything one wants to learn in this way.

V. Amulets

10. There are different ways in which one can procure a protective amulet:
If one can kill a raven, before he has a chance to spit up the Raven-stone that he has, you grab it, then you'll have an amulet of the best type.
If one has this, one can safely travel to warring lands and stand as a target

for all the rains of bullets and hellish machines, bombs and granades, without injuring so much as a hair on your head.

11. When Napoleon of France stood against all his enemies, he had a whole Psalm – number 91 – written out from the Psalter. And when he was dead, they found it inside his shirt on the left side of his chest.

12. The surest protective amulet is still, if one buys the left collarbone of the corpse of an aged man and this should be done during a Thursday night during the waning moon.

13. A good protective amulet is also if one takes a one crown piece and bores a hole in it and threads it with a black silk thread through it. Then one takes ahold of the thread without touching the coin, and lays it in the mouth of a suicide.
This is a good amulet which can even be used to reveal thieves and evil people and to draw money or other things, whatever one can wish.
[When one puts the coin in the mouth of the suicide, then one can wish three wishes. One can also have this amulet to reveal thieves and other people in liquor, if one puts the coin in it.

But when one some day then leaves the earthly plane then one should have notes afterwards. I have once seen such a person's journey into death and if I lived to the age of Methuselah, I'd never be able to forget it. It was probably the most frightening sight that I have seen in all my days. Foam came from his mouth and he wailed like he was in the greatest need and he heard and saw the suffering and trials of the damned.]

14. The left ring finger of a corpse is also good as a protective amulet (see "To show a thief in a glass of liquor"!)

Treatments – Advice – Examples

I. Treatments

1. Pour a shot of liquor into a liter of water. Go after sunset to a well or spring; take a pail that you have taken with you, and put it down into the well and put the pail's edge under the surface of the water, so that the pail fills. Throw a one-crown coin over the left shoulder into the well without looking back; then go home and don't speak to or greet anyone you meet on the way.

Before you begin the treatment after that, recite for loss of fortitude, madness, ache, "*rensel*," an Our Father and Benediction or otherwise as many prayers that you view as being needful.

Then you take six hollow-straws and blow three times through them into the water, whereafter you take a glowing red-hot knife or "*lie*"[75] and cut a cross into the water.

Then you dip your hand into the water and make a cross in the middle of the head [of the patient] and go then with the hand down over the left cheek and throat, down over the chest and out along the right arm and down to the tips of the fingers.

The second time you make a cross with the hand up in the middle of the head and go down over the right cheek and down over the chest and then out along the left arm and in that way a cross is built in the middle of the chest.

Three evenings in a row you should anoint him with water so well, that not even a single dry spot remains on the body. But at each anointing the sick should take a little sip [of water], for otherwise the sickness can go inside the body. Additionally, what is done with the water at each anointing, you should pour it out slowly in the morning wherever and spit three times: if you don't do this, the invisible ones are able to get power over you. The water is kept in a place where no one sleeps.

II. Procedures while reciting

2. After one has recited for either confusion or such into liquor, or when one has recited into loose sugar for blemishes, one always has a knife of iron or steel, the tang of which goes completely through the handle.
When one recites and comes to the name of the Trinity, one moves counter-clockwise with this knife in a circle and says: In the name of God the Father ☩ and of the Son ☩ and of the Holy Ghost ☩. At each ☩ one moves counter-clockwise with the knife.

You should never say "Amen" for then spells and conjurations don't have any effect.

3. To heal such chronic illnesses such as nerve sickness, or such confusion of the mind as arises from such illnesses, then these spells and "cunning men" have no power in this case; healing should be sought in some other way.

4. All conjurations in this book are read three times with devotion. For no one who doesn't believe do these spells have any effect.

5. When one reads these conjurations three times, one blows unnoticeably a little at each recitation. This is true for whichever spell it may be.

---

75 The words "lie" and "lia" recurr in this text. I've been unable to find an attestation in dialekt, though it may have to do with the scythe or other sharp edge, since its use is referred to in the context of harvest.

III. About throwing out Water

6. One should never throw out hot water after sunset, for then there can arise some ill. Therefore one should always say before one throws out the water: Move yourself! and thereafter you can throw out the water for one is protected.

IV. On preserving anointing materials [salves]

7. One may not keep materials wherewith one anoints, or powder or whatever kind of medicine it might be, inside the house where anyone sleeps, for then they lose their magical power and effect and will be of no use.

V. Examples

8. If one is frightened, when you staunch blood, there is danger on the way. For then it can happen that the person for whom one is working can fall dead right there.
Many years ago there was a girl here in Mo, who cut herself in the foot with a "*lia*." It was during the harvest, when one was outside and cut and raked the hay.
   Then they cried out to H.O., a farmer here in Mo who could staunch blood: - H.O.! Oliva has cut herself with a "*lia*."
   He staunched the blood in terror with the result that the girl fell down and lay as one dead for two hours, but awoke again finally then.

9. At the Bishop's estate there was a young fellow who went to Sollefteå for an operation during the autumn of 1915. But as it was a growth that was situated in a dangerous position in the body, the blood couldn't be stopped, but rather the boy threatened to bleed to death.
They telephoned then from Sollefteå to the boy's home, that he was bleeding to death and didn't seem like he could be saved.
   Then there was a man, who could staunch blood and he was notified of the boy's condition. Then he staunched the blood, so that it stopped right at that moment.
   But between the Bishop's estate and Sollefteå there are six or seven Swedish miles.

10. I was in Håsjö last year – the summer of 1915 – at the timber-driving in the Singså, Jämtland. There was a timber-driver there, who had cataracts (blemish) in both eyes and could hardly see anything. He was sixty years old and was from Moarna, Ragunda.
He sent word to me when he heard that I could treat blemishes. Then I came

and recited three times into pulverized sugar, the conjuration that begins:

Jesus stepped onto Christ's table, etc. and within five 24-hour days he began to see as fully as before with the right eye. The left, on the other hand, that had been without light for 15 years, there was no healing for, for he had lost the nerves – and such a cataract isn't able to be treated magically, if one doesn't immediately seek out healing for it.

11. During the time I was in Singsån, there was also another person that had eye-trouble. I examined it and found that it was blemish (cataracts).
I worked then in pulverized sugar and when he had had his eye treated three days in a row, he was completely healed within eight days.

In the month of April this year he wrote to me from Stugun, Jämtland, asking if I would send him a little powder, for he had begun to have pain in the other eye. I sent him then a little powder as well as directions for use and I want to hope that he got better from it.

12. In autumn last year I got a letter from a woman in Sundsvall with the request for help for her poor eyes; she was eighty years old.
I sent her the powder in a letter and received three weeks later the message that she was better; even so, she wanted to have yet more of the powder. That I sent to her. And now, last spring, she sent word that she was almost completely well in the eyes.

13. Last winter I was with a thirty year old J. N. in Östansjö and lived there for a while. During that time he was driving timber in the forest down to Östansjö. One day he was loading timber down there by the lake, when his back went out and he was completely unable to move. And had a person not chanced to come down to the lake and helped J.N. up upon the injury, then he'd have had to lie there.

Now when he came home and was put to bed, his mother, who knew that I was knowledgeable about twists and sprains, wanted me to cure him.

Then I took a little lard and recited in it the conjuration for sprain and massaged him on his tender back three times counterclockwise in the evening.

On the following morning J.N. was up at six o'clock and went out to the woods just as if nothing had happened.

14. A little girl – two years old – here in Mo had rickets and I treated her in such a way that I recited for rickets, confusion and pain as well as the Our Father and the Benediction three times and within a few months the girl was healed.

15. A person in Stöde, Medelpad, became completely unhinged in a second, and they had to tie him up.

There was a person there who knew me and when I traveled past that place, they asked me for death and suffering to help the sick one.

I went there and did a working – I fetched water from a well; while I anointed him, five men had to hold him down.

The morning after he was calm though, and when he had been treated three times, he was on the road to recovery.

Since then, i have heard that he is completely well. But people believed that he had come up against the Earth man[76] himself.

16. In Noveledinge, Graninge there lived about fifteen years ago a Lappman by the name of Kristoffer Kristoffersson who could do workings to drive off bears and wolves from a piece of land.

So, he was ordered to drive off bears from Vestanå- and Korså- mo forests, since at that time there were plenty of bears that did great damage in the woods.

It was as if the bears had settled in the Indal- and Liden- forests in Medelpad during 1856–1870. Not less than 27 cows and 50 goats were buried in Högland, Vestanå, Korsåmo and Bodasåg forests during the summer of 1867.

That's why they sought out Kristoffersson.

When he was going to fulfill his assignment, he had with him an eighteen year old boy who was supposed to follow him to the highest mountain within the area of the villages.

When Kristoffersson came to the first high mountain, he screamed as loudly as he could the spell no. 1 »To Transfix Predators«. This he repeated then as loudly from all the mountain tops.

The boy, who followed him, became ill at ease and several times threatened to lose his senses.

But after that day neither bear nor wolf has visited these parts.

17. A woman K.H. in Vike, Holm was healed by me. Seventeen years ago, she had been destroyed by a boy who she cared for.

To heal her, I recited conjuration no. 3 »send back« etc. – in water and liquor. As well, I recited for confusion, loss of fortitude, pain and the Our Father and the Benediction. She anointed herself three evenings in a row and took a sip [of water] each time.

She is now completely healthy. This cure was accomplished two years ago.

---

76 Interesting word usage: "*själva jordgubben*" can be translated as either "The Strawberry himself" or "The Earth Man himself." I'm of the mind that this is a reference to the "*tomte*" or land spirit of a locale. Otherwise, other than foodpoisoning, I'm not sure it would make sense.

18. A few years ago it happened that a woman here in Mo was going to go to the grazing meadow on a summer evening after the cow to lead her back to the barn.

When she was on the way back home to put the cow in the barn, she ran into a stump so that she wasn't able to go anywhere for a whole hour, but had to be helped from there; and after this day she remained in bed with pain and misery and she became crooked and twisted in her entire body.

She sought healing with the old man from Strömsnäs [Strömsnäsgubben] and he said that she stepped on the Earthman himself. If she had gone to the stump the same evening and "offered"[77] to the Earthman, then she would have gotten well again.

19. The fifty-year-old A.L. – mason – here in Mo, was in Edsele in May of 1914 and was building with brick.
Then one evening he was at the mason's craft and was about to go down and go to his lodgings. When he was about to undress, he had an itching over his entire body. When he examined himself, he had red bumps all over his entire body, just like one gets with stinging nettles.

When we came to Mo, he asked me if I would cure him. I recited into water with a little liquor the words for confusion, that begin with >>If from you is taken power and fortitude<< etc., as well as for pain, an Our Father and Benediction – everything three times. Then he anointed himself three evenings in a row and within a few days he was completely healthy.

20. The sixty-seven year old F. L. in Strömbacka Mine in Bjursåker congregation in Helsingland had become confused when he was out plowing the fields in the autumn of 1907.

He got such a pain, "*rensel*" and itching that he couldn't sleep at night.

He sought out healing with five doctors and was suffering for five years.

One evening I came there and wanted to rent the house over night. That I did.

He argued his complaint before me and talked about how poorly situated he was and believed fully and firmly that he had been met by all the evil powers.

- For, said he, I have besought all doctors, but nothing helps for me anymore.

- Yes, I said, have you any liquor, then perhaps I can help you.

- Yes, of course I have liquor, he said.

Then I worked a treatment and recited for confusion, "*rensel*" ache and enchantment. The Our Father and the Benediction. Then he anointed himself three evenings. The first evening he fell asleep at nine o'clock and slept

---

77 "Myta'" possibly "mata" to feed, and thence to offer to.

until eight o'clock the next morning, and he slept like he hadn't slept in the last five years.

Now he's completely healed.

21. To take off the strings from a fiddle I learned from a man A.K. in Berg's parish in Jämtland; he is now sixty-three years old and he learned it from his maternal grandfather in his youth.
This is the spell that is given in the previous (C – To Curse – III – 7.)

One time he was driving a wagon-load over to Haverövallen and then on his way back went to a dance.

He made an attempt with this spell. The result was that all the strings on the violin popped and since there were no more strings to access, the dance was over that night – to the great sorrow of all the dancing parties.

MANUSCRIPT B

Supplement

I. To staunch blood

1. NN., Jesus Christ bore his cross himself... then blood ran ... before I said three words the blood stopped ... in the name of God the Father and of the Son and of the Holy Ghost.
– Axel Svensson, 46 years, Hammarstrand, Ragunda.

II. For ache, toothache and other pain

2. The Virgin Mary stood at the Cross of Jesus and as surely as she stood there, so surely shall this pain go away, that say I N.N. in the name of God the Father and of the Son and of the Holy Ghost.
[This is for pain, toothache and even for all sorts of evil for people and animals.]
– A. Molander.

III. Bad Ache and *Ränsel*

3. For people who are lying in bad *rensel* the following is a good means:
Go to the cemetery to a newly opened grave, best to where one can find earth mixed with the remains of a human body. Take a water vessel full of this dirt as a loan, and leave a one crown coin in the grave. Then go thence in silence.

Upon returning home, empty the vessel in a bathtub or such and fill the bathtub with water. The whole takes place on a Thursday night.

In the morning remove all the dirt from the bathtub, whereupon the sick one is bathed completely in the water. And however difficult the sickness may be, it will disappear completely through this cure.

But you should take the dirt back to the cemetery and take back the coin. [So, with Graveyard dirt both helping and overturning; and each time one borrows from the graveyard, the one should be serious and have the thought and the wish inside that to use the dirt, then it will come to pass, whether for good or ill.]

IV. Pain and Infected blisters (poisonous pustules)

4. Jesus and Saint Peter went forth on their way; he met a riding running swelling.
- Where are you going?
- To the farmer's yard; bore hole and stretch the bone.
- I shall put on you nine of God's fingers and ten of God's angels: up on a mountain where no one dwells; there shall you have your peace, under an earth-fast stone, there shall you sit and burn no one, swelling, you damned heart of poison. You shall ride both cat and claw and all the dogs in Hell's dwelling, in three names: God the Father, Son and Holy Ghost.
[Recite three times over the aching place, spit three times and smear it with a knife over it three times.]

5. Saint Peter went on a road. Then he met a swelling.
- Good day, Swelling! Where are you going?
- I'm going to break legs and crack sinews.
- Turn around to a lake where no one rows, to a mountain where no one dwells, in logs and earthfast stones, there you can harm neither man or woman, in three names: God the Father, Son and Holy Ghost.

V. Incurable Illness

6. If a person hasn't become well, even if they've sought out all the cunning folk and even the doctors with finding respite, then on a Thursday night – best during the waning moon – go to a grave and have with you a piece of cloth that the sick one owns.
One takes the cloth and ties around the gravestone with it – counterclockwise – a knot and says:
- You N.N., who lie here, you know nothing.
Then tie with another knot and say:
- You can take this sickness from N.N.
For the third time tie a knot while you say:

– For you feel nothing – in the name of God the Father, and of the Son and of the Holy Ghost.
The sick one should then keep the piece of cloth, and untie all three knots, then he'll be healthy.

VI. For Sprains

7. Jesus Christ, God's son, rode on the Gullbrands-horse. Then he fell down, and turned his foot out of joint.
Then Jesus Christ, God's son, got down and put the foot back in joint, in the name of God the Father and of the Son and of the Holy Ghost.
[Recite over the sprain three times and spit there three times; then take your knife and stroke over it three times, then the sprain will soon be put right.]

VII. For stomach cramps

8. There came three wise men from the East. The one stopped pain, the other fixed sprains and the third worked for the pains in people's stomachs in the name of God the Father and of the Son and of the Holy Ghost.
[The above is read three times in liquor or coffee and given to the one who has stomach cramps. You should give it to the sick one three times.]
– E. Gärdin.

MS 10

NORDISKA MUSÉET #33.823
SVARTKONSTBOK FROM TJULA SOCKEN, SÖDERMANLAND

1. <u>To fix a shotgun that is hexed</u>.
Take the barrel out of the stock and take the loose back screw. Then take [*flogrund* (*flygrön*)] as much as will fill the barrel, and bore a hole in the end through it. Go then to a running spring that runs towards the south, lay the barrel in it and let the water run through it 3 times (<u>days and nights</u> in a row) then one will see how it goes with the hexing. NB. But before one does this, one must first shoot with loose powder into another's baking oven.

2. To protect a shotgun
Buy at the pharmacy "Sabenwood" and put it with an awl in the shotgun stock, then no one can hex the shotgun. This type of tree is similar to cork and is hard as [tunder].

3.
Another method.
Take the barrel out of the stock and the back screw out of it. Then hang a living snake with a thread approximately in the middle of the barrel. Then put it on the fire and toast the snake – and the one hexing will be so as well.

4.
Another method.
When one shoots any animal or bird, then one must take a little hair or feathers as soon as one has shot, and keep in the shotgun case. When one discovers that the shotgun is hexed, then smoke it with it, then the gun will be fine immediately.

5.
To temper good shot and bullets.
Take a peat pellet and grind it very fine, and mix it with the lead when you cast in this way, you won't need to doubt hitting the mark.

6.
If the fire is taken from you so that no spark comes out, then pour the priming powder out and dry out the flashpan with the left nameless finger and load anew in its place. Put the shotgun opening in the air and ask with these words "What kind of weather we have today!" then the fire will return again.

7.
4. To become strong.
The one who has a rat's heart on him, from this he will become so strong that no one can hit him.

8.
5. To know whether a woman is a virgin or not –
Take a flea and put it into a glass of beer and let her drink. If she's not a virgin, then she'll pee.

9.
6. To gather horsetail seeds:[78] Take three tin plates and nine pieces of clean paper on each plate. Put them under the horsetail on midsummer's night, but one may not say a word. –

10.
7. To know whether one will get a 'yes' from a girl or not.
Lay two sewing needles on the floor in a cross and have her walk forth – if you'll get a 'yes', then she'll walk immediately over them, if not, she will stop in her tracks.—

11.
8. To get a girl to love you
Take a dove while it is using its immodesty, cut off its secret thing, dry it and grind it to powder, and administer it to the one you want to have love you – another: take the eyelashes from a living wolf and give it to a girl, then she'll be smitten with you – another: take an apple and put it under your left arm so that it will be completely wet with sweat, take it then with you three Sundays in a row to church, and give it to the one you want to love you

12. To cause one to sleep
Take a wolf's heart and put it under the head of the one you want to sleep, then he'll sleep until you take it from him. –

13.
9. Divining rod that will find silver and gold –
It is cut two times a year, Christmas night between 11 and 12., and Midsummer day between 11 and 12, then one will seek out a flayed-round hazel or birch, all of a year old according to the figure's growth written below, but when one goes out cut the divining rod, then one should remain silent and cut it in three cuts without taking the knife from the tree. During the first cut, one says: "I cut you, divining rod," during the second, "in the name of the holy trinity," and during the third "that you will show me silver and gold," whereupon one leaves that place without looking back. – Then, one should have heirloom silver and gold that has been stolen three times and been returned. Bore a hole in the divining rod, in the end which is the head, and put the silver and gold into it. Plug it up again – when one now takes the divining rod in one's hand and seeks for treasure, then one should say to oneself "I swear you, divining rod, in the name of the holy trinity, that you show to me silver and gold" then one will become well-disposed towards that which one seeks.

---

[78] *Equifetum arvense*, medicinal uses included stanching bleeding both internally and externally (Culpepper, 9). Magically, it was used for invisibility (Huson, *Mastering Herbalism*, 272).

14.

10. To keep the treasure where it is –
Take a hazel staff that is a year old and draw a circle around where the divining rod is, in the way that is shown in the figure, to a width of 5, 6, 7 or 9 alns, and when one draws, one should say the words written below three times –

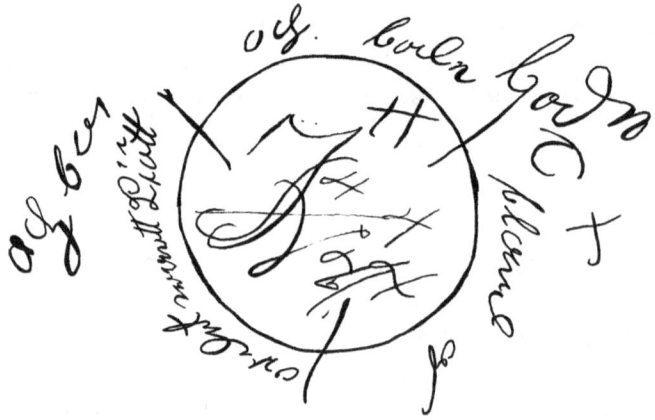

(And the Word was made flesh and dwelt among us)

15.

11. To take the treasure from the dragon without injury
First, one should dig until one comes upon the treasure. If there is a chest or something else, then one shall write with chalk three crosses. At the first cross, one says: "God the father." At the second "God, the son." And at the third "God, the holy spirit" whereupon one must hurry away from there – but first of all, before this is done, one puts a wooden cross in the pit, that one must have in readiness, upon which one hangs one's clothes so that it resembles a human being; because when one draws and hurries away from there, the dragon will come up, and will fly three times through the same simulacrum.

16.

12. Another method.
Take a few rounds of rope and put one end very slowly through the ring on the chest or the pot [of gold], then tie a dog to the rope, and take the other end and go a bit from there, and pull the dog down onto the treasure. When the dog now begins to scream, the dragon will come up and tear him all to pieces, and then he will fly his own way from there. When he has done the injury, then one can take up the treasure whenever one likes, and this without any danger of injury.

17.
13. To make a box that seeks out gold and silver.
One takes a toad which is male – and hangs it up by the back legs, and puts a water-bowl under him that he can't reach with his mouth, then he will release a stone out of his mouth that is called ONIX; put it in a box, and when next you go wherever treasure is, the stone will hop out of the box.

18.
14. Concerning the thorn-devil.
One takes the head from a "torndyfwel"[79] and puts it into a box along with "mastrikt" and quicksilver, and carry it in your hand. Then, when you go on rocks where some ore-vein is, then the box will knock very hard. –

19.
15. So that the ladies will do his bidding (lit., please him),
take an apple and put it under your left arm so that it will be completely wet with sweat, take it then with you three Sundays in a row to church, and give it to the one you want to love you

20.
16. If one takes a water-snake and boil it in water, and dip bread into it and eat, because it isn't poisonous, then one can know what other people are saying about one. –

21.
17. one who takes *ormgalla*[80] and put it in a nutshell and have it in one's mouth, that one will please the ladies. – another: if one takes a snake-sting and stick womenfolk with it, then they'll do his bidding.

22.
18. Concerning the bat
The one who takes the head of a bat and keeps it on him, when he goes to court, then he'll win. Item. If one finds a bat upon the fishing pole staff, then you'll get a good catch. Item. If one takes the left wing of a bat and stroke it on a woman, then they'll do his bidding. Item. Take three drops of blood from a bat in a linen cloth and carry it with you, then one will be able to hit whoever one wants. Item. If one puts the drops of blood into snuff and gives it to a woman, then she will do his bidding.

---

79 Thorny devil, a type of toad.
80 Ormhalla: *anguis fragilis*.

23. Concerning the hazel-hen.
The one who has a hazel-hen's heart under his left arm when he plays, then he'll win. G S SsG.

24. Concerning the raven –
The one who takes a raven's eggs which are red, and boils them until they become white, and puts them then back in the nest, then the raven will fly to get a red stone and put it upon them. One takes this stone and puts it on a lock, then the lock will spring open immediately. Another:, the one who keeps a raven's heart on oneself, he will not be sleepy until he puts it away from himself. Another: The one who keeps with him a raven's bill and his right little claw will get money for drink and favor from men –

25. Concerning the Owl.
The one who takes an owl's head and nails it onto a corner and shoots two shots towards the same head, he will ever after shoot accurately. Item. One who has such a head on himself is lucky in his doings.

26. Concerning the lapwing.
The one who goes to a lapwing's nest in the mornings will find a stone. The one who lays that stone on the breast of someone who is sleeping, he will become aware of what the other is thinking of doing. Item. The one who takes a white feather out of a lapwing's left wing and strokes a woman on the hand with it, then he will be loved.

27. Concerning the starling.
The one who takes a starling's heart and puts it under the head of one who is sleeping who one previously has wondered if they'd done something secret. Item. The one who takes a little starling's blood on his tongue, he will be so strong that no one will be able to hit him.

28. The one who has a rooster eat ants, then he will be drowned an hour thereafter. Then one will immediately chop chop off the head of him. The one who has it tight on one's person, he will not fall in love with anyone until he takes it off himself.

29. Concerning the mole
The one who has a mole's heart on him will become invisible. Item. The one who takes a drop of blood from a mole, puts it into snuff and gives to whatever woman one wants to love him, she will immediately fall in love.

30. To make oneself invisible and so that all shall please one (do one's bidding). In the month of August during the new moon one shall take an old swallow that is red under its head. Tear up the bush (misspelled *bröstet*?) on her and take out the heart. Cut it in two, then you will find two stones, one white and one red. When one has the red one on oneself, then one will be invisible. If one has the white one, then everyone will do your bidding.

31. So that men and women will do one's bidding. The one who takes the left forefoot print from a sheep shed and keeps it on himself

32. To shoot accurately
The one who takes a bat and shoots at him, then shall one take the blood that runs out and with it anoint the shotgun's muzzle.

33. Item. take hart's blood and anoint the barrel with it

34. To make oneself invisible
One shall take a raven and tear the heart out of him while he's still alive and then lay the heart within another raven's nest. Then the raven will perceive the scent of the other raven's heart. Then he will flee. A gold nugget, the one who has on himself the stone that is left will be invisible until he removes it from himself.

35. So that a woman won't dare to eat or take food.
Take green basil and put it surreptitiously under the dish, then the art will surely show itself.

36. <u>Concerning the Swallow</u>
Bind her feet together and hang her from the nest until she dies. Then one will find a stone. The one who scrapes off that stone and gives to a sick person in beer, he will get well.

37. Item. The one who has that stone on himself no one may hit, because the one who wants to hit him will injure himself instead.

38. To destroy lice and nits
He who takes honey and mustard seed, grinds it up and mixes it together and spreads it in the hair, then they'll disappear.

39. To become strong, one shall eat garlic three mornings on an empty stomach. That will strengthen the powers.

40. To carve a dowsing rod that finds water. One cuts a branch from a hazel bush that is a year old all dowsing rods should be greased with camphor, or the one who has garlic, *tjurbast*[81] and *bränsten*[82] on him, he will be lucky in all his doings.

41. To win at cards
The one who takes flax seed oil each morning and spreads it on his left little toe, he'll win.

42. To become invisible
The one who has the precious stone onyx, no one can see him until he removes it from his person.

43. To remove love for women
The one who buys 31 units of asafœtida and takes it in liquor (*brännvin*) during the waning moon, that one won't fall in love with any woman.

44. To have luck in obtaining money
Take a claw from a raven and rip a dog with the same claw so that it begins to bleed. Then, take half a weight of dogs blood and one weight of slaked lime, kneed from these a dough ball. The one who has this ball on him, he'll never be without money.

45. To stop bleeding
the blood
put your hand on the place and say: Jesus, he went over a bank, there met him the raging river; the water was dammed, the blood was stopped, both for woman and man – in the name of the father and of the son and of the holy spirit.

46. To place the runs on whomever one wants, take quicksilver (mercury) in a goose feather as well as the dung of the person one wants to unleash and stuff the pen with it, stopper it with magic.[83] Say: "Hereafter in magic, as long as one wants." If the feather remains there for three twenty-four hour periods, then the victim will die.

47. To stop the devil with the savior's word, In Jesus Name. got the longest three times in a row.

---

81 Alternate spelling for *Tidebast* or *tibast, daphne misereum*.
82 Alternate spelling for *bärnsten*, or amber.
83 The text reads "*mäd vit,*" and the only translation I have been able to reconstruct is "with magic," using Rietz's dialect lexicon who appeals to Hyltén-Cavallius's *Värend och Wirdarne* as a source.

48. So that no one will marry a certain girl, throw earth between in three clumps and powder, and "in the Devil's name you'll never be married," three times.

49. For shot, make a cross on the animal with your left hand and recite the following words three times, and the third time one shall say "amen." "You, God's creation, shall get healing for troll-shot, for *iorr*-shot, for sun-shot and for nine types of shot through logs and earth-fast stones shall neither folk nor livestock deny. In the name of the father and of the son and of the holy spirit."

50. For Troll-shot
Ture stood on the mount, and spoke to his mother Helena. Shot in the mouth, healing at the very same moment.

51. For Lapp-shot
The Lapp was going to go out to shoot, Our Lord Christ came;
What will you shoot?
I will shoot folk and livestock
and everything that is in front of me.
I will make you great,
while you'll be shooting at logs and stones.

52. For a cold-sore
Freeze the frost in the wide world
great rivers run and rage
cold out and hot in,
healing in the very same moment.

53. To hex wolves devastation among livestock, one takes the right foreleg from a wolf, and burns it and grinds it to a powder. Thereafter one takes three pieces of bread and puts a knifeblade in each piece.
Per kettle Psson

54. Concerning horses
To make a horse dapper (courageous) one shall take garlic and asafœtida, kneed bitesized bits with it, three times when one feeds, and give it a little each fourteenth day as well as a little [*säwenbom*[84]] and a little snake ash. which is taken during the winter. Dry it before one burns it to a powder, otherwise the powder will be essence-less and the sting should be torn away, otherwise the horses will be angry/evil. The garlic should be set outside for three nights during yuletide, but not [*iga*] it, because then the essence will go out

---

[84] Presumably this is the same as the Saben Träd on page one of this manuscript?

of it; rather, one shall take a box and put it into it and let it rot. The Christmas dry the stall, and the dung heap, and let it remain over him during Gold Night. The *sävenbom* will be for a stallion to stand, for a mare for the horse. [*sic*]

55. So that no one will be able to hex a horse when one shoes him for the first time, then one shall take a little from the end of the angle from all four feet a little of the grain on the legs a little bit out of the fringe and a little bit from out of the tail. Let him eat it in three bits of bread.
If he should then be found at some time to have not a mature courage, then turn up the upper lip, and three times cut him so that blood comes out, spread then a little fine salt into the wound, then he'll get his courage again.

56. For that which is broken, recite the following words three times:
Virgin Mary rode forth
there was frost on the flat-rock outcropping
the stone slid, the foot was twisted,
out of joint and out of bounds
but now it will be as it was before
in the name of the father and of the son and of the holy spirit.
    Recite then the Our Father.

57. For that which is broken out of joint, say the following words:
Virgin Mary rode over a bridge
and The Lord Jesus in her lap said
Then they came to a path where their horse broke its foot out of joint,
So surely shall I heal your foot or arm or whatever,
So surely as it was the Lord Jesus that sat in the Virgin Mary's lap,
raised the prayer.

58. To dull the pain, take hold of a cross with the fingers on that place where the pain or ache is, and recite these following words:
Out, ache, flee and wander,
for god's word are the same
and now Isaiah with God himself
the pain shall stop.
    Stroke with steel with your left hand and recite the Our Father.

59. For "torsk-bite" or pain, one shall ~~name where the pain is~~
For worm-bite
Virgin Mary goes her way down the road
There she meets a man
Where shall you go?
I shall go and bite

[then, one shall name the name of the person who has the injury]
They make out but rather
go under a bridge where no one goes
into a forest where no one dwells,
under logs and stones and no person or livestock to deny it.

Carl Petter Spång

Perersonn Ptr i Stan stan Geri sä gag A A minitt uhager ga a siel och sine min sonen Petter[85]

MS 11

NORDISKA MUSÉET MS# 33.824

NB: All code realized by G. Ericsson. Code indicated by [brackets] and *asterisks*

1. To take care of "acid upset stomach,"[86] one recites the following words three times and the third time one draws a five-point[ed star] over it. The words are these:
Flennar flena opos or flick you shall shrink, be subdued, and then one says the person's name and the father's name as a dead man under the ground far away in the woods in the name of the father and of the son and of the holy spirit

2. To win at court, then recite these following words as soon as you see your opponent before he has a chance to see you: "I shall go to court and all my enemies will be as much as stones." Recite then three times in the name of the father and of the son and of the holy spirit, amen, but one should have one's shirt on inside-out. [*put three unused sewing needles under your left foot, as well as a tongue of a swallow in your mouth under your tongue when one recites these words.]

3. [*To soothe ache one repeats "out, ache, fly and wander, for just as God's

---

85 Looks like a child's practice in penmanship.
86 *Flen* is a dialect word that, according to Rietz, means different things in various localities. In southern Sweden, it has to do with an upset stomach, pain or discomfort from acid indigestion, etc. In northern Sweden, it has more to do with a reddened and painful swelling of the skin.

words are true and you, ache, remain in the name of the holy trinity. Amen."]

4. For worm-bite[87]
[*Maria went on her way forth
She meets a man.
Where shall you go?
I shall go and bite the one
Either the man names then his name
Into whatever he will be
No, don't do that.
You shall go into the wood where no one dwells
Into a bridge on which no one walks
There you will bite logs and stones
And to the harm of no one.]

5. To make stomach ache go away, prepare so: one waves/greets backwards three times and each time one draws anticlockwise, but this should happen the last Friday during the waning moon, three months in a row. Draw it with the left nameless finger.[88]

6. To blunt a sword with words: our [*lord went] forth with "heda" (heathens?) blunt swords and knives; with their blade-edge [*broad] chops and firm, it shall not cut more than a mere bit.

7. To blunt a sword: kill 2 snakes, take their "stings" and put them in a box. Put it in a cross-road on three Thursday evenings. Go thereafter to it and take the box and don't look back, nor open the box, because there will lie 2 poisonous snakes. Go and put it in an oven where there is burning the most heatedly, and look …the box. Let it lie there until the lock burns up. Run to it and take the box thence, then you will find two stones. Sew them into the clothing that you have on, then no sword will bite you.

8. Against witchcraft. Bind on your person these names:

"A r s n o t o r f a t t a f a l"

9. If you want to win at cards, then take a lapwing heart and carry it in your left arm.

---

87 *Torsk-bett* is a complaint of pain as a primary symptom, and was believed to be caused by the bite of a type of worm (*torsk*).
88 According to Valter Forsblom, this means the ring finger, often of the left hand.

10. Defense. Put a swallow's tongue into honey for three days and three nights. Put it under your "Pina" (suffering?) "pinna" (peg or stick?), then no one will win against you.

11. Against witchcraft. So recite these names over a running stream before the sun comes up on a Thursday morning, and turn yourself to the east, to the west, to the north and to the south and recite these words each time you turn yourself: "I bind sun and moon, stars and planets, and all heavenly powers that You shall never shine over the ungodly person who has stolen from me."

12. You shall shoot through logs and stones, roots and branches, and you will not be of any harm to Gods created creatures.

13. Another way for troll-shot
Make a cross on the livestock with your left hand and recite the following words three times and the third time one should say "amen." "You, God's created being I shall heal for troll-shot, earth-shot and sun-shot, and for nine types of shot through logs and earth-fast stones; there no harm will come to people or livestock. [*in the name of the father and of the son and of the holy spirit. Amen.]

14. How to do for broken [bones]
"The virgin Mary and Saint Peter rode over a bridge.
Their horse went out of joint
In the turning, and out of the turning,
And into the joint again"
    This is recited three times. The first time one spits once, and stabs with the knife once. The second time two times, and the third time three times, and then it is done.

15. A method to take care of troll-shot
One says:
"[*Jesus] went his way forth,
Then he met a Lapp
Where will you go, said [*Jesus] to the Lapp.
I shall go and shoot a horse or cow or other livestock.
No, you shall go into a wood where no one dwells
Into a lake where no one rows
There you shall shoot at logs and stones
Roots and branches
And be of no harm to people or livestock.
In the name of the F a S athsn (*Father and Sun and the holy spirit's names*)
[*amen]

16. [* a method to take care of broken bones out of joint
One says:
"The virgin Mary rode over a bridge
And had the Lord Jesus in her lap,
Then they came to a path
Where their horse's fot was broken out of joint
I shall heal your foot, arm, or what joint whatsoever
As surely as the Lord Jesus sat in the Virgin Mary's lap."]

17. For that which is [*broken out of joint
One recites the following words three times:
The Virgin Mary rode to the well
On the rock the horse advanced
And the foot went out of joint and ou-joint
But now it shall be as it hardly was
Name the Father, of the son and of the holy spirit, amen.
Then recite the Lord's Prayer.

18. To heal very painful or so-called inflamed [*bones.
One takes a human bone and puts it in the hole and burns when one starts a fire in the oven. And then one takes it and grinds it completely finely, and then sift it together with fine flour, and then spread it in the wound,] but be very careful when you spread it because if any of it gets in the eye, then one will be really blind and without any hope to ever see again; that's why it's best to be as careful as one can be, it is quite dangerous, but in cases of need very useful.

19. [*about the secret
If there is swelling, so buy some turpentine and blood-purifying drops and take it in water, then it is healed soon. That which is called "dröpel" it should be equal amounts of each type.]

20. "Virgin Mary went forth in the grass
She heard then the snake hissing
Then she took a binding, in order to bind the snake
I bind you in the name of the Great One,
You shall never do any harm to that person, or livestock."

21. To [*hex a] gun. Walk in their lane with your feet (-*lyk*) and say these words:
"Your luck I take from f8[ive] traps
you, then they turn
the birds fly and the animals run
take the blood
and intestines wrap around your arms, feet and legs

your shotgun will bleed, and never more kill
as truly as Christ is risen from the dead
[*in the name of the father and of the son.]

22. To hex another, and heal oneself at the same time
Take up three turfs of earth counterclockwise which is his trap. Turn them inside out, place them towards the north, then in the same footstep again backwards and these words: "Now I heal myself and bind and fix you even there, you who have stolen away the shooting luck from me. I fix you and bind you by sun and moon and stars and all the holy angels and martyrs, and that it should not come down. Your blood will make you as fearful as Christ suffered transfixed on the cross, and you shall not have peace under my knees until I get my shooting luck again. [*inam]

23. For scabies one buys type-setters' salve and mix in a little cream and smear it on. It helps.

24. To staunch blood-flow. Write these words with their [*blood] and cast it into the fire on a piece of paper: Buria Balta Bloria.

25. His blood will make him fearful
As Christ suffered transfixed to the cross
His blood will run about his heart
And he shall never have more peace
Than this running stream under my knees
Until he has brought back that which he stole from me
[*in the name of the father and of the son and of the holy spirit.]

26. So that no one will be able to curse your shotgun, write these characters on the shotgun: *#SE‡OR +*

27. Same: write these figures on paper and set the same paper in an auger-hole and shoot through the hole; then put a plug into the hole and say these words:
    That one who wants to curse this shotgun
    Death will usher him
    That one who wants to trick it
    He shall bleed for three days
    As other thieves want to covet it
    He shall never come to an honorable end
    As long as this same piece of paper
    Sits in the same hole
    You'll have luck in shooting.

28. Shoot a raven pluck it of all its feathers. Cast all the feathers in a running stream. There you will find three feathers but two will be standing completely still. Keep these feathers when you see something you want to shoot, so walk there clockwise around and close them in a circle, then they must wait

ERIK LÄNMARK i Spånga
MMDCCCXXXVIII
Carl Lager Länna Bruk
Amanda Josefina
Län Am
Åkers socken

for you. If you see the track of that beast that you want to shoot, so burn a piece of leather to ashes, and spread the same ashes in three tracks, and say: "So I bind you." Then the same animal must wait for you.

29. Have these characters with you:

30. *Holio* (Vg. Considerable) when you have shot the animal as he is, then take three drops of blood in your mouth and spread it on your shotgun with it. Next, cut off his "secret thing" and spread it three times counterclockwise around the lock, then throw it over yourself and don't look back.

31. To curse a shotgun when the shot is heard
Stick a pin between the bark and the tree and let it remain. It speaks to your shotgun "Curse the pin, a man with a cross on a tree, and shoot at it there 3 rounds, then he will get his rightful wage for the shotgun.

32. Or, go into the woods a Thursday evening when the sun has gone down. Split a little runpole in three parts from the root to the top, however so that it keeps above and below. Creep counterclockwise three times through it. Have with you all of your shooting paraphernalia and each time you creep, then tie a red piece of silk around the middle part and say:
    Here I bind misfortune here,
    And that one who has injured me
    And together with him all the devils of hell.
Then spit three times under the left arm, and leave.

33. To heal the man who curses the shotgun
First, break nine Alder branches out of their joints from 9 Alder trees. Make

for yourself from these a whip with dry twigs. Use with your shotgun for ¼ hour and say these words: The Devil's witchcraft, take it back home to him who has sent 7,000 devils.

34. The one who bears these words with him is protected from all of his enemies both visible and invisible:

+ R 7 O V + V + + + V + O +

35. That no spirit will bite you, take a sting of an adder and have masses sung over it for three Sundays, and lay it in your left shoe under the foot, then it will happen.

36. If you want a girl to love you, then write on a red apple "orsa torsa tersa" and give it to her.

37. The same: Take a swallow's tongue, and have it under your own tongue, and kiss her if you have a swallow's heart with you.

38. Shoot a kite and take her heart and put it under your left arm, then everyone will love you.

39. The same: take 9 types of fruiting trees on a Sunday morning before the sun rises, one at each residence. Bind this together with red silk. Dry it and burn it to ashes on a Thursday evening on an earth-fast stone to ashes. Have this in a hare-skin between the shotgun and the "lås" then you will have good shooting luck.

Either that, or have a piece of leather on you when you set off to shoot, or fish

40. To put out an accidental fire, write these names on a wood chip and throw it through the fire [*"Fir den Eianae ar E bara da E barosen"]

41. To be free from (troll-)shot, have these characters upon you:

4 + 9 Casl ue 4 Lazjo
Doorset

42. When you have a shooting competition with someone, bear these words on you: + aba + sadla + gabra

43. To curse a shotgun when you hear the gunshot: take 12 green blades of grass under your foot, and throw them over your head and say these words: "humina sakmeria" then the flashpan becomes completely full of blood, and can't be fixed unless…

44. Take the blood of a virgin, with it write on the shotgun ⟨𝑡𝐻 𝑃 𝑃 𝑃⟩ and a + then put it under the threshold rock, then it will be fixed again.

45. Burn an oak-stick on one end. Sway there three times counterclockwise around your left foot, and say these words:
    I hear shooting
    Your shotgun shall get to enjoy
    Evil I want, and I can curse it
    In all the 3000 devils' names.

46. [Note: repeated from previous page] If you want a girl to love you, then write on a red apple "orsa torsa tersa" and give it to her.

47. The same: Write these words on a piece of bread and give to her to eat: siop gsgli

48. The same: take a swallow's tongue and have it your tongue and "*tigs*" her (if you have a swallow's heart with you).

49. If someone is angry with you, then fix it so you get a glimpse of him before he sees you, and say:
    I see you with my radiant eyes
    And I bind your liver and lungs
    In the name [*of the Father and of the Son and of the Holy Spirit, Amen]

50. The same: Go to a swallow's nest when the older ones are out, and stop up the hole with clay so that the chicks will die from hunger. Then, after two days open up the hole and the chicks are dead, then the older ones will come back, and, finding them dead, they will fly away and take a stone that his fire-red, and put it on the chicks so they will be living again. With this same stone you can heal each and every sickness, scurvy in a drink. If you carry that same stone on you, then no one can injure you. If anyone wants to stab you, then they'll end up hurting themselves.

51. To soothe pain, then recite the following words:
I pray to God for you, you image of God's creation,
That to yours he shall be
Neither pain nor ache

Neither swelling nor smarting
More than the wounds in the side of Christ
[*in the name of the father and of the son and of the holy spirit, amen]

52. To treat a pimple, or skin infection
One says thus:
A sore would travel over sea and land
There she met a man
Where are you traveling to, he said.
I shall travel to the north
The blood rushes, and the bone breaks
You I shall forbid!
You shall go under the earth-fast stone
In a wood where no one lives
In a lake where no one fishes or rows
[*in the name of the father and of the son and of the holy spirit, amen.]

53. To soothe pain, then ones says:
Out, ache, fly and wander
For just as God's words are true
And now I am sure with God's help
That the ache will stop,
In the name of the holy trinity. Amen.

54. A method for treating troll-shot
Pain/Evil stood on the mountain
There came forth the Lapp, walking,
What do you want?
I shall shoot.
No, I shall be to your detriment!

55.
1. To restore that which has been stolen away
cut away for yourself three chips or bits from that place from where thing thing was taken, which one should know. Carry it with you to church and put the same wood chips under [*the altar]. Leave them there for three Thursday evenings. Then take them first of all of all (sic) three times taken around your right thigh, and lastly put them in a grave or a coffin.

56.
2. To curse a shotgun so that it will never kill animals
As soon as one hears the shot, then take three steps backwards and in the third step, cut up a turf and turn it around so that the grass comes downwards

again, and let it stay like that. Then the shotgun will smell bad and not any animal. But when you want to make it good again, then turn the turf around, and put it back like it was before, then it will be good again.

57.
3. Another method
As soon as you hear the shot, then cut a branch from its joint on the nearest tree, however so that the branch doesn't completely fall down, then the shotgun is hexed.

58.
4. So that he must ask for forgivness
Take the shotgun barrel from the stock and take as well the screw out of the back, but when it is done, then take yeast and fill the barrel with it, and stop up both ends with two oak-props, and put it on the fire to cook. Then the same one who cursed the shotgun will surely get such a magical run that he must come and ask for forgiveness. When one takes the shotgun barrel off the fire, he'll be alright again, but if he has a long way to run, he might also lose his life for the same.

59.
5. So that one will never shoot and miss ducks
Shoot first a drake and take the heart out of him, and dry it well so that it can be ground up finely into a powder. This is mixed then with the gunpowder. Then you will never miss shooting a duck, as long as the shot makes it all the way to the target.

60.
6. So that one shall be able to shoot the bird one sees, seek out three pieces of hail that have been shot into a bird, and when you then see a bird that you want to shoot, then take the previously mentioned hail in your mouth. Then he won't fly away, rather you may shoot him for sure.

61.
7. If someone stole away a bird out of a snare or trap, so that you can plague him and find out who it is, seek out three pieces of down or feathers of the bird that has been stolen, and take them. Then look up a couple of trees that stand rubbing up against each other, and put the feathers in between there where the trees are closest together, then you'll see what effect it will have. But don't let them sit over three days because then the thief can die.

62.
8. To curse a fiddler so that his strings will break

Take quicksilver (mercury) and broken-off screws and put it where [*the fiddler] walks then his strings will break.

63.
9. To protect a shotgun so that no one can hex it
Take three cloves of garlic and a little quicksilver and put it between the lock and the stock, then no one can hex it.

64.
10. To take a shotgun when it is hexed and nothing will help when you shoot at any animal
Take the shotgun and carry it to the churchyard in the evening, and put it across a grave until the morning, and take it then from there. Then it will be as good as before, if not better. This has been tested often.

65.
11. Another method
Take the shotgun barrel from the stock and touchhole and prepare the barrel full of urine, and put the barrel well into the opening then, and strongly again with an Alder plug and put it on the fire to boil until the plug flies out of the barrel. When it makes a bang from itself, and then the shotgun will be good again as before.

66.
12. Yet another method
Shoot a skate however so that it is not completely dead. Take the heart out of it while it is still alive and put it in the shotgun and shoot it out again but so that one puts the shotgun under the arm and turns the opening backwards, and makes it then clean again, then it will be as good as it was before.

67.
N:o 1 To hex a shotgun of narrow T A O H.
Take three rowan berries on the north side of the tree and have them with you; and when you hear the gun's shot, throw them over your head. Then both the shotgun and the person is cursed.

68.
N:o 2 Protect a shotgun
Write these letters on your shotgun, then no one can hex it:

5# HK+ ʃ 3

69. Then you'll also have shooting-luck, take a viper's heart and a dog's heart, tie it to your shotgun when you want to shoot, and when when (sic) you have shot, then hide it until next time.

70.
N:o 3 So that birds will sit still
Shoot a raven and pluck the feathers off it and throw it into a river, then you will see three feathers going against the current, but the others standing still. Take these three feathers when you see the birds sitting, then go around them so that you enclose them in a circle, then you will walk counterclockwise around them, then they all must wait for you.

71.
N:o 4 To hex a shotgun by the bang
When you hear the shotgun shot, then you should throw yourself down and roll yourself three times around, and yell as much as you can, then it won't hit the animals.

72.
N:o 5 To heal it of this
Take the blood of a virgin and write with it these letters: *4†ℓℓ*
and put it then under a door threshold, and let a [*pregnant] woman step three times over it, then it will be unhexed.

73.
N:o 6 To unhex a cursed net or fisherman
Go into the forest where you will find a thick tree. Lop off the branches and twist it counterclockwise to a wicker. Put the other end in the ground. Creep then backwards under it, and drag the net or shotgun with you, then you'll be cured of it.

74.
N:o 7 So that no one may take the fire from the shotgun
Dig up a turf with your hands. Then take a mole in your fingers and put it in the flashpan and say: "I have made my shotgun better!"

75.
N:o 8 So that no one can curse your shotgun
Take the tack of a dipper and comb portion and a silk thread and put them through your shotgun three times. Do this during Sunday Services 9 Sundays then no one can hex it.

76.

N:o 9 To make a maiden be sweet on you

Put 9 straws of grain-hay that have borne ears, and hold them in your hand. Take one of them and make yourself a pen of it, write her and your names and between them these letters: M. S. S. U. U. A. S. O. H. A. B. 9 H O e s Then put the leather in the shoe and put it in its previous rune. Do so three times.

77.

N:o 10 To take the fire from the shotgun

Take the hoof-shavings around the left foot of a horse counterclockwise three times, and take the dirt (or a mole) between the fingers and put it between the shirt and the jersey. Then go to the one from whom you want to take the fire, then he'll not have any fire.

78.

N:o 11 So that no animal will catch your scent

Take some birch bark from a newly cut piece on the eastern side of the birch, that which faces from the south, and tie it under your shoes. Then no animal will catch your scent.

79.

N:o 12 So that a thief will bring back again whatever he has stolen

Take a coin in your hand and go to water that is flowing, and a river that is flowing towards the east, and say:

>I exhort you, winds in charge
>I exhort you, earth agony
>I exhort you Odin from Oders farm
>That you take my possessions back
>I exhort you, the devil of hell
>I exhort you, Nappa, with all your devilry
>That you let this thief have neither peace nor relief
>Neither sleeping nor waking
>Until he has taken back that which he has stolen
>To this I put him in motion.

And this shall happen on two Thursday evenings after the sun has set and is hidden.

80.

N:o 13 In order to find out who has stolen

Make yourself a cross of [*human bone]; put it under your head when you go to bed, then you will know in your sleep who has stolen. It shall be *omtärligt* (unavoidable?)

81.

N:o 14 To have a thief bring back that which he has stolen

If one knows in which room that which was stolen was kept, then cut from there a chip or shaving and write these letters on it with young swallow's blood:

B·G·D·H·V·L·Y·H·E·W·o

You shall take this shaving and put it in the woods under a creaking tree, so that the thief will never get peace until he brings back that which he has stolen, even if it was 20 or 30 miles away.

82.

N:o 15 For [*trolls] carry these letters on you:

h:H:n:s:a:n:z:a:o

83.

N:o 16 To get a spider-stone

Take the largest spider you can get and put him in a new unused glass. Seal it well with wax, and let it remain a full year. Around there on the day and the hour the yarn was balled, then you will get a stone. It is precious, and useful to carry for everything.

84.

N:o 17 To make a person tell all their secrets and everything they know

Take off one from his right foot and put it over someone who's sleeping, and he will say [*everything] that you ask of him afterwards.

85.

N:o 18 To make oneself invisible

Go to where a lapwing has its nest. There you will find a stone with many colors. Keep it with you, then you are invisible.

86.

N:o 19 To see that which others cannot see

Take a gallbladder and fat from a snow white hare, and smear both of your eyes with it, then you will see a lot.

87.
N:o 20 To make it so dogs won't bark at you
If you have a dog's heart on your left side, then all dogs will remain silent.

88.
N:o 21 To get an ant-stone
Take a raw egg from a young hen, the first she has lain. Put it in an anthill on the last Thursday in Spring when the sun has gone down. Let it lie for nine 24-hour periods. Be careful at the same hour that you laid it there, then you will find the egg empty and instead inside a stone that is useful for every matter if one has it with one.

89.
N:o 22 Take a turtle the first you find in the Spring. Impale it on an aspen stake and let it dry out. Carry it with you. It will drive away from you all poisons. Nothing can injure you or pass pestilence.

90.
N:o 23 Make it so that you get a raven either young or old. Bind its tongue and yank it out with the root, and when you go to court with anyone then wrap it up and put it under your tongue. If you have never been so guilty to plead, even though you'll win.

91.
N:o 24 For witchcraft take a dog's heart, wrap it up in paper on which you write these letters:

92.
N:o 25 To get a swallow-stone
Cover over the entry into a swallow-nest on a Thursday evening so that the chicks are inside and that the chicks die. After 3 24-hour periods, tear up the entry hole again, then the mother will fly after a yellow stone. Keep this same stone. What the stone is good for: when you speak with people then these words will have an extraordinary effect in matters of law and rights 2) if you quarrel with anyone, then you will win without hindrance; 3) you shall procure great riches; and 4) what you begin with shall be well concluded.

93.
N:o 26 So that no enemies shall injure you, carry these letters on you:

[magical characters]

94.
N:o 27 So that no enemies can injure you, carry these letters on you

[magical characters]

95.
N:o 28 If you have lost something, then write these letters on paper and put it under your head when you sleep, then it will be revealed to you in sleep:

[magical characters]

96.
N:o 29 To win at trial
First thing when you get up in the morning, you shall put in your right sock before you put on anything else, and when you walk to court about anything then one says two times:

    Today I clothed first my right foot
    All my enemies who have done to me
    Whatever Divine power and might
    And the power of spirits
    Even though I bound a virgin with force
    I undertake nothing on this day
    So freely I go to court and meetings
    Just like that man who stood in completely white (penalty?)
    Knew right, and did wrong.

97.
N:o 30 Write these letters on paper. Have them with you, then you won't be found at fault that day:

[magical characters]

98. *Påbolius* can be bought at the apothecary and [*gʒf?4: gif?o*][89]

---

[89] This looks like unrealized or distracting code.

MS 12

NM 40.034
"CYPRANIS[90] KONSTER OCH LÄROR OCH DES INRÄT"
ONSBY SOCKEN, SKÅNE, 1809.

*   *   *

"THE ARTS AND TEACHINGS OF ST. CYPRIAN AND ITS EQUIPMENT."

1. Trap a bird that is called "snow-king," tie it and shoot it to death. Allow three drops to drip from the wound, and then say: "Wolf's fat" over it, as a plaster on the wound, then it will be healed – the "snow-king" should be of the grey kind and not the yellow kind.

2. Kyrieleison. Lord, be merciful, Christ be merciful. Kyrieleson, Holy Lord, be merciful. [?] + + Jesus Christ our lord, Flee you devilishness. Praise the Lord. The Lord won the Cross from Judea's trunk, David's root, Jesus Christ, Eternal Word, amen #

I, Cyprian, the worshipper of the eternal God and Jesus Chris is only son, the pure and true Gospel, confess by the holy Spirit in Christ Jesus whereof here I exorcise you devilishness and exhort you by God who has created everything from nothing; heaven and earth and the pure from the impure; by god the almighty; by god's mercy; by god's fatherly goodness; by god's unearned righteousness, thus done by god's ways as god and forbade the evil angels to enter heaven, I exhort and forbid them by all that is holy that God has created. I exhort and forbid by heaven and earth, by sun and moon, by the planets and all the radiant stars, by all the 4 Elements, by all God's holy angels, by all the great predecessors and hell-fires, by the four Evangelists, by the twelve elected apostles, by all the holy Prophets and the martyr's confessors and martyrs, and all the holy people's faith and patience, by all the holy prayers on Sunday and litanies, by Saint Bengt's nobility, by the Virgin Mary's chastity. I exhort and forbid you by our Lord Jesus Christ's honorable birth and by the holy cross that Jesus died upon, by the crown of thorns he bore upon his blessed head, by the three iron nails with which Jesus became fastened to the cross, by Jesus' nails in the hands and feet, by the whip and scourge with which Jesus was struck, and by the spear that Jesus was pierced in his side with, and

---

90 Cypranis is an obvious misspelling of "Cyprianis," named after St. Cyprian, who was a mage in the Christian tradition, and after whom most Danish black art books are named.

by the blood that ran out of Jesus' holy blessed side, by the water and blood that Jesus sweated out in the Garden of Gethsemane, by the words that Jesus spoke upon the cross, by Jesus Christ's holy earthly journey, by Jesus Christ's resurrection and assumption into heaven, by the old testament and by the new testament, by all of Jesus Christ's works and miraculous deeds which he has done in heaven and on the earth and all that which is in heaven and all that which is on the earth, and by the holy Trinity's name God the Father and the Son and the Holy Ghost.

G F + and S + and H Gh +
IHS S.b.[91]

Our Lord Jesus Christ walked in his Garden of Gethsemane. He saw his enemies standing before him, and took up his blessed hand and banished all of them in Christ's powerful name, just as I bind you devils and all evil spirits and evil people, and all sorcerers and elves and insane horses and *pookas* that are now listed, who have done N: N: any harm, whether inwardly or outwardly in any way. I bind you with the strong binding that Jesus bound his enemies with. I [*utlider*][92] liver and lung, tooth and tongue, bone and belly and gruel and by mule and strength, and everything on them both inside and outside now and forever, that they never after this day shall do N: N: any more harm in day or night. I bind you with the strong bindings that Jesus bound the Jews with in the Garden of Gethsemane. I bind you in the name of the Holy Trinity, of God the Father and of the Son and of the Holy Ghost, amen: amen =

G F + G S + G H Gh +
IHS Sb

Our Lord Jesus Christ said to his holy disciples Peace be with you, the same holy peace I spell and wish now and always over N: N: and forbid the devil and all evil spirits and all sorcerers and evil people, all elves and insane horses and every other troll and pooka that now have been listed that they shall never after this very day do any further ill inwardly or outwardly to N: N: neither day or night, in any way. In Jesus' holy and powerful words and exhortation that now is recited, turn away from said N: N: and never harm you N: N: any more than a mouse does to an earthfast stone. Peace over you, N: N:. Body and body inwardly and outwardly peace over your flesh and blood, peace over your sinews

---

91 While "I.H.S." is a regular part of the Christian Tradition, and is a Low Latin transliteration of the Greek IHΣ, an abbreviation of IEΣOYΣ or Jesus, the meaning of the addition "S.b." is uncertain.

92 3 Sw. *utlida*, from G. *ausleiden*, to cease suffering. Could this be a copyist's error? More likely to *cause* suffering.

and bones and belly, peace outwards and inwards. Peace day and night. In the name of God the Father and of the Son and of the Holy Ghost. Amen, amen – over this servant of Jesus Christ N: N:.

G F + G S + G the H Gh +
IHS Sb

3. The Litany to exorcise sick people

Lord be merciful; Christ be merciful; Lord Holy Ghost be merciful to this sick person. Lord God Father in Heaven. Lord Jesus Christ God's son, the savior of the world. Lord God, Holy and Holy trinity. Eternal God, be merciful to him/her N: N:. Lord be graceful and preserve this mortal human from the evil spirit and from the devil's deceitful desire, from all evil from Hell's burning, Keep him, dear Lord God for the sake of your holy birth, for your struggle in death, and bloody sweat, for the sake of your suffering on the cross, and death, and for your resurrection and ascension, by your holy spirit's grace from his last end to the ending day of judgment, help him lord, lord god. We poor ones pray to you that you will answer.

Dear Lord God and God's Lamb who carried the world's sins, be merciful to him, o you God's lamb, who carried the sins of the world, bestow upon him eternal peace. Kiyrie Eleson, Christ be merciful. Lord Holy Spirit be merciful over this person in the name of Jesus of Nazareth.

Now is recited the "Paster Noster"[93]

Jesu Christi fili dei misereij mei est apud a frites mehi misero olatori qui promo quo brudat di natus. C S mori

4. A person who is enchanted should go on a Sunday morning on an empty stomach and silently under an [abul], cut up a turf and put it on his head, and then go three times around the [apulen] and say these words: "If I am enchanted and must wait until I go into the earth, then now I have earth both under me and above me and await healing now, in the name of the Father and the Son and the Holy Ghost." Recite that three times and put the turf in its place again and go home again, and don't look back.

5. A way the ache of gout so that they....

Sun gout, moon, you yellow gout, you blue gout, you red gout, you green gout,

---

93 "Paster Noster" is actually the "Pater Noster" or "Fader Vår" or Lord's Prayer.

you brown gout, you black gout, you white gout.

I conjure you in whatever limb you are, whether yellow, blue or red, whether you are in the head, or in the eyes, or in the ears, or in the arms, or in the bones, or in the back, or in the blood, or in the teeth, or in the tongue; by the power of the majesty of God the Father, Son and Holy Ghost, by all the true articles that I now have recounted in God's stead, I conjure you, you gout and ache that you now immediately turn away from and surrender from this servant of Jesus Christ, male or female, N: N:, and no gout any longer to trouble him or her to their sorrow, or suffering in the temples, mouth or hand, or any joint. I conjure you gout and exhort you pain that you now immediately leave this male or female servant of Jesus Christ, in the name of the Father, and of the Son, and of the Holy Ghost, amen. Recite this three times over the sick one.

---

6. When sheep or calves or bulls are unable to live, or thrive, then take from the cud in the cattle-shed and recite this three times over them, and spread some of the cud onto all the livestock, then it'll be better.

With the promise of God the Father, and with God's powerful words and holy exhortation, in the name of the Father and of the Son and of the Holy Ghost, amen. I request and forbid all the sorcerer's and other people's arts, and of all the farmgirls and forest spirits, elves and defilers and all mountain trolls and all types of spirits, earth spirits, fire spirits, forest spirits and all evil, and woodwives under the table and all types of spirits and pookas and ghosts and all types of poisonous sicknesses that affect the calves, bulls, sheep or heifers of this servant of Jesus Christ, male or female, N: N:, or cause any evil to them. This I pray, in the name of the Father and of the Son and of the Holy Ghost amen. And I forbid them very much [hard] on God's roads and God himself forbid the evil angels entry to heaven. I forbid them to do it by heaven and earth, by sun and moon, by planets and shining stars, and by the four elements and by the four Evangelists, and by the 12 chosen apostles, by all the holy prophets, patriarchs, confessors, and martyrs, and by their faith and their witness and by the faith of all people and patience, and all the holy Sunday-lectionary, and by S b: [ädrughet]: whatever bewitching, evil, sickness or bewitching, or whatever has been sent of sorcery or other poisonous scourge or illness and evil hauntings that want to destroy, devastate or kill this servant of Jesus Christ's calves or bulls, sheep or heifer, I forbid you, in the name of the Father and the Son and the Holy Ghost, amen. --------

and I forbid you it by our Lord Jesus Christ's holy and honorable birth, and by Jesus's holy death and suffering, and by the Cross that Jesus died upon, and by the Crown of Thorns that Jesus bore on his blessed head and by the scourge and shroud that Jesus was hit with, and by the three iron nails that Jesus was bound to the cross, and by the nail wounds in the hands and feet and by the blood that Jesus sweated in the Garden of Gethsemane and by the water and blood that ran out of his holy side, and by the seven words that Jesus spoke on the cross, and by all the all the proceedings that the 3 judges of Pilate Herod and derided Jesus, and by the deridable death of the cross that Jesus was able to undergo and suffer and by the Lord Jesus Christ's holy and honorable resurrection from the dead and all the saints who are in heaven and on earth, and by all the miracles and wondrous deeds that God has done in heaven and on earth, and by all the old testament and by the new testament and the holy Trinity's name, of God the Father and of God the Son and of God the Holy Ghost, amen. In the name of Jesus Christ, amen.

IHS: Sb.   +   +   +

Our Lord Jesus he went in his blessed Garden. He saw his enemies standing before him. He held up his blessed hand and bound them all in God's powerful name, and holy name, just as I bind all of you sorcerer's powers and poisonous hits, pookas and hauntings who want to destroy and devastate or kill this servant of Jesus Christ's N: N:'s calves, bulls, sheep or heifers. I bind them with the holy and powerful bindings of God with which Jesus Christ, God's and Mary's son, bound the Jews in the Garden, and with the holy bindings of God with which Jesus bound his enemies, I bind the enemies of this servant of Jesus Christ, N: N:'s calves and bulls, with the holy and powerful bindings that Jesus bound all the devils and evil spirits with, I bind them in the name of God the Father, God the Son and God the Holy Ghost, and in the name of the crucifixion of Jesus Christ I bind their teeth and tongue, liver and lung, mouth and snout, bone and belly, life and woodenshoes, power and will, and all that is within them and upon them, now and always, in the Name of the Father and of the Son and of the Holy Ghost, amen.

IHS: Sb.   +   +   +

Our Lord Jesus who said to his holy disciples: peace be with you, the same holy and powerful peace of God I bestow and wish upon you now and always, this servant of Jesus Christ N: N:'s calves, bulls, sheep and all types of heifers, in the name of God the Father, and of the Son, and of the Holy Ghost, amen.

+   +   +   IHS: Sb.

And in the name of Christ Jesus I forbid all sorcery, hauntings, and devilishness and all types of sickness that are recounted here, that they never after this day will destroy, devastate or kill this servant of Jesus Christ N: N:'s calves or bulls, sheep or heifers in any way, more that a mouse does to an earthfast stone, and by these powerful words and holy exhortations that I have recounted now in the name of Jesus Christ, these calves, bulls, sheep and heifers of this servant of Jesus Christ N: N:, they will have a good, whole and God's blessing to a good luck just as Abrahams, Isaac's and Jacob's, in the name of God the Father, and of the Son and of the Holy Ghost; amen. In the name of Jesus Christ, amen.

Recite the Paster Noster[94] as well as the Benediction, in M: H:[95]

Blessed be the fruit of my life; blessed be my blood just as the man was healed by the voice of the prophet, in this way I will also be, in the Word of the Lord in the name of the Father and of the Son and of the Holy Spirit, amen.

---

7. John Kolerius gives the advice: the one who by means of sorcery and milk-defiler and thief who takes their milk, that they take the milk and throw it into a [prevet? Outhouse?]

---

8. When the cow or heifer has had a calf, then feed her first rye-bread, malt, salt, garlic and sulfur, then no milk-hare will harm her. M M: na.

---

9. Again: to perceive if the butter has been bewitched. That someone has stolen butter, will be smelling badly and fall to the bottom towards the malicious witch [...] wants to do unto them injury again, will from the devil be powerfully inflicted and brewed when one's stolen butter or stolen cheese are put on the glowing coals, and so that they may come and request something back or for God's sake ask that they may no longer be tortured. Village parsons and schoolmasters have well known this art in previous times, to return the suffering back on them, but among others the doctor [*pommerens*] is the best: to afflict them with [shit], stir the same in their milking pail. That's what all the malevolent witches do stinkingly. Because when the milk is stolen from the cow, he immediately took down his pants and shot loose a warning shot towards the devil... full of milk and stirred well and said that now you devil and those with you may no longer take away the milk. Lutarius in his art.[96]

10. The breaking off of a divining rod, say: Honorable Rod.
(Spit) I break off now here from the trunk in name of: God Adonai, Tetragram-

---

94 See footnote 91.
95 Letters of the first two words of the Benediction, "Må Herren..." from Numbers 6:24–26.
96 This passage is corrupt – it makes no sense in Swedish, and so I'm recreating a possible translation, but the grammar may or may not support it...

ator⁹⁷ [sic] neagion hagiotaton and of Jesus Christ Adonai tetragrommator Eloah bon ais, and in the name of the Holy Spirit Adonai tetragramator Eloah Ruack hakedosak Elohim:

in the names of the three holy patriarchs Abraham, Isaac and Jacob; and in the names of the four evangelists Matthew, Mark Luke and John; and in the names of the 12 holy apostles of Jesus Christ, and in the names of the four holy archangels Michael, Gabriel, Raphael and Uriel[98]; and in the name of the 4 Elemental Princes Cerubim, Tarsius, Ariel and Seraph[99]; N.B.: Bend the rod down towards the east and then the breaking is accomplished. Then hold it still with the thumb stretched into an "N" and say:

You Rod shall always and forever say to me the whole truth about what will happen in the future, and what will happen in the immediate present, and what in the past has happened; and you, Rod, will now as well show to me all the treasures that are under or are within the earth, however deeply they are hidden and however rich they are in silver or gold or precious stones: all this you, Rod, shall give a sign to me as a quick, swift hit before me, and I won't carry you elsewhere until another time than that I require to know. That this you, Rod, shall do as truly as the Lord Jesus Christ arose from the dead, just as truly as God lives and reigns in heaven. And as truly as God has created you, and as truly as God has placed the sun and the moon, and as truly as God maintains the heavens and the earth, and as truly as our Lord Jesus Christ trampled the head of Hell's Serpent, then just as truly you, Rod, will do all this as in truth God has created you and me. Amen.

+ + +

N.B.: Just when you say "Amen" then break the rod off and at that very moment, then conjure it in this way: "I conjure you by the four Elemental Kings, Cherub, Thorsis, Oriel, Seraph, and I conjure you, rod, by God Adonai

---

97 Of course, this name should be understood as "Tetragrammaton" the Greek for the "Four letter name" which is the name of God as found in the story of the Burning Bush. Obviously the transcriber was unfamiliar with the Greek orthography, and spelled it as he does here.

98 This one reference belies the provenance of this text. The Four Archangels of the Revelation of St. John of Patmos did not originally include Uriel, but Uriel was used in the Western Magical Tradition to round out the "Magic Circle" and its four quarters.

99 The obsessive in me requires that I point out that these names are not in keeping with the western magical tradition: Cerubim and Seraphim are choirs of angels, while Ariel might be a spirit of Air, and Tarsius of Fire, but the Tradition assigns those rolls to: Paralda to the East and Air, Djinn to the South and Fire, Niksa to the West and Water, and Ghob to the North and Earth. Throughout, the Swedish word "Princes" is used, though in the tradition in English, the term is commonly "Kings."

Taakosik Tetragrammator = and by Aedonaij Jahabiel tetrammator and by Eloah – and by Schoked barschemod – and by Sehoakoh, and by Elohim – and by Bea Zach – and by Zerbiell that in the midst of this rod is such a power that I will soon be able to find out that which I wish to know, and that I may wish to know in all of your Elements' or in the Elemental Kings I order that through this rod, Tetragrammator.... that has created you and me and this rod, amen, amen, amen.

---

11. NB: If you wish to know something or wish to find a treasure, you should do this with the rod. [Sigil ~ H]
I conjure you Rod, by Adonaij tetragramantor Zebaoth, Eloeh, Abh. Eloo Elea, and I conjure you Rod by the Lord Jesus Christ: Siloh the adonaij tetragramator Elohim Ber. Lord of the wonderful name Skhadob mallo: and I conjure you Rod by adonaij tetragamator Elohim Ruach hakadosak hagion hagiotatum – and I conjure you Rod by the 4 Evangelists' name, Matei, Marki, Lukas and Johanis: and I conjure you Rod also by the names of the 12 apostles, and I conjure you Rod by the names of the 4 archangels: Mikaiell, Gabriell, Rafhaiell and Uriel, and I conjure you Rod by the [name] of the four Elemental Rulers Chrerub, Tharssis, Ariell, Serafhim, that you will provide to me the correct truth that I wish to know, by demonstrating a quick dip before me, as truly as Jesus Christ was born of the Virgin Mary, and as truly as Jesus Christ's resurrection from the dead, and as truly as God lives and reigns, and as truly as God created the Heavens and the Earth, and as truly as God has created the Sun and the Moon, and as truly as Jesus Christ crushed the head of the Serpent of Hell: So assuredly you, Rod, will do this. N.B.: name here the purpose and give the correct truth to know if it has happened. Then put the divining rod on the Elemental Kings Element where the thing you desire is hidden; and hit that place with it saying the previously mentioned Elemental King's name in the following conjuration:

N, I [name] conjure you , you King of the Element of Air, who is called Cherub, or the Element of Water who is called Tharsios, or Earth's by the name of Oriell, or Fire's whose name is Seraph, by Adonaij tetragrammator Eloeh Abh. and by the invisible Elo Elell, and I conjure you the King N., of the Element N. NB: here is mentioned both the King's and the Element's name, which has just been mentioned. By our Lord Jesus Christ Adonaij tetragramator and I conjure you Eoloeh ben Lord of the named names sadobmals: and I conjure you King N. of Eleor hakedosak Elohim Hagior hagiotator and I conjure you King N. of the Element N: 5 and I conjure you King N. from the Element N., in the name of the four Evangelists Mateus, Markus, Lukas and Johannes /:6:/

And I conjure you King N of the Element N, by the names of Jesus Christ's twelve apostles. ·7·

And I conjure you King N of the Element N by the 4 holy archangels Mikaiel, Gabriell, Rafhael and Uriell, and your name King N of the Element N., Steer and guide this Rod and lead it to your Element and help me through this Rod to discover and take up the expectation of my soul, so that I may find out through this Rod and come to the main goal and complete truth of my purpose and find it.

NB: Here you declare before the Elemental spirit that you have named your desire which the Rod will show to you. All this, you Elemental King N of the Element N. shall do without artifice or hesitation fulfill my intent through this Rod with a quick hit, and let it also show the true metal of the Element that I wish to know; and this I order you, King N. of the Element N. through God Adonie tetragramentore Elak and through the invisible Ela Eheo. This I order you, King N. of the Element N, through the Lord Jesus Christ Adonaij Maschiah Eloahben and through the miraculous name Schadob malo, the Saviour of the world; and this I order you, King N. of the Element N. through Adonaij tetragrammator Eloh ruack hackedoseh Elohim hagion hagiotator; and this I order you, King N. of the Element N., through the three holy Patriachs Abraham, Isak and Jakop, and this I order you King N. of the Element N., through the four Evangelists Matt: Markus Lucas and Johanes, and this I order you, King N. of the Element N. through the 12 apostles of Jesus Christ, and this I order you King N. of the Element N., through the four holy archangels Mickaell, Gabriell, Raphael, Uriel [Sigil ZH.]

+   with   +   red   +

Now in the usual way hold the rod with both hands and while holding it, then say: Now, being, stand up you noble Rod, in Adonaij Tetragramator: Eloah, abh's name and the invisible Eleo Elea's name, and stand up you noble Rod in the name of the Lord Jesus Christ Tetragrammator Eloah ben and in the name of the miraculous Lord Schadob mallo. Stand up, you noble Rod, Rod and in the name of Adonaij Tetragrammator Elah ruach hackedosak Elohim hagion Haepitator; and in the name of the four holy Evangelists Mateius, Markus, Lukas and Johannes; and in the name of Jesus Christ's 12 apostles [corruption] raphael, uriel's name! and in the four Elemental Kings' name Cherub, Tarsis Ariel and Seraps [sic] arise and show me without delay and without falsity show to me, Rod, the truth of what I wish to know, and therefore I request of you, you Rod, through the power and might of God Adonaij Tetragrammator Elohim, who has created you and me, that you will show me the whole truth.

NB: Say now here your desire or intent, as truly as our Lord Jesus Christ was born into this world by the Virgin Mary, so I order you Rod in the name of Adonaij Elohe abh and in the name of the invisible Elo Eloa, and that I order you Rod in the Lord Jesus Christ Adonaij Tetragrammator Eloah ben and in the name of the most miraculous Lord Schados Malo, and this I order you, Rod, in the name of Adonaij Tetragrammator Eloah Ruack hakedosik Elohim hagiotator, and this I order you Rod in the name of the Three Patriarchs, Abraham, Isak and Jakop, and this I order you Rod in the name of the four Holy Evangelists Mateius, Markus, Lukas and Johannes, and Jesus Christ's 12 apostles' name, and in the four holy archangels' name Mikall, Gabriell, Rafaell and Uriel, and in the four Kings of the Elements Cherub, Tharsis, Ariell, Seraph, Jetroragiom Fafhom alsagaos alla amen!

+   [this red]   +   +

NB: Have I taught you the entire manner: The method from the beginning to the end to be done with this Rod now I will teach to you; which is that the often named Elemental Kings and spirits Cherub, Torssis, Uriel [sic], Seraph are actually: good angels foreordained to rule over the stars or the planets. Cherub rules over the Air, Torsis the water, Ariell the earth and Seraph over Fire.

---

12. The Conjuration of the 4 Elemental Kings

I, by the name of G.[100] conjure now you all altogether, in the for Elemental Kings. Both you King Cherub and you King Tahrsis and you King Ariel and you King Seraf, by Adonaij Eloah Jehowa: Elior bora, melaikgadolah koll haaretz: asiken kadosik[101] bek holl saka dosian and I N. conjure you 4 Elemental Kings by the holy staddonayij Masihiach Eloah Ben Jesus Jehowa Eloe bora malak gados, alkoi ha'aretz Jehaia Elohim Emethku Elohim Kajim mikitzepesthira shatiirat håretz = and I N. conjure you all in the four Elemental Kings by Adonaij, Eloah, Ruack, Hakedosek, Elohim, Jehovah, Elion, rora malek, alkor haretz. Jehowa and Mersadosak bekol Nakedosikom Jehofva haparetz THAT:

You Elemental Kings will show to me and my comrades in this Circle the pleasant service of now and from this moment cast away all of the spirits of Hell and ghosts and all the parties of Hell, and those who from all directions facing us, so that I might evade any of the spirits who are from the Elemental realms which might be injurious to me or my companions as to body, and soul and life; and that which may be displayed in this circle: you may resist them so that none of them may be able to divine and bring to fruition, and that they also not be able to do any harm from their Hellish realm to me or my comrades in this circle, either to body or soul or life. With one word that no spirit

---

100 God?

101 A misreading of Kadosh? Could this all be badly transcribed Hebrew? cf the cabalistic banishing ritual "Ateh Malkuth, Ve Gedurah, Ve Gedulah, Le Olahm, Amen!" Roughly translated "For thine is the Kingdom and the Power and the Glory Forever, Amen."

of Hell or Ghost may infiltrate even for an instant into this circle which myself and my companions might be harmed. In the Kings of the Elements; you King Cherub; you King Tarssis; you King Ariel and you King Seraph, through this I conjure you: by adonaij, Jehofwa Elohim hael hakedosek hagibbos wehabbora, and I order you by Jehofwa Elohim takipk Le Olam daij skokaddaij and this I order you by Jehofwa baaretz astohar skhoker and this I order you by Jehofwa Elahim Zabbaoth tetragrammentom hagin hagistatum; and this I order you by Jehofwa Elohim Zuramwekl Econ boras malok gadollal, kolhart, goatam. Amen.

+   with   +   red   +

+   with   +   red   +

Here you have, friendly reader, a considerable artful and rare highly valued treasure wherewith you and your fellow Christians can take and praise the Lord God very well. Then you can, as in former times, and with discipline ---

+   with   +   red   +

B.   F.
HABHTNABOL:
JOMRYJOMARY:
OROAY:-MECNASABY:
VOrem VOREJwOM
MAREW?
T.   F
ÆREN:AOMY=
EROMAYO:AUS
DTRY:DUMUCM:
Dcemme mayoiAju
Jommeyo, Nimoy
Jammemo yoaygmmd
Roayooa, Vmeyoooy
B
Vormamiro;

Eromortuij, Furtis, Booa – Futoooa, oo, Jmmarreoooij = Jehofwa Zebaoth, Jah. Schaddai Jehofwa hael Skadaij, Jehowa, Schaddaij mallo Jehofwa Eloa Jehofwa Eloan, Bena', Mullek, gadol, al, K ol haare tz. Elohim jimloth, Jehofwa bolan Zion, Jehowa Elohim gibor Jehowa Zebaoth.

the first and the last which believe in me; he shall have eternal life and I shall raise him up from the Earth and he shall be before my face into Eternity.

Here is a drawing and the Savior Jesus's who is the Christ own transcription with the cross in the hand and the Devil about the Cross and stomps on the Serpent and his head, and the chains about his throat and feet with the right hand. That bound about by the chains and with this words should have these words:

and praise the lord God as well, then [...] and you disciplined. May live...

+   with   +   red   +

These are the letters that are at the writing of the Savior and the dragon and the serpent bound who is bound underneath.

Tues meus Lucifer in romire mei Patris et spiritus santi tale vinculum est meus sanctus sangwis qui sates facit pro omnibus kara Elohim Eloha Jehofwa Adonaijim sehim Certha,

that is,

You are my Lucifer in my God's my Father's and Holy Spirit's name; such a binding is my blood, the holy, which was shed for all, dear, Elohim, Eloha, Jehofwa, adonaim skheim Certtea.

meeh undi et spiritium N: Compesu utki obtem, hear me and force the spirit N: so that he will follow me and will be subscribed to me. NB, within the half circles! And Answer unto me, Jehofwa asker akadosek bekol hakedosekhim:

if the evil spirits hesitate to follow and lustrate to you, then pray continually with bent knee these words, that you see here!

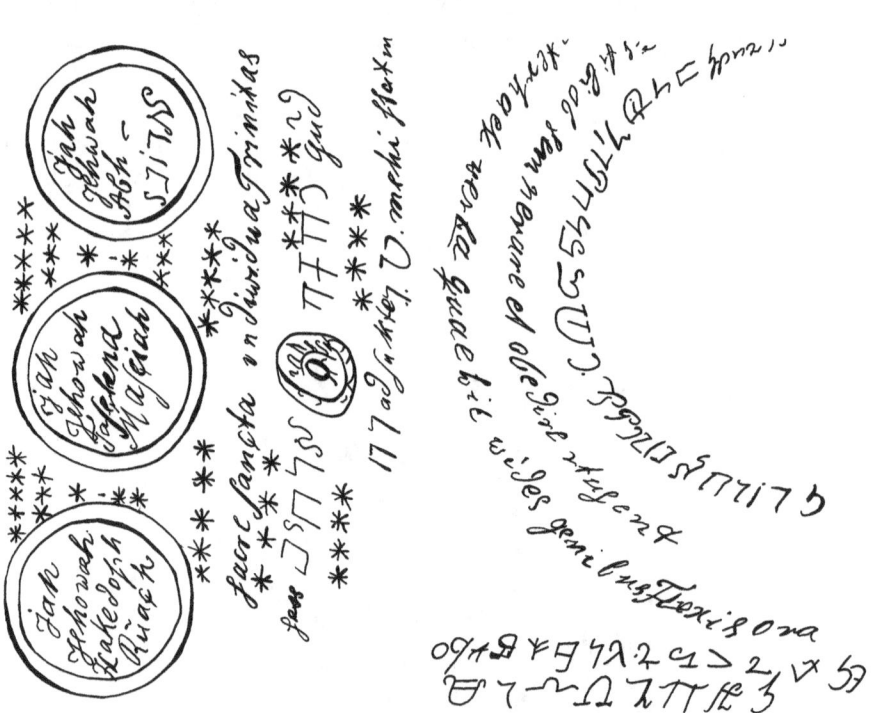

Hear me and force the spirit N. so that he will follow me and follow me and subdue the spirit N. so that he will follow me and listens to me, and force the spirit N. so that he will follow me and will be subjugated to me.

+ + +

and the spirit of Hell will quake before you and will gladly accomplish your intent.

+ + +

H --- --- mtapa sili maton[102]

Fehimotha Jehofwa Donaim Eloheia Schomackrin Zu Aradaij Clyomaij[103]

Now I will teach you, favoured reader, in what way you may force the Spirits of Hell to follow your intent and orders; a Sunday morning when the sun comes up and cut a Hazel or Oak walking-stick with these words:

+ + +

I by the name of N. cut you, you staff from this trunk, so that I may force all the spirits of hell with you – then cut it now in the name of the tetragramator, Eloah, abh, Elohim, adonij, and in the Tetrg: aloah ben Jesu Jetroschina.

13. To make a correct rod

The one who wants to have a correct rod that will attract silver and money, then he will undertake to seek out an Oak or Hazel tree, either a year old sapling or three year old both of a shape that both the length is equally long and equally grown, and the top is retained on them, and then it should be cut off on a Sunday morning before the sun comes up, and then the wone who cuts be completely naked. Then he will have a silver coin that was offered on the Altar, and put it in the end of the trunk. Then it's good. And otherwise it is good to take the silver that has been offered in the [klynan] and that is good.

This piece belongs to the one that has to deal with Treasures in the Earth and that which is almost [klögan]. Maschich Elohims Adaij name and in the name

---

[102] Once again, the ending "maton" leads me to believe that it might be a corrupt text, referring instead to "Tetragrammaton."

[103] Although I can't be sure, the original from which this is a copy might be mentioning Adonaij rather than Arakaij. Adonai, the Hebrew for "Lord" is a common occurrence in Hebraic magic.

of Tetragrammentor Eloach Ruach hakedosak Elohim adaij. Then write on a piece of paper the words that are at the end of page 67 Jehofwa Zebaoletz: tie the piece of paper around the walking stick; conjure it also in the following way in the middle of a circle: I by the name of N., conjure you in the name of tetragrammator takiph lalom daijsahaddaij and in the name of tetragrammator Elohim Emetz and in the name of tetragramattor Elohim Zaram weal Ehiom gaalam and in the name of Tetragrammaton Eloheka Elohaha Elohim adonaij haadonimka Elhagadol haibbor wehabora; and in the Almighty and Powerful name of Jah adonaij baaretz asker schokorad tetragrammator Zebaot hagion Hagiotatom, I, N. conjure you staff that you be as strong that you now drive away all the types that I strike of Hell's spirits, and the marks or the signs that I want to make, just as if I were standing in front of them and struck them personally.

So that you now in His spirit and in his spirit and over his spirit may thoroughly strike, break and thoroughly shake the head of the Serpent of Hell, who tried to tempt Jesus Christ in the wilderness. Just as our Lord Jesus Christ did with the spirit of Hell when he crushed his head. So that the spirit of Hell through its beatings may now follow me, and that you through this will force him as God's sword did the damned angels when the holy archangel Mikaiell deprived him of his power and might, and he was called with another name, namely Lusefär Satan. This might and power and strength that you all this may be able to bestow, confer the highest and strongest God Tetragram; tackif bolamdaij Schaddaij, this power and strength and might that you all this would be able to bestow and confer upon the highest and strongest God Tetragramator Elohim Emelkhu Elohim Kayim mitkitzep thor sechah widiral haaretx this might and power and strength that you are able to confer and bestow to the highest and strongest God Tetragramator Elohe hu ha Elohim reo Adonaij haa domien, haellhagadole, hagibor wekabora, this might, strength and power that you everything [from?] are able to bestow and confer to the highest and strongest god Sihoker and Tetragrammaton Zabaoth hagion hagiotaton

---

Pray now with bend knees

I pray to you Oh you Lord God you holiest god Jah Tetragrammatorn oscher, Hadosch bekol hakee doschim Eloah abh, bestow upon this staff NB: now with both hands hold the staff upright: with that might and power that I may be able to force and transfix the spirits of hell, especially the only [blota] spirit that your beloved son Jesus Christ out in the wilderness tempted that he should transform stones into bread, this spirit of Hell I want to know and be able to sustain all the beatings that I will make with this walking stick, in his name, and be afflicted just as if he stood personally in front of me.

O Lord Jesus Christ and God you Holy Spirit, in both holy persons and the same holiest trinity God the Father God the Son; God the Holy Ghost; Hear my prayers and the spirit of Hell for punishment for such vice and faithlessness against his God this Power and Strength that he now follows and submits to me; amen; amen; amen

Stand up now and take hold of the piece of paper on which you have written the name of the spirit into the earth and hit it with three blows and say this: I N:N:, I N:N:, you N: N: /: here you name the name of the spirit that you are beating, just as your God Tetragramaton Elohim who has created all creatures, now himself beats you in the holiest of all Trinity's name.

NB: no you can do according to your will as many blows as you want, but between each blow it is needful to say first: In the name of God the Father, and between the second in the name of God the Son; and between the third In the name of God the Holy Ghost, repeated, as often as you wish, or in such a way until the Spirit comes to you and with apologies asks you to listen.

NB: this I have, favored reader, for brevity's sake, in the previous given to recognize, so that you may be able to all the more cheerfully cause the spirits of Hell to come to your aid and to better compel them.

+ + +

[THUS ENDS PAGE 28]

[NOW BEGINS PAGE 29]

O, you most holy and highly praised God of the Trinity, Father and God the Son and God the Holy Ghost. I pray to you that this book that I have righteously and in the holy baptism have completed, is worthy to be borne out of God's temple and is right for you as my fathers brought me up righteously through the blessing of the Priest, through your holy names and through your holy laws from the sacrament of Holy Baptism back to my room again, so that this book may be just as righteous against all the spirits of Hell for the sake of you holiest name, in which it is written. a a a

H here the book ends.

[Amen] ꜱꜱ7ᵶ ᶞ𝑁 17 17 Mᵒ̣ 3ᶳᵒ
Ǝ ᵶ Ɔ Ǝ Ǝ Ŧ

Elohim Jehowa El
Nichawo Amen
G D G L So D N Mich
D F ✱✱✱✱✱

L L S O W F D. Heer
E S B Cⁿ ✱✱✱✱

M DDee G E D O G E H O
B R ✱ ✱ B F E S
Des alandi und das
morgens und 3♃♃ D n ß
D G ♃♃ D F L L Des
Nachts um 3 H J ♃ A
H F O auf D K. und dem
Fr: i H. m: und ♃
A A D H 3 D g H im und
L K.

14. to exorcise the dragon

In the name of God the Father and of the Son and of the Holy Ghost, amen. Oh, you old apadonius, who lies here on top of this treasure, and are revealed to me by God and mankind, and are given me to know, I put you down and exhort you to immediately depart and betake yourself to that space where I show to you with my created finger until the Day of Judgment, and release this treasure upon which you have long laid. All together: that you now depart from here and no more injure me, more than a mouse can damage an earth-fast stone in the name of the Lord Jesus, eo X X X

15. To see what is coming

[Go to] a horse that is sweating and take some of the moisture which is in the horse's eyes, and anoint your eyes, then you will be able to see how it is, but not see firelight. Also, you can do just like with a newborn foal that was born during that year.

16. When the dragon wants to grow

Then you should have ready [*spräng* – seeds] and then some earth that is taken first to a pulpit, and then by the Altar and then through the church doors. Throw it on him then he will fall and disappear altogether.

When you want to have your correct vision again, then wash your eyes with water from a spring. [This appears to refer back to the spell To See what is coming.]

17. When you want to attract money you should have on you 3 *öre*'s worth of asafetida and 1 *öre*'s worth of sulfur, and also from the altar cloth, as well as three splinters from the Altar and a little from the altar cloth [sic] and if you can find a knife with nine different types of steel in it, then no dragon can touch you or anything you have on you.

[…] to fasten the bucket or material which is in the earth so that it isn't taken away or is carried away […] and then you should have the [*spräng*-seeds] which are poured counterclockwise and they should be spread around the space before any digging takes place is even touched. These should have been in church.

And walk at the place or the area and take your knife in your left hand stab it three times into the earth in the name of the Devil, and walk then around the place 3 times counterclockwise and recite the Lord's Prayer correctly […]

and when you get the dragon, you should take out the first piece of cloth and strike towards him three times and say "I say to you, that you shall be dead and harmless as the dead man in the earth within 7 or 9 hours, and the third time, then give it in the name of God the Father and of the Son and of the Holy Ghost. Then he won't have any power, and then you should take up the hafwentorn [hawthorn?] staff that you cut on a Sunday morning before the sun comes up and with the staff you can compel the dragon away out of the place or out of your way. Then take away the materials and then throw three times some of it back, and compel him again, then throw three spades of earth over him == then you should have a cat with you when you want to take the treasure. Take him by the tail and drag him three times around it, and then let him run away, but look out that he doesn't run to any of the people.

Jesus

I see over you and I see over you and now I bind you who are, walk or lying here, with the bindings that our Lord Jesus Christ bound all the devils in Hell, and you shall eat of your own flesh and drink of your own blood and let me be in peace, by fosohaa Jeussum [sic].

     X   X   X

Our Lord Jesus Christ said to his disciples Peace be with you. == the same strong peace I wish over myself and these servants of God, namely in the name of Josohaa. And now I bind all kinds of trolls, sorcerers, elves and waterhorses[104] and all kinds of poisonous dragons, vipers and evil spirits; these I put down and bind and I exorcise by the power of God the Father, and the strength of the Son and the wisdom of the Holy Ghost, that you immediately turn away from this place where you are, and no more injure us than a mouse can harm an earthfast stone. And with these holy words and this holy [...][105] and all these exhortations then this servant of God will be freed from all evil in the name Fosohaa I H S X X X Jesus, the Lord's Son, our Lord Jesus Christ, went in his blessed Garden. He saw all his enemies standing before him: He lifted his blessed hand, he bound them all in the blessed name of Jesus, and with his same bindings I will bind all our enemies who are and stand against us in the name of Fosohaa X X X and in the name of Jesus Crist; in the name of Jesus Christ.

     X   X   X

---

104 Presumably the näcken?
105 Perhaps "staff" was left out of the original.

18. For freedom for yourself, use these characters 3 times and tie them then around your waist and cast a circle around you with X. Then take a [qvino tråd] around the entire circle so that you won't run into an accident == The exorcism:

Therefore in the name of God the Father and of the Son and of the Holy Ghost
X

I pay heed to neither sword nor shot

---

and and for that be my helper

belssebubs. ba; bal. wad

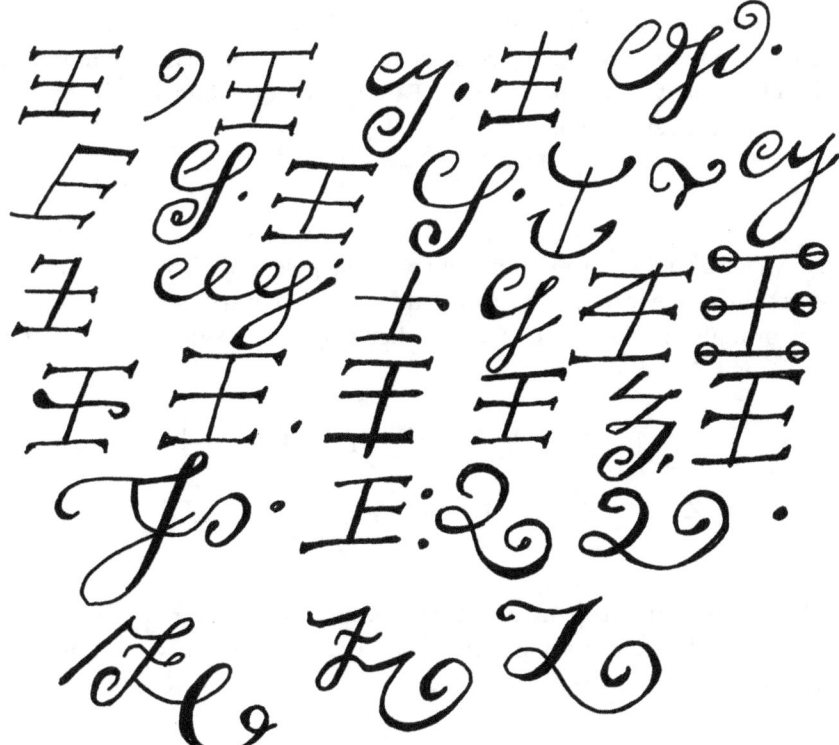

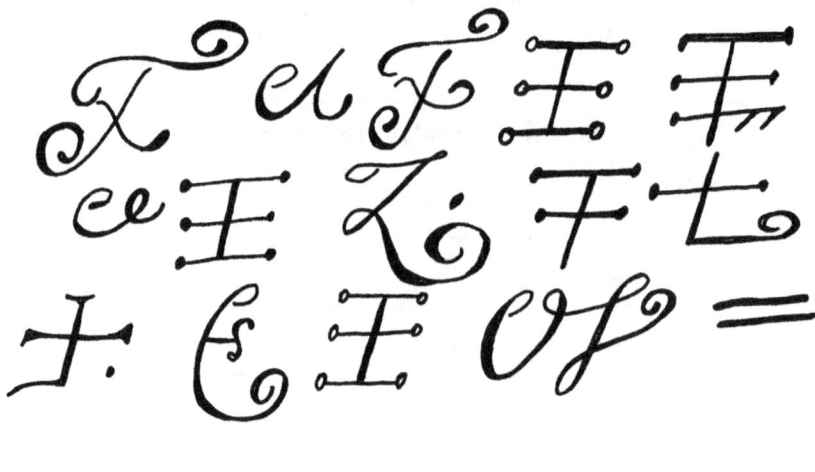

+ + + + + +

19. I conjure you, you unclean spirit by god and the holy trinity through Jesus Christ, that you turn away from this person, N. N. and leave him or her in the health of the body, in the name of the Father and of the Son and of the Holy Ghost, amen. Amen. Amen.

+ + + + + +

You devil with all the power I bind you with the power of Christ that you turn away from this person N. N. rose or gout whether flying or still, in his power that is brought by the name of the Father and of the Son and of the Holy Ghost. Amen. Amen. Amen.

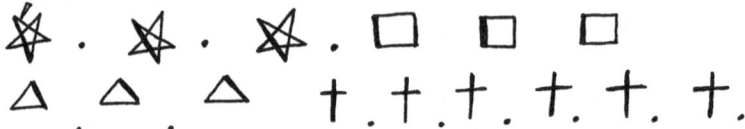

God help N. N. from his pain and suffering, save him for the sake of this servant of Jesus Christ, in the name of the Father and of the Son and of the Holy Ghost. amen, amen, amen.

20. Tried method proven and drink around...
I conjure you all evil spirits and every evil and all the devils [away] from this place this evening; a thousand devils' names and shall by Belssebubes court and Lussefärs court and the power of all evil spirits. With God's promise and

with the power that he taught them of in [*oly*], therefore I bind it to me and this place shall be free from vipers, dragons and all types of devils by God's Highest Commandment. I forbid all witches, mountain trolls, and sorcerers, woodwives and water sprites, all types of spirits and all types of poisonous hauntings I forbid by the Heavens and the Earth, by sun and moon and by all the shining stars and by all the saints and by the honorable birth of our Lord Jesus Christ and his resurrection from the dead, and by the sweet grace and goodness that our Lord Jesus sweated in the Garden, the crown of thorns that they set on the blessed head of our Lord, and by the nails and the spears that pierced through Jesus' blessed hands and feet, by the spear with which they pierced his blessed side, and by the water and blood that ran out of Jesus' side, in the name of God the Father and of the Son and of the Holy Ghost, I shall have my prayers answered. Yea, may God grant that this will happen.

Santa gar
Sante Hans
Santa rangett

Your strength will from this moment with be under my control, as a condemned person's soul in Hell, just so, all of Hell's devils are under the control, in the Devil's name, so shall your strength be taken from you, and with these words you shall have no power.

recited three times.

21. Against wolves.
The first wolfprint you see on New Years, then clip three woolen-threads from your clothes, and make the sign of the cross three times before your brow, and throw it in the track, and say: With this I clothe you, but you and your friends will take your meals at some other place, and not from my livestock. Rather herewith this is forbidden, by the Father's Strength and the Son's Wisdom and the Holy Spirit's Power. And each time recite the Our Father. To be recited three times.

22. Against predators in the forest and others

Wirack	21.
Red coral	21.
Bernsten	21.
åto Tantrafe	21.
Skutbek	21.
Allol	21.
Neggielis rot	21.
onthiemonium	21.
Human skull	21.
Mixed incense	21.
Asafetida	21.
Castor	21.
Pions bone	21.
Pione root	21.
Myrrh	21.
Bihor	21.
Sasafas wood	21.

All of these previously written herbs should be put together and ground into a powder to use as incense, and also to take internally eating a bit however your nature dictates to you, it is for use by a householder in his day to day work.

23. Eye salve is bought at the apothecary
white galmaja

24. For the brewing of liquor use this to cense the tin and the distilling tub

#	#	#	#

07 swam karat	8. öre
pione root	8. öre
pione stone	8. öre
male torne	8. öre
mineral oil	8. öre
asafetida	8. öre
angelica root	8. öre
antimonium	8. öre

25. To free your bees from all evil or what it may be, and that they won't travel off.

Take a little of a raven [*reesen*]¹⁰⁶ and bore into a bee hive so they won't fly away but the [*reen*] will be taken before the young one's fly away. This can be used for whatever.

---

26. A short exhortation for whatever, just use these words against all sorcery.

Just as God the Father by his majestic power and by his right hand on the cross, and by the cross here is bound the Devil Lussefärd, Bälssebub, Belial, and Asstor, with all their evil and angry company, that you may not enter that Heaven that God has prepared as is dwelling. Our Lord Jesus Christ got down off the cross and there and then bound all the power of Hell; In that way do I, a man of God, bind the small fiends, yea all the evil that flies and travels in the winds of the air. I bind all the evil that is in the earth and on the earth. I bind all the evil that is in the water and on the water. I bind all sorceries and evil people's sorceral arts. I bind the Devil in all his colors: both brown and blue, tawny and gray, black and white, yellow and green. I bind all the sickness of whatever type it may be, that I, a [male/female] servant of Jesus Christ N. N., may wish, that all the evil will not injure them, or theirs, more than a mouse can do to the earthfast stone that stands in the earth but never walks. But you all shall fly away to that place that God has ordained untill those days come that are the Days of Judgment, when the Lord of Grace, Jesus Christ, will become radiant in his holy Trinity, and I do all this together in the name of the Might of the Father X, and of the Power of the Son X, and in the child of the fully intended Grace of the Holy Ghost X, i Speritus filius sankto, Amen. San Jöra och här Per. Amen, amen, amen.

---

27. To put down into the cattle-shed's stall for sorcery and grounds where you have the cattle.

You should get out of bed in the holy trinity's name; and you should be fasting (on an empty stomach) and you should have washed clean your face and hands. Then you take an oak knob from the root, and whittle it to be four-sided as well. Then you bore 9 holes and write 9 Xs and nine types of fruit-bearing trees, and garlic, and hair from each of the animals [in the farm], and stuff this down into the holes, by Jesus Christ X. When this "pill" is ready, then recite the following words. "Dead and dumb are those who stand before me, but this "pill" I set down before me, in the name of the aforementioned people or animals, and take away all evil from this house. First a month, then a year, then as long as the world remains, this is ordered by Jesus Christ's own image, and by God the Holy Ghost. Amen.

---

106 Could *reesen* mean a few twigs from a raven's nest?

You should be fasting and silent except these words that are here and before the sun comes up on a Thursday morning or a Sunday morning.

28. Stopping Thievery

The one who has stolen this goose, I bind in the name of all devils, and by avoiding so many sufferings as the fire with which I burn up this paper, so that at this precise time and place you bring back ~ in N[ame of the Father and of the Son and of the Holy Ghost.]

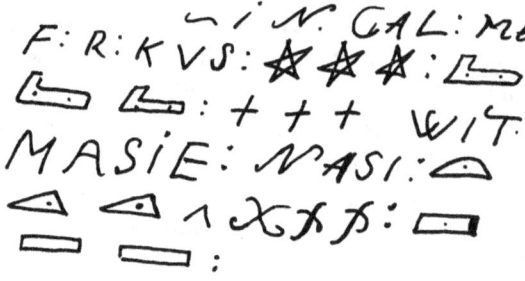

29. For constipation

Take a piece of Alum a half a finger long and as thick as the little finger, and anoint it with butter and stick it deep in the ass – and then at the same time afterwards stick in after it a piece of raw meat of the same size, and the sick one will sit on a chair and sit a good while. They he'll get up and walk around some, then he'll be loosened – this is a sure and tried means and written out from Hindrich Smit's Healing Book.

30. To protect horses over the winter from heaves

Cut a little from the mane and a little from around the genitals and a little from the rump[107] and mix it with oats or groats, and give to the horses during the autumn when they're just starting to be fed inside, but cut it really finely, or grind it. (untried)[108]

---

107 tail?

108 Based on the free alternation between the two, perhaps these rural healers did not know the difference between "proberat" or tried, and "oproberat" or not tried. Perhaps they were indicating their own familiarity with the method, or perhaps the Latin looked impressive.

MS 13

NM 41.652 SVARTKONSTBOK FRÅN NORRA SKÅNE[109]

*   *   *

Whoever recites this exhortation, should make the sign of the cross on the sick one with the finger that is called the gold finger, and it shall happen on a Sunday morning and on Thursday evenings nine times.

[Whoever ...cousin] then he should go, or another in his stead, to a church yard and ask for permission to take three bones and put them towards the fire, until they become warm, and then throw them into the water and put the bones in the same place, that you took them from, and wash the sick one in the water and recite this [...] then with God's help it will get better.

Kyrie Elleson Lord be merciful, Christi Elleson Christ be merciful, Kyrie Elleson Holy Lord be merciful: See God's cross, Jesus Christ our Lord. Flee you devilishness. Wash the wound + of Judea's tribe, David's Rold Jesus Christ God's word Amen. Christ lives, Christ reigns, Christ rules over everything.

I, Cyprian the Eternal worshipper of God, [...] Holy birth, by his holy circumcision, by his holy baptism, by his holy miracles and wondrous deeds, by his holy suffering, by his bloody languishing, by those ropes, wherewith Jesus was bound, by the kiss on the cheek that Mattheus gave to Jesus, by the scourging of his back, by those thorns and thongs with which Jesus was scourged, by Jesus' crown of thorns, by Jesus' purple robe, by the spear that was stuck up into Christ's side, by the five wounds, by the 7 (last) words that he spoke on the cross, by the sweat cloth, wherein he was wrapped, by Jesus' grave, by Jesus' burial, by Jesus' resurrection, by Jesus victorious ascension into heaven, by Jesus' Reign and Lordship at the right hand of the Father, by Jesus' return to judge the quick and the dead.

---

109 As this manuscript is one long conjuration, no item numbers have been inserted.

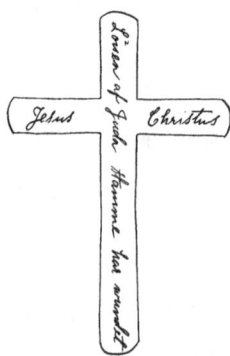

And by the Holy Ghost, that proceeds from the Father and the Son, by the Holy Archangel Gabriel [sic] and by the Holy Archangel Michael, by the Holy Archangel Rafael, by the Holy Archangel Uriel, by the holy Adam, by the holy Abel, by the holy Enoch, by the holy Noe, by the holy Sem, by the holy Jafet, by the holy Sett, by the holy Lott, by the holy Abraham, by the holy Isach, by the holy Jacop, by the holy Judam, by the holy Josseph, by the holy Mossen, Jossuam, Caleb, Tolle, Gedeon.

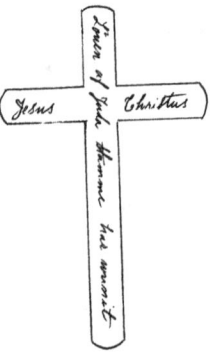

And by the holy King David, King Solomon, King Esechiam, King Josiam, King Wtriam, King Manasseh.

And by the holy high priest Jesus Christ. His only son's purity, and true Evangelical Witness, by the holy and within Christ Jesus our Lord I conjure you, you Devilishness, and exhort you by God, who has created everything from nothing, the Heavens from the Earth, the pure from the impure, by the omnipotence of God, by the Mercy of God, by the Goodness of God, by the truth of God, by the Righteousness of God, by God's single peace, that he has made with people through his beloved Son Jesus Christ, by God's invincibility, by God's indescribable honor of his Majesty, by the Holy Name of God, Holy Elohim, Emanuel, Jehovasg, the Beginning and the End.

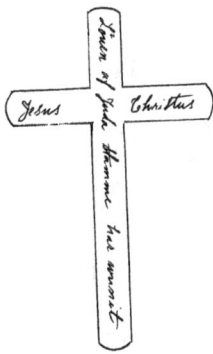

And by Jesus Christ, God's only begotten son, by his holy liberation, by his holy priest Aron, Finelsz Eleazar. To Jesus nane Jefunne Omie Simon Sachariam and by the holy prophet David and Eliam Eliseum, by the holy prophet Esaiam, by the holy profet Jerimiam, by the holy prophet Barrachiam, by the holy prophet Sachariam, by the holy prophet Joel, by the holy prophet Abdiam, by the holy prophet Sophoniam, by the holy prophet Michaeem, by the holy prophet Nathan, by the holy prophet Asap, by the holy prophet Nahum, by the holy Job, by the holy prophet Jonah, by the holy prophet Malachiam, by the holy prophet Daniel, by the holy prophet Ezechiel, by the holy prophet Habacuch

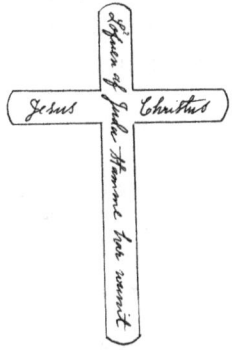

And by the holy John the Baptist, by the holy Apostle Paul, by the holy Apostle Peter, by the holy Apostle Matthew, by the holy Apostle Bartholomeus, by the holy Apostle James the greater, and by the holy Apostle James the lesser, by the holy Apostle Philip, by the holy Apostle Marcus, by the holy Apostle Mattheus, by the holy Apostle Andrew, by the holy Apostle Thomas, by the holy Apostle John, by the holy Apostle Timothy, by the holy Apostle Titus, by the holy Apostle Barnabas, and by the holy Evangelist Mark, by the holy Evangelist Matthew, by the holy Evangelist Luke, by the holy Evangelist John, and by the holy Patriarch Abraham, and the holy Patriarch Isach, by the holy Patriarch Jacob

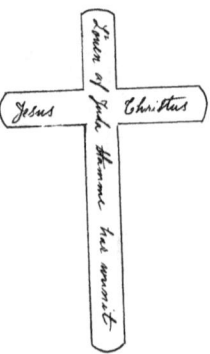

And by the holy Bishop Paul, by the holy Bishop Peter, by the holy Bishop Hilarius, by the holy Bishop Blasium, by the holy Bishop Ansgar, by the holy Bishop Anshelm, by the holy Bishop Valentine, by the holy Bishop Sigfrid, by the holy Bishop Eucharium, by the holy Bishop Gregorius, by the holy Bishop Hubert, by the holy Bishop Egidium, by the holy Bishop Godehard, Desiderius, Erasmus, Vedarius, Sixtus, Donatus, Paulinius, Lambertus, Florentine, Felix, Withadus, Martinus, Nicholaus, and by the holy Bishop Lazarus, by the holy Bishop Echardus, and by the holy church father Policarpus, by the holy church father Beda, by the holy church father Ireneus, by the holy church father St. John Chrysostom, by the holy church father Ambrosius, by the holy church father Augustinus, by the holy church father Bernhard, by the holy church father Jerome, by the holy church father John Husius.

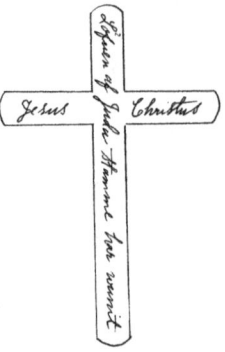

And by the holy confessor Professor martyr Cariutus, by the holy confessor Christophorus, by the holy confessor and martyr Severinus, by the holy confessor and martyr Antonius, by the two brother confessors and martyrs Fabianus and Sebastianus, by the holy confessor and martyr Vincentius, by the holy confessor and martyr Ignatius, by the holy confessor and martyr Simplicius, by the holy confessor and martyr Vitales, by the holy confessor and martyr Victorius, by the holy confessor and martyr Benedictus, by the holy confessor and martyr Quirinius, by the holy confessor and martyr Caudiaenus, by the holy confessor and martyr Georgius, by the holy confessor and martyr Isidorus, by the holy confessor and professor Constantinus the Great, by the holy confessor and martyr Olaus, by the holy confessor and martyr Stephanus, by the holy confessor Laurentius, by the holy confessor and martyr Rufus, by the holy confessor and martyr Marcelus, by the holy confessor and martyr Mauricius, by the holy confessor and martyr Dyonisius, by the holy confessor and martyr Galus, by the holy confessor and martyr Togerus, by the holy confessor and martyr Theodorus, by the holy confessor and martyr Julius, by the holy confessor Nicodemus.

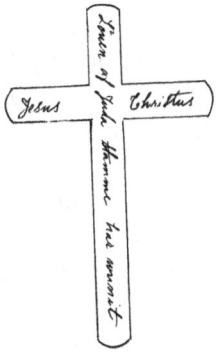

And by the holy woman Eva, by the holy woman Sarah, by the holy woman Rebeccah, by the holy woman Rachel, by the holy woman Abigael, by the holy woman Ruth, by the holy woman Judith, by the holy woman Susanna, by the holy woman Elissabat.

And by all holy virgins, by the holy virgin Piscah, by the holy virgin Agneta, by the holy virgin Birgita, by the holy virgin Agatha, by the holy virgin Dorethea, by the holy virgin Scolastica, by the holy virgin Euphrosina, by the holy virgin Rosina, by the holy virgin Gertrude, by the holy virgin Sabina, by the holy virgin Theodosia, by the holy virgin Euphenia, by the holy virgin Voltursa, by the holy virgin Petronela, by the holy virgin Bodil, by the holy virgin Margretta, by the holy virgin Gieitha, by the holy virgin Catarina, by the holy virgin Barbara, by the holy virgin Lucia, by the holy virgin Maria, Christ's mother.

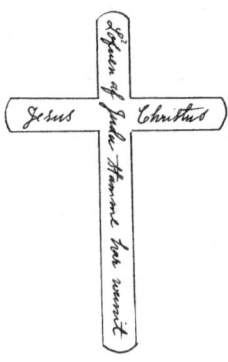

By all these articles, words and exhortations that I, now in God's place, have rehearsed, I exhort you all in the ten thousand regiments of Hell, and all of you who are under those regiments, that you may not any longer either yourself or by means of some of your servants, harm or hurt the place of this (male or female) servant of Jesus Christ, N. N.

I exorcise you, you uppermost and principle Princes in Hell, Lucifer, with all of your princes and servants in the 3 thousand principalities in the lake of death, the pit of fire and the land of shadows, 5 of whose names are Agron, Degel, Brisont, Avetzan, Frischop, Volan, Graga, Mulesa geres mefor Dorgant Candelux pison phlegton and Kings, with all their millions of consorts in mountain and in valley, in forest and the soil, in the air and water.

You, you Principal Prince Belsebub with all your princes and servants in the 3 thousand Regements[110] in the northern part of Tartarus, in the Earth in Oblivion, in the below by the names of Ragsepedes, Lucermin, Mempes, Averhan, Dole Dores Menergos.

And you, Prinicipal Prince Belial, with all of your princes in the three thousand Regiments in the South, in Gehenna, in Barratheo, whose names are Sersostenes, Slaudiens, Apolexis, Mesena.

And you, Principal Prince Astaroth with all of your princes in the 2 thousand Regements in the west, in Usisge and Lizeronttes, who are called nemores, Rephorsin, Aequiste, Parretemene, with all your consorts, wherever you can be.

Under God's highest commandment and the highest power and strength, that you not hereafter anymore injure and trouble this Servant of Jesus Christ, N. N., and this I conjure you by Sun and Moon, by all the shining stars, by the Entire Heavenly Host, by the rainbow, by the snow, by the thunder and lightning, by rain, by darkness, by [...], by the skies, by the Heavens and Stones, by

---

110 This term for a generic sub-group of the Heavenly Hierarchy is seen more commonly in English as Principalities.

Trees, by mountains, by valleys, by fish in the water, by birds under the heavens, in the name of the Father and of the Son and of the Holy Ghost.

ms 14

NM 41.674 LÖNSBODA, STRÖMHULT, FROSTENTORP
PER PERSSON "NERINGEN" (1759–1834)

*   *   *

[PAGE 1]

1. This lucky divining rod or "gore" which has grown out a ring a summer may be over 14 alns the bigger the better.

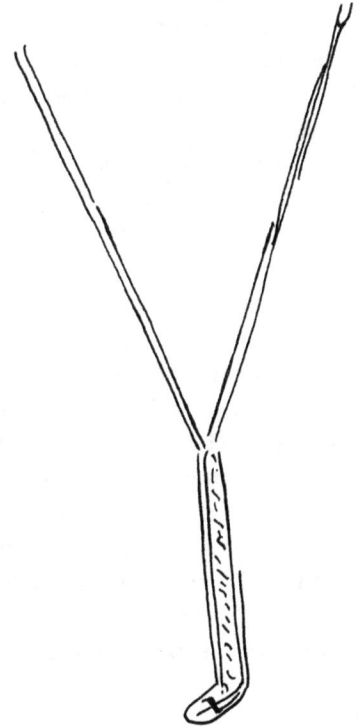

Per Svensson

[PAGE 2]

The fundamentals concerning buried treasure or walled-up treasure or sunken treasure, whether it may be of gold, silver or precious stones, copper or brass, so that these previously named can be opened and found by me according to the following art so that it is accomplished, it is the 2 August, 1674, during the process of Holy Testamonial the same year as af Ratzenborg ... under Wessen.

 Therefore, I beg you, my dear and faithful Eliam, that you do not touch upon this high and wise lore for that which is kept by the thief himself, and that no one wants that the same shall lie with me in the earth, but rather this must be relayed to you in writing since this high and wise art will finally come to effect, without the

[PAGE 3]

All-Highest's suffering or disgrace. God himself revealed this in a vision after the natural science, not now and again, but rather the one who on certain planets gives birth to worlds, therefore according to what your "Creulation" and planets so that you would be the same badness and together with (me?) therefore I relay this to you. Not like St. Anthony will you find any loathing here in the world which is to be relied on, and you hold to be worthy to reveal it on the earth so that that which I have done alone so that it isn't visible outwardly with limitations, or evil from twisting, remain under the ground without remaining hidden but sought out and for your own happiness, and you anoint to

[PAGE 4]

the enjoyment of prosperity and dug up the same may it be walled up, buried, or sunken, then I will show you in what follows how the same can be sought and have to come and pray as well, so that you take such of mine to your own. Those who you have previously tested their faithfulness that the same work with you according to the worth of the treasure, pray again to us that no one allows any wind to pass, or any water to be cast or a word spoken either. Hasten to pass orally what is to be done: when they have the same mind, then they see hastily if possible from the earth, or water, nine steps from the site he has dug, then he has three and makes then with it as you want. For then no one shall be able to snatch or take the same from you. Turn aside, I command you, to sit

[PAGE 5]

in God's hand and with faithful exhortation I wish to observe you in that in which you are made wise according to this honor. And in all High Wisdom to keep and will die, your Faithful G Rotter

2. For the first

When you want to break or cut a lucky divining rod or weak evergreen, then go to a plumbtree or a Thornberry tree, of the same sort that Christ's crown of thorns was braided, of which a split or a double tree grows together. And twist it off well, towards morning or sunrise and stand on the place so that when the sun comes up so that it is shining golden through them, and when you have broken off or cut the same, then cut three crosses in the larger end, and out on each side, and when these three crosses have

[PAGE 6]

ready ... and then walk three times around the same tree. Recite three times, even others, and recite the Apostolic Confession of Faith when it is done and for ... then make three crosses over the lucky divining rod. When you now want to look forwards and then look back, the second time, when you recite the Confession make sure you step in the same footsteps as previously. When you recite the Our Father and especially observe the touched place, and the last circumambulation you can break or cut such a one, any day, that is to say, on Sunday at sunrise or sunset; on Monday at 1 or 6 in the afternoon; on Tuesday at sunrise; on Wednesday between 11 and 12 noon;

[PAGE 7]

on Thursday between 11 and 12, if you know in advance where it is and have marked it the day before, since it will soon be ...; on Friday at 9 in the morning. Observe during the night when Christ prayed and sweated blood in the Garden, as well as was ... 9 hours driven to the mount of Golgotha and crucified

On Saturday between 4 and 5 in the afternoon. When the time and the day allow, this will succeed and it should be grown over 14 aln, a strong quarter, if it is longer or bigger, the better it is. For wherever a treasure lies, if the divining rod is small, then it will swing greatly in the hand, so that it will break.

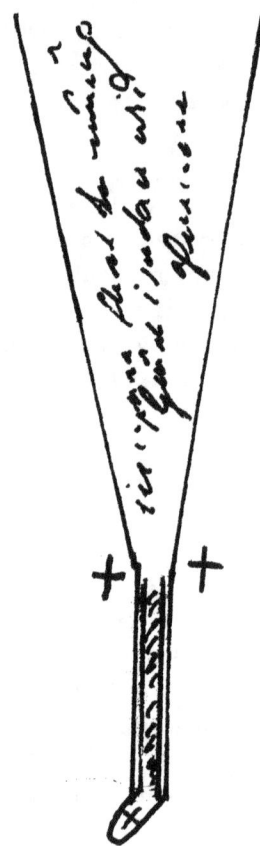

3. For the Second. Here follows the model to attain success and for the same

[PAGE 8]

the same shall according to the following words be broken off, as follows

I conjure you lucky divining rod, to display, and to surely and truthfully say wherever there may be hidden treasure of silver or gold, hidden or buried. I command and conjure you by the holy name Antony antoni antonj the Name Alay Alay Alay, that I so surely and knowingly can follow you as did the Wise Men from an impure country, Casper, Melchior and (Balthazar?) the star + + Christ's birth to Bethlehem which the wise folk also knew to have been found and further I command other by the highest

[PAGE 9]

by the four Evangelists – Matthew, Mark, Luke and John, as well as all the holy confessors, and angels and herewith I break you off, in the name of God the Father and of the Son and of the Holy Ghost, amen. B: here you may stand with your back against stones. Lucky divining rod and back over your head I break or cut the same off, and thereupon departed, you can quickly sow a few silver coins; it is better when you are under a branch or the lucky divining rod, and go towards the place where you perceive the buried treasure to be. You know and find then you take your divining rod in both your hands (unbygen no one) in each hand so that the end of the main trunk stand up in front.

[PAGE 10]

in this way

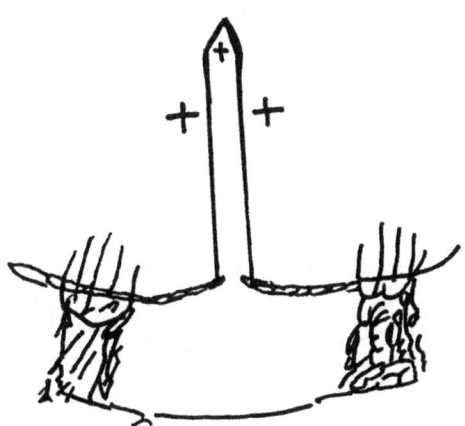

then then it will show you whether you should proceed forward or backwards, to the right or to the left, when you have a wooden plate, the divining rod will show that place and it will go immediately down with the end of the trunk towards the earth, and will turn itself around yet another time around and to the earth again. This is a sure sign for you and you can together with your helpers dig up that which has been hidden.

4. For the Third.

[PAGE 11]

that then the same burial remains firm so that it cannot be taken forth or can turn, then make three rings around about or crosses, as follows:

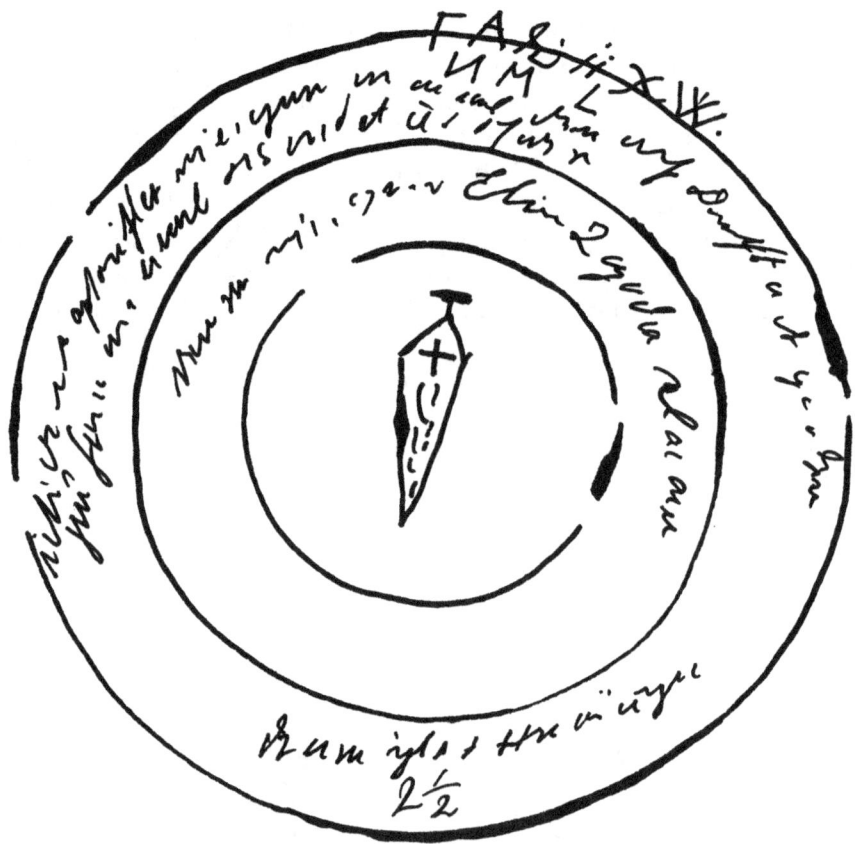

writing inside the graphic: in this outermost circle, the newly dug earth, the outer circle is 2 ½ ; this circle is two alns.

NB. note that in this previous outermost circle is written then 11 letters

[PAGE 12]

as one is outside, and one additional man who describes the circle. Then take your scimitar or sword and cut towards all four main directions (winds); so to the east, the west, the south and the north. When you have done this, then take your oaken bowl which also has written on a cross with three letters on each side, so on the first K:M., on the second the following B: R. X. on the third D W Y, on the fourth N: G: L, over a ... long ... should be of ironoak and in the sign of the cross a horseshoe nail or spike of iron one inch long and then let it stand in the innermost circle where there has been no speaking of people, no wind let, nor any peeing, as related before.

[PAGE 13] (LEFT BLANK)

[PAGE 14]

5. Greek and Syrian A B C

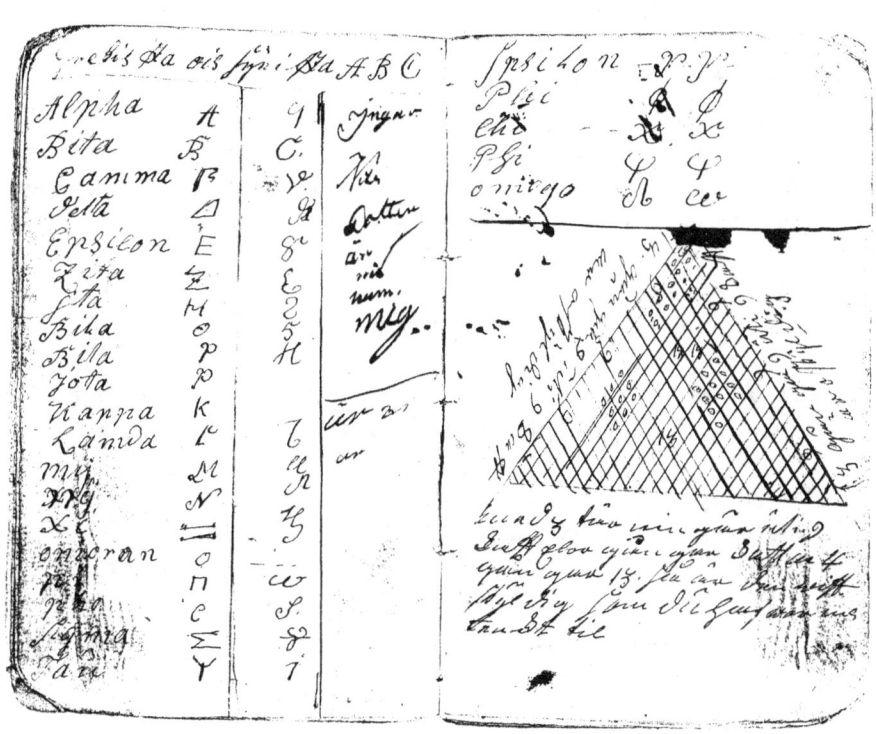

6. with three dice in 9 throws or the past cast 4 times, 13 then he is surely guilty that you have suspicions of.

[PAGE 16]

7. To take up treasure out of the earth
Emanuel's god with us, Jesus, the Lord's son, Jesus is a heroic name, the one who hangs before my chest, be my shield and sword, and disappear away as a dead man in the earth, in the Name of the f. and S. and the H. Ghost am.

"In wisar fajen wanett gen alpion rotas filius spiritus sancta fufs legostota + + +"
that you, old Abladanius of hell, who lie here on this treasure that has been revealed and assured to me by God and other people, thus I quell and exorcise you immediately to go hence and take your place until judgment

[PAGE 17]

day, there where I show you with my god-created finger, and let this treasure that you have for so long guarded stand with peace that you now immediately turn away from here, and not harm me more than a mouse can harm an earthfast stone, in the Name of the F. and the Son and the H. Ghost, amen. I H S + + +

Our Lord Jesus Christ said to his disciples, Peace be with you, the same holy and powerful peace I wish over myself and these servants of God N. and I damn all types of trolls and sorcerers and elves and watersprites and all types of

[PAGE 18]

And all types of poisonous dragons and other evil spirits, Those I quell and bind and exorcise: Help it, in the Might of God the Father, and the Strength of the Son and the wisdom of the Holy Ghost, that you turn away now immediately from the place where you now are, and harm us [no] more than a mouse can harm an earthfast stone, and these holy words and strong bindings and exorcism this servant of God should be liberated and free from all evil in the name of the F. and the S. and the H. Ghost. amen. I H S + + + + + + Our Lord J. C. Christ in his blessed Garden he saw his enemies and fiends

[PAGE 19]

standing before him, and he put up his blessed hand and bound them all in his blessed Jesus Name in and with the same bindings I will bind all types of trolls and sorcerers, mountain trolls, and forest wives, evil wights, elves and watersprites and all types of evil spirits, I bind them with their eyes and ears, their fortitude and their blood, their teeth and their tongue, their heart and their kidney and all that is within them, I exorcise in the name of J: Chri + + + in the name of Jesus the son, preserve me and help me and liberate me, Jesus, where you lead me ...

[PAGE 20]

Alpion Jesus may he preserve me, and help me, and preserve me, Jesus, may he kill you, and destroy you and decimate you and destroy you. Jesus + + +

thus do I bind all trolls and mountain trolls and sorcerers, magical serpents... and woodwives and watersprites and all elves, house wights, farm wights, and earth wights and all kinds of evil spirits and poisonous ghosts that are perceived here, and would do us any ill, those I bind firmly from us, by heaven and earth, by sun and moon, by planets and all the shining stars and by all the holy saints faith and patience. By our Lord Jesus Christ's accomplished birth and

[PAGE 21]

resurrection from the dead, by the sweat and blood that our Lord Jesus Christ sweated in the Garden, and by the crown of thorns that they put on our Lord Jesus Christ's blessed head, and by the nails and spear that they struck through our Lord Jesus Christ's blessed hands and feet, by the spear that they stuck in our Lord Jesus Christ's holy side with, and by the water and blood that ran out of Jesus' holy side, by the stillness of the Virgin Mary, and by Saint Benedict's glory and by the 4 Evangelists and by the 4 elements and by our Lord Jesus Christ's accomplished ascension into heaven from his holy grave with these words I quell and bind and exorcise

[PAGE 22]

I exorcise all evil spirits to turn from us and take the place that I shall show them with my god-created finger and by that which God has said in his holy word "the seed of the woman shall trample upon the head of the serpent." I do that in the Name of the Father and of God the Son and God the Holy Ghost. + + + Jesus, the Son of the Lord.

Jesus, I see over you and I see under you and I bind you with the bindings that our lord bound all the devils in hell, where you shall eat your flesh and drink your blood and let me be in peace in the name of God the Father and of God the Son and of God the Holy Ghost I H S + + +

[PAGE 23]

8. The Lion of the Divine Line has won
To research concerning knowledge to seek out hidden goods in the earth, take 9 spring-rye-thorns and amber and a hazel sapling that has grown for one year that same year and the day such as is possible at 12, you shouldn't go hang out with any person, or look at fire but rather hold yourself peacefully and go then as close as you want, and go 9 steps backwards and lie down on the earth, in the name of God the Father and of the Son and of the Holy Ghost, amen. A Helmet of tin this will show – thereafter, take yourself a flyrönn twig

either on Maundy Thursday or a Sunday morning before sunrise, just as night and day separate.

[PAGE 24]

Though, so that it doesn't fall on the ground, the same twig is best to get on a Maundy Thursday morning just as night and day separate. Let the bark remain on it, and carve the same with a sewing needle or a needle that is stuck through a black toad, these characters:

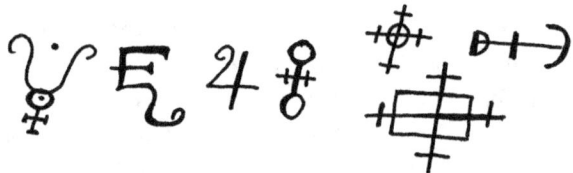

This should then be written when it is carried in the hand with the blood of a white rooster's comb, when it is borne in the hand over the place this it will show immediately a transformation to a snake, that you can hold in your hand. When you come there where it is, or ask the best time to take it up the contents of the goods.

[PAGE 25]

Goods out of the earth when between Good Friday and saturday as well as Sunday night between Saturday and Sunday and then at Midsummer night, for the whole time no sickness can be out on earth, then you should have something on you for protection, like *flygrönn* seeds, musk, sulfur and garlic, together the name with you, carved I H S in ironwood, ... or anything that has carried a cup, and stick this in the earth wherever the goods are, then no evil power has the ability to bear them away. ---------------- Some prefer to use sandal glass or perspelt?

[PAGE 26]

it, so that through the earth wherever they are, or how far down they are buried in the earth, as well as what type of metal they are, or may be –

The goods will come, and this surely through particular times of the year. Life's look during the year like a light burning up on the ark as white flames, and some as blue, and red. The white mark in silver, the red, gold, and the blue other metals.

9. To carve ... on a thief

Take yourself a wood shaving before having drunk or eaten anything on a Thursday morning or a Sunday morning and recite over it three Our Fathers and Holy Mary's prayer, write these following letters

[PAGE 27]

on clean, unused paper and put it in the water then you will see the thief in the water –

10. To conjure forth thieves with that which they have stolen – recite these words over the water on a Thursday evening and stand on your bare knees while you recite: Mirgo Esegregia pronebes S Appoliam Ferd prebes ad dominus pro nobrg.[111] Recite five Our Fathers and five Holy Mary's prayer that follows, for yourself and for your own liberation's sake, then blessed is the fruit of my womb, blessed is my blood which came to fruition by the voice of the prophet, then I shall also be, in the name of the Lord F. a. S. a. H. Gh. amen.

[PAGE 28]

11. another

Take a human bone at the churchyard and a little (skeft) under the altar and a little (flo) from the pulpit and a little from the church door, and put it under your head at night with the words and desire in a linen cloth, to get to see the thief, then you will see him. Another. Take a raven's feather, heart and topmost feathers from the left wing and put it under your head at night and when you sleep then you will see the shape of the thief as the feathers turn together in a ring --

[PAGE 29]

(This page contains writing in very faded ink, and the bottom has some troll characters, but the writing on the top half of the page is unreadable.)

---

111 Between the possibility of illegibility and a miscopied passage in the manuscript, this passage remains a mystery. Clearly, it is misremembered Latin, probably heard rather than read. *Mirgo* could be from the verb *miror*, to wonder, be amazed. *Pronebes* is likely *pro nobis*—for us. *Prebes ad dominus pro nobrg* could be *præbes ad dominum pro nobis*—supplicate to the lord for us.

[PAGE 30]

Nama på wirkmin
496 Österbergs lemd
Lönsboda[112]

[PAGE 31]
BLANK

[PAGE 32]
BLANK

MS 15

NM 63.180, "SAMLING AF UTOMORDENTLIGA MENNISKORS STÖRSTA HEMLIGHETER I FORNTIDEN."
URSHULT SOCKEN, SMÅLAND.
A HANDWRITTEN COLLECTION OF PRINTED MAGICAL TEXTS.

* * *

COLLECTION OF EXTRAORDINARY PERSONS' GREATEST
SECRETS FROM ANCIENT TIMES.

I. The magical Kabbala's spells or the Magic Art of the 6th and 7th Books of Moses, as well as the authentic Little Key of Salomon   p. 1
II. Prayers to the holy Corona Erke the Mistress of Treasures and over hidden treasure   p. 18
III. A Natural way to dig for treasure   p. 34
IV. Prayers to the holy and great Christoph, the powerful, the giver of all hidden treasure   p. 41
V. A well-known book to discover treasure and procure a Serving Spirit. Giving power over spirits.   p. 70
VI. Biblia arcana magica [page torn] after the treatment in the 6th and 7th Books of Moses, [torn] magical rules. [no page numbers appear on this page]
VII. Veneris little book to conjure spirits in a godly way.

---

112 Uncertain, perhaps it is an address.

VIII. The Algebraic Lottery: Kabbala of Rottilio Benincasa.
IX. Nigromancy's secrets and conjuration of evil spirits.
X. Planetary spirits
XI. Conjuration of treasures that are under the earth. Exhortation to the spirits that guard the treasures. A correct divining rod[113] – Solomon's true sigil – How one can summon a Spiritus Familiaris.
XII. The art of ordering the heaven's, the air's, the earth's and hell's spirits, as well as the Grand Grimoire, the black art of hell's powers and the correct secret of how to open them, and to discover all hidden treasures.
XIII. Arcanum arcanorum (The Secret of Secrets), mat[...] The Secret [...] of Secrets) That is: Jesui tisk Veneybook, or true power over all spirits.
XIV. Magic lesser powers secret school of art on, or the book about the true practice of the ancient divine magic.
XV. Selection out of the Kabbala in the 6th and 7th Books of Moses, translated from the cuneiform-semitic language.
XVI. The Holy Virgin and Abedirsan Gertraud's arch-mistress of treasures, (her) heavenly exhortation and prayers.
XVII. Alomonis Ladocki noteworthy nigromantic Magic – in the German Language.
XVIII. Almuchabota Ablegalim Alkakib Albaon, that is the summary of the unnatural Black Magic – By M. Seotis.
XIX. True location of treasures
XX. Complete method to discover treasures. Exhortations to good and evil spirits, that they must reveal the treasures.
XXI. The completion of an earth mirror, wherewith one can see all hidden things. Questions and divining rods for treasures, as well as the art of making oneself immovable, etc., etc.
XXII. Johann Kornreuthor's mighty exhortation and conjuration.
With a large number of illustrations.
Printed in Köln on Rhine at Peter Hammer, 1725.

I.
THE MAGICAL KABALA'S SPELLS
OR THE MAGICAL ART
FROM THE 6TH AND 7TH BOOKS OF MOSES
AS WELL AS A SELECTION
FROM
THE AUTHENTIC AND TRUE
ISRAEL'S KING SOLOMON'S CLAVICULA (LITTLE KEY).
WEIMAR 1505.
(See the other German: pp. 139–150.)

---

113 Sw. *slagruta*, divining rod.

Page 216.

N.B. the Exorcist can undertake the conjuration by himself, but if he has some with him, then it isn't so bad, while "three" is a holy number besides.

If they then are 3, then the one can carry the incense burner or even two incense burners, namely the one to pacify and lure forth the spirits, and the other to banish or dismiss them that one has had the occasion to require at that place. He shall even have with him a piece of chalk wherewith he can outside of the bounds of the circle in the four corners make the following figures:

Inside the circle is written:
The Circle, namely such as it is drawn on page 210–211.[114]

---

114 This figure is curious. In the grimoire tradition, there are many variations of circles, almost always found as three concentric ones with various names of power drawn from the Hebrew Cabalistic tradition written between them, stars of different shapes, sizes and constructions in the cardinal directions, etc. This figure stands out in its extreme simplicity, a single circle (not three concentric), with no names of power around it, and simple pentagrams drawn in the directions. I have not found a textual precedent for this variation, and yet the writer makes specific mention of the page upon which the model for his sketch is found.

MS 16

SVARTKONSTBOK FROM ÖSTRA GÖINGE HÄRAD, SKÅNE

* * *

1. For all types of sickness
If anyone becomes sick and begins to shiver, but doesn't know what kind of sickness it is or might be, he should take a *qvintin* (fifth?) of ground tormentilla-root (devil's shoestring) and a *qvintin* of *Theriach*, which mixed all together can be given to the patient in lukewarm drink of devil's shoestring water which is to be given to the patient all at once, whereupon he lies down to sweat between the sheets, and notices then that he is becoming quickly cool; he shouldn't go out either, especially in cold air that day. This helps assuredly, for all poisonous sicknesses and is used effectively on many.

2. For third-day's malaria, whether one has had it previously or if it is the first time for him.
Burn small swallow-chicks before they get their feathers and grind them to a powder, mix *bäfwergäll*[115] and vinegar, let it sit for 9 24-hour periods, mixed together, stir it with a spatula each day, so that it doesn't become bad. When it has sat for nine days (of 24 hours' duration), each is distilled from the water, whereof the sick one drinks it on an empty stomach each morning after he has had the chills 3 or 4 times. This is good also to massage into the scalp, to strengthen the brain as well.

3. For jaundice
Take the patient's water (urine), that he eliminates all at once, put it into a fresh cow-bladder, and hang it up loose up in the chimney in the smoke. It is best if the patient immediately urinates into the bladder, whereupon it is immediately tied up again. As the urine dries out afterwards, the jaundice will pass.

4. For headache and buzzing in the head
Grind *winrutta*[116] with rose oil and smear it on the head. It helps.

---

115 *Castoreum*, or beaver musk.
116 *vendelrot?* = valerian; *vinbärsrot?* = current root; or lastly, *vinsump* = the remains of grapes used in making wine.

5. For a headache that is completely too much
Tie lilies-of-the-valley-flowers that are large and put some of them on the pulses, just as tight so that no air blows beneath them. It helps.

6. For a tight and weak chest, as well as cough
By at the pharmacy from 12 to 15 (units?) of Balsam Sulp. Anis. and drop five or six drops on a bit of fine white sugar: thereafter, put it in your mouth and let it melt, and then swallow it down, which is done each third hour.

7. For chest sickness from a cold
It is excellent to wash yourself under the feet over a coal-dish or otherwise toward the fire with (*giädde*[?]-grease) especially fresh, as well as take two teaspoons of Tussilago Syrup, which is mixed up with cotton oil, equal parts of each, 5–6 times a day.

8. For eye sickness
It is very good to take a red beet and grate it, as well as add an egg white and cornflour to it, which is all stirred together as a soft dough, and is put then on the throat back in the neck in the evening when one lies down to bed. Smear the eyes with it every other or each third day with St. John's oil. (Punctuation in this item makes it difficult to know where the break in the sentence occurs in the last two directions.)

9. For colic: a little house-cure
Take blue paper as large as covers the stomach. Wet it on one side and spread on it completely finely ground pepper, but thinly, and put it on the stomach right over the navel. But Nota Bene if no fever is sought, this won't work.

10. For wind-colic in the intestines and the stomach
To be used: 4 measures of *mannaSabulata* and 4 measures of sweet almond oil which is mixed together with *fänkålls*-water, so that of it will be produced a thick pulp or paste, of which is taken 1 to 2 teaspoonfuls at a time 2 to 3 times a day.

11. For ringworm
Guasasi oil from the pharmacy is good to sometimes smear on as quickly as it dries. Take tar and wagon grease, the older the better, mix them together and smear it on the site a few times with it. Let that which has already been smeared on dry by itself. It helps.

12. For toothache
Take 7, 8 up to 9 grains of (Sassorgria? Sassafras?) which is bought at the pharmacy. Put it in a little linen cloth and stuff it on the tooth that aches.

13. Another secret "remedium" (cure)
Cut off the bark of a growing willow on such an angle that it can be put back again. Cut right out of the tree itself a splinter with which you put into that tooth that aches so that there comes blood on the splinter. Put that same splinter back after the blood has dried somewhat into the same place and then put the bark over it.[117]

14. A salve for scabies and pimples that break out on the hands
Take four measures Litargirium or silver glitter that has been ground up finely. Then, flour is cooked in a quart of wine or beer-vinegar, in a new crock over a slow fire. Stopper well this third part, if no more is cooked into it, then this is done. Then it is ready to swallow, and then you can cork up the bottle. Then is taken cottonseed oil, just as much as you have after this preparation. Put them both together in a mortar. It is well stirred and is crushed together until it is thick enough to be a paste or grease, if it doesn't thicken, put more cottonseed oil into it. Even though it is stirred it can be kept in a clay pot until you need it for the purpose listed above. This thickness is good to smear in wounds on horses.

15. To increase and improve the memory
Wash the head first with ordinary good lye, whereafter you immediately take 4 spoonfuls of rose water, 4 spoonfuls of Salvia water and the same amount of Poleije-juice, which is mixed together well and is smeared on the head which is then wrapped up with a warm cloth, then you shall receive the wonderful use of it.

16. For freckles
A type of grass that is called Maidens soap is put into warm water and then is kneeded into the face.

17. For sunburn
½ pitcher of water, 4–5 egg whites, a little bitter almonds finely ground and mixed together with the previous in such a way that one can shake it in a bottle for a ½ hour's time, this is really good to wash yourself with.

18. For headlice and nits
Take currant leaves, preferably of the black sort, as well as garlic, which are ground together and kneed the head with it then, then both the lice and the nits will die.

---

117 This may have some medical currency, as the willow is a natural source for the major component of aspirin, and might have been one method of administering it combining it with the magical operation itself.

19. For constipation
Take cat filth and Venetian soap together and grind, only a knife point's worth given internally, it will help very soon.

20. Constipated due to colic
Use crushed cumin salt and water, which is cooked an hour (or a while) and then strain, if you want to add to this a little chopped tobacco of good leaves it is more certain.

21. For diarrhea
Take liquor in a tin can, throw a spoonful of peas in it, and roast it over the fire so that the liquor takes fire, let the peas be roasted in it, whereof is eaten a little afterwards.

22. Proven treatments for toothache
One takes a red onion and roasts it, cut it then right in half and put one piece of it completely hot in each ear inside a swatch of linen. Then the ache will cease within a few minutes.

23. For toothache
Buy box-cottonwood-oil for 2 ./. and take some of it on a little cotton and put it against the tooth that has the pain in it.
Carnation oil on a little cotton against the tooth usually helps.
Camphor, weak, in cotton and put it against the tooth, also in the ear or both.
 Take wet soft *Samskat* or some other piece of "*sking*" as large as will cover the cheek or actually that part of the cheek where the pain is, spread on it *Conu Plåster*, and lie on it for a while. And then when it has a chance to warm up the aching place that before long it happens that the pain begins more and more to abate, so that it begins like to itch and tingle in the hole.

24. For bugs[118]
Take *Sabedille*-seeds and mix into green soap and smear the place where the assembly is.

---

118 One assumes this to mean lice or other human skin parasite.

MS 17

NM 271.600 15:1949 "KONSTBOK"

* * *

Then he won't only be healed but also the one who cursed her will be plagued by diarrhea.

to get womenfolk to say everything that they know. Take a swallow-tongue in your mouth and kiss them.

[119]shall give it to your cows, then the butter will never come together.
[40.] Another... Take the manure or something else. Do in the same way.

19. Means for healing of it.
[41.] Fix it so that you get the previously named things from the cow of that one who did the same to you, and give it to your own.

20. [40.] The same.
Take a wedding ring and tie it to the grain-tile, then the butter will congeal.

21. To procure for yourself the right unlocking stone.
Take a starling's nest and thread it through two holes, and insert a plug into the hole while the male starling is away. Put a red cloth at the root of the tree. Then when the male returns home, he will find that the hole to his home is plugged up and will fly away, but will come back and will have the lock-stone with him, and holds the stone in front of the plug. In this way he will get the plug out, and drop it onto the red cloth. Then you will be quick and pick it up.

---

119 There is obviously a page missing which gives the purpose for this procedure.

22. [13.] To procure a raven's stone.
Seek out a raven's nest in a tree. Hang up the chicks in the tree while the male is out seeking food. When the raven comes home, he will find his chicks hanging up and will become out of his mind, and will cough up a stone. This stone you must immediately pick up, but look out that the raven doesn't peck out your eyes.

23. [44.] To make it so that another releases feces with each word he makes.
Take hare's feces and put them in a drinking-pitcher, and let them drink it, or something other in which it has lain.

24. [25.] ~~To find out what another is thinking.~~
~~Take a swallow's tongue and put it in your mouth.~~

25. [21.] To make yourself invisible.
Take a pea from a black hen, and sweep the feather down. Put them in a manure heap as well as two peas and allow them to grow until they ripen. Take one of them and put it in your mouth and they'll say everything you want to know.

26. [14.] To make a virgin become in love with you.
Write your and her names on an apple or something else, and give to her to eat.

27. [45.] To get rid of pimples.
Count the pimples and take just as many peas and throw them into a burning oven or just as many grains of salt, but be quick to close the door to it, and say: "I burn my pimples and not my peas."

28. [46.] The same.
Go to a churchyard and wash yourself in the water that runs off a grave-cross.

29. [47.] To win at the lottery.
Go on a Thursday evening to the churchyard and take a human skull and write on it the numbers you believe will come out, and then go there the next day, and take up your human skull. The numbers that are then struck out will not win, but the ones that are not will win, and those you will put into your hat, and then you'll win.

30. [12.] To make yourself invisible.
Take a raven's stone and put it in your mouth.

31. To get rid of pimples.
Smear them with a pork rind and then put it under a juniper bush on someone else's property.

32. The same.
Take a fishing net and put it on the pimples and burn it with your breath....

[TORN PAGE]

47. [32.] ... and throw ...
To take the fat from a cow.
Take the hair of the fat one and put it in a piece of bread and give it to the other then the thin one will grow fat and the fat one thin.

48. [14.] To see who is fey in a household. Go Christmas Eve when everyone is sitting all together and eating dinner and look through the window. The ones who are fey that year sit headless, but look out so they don't notice.

35. So that roosters won't crow.
Give them something to eat that is fat, that has melted like melted tallow, then they'll not crow.

36. [??] (Torn) So that one doesn't get a bone that has lodged itself...

Kingslight (Staffans). Fish (Starsyna). Angelica (white). . Then you won't have him back. Three times for the stomach.

45. [30.] To put the diarrhea on someone.
Take a nail that has sat in a coffin. Nail it into his feces.

46. [31.] ~~Take cow bone and mix it with sifted grain flour. See to it that they are just as fine with the flour and give her one teaspoon, use it as dough~~...

49. To make it so that the bird that you want will stand still so you can shoot, and can't move.
Take a sewing needle and thread it through both the eyes of a snake and before the cuckoo sings in the spring, take the same needle and look through the eye at the bird you want to shoot, then it will sit still.

50. So that fish will come –
Take the juice of *Sterisaquat* and anoint your hands with it.

35. [37.] Thief. 34. the thief. 36. [illegible]. 37. h.e. 38. gunpowder 39 [illegible]

Musical notation of some kind. Time signature is 4/4. B – F agfdf

ms 18

NM 271.601 SANKT PETRI NYCKEL

* * *

Come to pass as is said, say outside your door when you are leaving.
I. Sankt Petri Nyckel (Saint Peter's Key)

1. Pass over with the knife or the hands. Say: Whatever is bound in heaven shall be bound on earth, you who intend to take ill-gotten goods, I bind with St. Peters Key, and then you are bound firmly, until you are let loose by that same key, this in XXX. P. oct. 39

2. For robbery.
You whoever you are who has taken a thing which doesn't belong to you, you shall just as truly as the sun and moon shone for Joshua, from Abraham's God and Jacob's God, acquire the worst troubled conscience until you personally visit the one you robbed the goods from. This will happen just as truly as the Red Sea stood for King Pharoah and as truly as Jesus Christ woke Lazarus from the dead. This in XXX.   P.S. oct. 39.

3. To transfix a thief.
Mary worked and bore the child. Three angels were the servants[120] of the Lord.

---

120 Sw. *tjänarinnor*, female servants.

The first is called Saint Michael, the second is called St. Gabriel, the third St. Peter. Three thieves revealed themselves in order to steal the child from Mary. Mary spoke to St. Peter. St. Peter said I have [bus...] there with iron chains with God's own hands, that they must stand like a stick and look around, like a goat until they could count all the stars, all the raindrops that fall in the ocean, all the grains of sand backwards and forwards. If they stand like a stick and look around, like a goat, until I see them and myself bid them rise and confess or ask for forgiveness * * * Give them 3 x 3 beatings, and bid them go in the Lord's name.

4. To make yourself insusceptible.
Take a nail or a knife, bite it without letting your lips touch it, and say: God shall take out of mine? Satan all wickedness out, in three names. XXX
K. Å. 39

5. To see.
S. Solam. S. Tattler.
S. Eckogardner.
Gematar.   K.

6. For Snakebite.
Jesus went out on the road. He saw the snake run, and the wound disappeared. in XXX.
K.

7. To write this on the door, they can not steal.
    Chamoka +
    Amacka +
    Amschala +
    Wagston +
    Alom + + Elast Lamach.

8. Write on the door for thieves.

+ Z + DIA + B + Z + SABZ + HVWF + BERS * * *

9. For contagious diseases over the door.

+.27..D.I.A.+.B.1.2.S.a.■ V.+
2.+.H.6.F.+.B.F.2.S. ✱✱✱+

1. + 2. 7. D. I. A. + . B. 1. 2. S. A. V. + 2. + . H. 6. F. + . B. F. 2. S. * * *   K.

10. To get strings to break.
As truly as David's Harp sounds, shall your strings break. in XXX.   K.

11. To Epilepsy.
Take from the patient all the clothes, and burn them in fire.   K.

12. To keep someone from leaving.
Take a sewing needle with which a corpse has been sewn. Draw the needle through the hat or the shoe of the one you wish to transfix, and this cannot be undone.   K.

13. To buy cheap and sell expensive.
Catch a white [lekatt] take its head. Carry it on you in the right smoking pocket.   K.

14. To stop shot.
Shot stand still in the Lord's name. Give neither fire nor [lågoz] as surely as the rock of Gibralter sits fast, in XXX   K.

15. When animals have growths.
I measure for needles, I measure for steel, I measure for everything that can harm an animal's life, in XXX.   K.

16. To tame (train) a horse.
Brown, Black, Fox-colored, or Grey horse, be so tame and calm that whenever I sit on your back and ride you, you will carry me, with great humility, as Jesus Christ was meek and humble. In XXX.   K.

17. Casper make you rise, Melchior bind you * Baltasar embrace you * * * * or Baltasar lead you home: K.

18. To transfix a snake.
Lie still, you horse of hell, while the Virgin Mary wraps her child.   X X X   P.S.

19. Against Envy.
I bind away all those who are envious of me, with these words: Stand as stand and stumble as stumble in XXX.

20. To recall thieves.
Under a rock in Hell, until you restore what has been stolen. in XXX   P. S.

21. To stop predators.
From a high mountain yell: As far as this sound is heard, turn away just as far. Through the name of the Trinity.   XXX.   P. S.
   Not many seek like the predator, Pelle said.

22. For those greedy for revenge.
Bite the left arm muscle and hit with the right fist under the left armpit strongly, and recite: I order you, Lucifer's Devil, that you turn away from me in the Triune God's name XXX. The one anxious for vengeance will get the blows.   P. S.

23. Incurable illness.
I, N.N. order you N.N., in the blood of Jesus Christ, God's Son and in the name of the Holy Ghost, that you, N. N. will become well, as long as you live. Recite 9 times. Our Father 9 times. Benediction 9 times.   P. S.
Obs! Everything you recite over should be fermented. If you hear something, then don't pay any attention to it.

[NUMERATION DISRUPTED, RESUMING WITH...]

28. The Power of All-Knowing.
I invoke you and ask that you, through this Crown-coin, make known to me if it will be lucky for me [us] in our mining. A Crown-piece, preferably a silver crown in a glass of water when, before you have recited the formula, you have decided on a Crown or doing snuff or throwing. Shall happen 9 times. And the Crown or coin is dipped in the water each time as well [XXX] but no "Amen." This formula. A knife is stuck down in the water onto the Crown while one recites the formula.   P. S. 39.

29. To See.
The one who will be healed holds onto the glass first. Then dip both index fingers in the liquor. Then I can see. Recite then: Just as well as I have seen before, so shall I see now, in the name of the Almighty. F.S. and H.G.   P.S.

30. To read over against evil.
Cast out [...] go backwards out through the door into the yard. Make a cross. Then sweep. Bury. Recite the Burial Ritual. Say: This will liberate me from all

evil wherever it may come from. This in XXX Amen. Throw with the right hand over the left shoulder. Pelle.

31. For everything.
As truly as I sit here, a poor servant of sin, and as truly as Jesus Christ hung on the tree, and as truly as the Sybil walked over the River Kidron, Just as truly and just as assuredly I order you who have taken ill-gotten goods of whatever type it may be, that by the salvation of your soul, you will bring back the same. This in XXX. P. S.

32. Against [Utkast]
I order you (in the name of the Almighty) that you turn back from wherever you roam. P.S.

33. To take m in a [strut]
Hair, nails, blood say: as long as these contents do not roam from here, then you will not be at peace. This I order in Satan's and the Devil's name, which evil powers you serve. + + +

When one takes m. say: 10 *öre* I leave for the loan I take for as long as this is with N. N., you will have no peace.   P.S.

34. Hexed shotgun.
Load the shotgun with [d.m.] if it is hexed. Birds, animals of all types. You get it when you shoot.   Pelle.

35. For insanity.
As Jesus Christ healed the man at the shore of Jeneseret, who was possessed by evil spirits, and the spirits asked him not to destroy them. Then Christ gave them permission to travel into a herd of swine that went into the lake and drowned, just as truly as that and just as surely I drive out from you N.N. all evil spirits that have made a place for themselves within you, and in the Power of Jesus Christ's deeds I permit you to travel into a fox in the woods. This in XXX Amen.

36. A bone flute from a churchyard or a branch from there to blow the spirit through.   P. S.

37. To put a silver coin out by the stairs, say: This coin shall draw to me coins of all types.   P.S.

38. For robbery.
You who have given yourself to Satan, the Devil and Lucifer, you I order that you bring back that which you have under the light of law and right have taken

from me unjustly. You shall not find peace neither day or night, for Abraham's God shall smight you, Israel's God shall force you, and Jacob's God shall rush you to fulfill this order. This in XXX Amen. Recite 3 times. P.S.

[UPSIDE DOWN] For cataracts: Lemon.

39. To drive away sicknesses.
I drive away all evil that is found under heaven, under the sun and under the earth, to a place where no one dwells, in a lake where no one rows, on a mountain where there is no end, that evil and the Evil One's purpose has done, may he travel to the very stomach of burning. i F. S. a H G name. In flax seed, recite 3 times. P. S.

40. Sending back.
I order you Satan and all your servant spirits, that you take your loan back from me and my animals, or person. This in XXX. P.S.

Stearine (candle-grease) instead of relatives who mooch. G.D.

41. For sendings.
This evil shall go back from E. A. G. Karl Oscar Eugen's name to the person who has sent evil. This person he will be a stone and not have bones/legs, and this as truly as the serpent drove Eve out of paradise, as truly as Satan was driven into the swine herd, as truly as Sebaot's Jacob's and Israel's God lives, and as truly the person who has done evil, his bones and his sinews and roots and feet and hair shall rot away and whiten as the dead in the ground. In + + + This after Berlin Quarp.

[UPSIDE DOWN] Red currant for hard belly.

42. Take away blisters on the eye.
Jesus went out on a path. There he met sand and little men. He made the path clean and the blemish shall go out of your eye, in XXX, use woman's milk. P.S.

43. For [iråk]
As Peter and John healed the poor cripple at the Temple in Jerusalem, So do I heal you, in 3 XXX   P.S.

44. For dragging under the earth for rickets.
Peter went out on a road, there he met Kväsa. Where are you going? I am going to break marrow and bone of a human child. That you will not – Go out and break in rickets and in root, and in log and in stone, but not in the marrow and bone of this human child. This in XXX   P. S.

45. The one who has done evil must show himself.
You monster and Satanic material, I order you as truly as a soul stands in heaven and knows truth and witnesses truth, and as truly as a soul is in Hell and knows truth and witnesses false, just as truly and just as surely you, who has practiced evil, will not find any peace for body or soul, for the fires of Hell will plague you both night and day until you show yourself and where you have done evil. This in XXX   P.S.

46. For pain.
Pain! under iron and steel, out of marrow and bone, out of bone and sinew, out of sinew and into Flesh, out of flesh and into skin, out of skin and into hair, out of hair and all the way to the heel. Which is through XXX   P.S.

47. To stop bleeding.
Stop, stop, stop blood in N.N., as did Noah's Flood. When Jesus Christ before. So truly you blood will stop, as the Red Sea stopped for King Pharoah, this in XXX. Stop, Stop, Stop Blood, in N.N.   P.S.

48. To stop bleeding.
Stop, blood, that runs from N.N. Stop and halt as truly as a man is in Hell, knowing right but witnesses wrong, it shall be so reluctant to run as Jesus Christ led the woman, who late on a Saturday night was spinning. This in XXX   P.S.

49. To get animals to thrive.
The Virgin Mary went to her blessed Son and said Up, my Son, and cure. What is the cause of your mood, my animals are sick also and are not thriving. May you be well in the same second whether they are near or far. Here you shall thrive and here you will dwell, and here you will have peace. This in XXX.   P.S.

50. Sprains.
Twist to wide, bullet to bullet, sinew to sinew and blood to blood. This in XXX.
P.S.

51. For wasp stings
Wasp, wasp poison spike
From Satan you are come
And you are like him.
Sting in the meadow and not in the stomach,
Sting in the dirt and not in the flesh,
Sting in a stone and not in the leg
and then you will die. This in XXX   P S Å.

52. For loss of fortitude.
Away Away Away loss-of-courage, and all evil. This as truly as a soul stands in Hell knowing right, but witnessing wrong in XXX   P.S.

Stroke with the knife from the snout to the back leg, even from underneath after the forelegs, also the knife is stroked on a piece of bread that is given internally.

53. Pain.
I stop the pain in the blood for you, N., [name, first name, the father's entire Baptismal name, repeat the name] as Jesus Christ stopped Noah's Flood. This in XXX.   P. S.

54. For evil sendings.
I order you Satan, that you take back your loan. This in XXX

55. To cause animals to stay in a certain place.
As truly as God said to man: Rule over the fish in the sea, of the birds under the heavens, and over all animals that creep on the earth. Just as truly and just as surely I instruct and order E.A.G.H. you all, all my cows that you won't transgress this area I have written here in the earth with my knife. From fence to fence with the knife counterclockwise, Here you, my cows, shall turn around to go to the woods and peace and enjoyment. This all the way to Rt. 6. In the evening when you all will have homesickness. This in XXX.   P.S.

56. For rats.
I order you Satan that you drive away from N. both rats and mice or what it may be. I went once over a churchyard, there met me a man. It was the Devil. There I say 3 paths. One went to heaven, and one went to hell, but where did the third one lead? Yea, into the Virgin Mary's dwelling. But stop here and stop there and stop in hell. But as truly and surely as God is good and as truly and surely as I am a human being, then I have the power to drive out all vermin from N.N. That I do in your name, Devil, as your servant and thrall P.S.
The secret power and wisdom of the Æsir Huld [...]come could see in the Well.

[UPSIDE DOWN] For outer steps, Beck Oil.

57. For cough and even whooping cough.
1 Handful oat [...]
1 ½ batten
25 öre chest [...]
Boil together
It will produce one quart.
Signe E.

58. For tuberculosis
To roll pills of pitch in potato flour.   Signe

59. For mosquito bite
Beck oil, peppermint oil.

60. For blood poisoning and wounds.
Peppermint oil to spread around where the poisoning is, then stroke it over. Signe.

61. Against hexes.
Recite three times. The last time, say Amen.
3 or 9 10-*öre* coins, throw over the left shoulder, look towards the south. Say: Here you may, and God preserve me, in 3 names.   F.S. and H.G.

62. To take away impurities in the home.
Urine of a girl that hasn't yet turned 12, in a quart bottle with the urine, as well as 25 *öre*'s worth of verdigris.   Signe

63. Lavender Oil
For mosquitoes, moths, flies and wasps.   Signe

64. For toothache and all pain.
Jese went over a churchyard, there he sought means to cure pain. And you, N. fell asleep, and the pain was gone. This I assure you in the three names of God, F. S. H.Gh. recite 1 time. Put the finger on the tooth as you recite.   Signe.
    If there is a lot of pain, then recite the Benediction, completely quietly, and as well take your left hand out of the bottle. R. M. Eriksson 12 July, 1939.

65. To stop bleeding over 10 miles away.
Christ Jesus went over a bridge, then he transformed the water into blood. The blood it shall stand. As truly as 12 men sit in Hell's court, to judge, but rule unjustly. This I assure you N., in the name of 3 Gods F. S. H.Gh. Amen.   Efr. Z.

66. To sleep.
Take of that which is between the large toe and the little toe. Spread it on where you feel uneasy, as well as go to bed on your socks.   Aug. 39 Sköndahl Watersson.

If you "fix" someone, then you can not do any evil to them afterwards.

67. To get rid of all evil.
1 coin in each shoe. Throw over the left shoulder, look towards the south, wish that the one who takes them will get it.   A woman gypsy.

68. Hex.
9 knots, blow in each knot. Name the name. Spit 3 times. A woman gypsy.

69. Ef.... S.....
P. stama Pigen 3d Pigen

70. To Draw
Mercury
[*Vetterljus*] Spirit light?
3 holes in the threshold
Crush W.

71. The Finnish method.
Get together 1 dr. 1 dr. 1 dr. 40 gr. water. Stroke n well at the pain. Take Back 7 dr.

72. To transfix thieves.
Stand, Stand, Stand, you thief. As truly as Absalom was hanged in a tree, as truly as Joshua ordered the Moon to stand still, just as truly as whatever Saint Peter binds in Heaven, is bound on earth, through XXX. P.S. Oct. 39.

Was there when he celebrated his 80th birthday.

Outside doors.
Let it happen just as is said.
October 39. Pelle S. G.

73. For hexed butter.
"*Skräsa* in the butter" 3 times. (clear in the butter?)

74. Protection
Obl. Wild anise in paper in [...]

80. Bringing back.
You, who have given yourself over to Satan, The Devil, and Lucifer, you I order that you bring back that which you under the light of the law and right have taken from me wrongfully. You shall not have peace either day or night for Abraham's God will smight you, Isaac's God will force you, and Jacob's God will rush you to fulfill this order. This in XXX Amen. Recite 3 times. in liquor get them to drink, otherwise pour it out on the lowest step. 1939 got from P. S. G---p.

A Prayer gotten from M...t Selma H.

With light from Heaven in dark times
Be still before God in the hour of worship
He brings to an end hot struggles
And makes all the sorrowful quiet.
                    Stockholm, 8 March, 1940

From Lolo
O God who is my strength my support
In the dark hours of life
Stretch out your hand to our protection
For you do great wonders.
Colis Colis i Laimie February 1940 A. K. Lolo. Selma

Boils
Anoint 5 twigs with the puss from the boil. Bore the twigs into a tree. Oriented north of the house where I live. Tomtegubben. 7 July 1940.

MS 19

NM 271.601 LÄKARBOK

*   *   *

<u>BOOK OF HEALING</u>
DEDICATED TO ELSA BY OLOF, YEARS 1920–1929
ALL THIS I HAVE LEARNED TO HELP THOSE WHO ARE IN NEED. OLLE SAID.

Mr. James Moore Hickson
Frisinhall Church
Braford England
Heals everyone.
Madonna in Capo di Monte Italien
<u>Near Naples</u>

Rudolf Skoljom på berget.

Stina Åberg died 2 December 1925
Olov Åberg died 10 September 1932 at 12 o'clock at night.
Buried Sunday, the 4 October.
Peace over their memories

Disciple Elsa

Play the lottery 292 –

Those who can
1. + Olof Åberg Gåltjärn.
2. Jonas Petter Småland
3. Fru Larson Holmöberg 9 Skilsåker
4. Fru Sofia Näs Sprängsvikare
5. Fru Stolpe Ortsviken, Sundsvall
6. Fru Strandin Fagervik, Sundsvall
7. Jonas Wallin Vestanå Maj
8. Upsala Gumman, Bävergränd 4
9. Israle Ofvansjö
10. Hemlings Gubben Björna
11. Seljen i Skulö
12. Olrika i Fors
13. Kaj Lova Sundsvall
+ 14. Rojås Hans Kårpåsen Boda
+ 15. Lars Larsgubben Kårpåsen, Boda
16. Morkäringa Örnsköldsvik
17. Olina Johansson Råå Ransnord
18. Hangen, Norway
19. Karin Jonson Boden
20. Carl Janson Uddevalla 3Run
21. Karl Karlkvist Sundsvall
22. Magnus Värme Solberga Njusunda
23. Sjölv Margareta Ljusdal
24. Husmo Gubben Bergsjö
24. Lumpjones Kerstin Östanbäck
25. Kristin Lundgren Hudilsvall
26. Run Peter Lund Forsasocken 4m From Maj
27. Erik Erikson Glanshammar
28. Petter Berglund Brusta, Njurunda
29. Tok Gertrud Tranås, Raka Tranås.
30. Fru Elisabet Enkronade Himmerdal.
31. Fru Lindenstein Roslags Näsby 24 Vallhallavägen 101
32. Fru Rikhard Vexsjö heals cancer.
33. Lapp Selma Lapp Sigrid Hopverberga Östersund
34. Lappska Frösön
35. Gubben Skog Söderhamn
36. Tim Edla Bäklund Ångermanland
37. Fru Anderson Solvarbo Gustavs

38. Fru Tilda Nelson Svärdsgatan 7
39. Hanna Bredson Oskarshamn
40. Fru Johansson sees in liquor Ericksgensgatan 5, Upsala
41. Fru Elfström Sysslomansgatan 40 Upsala
42. Fru Signe Söderström Marielund Upsala
43. Sidsjö vid Sundsvall Spår
44. Ryn Holm Siden 7 naal Rosenquist
45. Anders Person å Sjöström Bredsjön, Umeå
46. + Ernst Jonsson Edsta Ljustorp dead.
[LIST CONTINUES INSIDE THE BACK COVER]

1. Toothache.
I heal you, N. of Toothache, bitter toothache, rheumatic toothache. Jesus Christ came down from Heaven and healed 96 and 99 teeth ailments, and now I heal you even if it were as many toothaches as there are grains of sand on the beaches of the world. [L-a öfer s. eller br. ha i m.] don't swallow (Recite over the sick one or should have them not swallow) spit out into the fire. Boil s. in water, anoint outside. Go around with the tongue.

2. Against insanity.
I cure you N. for depression, for uneasiness, anxiety, tears and morbid obsessions, and I do this now in the name of the Lord and with the help of the Lord and the Power of Jesus and now I believe that your depressing thoughts will disappear and so I ask God now that you receive a happy mood with your parents and siblings, friends and enemies, acquaintances and strangers.

3. Troll shot
I cure you N. from the wiles of troll shot. 3 Norns stood in Jesus' Garden, the first cured finn-shot, the second cured lapp-shot, the third for pain and all evil, and I do that now through the name and help of Jesus Christ.

4. For [Förråkt]
I heal you N. of [förråkt] 3 Norns stood in Jesus' garden. The first healed for wight-bite, the second healed for pain and painful blisters, the third healed for every evil, and she healed best, and I do so now but through Jesus' help.

5. Against hexes.
I heal you N. of hexing. For the Lapp who dwells far up in the mountains and for a wicked enemy and for a Finn, if any out of these three have done me any evil or ill, in air or in wind or anything else, then I pray now to God my true Father Jesus Christ that my ills will disappear both inside and outside, so that that same thing will be buried in the churchyard. The Lord God says that what a man sows, so shall he reap, says the Lord.

6. Pain through fire, air and water.
I heal you N. of pain through Fire, Air and Water. If I have eaten or drunk that which is hexed, from man or woman, then I heal you of evil through Jesus' name and Jesus' help.

7. For all pain.
I heal you N. of pain, through Jesus' name, Jesus our Father and Savior, descended from Heaven and healed 96 pains and 97 that was death, and I do that now through Jesus' name and with Jesus' help, I do that now. And when you now taste the medicine which is prepared in Jesus' name and anoint you both inwardly and outwardly, and when you now go to bed to sleep, then I will pray to God that you will have respite from all your sufferings and pains. Then I believe that you will sleep with Jesus Christ's help, even if there were as many aches and pains as grains of sand on the ocean's beaches; and when you wake up from this good sleep that you receive from God, then I pray to God that your pains and sufferings will be missing from you forever forever forever. The remaining mercies you have left all through the name of Jesus and Jesus our Father and Savior.

Tight Milk (?)
Pinquicula vularis
Hosea – arter.

8. Depression
I heal you N. of depression, from envy, evil eye, envious tongue, envious hand and from all envy whoever it might be, and so I pray to our Father and Savior Jesus Christ who is our Father on earth and in heaven, and if I have eaten or drunk something deadly, or am trampled by something deadly, or hexed, then it will disappear out of my flesh and blood, out of marrow and bone, in this way it will disappear. In Jesus name.

9. Troll Shot
I heal you N. for winds of troll shot. Three Norn stood in Jesus' garden, the first healed for finn shot, the second healed for lapp shot, the third healed for troll shot and for all evil, and I do that now through Jesus' name and help.

When you cast salt from the south to the north, or towards the direction where they are.

All good comes from the South, Olle said. Look towards the South when you throw/cast.

9. Other views and to be authentic.
Hence you, N., will come, hence shall you go, hence you shall long for, hence you will yearn. I pray to God who is the Father of all the world, that you N. receive help and healing, to be with me M. and in my dwelling and not be outside, and live the wild life, but rather you shall find peace in living with me, have happiness, desire, and fun, and pleasant and so I pray to God that they should harvest what they have sown which was aimed at you. I pray to God that you, N., receive might and power to go through doors and gates, roads and paths, and receive courage and might and power. Thus says the Lord if you have eaten and drunk that which is deadly, then it will disappear in Jesus Name and through Jesus' help. So I pray to God that you receive enthusiasm and desire to read God's word and sing God's word and to go to church through God's power and help, in the name of Jesus Christ and no evil shall befall you.

And to receive courage and might and power in all your limbs to bed and bench. With salt shall all evil be salted down, for visible and invisible as well as evil thoughts.

10. To stop bleeding.
I stop your bleeding N. through the help of Jesus. Moses threw his staff into the River Jordan, and said, Stop river, stop river, stop river; and now your blood, N., stop blood, stop blood, stop blood; through Jesus' name and Jesus' help, I believe that your bleeding will stop and stand still. Stand, stand.

11. To get back stolen goods.
I pray to God for you now N., if you have been robbed, that for the one who robbed you there will be no peace, no desire for food, no will to work, and no sleep but rather a headache and uneasiness will befall you until you have restored that which you have stolen from your neighbor.

12. To keep what one has.
In Jesus' name I pray that I may have the cows I have and no one shall have the might to tough this, and they may stay here, and keep on until I roam and release them. When one roams say nicely "thanks for watching over me, now you may go."

13. Evil thoughts (or confused.)
The thoughts in flesh and blood which are not of any use to your body and soul, then I pray now to God that they will disappear out of the head, arms, toes, marrow and bones, sinews and skin, that they will disappear like a river that falls down from the steepest cliff, and disappears in the waves of the sea to return nevermore. In Jesus' name and with Jesus' help.

14. For [*Förråkt*]
I heal you N. of [*förråkt*]. 3 Norns stood in Jesus' garden. The first healed for wightbite, the second healed for pain and fever blister, the third healed best, and I will do that now but through the help of Jesus.

When Olle was going to scry in the glass, he said "In Jesus name, I command forth your spirit."

When you want it cold.
Go to an acquaintance's farm. Put a silver and a copper coin as well [ta.]

15. *Artina* also for all pain.
I heal you N. from pain through Jesus name.

Struma Hemoröjder (swollen hemorrhoids)
I heal you N. for swelling in the name of Jesus in through Jesus' help, that this swelling will now continue to disappear out of marrow and bone, sinews and flesh in Jesus' name. Take pig lard and spread it around the throat. The lard is heated up over a weak fire. Recited over, Preferably is should be one or a half year old. The swelling is also anointed with liquor lastly over the whole body.

For hemorrhoids anoint inside and out around the anus. Lastly, liquor over the entire body.

Put your money in your hands and say three times:
God preserve my money.

Good God, I, Elsa, ask about my health and that you who have done me ill may get it back again, in F, S. and H. Gh. name, Amen.

16. Legal Trials.
Now I command you, N., to the Just Doctor who is healer of everything here on this earth, and now I believe that you will receive help and healing for all your ills. Just as he is the judge over all judges here on this earth, so I believe completely and firmly that you will receive a just judgment from our Father and Savior Jesus Christ, our Father; He is the creator of everything here on this earth, and so I pray that you make them dumb who speak lies and that they will not be able to move their tongues.

When I cast out.
I pray to receive courage, might, and strength in all my limbs from bed to seat. With salt I salt down all evil, visible and invisible, as well as evil thoughts. God save me from visible and invisible evil thoughts, in Jesus' name. No one take

from me this might. When I work it doesn't work. They don't come out for as long as I am holding onto a glass or bottle.

17. For [krubbstulen] horse.

If you [sic] horse is bereft of courage, the I pray now to God that you have courage and blood and power to draw and run and a free mood, and so that you will rest in your limbs and that you will sleep whenever you want to sleep, all through the name of Jesus and so that you receive strength and power to go along roads and off of roads, through doors and gates and I pray to God that he will keep you from the evil eye, the envious hand and the envious tongue, and every evil.

To take courage and strength from an animal is to take them [i krubben].

Dissolve the salt in the water, give internally.

Hexed in the barn.
Recite over salt, go into a corner, cast to both sides and up to the roof, and say: I heal the barn from hexes and all evil both over and under through the power of the Lord. All evil will be salted down with salt now, through God's help and your help.

Salt, flour and [sådor mor i gålu]. Take these things three times with the left hand. You should also recite over just the salt as well as mixing it thereafter in the flour and *sådor*.#

18. For sheep, goats, cows, pigs, hens and all livestock.

I heal your livestock from stolen courage through the name of Jesus Christ. The Virgin Mary went out on a green meadow and picked flowers. Then came the Savior and went forth to here, and said, what do you want with these? Then the Virgin Mary answered and said I will have it for my livestock, for robbed fodder, for robbed courage, for robbed milk, and for robbed cream, and for robbed butter, and for all robbed fortitude. Then said the Savior, take back, and take the fruit that is grown on the earth, and give to your livestock, for robbed fodder, for robbed courage, for robbed milk, for robbed cream, for robbed butter.

Throw in a crossroad by the church, the church they in which they are parishioners, and in all the crossroads.

#if the animals don't come home, recite over salt and cast it in the crossroad near the Church, as well as establish the time when they should come. Olle.

19. Revelation of God.

I want to have the Revelation of God and courage and blood and might and power in all my limbs to cure all sicknesses whatever they may be, suffering and sickness, and those who are depressed and tribulations, that no power between earth and heaven can take from me as long as I live. All through the name of Jesus Christ, and the help of Jesus Christ, my Father and Savior.

I pray too that he will protect me from visible and invisible and in the name of Jesus that no one will take from me this power.
& as well evil thoughts.

When on builds a new house, then you should take 10 *öre* and put it between stone and sill of the first log. Olle said.

Recite over wares bought at the Apothecary, for those who don't believe it does just as well, Olle said.

Olle killed the Lapp. 1915. He lies under the large building in Hörnes towards the barn.

20. Confusion.
Those thoughts in flesh and blood, that which is no use to your soul and body, so I pray now to God that they will disappear as a river that falls down from the sharpest cliff and disappears in the waves of the sea to return nevermore. Olle.
In Jesus' name and with Jesus' help.

21. If someone has stolen courage, blood or warmth.
I pray to God for you, N., if they stole courage, blood, warmth, that the one who has stolen will not get any peace or sleep until they have brought it back on this day at this hour. All the might and power of Hell will disappear and now it will proceed. Said Olle.
    Twelfthnight, 1931.

1, 2, 3, 4, 5, We can't go further. Meaning that we can't recite more than 5 different spells for each bottle.

To approach the Altar and take the degree. To decide the time when it strikes 2, 3 or 4 there. Olle 1931.

22. If someone "walks again"[121] and you want it to be dead and still and to disappear. I pray to God that all the might and powers of Hell will disappear and that I will receive courage and blood and strength in all my limbs, 3 times.

---

[121] Sw. *gå igen*, to walk as a revenant.

May the Grace and Peace of Jesus Christ be merciful to me now, because I receive help and healing for all my sufferings and sicknesses.   Olle 31

23. Lord, Lord be merciful to me, both inwardly and outwardly and all evil will give way to me, through the name of Jesus and the help of Jesus. For lost earth, that I may receive healing and help on this day at this hour through the Lord's might and the Lord's Power and the name and help of Jesus Christ, and this steel and this silver. The grace and peace of Jesus Christ be merciful over my sins and sufferings.   Olle 1931 Twelfthnight.

Holy Mother of God, hear me.   Elsa.

Think sharply during all workings and upon casting out

For wallvermin.
Delris Derris powder.

24. Put a ring from them in the glas, then you see their entire life that has been and is now.   S. Jansson, Ljustorp.

If I want to teach someone to recite over them, say then [...] a piece of the ring. I recite then over their head.

25. My knife that Oli said he had
smithed from 7 broken steel points of knifepoints, over 7 Thursday nights.

26. For them to be healthy
Take a hazel staff, wrap it in silk when a snake comes, be patient, and fasten it by the stinger in the silk. Take a hazelnut, make a hole in it, put the snake stinger in it, then close up the hole. Have the nut in your mouth when you are kissed by the man you like, then he'll be yours forever, who has the nut.
Said over the Radio.

27. To be left in peace.
Take three buttons, recite over them, go to the churchyard. Throw over the left shoulder.
Say "I have not taken anything here."   Stokk. Anna Pr.

28. To be left in peace.
Take two horseshoe nails, put them in a cross under the building. Say: Kiss me Asolet (?) Recite first over it, so that all the might and power of hell will disappear.   Anna Pr.

29. For evil.
Take a pig's kidney, cut it in two. Hit the one half 7 times. Recite and burn. Recitation. [*varefrö*] sickness.   Anna Pr.

30. To be able to see.
Martall at HaljbasKea between Västmanland and Norberg. Take it up by the root, screams, don't be afraid. Put it in liquor, clearly see everything.   Anna Pr.

31. For hardening of the arteries
50 gr. Malört (*Artemisia absinthium*), 20 gr. extract of Belladonna, 10 gr. Natron (Sodium Hydroxide) 5 gr. nicotine.

Indian Nikodem.
8:10 am, Oct. 7, 1936

32. To put an end to love.
Go to the churchyard and take earth, say God allow me to take this earth to kill love between this one and that one. Don't say anything when you put it out. Take from a grave where a male is buried.   Alma, Upsala.

33. Cure for...
Take from a calf from q-u from the horn, smoke it. Norla S. J. Sångberg.

34. For sicknesses.
1 kr. mixed incense. light and move it around the head, and then the whole body, and lastly the foot.   Maria Lövestad, Skåne.

35. The white snake.
Boil it then eat it then you will be able to see.   Radio.

36. For a humid cellar.
Take from an anthill, spread it around your cellar as well as [*jära*].

For moles.
Lime the earth where they are. Oct. 8, 1936.   Selma said this, 8:30 pm.

Stagga. To stop bleeding.   Stag.
37. Jesus and St. Peter met a sinful and bloody man. The blood had bled out over and under him. Blood stop. Blood stop as the man in hell who knew right but witnessed wrong. In 3 names the Father, the Son and the Holy Ghost. 3 times.

38. To stop bleeding.   Ol. Oldberg. Kaxis.
Jesus is born, Jesus is dead. Jesus commands the blood that it shall stop. Jesus commands the wound that it will no longer give from itself, but rather be closed as the holy wounds did when he hung on the cross. These words I bind together in three holy names the Father, the Son and the Holy Ghost. This is recited 3 times, as well as the Our Father.

Old Olof Oldberg in Kaxis. The body of Arnsten Berge

If you [*staggar*] to yourself, or teach the art to another, then you lose the power, but this isn't so.

It is not sinful. It is the pure word of God that is recited.

Dr. Fritz Olsén, Stormman. Learned from Olof the recitation to stop bleeding. 3. 6. 9. 11.

39. Gammal Jesku in Graves. preserves plants, roots, stones, shots, lead slivers, protective medallions, dragging under the earth, stones around the neck for wishing fever. The sickness comes from the devil. It must be driven out. Melt lead, let the patient drink from the water, but recite the entire time he's drinking.

40. Kisamor had a book in which was written all cures. Then she would thumb through it until she heard a knocking on the heater, then she understood that it was the right cure that she had turned to.

Vingåkersgubben anointed and put his wedding ring under his tongue.

[*Den hornper den hornpär.*]

41. To pour molten lead.
Take a bowl with water and 9 matches and 9 buttons, a little liquor, have all of this in the water. Pour the lead over it, through the hole in a cookie. Throw the water into a crossroad, wish what you want will happen. Think sharply. Give a white horse the cookie afterwards.

42. To bind the nyxie when one swims or bathes. Say: Steel knife in the water. Cross.

43. Hexed well.
Say The Cross upon, the Trolls away. + + +

44. The Sunny side is on the right side,
there are silver coins.

45. Twelve mens eating [*tolvmansslukan*]
Tibast (*Daphne mezereum*), *Vendelrot* (Valerian root), it helps me but works against you.

46. For cows.
On Christmas night I cook peas, they go home.
On Good Friday mix it in the root cellar.

47. To hex.
Take asafetida, put it powdered outside their step, so that they have to walk on it. Recite also. Recited by the Lapp Adolf Lundblad, Härnösand 1935.

55. This is what Emil Melander did in my yard to hex me both the farm and everything. Put a cross from four buttons. Recited 7 names of Jesus Christ God's Son and of the Holy Mother, as well as the Holy Trinity's Spirit's name, I command you that whoever walkes on the right side of this cross shall lose his wits, in the name of the highest who has all power. And the one who takes away this cross has bad luck into eternity. Bow down you highest before the poorest. In the name of all the powers of the abyss. Make 3 + + +.

Emil took Olle's black art book. Has it in bed. In 1940, I got it amongst valuable papers in the writing desk.

56. To take O. P.
2 m. from the rowen to the step. 4 m. from there to the flagpole. 6 m. from the large building to the flagpole. Right in between these points it is 2 alns deep. Olle said after his death 25 Sept. 1936. Stockholm.

57. For anything in the head.
In the name of God the Father and of the Son and of the Holy Ghost, I command all evil out of this head shall come, you highest, before my might in the names of the holy Virgin Mary and her Son. recite 3 times.

58. Vallins recitation to be able to See.
In the names of all 7 of the spirits of the abyss, I command you to appear and tell me what this man or woman has for sicknesses. You spirits of the abyss tell me, and bow down before the most powerful God the Son the Holy Ghost and in the name of the Virgin Mary. Cross me 9 times, first head, then chest. To [kusma] this, go to a grave, take up a plant with the roots. Recite this while you take it. Keep it inside afterwards. Recite this: when I take you, the one who

lies in this grave, does not deny me this root that I take for many blessings. Rather give me your power and blessing. Rest heavily in your gave. I wish you no ill. Work peacefully in God's name. Vallin.

59. XXXXXXXXXXXXXXX
Stina in Rans drew this. It means "say."

[PAGES REMOVED WITH A SHARP EDGE]

66. This is what Petter recited before the raven's stone when he put under the big building to hex it. [mig med. stär 1 g.]
You, the highest, bow before my power. This moment, bring back I conjure you, follow me in all the names of all the spirits of the abyss. In the name of all the devils and of Satan. You the strongest [t…] I even so the most powerful is in the name of the Great Devil himself. Spit 3 times on the Raven's stone. This is what Petter did and said in 1935.

67. To live a lucky life.
The Cross and Nails of Christ Satan shall turn away from. I will live luckily in your name. No evil shall happen to me, for you are powerful, Great Lord, hear me. I am lucky in you, I, your humble, faithful servant in the name of Jesus Christ, God's Son and of the Holy Mother. Olle, Sept. 1936.

68. Earnings.
In the Cross of the Lord, Jesus Christ, I command that you create for me all the earnings and secure them, so that I may have prosperity. Bow down before my power, for your name's sake, in your holy, beloved and dear names. Amen. 9 times. Olle, Sept. 1936. Recite with bent knee until it takes.

69. Unjust/unrighteous people.
The Mother of God, Jesus Christ, and the Holy Ghost, I now place it all in your hand. You know what I have suffered, even while I awaited justice. Help me for your Holy […'s] sake, and don't fasten me to all the gold of the world, I pray only for justice. I say nothing. You see, for you there is no wailing. Bow down the stiff-necked. Punish the unrepentant, show your power. Put a stop to the hateful, make the lying ones dumb. Oh, you the king of all kings, to you alone I bow down in the name of the holy Trinity. Recite over liquor, give to him to drink. Recite 9 times. When he has drunk, then cross 3 times over what he has drunk out of. Fjellpelle, Stockholm 24 Sept. 1936. by Samina lu…

70. For robbery.
Holy God the Father in God's holy dwelling, I conjure and command you that Satan my take all those who take from me, in eternities' eternity. They shall

always suffer and will bear back to me everything and more, they will have no peace in this world I command in following the evil one's power. Fjällpälle, Sept. 36.

71. To get the Sight.
O Holy Christ, Holy Trinity, you who can give sight to the blind, hearing to the deaf, and wholeness in me by your grace, your humble servant at cows... I pray you make my eye's light sharp, let me glimpse you glorious [*pra..*] Let me sing among your angels. Let me go among your faithful, to the good of all, and to faith in you, in the names of the Holy Mother of God, The Virgin Mary, and the Holy Son's name. Amen.   Fjällpälle, Sept. 36.

72. To get power in a knife.
Sharpen (whet) it on a gravestone. Say: Whet out and whet in. The Power yours, the Power mine. And this will be united, in the Mother of God, Jesus Christ.   Ol Trac. Sept. 36.

73. Recitation for the farm over the cross.
In the Power of the Mother of God, Jesus Christ, and of the Son, No evil from this cross shall come. You who suffered on the cross and struggled for our wellbeing; You want no evil. Protect us now. Make this cross no evil spirits disturbance, you make us blessed. In the name of God the Father and of the Son and of the Holy Ghost. Amen. 9 times.   Kvastg. Sept. 36.

74. The Fence of Protection.
Recite and cross in front of yourself.
In the names of Jesus Christ, God's son, the Holy Ghost, and the Mother of God, I pray that this sign may provide protection from all evil thoughts and deeds. Let your saints of protection watch before this. I pray O Lord in your dear name on my bare knees, in the names of God the Father, Son and Holy Ghost. O dear Virgin Mary. Amen.   Finnish. Sept. 36.

75. So that they are unable to walk in the dark.
Holy Trinity, God, David's Son God's Mother, over this mercury no one can walk in the darkness. Their legs will be lame, the must turn. You have the power and you alone. Let me sleep in your care. Help me from all evil and evil people's mischief. In the name of the Holy Mother of God, Amen.   Recite 3 times.

76. Lucky Nail (Janson, Sept. 36.)
In the name of the Holy Kingdom of God and its inhabitants, this nail will have all possible luck, as a protection against all evil and for power for that one who has it, for one is Powerful, one alone, for you are the most powerful,

O lord, In Jesus Christ's Holy Nazarene's name. Recite 1 time. Cross with steel, 3 times.

77. Fence
The art of compelling. What Draugn? Coins, 93. 86. 80. 82. 90. 60.
Ensorcel together to brågden. What the lapp in the ashes? Protect?
Lure cows far out in the ground?
Speak to the Northern Corner.
Stop wolves? Threaten bears.
Turn your eyes back in. Naked? What arts of ...?
Must look at the one who can hex. Turn away the face.
Bone... Lapps have? Flugr."
Measure with the m. Skis, the curse can't take hold.
S. gave K. some of the r. to make him follow. S. gave K. some of the hair from a corpse, so that he would go insane. Olle 1928.
Then Olle took it away.
[upside down] Troll shot so that it will be fog in their thoughts.

79. To subdue others.
In the name of God the Father, the Son and the Holy Ghost, I command you to give me power to subdue all others, you, the Highest, no one can subdue, but all evil turn away from me. Not just the body, but power to destroy those who have done me ill. Bind their tongue, put out the lights of their eyes, stop their thoughts, make their feet lame, as I take refuge in your, the Highest. Only I bow down to me, for one and one alone has the power, in God the Father, Son and the Virgin Mary's name. Amen. Olle. Sept. 36.

80. Prosperity.
O Holy Mother of God, O Holy, Holy God, you alone have might. You alone can grant prosperity. I command you that you give it to me for my use. For your use and my use. For all the sick to use. For all the unlucky ones I pray and command you to bow yourself before my power in the name of the Trinity. Recite 3 times. Olle. Sept. 36.

81. To get fish.
Recite over the worms.
Onto this worm all fish will fasten themselves. In Jesus Christ's God's Son's and the Holy Ghost's Name. This fish will bring me a large catch, an overflow for the hungry and the poor, I share the blessing for your name and for my dear soul's salvation in the name of God Almighty. Olle, Sept. 36.

82. To get power.
Holy Virgin, Holy Mother of God, In the name of God the Father and of the Son, I pray and command you to give me power, power over this, power over everything, for no power shall overcome me other than you, the Almighty. I know I believe, I know I believe, I know I believe, You are the mightiest along, In the name of Jesus God's Mother. Recite 9 times.   Olle, Sept. 36.

83. For bugs.
In the Holy Ghost, God the Father, Son and Holy Virgin Mary, I command you to disappear from my house, for by this salt, you will not thrive. Go away, far, far away, as far as the road goes down into the abyss in the suffering, in the name of the Highest, I command you to turn before my power that is not created, to go and find a peaceful habitation but for those who do not listen and obey, instead one created for a punishment. O you almighty whose power has liberated me from this encumbrance. In the name of Jesus Christ God's Son and of his Mother. Amen.   Ernst Sept. 36.

84. Bell-ore
Gives power if you have it in the same room where you sleep.   The Finn. Gåltjäm, 35.

85. Hollertz.   Signe Sax.
In the name of the Holy Mother of God, I ask from my innermost that you, the Highest, bless this one, that it may protect from evil this one from the outer as well as the inner injuries. Give the power of the Atonement and show him also the strongest among all, the King of Kings, you the Highest are in the name of God the Father and of the Son and of the Holy Ghost. Amen. First make a sweep with the scissors 6 times, then back 6 times. Recite quietly the whole time so that the Amen is the last word recited.   Ernst Sep. 36.

86. Memory.
In the Holy Trinity, The Mother of God the King and the Spirit of the Son, your humble servant prays for grace and [*tukit*] command all evil spirits my memory, destroy, drive them out. You the strongest. My memory will forever be good. No one has any power over me. You alone have power and are the strongest, one alone in all my protective saints and the name of the Highest. Amen. + + + over your head.   Ernst. Sept. 36.

87. What Olle recited over my handkerchief for luck.
God Father Son and Holy Ghost, This that I twist in my hand, so sharply will Elsa's righteousness become in your name alone, only for truth and not for lies. May Elsa get justification, for everything in its time. I command you, the Highest of Kings in the name of the Holy Trinity.   Olle, Sept. 36.

88. The Lapp Adolf said to take three hairs from a corpse.
You who rest here in whose name you now sleep. With this you shall give to me power to hear what I wish, you shall only follow me, you servant of my spirit, you are in the name of all the Saints until the beginning of Judgment day. Recite but speak at 12 o'clock at night. Cross then + + + times over the coffin.   The Lapp Adolf Lundkvist Sept. 36.

89. Dragon's blood, Power and Might.
I will live until 13 August 1966, 30 more years, 88 years old. (The finnish woman, 1934.) Karl Hildur will live until 1997, 87 years, Språngviken

90. When Hollertz took a heart.
He recited this:
O Holy Spirit of God
O Holy Mary
O Holy Son of God
O Holy Name of the Nazarene
Give this being peace, the heart faith.
Give the Heart Power
Give the Heart all my wishes, O Lord, you alone are the Highest. Before you I will bow down. *   Ernst, Sept. 36.
   You shouldn't look at the one who is thinking about hexing you.
   You who are the strongest, give to me so that I may believe. In the name of God's Holy Holy Dwelling place. *   Ernst, Sept. 36

91. To protect people. [*Att (be)vara folk.*]
In the name of Jesus Christ God's Mother, Son and all the protective saints, I humbly pray for power to keep K. from going out. I know that you have Power. Give me of it, I your humble servant will always remain. O in the name of the holy Mother of God, O Holy God the Father, Holy Ghost, Holy Trinity. Amen.
*You now have power over your own limbs.

[PAGE CUT OUT WITH A STRAIGHT EDGE]

103. To See.
Go to a churchyard. Recite over a gravestone, cross yourself while I read. Your Sight shall be in my sight, in whose name you rest here. I would not disturb you , but hoped that you in the name of peace sleep so that I may discern the hidden and see its power, hear its celebration, and help in need. Could you, O holy Ghost, give to me of your power in the name of the Holy Crucified One, Amen. Cross my eyes. 3 times. each lid.   Forsgalen, Upsala.

104. Peace over all things living.
O Holy Lord crowned by a crown of thorns, in your name, you the purest you the wisest, wisdom's King, The Prince of Peace and Salvation, King of Israel who is of Saint Mary, in your name in your name I a poor servant pray for grace and peace for all living, my friends as well as enemies, for you have said Love your enemies, help the poor, support the stumbling. O, you who bear the crown of thorns who suffered on the cross and bled your blood for us poor beings that we might obtain peace, I pray now for grace and peace for mine and for all poor ...

105. Blessing.
O Holy Holy Father, O Holy Mother of God, O blessed and Highly placed Son of God, O Holy Ghost, give to me and all my dear ones you rich blessing, as you, O Jesus Christ, you who suffered on the cross so that I might live, give to me Power and grace and blessing so that all my dear ones as well as house, barn, and all my faithful friends. O dear, beloved Father, I seek your blessing for everyone now, humbly pray that I may also receive a crumb of it, in the dear name of Jesus Christ and in the name of the Holy Mother of God, The Virgin Mary. In your name, O dear Father, and God, and the Holy Ghost's name, Amen. Recite 3 times.   Sven, Sept. 36.

106. For the Dead.
O the Prince of Salvation's Salvation, you the Highest of all, over everyone give peace and grace for all misfortune, over all beings as well in consecrated as well as unconsecrated ground. O You who have power, give to me power to work grace for these ones, in God the Father and Son and Holy Ghost's name. Amen. recte 3 times. Recite over salt and throw over the roof three times, also liquor.   late Sept. 36

107. Counting recitation.
Protection, Power, Peace.
Recite over mercury. Throw over your head then the evil will go away.
13 God the Father, Son 18 Holy Mother of God and Son 21 The Holy Ghost 22 I command now protect 23 this house and inhabitants 24 You have all the Power 27 I promise to you, the Highest 31 You the Greatest give to me power 42 You are Mighty you alone 54 I bow before you 57 Give to me peace, give to me courage give to me power to protect myself and my dear ones from all evil 61 Holy God the Father, Son and Holy Ghost and all the Protective Saints' names. Amen.   Ernst Sept 36.

108. What Anna's mother recites.
O dear Savior, Dear Mother of God, Dear Savior, give to me as well as mine peace and salvation in your name. O Holy Mother of God, give to me and my

children your blessedness and perfection. Beings of earth in the names of Jesus Christ God's Son, Holy Virgin Mary, Holy Spirit of God, Holy Trinity, God as well as all the protective saints. O you crowed with a Crown of Thorns, + Amen.   Late Sept. 36.

109. May 15, 1927
Win on the numbers 2481 587.
5.000?
A.B. Laniskassa Norrmalmstorg 8
Buy there in January for 45.
Win 50.000 15 May.
N. 13976 Ser. 2471
1946 won 100.000
1939 Olle's P
1947 Dan. P.

To see olisag learned.
I the name of Jesus Christ the Son of God and Spirit, I pray for power to be able to see for myself, in your name, everything that happens in this world or behind the hidden scene that we all have in our family. O Highest, and in this time without a spell or anything else, now I pray in your name O Dear Father Dear Savior, let my son also inherit it, do not be provoked to anger, but rather show your grace, I pray in your dear name, the name of O Holy Ghost and Holy Virgin Mary, God's Son and the Spirit. Amen.

110. Water, to recite over in salt, for plants.
I the name of the Father and of the Son and of the Holy Ghost I pray that you bless this water that it may receive power to grow and propagate, for you, the great Creator alone have all the power. In your care I leave these flowers and trees and everything on my farm to grow, O dear Lord, in the name of Jesus Christ, God's Son, and God's Holy Mother and the Holy Ghost. Amen. Cross three times over [PAGE CUT OUT]

[ONE PAGE CUT OUT]

113. Plan of Study
The Law of Similarity. Similia Similibus Curantur. That's like heals like.
Materia Medica
The doctrine of Cures.

114. Faith healing.
Paracelsus, lived in the 1600s.
Urine, excrement, spit, each hair, blood, AntuTrapati is by him, himself.

Cancer, Tuberculosis, Venereal Diseases. The lowest 200 potens, Others, lowest 30 potens.

115. Medicine.
Milk sugar. A postluis morat.
Removal of blood, urine anointing. A flat bowl to keep it in, put it on the stove fire, burn to ashes. The ashes are called *mumia*. 9 parts milk sugar in the mortar, 1 part *mumia*. Decenepoteus. But if we take a 99, then we have the centisimalpoteus, compare with 6/24, it is maintained during two hours in the mortar and then I take from it one part to 99 parts alcohol and one part of the thick mixture, for 30. The first potensen, a button-hole's size of one part, give 2 parts.

116. The Homeopath, Count Mathe, Italy.
What Mathe whispered into the ear of the Pope "I believe in you!"
Bhia-root, [*stenört*], [*ögonblomma*] [*Esi-*]root, Ginger. Boiled in a half liter of water for 35 minutes. Mixed cold with a half liter of liquor.

117. Protection from suffering. [*jndeby Uliv*]
O dear, dear, dear God, Father, O holy holy Son of God, O Holy God Dear chaste, Mother of God who is worthy of worship, you the Sweetest, Purest, Most Peaceful and Sanctified, give to me power to be able to withstand all suffering, be equally patient and joyful as you were, O holy Virgin mary, who who have power, give to me from your grace, your dear grace, to be able to heal all sufferings so that many souls will be saved, in your name alone, I recite this spell. Amen.

The Ring of the King is engraved I. P. C. M. B. I.: International Companies for the care of humankind. Only 9 rings were made of copper from the roof of a church. Only the highest bishops and in the name of all the protective saints. I humble myself, and bow before you, O saviour mild. Sven, Sept. 36. Amen.

118. To not go again[122]
In the name of the Holy Mother of God, and grace for the being who wanders here, thou Virgin Mary, give peace to all, that peace that you most peaceful of all beings on earth, in your name and in the name of Holy God the Father and the Holy Son and all the protective saints.

119. Power.
In the name of Jesus Christ Crucified, and the purest on our earth, and heav-

---

[122] To "go again" or *gå igen* is a way of talking about coming back as a revenant. This spell purports to prevent that from happening.

en, O Holy Mother of God, Virgin Mary, you purest of all mothers, blessed by God. O you Holy Dear Father, give to me, a poor and unfortunate being, grace to receive a portion of your power, for the good of all the poor ones as riches. For before you are all alike. Your grace is great and Dear Saviour, your grace alone is dearly won, in your name I would only work with the power. I pray for my [...] and should I misuse this dear power that I receive from you, punish me the hardest you can, for alone when I dare to pray for grace in Jesus Christ the crown-of-thorns be-crowned, my Dear Holy Father, the High Virgin Mary the Holy Ghost. + +

120. To become people [*att bli folk*]
In the name of Holy God of the Son and the Father, I command that from this moment those at home will find the dearest resting place. He always stays home. He will always have home first in his mind. He won't go out, and he will conduct himself following me. You have the power, you alone, you the Highest on our earth, in your name I recite and pray in the name of the Holy Ghost and the Holy Trinity. + + +

121. For hard stomach.
In the name of God the Father, Son and Holy Ghost, I command you to bow down before the most powerful. All evil spirits out of this stomach. You will be from this moment in your holy name I know everything, Blessed be in the name of God the Father, Son and Holy Trinity and the Holy Mother of God. Amen. Recite over, spit three times, take in three times, *tjälspälle*. Sept 36. Blessed that which you take in, but without necessary [*uppe...*]
In Jesus Christ God's Son's and Spirit's name, bless this one to your glory. E.g. Sågberg.

122. To get cows to stay. recite three times.
You who call yourself the Highest, now I command you to bow down to the strongest in God's name. When I say a casting, lead me. I am the strongest. Lead my + + + Helmer. Sept. 36

123. The Seraph of the Jewess.
In Jesus Christ, The Mother of God, you are baptized I now take your head so that I may have wisdom through you. You may answer everything I ask, otherwise you will have no peace. I want to know everything and you are forced to answer me, I who am the strongest, who dares to go against death, for as long as I live, your head will be with me. Bow down before my power in the name of the Cross. Hold the hand on the head while I recite in the name of the Cross. Jewess.

To gargle with.
[*Kolsgrad kalilösning.*]
Vålhems-stone is a stone that lightning struck. If you have one, then they can't steal.

124. Whatever can happen in the world no one can know more than He, who has created it. His powers are unending and we humans know hardly a single perfect, among the many turns there are. That what happens through God's powers is natural and completely natural is Godly. There are more natures than there are stars in heaven and that which can happen according to a higher nature's plan no one can know, foresee or understand, with the exception of the one who has been given some of the Lord's powers. Our Lord is All powerful, and is able to do what He wills.   Elsa Stockholm 25.

125. Salomon's 6-pointed star drawn with two circles each within the other. This sign has power against spirits. Draw it so that you begin at the upper left, and second from the top, over the door, all within will be at peace then. Give me courage and blood to perform this.

132. The Other I. Elsa Stina, 25.
The so-called conjuration of the soul, this consists in that one at midnight in a church or open ruin or other lonesome place or solemn place and there three times with a minute's pause between each time the name is named, equally loudly. Which calls to me. When this was done a picture of the conjured being should like come forth out of his soul and suddenly appear before his eyes. His appearance should be so terrible that few humans would have the strength to survive it.   Elsa Stockholm 25.

133. Carrying under the earth for scurvy.
Immediately in front of [...] a hole through a earth mound, from the south to the north. When it is made, cover it with pieces of turf so that the earth vapors won't dry it out before the child comes. Take off the child's clothes inside and wrap him in a sheet in which there are no knots. All must remain silent. Quietly go to the earth mound with the child. Take away the turfs. The one who is able shall stand at the Northern hole, stuff the child in headfirst, say: I send you a well-bound girl or boy. I release her or him again in the name of

Jesus Christ answered the mother, gave back. This is done 9 times. Don't say anything until you are back inside.   Fru Kerstin Fjäll Fyrås, Oct. 1936.

134. If you want to sharpen your understanding, increase your riches, glimpse into the future, then you should carry with you an emerald. Albertus Magnus from Laningen i Schwabia, lived in the 1200s. Says that a hand full of precious jewels can help one forth through the whole world. If you want to make yourself invisible, then take an opal, wrap it in a bay laurel leaf, then all those present will be blind. If you want to survive all dangers and triumph over all earthly things, then take an agat. It sweeps out all dangers and difficulties from your road in life, and makes people strong and in a good mood.

135. To come inside the church.
You Holy, who dwells in this house, I conjure you in the power of the abyss, show your power and open this door. If it doesn't open, then he will free them from all evil spirits and they will fly up with a rush.   Nils Nov 9...

136. Go on graves, fall upon your knees, and pray to the dead. Receive protection so that they have peace, those who do it.

Worshipped, Pure, Wise, Humble Picture of the Mother of God, of Bronze is from the 1200s.

Helmer works in the sun. After 9 am and before 9 pm Helmer blows out the salt where they are after 9 am and before 9 pm. Think sharply (concentrate). 9 times.

Strong medicine in three places Pillow, Moss, Shirt. Think --- 9 times.

Don't have it inside while you sleep. But Olle said that he had seen that it didn't make any difference. No air should come in. It doesn't matter as long as I have the coin in my mouth. Olle put the knife point under the glass, as well as the point under the bottle 1 ½ hours until it was ready. Stroke on the bottle to make it electric.

[CONTINUATION OF NAMES FROM INSIDE THE FRONT COVER...]

45. Kronotorparen Gustav Karlson, Adolfslund, Stensele.
46. Fru Ramén Strömsund
47. P. S. Kerstin Västansjö, Kavland.
48. Mr. Nils Olof Söder Tanbyn Slättån
49. Mr. Åsen, Samamon Bergeforsen.
50. Fru Åman Skönsvik, Sundsvall

51. Fru Ing Söderlund. Stöde.
52. Anders Andersson Färila Ljusdal
53. Törnblom Holmsveden
54. Fru Hellkvist, Sundsvall Her husband in Tullen
55. Fru Hallberg, Alsta
56. Fru Jonson Krötesta, Sundsvall
57. Kron Alfta Skålsjö, Viksjöfors
58. Indals Prästen Berggren Berjeforsen.

Hj. Kroksta. Gullänget, Örnsköldsvik
Tysk Anders Ruk Kärfsåsen
Marisfar
Lis Olle Boda
Erik Arnsten Berge
Gammal Jerker Grava
Nils Emanuel Jonson Töva

In the Holy Ghost's name you have promised me.

When the moons in the nails can hardly be seen, then there is sickness.

Fru Karin Strand, Hedesunda
Kron. Alfta Glason Stret Aveny 37 Flenos, Cikago Have bank 1.789.

MS 20

NM 271.601 "UPPLYSA DE OKUNNIGA"

*   *   *

To enlighten the ignorant is to accumulate merits.

Carrot juice.
Good for kidneys
Prayer to our Father in need.
O Holy you, the first ... help these poor ... be merciful to them so that they might have in their reason ... away all desires of Satan, ... pure spirit in them in ... these small spiraling ... flames forth to faith, certainty. God Father you the ... God's peace over them...

For eyes.
Coffee without cream, good for eyes.   E. H.

For kidneys
Dandelion root, boil, take.

Conjuration can release powers unknown up to now. It can also [...] the power.

Light a candle.
Say with a soft voice. Look at the flame, a slow, peaceful tone, monotone. Look at the flame. It burns higher, higher. It is becoming clearer, clearer. Look at the flame. Look at the flame. There is no other light in the whole world. There is only darkness all around. There is only darkness all around you, darkness. And the deep hole of sleep. Look at the flame, it burns high above you, high, high, you sink down – deep down in the darkness in deep, deep sleep. Look at the flame. It burns, burns higher, higher, and clearer, clearer, completely high, completely clearly. It blinds your eyes, you can not see. Put out the light, close your eyes. Soooo.

To wake up.
You have been deep down in the hole of sleep, much too deep. With a deep voice so commanding that I thought you would almost reach beyond the portals of sleep. Too deeply to hear you – too deeply to think – to deeply to want to turn back. But not too deep to obey. You will arise out of the dark hole of sleep – up, up to the light of day – and awake!

MS 21

NORDISKA MUSÉET #271.602
"NEGROMÄNLISKA SAKER"

TITLE PAGE:
NEGROMÄNLISKA SAKER – FÖRFATTADE I TRYCKET AF
UPGIFVAREN ÅR 1315
ÖFVERSATTE FRÅN EBREISKA, GREKISKA OCH LATIN PÅ
GÖTISKAN – 1410 – OCH SIST PÅ SVENSKA UTSKRIFVIT.

*NEGROMÄNLISH MATTERS – AUTHORED IN PRINT BY
THE AUTHOR IN THE YEAR 1315
TRANSLATED FROM HEBREW, GREEK AND LATIN IN
GOTHIC – 1410 – AND FINALLY WRITTEN OUT IN SWEDISH.*

Jesus, God's and Mary's son, halleluja!

Marbuel's conjuration
\#   \#

1. I, C. B. entreat you, o Marbuel! Bring about for me Aroraen ⚡, Lasunabula ⚡, and upon Jesus Christ + the power of the winner of victory and the power of the sun ⚡, now come, come before this my circle in this moment.
  Marbuel! Amen! Amen!

Marbuel's general conjuration
\#   \#

I, C. B. invoke you by the Almighty God, the creator and ruler over heaven and earth, in the water and in the air, over the fire and Hell and outside of Hell – yea, I conjure you with the word that was in the beginning with God, that is Jesus, the savior of the whole world, the hero ⚡, by him, who in his victorious descent to Hell forced you, you M a r b u e l, who trampled you M a r b u e l under his own feet and made all your grandeur into a mere loan; he placed you by means of his own suffering to be obedient to people, and to do their will.

  By his suffering, blood and death I conjure you, that you appear here at this very moment before my circle.
  Amen! Amen! =

General conversation with Marbuel
# #

I, C. B. invoke you, M a r b u e l by God, the Highest Ruler of All, that you open for me all the "grundfästen" of the earth, and that you, for the sake of Jesu Christi the highest victorious one's sake, send all the usual spirits, as many as there are, here away from the earth, that they make themselves ready in this very moment and let themselves be seen before this my circle in visible human shape (for me and no other) so that I can speak with them and give them orders to each one according to his specialization, to which end I absolve and herewith set them free from all other "förruttningar" during the same time.

N.B. I invoke you, M a r b u e l, by the holy and great name J e h o v a h + A o l a 𝒵, A o l y 𝒵, A o l a n d 𝒵, J e h o v a h + A d o n a i j 𝒵, A t h a n a d o i 𝒵, God of the heavens; yea, by Jesum Kristum + and his holy word I invoke you, M a r b u e l, that you fulfill my desires. Hear, J e h o v a h + the heavens' 𝒵, the firmaments' 𝒵, the planets' 𝒵, and the earth's lord.

I, the son of earth, consecrated by God and people, invoke you, so that you perform my will, which I order. Amen!

The 1st Chapter.
About spirits.

Here is presented exclusively a good chief or spirit, who is in the southwest and has under himself many millions of serving spirits.

Invocation or Calling upon the Chief or the spirit Marbuel
+ + +

O Marbuel! I, N. N. Invoke and call upon you, Marbuel, by the great triune God and Lord Jehovah Dei Schadei, by Jesum Kristum + Siloh Schadole Mallo + + +, by God the holy Spirit Hagion Hagiotaton + + + and by the four holy evangelists: Matheus, Markus, Lukas and St Johannes names, and by the three holy Patriarchs Abraham, Isak and Jakob's names, and by the four archangels Mikael, Gabriel, Rafael and Uriel's names, and by the four elemental chiefs Chirub, Tharcis, Ariel and Serafim's names' power, that you, Marbuel, without failure/neglect immediately in an attractive human shape without a racket or causing any harm, shall appear before this my circle, so that I may speak with you regarding those errands I desire.

# # #

The Second Exhortation

I, N. N., call you, spirit Marbuel, for the second time, by the great triune God and Lord Jehovah Dei Schadei's name, by Jesum Kristum Sihlok Schadol

Mallo names + + + And by God the Holy Spirit Hagion Hagiotaton's name, and by the four holy evangelists Matheus, Markus, Lukas and St. Johannes' names and by the three holy Patriarchs Abraham, Isak and Jakob's names, and by the four archangel's Mikael, Gabriel, Rafael and Uriel's names, and by the four elemental Chiefs Chirub, Tharcis, Ariel and Serafim's names, that you, Marbuel, without neglect immediately, without noise or causing harm appear before this my circle in an attractive human shape to answer me those questions I put to you and wish to know.

#   #   #

Third and last Exhortation

I, N. N., call and invoke you, Marbuel, a third and last time, by the great and triune Lord God Jehovah Sebaoth Theschua Dei Schadei's name's might and power. I, N. N., call and invoke you Marbuel by Jesum Kristum Sihlo Schadoll Mallo the lord the highest's son's might and power + + +. I, N. N., invoke and call you spirit, Marbuel, by God the Holy Spirit Hagio Hagiotaton, the most holy lord's name's might and power, that you in this very moment appear before this my circle in an attractive human shape, without noise or causing harm, to give me answers to all those questions that I put to you, and accomplish what I desire to know.

#   #   #

The Arrival of the Spirit.

Now when the spirit Marbuel comes, speak to him in the following manner: To be said three times after each other.

O Agland! + Jesus is before me and at my side. + Morsala 𝒵, Quamdam Sola + o, Jehovah + Dorsat + I am that one whom Kristus + preserves + Soland + and the one through whom Jesus + works, here Jesus is with me + Amen!

#   #   #

The spirit is bound in the following way:

God the father binds you 𝒵, Jesus holds you + God 𝒵 the holy spirit 𝒵 binds you the chief of peace Mikael binds you.

O, Annad! Bind this spirit through your peace +
P. Gabriel! 𝒵 You power of Christ 𝒵 bind the spirit Marbuel!

#   #   #

The departure of the Spirit back

O, Milias Gudi praise + Jesus + be blessed, I want to bear your holy cross +; o, Marbuel! Be departed +, go back to the spirits, without causing harm +. Jesus + be with me. Amen! +

    N.B., This exhortation should most certainly happen on Thursday mornings before the rising of the sun, at a crossroads, or one walks or makes a cross with the feet, wherever one is standing, until one gets to speak with the spirit for the first time and arranged regarding one's errands.

The following circle is made of weave or paper.

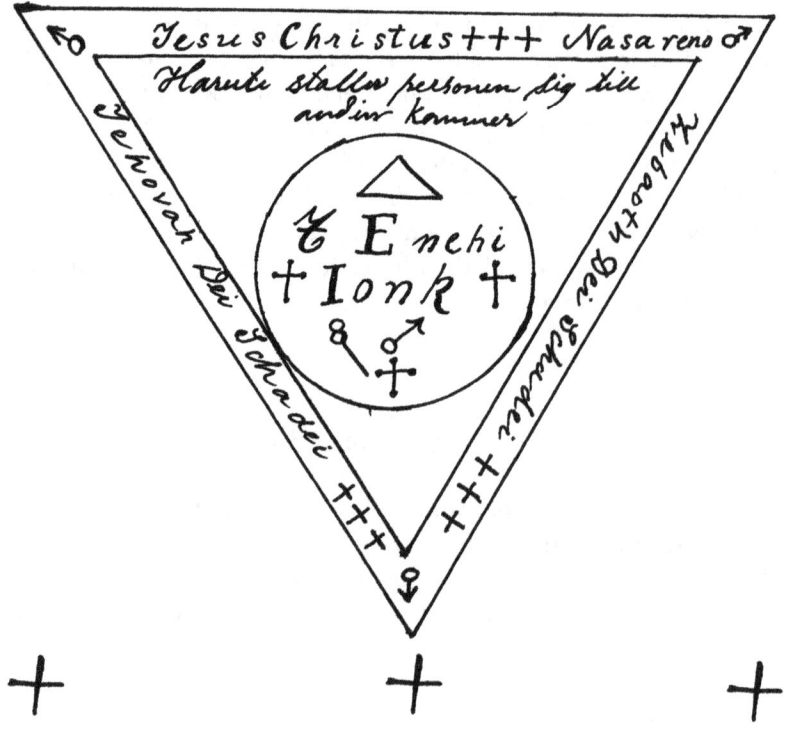

Untried.

The 2nd Chapter.

2. To show invisible spirits and to be able to speak orally with them in whatever parts one desires, to find out hidden things. Write these words, which are written below, namely. Put your name and then this:

Filx Gackte ol hordea

OSS. YQQ Pelock Bjelsebubb.
Behov vara. [need to be.]

1°/ Write this with red letters on an old spruce chip and go to the cemetery and put the chip under an earth-fast stone. When you set out, it shall be a Thursday evening. When you come back there the second Thursday evening, then take the chip and say their name as well as say: I order you spirits next Thursday evening to come and meet me and this in the name of Domine Pater Filius Sanct Spiritus or in the name of God the Father and of the Son and of the Holy Spirit. Then, go thence the third Thursday evening, then the chip is gone and a little round stone in its place; take this stone and keep it, then they will come to you and then you can get to know whatever you ask of it; but don't ask too much all at once, because then they get too tired, but then further. When you have the stone in your pocket, you'll never lack for money; 2°/ take the stone in a bottle and drop it a drop for each spirit you want to speak with; 3°/ they shall procure for you in this way whatever you order, as wide as the whole earth extends.

The 3rd Chapter.

3. To in another way procure for yourself spirits.
Take an unleavened bread, baked on a Sunday morning or a Saturday evening before or after the rising of the sun, no larger than a crust and three new thorn sewing needles; put them in a triangle in the bread and put three shillings of quicksilver (mercury) into a previously sewn tight leather pouch, put together and well closed-up. Go then on a Saturday evening late to the cemetery and lay the pouch under a headstone and say slowly to yourself: up and meet me in the way that I shall order next Saturday evening! Go there and move the pouch, as was said, and say next Saturday evening the invocation above. The third Saturday is said: "Up, in the name of God the father, of the Son and of the Holy Ghost and come to meet me here next Saturday night at 12 o'clock in the appearance of a fly on my window, when I shall take you into my service." Have a fitting little bottle at hand, cork it well and wrap it up and have it with you! When you want to know something, take the bottle in your hand, put it to your ear and ask slowly for yourself, then you will immediately

get the right answer to what you ask; don't ask too much at one time, because then the fly will suffer and get tired of it. It is preferable that the leather pouch is put under a headstone under which a man is buried.

N.B. Look out, that the bottle doesn't break, because then the spirit will get loose, and that will cost you your life.

When you die, if you keep the bottle that long, take it in your coffin to the grave, then it will break; but it may not be transported by another during your lifetime.

Untried.

The 4th Chapter.

To hinder thievery (*tjufwahand*) and fires (*eldebrand*).

4. Go to a cemetery when graves are opened and take a dead man's skull and put it aside in the cemetery; go then to the cemetery on a Sunday evening, silently, and say: "I take you to use for my allowable needs during my lifetime." When you want to use the above-mentioned errands, then take the dead man's skull between your hands and say, as you go around your belongings as widely as you want: "You unnamed man, I invoke you by the power of the name of the great triune God and lord Jehovah, and by the power of the names of Jesum Kristum and of God the holy spirit.," or only "By the name of God the father, of God the Son and of the Holy Spirit, that you bind and keep the hand of the thief in its place at my wares until I get the same, and keep away fire from my belongings and house and farm in the same power of the High Names, who created me and you. Amen."

N.B. This is said three times, as you walk as many times around your belongings and hold the skull between your hands. Then put the skull in your cupboard or trunk on clean straw under lock and key when you use it. This shall be done with good respect.

Untried.

The 5th Chapter.

5. To produce stolen goods that are not too old.
When there is something stolen from you at night, or even in the daytime, or at whatever time it happens, before you walk over the place where the thief exited, remain silent, take a knife in the hand and put it into the thief's footprint and say: "This knife I put through your foot, you damned thief, who has stolen my wares, wherever you may be, and this in Satan's name." You say this three times in a row, and the knife remains in the thief's foot, that foot you hit in the track; and he will come soon to you with the stolen goods and asks for forgiveness …

6. Binding of the Spirits of Hell.

Helvetis-andars band

u, k, n, a, t, l, m, i.   k, s, t, l, m, k.

Tsudninter Drusuon
Tsudninter Thraison   f, u, r, o, b

lit   rita   stin   thina
låt   resa   sten   denna   f, th, n, a

ah   bui   girdi   fli
och   hög   gjorde fler

A book, in which is shown that with it one may call forth all the spirits of hell, who watch over the hidden treasures.

To discover with it all those treasures that are on the earth, or in the earth or under the water or in hidden rooms lying hidden.

In the preface it is warned: to pray holy and live chastely, to not go astray or neglect anything, so that you might not cause yourself or your assistants any danger and injury to either body or soul, so that you through God's grace and blessing do not receive ill etc. is employed Defect that if you are near to some treasure, in whatever way you dig it up or procure it, then through God the treasure is brought forth by that spirit who has guarded it or has caused it; when you listen to his words, if you shall make some contract or promise, it should be a promise that some of the treasure should be distributed to churches or poor people, then you must do that, but if you will give to the spirit some pledge, then don't do it, rather say to the hellish spirit, who is standing before you, like so: "I want to leave a pledge to give obligation or promise to him, to whom I am indebted, namely the most high God, who created that thing, but to you I shall give nothing; you have received your recompense etc., turn etc.

N.B. + Take now in, but how you, friendly reader, will do if you want to take some treasure and that, that people may not see your doings:

Buy virgin-parchment, pay for it immediately with money, make for yourself thereof a girdle, wherewith you can gird yourself and write on it the following names which are written here and divided into three parts.

<u>The blessing of the girdle around the body.</u>

I, by the name of N.N., bind myself over you, earthly and elemental creature, you earth, with this threefold girdle, decorated with the names of God. Jehovah Zebaoth (Lord of Hosts) Aloa (God) Abh (father) Jehovah El Schaddai (Lord God the Almighty) Jehovah Dai (Lord, you Absolute) Schaddai Malloch Jehovah Ales Alæ, Jehovah Alion (the highest) Bora (creator, Mâlâk Mâlâk gadol alkol haÿretz (a great king of all the earth) Âloh im Timloch (God who shall reign) Jehovah leolam (the Lord in eternity) Âloa Zion (Zion's God) Jehovah Happuratz (lord the layer of wastes or the one who breaks down) Jehovah Zidkenu (the lord our righteousness) Jehovah Elohim Gibbor (the Lord God the Mighty) Jehovah Zebaoth (Lord of Lords).

+ + +

I by name N.N. (ut supra, as before). Jehovah Goïl (the Lord the redeemer) Âloa ben Jesun (the Son of God Jesus) Jehovah adonai (the Lord) Mabiach (anointed) Jehovah Ichchua (Lord Jesus) Jehovah Ichchu Ichchua Ichosehua (Savior) Jehovah âla Adonai (Lord) Ichovah Bazza Iehovah Ichchu (the Lord Blessedness) Zidkenii (our righteousness) Jehovah Elohim (Lord God) Gibbon (Mighty) Daliova Jehovah Theos (God) Tetragramaton (the four-lettered).

N.B. יְהֹ Jehovah Theos (The Lord God) Hagion hagiotatos (the Holiest of the Holy) Jehovah Masciach (anointed) etc., etc.

+ + +

I by name N. N. etc., ut supra the first. Jehovah Aloa, Ruah Hakedosch Jehovah Zidkenu Elohim, Gibbor Jehovah Zebaoth, Malloh rich Âloh, Jehovah Âlohim Âmat hu, Elohim kaijm, Michizzepho reaschol veal Laasetz. That is: Lord God Holy Spirit + Lord of Hosts. – God, Lord God, who is the Truth, the God of Life, before his substantial wrath they tremble also on the earth + the lord our righteousness God Mighty

+ + +

Within which I N. N. with the power of the highest God, Jehovah Âlohim (the Lord God) indicated to be freed on earth from all spirits of Hell and ghosts and from all of Hell's provocation and collusion, that they shall not dare to appear before me before my eyes nearer than three paces, and that they shall not be able to cause me any injury to either body or soul, neither to approach me closer than always three paces from me, so that I may remain assuredly uninjured, but in front of me, behind me, with me, under me and over me the holy spirit etc., I remain three paces away from all the spirits of Hell and ghosts and the entirety of the root of the Abyss, so that I am just as safe as the Lord Christ was safe and uninjured before the tempter from Hell in the Wilderness, who could cause no injury or pain to him. Amen!

7. Letters to administer to both people and livestock when any pain occurs, as a remedy of it; are written in this way:

KORBORFABOR
METARLLIΨNF.
KORBORFABOR
METARLLIΨN.F.

8. So that no one has the power to do you any ill, so no one has any power, carry these words on yourself:

HABLITETTBN
LABOR EBOR ORFIDIVMAW.
HABLITETTBN
LABOR EBOR ORFIDIVMAW.

By the crown of thorns that they put on our Lord Jesu Kristi blessed head and by the nails and spear, that they struck through our Lord Jesus Krist's blessed hands and feet and by the spear that they stabbed our blessed Lord Jesus Krist's in his holy side with [and by the water and blood that ran out of Jesus's holy side, and by [I U N G F R U M A R I A] chastity, and by [S A N T E A P O S T L A R N E], and by the four evangelists, and by the four [E L E M E N T R], and by our Lord Jesus Christ's joyful ascension to heaven from his holy grave.

With these words, I silence, and bind and exhort all [O N D A A N D A R] to turn away from us, to take that place that I will show with my [S K A P A D E F I N G R], and by that which God has said in his Word, that [T H U I N O N E S S Ä D S T A L S Ö N D E R T R A M P A O R M S E N S H U F V U T] *(because ?? speech stomp to pieces the head of the serpent)*, this I do altogether [I N A M N G U D F & S & D H A . A M E N, I E S U S H E R R A N S + + + I E S U S] *(in the name of God the father and the son and the holy spirit. Amen, Jesus the Lord +++ Jesus)*. I see over you and under you and I bind you with the bonds which our Lord were bound [A L L A D E D I E F U L A R S O U] *(all the devils SOU)* in [H E L F V E T E] *(hell)*, and you shall eat your own flesh and drink your own blood and leave us be in peace. [I E S U S N A M N G U D F A D E R S & S O N S & D E N S H E L I G E A N D E S A M E N I E S U S H E R R A N S + + +] *(Jesus name God the Father's and Son's and the Holy Spirit's Amen. Jesus the Lord +++)*

---

9. En Dracka Dracka Maning (a Dracka Dracka Conjuration)

Ut [D R A C K E F I O F A N D M E N F A N D T O G D I G , G U D B E V A R E M I G] *(Drackefio the Devil but the Devil took you, God preserve me)*

---

10. [A V E P A T E R N O S T E R]
[N E M A T H G I V E I N E T E H G I L R Ä H H C O N E T H C A M] Hco ttid rä tekir yt; odno nårfi sso slärf natu, esletserf i ekci sso delni hco, orä egidlyks sso med etålröf iv kco mosås, redluks aråv sso tålröf hco gad i sso fig dörb agilegad tråv enedroj åp kco ås, nelemmih i mosås ejliv nid eks, ekir ttid emmokllit, nman ttid edrav tagleh, molmih i tsä mos, råv Redaf.

(This is the Lord's Prayer written backwards, with the first line within brackets written in runes.)

11. Romani A. B. C.

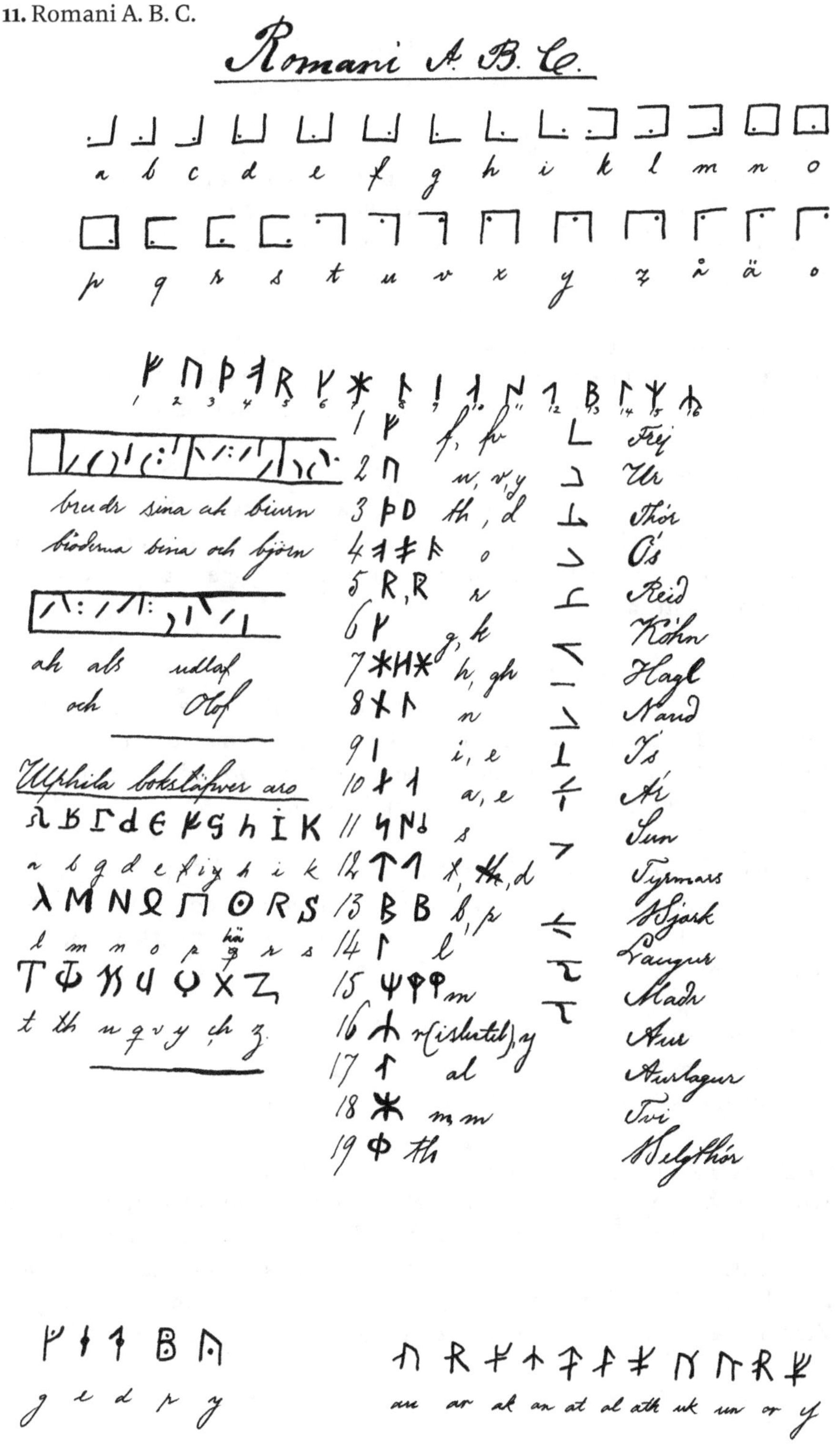

Romani A. B. C.

[alphabet chart with symbols for a–o and p–ä, o]

[runic characters numbered 1–16 at top]

1 ᚠ		Frej
2 ᚢ	w, v, y	Ur
3 ᚦ D	th, d	Thor
4 ᚨ ᛅ ᚨ	o	Os
5 R, R	r	Reid
6 ᚴ	g, k	Köhn
7 *H*	h, gh	Hagl
8 ᚾ ᛐ	n	Naud
9 ᛁ	i, e	Is
10 ᛆ ᛐ	a, e	Ar
11 ᛋᚾᛑ	s	Sun
12 ᛐᛐ	t, tt, d	Tyrmars
13 ᛒ ᛒ	b, p	Björk
14 ᛚ	l	Laugur
15 ᛘᛘᛘ	m	Madr
16 ᛂ r (islutet), y		Aur
17 ᛐ	al	Aurlagur
18 *	m, m	Tvi
19 Φ	th	Belgthor

brudr sina ah biurn / bioderna sina och björn

ah als udlaf / och Olof

Ulphila bokstäfwer äro

Λ B Γ Δ E F G H I K
a b g d e f y z h i k
Λ M N Ω Π Θ R S
l m n o p kun r s
T Φ U Q V X Z
t th u q v y ch z

[bottom runic inscriptions]
ᚠᛁᛐ B ᚾ
g e d r y

ᚢ R ᛅ ᛐ ᚨ ᚨ ᚢ ᚾ R ᚠ
an ar al an at al ath uk un or y

13.

83994718132
[N D I I O H F N F D U?]

14. <u>To overcome one's enemies</u>.
So go silently and rinse your hands in the morning in the dew and say like this: "I see you and you don't see me; all the hate and envy you bear for me, that I push away from me to you, in the name of the Father and of the Son and of the Holy Spirit. Amen."

15. <u>To find favor with your master</u>.
So take a mole and take the heart from him, and to that you take a "seal-clamp" and you bind this on you or sew it on the clothes that you use.

16. <u>So that dogs won't bark at you</u>.
Arrange that you get a black dog, that you take the ears off of and carry with you, then no dog will bark at you, but notice this first, that the dog should be only one color, and for the second thing you can see (papers) that no one else can see at nighttime.

17. <u>To make a shotgun to shoot lucky</u>.
Shoot yourself a raven, and when you have shot him to death, then take a white feather, that is sitting under the right wing; but in case he isn't shot to death, he will swallow that feather, when you cut him up and find it in its gizzard, put it in the gun barrel so that it can't be seen.

18. <u>When a shotgun doesn't want to kill</u>.
Now take the heart of a skate and put in the shotgun, shoot it out towards a clay wall. Do this each time you clean your shotgun, then it will kill, whatever you want to shoot.

19. <u>Another way</u>.
Take a snake and whip in your shotgun and put the ammunition in front and shot him then out into the air. This is tested and helps.

20. <u>To cause a shotgun to be silent</u>.
When you hear a shotgun shot, then take your knife and cut a turf under the right foot and put then three pieces of steel-wire points into her. When you have done this, you run three times backwards around a (*lycka*); but notice this, that when you do this, the shotgun won't be good to shoot with, and you should probably be careful that you don't yourself get injured through it.

21. To cause wild animals to gather at a spot.
Shoot yourself a raven and take the heart from him and make a hole all the way through the heart so big, that you can in a hurry see whatever you want. When you see something wild, look through the heart, then it will be where you aim to shoot. Probatum.

22. So that no person shall hex you.
Write these words and have them with you:

"Karbeox Sabox melars."

23. When a snake creeps in someplace and you want to have him out from there again.
Say three times: "Out again in the Devil's name at this hour to change life and blood with me in a sinful way at this place on earth in all devils lengthily in a sinful way this substance in "*tigrar*," which by god my soul appointed that you (*eder*) offended and show many long way forth that while she may know of Christ's burial, that you even so never attain you shall not rule this treasure so that my health vein is taken blood to write and that on the place in the name of nine devils and in nine names of Gods godfather's names, so that they on both sides are fighting against each other."

24. When you see a ghost or revenant flare up from money
Take a silver coin, little or big, and through the same coin toward the ghost and say this three times: "Flare up in the devil's name, for I give you chastity and by St. Bengt's "*edroghet*" all evil spirits' magic and all anxiety and haunting shall be forbidden to do to this Godly person N. N. any injury by our Lord Jesus Christ's holy honorable birth and by our Lord Jesus Christ's death and suffering and by the crown of thorns Jesus bore on his blessed head and by the blows that Jesus was hit with and by the three nails that Jesus was nailed to the cross with.

_____

_____

25. A sure release for cattle from the arts of magic
When the cattle come out to graze for the first time of the year, notice carefully that place where the very first one bites, there one pinches three times from the grass and keeps it until evening, when it comes back in; then one takes three times the hair from the cow, first on the shoulder, then on the back and lastly on the hind part of the back. With this cense the cow with the grass and with the hairs, but be careful that when there is more than one cow, that each and every one gets its own, so then no one has power to injure them that year.

_____

26. Finally is this following recipe:

Incense.

To be bought of each sort

Castoreum – 4
Red Coral – 2
White Coral – 2
Black Coral – 2
Sasealans – 1
Mixed Incense – 2
Lovage – 1
Asafetida – 1
Garlic – 1

MS 22

NM ONUMRERAT
"1. ATT LÄSA MOT VÄRK – 10. ATT FÖRGÖRA EN FIOL"
GRYTS OCH GÅRINGE SKOGSBYGD, SÖDERMANLAND

* * *

1. To recite away pain.
You hold some liquor in a glass and draw a cross in it with a knife and say: The Virgin Mary promenaded across the churchyard. She stopped pain, she healed sheep. Jesus fall asleep, pain be anesthetized; Christ *waktnas vakna, wärken fakta*,[123] in the name of God the Father and the Son and the Holy Ghost.

2. To stop bleeding.
Then you say: This blood will run for the time that God has ordained for man and woman, who goes to the court and knows right, but swears falsely. In the name of God the Father and of the Son and of the Holy Ghost.

---

[123] This string of words is unclear. It could be "Christ is watched, awakens; the pain… If *fakta* is a misspelling for *fäkta*, then "fights the pain" could be inferred.

3. To bewitch girls.
You take a frog, then you take a box and bore nine holes, three in the bottom, three in the top and three in the sides. Then you put the box and bury it down in an anthill. A Thursday night you go there and look for it, then a second Thursday night you return; the third Thursday night you go there and take back the box. Then you find in the box two bones resembling it, the one a hook, and the other a shovel. Then you take the hook and take it towards you and name the person's name that you want to have come to you, and with the shovel you shoot the person away when you want them to leave. In the name of God the Father and the Son and of the Holy Ghost.

4. The same but in another way.
You take a sugar cube and put it under the left arm three Thursday nights, and then chop it into three pieces, and put them in coffee without the person you want knowing it, and say: "As truly as God lives and my soul lives, just as truly you will (by name) become in love with me, in the name of God the Father and of the Son and of the Holy Ghost."

5. To cause a traveller to be transfixed.
Then you take blood from the left little finger and draw a cross over the road and say: "As truly as God lives and my soul lives, so truly shall you stop here. In the name of God the Father and of the Son and of the Holy Ghost."

6. To cause a sitting person to be unable to rise.
When a priest stands over the grave of one whose funeral it is, you take a little earth from the grave, as well as go with it outside the door, and swing yourself by the left heel counterclockwise three times and say: "In the name of the Holy Trinity." Then spread the dirt in the head of someone who's sitting down, and say: "Here you will sit as long as I wish, in the name of God the Father and of the Son and of the Holy Ghost.

7. To write away the Nightmare (*Maran*).[124]
Then you cut yourself in the left little finger and write with blood: "Mara, mara, mara! You wish to travel here during the night; but if the thing you desire wishes to travel to your home, or if you want to travel to Hell, you may have that which you'd rather." And then cut yourself in the little finger of the left hand and write: "As truly as God lives, and my soul lives, then just as truly will by heart's blood be a witness to it." Then write with ink the name of the holy trinity.

---

[124] *Mara* was a being that was often thought to sit atop the chest of a sleeping individual, and caused them the anxiety of being unable to breathe. Whether it was in fact a nightmare or a spirit that caused certain symptoms isn't clear from the tradition, but this spell aims to exorcise it.

8. A walking stick to "try" women.
Pay attention to when a rooster mounts a hen, and twist off a feather from it's hindquarters. This feather, as well as a little mercury you should immediately put into the base of a walking stick, and with this walking stick you stick under the dress of the one you wish.

9. On the runs (Diarrhea).
If you want this illness to affect someone, then take a little of their feces and put it into a goat's horn, which is then sealed and is fastened floating in a running stream or river – OR – the same thing is taken as well as a little yeast, and put it into a well-corked bottle and put it down into a warm pile of horse dung.

10. To bewitch a fiddle.
You take a snake sting and carry it four times around your fingers counterclockwise and say: "As truly as I have carried this snake-sting four times around my fingers, then just as truly you won't get any more sounds from your strings than from my fingers. In the name of the Holy Trinity.

MS 23

SVARTKONSTBOK FROM MÖNSTERÅS, SMÅLAND
NORDISKA MUSÉET, UNNUMBERED MANUSCRIPT

1. <u>To have luck in shooting</u>
Shoot a raven with the shotgun you want to use, and while it is still living, take its heart out up through the back, dry it, and when you want to go out hunting in the morning, then put that same heart into a bowl of water, wherein you wash yourself; and wash your eyes in the bowl three times with the back of your hands, and then few can harm if one dries oneself; Then, when you go out through the door, then grind the "touch" (trigger?) on your shotgun, without anyone noticing, 3 times in the threshold, and say to yourself: Help, God; and when you come out, then break for yourself three branches of fir, ones that are three-branched, like a birds foot ⤚⟨. Cross yourself with them, one time over your chest, and throw them away from yourself, over your left shoulder, and go your way quickly. If you can be careful, when you go out, so that no one catches a glimpse of you, then this is much better, because not everyone has "good eyes." Be careful and when you sight a bird or animal, that you always walk against the wind, and not with it, so that the bird or animal

won't have any scent, and so escape from you; because all birds and animals have the scent of human beings.

When you want to hunt, and your shotgun won't fire, then screw out the flint that sits in it, and throw it away over your left shoulder; put in a new one again, and moisten on the stock with the nameless finger. If it still won't fire, then remove the lock, stop-up the "touch hole"/"flash-hole," and piss out through the barrel, and when it has stood for a while, then rinse it well and clean.

If the bird won't die quickly from your shotgun, then shoot a *stensprätta* (stonesparrow?), and while it is still alive, drip three drops of blood from it into the shot-gun barrel, it helps; and if one can't get hold of a *steensprätta*, then other birds are also good. If one singes the head or the feet of a shot bird in the fire, then all other birds will bear a terror towards him, who has shot the bird, and will become tremendously timid or skittish.

2. <u>On the time in which the birds mate.</u>
<u>The capercaille or wood-grouse</u> begins to mate immediately after Our Lady's Day (March 25), and continues until Erssmässa;[125] if one wants to shoot it while it mates, then one should be careful when one comes up to their mating place, that one doesn't move, until the grouse says: bällä, bällä, bällä, bällä, bällä, bällä, klickop: gigi, gigi, gigi; /: but the hen she clucks with a coarse voice ock, ock, ock, ock, ock, ock, ock; and one can lure her to you, if one starts to "ocka" :/ then one should run two or three steps forward to the very highest, /: because then he'll neither see nor hear :/ and then one shall stand still again, just like one was a tree stump, /: the hunter should always be clad in grey :/ one should not shoot the largest or the oldest of them, because as soon as he is shot, then they all flee from that place together, until they find another comfortable place, where they are able to have their mating grounds, and they'll never come back to the previous place; that's why if one wants to track them, then one must seek them just southeast from that place where their mating grounds were, because that is their customary flight pattern.

Nota Bene. Where the old cocks are, there the young don't dare to mate; but sit and make a sound like if one strikes two staves together, but make it a long time between each sound: but when the old one's are all hunted out, then the young one's will begin to mate: But there where all the cocks have been hunted out, then the hens will remain there yet one more day, but when they see that they aren't finding any cocks, then they fly away from there, and settle at another place, where there is mating going on, and where some cocks are able to be found.

---

125 This peculiar spelling makes it unclear whether this refers to Irje's feast day, April 4, or Erik's feast day, May 18. Either is feasible.

3. _Årn (årr, alfågel)_ Long-tailed duck also begins its mating immediately after Our Lady's Day, and mates until the rye forms ears. The one who wants to hunt it during mating, he must carefully watch that he doesn't run towards it more than 3 steps before he coos, and there he should stay still again, before any movement; because /: he neither hears nor sees, when he "hisses" :/ when he clucks he sees well, but because of his own noise and clucking, he can't hear very well. If during a duck-mating one encounters an uncomfortable place, where it is difficult to approach to shoot, either because of some large boulder or exposed area, or some other inconvenience, then one can lure them with beginning to cluck, like a female duck; then one will with pleasure and gladness see how the mallards come flying to that place where they heard the clucking, since they will be expecting to find hens for themselves there. One can also build for oneself fir-huts, to which one must repair, an hour before dawn, and there await as long as it take for the ducks to come, and when they have well begun to mate, then one shall shoot, and then completely silently load again. In such a manner one can remain completely still in the hut, and shoot 6 or 8, and even 10 in a row, which he /: after the flock has flown :/ can gather together. NB. In the Spring or late in the autumn the huts should be built at the mating grounds, in order that they may all the better be accustomed to them, where they otherwise are timid, they'll fly away, and chose another mating ground: if is a highland and no stone underneath, then one can dig down in the ground up to the knees, and then build with fir or bushes over it.

4. Järpen, The Hazel-hen one can have the best chance of shooting towards Easter, because then he sounds the pipe, and allows himself to be lured, so that he often comes so close to him, that one can almost take hold of him with the hand.

NB. The pipe is made of owl-bone, which is held to be the luckiest.

5. Of seafowl there isn't much to be remarked upon, except this alone, that one should aim low at him, that it to say, down at the waterlevel, in that place that one aims on the legs, on a forestfowl, if he is close to one, and sits right up straight. Young ducks are best to track 8 days before Midsummer, because they are full-grown, but still are not able to fly, but rather the whole brood follows the mother wherever she swims.

NB. All birds have scent, and especially seafowl; if you come downwind of a duck, then she'll get wind of you, then she'll wander her way. The swan does the same thing, and all other sea-fowl, great and small.

6. If one shoots after a bird or an animal, and one hasn't killed, but rather it just stays still, then that same animal or bird is "liberated by the _skogsrå_." This one can fix in the following way: One loads one's shotgun anew, and if it is wintertime, then one scrapes away the snow from oneself, and pound the muzzle on the ground three times, and ask it to bite in Jesus' name, then one spits into one's hand and smears it over the lock, /: namely from the muzzle towards the trigger :/ three times, and shoots thereafter, then one will kill.

Or after one has reloaded, one throws a crumb of sourdough bread in the barrel and shoots; Another: a saltkernel helps as well. NB. A little crumb of unfinished steel, is better than all of these together. If it is a lead-shot gun, then one can stuff a little piece in the bullet; and if one wants to hit game, then one ties a little piece of steel in the dog's collar, then it can't escape. Prob. ab Ad. Wachtmeister. [Probatum = tried, tested; ab = by; Ad. = advokat?; Wachtmeister = name].

To shoot all kinds of animals, and first

7. about Hares.
One can find hares easily with it gets on to fall, and before the snow has fallen when it should have, then they will become white and the ground is grey. Between *Mårmässa* (*Mårtinsmässa* = Nov. 10 – ?error? for *Mikaelsmässa*, Sept. 29) and *Helgonmässa* (Nov. 1), then the hare is docile, and lies still, just as if he were blind; when one tracks him now, and one comes upon him too quickly where he is lying, then one mustn't stop, but rather walk past, just like you haven't seen him, when he sees that, he is convinced that he has not been seen, and thus continues to lie still: But then one shall walk around and come in this way unnoticed and right up to him, on another side, which he would never think. But if one stops while one is tracking, then he'll run off hastily from his nest. When one happens upon hares in the summer, either out in the woods or in a field /: as in when they are usually in the rye fields in the morning before the sun comes up :/ and they begin to flee, then one shall either whistle sharply, or blow into a key; when they hear that they'll settle down and that's the time; or also if it is sufficiently close to one, and he jumps past one, if one then lets a glove fall, then he'll settle down, because he will want to find out what it was that was glimpsed. More about hares and their nature, is found in Adeliche Waidwerck from page 165 to folio 190.

8. Foxes.
They can not be shot other than up on a ridge. And in order that they not get the scent of one, the one must chew on pine needles, and have a mushroom on one, that grows on a type of tree that is called Siälk, it is yellow, and smells terribly strong. For whatever type of animal one will shoot, which might have one's scent, then one must always have this mushroom on one's person, and constantly chew a little evergreen, as has already been said.

If one squeaks at a fox, like mice squeak, then one should slow in one's gait, and listen, and even stop is best, and when he hears, to continue, then he'll come to that place where he hears the squeak and then continue, then he'll eventually come to that place where he hears the squeak, in front of the hunter where he stands in wait, where he won't get a scent or wind from him.

9. Wolves.

To hunt wolves, is little different from foxes, except only this, that a shotgun never easily goes off for a wolf. Then one must break of a little three-branched fir branch that is formed like so: [a. ⤙ b.] stick it into the shotgun muzzle, so that the end (a) points in, and end (b) outwards, then the shotgun will be fired without any hindrance.

10. Moose.

The one who wants to shoot a moose, should first load his shotgun for [the moose] as one would load it for a bear, and after one has loaded, then one should not aim higher at it than about 1 or 1 ½ quarter from the lowermost, up on the buck; because the moose has that way about it that one does not easily down it; because when he sees the ammunition fire, he sinks his back, just as the wolf does, so that the bullet has to go over him if one aims high up.

N.B. almost all animals have this manner about them.

11. Lynx.

He who has ash, which is burnt, from three bats (from nine is better) and can walk one time around the place where a lynx has its den, then the same animal will be unable to survive. Or strew a little bit of that same ash in its tracks, namely into three footprints where it has just walked, then it must bide. I mean that the grip (powerful effect) will also work with other animals as well, which will remain for hunting. N.B. The bats should be burned on a hot iron, or in a frying skillet.

12. Bears.

When one wants to hunt a bear, then one shan't make any calls about it, or talk trash or boast about how one will go about hunting him (so with all hunting). Rather proceed with all silence go forth, and when one catches a glimpse of him, then one should say the following words, one time to oneself, and thereafter in Jesus name go about 18 to 20 steps away from him, and fire. ://Åchtene messan omain, willa suus, willa päs, willa wijes hambastans, Kätta Kynnet Karwais, hamba tyckeunis, täcke törhen tienolet, uhle siwalles, silmet korwan lummien tukihielkutu, uhlen siwallas silmet.//:[126] The more there are, the better to shoot, because the one who gets shot doesn't know what it was that caused the pain, but instead in the fervor he runs to the the bear

---

[126] It seems clear in this case that this is an attempt to represent with Swedish orthography some other language.

that is closest to him, and fights with him until he becomes unconscious and falls down. NB. When one has said these words on time to oneself, then one is sure that the bear neither sees nor hears him, neither can the bear do him any harm with clawing or biting if one unexpectedly comes up on one. Therefore for that reason one can safely go up to him completely alone on level ground. If you have a friend with you, then he's not free, unless he himself can say these words. NB. When you've shot, then you should immediately run from that place where you were off to another place, and don't delay where you shot.

If you want to load for a bear, then you should get some bear skin, then take 2 measures of powerder in it, and and put 2 or 3 chewed weights before, then you'll be sure that when you aim for the heart, it will not hit the shoulder blade, and that he will fall with the first shot. If you shoot with a Danish "*Haka*," then you don't need to use more powder that it is ordinarily used to have than when you should with gunshot; rather put a good load before, and then to that add a medium bullet that perhaps weighs 1 mark with a medium wide cloth, then it will go through, although there'll be a hole of 150 "schritt" (tears?).

If you want to shoot a bear on a mountain, then you have to build yourself a ledge up in a tree, with over two or two and a half "*famn*" (thus, four or four and a half yards) up from the ground, and have yellow mushrooms and firs with you, that are discussed before under the heading Wolves,[127] and then one doesn't need any words, but rather only a good axe, with which you can reach his paws, when (if?) he isn't yet dead but comes and wants to climb the tree.

13. How a shotgun can be hexed
[If one is] Present.

a) if you kill a louse on the gunbarrel
b) if a bug comes into the stock (burrows into the stock?)
c) if you hit some person with your shotgun so that there is blood afterwards, then it isn't just hexed, but now it is completely and irrevocably destroyed, so that it is unable to be unhexed
d) when you've shot an animal or a bird, and when you want to take it up from the ground, and disturb it first with the left hand and then with the right, then it's hexed
e) earwax smeared in the muzzle destroys; also arm sweat if it comes on the barrel

---

127 While the fir branch was mentioned, there was no mention of yellow mushrooms in that subsection.

14. [If one is] Absent.
a) if you point with a drawn knife to the direction you hear the shot go off
b) if you say: Devil take your shot
c) if you quickly cut and raise a turf of earth under your left foot, and overturn it
d) wherever you throw three wheat grains over your left shoulder, one after the other, and don't look back but go your way

15. How to make a hexed shotgun right again
When you shoot a bird and you see that your shotgun is hexed, then immediately make a fire, purify your shotgun quite well, and burn up the shot. Then take either the feet of the bird or a bunch of feathers and carve loose a shaving from a pine tree or another large tree on the north side, just in a way that the shaving remains attached at both ends, and it tight in towards the tree. Put the feathers or the feet in between, hit three times on it with an axe-hammer and say: You shall not escape your previous deeds until these feathers/feet come from here. Then the one who hexed your shotgun gets as repayment that he will never have luck in shooting anything as long as he lives.

16. Seek out a tree that is burned all the way through from a forest fire, so that there is a hole all the way through it as big on both sides, whether it is dry or living, put your shotgun as well as powder and bullets three times through it, then it will be better, but the one who hexed it won't receive any injury from it.

17. Load your shotgun and shoot it off under your left arm backwards, in such a way that the muzzle is turned towards your back, and don't look back. Then it will be good, and the one who hexed it won't receive any injury from that. When you shoot animal or bird and you see that your shotgun is hexed, then cut it up and take out the heart immediately, put it in front of the ammunition and shoot it off.

18. Shoot a squirrel, flay it and spit or spike the skin on a wall in such a way that the back feet stand up in the air and the head down. But notice, that the one who hexed the shotgun will pine and languish away and will never see a healthy day again as long as he lives. If anyone comes and takes it down off the wall, then he will get the same sickness.

19. Split a Rowan that you find standing out in an anthill; crawl three times around it, and take your shotgun with you as well as powder and bullets.

20. Take a fire arising from friction (either flint or from wood), and let the smoke go up the barrel that it goes out the touch-hole.

21. In the Springtime when the leaves are just coming out, take branches of 9 types of fruit-bearing trees, and especially from those that leaf the first of all when now your shotgun has become hexed. Put these said branches in a strange or odd place, light them on fire, lean so the shotgun is over them and so the smoke goes up the barrel, then it will be good again, and he will get as payment whatever harm you will place upon him. NB. Alder buckthorn, black dogwood [*brakvedsträd*] must be one among the nine types, otherwise it won't work.

22. Drive a snake into the shotgun, and shoot him towards a tree, or shoot the snake where it lies on the ground.

23. Take your shotgun in hand, move it in back of you, around your right thigh, stick it then between your legs with the muzzle in front, and grab it with the left hand. Move it in the same way around the left thigh and take it by the right hand, and back (as was said before) around the right thigh, and after you've turned it around, then hit yourself slowly with the barrel end, first on the inside of your right, then your left then back to your right knee. Then put your right hand on the muzzle so that the middle finger and the nameless finger are lying to either side of the barrel. Put the same fingers of the left hand in a cross over the others, and blow a short breath into the barrel. Put both hands backwards back up there, blow again. Lastly turn them back forwards again, and blow, then it'll be good. But the one who hexed it won't have any injury from this. NB. The right hand should always lie nearest the barrel.

24. If you want to shoot almost two times as far with common ammunition as you usually do, then you have to make yourself a wax bullet, that fits just past the muzzle, and put it quite hard next to the powder, and then the lead bullet going over it.

25. For a Shot shotgun it's best to put over the ammunition of powder a turned wooden prop that is as high and wide as the muzzle, yet so that it runs easily out in front, and is a little bowed-in or turned out at both ends, put the shot or the bullet up on it with a little powder before, then you'll see a miracle.

26. Dry a bat, and carry it on you into the woods, then no one else will have any luck hitting anything in that forest, more than just you alone. NB. In all hunting, that happens on the ground or in flight, you have to aim always at the head, and not at the body itself; the bird and animal may be approaching or departing: yet, its sometimes better to shoot with them facing away than facing towards, especially with those birds that have large and stiff feathers and thick down, where the shot doesn't easily penetrate, such as eagles, swans, geese, ducks, etc.

27. Go out early on a Sunday morning, take a knife and split a little juniper tree but so that it is not split up at the top and down by the root. Stick your shotgun three times through that opening, with the touch-hole foremost, and spit one time after it, upon each time it's put through; Go away afterwards, and don't look back.

28. If you know a type of animal is present, that was let out by the *Skogsrå*,[128] then go out early on a Sunday morning, unwashed, spit in your hand and spread it along and afterwards to the lock, from the muzzle to the touch-hole three times, then you'll have no hindrance in meeting the same animal; in the same way you can also do, when you otherwise go out to hunt, it is said to be lucky.

29. If you can't shoot down such an animal, then take only an alder-branch 1 finger long and three-branched and put it around in front of only the ammunition, in the shotgun-barrel, then you will get to see the effect, even though the animal is shot with neither bullet or buckshot.

Stämma djur. (To summon animals.)

30. When you become aware of an animal, then take immediately up your knife, and quickly cut up a little piece of turf, and turn it upside down, and stab the knife through it, let it stand there in the turf for a while, then you have thirty steps free to go without the animal or the bird seeing you. Another: if you take a sewing needle that has been used to sew around a corpse[129] then stick it down into the ground where you find a foot print or track of that animal you see fleeing, then you sit down quietly and hidden around 60 or 70 steps from there, then the same animal will come forth to the needle again, within one or at most two hours time. NB. You must not stick such a needle in your clothes, but rather keep it in a clean paper or pincushion; This works especially well with hares.

31. Another: If you find a horseshoe on Good Friday, then take it the same day to a smith, and have him smith from it as well as from all the old horseshoe-nails or spikes that are in it /: so that nothing falls away :/ a large nail or spike, and pay the smith according to his desire, nothing deducted, and keep that spike in a clean paper: When you want to hunt and find a fresh track, then cir-

---

[128] The *skogsrå* is a Swedish forest spirit, often with the appearance of a lovely maiden in front, and a hollowed trough in back accompanied by the tail of a fox.

[129] For corpse clothing such as shrouds and head-coverings, see Sigfrid Svensson, "Likklut," in Åke Campbell, Waldemar Liungman and Sigfrid Svensson, eds., *Nordiskt folkminne: studier tillägnade C. W. von Sydow 12/21/1928*. Stockholm: C. E. Fritzes Hovbokhandel i distribution.

cle the track counterclockwise, and stick that nail into the footprint or track, then the animal must turn around and stay still, then you can track it down.

32. You need to carefully observe during the Harehunt, that the colder it is, then the higher up in the mountains he is, or has his den: and the more it thaws and is nice weather, the more he will be found in the valleys, and in small bushes by fields and meadows.

33. Foxes go mostly to the woods to scavenge in the evening an hour after the sun goes down, and you can get the best situation to shoot them if you climb up in a thick tree, when one can sit hidden. They'll come easily forth, when they have not seen any cabin or hut, they won't fear any ill; they'll also not be able to get a scent easily, since you'll be up in the air; the wolf has that tendency more, even if he doesn't disdain to come back at nighttime.

About all types of traps, and first about Fox-traps.

34. All traps must be begun upon, or also immediately finished being smithed either in the Autumn during the waning moon of Martinsmas, or especially on Martinsmas-day, or also in the Spring on Good Friday. When you set up the fox-trap, you should cover the bait with honey, because the foxes are terribly fond of it. For bait for foxes you use either small herring heads, or a dead magpie, or a hen, or some other dead bird.

35. You put the fox-trap under the water for ducks, geese and swans, and put two or three small bundles of reed-roots onto the bait; the roots are small, white and tender.

36. If the trap is hexed or stolen, you should put it out three 24-hour days on the floor of a sheep-shed, then piss all over it, then put a tree in between so that it stays open, cense it with juniper so that it becomes warm from it; Smear it with a tallow candle /:because other tallow or fat, won't do for this :/ and finally your should rub it with spruce twigs, then it'll be good again.

37. The trap should always be placed on a three-branched tree, so that it won't sink deep down in the snow or sand, you must always cover the lock with a little piece of birch bark.
    NB. when you see an animal in the trap, then you should take it out through the trap, and not back out. For otters you put the trap or otter-iron under $\triangledown$ (water) where you know he has his escape, how this is done, refer to the foregoing.

Traps for hares and lapwings.

38. With these types of snares there are many points to observe. You should carefully prick a hole, 1.) it should be carefully observed and marked that the iron, that shall be spinned into these snares, must be spun when the New Moon is 7 days old, and when there is a wind from the south, and especially when some sign of the blood rules. 2.) The one who is going to spin it, must not take up more line in their hands than they believe that they will spin up, until he gets up from the spinning. 3.) You should also be very careful that one not wet the iron with spit, but rather with clean water, during the spinning; you should also not chew the line with the teeth either, but rather break it with the fingers. 4.) When one measures out and makes the snare, one should not bite off the iron either, but rather cut it with a knife. 5.) You should take 3 juniper branches, that are three-branched just like a birds-foot and put them under your left heel and drag each snare alone three times through it out towards your left side, then the hare can't bite off it as easily. 6.) The pole that should be cut for this cannot be branched down towards the root, but rather up from the roots towards the top. 7.) If you aren't going to chop up the same tree, that you chop the pole off of, with an axehammer, though there shouldn't have been as much snow on it. 8.) The snare, after it is fastened to the pole, should be rubbed back and forth with a linen-cloth, upon which is sheep-tallow and garlick, surely, with each other well chopped and mixed together. 9.) The snare must stand a good span from the ground. 10.) When you have caught an animal in the snare, then you should first before moving it, take a branch of a leafy tree, and with it hit the animal three times, then loosen the snare, and take the entire animal out through it, and don't take the snare off back over the head. 11.) You should never set a pair of snares in the woods, or up on a path, but rather always prepare it so that there are odd numbers, 1. 3. 5. 7. or 9. etc. 12.) Then, when it is strongly raw, then you must, the first you should never spare or save, but rather immediately cook it and eat it up. 13.) The one who goes around the snares and sets them up, must always eat up the kidneys, whether the hare is boiled or broiled, then no one can injure him, even if they steal out of his snares. 14.) No one may eat of the broth, or tear or cut off the meat while it is being boiled or is in the pot, before it comes to the table; but the one who cooks, may taste the soup and the meat; if someone else does it hardly a hare will come into the snare before the foxes and crows are present to eat it up. 15.) You should not stamp your feet either in the woods nor when you return home, or hit your mittens together to get the snow off of yourself, but rather brush it off yourself with a broom. 16.) you should not come up to any trap with "*skiählspeck*," that you have up on your shoes, or handle it at least. NB. No birds or animals, that can be carried, should be carried with a horse, but rather should be carried on your back.

To recover that which was stolen.

39. On a Maundy Thursday morning you should buy a mirror, and not haggle for even a coin. This you should bury on a Good Friday morning before people go to church, then you should go there and dig it up again, but don't look back; It should be buried at a crossroads, in addition you must make a cover for it, and never open it unless you want to see who has stolen, and that must happen on a Thursday morning, then you will see the face of him who has robbed.

To train a riding horse.

40. Cut the horse a superficial cut across the muzzle towards the leg with a sharp knife, or stab him with a [*lija*?], and when it has finished bleeding, then spread ground glass in the wound, in such a way that it will never fully heal again, but rather always be painful, then put a halter/bridle on him into the cut, and curb him until he becomes used to being ruled and steered with the bridle, next he should be bound underneath with the harness that is done in that way; let the horse stand and eat grass or oats from the ground, and lead his head through the harness, so that the iron (a) remains situated over the forehead up by the ears, and put the large [*wahlknuten*] (b) snug around the neck, and tie him firmly with a strong strap (c) so that he won't slip back, let all four reigns run between the forleg under the breast, so that the small [*wahlknutarna*] (d) /: which each hold two reigns :/ are are shoved sufficiently far back that they remain behind the forelegs, two finger-widths away, and then then immediately take hold of the [*gördelen*; saddle?] (e) which is thrown over the back of the horse, and is fastened loosely by the saddle belt (f) then the [*wahlknutarna*] are moved (g) so close to the knots (d) that the horse can be belted quickly /: too quickly isn't good either :/ but just so that they are equally far from the knot (b) /: because if the one reign is fastened shorter on the one side than on the other, then the horse will become used to walking or driving towards that side on which the reign was longest, and they usually are fastened shorter on the right side than on the left, when you want to use them to drive partridges inwards :/. Then the reigns are bound (h) tightly around the thigh over the forelock, as many times as it can reach, and with each round a simple knot, and lastly a whole knot, and the ends are bound (k) strongly together with the saddle belt (i) so that the knot won't come untied, then one takes hold of the bridle and drives him fast, then he'll begin to kick and hit, so that oftentimes he'll fall down, or probably will remain lying down from all the liveliness, but then you should raise him up again with a good whip, then he'll be forced to finally from the material, that he whistles like a power, and begins at last to walk slowly, and allows himself to be led with the bridle. When he has in this way been trained in the [spännetyget] for three or four hours, then you take it off and put instead over the forehead a narrow cord, decorated with (o) /: a year-old boar [hijsing] :/ in which in the same way are tied three knots, of the same distance apart as the rivets are on the headiron (a), and is tied or laced in the same way with a [wahlknut] under the chin, and is led under the breast between the forelegs, and is tied firmly on the back. If he still doesn't want to do well, then one can bind him underneath again for a second time. But if the material is strong enough, or any knot loosens so that the horse escapes, then he's ruined from that, and will have a bad disposition, and won't let himself be easily saddled again. It is also something to be careful about, that when they are thus tamed, a strap (g), that sites with a head-piece (p) should be buckled on their nose, so that they aren't able to eat; but when they are broken and you want to track with them, then they should have their mouth free. NB. No horse may be buckled under the first time, even less when the wind isn't coming from the west and is during clear and sharp air.

41. In the same way you can break oxen and cows, as long as you notice just this, that the iron (a) should be made more flat for the forehead, because the ox has a flatter forehead than the horse; They say that an ox is better to track birds and animals with than a horse, because they are more used to seeing cattle, and wait much sooner than a horse. You can also hide better behind an ox, since he is big-bellied and low. That's why a big-bellied horse is much better than one that his tall and straight.

42. When a horse is trained, then you may not use on him anything other than just the bridle, and so that such a newly trained horse won't be shy for the shot, one should track with him in the ordinary way, as one would otherwise do when one tracks something, and shoot of 20 or thirty loads of powder on both sides of him at his tail, and then when you've done that for a few days, then at his side, as well as forward by his neck, so that he won't be shy because of it. Then shoot a shot 3 or 4 times a day in back of him, and at his hindquarters, just so that they turn from the back forward to the head, and stand at his left side /: because if you stand at his right side, then he'll be burned from the powder that has come out of the touch-hole, and will become 10 times as shy as he was before :/. After two or three days time, place yourself at his right side and place the shotgun over the neck at the mane and shoot /: which is what you should already be doing when you are tracking something :/ then he'll get used to it, and will stand as still as a lamb when you shoot.

In another manner.

43. When a horse has first gotten sore over his snout, as was described before, then you should put the bridle right into the sore, and take the reins under the breast towards the forelegs, even just so that they will be lying outside of the thighs. Then you can break him and train him, so that he will always bear his head down towards the ground, because he durn't raise his head, since it will cause him bad pain, and he pulls on the bridle, and in this way you can break those horses that don't kick, and are shot-shy. Those that are, you must break with the buckle.

When a man becomes hexed by an evil woman.

44. Take the poop or uncleanness of that same woman who has aimed some evil at you, or hexed, put that same poop in your right shoe, when you feel the smoke, then you've been healed in return. Another: Take a goose-quill or a hazelnut with a hole in it, stuff in it some quicksilver, plug up the hole well with wax, put the same under the pillow or the threshold, then you'll be healed. Or smear your entire body with raven's gall,[130] then you'll be saved.

To walk without getting exhausted

45. Take 8 days *gråbo*[131] or iron-root, or that, which 8 days after St. Bartholomeus' Day is dug up, then you won't become tired.

To make it so that no one may put a spell on one's Shotgun.

46. Buy from a Dalekarlian some *Tidbast*,[132] and bind the same to the rifle, then the sorcerer will no longer have power.

For a colorless complexion

47. Take oatmeal and white lead and mix it proportionally with water and wash with it often, then you'll be clean and white in the face.

---

130 *Empetrum nigrum*, fam. *Empetraceæ*?
131 *Oniscus asellus*?
132 *Daphne meserium*.

Recipe/Prescription for heartburn

48. Take a bunch of *skabbrosor*[133] burn them to a powder, and take a little bit in at a time, and exhort Michael Hermonius that it will go away.

For toothache.

49. The juice of the *groblad*[134] either from the root or from the other parts surely helps for a toothache, when one dips cotton in it, and puts it against the gum. If one washes and rinses the mouth with *groblads*-juice or water, then it will take away the ill smell, and stinking breath.

For "Third day's *Fråssa*"[135]

50. For third-day's *Fråssa*, you can take *groblads*-root, grind it to a powder, and take that in wine, water or drink, before the shivers and shaking begin, then it will hardly come back more than one more time.

For throwing up blood or blood in the urine.

51. If one drinks *groblads* water, it will be stanched.

For red eyes.

52. The one who has hot and red eyes may drop a little *Groblads*-water in them, that will cool it and take away the redness.

For toothache.

53. The root of the *Groblad*'s herb boiled, and held at the gums helps for toothache. If one wants to distill water of the *Groblad*, then it should happen some-

---

133 Skabberosor, acc. to Rietz, this is either *Scabiosa* or *Knautia arvensis*, and has the other folk name "åkervädd," though an English equivalent I could not locate.

134 Grobla[d], acc. to Rietz, this is *Plantago major*, Riksspr. *Groblakka*. According to this, the plant was so associated with healing properties that *läkningen* or "healing" was often expressed *groningen*.

135 Valter Forsman gives the following regarding Frossa: "*Frossan är av tre slag: 'våran', ältfrosa', and tridjidas-frosa'. Den sistnämda är värst* (EC-HA:90, s. 123)." (Forsman, 441) [Frosson is of three types: the springtime, high-frossa and third-day frossa. The last is the worst.] By the description, it sounds like a form of bronchitis, or perhaps some influenza, though a translation is not given.

time before midsummer from its roots, leaves and stalks, but in the month of August it's time to take the herb's seeds.

54. *Libbesticka*[136] Water.
Water distilled from *Libbesticka* is good for stitches in the sides, if one drinks of it both morning and night 3 spoonfuls in a row. Also drinking the same amount of the same water is good for "*stenplågo*."[137] If someone has become hoarse, he should drink *libesticke*-water morning and evening, 2 spoonfulls in the same way. If one washes one's face with *libesticke*-water, then he'll have a white and clear skin. This water has also a great power to drive away and heal *kräfwetan*[138] if the patient washes himself with it. It is also good to wash the feet for gout. To boil water from it, one takes the leaf tops and stalks.

55. If one gives cows dill-seeds, they'll have a lot of milk thereafter, that is for sure.

To quickly drive away Colique for men;
and passing blood for women.

56. One takes *libesticke*-roots and cuts them fresh with a grater, and force the juice through a fastened linen-cloth, and keep it completely for the future. A half a spoonful of it with ½ finely ground nutmeg in tea or liquor taken internally drives it away.

To sleep.

57. If one take white *walmoge*[139] poppy-seeds and grind it up small, mix it with cotton oil and bind it at the temples, then it will make it so you can sleep.

To take away aches out of a limb.

58. You may dip a linen-cloth in *cardebenedicte*[140]-water, and massage with it so that the limb begins to get hot, then the ache will before long go its way. The same water drunk two times a day, breaks the "stone"[141] so that it will go its way before long without great difficulty.

---

136   *Libbesticka*, also *Limmburr-stück*, *Ligusticum levisticum*.
137   Could this be Forsman's "*Steinälton*" a malady in which the stomach swells, and one cannot urinate. Alternately, it could be a reference to either kidney stones or even to constipation.
138   *kräf-wetan* could refer to cancer, though more likely a canker sore. Unable to find a gloss.
139   *walmoge* = vallmo, poppy.
140   Cardamom?
141   This could be a reference to a kidney or bladder stone, or to constipation.

Strong Teeth.

59. The root of *cardebenedictæ* chewed makes good and firm teeth. If you boil water from cardeben: it will also happen from its leaves and tops either at the end of May or the beginning of June.

For a good voice.

60. Boiled together in water and drunk gives a good and a clear voice. (That is: *cardebenedicte*-water).

To keep bed-clothes (sheets, comforters, etc.) away from mice.

61. Put dry *malört*[142] among the down-clothes, then no mouse will touch them.

For the worm[143] in the teeth (caries).

62. Take verdigris[144] 1 fifth, honey 1 weight, mix them together, and smear it on the tooth that the worm is eating, then it will die immediately.

To play a prank on women, so that they won't be able to get butter when they churn.

63. If you throw a little piece of sugar in a butter-churn that the cream is in, then you won't be able to get butter from that same cream.

To make oneself strong.

64. Take a quart of wine, bury in in the earth, let it stand in a bottle until next spring. In the month of March take it up and drink it up, then you'll be terribly strong.

"Ut a virginibus carus sit." [In order that you would become loved by virgins]

65. Take *Jungfru Mariæ* herb, or /as it is more commonly known, God's and Devil's hand/ out of the earth. This herb has a white and a black root, and

---

142 *malört* = Artemisia absinthium.
143 Sw. *masken*, "worm," was commonly thought to eat through teeth, and produce dental decay.
144 *spanskgröna* = verdigris.

when one throws it into the water, then the black one floats but not the white, and if you take the prepared black root and give it to a *puella* [girl], then that one will hold you quite *carus* [dear]. This herb doesn't have more than two green leaves ... remain silent, and in the middle stands a straight stalk up in the air.

"Secundo" [Another]

66. Take two frogs and a box with some holes in it. Put the frogs then in the box, and bury the box in a large anthill. Let it sit there for 8 days from the first Thursday evening until the second, and don't look back when you go there and from there.

To transform one's appearance.

67. Take a cat and kill it, and put peas in its eyes, bury it down in the ground, and when you then have peas from the plants that grow up from the one's you sowed in the cat's eyes, then you will be invisible.

MS 24

NM ONUMRERAT, "OM FISKERI Å DES INEHÅL"
SKIRÖ AND VIRSERUMS PARISHES, SMÅLAND.

[PAGE 1]

1. So that a girl won't get pregnant. Scrape off a little from the big bell at the church, and smear under the shoulder blade with mercury and *säfbom*[145] and glass crystal added to it, with put into hard cakes that she eats up. To heal a wound from an injury with mercury so that it heals right in the flesh and then cut ... for the nose when she indulges herself.

---

[145] Here and throughout, I will err on the side of transcription rather than translation – many of the plants are named in dialect, and cannot be confidently identified. Oils, Waters and Drops may be brand names rather than a tincture, tea, infusion or lozenge of one herb or another, and are left in their original form. Where an intelligent guess can be made, a footnote will present alternative readings.

2. To know how many children a woman will have when the first child is born. Look at the umbilical cord and see how many bumps there are. That's how many children she will have. The caul means a lucky man. The umbilicus tangled around the throat means he will be imprisoned: the sign if a child ... outward will have luck, but inside is an evil sign.

3. For excessive blood in giving birth, gather together a lock of hair from the bleeding one. Rock coal grains and salt, in vinegar together with *grovblads* water ground fine. In weak beer it is drunk. Let sleep. Around the upper thigh on the leg and put sour dough in vinegar under the left armpit.

4. To test if a girl is a virgin. Have her ... three times on the knob, if she sneezes then she is untouched woman and high minded.

[PAGE 2]

5. If a woman has missed her period. Make the woman a bath of those herbs that follow, and that open up the rose-artery.

6. Boil *tusvin*, put it in wine, and drink. Grind *rölö*[146] and pepper into beer and drink.

7. *Bakablad* and white root, boiled and drunk.

8. To void a dead fetus, bake beans and molasses, and rinse in spring water and then drink.

9. *Kiörlfvel*[147] and *matram* boiled under cover. and in beer, encourage a woman's period and ....

10. *Tormele*[148] root and *brusapastors* root are boiled in beer with white clover, the mixture is drunk.

11. How a child is first engendered in the mother. The boy child is quickened sooner than a girl-child and so is born sooner. On the sixth day the blood and such is ordained to come together. But the 9th day it improves and one begins to see a liver and heart and brain. 12 days and up to 20 days is the shape. Thereafter the upper limbs are created, and after 45 days the child is ... but after 90

---

146 *röd lök* = red onion.
147 3 chervil?
148 Any permutation beginning with the first four letters "torm" can be seen as misspellings of Tormentilla root.

days the weak women, suck from 90 to the 9th month when the child is born, and the shift to girl-child first gets its...

[PAGE 3][149]

12. *mum* oil and *mantram* for stomach ache.

13. quintin oil for a swollen stomach, take internally and apply externally.

14. [...]acid drops heal bad wounds.

15. oil: and spiced vinegar: for ...tooth, deadens the pain.

16. *Romasi* salve is for serious illness in humans, take internally. Romasi salve, and long peppers and yellow ... are given internally to the sick one.

17. ... salve for bad swellings.

18. For pain and deafness... buy: bitter almond oil, tincture of *myrå*, mixed together well, and apply inside the ear: Further – buy essential *kulkis* oil: and soak cotton in it and then put it in the ear. HAM oil is also good.

19. Fetch spring water, boil *bakablad* covered: and wash .. the face .. make ... the eyes. Hazel herb and roots. *Riklagen* increases the memory.

20. Calcium drops: for colic, taken internally.

21. BARBORENS WATER. to obtain a good memory.

22. Buy rose water, for all bad wounds and ... drops, walnut oil is massaged onto the navel of a child with a loose stomach (diarrhea).

23. Be careful to boil Saint Peter's Key and the red clover in juniper... and *pimenela*,[150] and tie it on a skeleton, and *bolm*-herb[151] as well. Juniper oil: Peter oil.

24. Lily of the valley and garlic, put in water is for the eyes.

25. Lily of the valley put it on the pulse points and it will stop a headache.

---

149 17 items. Only partial items are readable.
150 Any item beginning with *pimpen* can be assumed to be Pimpernel.
151 Cotton, balm?

26. ... drops of water on a boil and such.

27. ... on a burn, and take betony water internally.

28. ...oil buy on the side. to take internally ...

[PAGE 4]
9 ITEMS

29. Recite if someone gets *durklop*: Jesus stood in Noah's flood, there he dammed both water and blood; with the same I stop this sickness so that it stops and stands and doesn't go now. With words three times in F., S., and the H. Ghost's name. Healing as good as done.

30. *Durklop* to prepare in water: Salt, and prud and Elm. Give to the sick one: and three pieces of bread soaked in the impurity.

31. Further. Cherry, oak-alden, Tormentilla erecta, bl... wood, bolus, buckwood, burnt ribs, quiet seeds, diublo: sakersti-lime, rock coal: way-bread or plantain...

32. For blood in urine: take onion, blueberry, red onion, vervain, plantain-herb, seeds of grain: Tormentilla erecta sakersti-lime, and this is pulverized: and given internally.

33. Then go around the entryway. Administer internally a little mercury in bread. Prick a hole in the ear, and take white sneeze-root, cut a bit of the ear and give them the blood together with the bread.

34. Balsamic oil for lung ailments: smear on the chest: rosewater for burns and bandage with bracken roots.

35. Mint water taken internally for those who throw up their food.

36. Rose powder stops nosebleeds. Snort it.

37. Bay Oil for horses, apply it to the navel: and administer internally pimpenele water.

[PAGE 5]
5 ITEMS

38. Horse for pissing on the sick, prepare a ... stirred, and twist, and running water into a bottle: and recite the horse prayer so that it will go through the bottle as through the ear, 3 times. or a nice pair of pants and then administer internally to the sick one. It helps. Don't forget the *sofite* water.

39. For blood in the urine. grind oak, alder, house leek and tormile root. Ring flowers. Grind together or boiled in a juniper preparation and *tidlösa* and red onion.[152] Administer internally to the sick one. It helps. Further – sakersti-lime and hazel-hen help. They are best.

40. For *Durklop*: put a pig's gallbladder in liquor. Wring it out into the liquor. Put in a raw egg flower and a burnt rib from a mare. Further: boil juniper, birch leaves, cumin grains, salt, wet mushrooms,[153] rock coal and sakersti-lime.

41. Or: Scrape the bark upwards on a trast tree and boil it under cover. Pour it into a bottle, carry it three times through a pigs ear, as well as recite three times over the bottle, and administer internally.

42. If the sheep gather around the entrance, then administer internally first mercury in pieces of bread. Pierce a hole in the ear and put sneeze-root in the ear, and the blood that runs out give to them on the pieces of bread....

[PAGE 6]
4 ITEMS

43. When the cows are not getting calves: then administer internally [*jort-språng, iortamego, jort bruska*] from a cut rear end; rose-herb and when the cow rises, give her three strikes on her rear end with a snake... or a pair of bride-groom's pants. Now have the bull, and give him *topabala* and ... herb...

44. The lord-bird and stream-star's beaks and ... is put into the lock under the fence, The sick one will get worse each day.

45. To liberate the cattle-shed and calves from hexing: Take three fist-fulls of consecrated earth from the churchyard and ask for it. Go around the cattle shed, preferably on a Maundy Thursday morning. Throw one fist-full of earth

---

152   Sw. *Rölök* could be "red onion" i.e., *röd lök*, or yarrow/milfoil, *rölleke*.
153   Sw. *föksvamp*, literally moist mushrooms, probably a genus.

on the roof over the calf pens; then go three more times and throw the rest of the dirt on three places on the roof. Cure as good as done.

46. When the sheep have been hexed, make a drink out of well-boiled *legusticum levisticum* (lovage) and roots and administer internally and put a little lovage in the fodder.

[PAGE 7]
5 ITEMS

47. If you put a block under your beer-barrel, then you will sell more beer than others.

48. So that the beer will never sour.

49. Get some springwort. Where a white mare has foaled, after a year there will grow a plant that is called fetter-herb or lock-herb. If you find that herb and take it in your mouth as well as blow on a turned lock, then the lock will open all by itself. If you plug up the hole to a black-woodpecker's nest, the woodpecker will seek out that herb and hold it in front of its nest and the chicks that are stuck inside, with the result that the plug will ease out of the hole.

50. ... Cow grass, where a thief is hanged, when he dies he pees. And then the year after there will grow a seeding herb-grass: the one who finds it and carries it with them – he will have luck no matter what happens to him.

51. So that a child will be well... If a pregnant woman creeps through a ... the second morning after giving birth, then the child will be untimely in .... Four leaf clover is a giver of luck especially in playing cards.

[PAGE 8]
3 ITEMS

52. To hex a fruit tree. When you first hear the cuckoo in the spring and you are sober, then bite off 3 branches of the tree and speak harshly to it. Further: if you hit the tree with a splinter of a church window or you bore a hole in to the core and pour in strong liquor and then cover the hole up: and steal the fruit from it instead...

53. When a woman dies in childbirth, or a time thereafter, and the child may die with her. When they carry her to the church, and leave the farm, take the child on your arm and stand before those who are carrying her out, saying quietly: N. N. take this child immediately with you .. when they come out of the church and are going home, go to the same mother, and say You, N. N. I conjure you in God the Trinity's name, that you go home and take a child with you. Don't cry after you say it, and call slowly upon her three times.

54. If you cast mercury into a well, then from that water you will never be able to get liquor.

[PAGE 9]
3 ITEMS

55. J.M.H. (Jungfru Maria Hand?) is called in Latin Satyren, in German *stendel* and ivy in Swedish. It comes in two types, a purple-colored flower and the other white.

56. The way in which a woman can hex a shotgun so that it can hardly be fixed again: when the cows are going to sleep, then she takes a knife, and on the knife some of her moon-blood: and when the shot goes off, then she stabs in the middle of the air towards the shot, and says: the Devil take the next one: You and your shotgun will be hexed and never be cured, until you are cured by me. With this, she stabs three times in the first tree she sees.

57. For excessive bleeding after the birth of a child. Temper together *musgot* with walnut and the upper part of the double white herb... in walnut oil, taken internally in ...water, and wind around the thigh and leg and the left arm as much as can be tolerated with a ...

[PAGE 10]
7 ITEMS

58. the mother ... and cense yourself with amber: it will stop the malady.

59. To drive out the afterbirth from women and such. Boil grey beans and *låka* leaves, covered, in water and reduce by half and give them to drink. It helps.

60. Those who get blood blemishes and infections in bumps. Make a sour dough from wheat flour and ground salt and put something dry on it. Take them for warts. Salt and red onions.

61. Parsley roots ground and taken internally in wine give red blood. Drunk three mornings in a row. It improves the memory. Pimpeneles virtue helps. Heart pain. and comes quickly ... piss. Cut on the head stops real pain. Bowel

obstruction and pain in the anus and become free of ... sores with pempenele water.

62. A juice that is pressed fresh from bitter almond oil is mixed and applied to ringing ears. It helps the hearing... oil is also good in cotton put in the ear.

63. *Maleört* is a good herb for those who are sick and... take *tormele*-root powder. ... is taken with licorice. And go to bed to sweat... bed clothes, drives out the sickness.

64. ... eye pain: wash them in *torme* water and juniper oil.

[PAGE 11]
8 ITEMS

65. A type of tree that is called *hyler*-tree or ... looks mostly like *könd*: with white flowers and red berries but that become small black ones when they ripen, from this boil a bat, and it will rot ...

66. For water sickness: dig up the lake-root and chop and boil and drink the mixture, now a month away, always helps.

67. So that a cow will get with calf: rhubarb root recently sprouted-seeds... heal skin and travel-herb:

68. For a bad sore throat: prepare together *krobel*, and honey in vinegar: and if you have it, good beer: leave off... take internally. Pour out to apply externally and cover.

69. ... like wheat-root: administer internally in rolled spear: sugar lime: and from its blood urine comes out. Sheep's heart is best.

70. The yellow lake-root for water sickness: and the herb for bad illness... for life.

71. For a harsh cough in the throat, a half spoonful St. John's oil in warm beer and buy *valra*, ground and dissolved in a quart of beer, and drink it on an empty stomach: It will surely help.

72. For stubborn illness: are not good to cure. Without the one who remains without a cure from them, one would prefer to die or shoot them. Then recite the cure for all evil beasts.

[PAGE 12]
5 ITEMS

73. If the colon ... recite: -- they should drink burnt *ålans* water 2 or 3 spoons to drink per day and soak a linen cloth in it and put lay it on them. Ditto. Soak oak leaves and oak bark in water and wash it, it helps them. back into the stomach again.

74. if the fish are shot by the lake-spirit (*sjörå*), then put blood on the fish hook.

75. the mole. If one takes a living mole and puts it in a box with dirt in it, and lets it sit until he suffocates: keep that dirt and give it internally to the horse, it helps for *kvekdrag* (a cough in horses) and such. But you can throw away the mole. Further: *skolemodis* on bull powder is for cough in horses.

76. ... : it will get fine calves...when you ... a bull. Put bare in a hole pole... and put into a strengthening ... in three circles. Take the ... and look for bare then it is forced to ... them in a powder and give the cow a little ... then she will have carried. With ... such, and from this you will have a beautiful calf and the cow will be beautiful and ... for milk and more.

77. For horse lice. Boil lice ... Sylvester, rowan bark and boy-death-root and bark ashes and wash the horse with the mixture, then the horse will be lively and free from lice, and put a wolf's tooth in its mane then you'll not believe...

[PAGE 13]
6 ITEMS

78. When you go fishing and have previously prepared those things in a bag and carry it with you. Which was mentioned in the previous section. Then you are protected. Hang the bag in the lake where you are fishing, then no enchantment will harm you.

79. To make fish drunk: prepare small pills of liquor, honey, "*fenkols* pith" black henbane seeds, valerian root; throw these pills and for curiosity's sake and they become drunk and then in their stupor they rise up in the water, so that you can take them with your hands.

80. If someone steals your hooks or such from you, borrow a bone of a human corpse, tie *flogrönn*[154] to it and hang it in a stream that runs strongly to

---

[154] Defined elsewhere in Part Two, *a flygrönn* is a young mountain ash that grows from the base of the trunk of a more mature tree.

the north, and command it in 18,000 devils' names that they should go home to the thief that night and beat him up and down and give no peace until he returns that which he has stolen.

81. To protect yourself from malevolent witchcraft, and to keep your luck, over three Sunday mornings take three silver... on an empty stomach in a piece of bread, then you will have your freedom as well.

82. Sit at your stove with your spinning shuttle during vespers on Christmas eve, when the priest is preaching, and spin a thread counterclockwise. This thread will be good for fishing with.

83. Birch and *tidebast* (*daphne mezereum*) and unmixed vitriol are ground and mixed together and sewn into the net and basket traps.

[PAGE 14]
3 ITEMS

84. The fishless prayer: Listen, you fish, who are bound here, you shall now be loose and shown away; now you are loose; now all the birch forest is burned up; all nets and notes and basket traps and hoop nets are broken and bottomless, and all the fishermen are dead and hanged. Come back and go towards the land, to me and my progeny, for the use of humankind, in the name of the Highest Trinity. The God in the Highest Heaven, who ordains all, releases and gives you to me and mine for our use. In the power of the Father, Son and Holy Ghost.

85. To drive out a witch from the lake: You procure some consecrated earth and spräng seeds that you sow in a string around the lake. Also have on hand some *salmiak*,[155] masile bone, filings from the great church bell, asafetida, juniper berries, round *hålört* root, tiobom, flogrönn, valerian root, a piece of a seal skull, grey sulfur and throw this all tied together into the water. Hurry away from there afterwards, and don't look back. Be careful and protect yourself well.

86. The day after this take the landowner with you and walk around the same lake or pond and recite the fishless prayer as well as the Our Father with the hands in the water, then the malevolent witches and lake spirits will disappear.

---

155 *salmiak* is a white powder, possibly ammonium.

[PAGE 15]
4 ITEMS

"On fishing and its equipment."

87. To begin your nets and fishing baskets and such fishing hooks: In whatever parish and district you live in, take note of the first day of District Court when the district judge first starts the court, then it is good to begin your nets and basket traps.

88. Also on a Sunday when they ring the bells for church, to begin your net is good. Further it is the best of all to start your net when you see the figure of the fish moving, and the wind blows from the south: and then *helsinge*-hemp is good to weave your net with.

89. If you can make a fishing hook during lauds on Easter Sunday, when the priest recites the Benediction from the pulpit, that hook is said to be tasty to the fish.

90. To get lucky fishing hooks, take firm hold of a many-colored snake, put sewing needles between the flesh and the skin of the snake, until it dies. And make from that the hooks during the new moon and in the shape of a fish, if they can be made to agree.

[PAGE 16]
5 ITEMS

91. It has been told to me that if when you go fishing you spread in the water a little earth that you have take partly from the south church road and partly from a rotten coffin which you have kept in a little purse, then the fish will come forth.

92. It was told to me that if you fish on Maundy Thursday and Holy Thursday, Christ's Ascension day, the entire day, then one will have a good catch all summer.

93. The first frog you catch in the spring, take the heart while it is still alive and catch the first hooked fish, and then you release it in the lake.

94. When you come to the lake to fish, when you arrive, greet it and say "Good Morning, Good Morning, my dear lake, I set out early and I arrive late. K-lake, give me fish. In the name of the Holy Trinity."

95. In the morning take and drag your nets under your left thigh and take it around you. If they steal from you, steal it back and cense yourself with a flint fire, and creep under an earthen turf.

[PAGE 17]
6 ITEMS

96. To hex a fisher: place yourself secretly and stab at him with a knife, an axe or a rib of a human corpse, three stabs in a birch, and spit towards him as well as say: You, N. N., will be hexed in the name of 18,000 devils, you and your fishing gear, and will never get fish.

97. To take luck from a fisher: Take three stomachs from another's cleaned fish, and steal this. Put it under a stone and spit on it, and say: You, N. N. will never get fish until this is completely rotted away. Take three net-worms from the hand net and ... as well, and three hooks and spit on this and say: you, N. N. will never get fish as long as this lies here, unlucky ... N. put the stone on it and ...

98. Stick a feather filled with mercury in his net-bag and spread hen's droppings in his net and menstrual-blood.

99. If you get a hair from the head of another for your gear, and you carry it on you, then that one cannot hex you.

100. Steal a fish from his gear and dry it and grind it to a powder and spread it on the ground.

101. If you anoint your net with drop-sulfur, it will transfix the thief when he steals from you.

[PAGE 18]
8 ITEMS

102. Anoint the fishing hooks so that fish will come to you the following materials: *mormos misdes mumuskus*, honey and camphor, heron oil, *Colipe* drops white *hopmans* drops, whetstone oil, lard. *Lefverins* oil, bayberry oil, and heron lard. The best for all is filasers oil.

103. Make the fishing net from gallows rope and snake threads, the throatbone ring from a raven and heron feathers on the hooks.

104. If you can get a piece of a gallows rope for your net and basket traps and tie it to your boat, then you will get lots of fish.

105. Yellow and white olive heals: fish and women to you, anoint the hooks, for fish. Put it on yourself for women.

106. When you have prepared all your fishing gear, don't let them lie on the bare ground.

107. A net recipe: Buy cinquefoil, nettle seeds, five-finger-grass, onions, make this into a salve and put it on the hooks, and on the nets when there is a little sunny weather. Cut the fishing line up and towards you.

108. Knead drop-sulfur and anoint your fishing line. Knead hartshorn and living ... on the hooks and knead snakegrass onto the fishing line, and consecrated earth --

109. Pure heron's lard, smear it on the hooks. It is good to smear on everything. ... ... buy a little of all of these at Lidgrens Apothecary in Stockholm. *Tasma* musk balsam and heron are lucky: for fishing.

[PAGE 19]
2 ITEMS

110. To deny a girl from getting married: Make a hen, three small eggs and a nest of clay, put this nest with the hen on the eggs under the foot-sill of the house, where the girl has her bed, and say: You, N.N., will never be married or stand as bride, until this hen has hatched these three eggs to chicks. I determine and bind you to loneliness.

111. To make party-goers easily against each other (i.e., to sow discord), give them of a ring that is found and has been cut, and three pinches of .... from an angry dog at his ... foot, and then take a corpse tooth and put it in liquor and say: you, N.N., will be as cold and mute as the person whose tooth this is is dead, and in the name of 18,000 devils. Further: if you get some of their ... and put it in the liquor or similar, and get them to drink it, then they will be ill and be unable to sleep well

[PAGE 20]
3 ITEMS

112. To cure yourself for enchanting witchcraft who are in the way of birds. Catch yourself a sparrow. Immediately cut it in two and swallow its heart while it is still alive, and anoint your secret limb with raven's gall and hidden herb and cense yourself with hair of her head, then it will be better for you.

113. To draw girls to you. Take hold of a many-colored snake and with a sewing needle and red silk thread sew three stitches in put in it a nut at its protuberance. When you take that nut in your mouth and kiss a girl, then you will have her with you. The needle and thread you sew three stitches through her undergarments and in ... with the needle.

114. Carry on your person a hare's heart, a hedgehog's foot and a bat in your handkerchief, which is drawn through the church key handle at Christmas eve services, as the priest recites the *vangelmet*.[156]

[PAGE 21]
4 ITEMS

115. Cold fire on a boil. First it is destroyed – then put on it some excrement on a linen cloth and let it lie over night, do this three times over three nights.

116. If pain occurs in the chest and the heart, boil in spring water, rinse cloth and herbs and spear root, boil with yellow stone[157] and then strained clean. The mixture is mixed together with Johns oil. Drink on an empty stomach for a time, a virgin as well as a devilishness and wild saffron as well. (?)

117. About old wounds. Take carrot greens, 5 finger grass, with honey and salt, and boiled in beer until a thick salve and apply. Take a little internally.

118. For throat sickness. Boil *rysmarissyl* and after together Garlic, annis, honey. This is cooked in vinegar and tied around the throat and drink the mixture: and hold in the mouth and gargle with it.

[PAGE 22]
6 ITEMS

119. For vomiting. Take fivefinger grass and the white of an egg, in mint water and bake an egg-cake and eat it on an empty stomach, and put into it three drops of blood:

---

156 Evangeliet? The Annunciation?
157 Sulfur?

120. For spitting up blood, take up *salvantela* to the right and glowing steel in goat's milk and drink five finger grass and *grovblad* oak-mistletoe, this is boiled and drunk.

121. For boils. Grind baked beans with bran in urine. From this is made a salve with *finnish soap*. Let it cool and apply. It helps to put it in a bandage.

122. For boils. Grind *grovblad* and mix in fresh butter and honey, German soap and barley flour in turpentine oil to a dough and apply.

123. For boils. Grind *grovblad* with barley flour and sweet cream, spread it on a flat stone and ...

124. ...Take henbane and boil it up in sweet milk and apply externally.

[PAGE 23]
7 ITEMS

125. Anis and mustard oil for tender pain – grind the anis and inhale it into sore nostrils – anis, hyssop and honey in vinegar. Helps the sick one.

126. *Skrape* roots, grind in vinegar, prevents all scabs and drives away Saint Anthony's Fire.

127. Almond oil and a little honey in it prevents ... in children and flakes in the face.

128. Cotton soaked in balsam oil for painful teeth.

129. Valerian root cures for three kinds of *frossa*, administer internally to the sick person, and first ...

130. *Mosgot* pepper, poppy seeds, and *Artemisia absinthium* in wine tempers women's sentiments.

131. St. John's oil's virtues. Keeps for a long time. A good cure for burns. and for measles, for chest pain take internally, calms ... and loosens the arteries. Massage it onto the temples for women, and for children, cut the dose in half.

132. The one who carries sulfur on them with more... no one can hex them.

[PAGE 24]
3 ITEMS

133. ...may; then he is bandaged: 4. makes a foot soak for pain in feet and legs; 5. it makes them sleep, and for toothache. The seed in wax on a break, cook it through with a ... on the tooth; 6. Poka root in vinegar and wash now and the teeth as well. It stops the pain and kills the worm. 7. soak a linen cloth in henbane water and tie it around an aching head makes a good comfort: with others.

134. Cuckoo herb is called five-finger grass and Virgin Mary Hand, bears a flower and has that power that if a man puts it in a pitcher of beer and drinks to a woman, then they will have desire for each other. Further: if a pregnant woman is given the root internally, then no one can curse the child within her.

135. For *torvar killemarna* then you boil gall-wort, henbane, and 9 types of fruit bearing trees: A. Saint Peters Key is boiled in spring water, covered. The mixture is drunk, the herbs on the painful place. Helps. Finnish soap and sour dough and pig after in liquor, put it on the pain.

[PAGE 25]
10 ITEMS

136. For boils. Grind fine and put on boils, ... soaked in goat's milk with honey it drives out cough and chest pain. The mixture is drunk on an empty stomach.

137. The one who cannot release urine take internally lingon and leek juice. If you apply to the head it stops pain.

138. Annis: ground and drunk often in beer do it often when women have desire for each other.

139. Saint Anthony's Fire, grind *skrepe* leaves and apply.

140. Apply *kartosta* oil then you won't get bitten by insects.

141. boiled and ground pineapple and soak in vinegar and ... with beer to a salve and apply.

142. *Tormele* root cures for infected sores. fistulas, and swellings. Its water and powder ... thinly and apply.

143. *Tormele* root soaked in wine and drunk often is good for barren women.

144. If someone is sick with *frossa*, take *tormele* root powder internally and drink its water and pressings. Then go and lie down to sweat:

145. Those with blood in their urine take *tormele* water internally ... and rosewater for women.

[PAGE 26]
8 ITEMS

146. Juniper oil and parsley water is taken internally evening and morning for tar- stone passion and massage it around the navel, it will give back the appetite.

147. *Gnebers* oil is good for pain associated with motherhood, when she falls over, or stumbles. A little beer is taken. Juniper oil is good in cotton to put on sore teeth.

148. For tuberculosis. Massage the chest with balsam oil and take internally together with wine.

149. For bites and stings, and for constipation in the belly, take juniper oil 4 drops and massage the place.

150. Dill juice and bitter almond oil together and massage in the ringing ear...

151. brud soaked in water and wash the aching ear: the mixture drives out and flushes the intestines.

152. For burns take fresh bracken root, linden flowers in rose water. Heals well.

153. Pimpenele water heals a scurvyed head ...

[PAGE 27]
9 ITEMS

154. For a thick and hard chest, soak *hjärtansfröjd*[158] in wine and drink on an empty stomach. It cleans and makes no sweat and digests the food.

155. [...] oil and quinine oil for a swollen stomach to apply externally.

---

158 Heart's joy, an herb, *Mentha sativa*.

156. [..] *vannleks* oil and water helps those who have experienced loss: and juniper oil.

157. Warts: grind red onion and salt and apply. This mixture also removes flakes in the face.

158. Juniper, in Latin iuniperus, in German alkolder. It's oil is good for throats and for women who have heavy bleeding. Take 5 drops internally morning and evening.

159. Natron seeds taken internally in wine quiet the womb.

160. ... the womb make a plaster of flax seed. Flax seed, put this on the woman's belly.

161. For (hoarseness or cough?) soak *tidlösa* in beer and drink.

162. Loose roots and put on a swollen "secret member."

[PAGE 28]
6 ITEMS

163. *Ålans* root water for a stuffed member, helps and strengthens him.

164. For hoarseness, mix together honey in vinegar and drink evening and morning. Helps.

165. Leek for dry heat. Leek and rose oil for dry head ache. *Skråpe* root in vinegar drives out scabies and Saint Anthony's fire.

166. *ålans* root is cut and boiled and administered at the woman's time.

167. For hoarseness: pepper honey and mustard seeds, drink and gargle.

168. If the colon slips out.[159] When he drinks *Ålans* water, three spoons three times a day. And bleed a little and bind up the anus.

169. The first oak leaves that come out in the Spring and fine oak bark, apply externally to fresh sores, it will close them up. Pick oak leaves and oak bark and put it over where the end colon was seen.

---

159 Sw. *Om ändatarmen utskrider* – sometimes hemorrhoids can be so severe that they rest outside the anus rather than within it.

[PAGE 29]
5 ITEMS

170. To see if the sheep are healthy or not: If the sheep have red eyes and they are runny, then it is not safe to put it on them: In the month of January give the sheep alder leaves to eat. If they eat the leaf then they are healthy, but if they refuse then they are sick. Then put a mushroom in water and have them drink, it is best to tear apart the mushroom in the water and have them drink.

171. For hot fever boils (blisters?): take internally sulfer wood and *fläksebesbärs* oil, and apply.

172. To get long hair. Apply to the head hen's brains.

173. So that lice will not thrive on a person: carry a finger bone of a human corpse on you. ...

174. To take away hair and make a head bald: Take three swallow chicks and burn them to ashes; mix this together with musk in woman's milk and apply over the head, then the hair will fall out and the head will be bald. You can do the same with ant eggs that are ground up and applied to the head, there will never grow any hair.

[PAGE 30]
6 ITEMS

175. For obstruction in urinating. Take a cockroach and a piece of a rooster's comb, and a fish that is found in a frog. These are ground to a powder and prepared in food so that the patient eats it up all together. It helps.

176. For obstruction in urinating:
Take a goat or a sheep bladder, and burn it to ashes with hare sinews. This taken in fresh water helps.

177. For obstruction in urinating, take three hairs from his head and cut them small, and put them on three pieces of bread and administer to the patient. And drink Verbena and *grovblad* water.

178. For blood in urine: cense with verbena and *grovblad*, Tormentilla erecta, salt in vinegar or beer.

179. For tenderness and sores: if the limb is whole, wax oil. If the sore is open, put a linen bandage with wax oil on it. If you put on a fresh mouse skin, it will heal.

180. For sore throat, boil together annis, garlic and honey in vinegar: hold the mixture in your mouth, and you can apply it externally by putting it around the throat and tying it, or fresh ...

[PAGE 31]
5 ITEMS

181. For blood disease and *durklopp*: Cook together cherry-resin, Tormentilla erecta, blood wood, *stille*-seeds, *kardborre*-root, moist mushroom, sakerstilime, the burnt rib of a mare, a predator's blood-bread,[160] plantain-seeds, *brusapastorus* seeds, bolus, lime, rock coal, a seal from a letter, a pheasant heart is best, and a little living frog and take from the impurity[161] and give to the sick one.

182. Further: Take water, *elmörja* and ... and the white ... ... root moist mushroom, mix, and administer to the sick one.

183. Or scrape the bark from *Rhamnus frangula* upwards on a growing tree, and boil in water; pour it into a bottle, and carry the bottle through the ear of a water sow, and then recite the pray to stop bleeding.

184. For the one who has missed his target. Boil beech leaves and *alon* ... and take the mixture in the mouth and gargle in the mouth and throat and spit out..

185. Crabapple is ground and applied to sores, as well as cherries drive out as well as hellstone powder and three ...:

[PAGE 32]
9 ITEMS

186. If people's member is left "lame" after a serious sickness, wash and wrap the limb with *Ålans* water.

187. If a woman's breasts are swollen: wash them with *ålans* water and its root rib.

---

160 This may be brains, though I was unable to find a gloss.
161 Sw. *orenligheten*, impurity, probably meaning defecation.

188. *Ruta* and rose oil drive out Satan.

189. For cough. Soak *tidlösa* and drink. Loosens.

190. To stop a nosebleed: snort in rose-powder and make a plug of sedge grass and stick it up the nose.

191. Sedge grass heals sores if you apply it externally.

192. In the same way take linden leaves and put them on a fresh sore.

193. For a mother who is torn up inside. Make a paste of flax seeds and put it on the belly.

194. For horses: Massage a little bay oil on the navel: also for a loose anus.

195. Usually have the cows for milk healing instead of *flogrönn*[162] and that you should know.

[PAGE 33, PARTIAL]
8 ITEMS

196. Make a broth ... prepare: take ... large bits of ... in verdigris and fine... well together and the root of the same should be... skin, in case blue paper...

197. to stop a nosebleed, cense them with... in each artery and tie a thread around the little finger...

198. For sick eyes. Saint John oil, rose oil and ... vinegar water, and an incense of these. Don't apply externally, put in water. Drives out the ... blister and *alon* is good help for bad ...

199. Boil goatsblood and wash sick eyes.

200. Name on the plaster (bandage): *Sarbetina for... savase die til sa. x.a.x.: Serdes is usuallyl... bandage. Revasia, di, di, di, sesia.* This is mixed. The salve together onto a plaster, will heal... bandage, Lemon bandage is a dry plaster...

201. Take *estins* powder internally for letting blood. In the blood it separates the evil from the good.

---

162 *Flygrönn?*

202. When a limb must be cut off: take opium instead with hemlock juice, ... there is no doubt.

203. To stop bleeding of a wound. First censed with ... and spread some yellow-applepowder.

[PAGE 34, PARTIAL]
3 ITEMS

204. ... to be free from malicious witchcraft and ... put together, namely .. a round henbane root, a knob of asafetida, mercury water, sulfur, grey sulfur, ... nail and a bat ... skull: have a little bit of all of them in a pouch and put the clover with it, when you are to undertake something sure ... then both protect you and make ... and turn around... spread it where you... surely.

205. To discover some name like Satan and the ... in hell... Biälsebub their prince, ... against Satan and the Serpent.

[UPSIDE DOWN]
206. So that they are not able to take... put bread under the gunpowder ... as you have had... 3 whole shots you have well.

[PAGE 35, PARTIAL]
5 ITEMS

207. For a bad fever, evening sickness. Apply "*flåck*-fever" oil: take sulfer internally with raspberry water: and sweat.

208. For diarrhea take walnut oil internally, for children apply the oil on their navel and then it will stop.

209. For obstruction in urinating, take a male fish-stomach, and a fish that is in a ... this is pulverized to ... Take in water, it will surely help.

210. [...] take or sheep bladder and ... powder and burn hare-sinews, grind to a powder.
This is taken internally: Further, take three hairs from his head. Put it on three pieces of bread and give internally.

211. Boil verbena and *grov*-leaves to drink.

[PAGE 36, PARTIAL]
6 ITEMS

212. To drive away warts, knead the wart with meat until it bleeds. Put the meat under a stone. Then the wart is forced to go under the stone.

213. For warts: knead together red onion and salt to a salve and apply ...

214. For pain in the limbs: soak flax seeds ... with heron's lard together in a sourdough. Apply this and cover it with bandages: lily of the valley flowers are gathered and applied. Boil ... apply where there is the worst pain and ...

215. For dry pain: Elfberry oil, *tårs* oil and juniper oil for authentic ...

216. Spick oil is good, but it is too strong.

217. For dry pain, in wine take internally cinnamon. Apply externally raw ... and lead and beech *tör*'s oil and put some monk oil. We... boil lemon juice in beer and bind it on the swelling. Saint Peter oil, scorpion oil and blue lilies... herbs. White Renefana and ... in juniper...

[PAGE 37, PARTIAL]
6 ITEMS

218. Cuckoo herb is boiled in water and wash the eyes: which have the cateracts. And wash the hands, and take internally for the one who is hoarse...

219. Apply almond oil on the temples and the ... when you lie down to go to sleep.

220. Grind Satyr's herb to a salve, and apply to your testicles: if you have ... then you will regain your manhood again, and take the roots internally in wine.

221. For dry pain: take internally ... things in wine and apply externally over it. Bone oil, boil lemon juice in beer and mix it with ... 2 and apply. Boil pure ... in good juniper, apply it and cover with a bandage. Often helps.

222. For obstruction in urinating: take a goat or a sheep bladder and a male... and hare sinews, afterwards dry it hard so that you can grind it to a powder. This should now be taken internally in a ... the root ... water and give internally an evening ...

223. Further: take three hairs from his head and put it on a piece of bread and give it to him unawares ...

[PAGE 38, PARTIAL]
8 ITEMS

224. For excessive bleeding in childbirth – take walnut oil and *musgot* and white ... seeds. This in weak beer: and wrap the left thigh and leg and the left arm tight, then it will stop.

225. For colic ... blister: then take yellow ... three drops: just like the Prince's yellow drops and licorice in liquor: in case pepper... ground and then given internally in liquor. And recite the prayer for them, they see the oils, it helps for the attack.

226. For mothers: take internally *sederfångs* powder in wine: and the queen's mother drops: and almond oil... take internally: also take *bilsten* water that has been set out, and cense them with amber: recite over them: make them a ... of their hair with ... and sulfur and musk and amber: take internally ... remove their clothes as well, and henbane seeds and approach:...

227. [...] Oil, massage it into tired limbs, then they will lighten again...

228. For ringing in the ears: egg flower oil, dill oil, hemp oil, bitter almond oil, tincture of ... and *endys* oil.

229. [...] ... foot for swollen ache and aged salve...

230. [...](*Durklopp?*) is massaged on the navel:

231. [...] put it under the core out of a ...:

MS 25

NORDISKA MUSÉET, MS ONUMRERAD
ÅKERS HÄRAD, SÖDERMANLAND
"ATT BOTA EN BÖSSA SOM ÄR SKÄMD."
(TO FIX A SHOTGUN THAT IS HEXED)

No. 1
To fix a shotgun that is hexed.
Take the barrel out of the stock and take the loose back screw. Then take "flogrund" as much as will fill the barrel, and bore a hole in the end through it. Go then to a running spring that runs towards the south, lay the barrel in it and let the water run through it 3 times (days and nights in a row) then one will see how it goes with the hexing. NB. But before one does this, one must first shoot with loose powder into another's baking oven.

No. 2.
To protect a shotgun
Buy at the pharmacy "Sabenwood" and put it with an awl in the shotgun stock, then no one can hex the shotgun. This type of tree is similar to cork and is hard as "tunder."

No. 3.
Another method.
Take the barrel out of the stock and the back screw out of it. Then hang a living snake with a thread approximately in the middle of the barrel. Then put it on the fire and toast the snake – and the one hexing will be so as well.

No. 4.
Another method.
When one shoots any animal or bird, then one must take a little hair or feathers as soon as one has shot, and keep in the shotgun case. When one discovers that the shotgun is hexed, then smoke it with it, then the gun will be fine immediately.

No. 5.
To temper good shot and bullets.
Take a peat pellet and grind it very fine, and mix it with the lead when you cast in this way, you won't need to doubt hitting the mark.

No. 6.
<u>To fix it when it misfires</u> –
If the fire is taken from you so that no spark comes out, then pour the priming powder out and dry out the flashpan with the left nameless finger and load anew in its place. Put the shotgun opening in the air and ask with these words "What kind of weather we have today!" then the fire will return again.

No. 7.
<u>To get a rifle flint that won't misfire</u>.
One takes a new flint when one takes communion in the mouth, then it will surely be good.

No. 8.
<u>To shoot that which is bewitched</u>.
One takes a peat pellet as well as a little gold and silver from a wedding ring and put it in with the ammunition, during these words: "In the name of the Father and of the Son and of the Holy Spirit."

No. 9.
<u>Another method</u>.
Take the moss that sits on a dead man's skull and add it to the ammunition for the shot, which is safer.

No. 10.
<u>So that no one may take the fire from you</u>.
Prop up a turf of earth with your right big toe and put it in between amongst the ammunition, while you say these words: "I have done this to heal my shotgun, in the name of the Father and of the Son and of the Holy Spirit."

No. 11.
<u>To heal a hexed shotgun</u>.
Go to the woods on a Thursday evening, when the sun has set, and take all your shooting paraphernalia with you. Cleave a little round stake with a knife from the base to the top drik so that it holds above and below. Crawl then sunwise three times through it and say these words: Here I bind the bad luck behind, and the one who did me ill, and all the devils of hell are with him," spit three times under your left arm and then go home.

No. 12.
<u>Another method</u>.
Load with a magpie-heart and shoot under your left arm, and say these words: "For all the devils who are in hell, also drag him who has given you between the eyes. U Capolia"

No. 13.
Another method.
Put nine grains of salt under the barrel in the stock, then it will be fixed.

No. 14.
Another method.
Take branches with leaves of nine types of fruit-bearing trees, and strike the shotgun with it – and during this whipping one says: "In the name of the Father and of the Son and of the Holy Spirit. Amen."

No. 15.
Another method.
One takes one's shotgun, puts it in both the hollows of the knees, and while it lies there, do both your needs –

No. 16.
Another method.
When your shotgun becomes sorely hexed, then do the following: namely: take out the back screw, and screw in a "käll-seed," then load it with loose gunpowder and shoot, but say to yourself "after this hour of the night you shall never – and here is said the name of the person – do any more. In the name of the Father and of the Son and of the Holy Spirit, Amen – this should be done at sunrise on a Thursday morning.

No. 17.
To preserve your hat so that no shoot will hit it.
Take the hat and wipe the ear wax out of the left ear with the left nameless finger three times on it, then the shot will miss it.

No. 18.
Another method.
Take a piece of bread and put it between the lining and the hat, then the shot will not hit it.

No. 19.
To get as close as you want to an animal.
Shoot a magpie on a Thursday evening after the sun has set – take the heart out of it in the middle of the back put a loading-stock in right through the middle of it and dry it. Now, when one wants to go near to an animal, then one looks at it through the hole where the loading-stock was put, then the animal won't see the shooter.

No. 20.

<u>A better and surer/safer way to come as close to a bird as one wants.</u>

Take the foremost part of a skull. Make then three holes in it, one each Sunday during the sermon. View then the bird through the hole and say these words: "Little bird on the next branch, as the dead man in the grave, in the name of the Father and of the Son and of the Holy Spirit.

No. 21.

<u>Another method.</u>

Go to a cemetery on a Thursday evening after the sun has set. Take a bone by the ear of a skull. Write thereupon with your own blood and say – I bind you, bird, with my own blood, and this in the name of the Father and of the Son and of the Holy Spirit. This is said three times. Further, I bind you by heaven and earth, by the sun and moon, by the stars and planets and everything that God has created in heaven and on the earth, and by all the holy martyrs and angels, that you shall not escape from this circle/ring. And walk then three times around the bird.

No. 22.

<u>So that whatever animal you desire will come as close to you as you want.</u>

Make for yourself a knife in the name of the *Skogsrå*[163] before the sun rises on a Sunday morning, Temper it in blood, half of your own and half from an animal. Then take the knife with you and go to the forest on a Thursday evening after the sun has set. Make a fire, then the *skogsrå* will come to you with a sparrow's tail-feather which you will put with the knife.

No. 23.

<u>So that you will have hunting luck</u>

Go to the woods. Shoot the first bird you find. Cut it up into 200 pieces. Shoot with each piece at a point/target. At the 30th piece, a pea is put into the shotgun; and shoot at the same point. Then there will appear three drops of blood out of the point. With these one smears the shotgun, then one will have luck in shooting.

No. 24.

<u>To win a shooting contest with someone.</u>

Habas

Carry only these words with you + Nabba + Sadla + Gabla, C ---

---

[163] Here spelled "skogsråd," but more commonly in this century "ett skogsrå," and is one of the supernatural fauna of the forest. See Gunnar Granberg, *Skogsrået i yngre nordisk folktradition*. Skrifter utgivna av Gustav Adolfs Akademien for Folklivsforskning 3 (1935).

No. 25.
Another method.
If you are in a shooting contest with someone and don't want him to hit the mark, then write on your left arm these characters:

No. 26.
To hex a shotgun.
See that you are able to pull a hair out of the shooter.

No. 27.
To take the fire from another (to cause them to shoot blanks)[164]
Go to a horse. Draw a ring three times around his left foot sunwise. Take a pinch of dirt and bind it in a rag. Put this same rag between the jersey and the shirt, right up against the heart, and go to the one who is shooting.

No. 28.
To be able to shoot in front of another
As soon as you come into to the woods, then fix it so you can take from the first tree a grasshopper ["*stritta*"] unnoticed. Then put it in your shotgun then you will be able to shoot in front of your friends.

No. 29.
To protect your shotgun
Take wine that is left over after the Lord's Supper has occurred – and take 9 types of leafy trees – keep it on Michaelsmas until Walpurgismas. Burn it up then to a powder and mix it with liquor, kneed your shotgun inside and outside. It helps –

No. 30.
All types of remedies useful for many circumstances
The moss that sits on a dead man's skull, peat pellets, a bell that is found in a flowing stream, earth that is dug up in a left shoe while the priest buries a body, that happens in the following way: When the priest says in the name of the father and of the son and of the holy spirit, each time one takes up some earth with the leather from the left shoe – further, the remains of a "*hvepning*" that has lain in the earth, snakeskin that lies at a crossroads, a wedding ring,

---

164 See NM33.824, page 11, No. 10, for a spell so similar that it suggests a common tradition.

dyfwelssträck,[165] garlic, *bäfvergäll*,[166] *wändört*,[167] *säfvenbom*,[168] three drops of blood from a *läderlapp*,[169] nails from a corpse's hand, or its nameless finger, as well as the claw from a cuckoo's left foot –

No. 31.
To protect yourself from witchcraft
When one secretly [???] carries on oneself and keeps together garlic, *Bergsöta*,[170] *tidbast*,[171] and *Wändelört*,[172] no harm will "blow your way," but it must be gathered on Midsummer night between 11 and 12 o'clock.

No. 32.
Another method.
Recite these following words over a running stream before the sun has come up on a Thursday morning and turn yourself to each of the four directions and say wherever you turn – I bind you sun, moon, stars and planets and all the powers of heaven, that you all shall shine over the ungodly person who has hexed me, his blood shall make him fearful, as Christ suffered bound to the Cross, his blood shall run around his heart, his hand shall never have more peace than this running stream under my knees, until he has brought back again that which he has stolen from me – in the name of the father and of the son and of the holy spirit.

No. 33.
Another method.
The following is useful as well for people as for shotguns, fishing paraphernalia, fiddles and whatever else. When one secretly either one oneself or on the shotgun, instrument, or whatever it is keeps a *fyrsten* (firestone?), it helps for all kinds of witchcraft. Such a stone is also useful to mix together with shot, because then one can shoot with it all enchanted animals, the same stone is also good to have on horses.

No. 34.
Another method.
When you go to communion, then shave for the first three (?) small shavings

---

165 Asafœtida, or Devil's Dung, *ferula fœtida*.
166 Lit. "beaver's balls," but may be musk, or castor oil.
167 *Valeriana officinalis*.
168 Rush-rhizome?
169 Bat.
170 The rootstalk of *polypodium vulgare*.
171 Tidebast: *Daphne Mezereum* according to Valter Forsblom.
172 alternate dialect-form of *valeriana officinalis*.

from the chair where you're sitting, and hide them on you – Then, when you go up for communion then take the host out of your mouth and stuff it away on you – when you then go out of the churchyard, then take up earth three times with your left hand and add it to the other ingredients, and keep with you –

No. 35.
<u>Another method</u>.
Take a human bone from a cemetery and keep it with you, namely on your bare skin. NB: the bone must then be put back at the same place from which it was taken.

No. 36.
<u>Another method</u>.
Bind these names around your throat – amot – Orfatt – afal –

No. 37.
<u>To prevent another's wrath</u>
If someone is angry with you, then fix it so that you catch sight of him before he catches sight of you, and say – I see you with my two wise eyes, I bind your mind and tongue in the name of the father and of the son and of the holy spirit, amen –

No. 38.
<u>To slake a wildfire</u>
Write these characters on a woodshaving and throw it into the fire –

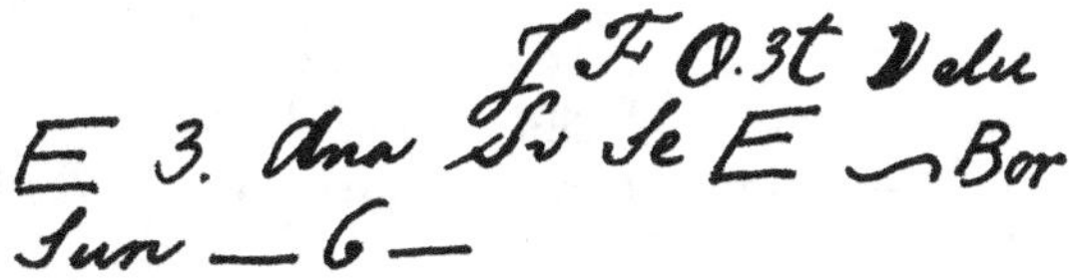

[handwritten characters]

No. 39.
<u>To win at court</u>.
As soon as you catch a glimpse of your opponent before he sees you, say these words – I shall go to court, and all my enemies will be just as stones – say this three times, in the name of the father and of the son and of the holy spirit amen –

No. 40.

Another method.

Before you go to court, *smöjj*[173] all your clothes that you have on that day three times counterclockwise through the hole in a fore-ring (*framring*), then no one will win against you.

No. 41.

To win at cards

Take a lapwing's heart in your left shoe, as well as a swallow's tongue in your bed for three days and three nights, put the tongue under your [mist, vapor?], then no one will win over you.

No. 42.

Another method.

The one who has a heart of a hazel-hen under his left arm when he plays, then he'll win.

No. 43.

To become invisible

Prick out the eyes of a swallow-chick and let him remain in the nest for three days. Then you'll find a stone in the same nest. Take it in your mouth and you'll be invisible – The swallow has three stones with it, red, white and black. The one that has the red one in its mouth and kisses someone, he will get everything he desires. The one who has the white stone in his mouth, he can never fare poorly. The one who has the black can never be cursed nor be destroyed.

No. 44.

So that one may without injury in haste become drunk.

Take Paradise Tree,[174] and grate it to a pulp and give to him in his drink.

No. 45.

So that womenfolk won't be able to "take to the dish" (each as much?)

Take green basil, put it secretly under the dish, then she'll not be able to taste anything.

No. 46.

Underline: Diverse ways to make girls notice you –

Take blood from out of your left nameless finger and give it to her in bread

---

[173] Sw. *smöjning*, a magical procedure of drawing something through a hole, natural or artificial, to imbue with a magical quality or bestow supernatural healing.

[174] Siberian crab-apple?

or drink – and carry a swallow's heart with you – write on a red apple her and your name and hold it under your *right* arm until it becomes quite warm, then she'll come to you. NB: this apple shall then be taken on a Thursday before the sun goes down – If you want a girl to love you, then write on a red apple with your own blood her name with these words – Orsa. Forsa. Forsma. – another: Take a dove, tear its heart out and burn it on an ax so that it becomes evenly brown, then her heart will burn for you – another: take a hare's heart in your left shoe and tromp on it with your foot when you talk to her, then she'll follow after you – another: if you want to win a girl's love, then take three flax seeds and plant them in a snake's head in a certain place – from the three flax plants that grow up there and ripen, a linen thread is made that is bound about the left arm, as long as it stays there, you'll not lose the love of the girl. – another: have with you a turtledove's heart, then you'll be attractive to every girl – another: take blood from a bat and smear it on a handkerchief and afterwards, dry a girl's face with it, then she'll fall in love – another: take a dove while it is using its immodesty, cut off its secret thing, dry it and grind it to powder, and administer it to the one you want to have love you – another: take the eyelashes from a living wolf and give it to a girl, then she'll be smitten with you – another: take an apple and put it under your left arm so that it will be completely wet with sweat, take it then with you three Sundays in a row to church, and give it to the one you want to love you – another: one who takes *ormgalla*[175] and put it in a nutshell and have it in one's mouth, that one will please the ladies. – another: if one takes a snake-sting and stick womenfolk with it, then they'll please him. – another: if one takes the left wing of a bat and rub a woman with it, they'll please him. – another: take three drops of blood from a bat and carry it on a linen cloth on you, then one will be able to have whoever one wants. Another: if one takes the same drops of blood and puts it in snuff and give it to a girl, then her mind will turn favorably to him –

No. 47.
So that a woman will express her true feelings and her secrets.
Take hare's blood and write with it her name on a cloth and put it under her head when she sleeps – another: take a raven's heart and lay it on her breast, then she'll say her true feelings in her sleep – or lay a new whisk or broom under the head, then it will happen –

No. 48 and No. 49 are natural substances and not worth transcribing.

No. 50.
To cause diarrhea in another.
One takes a lush fir-top and tie a loop firmly to one end, then one puts the top

---

175 Ormhalla (?) *anguis fragilis*

with its fastened loop in a rushing stream that runs toward the north – thereupon one sits and does one's needs through the loop and names the one who is to receive the diarrhea. Then it will happen immediately. Another: one goes to the churchyard three Thursday nights in a row, the first night one should seek out a human bone through which there is a hole. The following Thursday night one should go to the same place and see if it still remains there. The third Thursday night one goes and takes it away. Then, one puts it into a rushing stream, so that the water has a chance to run through the hole, and when one puts the bone into the stream, then one should think upon it, and name the name of the person who is to get diarrhea, and as long as the bone lies in the stream, then that one will have a strong case of the runs – one can even use the same bone more than once, but when one first takes it at the churchyard, one should determine for oneself within a certain amount of time that you will carry it back, and if one doesn't do that, then the owner [of the bone] will come to the bone himself and will want it back again –

No. 51.
A preservative against a suspected person.
When you see someone that you believe will hex you, then say these following words: – I see you first, I silence your voice, your liver and lungs will confess everything to me, in the name of the father and of the son and of the holy spirit. Amen. –

No. 52.
On the hedgehog
If one takes a hedgehog and cuts up its chest, one finds in its heart a little stone, white and angular. The one who carries this stone on his person cannot be hit by anyone – and the one who puts this stone right over the middle of the heart, he will be lucky in everything he undertakes. – If one takes 6 drops of hedgehog blood and a half weight of slaked lime, 3 weights of potash, grind it up well and knead of this a dough from which you shape a pellet or bullet, and dip it often in oil, – the one who carries such a pellet on his person, he will never be without money. –

No. 53.
To become strong.
The one who has a rat's heart on him, from this he will become so strong that no one can hit him.

No. 54.
To know whether a woman is a virgin or not –
Take a flea and put it into a glass of beer and let her drink. If she's not a virgin, then she'll pee.

No. 55.
To know whether one will get a "yes" from a girl or not.
Lay two sewing needles on the floor in a cross and have her walk forth – if you'll get a "yes," then she'll walk immediately over them, if not, she will stop in her tracks.—

No. 56.
To cause one to sleep
Take a wolf's heart and put it under the head of the one you want to sleep, then he'll sleep until you take it from him. –

No. 57.
Divining rod that will find silver and gold –
It is cut two times a year, Christmas night between 11 and 12., and Midsummer day between 11 and 12, then one will seek out a [flaying ground or flayed round] hazel or birch, all of a year old according to the figure's growth written below, but when one goes out cut the divining rod, then one should remain silent and cut it in three cuts without taking the knife from the tree. During the first cut, one says: "I cut you, divining rod," during the second, "in the name of the holy trinity," and during the third "that you will show me silver and gold," whereupon one leaves that place without looking back. – Then, one should have heirloom silver and gold that has been stolen three times and been returned. Bore a hole in the divining rod, in the end which is the head, and put the silver and gold into it. Plug it up again – when one now takes the divining rod in one's hand and seeks for treasure, then one should say to oneself "I swear you, divining rod, in the name of the holy trinity, that you show to me silver and gold" then one will become well-disposed towards that which one seeks.

No. 58.
To keep the treasure where it is –
Take a hazel staff that is a year old and draw a circle around where the divining rod is, in the way that is shown in the figure, to a width of 5, 6, 7 or 9 alns, and when one draws, one should say the words written below three times –

The word was made flesh and dwelt amongst us.

No. 59.
<u>To take the treasure from the dragon without injury</u>
First, one should dig until one comes upon the treasure. If there is a chest or something else, then one shall write with chalk three crosses. At the first cross, one says: "God the father." At the second "God, the son." And at the third "God, the holy spirit" whereupon one must hurry away from there – but first of all, before this is done, one puts a wooden cross in the pit, that one must have in readiness, upon which one hangs one's clothes so that it resembles a human being; because when one draws and hurries away from there, the dragon will come up, and will fly three times through the same simulacrum.

No. 60.
<u>Another method</u>.
Take a few rounds of rope and put one end very slowly through the ring on the chest or the pot [of gold], then tie a dog to the rope, and take the other end and go a bit from there, and pull the dog down onto the treasure. When the dog now begins to scream, the dragon will come up and tear him all to pieces, and then he will fly his own way from there. When he has done the injury, then one can take up the treasure whenever one likes, and this without any danger of injury.

No. 61.
<u>To make a box that seeks out gold and silver</u>.
One takes a toad which is male – and hangs it up by the back legs, and puts a water-bowl under him that he can't reach with his mouth, then he will release a stone out of his mouth that is called ONIX; put it in a box, and when next you go wherever treasure is, the stone will hop out of the box.

No. 62.
<u>Another method</u>.
One takes the head from a "*torndyfwel*"[176] and puts it into a box along with "mastrikt" and quicksilver, and carry it in your hand. Then, when you go on rocks where some orevein is, then the box will knock very hard. –

No. 63.
<u>To know of hidden matters</u>
One takes a water-snake (here is probably meant a white snake; see my comments on superstition) and boil it in water, and dip bread into it and eat, because it isn't poisonous, then one can know what other folks are saying about one. –

---

176 thorny devil, a type of toad?

No. 64.
Secret knowledge regarding the raven –
The one who takes a raven's eggs which are red, and boils them until they become white, and puts them then back in the nest, then the raven will fly to get a red stone and put it upon them. One takes this stone and puts it on a lock, then the lock will spring open immediately. Another:, the one who keeps a raven's heart on oneself, he will not be sleepy until he puts it away from himself. Another: The one who keeps with him a raven's bill and his right little claw will get money for drink and favor from men –

No. 65.
For trollshot.
Ture stood on the mountain and spoke to his mother Helena: Spit in the mouth, out of the mouth, healing in the same moment. (rhymes in Swedish).

No. 66.
For Lapp-shot.
The Lapp was going out to shoot, our Lord Christ came, what are you going to shoot? I shall shoot all the folk and all the cattle who are before me. – I shall make you great, but shall shoot logs and stones. –

No. 67.
For a feverish wound. –
Chilliness, frost in the wide world; great rivers run, rush, chill out and heat in, healing in the same moment. –

No. 68.
A short remedy for jaundice.
One takes a white-beam tree's[177] gall and cut off its beak, pee on it and hang it up in the chimney, then you'll find healing.

No. 69.
Another method.
One takes three rags of linen, upon which one pees and put them up in the eaves, then there will be healing.

No. 70.
To dull pain—
Just as truly shall you stand still as 12 men in court who judge rightly, and never unjustly. It is said nine separate times.

---

177 *Oxblåsa*, *Oks*: Cotoneaster vulgaris, *blåsa*: common term for a leaf gall. Alternatively, it could be a dialect word for a type of bird, since reference is made to a "beak."

No. 71.
To get an animal to follow you constantly
Stomp three times with your left foot on each of the animal's feet, and say: "You shall walk after me as the Evil One followed after the unjust sheriff."

No. 72.
For "*fulslag*"[178]
Goda goes on her way forth, Then she met Oden, "Where shall you go?" "I shall go stand and "*röta*" | "smoke" appears in another formula | meat and break bones, under both logs and stones, no one shall deny me, in that forest where no one dwells, in that lake where no one rows" This is said 9 times.

No. 73.
For shot.
The Wolf stood on the wolf's mountain, and asked the rock-peak, where shall you go? I shall heal shot, water-shot, accident-shot, lung-shot, foam-shot (rabies?) and for all nine types of shots. This is said 9 times.
[Up to this point, reproduced to the letter and punctuation, the rest summarized.]

No. 74.
Of geese and hens.
When a goose or hen has hatched, one takes the nest with the eggs and the hen and weighs it and records the weights on a [sledge? Beam?]

No. 75.
When children are unhappy
One takes the branches of nine types of leaf trees that hang over or next to the churchyard, and smoke (cense) the child with it.

No. 76.
"*Witrång*" for foxes...

No. 77.
To protect oneself from epilepsy/dropsy.
Each morning take on an empty stomach the [?*medlerita*?] of the urine, and drink out of the left hand. This helps.

---

178 Rietz Dialect dictionary gives "a swelling on the fingers accompanied by insufferable pain (panaritium); another entry gives "lice"; and I grew up with it meaning "pimples." Literally, it means an ugly affliction.

No. **78, 79, 80.**
Natural materials about tempering of steel as well as childbirth – not worth transcribing.

Thereafter follow Nos. **81–86**, which are taken out of Sven Samuelssons published *Horse Book*.

Here follow some tips about the art of marksmanship gotten out of a Black Art Book!

No. **87.**
Take a bit of hare's heart, a bit of the lung, a bit of the liver, none larger than a half a little finger – dry and grind it to a powder as well as 7 shot pellets and a hail stone, which is mixed with gunpowder.

Another: When one comes to the woods, one takes a birch or an alder branch with the two foremost fingers of the left hand, and pull them out of their sockets. Sharpen them on two sides and put them in a green turf, whereupon one says to oneself: "Bird and Beast."

Another: One scrapes off and eight-farthing piece three Thursday evenings in a row, some silver with 6 unused common pins which are crooked, as well as three drops of blood of the first bird one shoots which is dripped in a handkerchief as well as a fresh feather from the same bird, which, all put together and wherewith one kneads the shotgun barrel and which then is kept in the shotgun case –

Another: If someone has hexed a shotgun and one wants to punish with such a strong case of the runs that his life will only be for 3 or 4 [24-hour] days long, then go to a spring that runs either towards the north or towards the south, and put the shotgun barrel then down until the tail-screw gets wet with the big end or the [*gevinderna*] towards the current – a bone in which there is a hole should be taken from the churchyard and put with the hole against the muzzle and a red silk thread taken through the barrel and the bone as well fastened to the upper end – In the other end of the silk thread, is bound a fir-shaving that should have free movement in the water. This must be done on a Thursday eve (Wednesday evening?) during sunset, whereupon the bone must be put back in its place again.

Another: To get the shotgun to kill without fail. When one has shot, take ahold of the shotgun with the right hand and strike the barrel with the left free hand, support it with the nozzle under the left foot, and before one has taken the game in one's hand, one should touch it with the shotgun –

Another: If one takes wax from out of the ear and strokes it on the target, one will not hit it, or if frog-spawn or earwax is spread on the shotgun muzzle, it will do the same thing. Another: If one wants to forestall another's greater shootsmanship, then one can take the stock with the thumb and the barrel with the nameless finger and say: Iron and steel, you shall stand as Judas Simonis Iskariotz stood when he betrayed Christ.

Another: More reliable method: Out of the footprint of the shooter you are jealous of is taken a little snow, earth or grass with the thumb and the nameless finger, and in just that same hole which is let out inside-out again, and continue three times, while one says "(Person's name) may it be for you just as backwards today as that which I have turned inside out" –

Another: If a hunting hound becomes hexed, then go to the woods and break off 9 juniper saplings, pee on them and then with them whip the dog nine times, then he will regain his former goodness.

No. 88.
To hex severely a shotgun ---
Take a nail from the churchyard and file the muzzle with it, but if one files all over, then the shotgun can never be fixed – the nail must be put back in its place again – Or: smear your defenseless finger in the left ear and draw a circle with it counterclockwise three times around the aim/target.

No. 89.
To make sulfur steel.
Heat a steel pole well and hard, and pierce it with sulfur so that the steel melts into drops, which must fall through a funnel upon which a wedding ring is fastened. Uses: if one grinds this to a powder and puts it among shot, it will hit without fail, and if one puts it in a shotgun to be kept, then that shotgun can never be hexed.

No. 90.
To make birds come to you: When you see and hear birds then say: "You sound and no one answers, and all who hear your voice go away in the other direction, in the name of the father and of the son and of the holy spirit, amen. Repeated three times.

Nos. 91, 92, 93 (Common superstitions about cattle)

No. 94.
To conserve/preserve your pigs: Take the intended Christmas [?] which is hidden until Valborgsmässo- day and give to the pigs on an earth-fast stone before the sun comes up.

Variously strewn arts

No. 95, 96 – not worth noting

No. 97.

To gather horsetail seeds: Take three tin plates and nine pieces of clean paper on each plate. Put them under the horsetail on midsummer's night, but one may not say a word. –

No. 98.

To conserve or save a hexed horse:
Cut some of the Devil's Eye on the horse's leg and take each bit clockwise around the horse three times, and administer some of the same to him – three times in pieces of bread.

END.

To me the year was 1819, but the title page is lost. It is written in a better penmanship such as that used by the period's cunning folk or well-placed parish constable – Up through No. 73 the items are exactly as in the original, but many thereafter are summarized with main sentences. It represents the practice in Åkers District in Södermanland, and is kept still with care within a certain family, copied by Gustav Ericsson, Södermanlands Antiquities Collection's representative.[179]

---

[179] "å mig har varit årtalet 1819 men titelbladet är förkommen. Är skrifvet med bättre stil såsom af den tidens klokarna eller välbestäld fjerdingsman -- Är tiu ö:- m:- No 73 original fullt lik mm sedermera sammandragit hufvudmeningar – Har varit praktiß utöfning innom Åkers härad i Södermanland och förvaras ännu med omsorg innom en viss familj, afvskrifen af Gust. Ericsson Söderm: Fornminnesförening ombud in ..."

MS 26

PER BJÖRNSSON
LUNNOM, BROBY, SKÅNE, 1690

* * *

In the name of Jesus Christ.
Begins this holy conjuration.
Kyrie Eleison, Lord God Father in Heaven, be merciful unto N: here.
Kyrie Eleison, Christ be merciful unto N: here
Kyrie Eleison, Lord Holy Ghost be merciful for the sake of God's cross +
of Jesus Christ our Lord's + and the Holy Ghost's + A. N. Flee, you devil and demonic presence, the leaves from Judah's stem and David's root have triumphed, the word of God and Jesus Christ. Amen.

I Cyprianus, worshipper of and beloved by the Eternal God, Jesus Christ his only son's pure and true proclaimer of the Gospel, I, by the Holy Ghost and by Jesus Christ our Lord conjure you demonic presence and the Devil himself I exhort, by God who has created all things in heaven and earth from nothing, the pure and the impure, and with God Almighty's goodness and by God's righteousness. –

Sunday with God's promise, in the name of God the Father and of God the Son and of God the worthy Holy Ghost. Amen.

And by all these holy and powerful words and exhortations, I forbid all types of devils, both small and the big ones. Who are here in this sinful world and those who are in the realm of Hell, all Farm pookas, woodwives, elves and waterhorses, all mountain trolls, all evil wights and evil spirits, all hazelwives and trollwives under the earth or rocks, and revenants, water sows and all hauntings and every type of wight, fire wights and all other unwholesome beings. I exhort them and forbid them all under the highest praise of God and [hidelse] that they never after this day will do any harm to this servant of God N., neither day or night in any way. I forbid them from all that is within him or that is upon him, and both within him and outside him, I forbid them just has strictly in God's ways as God himself forbade the evil angels from entering heaven. And I exhort and exorcise them by heaven, the shining stars, and by all God's holy angels, and by the great [tordönnen] and [liuneld], and by the four Evangelists and by the 12 chosen apostles, confessors, martyrs and by the

Faith and Patience of all the saints, and by all the the Sunday morning lectionary (reading of the scriptures from the pulpit over the course of years), and prayers. And by Saint Benz faithfulness and by the Virgin Mary's holy chastity. And I exhort and exorcise them by our Lord Jesus Christ's holy and honorable birth and Jesus Christ's death and suffering – cross – and by the crown of thorns that Jesus had borne on his blessed head, and by the 3 nails of Jesus – and by the wounds in Jesus' hands and feet and by the scourge and bindings that Jesus was hit with, and by the spear with which he was pierced in his side.

Our Lord Jesus Christ was walking in his blessed Garden, he saw his enemies standing before him [...] he them all in the powerful name of Jesus; just so I bind the devil with those needles and strong bindings, and speech, and all that is within him and outside of him [...] the bindings that Jesus bound the Jews with in the Garden [...] God the worthy Holy Ghost's name Amen.

Of God the Father + of God the Son + and of God the Holy Ghost + and of the Three Persons and Single God + amen. J. H. S. Saint Bengt's faithfulness.

Our Lord Jesus Christ he said to his disciples Peace be with you. That same holy peace I radiate and I wish always be upon N., his soul and spirit and body and body, and I forbid by God's ways the Devil and all evil spirits and all sorcerers and all evil people and all elves and waterhorses, and all other troll and unwholesomeness, that is now listed here, that they shall never after this day do to this servant of God N. any more harm to his body or body inside or outside, neither day nor night in any way, and with these holy and powerful words and exhortations that have been recited now, they shall after this day depart from him and never harm him more than a mouse does harm to an earthfast stone.

Peace over N's body and body inside and outside, peace over his flesh and blood, peace over his sinews and bones and belly, peace over him out and in, peace day and night. Peace, in the name of God the Father and of the Son and of the Holy Ghost. Amen.

Turn away, you demonic force. Of God the Father + and of the Son + and of the worthy Holy Ghost + JHS and Saint Bendt's faithfulness. Amen.

In the name of God the Father Amen.

In the name of God the Son Amen.

In the name of God the Holy Ghost Amen.

[Here ends the written portion of the manuscript. A few inserted pages from a Danish prayerbook were included at the end, which included the following prayers:

A prayer against the temptations of Satan.

A prayer against the temptations of Sin.

A prayer against the temptations of Hell and Death.

A prayer for Hope.

A prayer to ask for a new life (attributed to Cyprianus)]

ms 27

PETTER JOHAN JOHANESSON, 1841
VARUTI JAG SKRIFVER VARJEHANDA

* * *

PETTER JOHAN JOHANESSON, 1841
IN WHICH I WRITE OF ALL KINDS OF THINGS

THIS BOOK IS TO READ IN ORDER TO LEARN MANY
DIFFERENT TYPES OF WOUNDS BOTH TO HEAL MAGICALLY
AND IN OTHER WAYS TO LEARN TO HEAL.

1. Fever: when you become ill with a fever blister (swelling) then take a clay stone (marble?) in a baking oven and a little tallow and put it on the fevering sore, and hold your hand on the same, and say, "this oven is made from clay and stone, out of clay and stone, take this blister to you in 9 weeks and a year, and as long as the world remains, in God the Father's et cetera" this is recited. 9 times and spit between each third time, and say the three names "In the name of God the Father and of the Son and of the Holy Ghost" three times and then anoint on the sore with the tallow.

2. Snakebite! When you have been bitten by a snake, then when the sun has gone down then sit down on an earth-fast stone and stroke your hand back and forth on the bite-wound and say "In this way the Snake lies in a ring, bite me on my foot or leg or whatever it might be, but I, by the devil, set myself down on an earth-fast stone and say. 3 names God the Father and God the Son and God the Holy Ghost." – this is recited three times and spit between each time!

3. When you begin to harvest, then betake yourself to some bush and bend it down to the ground, and put a stone on the top of it, and say "here you shall lie and bend rye for me while I harvest, -- and when you are not harvesting, then immediately take the stone off of the top of the bush, and you should do this each year. –

4. If you have a cow or oxen out on a journey and someone comes up who you think might hex them, then inside yourself in silence then you kiss the cow or the ox whichever it is [--- * ---].

5. But if it should happen that your cattle aren't healthy in your farm, then buy yourself at the apothecary for 4 crowns worth of coral, *Swaggel*[180] for 2 crowns; gunpowder for 1.5 and cut off a little hair over the hooves on all four feet and a little on the snout on all your animals that you have in the cattle-shed, and take these things that you've bought and the hair you've cut and divide up into three parts with a little bit of each substance in each part. A Thursday evening then go to your barn and take ashes and fire in a pan with you and put it on a chair in the middle of your cattle-shed and shut the door and seal all the holes so that the whole cattle-shed is closed up tight. Then take the two parts and put it on the fire in the pan so that it will burn up and so that all your livestock will inhale the smoke that issues from that. But guard your cattle-shed during the night until daylight. On Friday morning take the third part and wrap it up in a paper and in a linen cloth, and bore a hole in the threshold of the cattle-shed and put it inside. Then put a nail over the hole and nail it in. Then make sure that it is all the way in, and that it can't be seen.

6. When you go to market or whatever it may be, and buy a cattle-animal that you are aware isn't familiar beforehand, then when you take it home then when you take it onto your land, then look at the road after the first feather that you find on the road, take it up and throw it three times back and forth in front of the newly purchased animal and then hold it as far back from the newly bought animal so that it will jump into your fields and let it go over it, and say: "You shall not go into this place through the opening of the gate or earth's containment, higher than so, while you are with me."

---

180 *Svavel?* Sulfur.

7. When you buy a sheep when you come home with it then spit in its ear and say three times and spit between each time, "You don't need to be troubled, whatever the farmer is hanged up, and the farm is burned up, you don't have anything to follow after," recite this 3 times and spit between each time.

8. And when you have a calf born or a bull, and it starts to swell up, then buy for 2 Swedish crowns shaving soap and take a piss in an old pot and knead the soap apart and then wash in a cross as long as it takes to go away..

9. At the time you injure yourself by cutting or by a blow, then boil together 1.5 measures of wax, .5 measures maple sap, 1 measure goat tallow, 1.5 measures pitch and boil these four types together slowly. Then take a put it on a cloth large enough to cover the entire wound, and put it on until it heals – if it's not enough, then cook up some more.

10. When you have hens then when you get up before sunrise on the first of May, then take your hens and weigh them in the oven over the fire, and put a little salt in the fire, and when it sputters, then weigh them then, and say: "Now grocer, you are good to allow to aim my hen this year" and you do in this way each year on Valborgsmässa morning or the first of May.

"**9.**" Fish. If you use hooks then shake [...] to Carlshamn for 4 crowns worth of Black Bedset and anoint your hooks with it, then you sure to have them bite.

"**10.**" If you want to scare a horse, then when you're out on a journey and meet up with someone, then when you and your friend are about to eat, then take a piece of bread and with some of the froth from his horse's mouth, spread it back and forth, then give your horse the piece of bread then, and his froth will come out of your horse.

11. If you want to hex a pair of oxen, then take 2 onto marking-threads, and put three doubles, and tie three knots on each of them and then tie a knot each morning on the pair of oxen, and spit while you are tying, but tie them so that it isn't seen.

12. If you want to know if your sows, lambs and rams will survive the winter, then [*såinna mekellig*] then wipe both their upper and lower eye-lids at once, as well as you can. If the eye runs and trickles, back and forth, and it seems that they're not healthy but the eye doesn't run but rather it is just as clear as before, then you are sure that you will have them over the winter – but if the eyes run, then let it be, and you can slaughter them towards the winter.

13. If you are plagued by moles [or rats?], then during the summer when there is rain early in the morning, take a can [?] and bore a hole in it just like a shotgun with a little touchhole but bored so large that the hole is big enough, and then buy for 3 shillings worth of sulfur and likewise load it into the can. When you have rubbed it apart and then take some dry tinder and *raspefnas* that is dry, cut it small so that it will fit in the touchhole, and when you have loaded it, then put the piece of *berk* in the mole's hole and light the sulfur in the little bored hole. When it has taken light, then cover it over, bury it in such a way that it covers it, but bury it so that it will be tight so that the smoke will go into the Earth, into the mole's hole, until the smoke has time to get to where he is, for he'll either die or will roam away from the smoke that is so poisonous, bu it may be that he'll jump up onto the ground. Then you should be ready to smash him dead at once. Then you'll know where the mole has its entries.

14. For stomach ailments. When you have stomach ailments such as vomiting or diarrhea or whatever stomach ailments it may be that troubles you, you should send a message to the apothecary and buy for .8 crowns Bco: [bicarbonate?] and take internally both morning and evening around 10 or 12 drops each time from a standard dropper.

15. If you want to take away liquor! When you come to a house where they distill! Then take care that you have *Makorge* tied up into a fine cloth, and tie around it with a fine thread, then hang the cloth in amongst the pipes, in the *stånn*, in the thread that it is tied up with: you do it so that it isn't seen.

16. If you have a fiancée, and you want to know if she is keeping on with another dear friend: Then on a Wednesday morning, if you happen upon a grey snake, then kill it; and if you have a knife on you, then when you have killed him, then cut off of him both the tail and the stinger,[181] and wrap them both up in a piece of paper, and put the blood of the [*Natblake*[182]] and anoint it three times with the blood on these [*sotter*] and say now you will get to see something else and spit once each time you anoint with the blood. When you have done this, that is written here, then you have also bound it. Then put it under under the bottom of your home's threshold, but do it in such a way that it isn't seen. Then ask her to come to you, and when she comes to you, then you will see if she holds true or not. If she [--- --- *][183] on the floor then let her

---

[181] Stingers were generally considered to be in the forked tongue, so here, the tongue is meant.

[182] Sw. *Nattblakka, Caprimulgus europæus*.

[183] Though this was blanked out in the transcript, other similar spells suggest that the word here being omitted is "pisses."

go from you, then she is a [-- --*]¹⁸⁴ but if she is staying true, then she is gifted with her pure maidenhood, without her even saying anything. Then you can do with whomever.

17. If you are fond of a girl, and she's not fond of you, then put a bat that is still living and cut off its left wing, and keep the blood that runs, but keep the wing and buy a cloth or gloves and put the blood that you have kept onto the cloth, and say: "You will become my beloved friend." and you should anoint 3 times and spit each time, and then from the wing you took to keep, you should scrape a little of the bone from the wing and take it and lay it in a little sugar cube, and when you buy an apple then stick a hole in the apple and say the girl's name or say "Anna Karin i Brosstorp, my beloved friend" and stick into the apple the sugar cube, and name her name, and do it so no one sees, and then give to her both that one among a bunch of apples and say here, "Karin, here you have some apples if you'd like."

18. As is said here about boys of 17 seventeen then girls can do with boys, but the girls should buy a little *Stånpas* and kneed it apart fine and put it in a fine *goro* and say his "N. N. Petter Carl. in the grips of my in the lifelong dearly beloved of my heart friend." And when you you are are [*sic*] out at the market and want to give him food, then put the *goro* and others and then a little on them like sugar and say: "Here you will have a little food, you might need that perhaps, such that you haven't had any food today." But look out that he eats all the *goro* that you put on it.

19. For both boys and girls who are unmarried, if you get some hexed liquor from each other that can hex you. Then when you take a little drink, then don't drink everything that if offered to you, but rather leave a little drop, and say inside yourself in silence "If you want to kiss me [--- ---*] then the poisonous [material] has no effect, but don't let on that you know anything, but rather just be mild and friendly towards the same even so.

This is written the 13th of Octobber [*sic*] 1841, both 16., 17., 18., 19.

20. To wit, given to aid in the cultivation of potatoes. So that you can cultivate potatoes so that they can become fully-grown in a month earlier than usual, namely, -- during the fall when you dig up your potatoes, sow the one's you want to place the pears [?]. Then arrange it so that you have like a large malt barrel and throw them into it, but it should sit at the south side of a wall, so that the sun can shine on it as much as you can manage in the fall, when there is beautiful daylight. But at nighttime you should cover them so that they are

---

184 *frilla*? whore?

free from the cold, and when it rains then cover them from the rain, but dry them as much you can manage and then keep them over the winter, well and safe from the cold. The most important is: in certain holes or in a cold cellar – the one after the other - --

When it comes to the first of May, or 8 or 14 days before, when it comes to be more beautiful daylight, then you may take up the potatoes that you kept from the fall, and dry them in the same way as you did in the fall, until you think that they will be like mill-balls, then you keep them inside until they've crawled (sent out shoots) a little, at the most in the beginning of the 10th week, then you put them in the driest field you have, or in a new field that is well prepared and *jypp*. And when you see the first sprouts come up then you tangle them. And then as quick as you can then dig them up with a little digging hook and then a few days before Midsummer then re-plow them with a single horse or a pair of oxen, but put them in heavy earth. Then you should fertilize with horse manure or sheep-shit, but if it is dry earth, then you should fertilize with hog- or cow manure. And the 26th or the 28th of June you should plow under the potatoes a third time and clean off the sprouts so that none of the manure comes up around the potato stand, but that they get fresh air around them and no grass roots should be in the shoots that will strangle the growth of the potato in the earth – this is written for the edification for each and every person who wants to enjoy potatoes and have the enjoyment of both the earth and in planting potatoes. The one who does this and doesn't spare his efforts with work that is spelled out here, his work and his travail will be blessed by God to his greatest benefit – and when you have herewith planted your potatoes as is revealed here, and you have pulled them in the best way, then when it comes around to the 9th or the 10th of July then you may begin to look at the so-called Planting Almanacs and then you can harvest your potatoes and then also your fall rye, in the well prepared potato-land in a good time of year in the middle of the month of August.

the 13th of October, 1841.

21. When somebody hexes your shotgun, then when you become aware, then set them right again, then you can take some grease and load it in your shotgun and as quick as that grease restores, then the one who has hexed the aforementioned shotgun will get a stitch until he talks with you and then you can bring him to fix it again. And when you take that grease out of the shotgun if you want him to get the runs [-- --*] then if you take yeast and put it in the shotgun, then he'll get [-- --*] until he comes to you. When the yeast first starts to have its effect in the shotgun, then he'll have the same in his stomach.

22. To hex a shotgun, here's how: you take a common pin that has been over a corpse and put it into the barrel of the gun in both ends, and in the lock, or you only stick a finger into the mouth of a corpse, and then stick your finger into both ends of a shotgun barrel, and into the lock, then it is probably hexed.

23. The one who has hexed your shotgun. You can load your hexed shotgun with gunpowder and spit three times and a bullet and spit three times. Then take your shotgun and go to an ant hill and shoot the shot so that the bullet remains in the mound. Then take a medium pen (feather?) and put it in the hole. Then the one who has hexed the shotgun will have a stitch until you remove the pin from the hole.

24. During Holy Week[185] you shouldn't grind either grain or any flour because your sheep will be wandering about so that they will be running in circles.

25. When you dry-burn yourself then right away take some fresh cow manure and put it on the burned sore for two days. Then buy some bluing and put it all over where the sore is burnt. Then there will be new skin. It will be completely healed in fourteen days if you keep it out of the cold.

26. If you want to hex a horse. When you are with someone on a trip, when you graze the animal either from in front or back, then say: "You shall not ride or drive farther than there, or else the Devil will sit in my heart.-- "

27.th When you get mealy bread then when you get it and see that it [*myglar sig*] put it in water for an hour, then you can bake it hard.

[28.][186] When you get lice, then buy *sabbadil* seeds and have them on your body, and they'll disappear – for sores, put rancid lard in water and smear it on until it heals – for rats take crayfish in the month of August and let them sit until they go bad, then take a cup and grind them up to a powder and spread it on the floor where you want to get the rats to leave.

[29.] To wash an animal, buy a measure of [*stansip/salläbb*.]

[30]. To dull pain.
Grab hold of the limb that aches and then say both the person's name who has the pain as well as his father's name. Then recite like so: "Your limbs shall neither suffer nor ache since Jesus Christ is supposed to have suffered pain and ache for you and your limbs and for all the sinful people in the world, suffered

---

[185] Dymbeldaghar, or modern Sw. Stilla veckan, is the week immediately preceding Easter. This is called "Holy Week" in English.

[186] From here on, the items are no longer numbered in the manuscript. I have continued numeration for ease of reference.

pain and ache, suffered pain and ache, in the name of God the Father and of the Son and of the Holy Ghost amen. In the name of God the Father and of the Son and of the Holy Ghost amen. In the name of God the Father and of the Son and of the Holy Ghost amen. Then the one you're reciting over will leave you for a walk, and you should thank him, but he shouldn't thank you.

[31.] For someone who is extravagant with drinking liquor, then one can do in this way, that when a woman dies, then take yourself [*vid Pas*] a virgin liquor and pour down the corpse's throat three times, and then take the same liquor and give it to the one so that he drinks of that which has been in the corpse's mouth, then there'll be no liquor in him as long as there are any of the corpse's remains. But don't let the one you're giving this to know it, then it won't help.

(Grönnelid, the 5th of February, 1846 Petter Johan Johansson, written in my own hand.)

[31.] When you have to beg for food – when a male person has to beg for food, then ask a lady to beg. Then instead of eating it up, it eat in three portions, and spit between each time, and say after you have eaten it all up "I believe that I am so stingy that I've eaten up the whole bagful" and you say this three times. Do so with a woman --.

[32.] If you want to know who will be your trusted friend for all time, then on a Wednesday you shouldn't eat any other food other than fried potatoes and salt. That whole day you may not eat anything else than this. If you dream that there has been someone with you during the night, and has given you something to drink in a silver vessel, that will be your beloved friend, -- but when it has been made ready, then they will boil eggs in sweet unpreserved milk in which there is no water, and eat them and herring and salt during the day. If you eat anything else, then it won't work.

[33.] When you hit or cut yourself, if you pick vetiver and put it in liquor then anoint the injury until it heals.

[34.] When you get a headache then buy some vinegar and apply it to your forehead and on some places on the head, then all the ache will go away.

[35.] To put a curse on a girl. When the girl sits and has a little child, then you should watch so that you take three hairs from her head, but you should do it such that she doesn't notice. That you take these three hairs from her head and weave them about a common pin. Then you bore a hole in a piece of oak and put the needle in it and then you plug up the hole. Then you go either on a Thursday night after the sun goes down, or on a Sunday morning before the sun comes up and put that bit of oak under a stone at the door of the church, so that when she goes to church she steps over that stone. Then she'll not get married, but when you go back and forth, you shouldn't look behind you, and you shouldn't tell anyone about it.

[36.] For the cough from a cold. Take and pick a juniper sapling and boil it in sweet milk and drink it as warm as you can tolerate, then the cough will loosen. You should cook it and drink it until it loosens.

[37.] Balsamic oil you take one or a few balsams and put them in a bottle until it melts to oil.

[38.] When you want to protect your horse so that no one will hex it. On Maundy Thursday morning cut yourself a [selltampar] from rowan (mountain ash) before the sun comes up and keep it in the stall, then no one will be able to hex that horse as long as you have such [selltampar][187]

[39.] When you get warts, then take an apple and [cut] it right in half, and rub it so that it gets soaked with blood. Then take and put three spits in the apple, and put it together again. Then put it over a door and don't look back at it until it is completely consumed, and when it disappears, then the warts will go away.

[40.] To hinder tree-growth, or to whither it away. This is accomplished by boring a hole in the tree trunk a little bit away from the root into the core, and put in three bits of vikterjol in the hole but bore it pointing downwards so that the bits run down to the core. Then plug it up with a solid wooden plug in the hole outside. Then that tree will wither away soon enough.

[41.] To take away the water out of wells or springs. This is accomplished through dropping a pan of mercury down a well or spring. If it isn't accomplished, then for a new thing – (?)

[42.] To conjure whoever you want to come to you in the night – This is accomplished like so: if you write the Our Father backwards in a circle, and say the person's name as well as the father's name "in the name of the Trinity in the name of God the Father and of the Son and of the Holy Ghost, you will come immediately tonight to me, you will be in a solitary room and never tell anyone about it."

---

187 *sel* (*sil*) is nostril, so perhaps nose-gay?

[43.] To shoe a misbehaving horse. This is accomplished if you smoke off a tile of the horse's tail, and tie a piece of shot to one end of it, and then put the shot into one of the horse's ears, but not all the way, but tie the other end around the horse's ear, then he'll stand still while you shoe him but make sure you don't let the shot go all the way down his ear, and get stuck, otherwise he'll be hexed.

[44.] To make yourself beloved by women. – You should be careful when a rooster loves a hen then grab both comb-feathers, the left you take and clip off the down of the feather, but the actual feather you take and shave it to a fine powder, and then mix it in with some fine spices so that it can't be seen. Then make something small to give your lover, but arrange it so that she eats it all up at once – back again to the right feather you prepare it so you keep it safe and put it someplace against your skin when you want to meet your beloved. But not when you are going to see someone else, but only to that one, for it doesn't work for more than one, because then it is all accursed.

The same means can be used only that the feathers are switched around, and in the same manner as before for boys.

[45.] To send "shot" onto a person whoever you wish.[188] – It is a useful item if you can arrange to get a human skull in the beginning of the month of May. You plant peas during the Summer, and it a sure secret hiding place, when the peas are well ripe in the Autumn you take them to keep for yourself, so that they won't be used for anything. When you want to soon at some person, then you load your shotgun as usual with gunpowder for ammunition and take then some of your planted peas instead of shot to load with, but before you shoot you should draw that person's picture in similarity and form, and then you say his and his father's name, and the three great Old Guys names,[189] and at the same moment you intend to shoot and have the shotgun in your hand and let off a shot fearlessly. Then that person will receive that shot in the place on his body that you hit on the picture.

For this means, you borrow a human skull at a certain time during which you are planting the peas, and with the condition under the plant that no one can take from it except he will remain standing there and will leave it thereafter the appointed time, surely.

---

188 The motif of using a human skull and planting peas in the eye sockets is common enough, though no mention is made here that the pea must be planted inside the skull to impart the efficacy.

189 The more common and religiously toned reference to the litany of reciting the "Three Holy Names" is substituted with the rather less formal, some might even say irreligious "de 3 stora Gubbarnas namn," "In the name of the Three Big Guys."

[46.] A means by which you can go wherever you want invisibly. – This can be accomplished in such a way that you take care to find a raven's nest that has eggs in it. Take care when they are hatched out and the chicks are a little stronger, then you take one of the chicks that is in the nest. Hang it on a branch in the tree for 2 days. Go back to the nest thereafter, but look out that you don't become afraid or quake at whatever you see. It isn't dangerous. Then you'll find a little stone in the hanging chick's mouth. Take it to keep and don't let anyone know it. When you want to go invisible, then take this stone under your tongue, then you will be successful.

[47.] To stop nosebleed. This is accomplished by your taking a milking stool and going behind the barn. Hit all four legs off of it, and let them lie there. Then let the blood that is flowing run through all 4 holes of the stool. Then you go in back of the barn and slam the same all four legs back in the milking stool in the same manner as the feet sat before. If it isn't accomplished, then repeat it.

[48.] To hex a horse. This is accomplished if you slip one or several shots, or mercury in the horse's ear, then he is probably thoroughly hexed so that he will die in time.

[49.] The art of shooting a troll-hare. This is accomplished by putting a little silver ingot into a bullet casing, then you load your proper shotgun with gunpowder as usual, and then the filled bullet, and then you shoot at the Troll hare.[190]

[50.] The art of throwing your cap so that no one can shoot a hole in it.[191] – This is accomplished by previously putting in 3 lice inside it, then no shot will hit it. The same thing is accomplished if you slip some barley grains and a crumb of bread into the rim.

[51.] To protect your sheep so that no fox, or bobcat (lynx) or wolf will take them. This is accomplished if one boils together Russian oil (?) and gunpowder on a slow coal fire and put into the same some rusty iron, so that it becomes like a thin porridge. And when it has cooled, anoint the sheep under

---

[190] Though the manuscript doesn't define "trollhare," Jan-Inge Wall's two volume work on "Mjölktjuvande väsen" gives many examples of them. Often, when shot, the *trollman* or *trollkvinna* who was thus transformed in order to steal the milk retains the injury thus inflicted, which in turn implicates them the following day.

[191] At first this seems a curious aim of a magical working, until one considers that when out hunting, one needed protection from the inadvertant fire of a companion or a rival hunter.

the shin and around the middle and over the back parts under the rump one time each month. Otherwise, it will be washed away in a lot of rainy weather.

[52.] To hinder things so that a girl can't decide to get married.
This can be accomplished if you take some hairs from her head and take 3 or 9 hairs and weave around a common pin, and wrap it up in a cloth, or in a piece of wood, and then put it someplace on consecrated ground, and say her name and her father's name, and then "You shall remain unmarried until I take this from here, in the name of God the Father and of the Son and of the Holy Ghost, amen." This is repeated 3 times and spit between each time. This will also be accomplished if one places it at the bottom of a stream that is running, because then the girl will be much more uneasy.

[53.] The art of winning a girl's complete love – This is accomplished in this way: that the first snake you see in Spring, you take it and put a little weight around him near the head. Then cut of both its stinger (here, the tail) and its tongue to keep. Then when you come together with your girl, then take and put the snake's stinger and tongue under your own tongue in your mouth, then give your girl repeated kisses. Then your wish will be accomplished. If it doesn't go like this, then renew your efforts.

[54.] If there is too little or bad butter when you churn. – Arrange it so that you get butter from another cow, and give it to your cow, then the butter will come back soon.

[55.] Means of healing those animals who eat wood. Buy at the apothecary some pulverized bonemeal for each animal, 25 *öre* for each, and a little less for smaller animals.

[56.] If sheep or other livestock suffer when you have purchased them = Then let the lady of the house herself give them their fodder to eat a few times dressed in just her apron. This is repeated several times until you accomplish your wish.

[57.] To hex away a fruit-bearing tree so that it withers away. This is accomplished if you carve away the bark all the way around the trunk into the tree's sap, so that the bark loosens from the trunk of the tree, then your wish will be accomplished.

[58.] To stanch bleeding. The Virgin Mary she stopped all streams and all the rivulets, just as surely I will stop the bleeding for you, N N, that wants to run so badly. In the name of the Father and of the Son and the Holy Spirit's name amen. – This is repeated 3 times and you spit between each time.

[59.] To hex good pigs. – This is accomplished if you drop down a vial of mercury into the ear. Open the vial in one end, put it then down into the ear, then the pig will be completely cursed. Mercury costs 8 *öre*. The same thing works to curse a horse.

[60.] For hens who lay and no one knows the place where the eggs are – You should pulverize a little fine salt. Then take the hen and open it up a little in the back end. Strew a little of the fine salt. Let it go again. Then when the salt begins to burn, then the hen will run quickly to where the egg is. Then follow quickly after it, and your wish will be accomplished.

[61.] To escape being hexed - This is accomplished if you recite this prayer entirely: "The Lord bless me and keep me. The Lord let his countenance shine upon me and be graceful to me. The Lord turn his face to me and give me eternal peace. In the name of God the Father and of the Son and of the Holy Ghost. Ammen.

[62.] To conjure so that a horse becomes so un-trainable that no one can train it but the horse is just un-trainable – This is accomplished by putting garlic into the nostril or the snout, so that it isn't seen. In the same way it works if you put a little human bone in the same way.

[63.] To see who of a couple will survive the other on a wedding day – This is given as a sign whichever of the couple first walks in under a turf roof, that one will be the first take with earth in the grave.

[64.] When someone has hexed the cow milk – Go about lighting up your baking oven as hot as you can. Then throw in some of the hexed milk into the hot oven and say the name of the one who has done this together with his father's name "You have hexed my milk in the name of God the Father and of the Son and of the Holy Ghost." Repeated 3 times.

[65.] To the one who has done me injury and I don't know who it is – For this you put a black cat's skull then 7 peas, and put one pea into each hole in the skull. Then bury in the earth and say: Who you are who have done this to me, will have no peace until you come to me and confessed it before me, before these peas grow.

[66.] For livestock that eat wood – It's a good thing to ask to get some wood from a church bell steeple, and file it to a fine powder, and then buy some pulverized bone-meal at the Apothecary for 12 *öre* for each animal. Then take the powder from the bell steeple wood, and mix everything together. Then divide it out to each animal in the evening towards night.

[67.] For drum-sickness[192] with horned cattle and sheep – Administer fresh yeast to the animal, and some human feces, and cut some of the hair around its "secret thing" but from an animal of the same sex as the suffering animal. Then administer internally a drop of some of the stomach contents of a newly slaughtered animal, and sometimes human urine and some paraffin oil. It will be better. Or renew your efforts or repeat –

MS 28

"SIGNERI OCH VIDSKEPELSE – 1751"
VÄRMLAND, FILIPSTADS BERGSLAGS DISTRICT,
PRESENT FERNEBO DISTRICT
SPELL-CASTING AND SUPERSTITION – 1751

I.

1. Excerpt from the judicial records, held at Philipstads-Bergslags Laga Winter Court in Philipstad, on the days recorded below in the year 1751.

January 24.
§ 66.
The same day: the Crown's Landholder the well respected Arvid Lundbeck accused the Farm Hand Annika Mattsdotter in service at Saxån village in Fernebo parish and district, because she shall have had much to do with spells and superstition, and therefore subjected to the duty according to the Law; and the Court found reasonable to demonstrate to the populace while this matter was held forth.

Annika Mattsdotter confessed her crime, which she had committed from ignorance, and to have learned such superstition in her childhood when she was tending her flocks, from another girl at Tomsjön, a farm in Gåsborn parish, in Fernebo district, who was called Brita and was living at the farmstead Sandsjön in Helleforss-Bergslag (Hellefors parish in Grythyttans village in Örebro county) who is now dead.

Upon examination, she said that she had not taught this to anyone else.

---

192 This could refer to an abdominal malady (*trumma*); a type of falling sickness (*trumla*) or something entirely different. I was unable to find a gloss for *trumsjukan* in either Rietz or elsewhere.

Was asked, upon whom she was used to put spells?

Answered: on the wife of the Collector Staffan Jönsson, Lena Johansdotter, at Saxån; but upon no one else, after she had come back into service at Saxån at Michael's mass; Continued also, that when the livestock had been bitten by snakes (hexed) she healed them, as she also did now with the livestock of the now deceased Johan Olson of Bergslag, at the time when she was employed there.

The court summoned the Dean the right venerable and widely-read Magister Mr. Christopher Risell[193] after, upon the estate inventory that year, this matter was raised, and Annika was quoted that she was more known to the Lord Dean, than she had done, and the Lord Dean has recorded everything that she had confessed. And her conjuring went like this, word for word as follows:

For Sprain: Christ traveled through the trail, his foal got a sprain, joint to joint, bone to bone, blood to blood, that say I in three names, of the Father and the Son and the Holy Ghost. Then, the Our Father, etc.

For shot: The evil one went on the mount and tightened up his bow, what will you shoot? Folk and Cattle, whatever comes before me;

No, you shall shoot logs and stones, said as well in three names, Father, Son and Holy Ghost. Our Father, etc.

To quell pain: God, do not allow more pain and suffering to come over this wound than came over the wound of the Sodomites, this I say as well in three names, God Father, Son and Holy Ghost. Our Father who art etc.

For "worm" bite: You "worm" you "worm," you shall go into that wood where no one dwells, in the lake where no one rows, you shall go under an earthfast stone, you shall be no harm to any Christian person, this I say in three names, of God the Father and of the Son and of the Holy Ghost. Our Father who art in heaven...

For snakebite: A little child lies in a maple thorn, little done, little found out, then to completely nothing. – but for snake bite, you don't recite the Our Father.

The Lord Dean entered, handing down the following decision: that, when this matter was first brought to the attention of the catechismal inquiry, Annika Mattsdotter was of the opinion that she did not sin in the matter, since she used nothing other than God's word and prayers. She can of course read in books and her lessons in Christianity, has and now become educated in this circumstance, so that she now has other ideas about this than she did before. She was exhorted to say who else she had helped with her spells?

---

[193] C. R. born in 1687, pastor in Philipstad in 1743, dean over Näs county's contract in 1745, died in 1745; the son Olof, a lawyer, was ennobled in 1788 with the name Risselschöld, according to Carlstad's Bishopric's Notes by Johan Hammarin, II. Carlstad, 1847, 18 ff.

Answered, the Smith Clas Hero at Saxån, who had sprained his leg, which also became healed.

Addended that the shoemaker Lars Håkansson at Dalskogen (a village in Kumla district, Örebro county) shall have asked her to perform spells, since the Lord Dean had educated her regarding this sin; -- but she had not done this, but rather shown him the door. --

Was asked: if she had done harm to anyone using her spells, either to those who worked against her, or others, who asked her to do ill to folk or cattle?

Answered: I would not know how to do it, and I have not done any harm to folk or cattle either.

The aforementioned explained, that she was not known for such, which the Dean also explained.

County-man Lundbeck maintained, that Collector Staffan's wife and the smith Clas Hero should be fetched, that the legal case might be advanced.

The 26th of January.

§ 75

In the District Court the 24th of this month the case was advanced against the Farm Hand Annika Mattsdotter, accused of using spells; The Smith Clas Hero and the Wife Lena Johansdotter came forth, and the former alleged that Annika had not recited or conjured over him, as far as he understood; but, in the act and with the intent, he sent for her that she might heal him, since she had the reputation that she could do spells and heal sprains, and she took hold of his foot and anointed him, but even so, he lay for a month unable to rise.

Annika Mattsdotter maintained that she anointed Hero with lard. Lena Johansdotter said, that she had heard tell, that Anna Mattsdotter could conjure away pain; and as she had pain in her chest, then she sent for her, and she looked at her chest, but she was not heard to recite anything, and she didn't give her anything for the trouble either.

Annika Mattsdotter maintained that she never received anything for doing spells for anything, and that she didn't previously know that it was forbidden, since she did no harm to anyone with it.

It was inquired of her, if she hadn't recited spells over shot, as she had elaborated that she was knowledgeable about?

Answered: no, for that I have not been sought out. But for Snake- and "Worm-" bite, she maintained that she had conjured, when she tended her flocks with the now deceased Johan Olsson's cattle at Saxån, without the knowledge of the people of the household.

Was asked: how can the cattle get "Worm-" bite?

Answered: the animal rots them away.

Read and witnessed.

For further confessions neither Annika Mattsdotter, Hero or Lena Johansdotter was able to do so.

The inquiry was read out, and neither the accuser nor the accused had anything to add. Wherefore the Court considered the case, and rested with the following

Result:
Since Annika Mattsdotter is convinced to have performed spells and superstition, as well as used both on people and cattle, then she should, according to Chapter 2 § 2 "Misdeed's Code," fine twenty-five dahlers of Silver coins; but in case of inability to pay, according to the Punishment-Code, Chapter 5, § 4, to be punished with eight days imprisonment on water and bread. And since both the Smith Clas Hero and the wife Lena Johansdotter were not able to deny that they sought healing with Annika Mattsdotter, who was sentenced for Conjuring; then they should, according to the previously named Law, be fined 5 dahlers in silver each. Thus according to the Legal Code Chapter 25, § 5 this legal matter and judgement of His Royal Highness and the Götha Supreme Court of the National Most-worthy Court is attested by the undersigned. Year and days as were recorded previously

Upon the District Court's ways: Sture Sandelin, (Seal and Counter seal)

Göta Supreme Court's resolution – in the form of remarks (with two handstyles) on the first page of the record in the middle and at the bottom on the same page:

(1.) done April 16th, 1751 in the morning.

(2.) Performing spells while set free,
7 p. of rice instead of water and bread. In accordance with H-br., November 16, 1748. Without signature.

Recorded from Göta Hofrätts arkiv. Handlingar rörande trolldom och annan vidskepelse, 2, 1720, 1731–1754, i RA-s Östermalmsavdelning.

MS 29

SKARA VETERINÄRBIBLIOTEK MS 1051

When the pall-bearers are at the place that's dug out, put this letter in the grave.

I, Anders Olofson, make here, with full knowledge and of my free will, that I sell both body and soul, and deny the holy Trinity and baptism thirty six is here after the fourteenth of April at 10 o'clock in the morning, if I receive that which I wish for: First in Stockholm these numbers will win the highest prize that can be won Nr. 5, 8, 34, 39, 45, 53, 54, 58, 52, 63; and for the second, that I will be well liked by all, both high and low, and all girls will be enamored of me so that I get that which I wish for, and luck in all that which I undertake. If I get all this, then it is and will be as written, then I give to you Billiam your belongings; but if I don't get it, then I deny you completely. The 26th of June, 1785. Anders Olofson

Outside the writing:
For the manuscript, Lord Billiam, the Over-devil of Hell.

NB. The letter was written in blood.

MS 30

ULMA 984, JUGAS OLOF JONSSON, 1873–74 DAL
NÅS SOCKEN, WESTERN DALARNA

1. For snakebite.
"The grass snake lay in the tuft of grass with a poisonous thorn from the poisonous tongue. That's how quick God's word drives out snakes, as the sun drives out dew and fog. In three firm names: God Father, Son and Holy Ghost."

2. For predators.
I put my cattle under a tree, that Mary put hers, in the name of three persons: God Father, Son and Holy Ghost. God preserve them from all clawed animals

that are in the woods. Count them up, then Our Father, everything recited three times.

3. In another way.
Your mouth will be so totally shut as Jonas, when he lay in the whale's belly. This shall be recited three Friday evenings before May Day, three times each evening.

4. To get fish.
One dips the bait-hook in bat's blood or takes a bit of a white snake and stuff it into a purse or anoint the hook with black-water.[194]

5. For envy.
Jesus went on the road. Then he met the Devil and the one suffering from envy. "Where are you going?" – "Up to the farmer's farm to suck people and animals to the ninth knee." – "No, I shall show you another way, to him who has sent you. There you shall crouch and bow." In three firm names: God Father, Son and Holy Ghost.

6. To stop bleeding.
You blood of man shall stand fast, as Christ stood at the River Jordan, where they baptized Christ, and where the Devil stood at the portal to Hell.

7. To take the strength from others.
One has them cut their nails with a knife, but they may not carve anything afterwards with the same knife, and buy the knife from them, and when it has become dark, one walks three times counterclockwise around their house.

8. To transfix someone in a field.
One walks around an earthfast stone counterclockwise three times and says then by name the person you want to transfix, and say where the field is located where you want to transfix him, and at what time.

9. To get girls to come to me.
I take a bat and put it under a salt pile for 24 hours, and then I take it and rip it up and take a drop of blood from it which it has, and throw it on the one I want, and say that she will come to me at whatever time I want.

10. To get hens to lay.
You take hare feces in the month of March and give them or give them half of a lung from a many-colored horse.

---

[194] According to Sjödahl, this is a substance found at an apothecary.

11. To retrieve stolen goods.
One takes a newly laid egg and ties a green silk ribbon around it, and then one puts it on glowing coals and says the name of him who one thinks shall have stolen it.

12. If the horses fall on their knees.
You take a three-sided piece of bread and cut a hole in the rump (tongs?) and let a drop drip on each corner and give it to them.

13. To get cattle to follow you wherever you want.
You take a triangular piece of bread under the left arm and let it remain there, until it becomes warm, and then you take it counterclockwise around you three circuits and then give it to them.

14. To get money.
On New Year's Morning at dawn you go to the barn and take a sharp knife with you, and put a cross in the back of the un-castrated ram, and then you shave a cross on the scrotum and take the wool and put it in a place so that it won't be lost. And when you put it there, you should wish for as much money as you want, and then at sundown you go back and take the money.

15. To create discord between people.
One takes three old brooms and walks up to the roof right over the bed where they sleep, and tears apart the brooms and throws bits in every direction, and says: "Now the devil will haunt, and between you be quarrels and discord."

16. In another way.
You have two cats tear at each other, and take the hair that they tear out, and put between them between whom you want to sow discord.

17. To get someone (women) to become exhausted, when she lies near any man.
To dip a morsel of bread in baptismal water and give it to them, or to give them sow's milk, or touch them with a stick with which one has killed a snake.

18. Another way from the one previously mentioned to get cattle to follow you.
You stuff a piece of bread on you, when you go to "*skrift*,"[195] and then give it to them.

---

[195] "*när man går till skrift*" sounds to me like an idiom.

19. Cure for water sickness.
When water-sickness begins to show itself, then you take aspen sapling roots and boil them in a kettle of water, until it becomes a quart. Drink it then a little at a time.

20. To catch fish.
One dips the hook in heron's grease.

21. To create discord between people.
One gives them liquor all at once, or turns the footprints backwards after them.

22. Another way to get money.
One writes on a piece of paper, as much money as one wants, and puts it in the woods, where there are many stones, and then the third day one returns and takes the money.

23. To cure all sicknesses.
One takes from the sick one's clothing and goes to a crossroad and throws it there, and says: "Tevo salvo go. Pauli salig go. Feberaktigo. Ack enoliam, that is to say Health cure, travel cure, the Savior's faith, Botobo," or take three hay straws from the sick one's bed and throw it at the crossroad.

24. To dream.
One ties a morsel of bread and some garlic to the left arm, or boils a hedgehog in a gruel and takes it with him to bed.

Belongs to Jugas Olof Jonsson in
Nås and Öfverborg 1874

[BEGINNING OF SECOND QUIRE]

25. For Finnshot.
"There stood an old man on a high mountain with an 'arm-brush tree.' Don't shoot people, and don't shoot cattle, and don't shoot backwards." Then one recites the Our Father.

26. For snake-breath[196] and snake-bite.
"Poison, tongue, pus and tooth, all poison will disappear, before the sun runs down."[197]

---

[196] Sw. *ormblåst*, the snake has blown its venom on its victim as opposed to having bitten them.
[197] According to the editor, Jonsson gave the following oral instructions: "One takes a buttonhole, and sticks through that hole into the blisters that the snake's venom has produced, while

27. For sharp things.
The bear he was the first originator, who discovered iron and steel. In the Holy Trinity: You chaff, you shall not sting anymore, you shall go away like chaff.

28. In other way.
I will measure for needle: it won't sting, it won't burn. In the name of God the Father and of the Son and of the Holy Ghost.

29. For envy.
The cows stood there by the path and mooed. Then Jesus came and asked her why she was bellowing so. "How can I not bellow, when they have sucked the marrow out of my bones and the milk out of my udder."

30. To stop bleeding.
You shall stay, as the woman stayed in Hell, who made lye on Saturday.

31. To take away boils.
Blue worm, you will wither and fade like a straw. I put you in stone, and you will be a danger to no man.

32. To transfix snakes.
The Virgin Mary sent me a wrapping to bind this naughty snake to all liver and all lungs and in all his tongues.[198]

33. To set boils on someone.
To give him, something to eat, and recite: "I put on N. N. one, two, three or four boils. He shall have them for three weeks. In three firmaments' the Father's, Son's and the Holy Spirit's.

34. In another way.
To go to an earthfast stone on a Friday evening and take a hammer with you and say: "I put on N. N. one, two, three, four boils; he will have them for three weeks," and then strike three times with the hammer.

35. To never be without money.
Take a swallow egg and hard boil it, and then put it back and let it lie for two 24-hour days, then go back and take a root and stick it into the pouch.

---

one recites this."
198 Jonsson gives the following instruction: "One goes three times counterclockwise around the snake and recite each time the following:"

36. In another way.
Go to the swallow's nest and take a stone and tuck it in you. (?)

37. To get the cattle to eat the fodder.
Buy 25 *öre* of fenugreek, 25 *öre* of crab powder and 12 *öre* of ambergris.

38. In another way.
The noble and cattle powder.[199]

39. To become invisible.
Go to a snake pit and take a snake stone or shoot a crane before May Day and look for a stone in its head.

40. To get the animals to eat.
Take flour three times out of each flour barrel, take glowing coals three times out of the oven and take nine mouse feces and pluck hair from the left shoulder and burn it up over the other.[200]

41. To liberate them from trolls.
Take flour three times out of each flour barrel, burning coals three times (from the oven) and pick nine kinds of flowers in the summertime, then pull hair from the left shoulder and burn it up over it and recite the Our Father, then take a page from a book upon which is "father" and put it in the barn.

42. If the animals shit themselves (i.e., have diarrhea).
Take birch bark and give it to them.

43. If anyone milks with a nipple. (?)
Wash them about the belly and animal skin.

44. For a cough in animals.
Give them cheese.

45. For a cough in people.
Ginger, tallow and drink.

---

[199] Sw. *ädla och boskapspulver*. *Ädel* is a generic name, called so for its considerable properties, though seldom identified as any one specific substance. *Boskapspulver* or Cattle Powder "*pulvis pecorum griscus*" is another such substance.

[200] According to oral information given by Jugas Olof Jonsson to Sjödahl, "Ashes of the burnt hair are stirred with a knife in the rest of the mixture. After this is recited the Our Father. The recitation happens in the same way as when conjurations are recited over "flour and salt."

46. Two methods for toothache.
When the toothache starts in a tooth with a cavity, the first simple means to make use of is a filling of *gutta-percha* paper.[201] It is softened in boiling water, and the soft mass is pressed into the tooth. It hardens soon and can remain there for years.

A good material is Spanish Fly boil until a brown liquid with a sharp odor. Not more than moistening the painful place with this liquid is needed, and the pain will often abate for a long time. With weak people this means of healing induces a somewhat feverish condition, but its effect against toothache is good.

47. To stop bleeding.
One has a 6-öre that one shouldn't have to look for, and puts it on the bleeding wound.

48. For Finnshot.
"I conjure in nine brushes for troll-shot and for finn-shot." Then the Our Father. Everything is recited three times.

49. If the cattle are hexed.
Cut a cross on their rump and take blood onto three pieces of bread and give to them.

50. So that they won't be hexed.
Take tar on the ring finger and with it draw a cross inside the left nostril.

51. To become strong.
One takes a half-quart bottle full of wine, and put it in an anthill. Then one goes back for three Good Friday evenings and takes a nip each evening. Then one takes up the bottle and drinks as fast as one can. In the end, one will become as strong as the Devil himself.

52. To open locks.
You go to a woodpecker's nest and stuff inside it moss that grows on exposed bedrock while it is out, until he comes back again. Then, when he flies off again, you should wait until he comes back when he will have a straw in his mouth that he carried with him, he'll put it in the moss, then drop it. Then you should take it and stick it in a keyhole, then they'll open all by themselves.

---

201 A tough plastic substance from the latex of several Malaysian trees (genera Payena and Palaquium) of the sapodilla family that resembles rubber but contains more resin and is used especially as insulation and in dentistry.

MS 31

ULMA 36365
"SALOMONISKA MAGISKA KONSTER"
NOTTEBÄCK-GRANHULT PARISH, SMÅLAND

* * *

1. To transfix a bird in its place.
First you can look for the tree wherein the bird has its place to play or the place where it stays over night; then when the bird has flown away to its nest, take earth from three graves of stillborn children, and a little out of the mouth of one of them, and mix it together; and when you go around the place where you want the bird to be transfixed, then you should draw a four-rimmed circle, and on it spread a little of the dirt, and say: I (with both your and your father's name) bind you to this place before 8 o'clock with words and earth, with my 10 fingers and with 12 of God's angels, and then recite the Our Father in the

four corners backwards four times; but whatever you do, don't look back when you leave there; this must happen in the name of God the Father and Son and Holy Ghost, Amen. 3 times.

2. To be able to triumph over them who say they are untouchable by sword or blows. Then you should, wherever you find such a man, prepare yourself with a ring that is used in the consecration of three couples, which is put on the long (middle) finger of the right hand, and a key that has gone on in three generations and a little *Ligusticum levisticum* root; if you want to hit with a sword or saber a hard person, then you should look for a man who is dead by sword or if it was a bullet, and taking hold of the glazing off the body, and the clothes, and put it in the hilt and take as well 3 or 9 hairs from his head and tie around the saber-hilt, then one can order one's saber to make as deep a wound as you want; beforehand you can dig up a hole between two walls that are quite near to each other, and drag your saber under it, but whatever you do, don't touch the dirt, that should remain untouched.

3. To get your shotgun to be able to shoot far and so that no one can hex it. Then you should take from the dirt that the priest with his spade has thrown on a wife, who had identical twins, to that add ashes of a juniper tree as well as the heart of a bat and three snake-stingers, as well as prepared mercury and three grains that are whole and unharmed from the mill, and then a hole is borred under the point of the Swan-screw, and this is put down into the Stock, sewed in a piece of cloth from a cap of one who has been decapitated; in the same way a cloth from the right glove on the flint, and a little of the star from the tree ashes, in the name of God the Father and of the Son and of the Holy Ghost. Amen. 3 times.

4. For good memory.
Take the gall of a frog, dry it in the sun together with these Wittenberg Letters, written in rooster-blood:

tie it under your left arm, then you will have a good memory, as long as you let it remain under your arm for over a half a year.

5. If you want to have strong hair growth.
Take the brain of a black cat and mix it in vinegar and mix it well together and smear it on the hair and head one time each month for an entire year, then you will find that you have long, beautiful hair, that all will admire it.

6. To receive a beautiful and lovely face.
Take blood of a nixie and boil it in horse urine and sweet milk together, then wash yourself with it. Then you will see with joy your white and beautiful skin.

7. For a man to get a woman.
Write you and her name on an apple, cheese or nutmeg, with these words: Obera mater Dulcans tibi [symbols] qveror julus.

8. To get a good voice.
Take mercury and saffron and the jaw of a cuckoo, and grind it together and anoint your chest each month for an entire year.

9. To get white hands.
Take *Ligusticum levisticum* and soak in old beer, and wash your hands with it, then you will find that they will become white.

10. For cough.
Take hemp-seeds and garlic and soak them in milk and drink it warm – helps.

11. For wounds and stings.
Take fire-ants and boil them in vinegar, and tie on the side where the bite is.

12. For randiness.
Take linden bark and put it to soak in juniper-drink (gin?) for three days, and wash the limb with it, and drink a large mug of milk with poppy seeds.

13. For wisdom
Write these Wittenberg Letters with rooster's blood

and put it under your left side, when you lie down to go to sleep, then it will be revealed to you what will happen and occur in the month following.

14. To drive away tuberculosis.
Take [gråbo], milk and bloodroot and sweet raspberries. Boil them in water for three hours and mist a little white honey in it and drink it as hot as you can tolerate – helps.

15. To stop a nosebleed.
Take borax and soak in water and make yourself a plug of linden shavings, and soak it well in the same water, and stick it way up your nose. Then recite the Our Father 3 times backwards and make yourself 3 [blogdar] of juniper wood, and let it bleed on it and put them on a hard stone, hold it over a fire until it is dried, then put them up on a ridge pole, then it will stop. [Hagon.]

16. To have female companionship at night.
Take a snake stinger and a sewing needle which hasn't been used before, and put the stinger into the eye of the needle and keep it in a cat skull; or lobster blood and keep it in a mare's skull until you need it; when you want to have her come to you, then take the needle with the stinger and stick it through her girdle, then she will come to you at whatever time you set your mind to, and say: Ram. grin fil.

17. To recite away toothache.
I stop your toothache N.N. that you have, I bind you to the shore of the ocean, as Our Lord bound all unclean spirits at the shores of Hell, and this in the name of God the Father and of the Son and of the Holy Ghost, Amen. 3 times.

18. To retain a bird area, so that no one but me will be able to shoot.
When you come out into the middle of the area, then take the knife and cut up a turf under the left foot and turn the same turf over; and then say: No one will encounter any life in this bird area and this for as long as it takes grass to grow on this turf." And then put your right foot on the same turf and recite three times the Our Father; then no human being on earth will encounter life in this area other than me.

19. To have good luck in hunting.
Take a porcupine or hedgehog and cut it up and take the lard out of it, and anoint the shotgun with it, both the iron in the barrel and outside, then you will have good luck in hunting afterwards.

20. To reserve a fishing place on land.
Take three stones from the vault in the church and a little mercury in three

feathers, and tie one feather to each stone with a fiber, and then you drop the rocks out before the fishing spot. As you drop the first stone, say: Sexeren!; when you drop the second, then say: Hagelton!; when you drop the third, then say: Gnugul!

21. To catch fish with a hook.
Take worms and put them in dirt, which is taken under the floor of the pig-sty, and let them lie overnight and skim the cream from sweet milk and pour it on them, which the fish will gladly take.

22. To catch fish with your hands.
Take heron lard and melt it in a pan and take woman's milk and let it sit until there is cream on it, skim off that cream and mix it with the lard and stir together and soak your hands in the woman's milk, and allow them to dry in the sun; and when they become dry, cover them with the lard and then go into the water, the fish will come.

23. To catch fish with a net.
Take a piece of cloth from the cloth that lies on the altar and tie it on the net with a [*fixsa*] in it. Then go to the lake on a Thursday evening; and when you put out the net, then say 116 to 119 Ramgrubi Gardi, in good faith I cast out my net, as the poor chosen apostles of God did, and recite in good faith the Our Father 3 times.

24. On robbery.
If someone steals something from you, then take a shaving of where the stolen goods were sitting, or from the room, and write these characters with snake's blood:

go to the woods and put the shaving under an evergreen root, in the name of God the Father and the Son and the Holy Ghost, Amen, 3 times. on a Thursday morning before the sun comes up, then the thief will have no peace either night or day, walking or standing, sleeping or waking, until he carries back that which he has stolen.

25. To make yourself invisible.
Take a water rat (*Lemmus amphibius*) and cut it up, take the heart out of it, and cut these characters and put it three Sunday mornings on the altar, and then tie it under your left arm, then no one will see you.

26. To poke out the eye of a thief.
Make yourself a copper nail, before the sun comes up and paint an eye on the wall, and hit the nail into it, and hit three strikes and say: "I conjure you forth from Hell and chamber of sufferings, Bjälsebub, I conjure you Lusiferd will all your company, as well as friends and kinfolk, and this in the name of God the Father, Son and Holy Ghost, Amen. Hit the nail again, then recite these words: *Saluk osta bore helken talis Biälsebub* is a prince for all devils. I conjure you up all you devils in the name of the Highest God, and by his righteousness that is the holiest of all, and by the foot of the sun, and by the coming judgment on the last day. Then genuflect for these words Eli Eli Eli. Hit the nail and recite the same words: Saluck osta bore helken talis Biälsebub. When this shall happen, it should be on a Sunday morning before the sun comes up.

27. So that a virgin will love you.
Take a swallow tongue and put it under your left foot, the virgin, that you trample back on your heels, she will love you excessively.

28. To get a woman to say everything that she has done. Take the head of a snakeskin and the dung of a flying bird, burn it all together to ashes and spread the same ashes on her head, then she will say everything that she has done.

29. To hex a shotgun. Take lovage, cow dung and stuff it into the shotgun barrel, then the shotgun will never shoot right or take a life.

30. To keep a bird hunting ground so that no one by I will be able to shoot. Go out on a Sunday morning before the sun comes up, go to where the area is, take an oak stake and put it under an evergreen bush, write these words on the stake with blood from your right little finger O O O ♍ F ☉ △
and when you put the stake in, then say;
    Salten Filer Kamus
then no one but I will be able to take life there.

31. To make her sick.
Write these words on bread and give to her to eat:

gamler Vargax anagax Sargengax." The person must eat these words on bread and the dog these four-sided pieces of bread.

| Aron Hagon | Norgon Bargon | Bragon Fragon |

32. To find out in which room one's possessions are situated.
Take a juniper shaving or a rowan shaving on a Sunday or a Thursday morning, before the sun comes up, right at the moment when night gives way to day. If you take a rowan shaving, then it is best to get it on Maundy Thursday morning, right at the break of day, but if you take a juniper shaving, then it is best to get it on Easter day, before the sun comes up, and let the bark remain on it, and draw these characters with the blood from the comb of a white rooster; but first is should be written with a needle or sewing needle, which has first been stuck into a black toad, and draw these:

then this should be written with blood from a white rooster's comb, but on the juniper shaving, 9 points of regret should be put on the outside of the shaving. This shaving should not be cut with iron, knife or steel, but rather ground or broken off, and fix it so that it doesn't fall on the ground. When you come to the place where your possessions are, with the aforementioned shaving, you won't be able to hold it in your hand. But best to dig up your belongings from the earth between Maundy Thursday night and Good Friday, as well as Easter Day or Midsummer night, preferably between 12 and 1 is the best. Then you should have on you along with the shaving: genuine good musk, garlic, and the name I. H. S. written. Otherwise a type of powder for the sick is used, to spread around the room by a silver ring that has been through a wedding three times, then the shaving is filed together with the garlic, and sulfur is ground together with the silver, and spread around the room where the belongings are kept. In the same way you can make a circle around the room with a sword, that a man has borne, and then stick it down into the earth, then no sickness has the power to take it away.

33. To get whoever one wants as a wife.
Take a bat (*Vespertilio murinus*) and cut it up. There will be a drop of blood in the heart. Take it along with the drop of blood on your little finger, and mix it together and write these words on your right hand.

the virgin you take into your embrace, she can never leave you.

34. So that a virgin will not become pregnant.
Take mercury for 4 *öre* and two snake skulls and grind up the snake skulls to a

powder and take 3 hare droppings and the powder and the mercury and mix it together in beer, and let her drink, then she won't become pregnant, that you shall be certain of

Hagon Hergon

35. So that a virgin will undress you.
Take a piece of her under-bindings and dip it in hare's blood along with three hairs from her head, and fold it into the cloth, and put it in a lamp until it burns. Then she will take off your clothes.

36. So that no bug will have the power to bite you, even if there were never as many.
When you go to rest and lie down, then take up your knife and stab it over you in the panel, and while you are stabbing the knife, then say:
Branus bites.

37. To free yourself from fleas in the bed.
Take a bridle ring and a horse-hoof and throw them under the bed then the fleas will have no power to sting you.

38. To drive out lice from clothing.
Take some mouse-soap, which is a plant that grows on a coffin board, and go to the lakelands on a Sunday morning before the sun comes up, and wash your entire body with the same mouse-soap, then no louse will be able to thrive on your body.

39. To administer to a dog, so that he will be good to take with you in the woods.
Take a calf lung and cut it into four pieces as well as four square pieces of bread, write on the bread the following words:

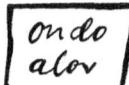 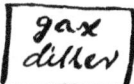  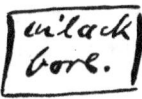

write on the bread with hare's blood and give the dog a bit of lung, tease a little each morning for 4 mornings, begin with a Thursday morning, then the dog will never tire and never let the game loose until he get a hold of it.

40. To shoot to death your enemy, as if he were not far away.
Load your shotgun with saltpeter and sulfur and water and take a little of a [äfläte] and take hair from your head and fold the [äfläte] into the hair, and put

it down into the shotgun and go to the woods and shoot three shots; the last shot that you shoot, the one you are shooting for, will be dead.

41. To reveal game in the woods.
Then you should first shoot at the target of 3 of your salvation treasures;[202] when you shoot the last shot, then you will notice three drops of blood on the place. Take them and smear them on the shotgun barrel, then you will have any game you wish come up to you; but don't take for than three animals in a day, otherwise the art will tire.

42. To bind the animals in the forest.
Take a feather quill from a turkey and pour some woman's milk into it and mercury, and stop up the hole with some wax that has run from the altar candles, and fasten a claw of a cat; when you find out where the animal is, then fasten the feather with the claw on a hurdle-pole, then the animal will stop.

43. For good luck when playing either the dice or with cards.
Take a bat's blood and mix into [your?] blood, and write these words:

[handwritten symbols: ⁊ ⌐⁊ ꝗ 4 ♃ ♀ anex 9.9.00]

44. To win at the lottery.
Take money that a whore has earned on a Sunday night from men, and put it into the lottery, then you will win.

45. For good luck with horses.
Take lard from a hedgehog and mercury together and bake into a cake and give the horse to eat, then he will thrive well and no one can hex him.

46. To give a horse strength.
Take a nail that was in a gallows, and make a ring of it in the kiln, that you can put on your thumb, then he will be straining and lively, so that you can hardly sate him.

47. To cause thieves to bring back home.
Take a coin that a whore has earned on a Sunday night with a man, and go to the water, that runs from south towards north on a Thursday evening and throw the coin into the water and say: I conjure you water *olansgält*, I conjure you *lusiferd*, with all your company, so that you take my gift so that the thief

---

202 Could this be the Bible, the Psalmbook/Hymnal and the Confession (curriculum for confirmation)?

will have no peace night or day, sleeping or waking, riding or walking, or in any way whatsoever, until he takes back home that which he has stolen.

48. For wisdom
Take a snake, that is black and burnt to ashes Simoniada, take walnut bark and burn it up also. Spread the same ashes on your head, then it will be revealed to you what happens and will happen, and what your end will be.

49. To catch a *lindorm*[203] or a white snake.
If you find out where a snake has its nest someplace, at a mound where he keeps himself, then go there on a midsummer night and arrange a meeting with him, saying: here in this meadow I arrange a meeting with this snake and in this place, and at that moment, put a knife in the ground. At the hour of 12 o'clock and no later, you will meet me and that in the name of God the Father, the Son and the Holy Ghost amen. 3 times. Then arrange it so that you have a cloth that has been on the head of a child, after the priest or immediately after the priest poured water on it, and when the snake comes then grab it with the cloth, then it will have no power to move; then go home with the snake, but be careful that you don't let him go. Then take a cooking pot and put it on the fire with water in it, and put a lid on it. Then let him cook for as long as you think that the broth won't be too much – look out that no one comes and lifts the lid on you. Then drink of the same broth, then you will be so wise that you will know what happens and what will happen in the whole world, and how long you will live, and as well what is happening in Hell and in the Kingdom of Heaven, and what will be.

50. A very useful herb (*Herba serpentina* filis mas)
Ormbonke, that is an herb that has nine virtues.
If a person has its seeds on them, then the impure spirit must turn away from that person who is afflicted. If anyone has it on themselves, then they will not get beaten or hit, he will never lack money, that everything he wishes and wants to have he will get, and he will appear as highest among all. If he goes to court with someone, then no one wins against him, and more.

This same herb should be taken up on Midsummer night between 12 and 1, and you should have a shirt that a newborn child has had on, before it has been bathed, and a sword or sabre which has been used to injure someone with. Hang the same shirt under and around the sabre-sheath, and make a circle around you of 4 alns around, on all sides, and sit in the middle of it, and sit silently and don't talk, for you must withstand great temptation. But don't allow yourself to tire or be frightened, for it will do you no harm.

---

203 Sw. *lindorm* is a snake with mythical qualities, such as the white snake, which when boiled and eaten, gives the operator magical abilities.

51. If you want to win, when you fight.
Put a corpse tooth and a "rooster's egg" and carry in your clothes, then you can never be hit, even if you fight with someone.

52. For eye-ache.
Take lard from a squirrel and anoint your eyes with it, then they will immediately become better.

53. To be loved by every man.
Take 4 lark-chicks and take the longest of the two and carry them in your clothes, then you will be beloved of every man.

54. To turn the sight (to appear invisible).
Take an owl's skull and two of the longest claws, and one from each foot, and put one claw in each eye of the skull, and draw an owl's head on a piece of paper and these words with blood from your little finger:

OOQ e e Ey Haken Gardi Nialagues t △ 9.9.27

then put the piece of paper into the beak of the owl's skull and tie it into your left armpit, then no person will see you.

55. To work the art of women.
Take two frogs (*Rene temporaria*) in the springtime as they are mating, and take then when they are lying on each other, and put them in a box with many holes in it, and go set out and put it in an anthill, and it should happen on a Thursday evening. Then you should let it remain there for 3 weeks, but you should look in on the box each Thursday evening, and the third Thursday evening then you will take up the box, then you will find two bones. Take them, the one is like a fork, and the other like a hook. Put them in a box until you need them. When you want to have a woman, then you take the bone that is like a hook, and move it toward you, then she will come. When you want her to leave, then take the other bone and thrust it away with you, then she will go her way.

56. To get a thief to bring back what he has stolen.
Take the same bone, which is spoken about, and go to water that runs from south to north on a Thursday evening, before the sun goes down, and move the hook toward you and say: I conjure you full of water, and you, devils in hell and Pluto and Bjälsebub, and say: Damn yourself over me[204] and six times

---

[204] Sw. *förbanna dig över mig* is a deliberate corruption of *förbarma Dig över mig*, the first meaning to damn, the second meaning to be merciful.

pederolem anam and these words *Vilack osta Borr Bjälsebub* and the devil in hell, that the thief that stole from N.N. shall find no peace riding or driving, sleeping or waking, walking or standing and in all its business and movement, until he has borne back that which he has stolen, in the name of the Father and the Son and the Holy Ghost. Amen. 3 times.

57. If you want that no legal case will bite you.
Take three snake claws and put them on the altar under the handbook for three Sunday mornings. Then put them in your right shoe, then no case will bite you. (*rätt = råtta?*)[205]

58. To make yourself invisible.
Take a dead human skull and bury it down in the earth at a place that is wise, and put a pea through the eye in the skull, and let it grow and ripen. Then take it up and break all the pods, but be careful that you don't lose any. Then take a pea at a time and put it in your mouth and look in a mirror until you find the right one, then you will not see yourself in the mirror.

59. If you don't want a court judgment to bite you.
Take a snake-stinger and put it on the altar for three Sunday mornings. Then take it in your left shoe, then no court judgment will bite you.

60. If you want it so that no man will be able to arrest you.
Go to the church where you were christened, go there on a Thursday evening after darkness has fallen, and drip three drops of blood from your little finger, then no person can arrest you.

61. If you want it so that you'll never run out of money.
Carry these characters on you, that are written with your own blood:

carry these in your purse, then you'll never run out of money.

62. To transfix a person on the spot, so that they are unable to move hand or foot. Take snakeskin and one of the oblates (wafers of communion) that the

---

[205] The text is not easy to make out the difference between ä and å, and while rats biting might make good sense, the formulas are typical of spells for going to court, and so "*rätta*" could actually be the appropriate word here – "if you want it so that the judge won't adjudicate against you."

priest has blessed, and rub them together, and spread it on his head. When you order in three names that he should stand or sit, then he must be bound hands and feet until you say: go freely, my friend. NB. don't let him be bound for over ten minutes, for then he will explode.

63. To stop pain.
Our Lord C. had five wounds,
No flesh and no pain,
No boil and no bursting.
In the name of G. F. S. H. Gh. am. 3 times.

64. For erysipelas.
Take warm pig feces, and squeeze the juice out, and mix with a little red-beet-water, and apply to the sore. – helps.

64. b. To know who is a witch.
Take a bat and bury it at the doorway to the church on Midsummer day just as the sun comes up, then they will yawn as long as they are in church.

65. To test if a maiden is a virgin.
Take hare gall and put into a beer pitcher, and let her drink of it, and if she is not a virgin, then she will yawn immediately.

66. To never get drunk from liquor.
Then you must eat of a goat's liver, when you have drunk a few shots and then a little licorice and musket-flower, then you will never be drunk, even if you are as long as you've ever been at a party.

67. To be well liked by great lords.
Carry nine snake-stingers in an amber box on your chest, then you will come into great favor with all the great lords you speak with.

68. To have good luck in all jobs.
Carry these Wittenberg Letters around your neck.

amortil ⌗⌗⌗ ⌗⌗⌗⌗ ⌗ all oll

tusenbold hagelon vilion hägelon.

69. To receive a swallow stone.
Take a swallow and hang it over its own nest until it starves to death, and then you will find three stones, one black that hinders sorrow, the second is

red and if you have that with you, you will never be thirsty, and the third is white, and if you have that one, then you will get everything that you desire and wish.

69. Of the natural black art, and its procurement, which is found written down both before and after this book.
To fulfill and use all these arts correctly and in their entirety, then you must have the confidence of a spirit first, before you do these arts correctly. For those pieces, in which there appear no signatures do not last, because those pieces in which there are signatures are complete without any further aid, because it is their dear faith's seal, and therefore they accomplish it without further request. But for the others, you should address these spirits, that they might do what you command, whether it be for evil or good, near or far.

70. To be able to get one of the Spirits to serve you.
Write on a short piece of paper with your own blood these words: I give to you this as a proof, you impure spirit, then write your name and then put the short note under the church threshold. When this should happen, it should be a Thursday evening, but be careful that no one catches up to you or meets you. Then go back the following Thursday evening and take hold of the lock and say: I give you this as a proof, you impure spirit, so that you will meet me on the next coming Thursday evening. Then go home again, but be careful that no one catches up to you or meets you, for you must be all by yourself.

[Written with a younger and more modern style] *These spirits serve those who are first lifted up, or touched at birth by those who are secret sinners, especially whores. But if an honorable wife or maiden, then she cannot serve or obey the command in any way, either for good or ill.*

Then go back the third Thursday evening and then it should be just as day gives way to night, then the short note is gone. But remain there at that place until a spirit comes forth and gives you a box, then he will go his way, but you must not be frightened, for he will say nothing to you. In the box is a little bell. When you ring that little bell, then the spirit will come forth to you, and will be visible to your eyes but not for anyone else's. This spirit must serve you and do what you command him to, whether for ill or good, and he must procure for you everything that you desire of him, whether money or other goods, or even other arts that you want to try out. But as often as you want him to serve you, then you have to ring the bell, then he will come forth to do what you command him. If you want to dispute with someone, then write this on a paper and put it under your tongue

then in no way will you be defeated.

71. If you want so that no one will be able to steal from you when you are out on some journey.

Now take a sewing needle with a white silk thread and sew three times counterclockwise through the nose of a dead person, and then put the needle into the wagon before you load it.

72. To get a thief to bring back stolen goods.
Pour yourself a little image of a human being out of lead, completely like a human, name it and put it in a place where you know that this person will travel past, then an accident will befall him, so that he has to carry back that which he has stolen. If I only will it, I can take his life. If I only wish to pierce the image with a sewing needle and put a little copper nail in the arm, thigh, leg or if I want to make him limbless or completely kill him, if I stick right through the body of the image and put a copper nail in it, or if you want to poke out the eye of the image and put a copper nail in it, then his eye will fly right out of his head, and then there is to say when you bury the image.

73. To conjure forth invisible spirits to speak orally with them to find out hidden things. Write these letters, which are printed here, and put your name and then this:

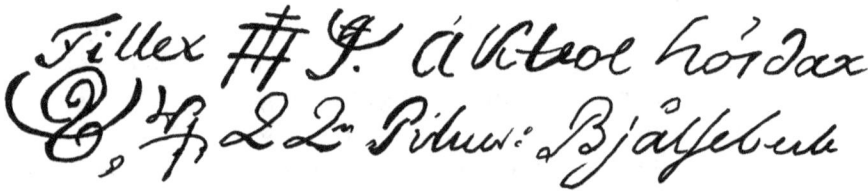

Write this with your own blood on an old evergreen shaving and go to the churchyard and put the shaving under an earthfast stone; when you set out it should be a Thursday evening and put the shaving there, and say your name and ask them to meet you on the next Thursday evening. When you come there for the second Thursday evening, then take the shaving and say their name as well as saying: I command you that you come to meet me on the next coming Thursday evening and this in the name of G. F. S. H. Gh. Then go there on the third Thursday evening, then the shaving is gone and a little rune-stone is there instead. Take this stone and keep it Then they will come to you, then you can find out all that you wish to ask them about, but don't ask them too much the first time, for then they will become sorrowful. But thereafter, you may know of the nature of the book.

    1. When you have this stone in your purse, then you will never be short of money.

    2. When you put the stone in a glass bottle and stir with the stone, then the spirits will come to you wherever you are; but if you don't want to

have more than one, then just stir it once in the bottle. But if you want to have several, then you should stir the bottle once for each one, that you want to have appear. For as soon as you have that stone, then they are bound to serve you and do everything that you order them to.

3. They will say to you everything that you wish to know, as far as the world streches.

4. If you want to fight and have this stone in your clothes, then you will never get a lashing.

5. If you have the stone in your purse and hang the purse under your left arm and then want to go and gamble with some others, then you will win as often as you want.

6. If you want it so that no court will bite down on you, when you go before the court, then have the stone in your left shoe, then no judge and condemn you, neither can anyone witness against you.

7. If you have the stone in your mouth and wish for something from someone, little or big, then he will be enchanted so that he cannot deny you what you wish of him.

8. If you dispute with someone, then put the stone under your tongue, then you cannot be defeated by any person.

9. If you have the stone on you and want a maiden to love you, then take her in your embrace, then she will love you excessively.

10. If I want to shoot, take the stone and put it into the shotgun case, then the animals will come forward to you, and you can shoot as quickly as you have time to load.

11. If you want to win the lottery, take the money out of the purse and put the stone in it and let it lie for 3 24-hour days. Then take the same money and put it into the lottery, then you'll win.

12. If you take the stone and put it on your head, then you are invisible for all people.

13. As long as you have that stone, then you will have luck in everything that you will begin, whatever it may be.

14. If you put the stone under your left foot and want to walk on water, then you will be able to go dry-shoed. If you put the stone at your knee and then go on water, then you will go down into the water to your knees, and however far up you put the stone on your body, that's as far as you will sink in the water.

15. If you are never so far away, and you want to get home in an hour, then you take three drops of blood and anoint the stone and say: I wish that I were home, then a spirit will appear and carry you home, so that you don't know how you got there.

16. This stone is red of color, and no larger than a nut, and when you have had it for a whole year, then it will not leave you. If you want to throw it in the lake or onto fire, then it will come back to you again. But when you have had it for fifty years, then don't keep it longer. Then you can be rid of it if you sell it to someone else. Otherwise if you bring it back to the place you got it from, then you will be through with it.

74. To be able to cure a horse of heaves[206]
Give a hen some grain to eat so that its gizzard is quite full. Then cut up the gizzard and take out the grain and give it to the horse to eat, then it will be free from it.

75. So that a horse will not tire, when you are out on a journey.
Go out on a Maundy Thursday morning and get a fly-rowan staff, take it right when day and night divide themselves, Make harnesses from it. As long as you use the same harnesses, then your horses will never tire.

76. For a woman who [qväls] with child.
Grind amber to a powder and take in wine. This has a mighty power.

77. To hex a shotgun.
Take your middle finger on your right hand and stick it in your butt. When you take it out of your butt, then put it into the muzzle of the shotgun. Then that shotgun will never shoot right, until it is completely scoured out.

78. To have good luck in hunting.
Anoint the shotgun with woman's milk, then the animals will come before it, or: Take a fly mushroom[207] and boil it in a quart of vinegar with a little bitter-

---

206 *Qweckdrat*: A veterinary malady that is characterized by coughing in horses. Also *kvickdrag*. English: heaves.
207 Sw. *flugeswamp*. Fly agaric mushroom?

orange peel, and boil it covered in a pot and with that, anoint the entire barrel, and the remains are put into the barrel and a cork is put in the end, and let it sit overnight, and then dry it well,

or, Take lard from a heron and apply to the lock two times, then it will obey so that no one can do ill to your shotgun.

[a shield with the word Victor beside it]

79. Another.
When you take your shotgun and go towards the woods, then don't load the shotgun before you come into the woods. Stand under an evergreen, that has most of its branches on the south side, stand under its largest branches while you load the shotgun. But when you put the shot in, then you should say: full fifty-eight hit Gardi, and put a little of it together with the shot, and stamp the shot down well, and take the powder outside of the shot from a girls linen cloth, and write these Wittenberg letters with blood from the little finger and put under the powder chamber of the shotgun.

[Rafel Fili Tull 52 & 6 ... ene/ana +]

Then you will be able to shoot as much as you wish.

80. To regain the fire.
If the fire is taken from you when you are out hunting, and when you notice it, you should take the shotgun between your thighs three times and with the left hand three times back, then it will be as smooth as the one who took it, and each time say: hupti siact 53 tuli fort

81. Another method.
Take a snake stone and keep it in the shotgun case, then no injury will ever be done to it, even if it was the most artful of all.

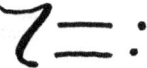

82. How to capture a snakestone.
Take a water snake and hold it with a forked stick, and take a string of black silk that is made from 13 threads, and tie it up at the navel so hard that it can't get out of it, and hang it up in a tree. And when it is hung up, then take the forked stick off it, and then look out, as he will have birthed a stone, which is as big as a large nut. This you should immediately pick up and put in a paper and put it on your left nipple on your chest, then then take the same away, and turn yourself to the north and say: Så så Durcht flemtis gaden 74

83. ... to this stone ... to its ... that .... to win in gambling, if it is the lottery... so that it is in some ... then you will ... follow after.

84. To win at the lottery.
Put three turkey feathers in a cross into a feather tip that is cut off, and put it where you sleep under your head, and a raven's heart and sleep on it overnight, then you will find the numbers to play in a dream, but when you wake up, say:

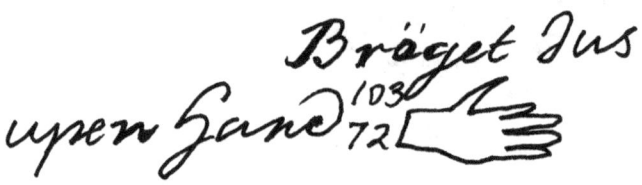

Bröget dus, open hand 103/72

85. To take away warts, corns and moles
Greet them [: morning, evening, and then contrary:] and say while you pinch them crosswise:

> Disappear, disappear, as coal into ash,
> man in earth, snow before the sun,

You shall become as small as a mustard seed
And then naught.

This is said three times.

86. So that a wife will become pregnant.
Take dirt from a churchyard, drop it without them knowing between their body and their underwear.

87. For miscarriage.
Take a dress that she has had, and go to a crossroads on a Monday morning, and wrap a silver coin in the dress, bury it at the crossroads, and say three times:

> Toni, Maxoni, Lime
> Wacka, Kalma, Lina,
> Kansa, Tuttra, Meijkoijen.

88. When animals are sick.
Then you cut a little hair from the animals left forefoot between the hooves, and then on the right forefoot and the left back foot, a little hair from the nape of the neck. Each animal is cured with its own hair, and the ashes are given to them internally.

89. If your shotgun doesn't kill.
Put two rye-, wheat- or barley grains on or inside the flash pan on the powder, then it will kill.

90. To know who it was who stole.
Take a [*grynasåll*]208 (deep sieve) and put into it a louse-brush, a psalm book, a wool shear, and in a piece of wood into which is put three new sewing needles. Two people hold this sieve across from each other over a waterway on their index fingers, then all the suspects' names are called out, and when the true guilty one's name is named, then it will turn.

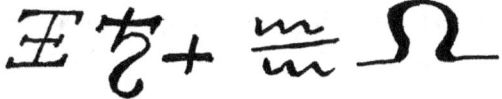

91. Harrowing or falling with cows.
For this, procure: a weaving reed, a card, three [*sylf*], a bridal gown and stockings and a tanning tin, and when you are going to cure the cow, you stand on

---

208 *Grynna* – bottom, deep. Not found in dialect lexicon. *Såll* = sieve.

the left side of the cow, and the one you have with you on the right, then take hold with the left hand these things and move them under the cow's belly, say:

> Jesus and I are two,
> The Virgin Mary is the third.
> It may be something that a dog and cat disturbed.
> It will go away and disappear to the haystack.
> Then nothing at all.

This is done three times and this in the name of G. F. S. H. Gh. Then it is thrown over the cow's shoulders, then back and lastly over the rear end with the reed, the card and the tanning tin. These things lie for 24 hours untouched in the cattle-shed.

92. To prepare a nail with which one can call animals to oneself.
Right in the middle between the new and waning moon, take a little rowan or hazel stick, that has a split Y in each end. The one end will point north, and the other towards the south. This stick shouldn't be brought under a roof until it is ready. When it is stripped, then knead it with garlic thoroughly all over, then you put it into the earth, so that the fork points north, and leave it for three weeks. Then it is anointed with hare gall, is put back into the earth for eight days, then you can apply to that same stick some fox- or wolf-lard. Continue according to the previous with putting it in the earth, then the animals will come to that place.

93. To transfix a thief to the place, when he has robbed.
You leave home silently and the whole way paying attention so that you meet no one or be greeted either leaving or on the way home. When you have come to the churchyard and found that which is sought which is a human skull, then you say: I, N.N., pray to you for forgiveness that I take you for such a long time, so that you will guard me and mine from thieves. When the time is up, I shall with reverence carry you back and bury you. In the same way he should be brought back silently and be buried, but then you may talk to whomever you want. When you have it with you, put it in a leather bag with a piece of a chasuble and a communion wafer in a secret place. You may not speak harshly to the thief.

94. To cure it when rye is cut or eaten up by worms.
You go to that swath that is eaten by worms, and notice where you find the first worm. Then the worm is pierced with a knife or some other sharp object, which is made from a gallows-nail. From there, you begin to walk from that place counterclockwise around the swath a little bit from the fence, holding

up the knife that is piercing the worm and saying all the while: I command all those worms, who are here, eating and munching, to turn away from this place, in the name of G. F. S. H. Gh. amen. Now when you get to the mark, you take a club from a tree, wherewith the worm is hung with a hair from the head. – learned from Johannes at Nordgjerdet.

95. So that a thief will carry back the things he has stolen.
After you have ascertained who is truly guilty, then write his name on a piece of paper and under that:

> S a t o r
> a r e p o
> T e n e t
> O p e r a
> R o t a s

And then the thief's name N. N. This is put under the smithy, and then it is smithed over when the suspect's name is mentioned.

96. To reveal and cure that which is hexed.
Write these words on a piece of paper and carry it with you, when the hexed is used, or bind it on it, so that it will then disappear.

> Haber, Avasex. Orel.

97. If someone overcomes you before you can gain a defense.
So that with these words with you, saying: *Ego Dam Barbiel Masa catist est Jesum Prucatum Barbielis.*

98. To make a horse lame.
Take a nail out of a rotten coffin, and three nails out of a horseshoe, which is found with the nails still in it. Smith it with the horse-shoe nails. And when you hit it, then say in Belsebubs, Lucifers, Belials and all the angels of hell's name --- --- ---. The nail is struck without a head. It is made on a Thursday morning when the sun comes up. Put it where the horse has trod with its foot, then it will become lame. When it is removed, then the horse is no longer lame.

Observe: when the nail is taken, you should be silent, even when it is ready in the smithy.

99. To bring back that which was stolen.
Go on a Thursday morning before the sun comes up, and take a glowing coal

and put it into a hand-mill eye, and then grind counterclockwise with the left hand three times and say each time the mill grinds: Titum I order you to bring me back the thief who stole from N. N. (a sum or goods is named) in your powerful name G. F. S. H. Gh. amen. The mill is turned in such a way that one starts at the chest and returns to the chest.

100. To stop bleeding (p. 22)

> Jesus stood at Noah's flood,
> ladled the water and stopped the bleeding.
> As surely this blood will stop running
> as the committee-man who goes to the meeting,
> knows right but witnesses wrong.

or:

Hold the word, stop the blood
As Jesus did with Noah's flood.

101. Childhood scurvy.
If a wife who is pregnant climbs over a fence, which is around and within which is a living pole [:an evergreen or other tree is bound with a border, then the sick one is called *wålbunden*:] if that same wife finds this pole and chops off the branches, then the child will be well within a few days.

102. For overindulgence in strong drink.
Take from three anthills, 3 gravestones, this is boiled in urine for a while, mixed with sweet drops and given internally.

103. So that bees will not fly when they swarm.
You observe when the swarm heads out, then you take three pig-feces, throw one at a time over the swarm, so that it comes over the queen bee, then they must stay still.

104. If a horse has his fortitude stolen.
Take from a decayed coffin, give it to the horse in its oats, but it shouldn't come under a roof.

105. So that a fox will not take sheep, lambs or geese.
Take flesh from a murdered person, give it to them in their feed for sheep, geese and lambs, before they have been weaned from their mother.

106. So that a shotgun will kill what it shoots at.
Take a decayed bone at the churchyard, shave a little off with the nail, and then put it under the shot.

107. For moles
Take a piece of linen cloth, that a person has died in, under the arm and the rear end, put it in the earth, then he will not move within a circle of 7 alns.

108. Another.
If a woman pisses in the hole, when she has her bleeding, then he will flee away.

109. So that a horse won't jump.
Take hair from the leg, tie a cross to a pole down by the ground, and put moss on it in the meadow where the horse is first put out in the spring.

110. To transfix a thief.
You take a thread, which is spun to the right, and counterclockwise wound and measure a body's width from middle finger to middle finger, which is a "fang," that length. Upon each measurement tie a knot. Then the following words are used: <u>Everything that is within this property , it will remain until I see what the thief has stolen, in the name of G. F. S. H. Gh</u>. NB. That which you want to protect is measured on the outside with this thread, while one says the underlined.

111. To hinder it so that the seed doesn't fall.
Take dirt, that is dug up with the heels of the shoes, make a little pile, put it on a seed of the type that you want to sow in the field. This is put in the field so deep that it won't be plowed up.

112. To cause an inability to thrive in a field, so that the seed doesn't grow.
Pull up three stalks, turn the roots upmost and say: never more shall any seed grow in this field, and that in the name of G. F. S. H. Gh.

113. So that seed and linen will grow.
Mix in all the types of seeds, grind them fine with *Antimonium crudum*, when it is sown.

114. Luck for pigs. (Swine-luck)
When you sell a pig, then throw a horse-shoe nail and a hair from the pig in the crib and say: Luck for me too.

115. So that the livestock will not wander.
When the animal comes to the cattle-shed door, put a little liquor in each nostril and a little in the mouth too, then you take a little hay, and let the animal sniff it, it is put on the threshold that the animal goes over. In the ear you whisper to the animal and say: hence shall you come, and never thence in the name of G. F. S. H. Gh. 3 times.

116. So that the cuckoo will not take any hens or birds from your farm.
Take a log that is used for linen breaking, put a stone between the shafts and the log. As long as this stone sits there, the hens and the birds are free.

117. For those who are unable to distill liquor.
Take musk, asafetida, sulfur, [*olsten*], [*wättaljus*], garlic, lovage, equal parts of each. Some is sewn into a fine cloth. Each time you want to distill, it is stick with a needle 9 stitches in three lines. Then it is put under the grain, but between times it is kept in a box until needed.

118. Remedy for tuberculosis or blood sickness or ...

> Our Lord and Saint Peter
> went forth on their way;
> they saw where the tuberculosis came from.
> Where are you running, said our Lord then?
> I will run to the house of man,
> Reeve his blood and break his bones.
> No, said our Lord,
> You shall go into that wood where no one dwells.
> In that lake where no one rows;
> into an earthfast stone
> there you will go quickly and be no threat to anyone.
>
> Lars Nilsson-Berg.

119. To drive away rats.
Malt is ground to flour, wherein is mixed finely ground human bone, taken at the churchyard. This is put out for the rats, so they flee away.
    Given by a traveler from Lappland to Karlskrona for Præpositus P. Starck.

120. To buy livestock.
When you have bought an animal, you should then take the seller by the hand and say: I hope that you do not begrudge me that which is purchased. If someone after you have bought or the seller hits the animal's rear or strokes it, then

he will have taken the luck from the purchase. Give him in the mouth, then your luck will remain.

from Jöns at Sjörenet.

Another:
If you take up a little dirt or a stone under where the animal has stood, stopped, and thrown it, when it lands in its crib, then it will not wander.

121. For painful bite.
First of all, you go to a well or a stream, take water in a wooden bowl, pour 9 drops on your back. The tenth you keep in the bowl until it is needed. Then take a jackknife, take water in the bowl with the knife and pour it on the limb that aches, counterclockwise around, and then make a cross, and say:

> Our Lord Jesus Christ
> Himself traveled on his way
> A Pain Maiden[209] he met
> Where are you going?
> His bones to break, his blood to suck.
> That will God forbid you
> In the holy names:
> father, son and holy ghost.

This is said three times. NB. the sick one should sit on an earthfast stone while this is done.

122. To stop pain.
To stop dry pain on someone who is not present.
Take a four-sided turf, after it is cut up (NB. on the underside) make three crosses with the same knife that it was cut up with, and say: The pain that you are plagued with will transform in the same way as the harsh sufferings on the tree of the cross. Then it is put in its place again with a stone covering. The crossing happens above – or toward the side of the painful place. Baptismal and father's name is named. When the patient is present, this it is burned up.

Silfversvärd.

123. For nail in animals.
Take a branch that has grown towards the north out of a trunk on an alder tree. Cut off one twig, off of which is cut three sticks when the cure is to be

---

[209] *Torska Qvinna. Torsk* is a pain causing agent, glossed as a worm in dialect.

performed, and upon each cutting, say: I cut away the nail in N. N.'s animal, the color of (reddish, black, white) – the right or the left side is named – in three names. Then the sticks are burned up and the twig. *Probatum est* (this is tried).

124. To recite away [*vättan*] (the wight)
You evil, wicked nit, who promised N. N. that he (she) could not get better, for now he (she) has earth on her, and water under her. In the name of G. F. S. H. Gh. This is recited 3 times and spit three times for each.

A turf is cut up with a knife, this is taken up and put on the bare head during the recitation. Standing over water can also be good. After the turf is put on the head, it is put on a fence post to dry out.

from Måns Månsson in M. Lida.

125. To get rid of worms.
You take some worms from each tree and go to the churchyard on a Thursday morning before the sun comes up. Drop them in an open grave – if you can't find one, make a hole in a closed grave with a staff – which should be done silently, and think or say: Hence will all worms go, that are in N. N. garden in the name of G. F. S. H. Gh. You don't look back, when you go to and from the churchyard. Then you go back to the garden again, put in a tree that is in the middle of the garden in its leaves and new shoots a needle with a thread through it, which has been used before to sew through a shroud or a sheet that a corpse has been wrapped in, though washed three times.

126. To drive away rats and mice.
You go three Thursday evenings in a row at 11 o'clock or at 2 o'clock to the place where the rats are to be found. When you go, you should leave home silently, and when you come to the place, you should say: Dirtom Mirtom Poss Bits. This I will send to you if you don't move within a month's time. Then you say to what place you want them to depart. For the second: "there you will have better food than I have here."

Be careful to bind well whatever you find, otherwise they will eat it up.

MS 32

SUPRIANIA
FRU ALSTADS SOCKEN, SKYTTS HÄRAD, 1858

SUPRIANIA

IKfZrpryvQQ22S.

dεττα vηp δv ταππαρ ἐvvη φωρ σιστ

EiPf.æ.bb.iℋikif.

στρvπ vvδερ Σκαv

This is when you thank her for last time, and rub under your chin.

1. To Stop Bloody Nose
As Father Johannes stopped the River Jordan,
    [the blood shall be required to run
    for you N.N., who can win salvation
    you who go to the court and witness to lies but know the truth][210]
    In this way I stop your bleeding N.N. in the name of God the Father and of the Son and of the Holy Ghost. (Our Father.) (Recited three times.)

2. Bleeding wounds.
As Jesus Christ stopped the vein of sin, in that way I stop this blood for you N.N., in the name of God the Father and of the Son and of the Holy Ghost. (Recited 3 times). (Our Father.)

---

[210] The original found within brackets was crossed out in pencil in the original, and the following change was made: the blood shall run no more than this person can win salvation who goes to the court and knows right but witness to wrongs.

3. To alleviate venom.
I bless you N. N. for mouse bite and worm bite and all the bites that are on the earth under the sun

> and in the forest where no one dwells
> and in the lake where no one rows
> in logs and in stones
> this no one can deny me

in this way I alleviate this for you N. N. in the name of God the Father and of the Son and of the Holy Ghost. (Recited 9 times.) (Our Father.) Stroked with a knife counterclockwise 9 times, and then apostle-salve is applied.

4. To alleviate snake-bite.
There stood a stone, where a snake lay

> He bit that one's horse in his heel
> Jesus Christ dismounted and healed it
> In this way I alleviate this bite for you, N. N.

in the name of God the Father and of the Son and of the Holy Ghost. (Our Father.) It is massaged three times counterclockwise around the wound with a handful of water, whereafter the one who is bitten drinks it. Apostle-salve, "Tilli" drops and a Beck's Bandage is applied. [*Tilli droppar*] ("Tilli drops")

5. To conjure up a dead person.
With a year old hazel branch is made a circle around the grave, from which you take dirt three times in your left hand. Say in this way: "I conjure you, you dead body with your spirit, by Christ ☩ by the Virgin Mary's birth and the holy evangelists' and apostles' earthly path, that you rise up and meet me here at this place before the hour of twelve, when I shall ask you secretly; and you shall answer me 3 words, which I shall not reveal; and I conjure you that you will not go outside this circle, and neither harm a hair from my head in the least, in the name of the holy Trinity and of Maria's birth, and the earthly path of the holy evangelists and the apostles. Amen.

Write then these signs around the circle: ☩☩☩ ✡ ⊐ I ☩☩☩. then put the branch into the earth and go 2 or 3 steps backwards outside of the circle.

When he has spoken with you, he will run counterclockwise around the circle. Then throw dirt three times at him in nine circles, then he'll go down immediately.

6. For pain.
Our Lord Jesus Christ, Your red cross, with which you triumphed over all the power of the devil. In his power I bind all evil, that which flies in the air as well as the wind; I bind all evil in the earth and on the earth; I bind all evil in the water and on the water; I bind with a binding, which our Lord Jesus Christ bound the inveterate Jews in the Garden; I bind all the devils in their

colors, both red and blue, spotted and gray, black and white, that there will be no more harm done to this person N. N. than a mouse can do to an earth-fast stone, and I do all this in the power of the Father, the power of the Son and the wisdom of the Holy Ghost; in the name of the great Johannes and Petrus. Amen, amen, amen. Our Father 3 times, benediction 3 times.

7. (For Pain.)
As truly as Jesus Christ stood on the Cross and took upon himself the suffering and pain of the whole world, I also do that with you N. N., in the name of the Father and of the Son and of the Holy Ghost. Amen.
  This is recited with devotion and is taken into that limb where the pain is.

8. (For Pain.)
For pain that settles in a place in whatever limb it may be, then take hold of it with the hand and recite these words: "No shall all you pain, N. N., disappear as straw disappears before sun and earth before fire, in three names: of God the Father, of God the Son and of God the Holy Ghost. Recited three times and take hold of the swelling with the hand, then it will be healed.

9. (For Pain.)
I will anesthetize (lull) this dull ache for you, N. N., as our Lord Jesus Christ alleviated his own dull ache. He shall turn aside before my power as Herod was turned aside by the Holy Ghost and this in the name of the Father and of the Son and of the Holy Ghost. Amen.
  Our Father and Benediction are recited.

10. (For Pain.)
I ask now for permission from God the Father to alleviate and stay and cast away this pain; it shall no more ache nor cause suffering. This I desire to do with my 10 fingers and the twelve holy apostles, in three names, of God the Father, and of the Son, and of the Holy Ghost. Amen, Amen, Amen.

11. (For Pain.)
I sign you N. N. as being free from heat, I sign you free from cold, I sign you free from susceptibility to pain, in the name of the Father and of the Son and of the Holy Ghost, and in Jesus' name. Amen, amen and in the name of Jesus the Nazarene. Amen, amen, amen.

12. (For Pain.)
Write in chalk a "five-point-cross" ☆ and say: Now I shall work for this pain for you as our Lord Jesus worked the River Jordan with his foot.

13. (For Cramp or Sprain.)
To sign with four hay-straws that have three joints in each straw: Saint Peter and our Lord they went on a road. Saint Peter said to our Lord: I have a sprain. Our Lord said to Saint Peter: Take three straws that have three joints in them, and if there's a sinew break lay the fourth on top; in the name of the Father and of the Son and of the Holy Ghost, Amen.

Our Father 3 times, benediction 3 times.

14. For toothache.
Take 9 oak twigs between the teeth, so that there issues blood from them, and put out 3 between the bark and the tree in an oak and 3 into running water and 3 into a stone cliff and say: Now I work away the toothache for you N N as our Lord worked away the toothache for Mary; he drew the toothache out from her blood, flesh and bones; but I draw the toothache out of your blood, flesh and bones and into logs and stones, and in the names, three names, of God the Father, and of the Son and of the Holy Ghost. Amen, Amen, Amen.

15. (For Toothache.)
As the paths in a ["*råglycka*" = rye path, or opening?] goes and disappears, in that way your toothache will perish and be as nothing.

16. (For Toothache or similar.)
You shall ache in stone and clay but never in a person's bones. Turn away, Satan!

17. (For the Rose.)
You yellow rose, you blue rose, you red rose, you green rose, you brown rose, you black rose, you white rose! I, N. N., conjure you in whatsoever limb you are, or in bone, or in blood, or in lung, by the names of God the Father and of the Son and of the Holy Ghost, by the power of God's majesty, by all of the twelve [*artiklar* = *apostlar*?] articles, by that which Jesus Christ accomplished, that you may not remain anywhere in the flesh. I, N. N., conjure you, rose and pain, that you immediately turn away and forgive this servant of Jesus N. N. and no more harm or break him or her by pain or suffering in head or teeth, or hands or any limb. I, N. N., conjure you that you immediately turn away from this servant, male or female, of Jesus Christ.

MS 33

TROLL-MARKSENS SVARTKONSTBOK
GOTTHARD WILHELM MARKS (TROLL-MARKSEN)
VON WÜRTENBERG (1758–1822)

*   *

*

N. 1. Toothache.
Then is written on an old wooden plate "Beelsebub" and is taken nine small nails or horseshoe nails with which one at a time is taken and put on the first letter and is hit on it three times with a hammer so that at the third strike the nail goes clear through. If the complaint isn't changed upon the first, then continue with one at a time of all the rest of the eight. Then one is assured of help.

N. 2. To stop a bloody nose.
A hole is bored in a threshold and three blood-drops are dripped into it. Then it is immediately plugged up again with a tight plug. Then it will depart and will stop.

N. 3. A sure cure for the Rose (a red swelling) even if it is open (purulent).
Take the most rancid lard or meat that you can get and to that a good portion of garlic that is pealed and put together in a mortar, and grind it together until it becomes like a paste and then it is applied to the wound or that injury. Then one will soon find relief and will begin to heal without delay.

N. 4. To soothe and take away a cough.
Make out of good pitch small pellets the size of white peas, and ten of these should be taken on an empty stomach each morning. To be continued for several weeks.

N. 5. To take away corns with garlic.
From a garlic plant is chopped slices which are bound fresh on the corn. When one has continued with this for several days, before long one will experience that one is dragging off the corn with its roots, so that it will completely disappear.

N. 6. The best method to cure trollshot.
One should immediately take that animal and stretch out the tongue and put on it fresh human feces in the throat and try to keep it on the feet for so long so that there is sweat, then one releases the tongue to its place.

N. 7. When a horse tires out.
Then it is best to give him immediately in haste chopped garlic in hay or grain, and from this its strength will be brought back.

N. 8. A nutritious water one can prepare.
On midsummer eve before noon, you shall gather of every type of flower you can find, which are taken up both root and plant and kept, and then dried and chopped finely and strewn in a liquor tub and allowed to remain there until is fermented and is stirred. When it has stood overnight, the second day it is brewed like other liquor and then distilled in a smaller pot whereupon it is kept in bottles and is well-corked.

N. 9. Urine of cows is collected on Midsummer night and boiled together so it thickens which is then stored in jars and with which one can grease up all sorts of broken bones and injuries as well as swellings.

N. 10. To help someone who is constipated in an emergency.
Lay upon his bare abdomen a cloth or Napkin that is soaked in cold or ice water, as cold as you can get it, and let it lay there a while, this can also be tried several times if the first doesn't get through. Then the patient will be helped without any doubt.

N. 11. For severe diarrhea and a mixture of dysentery.
On the other hand, here is a sure and sovereign means if one gives the patient a half a quart of good Pontak[211] and then in a while a glass of good linseed oil, then the dysentery will stop. It doesn't hurt if he takes two times daily a glass of beer with Pontak.

N. 12. A technique of stopping nosebleed.
Take a living spider and dig up a little pit or hole in the ground or sand especially where you can hold the spider with a stick but careful not to kill it, and drip some drops of blood on it. Bury it then with sand or earth, then everything is helped.

---

[211] Pontak is capitalized in the manuscript, which leads me to believe it is a brand name, either a liqueur or a wine.

N. 13. To anesthetize toothache.
Rub apart white ginger thoroughly fine, and take a living spider and put everything together between two flat stones and rub together, with which take a knife tip's worth and put it on the tooth. Then one lies down on that same side and allow the mouth to face downward, so that it is possible to have a bunch of saliva run away, then it's done, and everything will be better.

N. 14. Against the rose (a red swelling accompanied by pain).
if it is on the body or open on the legs. Take a piece of "finis"[212] soap and put it into a fine cloth. Then bandage around and hang it around the throat, then the "rose" will disappear. You may also carry it on your chest for a time.

[N. 15.] That a horse will be free for an entire year from "*fibel*" (a swelling in the tonsils of a horse).
The pit that is inside an elderberry that has grown that year, tear it apart, and throw it in a new pot. Put it over fire so that it will become dry enough for you to pulverize, and give this to the horse about the size of a walnut in his fodder or on a slice of bread with ground salt. It helps and keeps him for an entire year.

[N. 16.] So that he will never again get that sickness (*fibel*?).
Feel between the back of the chin and the throat, there sits something hard like a swelling. Cut it out with a "*åderjern*,"[213] and stick sharp glass almost as big as a bean in it so that it bleeds out by itself. Wash him all the time with wine, then he'll never get that sickness again.

[N. 17.] So that hair will soon grow on man and horses.
Take fodder in which crabs are caught, clean it and soak them in linseed oil in a new pot. And when they have soaked for a while, let it cool so that it is lukewarm. Then take a piece of honeycomb that the dead bees are still sitting in and put it in it. With this, apply it to the person or horse. There will soon be hair growing there.

[N. 18.] To get rid of hair.
Take the milky juice of *Daphne mezereum*[214] and of *Euphorbia helioscopia*[215] and mix them in cottonseed oil and apply to the area.

---

212 "Finis" soap. Can't distinguish if this is "fine soap" or "finish soap."
213 Literally, "vein-iron," but perhaps here a scalpel?
214 Swedish here is *Kiällarhals* (cellar throat).
215 Swedish here is *wargamiölk* (wolf's milk).

[N. 19.] If a horse is found to have worms inside him.
Good vinegar, ground garlic and human feces: stir well together and administer to the horse.

[N. 20.] A beautiful way of stopping bleeding.
Two parts resin of *Boswellia serrata*[216] and one part *Algopaticum*, pulverize each with the other, mix with an eggwhite and put it on the vein.

[N. 21.] For a nasty injury to a horse.
A little honey, a measure of verdigris[217] and grind it fine, mix together and let it soak in a half quart of vinegar. Soak it until it becomes brown. Apply to the wound. It'll heal soon.

[N. 22.] Another means.
Take a piece of pork rind that some of the meat is still on. Make it well heated and apply to the horse's injury. It will heal soon.

[N. 23.] A salve for burn wounds.
Pine cone (?)[218] from a white spruce, a kernel of sulfur and sheep tallow. Mix these things together and let it dissolve until the sulfur is loose and melted. Then take linseed oil and put it in and stir it together until it becomes cold, then you have a good burn salve.

---

216 Swedish here is *wirak*, the hard resin from the East Indian plant.
217 Swedish here is *spansgrön*. *Spanskgröna* is verdigris.
218 Swedish here is *Hwit grankåda*, and *kotte* is a cone, thus a cone of a white spruce. I am assuming the medicinal value here is from the pitch left on the cone.

MS 34

ZIMPARTIER WETTENSKAP
PERSTORP, NORRA ÅSBO HÄRAD,
KRISTIANSTADS LÄN, SKÅNE

SYMPATHETIC SCIENCE[219]

[1] For toothache, write these words on a slice of bread and eat it up when one lies down to go to bed.

AraGon	x	waragon
Atagon	x	watagon
Saragon	x	Satagon

[2] Examples -- -- --
  KORBORFABOR
  METARi.i.i.i. N.F

Letters to be given internally both for people and animals, as well as when any pain/evil has happened as a "liberation" therefrom; and with it is used incense. This is used for all pain/evil and helps next to God's help.

[3] So that none has the power to work evil on you, carry these words on your person. You have HABLITETTBAN no power to cause you harm – and KORBOR as well.

[4] So that a horse will not tire for 30 [Swedish] miles, procure for yourself a wolf tooth, and bind it under the mane or some other place, so that no one sees it. Then he won't tire as quickly. -- -- --

[5] The Heaves (a veterinary term) with horses. To an old horse is taken one spoonful with ground mustard, two spoonfuls of cotton oil, and two to three spoonfuls of good vinegar, which is mixed and is poured into the nostrils, whereafter the horse is ridden warm, the strangles will go away, this is used three times and on each third day.

---

[219] Such is my attempt to make sense of *Zympartier*. *Sympatiska* would make more sense in this case, as many of the cures are examples of "sympathetic magic." Cf. "Supriania" for Cyprianus, and NM 271.602 "Negromänliska Saker" for "Negromantiska Saker."

[6] For colic with horses, take six measures "shiny soot" (charcoal?) that has been ground finely and mixed with a pail of sweet milk, that is given internally all at once every other day, if needed until it helps, if you want to mix a measure of aloe with it, then it will have a better effect.

[7] For the horse that cannot be held in a stall. Boil a pot of water with a handful of Linseeds mixed in. Give it to him three or four times per day and along with it, let him out several times, all while the effect and the heat is strongly in evidence – also, lead him into a sheep pen that is warm, this can also have an effect. Or dip a piece of cloth in cold water and tie or hold it around its waist (*"skapet"*) that can also help. You can also cram three lice into the *"skåppet"* that has some effect.

[8] Scabies with horses. Grind finely "Sulfur Jallap Puckenhults Powder," of each type, equal amounts, mix together and administer. A powder of four measures weight each morning. Along with that, the horses is washed on the diseased places with a water that is boiled in this way: take four measures of tobacco leaf, boil in a pot of water that is strained, and this is mixed with a lime water that is can then be used with it. Continue until it is healed.

[9] To increase milk with cows. Chop up [*hinbärs*; ?misinterpreted? from "*vinbärs*"] currant-roots finely according to taste, and take some "*fankå*" approximately 8 measures. Boil in water and pour up the broth and let the cow drink. It opens the milk arteries.

[10] For the brewing of "liquor"[220] that is being magically affected for you. Incense (or smoking) is used in the boiler before one puts the water into it for the mashing, also into the tub before one mashes,[221] as well as in the boiler/pot before one has begun to brew. Or clear out the vessel which will be used

---

220 The original title of this section, "För brännevins bränningen för tiust för Dig." Firstly, Swedish *brännvin* is a generic term, and includes everything from a simple vodka to a liquor flavored variously and of various consistencies. Because it is home distilled, it could well be translated as "moonshine" or "hooch," though these American terms indicate a familiarity that is misleading. I have chosen the term "liquor" here, since this term generally indicates distilled spirits. Brännvin was commonly distilled from the potato, but it included grain alcohols as well, such as malt liquors and gin. This section deals with the treatment of the distilled liquor for taste as well as success in the distillation process, though the term "*bränning*" can mean either distillation or brewing. I will choose to go arbitrarily with brewing for simplicity, though technically it is process of distillation.

221 "*mäska*" Rietz gives the following: "*med hett vatten öfvergjutet malt till bryggning och brännvinsbränningen.*" That is, "the malt that has had hot water poured over it for brewing or the distillation of liquor." Malt and Sour-mash are both terms used in English to describe distilled liquors.

as needed, cense it before it is used, the evening before one begins to mash, a bit of "Master root" (bot. unknown) a Lord's Hand (*Orchis maculata*) into the burnt mixture; if you want to pass it to another, then it is ground finely with this, and also is thrown in 3 burning coals into the mix. If more is needed to be made, then you can take 9 small nails/pegs from another's fence and put sulphur on them and start the fire with them under the boiler, three each time for the mashing, the brewing and the distillation. You can also take a piece of "*likramma*"[222] that you find at the cemetery from which you cut three wedges and position at three angles under the cooling barrel with the ends toward the center so that the notches or grooves will actually stand on top of them. But all of the shavings that are cut off are burned up. Also you can procure a horseshoe with 8 holes in it. Put it under the mashing tub in the fire so that it becomes red. When the last of the water is put in, then throw the shoe, as red as it is, into the mash when you have emptied the tub. Then take the shoe and keep it for another day, and it will bring luck. Then you can also when you can throw in a little "Master root" a "Lord's hand" (*Orchis maculata*) and one or two garlic cloves (*knoppor*) buds into the mash. In the barrel board, those you can immediately bore three . ' . holes. Bore into the board as the dots illustrate, and put into them a little note of paper with the letters KORBOR into the first hole, and into the second hole a little bit of Master root. In the third hole put a little bit of silver and a Lord's Hand (*Orchis maculata*). It can be whittled finely from a little *flyrön* of Black, white and Red Coral Stone (*Coralia rubra*). If there isn't enough room, you can bore more holes that are then stopped up with dough. In stopping it with dough, some take a little hay from the roof thatching over another's door on the handle, or also to start the fire with.

[11] About the production of liquor. If the brewing of liquor is being charmed for you through the Devil's people or evil witches, cense immediately all the tubs three evenings in a row, and begin especially on a Wednesday, Thursday or Friday after sunset and quickly. If this doesn't help as before, do it nine times with it, and remain silent. On the following evening, go to that place where you and your people do your necessities (obey the call of nature) and take a clean staff and stir the filth around and say: See here, you devil, eat and dine on this, Let me have mine. Lastly, take a little on the twig or staff. Go in and stir in the mash tub, put in a little holy earth into the mash, and into all the tubs and then put the stick into the fire. In God's name, you'll most likely get liquor. Don't let anyone borrow anything from you during the time during which you will be working, anything that is needed in the production or whatever else. In the same way with the drink, when it doesn't want to be

---

222 "*lik*" is the word for corpse, "*ramma*" or "*ramme*" is *Scirpus cæspitosis*, yet more probably a corpse shroud.

made, cense the tub and put a little holy earth into the mix, then you'll get drink. Drink!

Rc[223] 9th Chapter[224]

[12] About people and their preservation against all injury and more. To protect and preserve people, second only to God's help which is the best, I will first write out a recipe for incense that can partly be bought at the Pharmacy, and partly be taken from Our Earth, namely:

PHARMACEUTICAL NAME IN LATIN AND SWEDISH

Caralia rubra for	2 spoonfuls	Rödcoralesten (Red Coralstone)
Gumiasa folida	2	Dyvelsträck (Asafetida)
Olibananum -- --	2	Wirack
Mastrick --	2	mastrick
Horba origanum	2	kalfhufvut eller konkar (calveshead or ?)
anterinum --	2	Spansk humle (Spanish Fly?, lit Spanish bumblebee.)
Pulfris fumalis	2	fluss pulver (rose? powder – Rietz)
Ginnisuk sirnum	2	berensten eller Raf (bernsten: amber, so Ambergris?)
Sulphir Carin	2	Gult Svafvel (Yellow Sulphur)
Hüpericum	2	St Johannes Gräs (As opposed to St. John's Wort?)
Kastorium	12	Bäfvergiäll (Beaver musk, also called castorium)
Saxafrax	4	Christikors trä (Christ's Cross tree, Saxafrage?; Sassafras?)
Rudallij		hvitlöck (garlic)
mäster rott	4	mästerrott (translated here as Master root)
Svart Coralsten	2	[no Swedish given] (Black coral stone)
hvit Coralesten	2	[no Swedish given] (White coral stone)
Tybast --	2	[no Swedish given] (Daphne mezereum)

sometimes a little holy earth.

This earth is taken in the evening in the name of God for healing and for a warning against all ill, and a pair of common pins is put into its place in payment/pledge for it, and it is mixed together with the incense. The dose for the fat bags which are prepared for the incense, the dose into 9 or 12 pieces of paper.

[13] When you have encountered something ill, of the magic of those on or under the earth, or evil witches, if you're suffering, which can be seen on your

---

223 I assume the letters "rc" here refer to "recept" or "recipes/prescriptions."

224 Since there have been no chapter headings previously in the manuscript, there may be reason to believe that this portion was copied from another manuscript *with* chapter headings.

nails, when the white half moon, the White half-moon is away down at the root of the nails, then it's high time for you to crush the incense and mix the bunch together and put, as was said, 9 doses each divided up, and cense yourself in the following way, on a Sunday, Saturday or Thursday evening stand facing north in the house, naked, with a sheet over you, take pure coalfire in a pot or brazier, stand over it and put the incense on it until it burns out. Then, afterwards, take the brazier around yourself five times to the right and the same number to the left, and put it down away from you. Go three times back and forth, spit from you all ill. Go then to bed in God's name. You can have a shirt on you, but no knots on you. One may not take it off, or change the sheet during the time of the censing. This can be tried three times in a row, and be kept up for 9 24-hour days, and see how you feel, and check out your nails and see how it goes. If you don't notice an improvement, but rather that the ill is as strong as it was, then you are hexed. Then begin the censing with full seriousness 9 times, and when you have accomplished it, go to running water and take approximately a pail of water against the current, but spit first into the water. This happens on a Wednesday morning silently. Put the water on the tile oven, so it can become lukewarm on Thursday morning. Go to a churchyard and take a little earth in God's name for healing and preservation against all ill, and put a pair of common pins in pledge. Take this dirt which is holy and mix it in the water, and spread it all over your body, each joint and limb, and each time taste a little of the water beforehand.

N.B. Keep some of this incense always on you, then no one can do any ill to you, or bewitch you, and if you may lose it, then immediately take another one in its place again, then you'll be free of all ill. Take also holy earth and, as is already said, and put it down in the evening into all your house under the thresholds at all the exits and entrances, as well as under the chimney's brace, then no devil or evil person will be able to inflict on you or any of your livestock any injury, or take even the slightest from you. Put this earth so deep down that it can't be dug up and taken away.

[14] When your wife churns the butter. Put a little bit of Asafetida as big as a seed of the calla-lily, then you'll have butter. If it's hexed, do as stated before, cense the tub and put a little on the churning stick (technical term?) also on it, sulfur drops in the churn and in your milk-tub, and wash them also with that is mixed with holy earth. Bore some earth out of the same, and throw in a *flyrön*'s pegs into it, or torn thorn's pegs.

[15] On the care of Livestock. Whenever you get a new farm animal, your own or bought or traded, then mark (brand?) them immediately and give them internally some of their own blood as well as your own blood, the third finger or the thumb, in addition to three whole grains that are found in the bread, and a little clay taken from the mouth of the oven, on a Thursday morning

before the Sun comes up, then no one can bewitch them, and then they'll stay with you.

Water your livestock on Maundy Thursday before sunrise, then they're free that year from scabies, even if they graze together with scabby livestock. It also helps for other afflictions. Mark your newborn piglets and other livestock as soon as they emerge and give them internally, as was said, some of their blood. Also, dock its tail and throw it in the place, then no one can harm them, but rather they will thrive and grow well.

| Am (Arn?) | + | pam | ++ | unter (unten?) | +++ |
| Fax | + | pax | ++ | malabax | +++ |

C. O. SWAHNS SVARTKONSTBOK
OWNER (1918): COMMERCIAL COUNCILOR CARL SAHLIN, STOCKHOLM
POSITED ORIGIN: TVETA SOCKEN, ASPELANDS LÄN, SMÅLAND

[HANDWRITING #1]

N:o 1.
WHEN ONE GETS an ear infection, then you should fry a red onion and put it as hot as one can tolerate in the ear, then one will be well again.

N:o 2.
WHEN YOU ENCOUNTER a haunting, then you should take a little gunpowder in water, then you'll get better.

N:o 3.
WHEN YOU GET severely ill (diarrhea), then you should take a little seed of *Sisymbrium sophia* in water and then you'll get better.

N:o 4.
WHEN YOU ENCOUNTER elves, then you should cense yourself with the so-called *Marchantia polymorpha* (a type of livermoss), and if it doesn't help, then you should go to the place where you believe you got too close to them, and ask for forgiveness, and offer a little silver at the same place, and then you should have an innocent woman who is single blow into a forge-fire and throw fire made from flint over herself, then you'll get better.

N:o 5.

IF YOU FIX it so that you can get a maiden's monthly flow and anoint your shotgun with it, then you can shoot whatever you want.

N:o 6.

IF YOU FIX it so that you get yourself a human skull and look through its eye sockets, then you can go as close as you want to birds.

N:o 7.

IF YOU WANT TO SHOOT a magpie or a starling and a lapwing, and take the heart and put it in the ammunition next to the powder, then it will shoot well immediately.

N:o 8.

TO CURSE THE ONE who hexed your shotgun, take snake fat, screw out the tail screw, smear it with it, screw it in completely, then he'll die within 24 hours. If he comes and asks you to stop it, then unscrew the screw and wash it, then the sick one will become well again immediately.

N:o 9.

WHEN THE SHOTGUN IS HEXED, pour it full of fresh yeast, tap it well in, put it in the oven so that it rises, then the one who hexed it will get diarrhea from it.

N:o 10.

TO MAKE it so much that the one who is along on the hunting trip doesn't even get to shoot, take 2 alder twigs or pegs, break them off, stick them into the earth, the one in the right the other in the left footprint of the one who accompanies you; then he'll not get to shoot that day; say when you stick it down into the earth that "you shall not shoot today."

N:o 11.

BE CAREFUL that after the left footprint, then take up your knife, cut three lines lengthwise in the print, and one crossing it. Spit in each time, and say "Thus shall you shoot," then he'll not get to shoot.

N:o 12.

TO HEX shotguns, when the shot goes off, twist a year-old evergreen, or its branches, counterclockwise, and tie a knot in the same. As long as that knot remains, then that one with the shotgun won't hunt successfully.

N:o 13.

TO CARE FOR shotguns, take up a piece of turf in a stretch from north to south, and shoot under it towards the east or the west, then the shotgun is good. You can tramp down the turf again.

N:o 14.

THE ONE WHO wants to have a shotgun that won't miss its mark should take earth from a tomb and shoot three times into the air, and one time into the earth. Then take some of that same earth and put it into the barrel and into the ammunition and shoot the bird that you see in the south, and hold the shotgun on him until he dies. Then it will never shoot amiss.

N:o 15.

A PERSON has three things in his body, and they are all evil. The first is the nails, the second is the lice on his head, and the third is earwax, or crust. Put the lice and the nails into the barrel, and earwax into the flashhole, then it is magically destroyed immediately.

N:o 16.

IF THE SHOTGUN is thus destroyed, then put it under the threshold in the sheep shed, and drive the sheep over it, then it will be good immediately.

N:o 17.
ABOUT BIRDS.

As the birds play, take a sharp pipe and put the bird-gullets outside and blow into the pipe and, when you want to shoot then they'll come to you. And be careful to cut both ears off a squirrel and put on the lid to the pot, then the dog under the window, then you will have as many as you want to have before one returns home.

N:o 18.

IF YOU HAVE a bullet in your mouth and chew on it, and say this: "I chew on this bullet, I to my advantage, and not to yours, in this way I have luck in my shotgun and you won't even shoot a living tiny animal with your shotgun, in the name of the Father, of the Son and of the Holy Spirit.

N:o 19.
TO SHOOT WHATEVER YOU WANT.

TAKE a lapwing chick in its nest before it comes out onto the ground, dry it in a pan and grind it up to a powder and mix it in 5 measures of gunpowder. Take and cut out the heart and the liver of a bat, and dry it to a powder, and pour it into the lead when you load the bullets. Then you'll see the use of it.

N:o 20.

IF YOU LOAD bullets on Pentecost morning before the sun comes up, then you stick a hole into the finger next to the little one on the right hand[225] and put the bullets in the blood, then you won't shoot amiss.

N:o 21.

IF YOU WANT TO HAVE luck then take the loose splinters/flakes from the bells/clocks[226] and have it by your shotgun, then you'll have great luck.

N:o 22.

STEAL three Malt grains, three salt grains, three bread crumbs from 9 households, a grain or crumb from each household, and have in your shotgun in the Sign of Sagittarius,[227] then you'll have luck in everything.

N:o 23.

ABOUT BIRDS or animals, take from the hair on your head and wrap it around the bullet or the shot and shoot, then it will hit.

N:o 24.

IF YOU WANT TO HIT WHAT with someone then you should load a shotgun without powder, and shoot out, then have 2 unloaded and load the one with loose powder and shoot in the flashpan on the other, then it will go out with the same shot.

N:o 25.

TO MAGICALLY DESTROY the shotgun, take a nail from a coffin and put it in the shotgun. As far as you put it down, then it is cursed, and no one can fix it thereafter.

N:o 26.

TAKE earth from three cemeteries and put under the altar for three Sundays. When you have it in your shoes under your feet and walk around any animal, then it won't walk over your footprints. If you walk around a fire, then it will be contained within those bounds.

---

225 The "right nameless finger."

226 It is impossible to tell from context whether this is the flakes from a church bell, or the splinters from a home clock. *Klocka* is both bell and clock. *Flåra* is both splinter and filing.

227 While Sahlgren writes that *skytten* here means the sign of the marksman, i.e., Sagittarius, it isn't really clear that it might not mean the marksman who owns the shotgun.

N:o 27.

TAKE a black cat and cut out its entrails and bury it at a place where three roads meet on a Thursday evening, go and see after 9 24-hour days or after three Thursdays, then you'll find after the same deed a ring. Keep it on your finger then no one will see you.

N:o 28.

IF ONE STABS out both eyes of Swallow chicks – then the mother will fly after a stone, with which she will anoint her chicks' eyes so they'll see. Then you go there after the ninth night, then you shall see that the chicks have their sight. Take the same stone and keep it on you, then you will become invisible.

N:o 29.

TAKE a black hen, twist or crush it to death. Take all the feathers from it and take the entrails from it and boil it, as complete as it is put it down, and put it into a new dish in which food has never been before. Then buy 3 knives at a street vendor's, all of which were made by a single smith and put all three knives into the same dish in which there was never food before. Cover it with the second dish.[228] Go then to a crossroads and bury the same food and three knives in the ground. Go back then after 29 nights to visit the dish where you will find in the same dish a bone with which you can see through earth where there are hidden things, and the best piece that you see in there, take it away or another that you are thinking of taking, but you shouldn't take everything. In this same dish you'll find a dice-piece, and when you have it with you then you'll have luck in games of chance. In the same dish you'll find also a stone, and when you have it with you then no one will see you. But out of all these three things that you find in the dish, you shouldn't take but one single thing.

N:o 30.

IF YOU WANT TO RACE, then take a ball of tallow and soak it in pure blood. Tie it at the horse's left ear, and recite these words before you sit down: "*påleta pelr a sa alsa.*" Then no horse will pass you.

N:o 31.

TO TRANSFORM YOUR APPEARANCE, – take a rotten tree that shines at nighttime, that one calls flying rowan,[229] grind it to pieces and mix with mercury and make from it a candle, and when you light the candle, no one will see you.

---

[228] Though the text is not clear on this count, I believe that there should be two dishes that have never had food in them, the one containing the chicken and three knives, and the second to be placed over the first.

[229] Flying rowan is a rowan that has taken root in a tree trunk of another type of tree.

N:o 32.

THERE IS an herb that is called *Platanthera bifolia*, the one is white and the other is black. The black is good for the one who wants to give himself into the power of women. Then one takes the white of an egg and the white of hen droppings, and hen's blood, and give to him who never has love for the womenfolk.

N:o 33.

TAKE the swallow and cut the heart out of it and eat it with honey. He can everything that he hears to be recited. (He can recite everything that he hears? He understands everything that he hears or is read? unclear.)

N:o 34.

IF YOU WANT someone to fall in love with you, then write these letters in your hand before the sun comes up: *Toogras*.

N:o 35.

WHEN YOU ARE LOVED by someone then take a swallow's tongue and put it under your tongue, and kiss the girls that you love. –

ANOTHER, take a swallow firmly and tie up its nest for three nights. Hook its feet and tie. After three nights, take it out and cut up its abdomen. There you'll find 3 stones, a red, white and black. If you hold the red one in your mouth when you want something from someone then you'll be receiving everything that you want to have; if you hide the white one in your mouth, then you'll not thirst or hunger either; if you hold the black one in your hand and speak with a troubled person, then they will become glad.

N:o 36.

IF YOU WANT to have meat springing up from the pot, then write these letters on the pot before you set it on the fire: "Grylista beta trixvit tryligen."

N:o 37.

WHEN ONE IS out hunting, even if there's lots of game, you should first shoot a hare, then be careful to dip the finger next to the little one on the right hand in the blood of the hare three times, and lick it. Then the one who does that will hunt successfully the whole day, and no one else.

N:o 38.

TO GET A MAIDEN to love you, take a serpent's sting and hang it in the back of your belt, then she'll love you.

N:o 39.

TO GET a faithful maiden as a friend, take your blood and her blood and stir it together in a quart of beer, and give her to drink quickly --.

N:o 40.

SO THAT A MAIDEN will fall in love with you, write both your names on an apple, some cheese, or whatever, and these words: "Abrautis, Atalulia," also write in an apple these words: "D. O. g. T. e. h."

N:o 41.

WHEN A MALE is hexed by an evil woman, take a corpse tooth, cense yourself with it, that will help.

N:o 42.

IF YOU WANT to be invisible – inside a lapwing's breast is a stone with many colors, keep that with you, then you'll be invisible.

N:o 43.

FOR HOLE,[230] take *Artemisia vulgaris* in milk, then it will pass.

N:o 44.

TO TEST a girl's maidenhood, take garlic and give to her, if she sneezes then she doesn't have her maidenhood.

N:o 45.

FOR COUGH, take nestle roots and soak them in water or beer, and drink each evening as you go to bed.

N:o 46.

TO KNOW who is a malicious witch, beat a snake to death before Our Lady Day,[231] put that cane by the Church door, and let them walk over it. The one who goes into the church and is impure, then they'll yawn as long as they're in church.

N:o 47.

TO MAKE a maiden come to you, take up out of the earth *Orchis maculata*, which has a white root and a black. If you throw it into water then the black will float. You take the black and administer it to her, then she will be more fond of you than of all others.

---

[230] This could be an ulcer, or perhaps a hernia, though the text isn't clear.
[231] Vår Fru Dag, Our Lady's Day, also known as Våffeldag, March 25.

N:o 48.

TO RECITE over colic for horses, "The troll sat in camp, the horse got colic, spit in the hand, hit in the mouth, healing in the same moment!"[232] this is recited 3 times.

N:o 49.

TO TEST a maiden's maidenhood, take the root of "Hedera"[233] and burn it in front of the nose. If she's impure, then she'll wet herself immediately.

N:o 50.

TO HEAL peas from the lice,[234] a suckling woman should walk around the pea fields, and milk around them and up among them, then the lice will disappear from that.

N:o 51.
LIQUOR SOAP

PREPARE 4 measures of soft soap that is dissolved in 3 quarts of strong liquor. This substance is useful to bathe with for stretched muscles and swellings that one wants to dissipate. One can make it more dissipating, but to mix it with 100 drops of terpentine oil in which case the Spiritus is useful for driving out gallstones, swellings of the horse's hamstrings and other such cold swellings. If they are not too old, you want to use it to dissipate heat and painful swellings. You should instead of using terpentine oil, mix 1 measure of Camphor to it. This medicine is very good for animals.

N:o 52.
ABOUT DIGESTIVE SALVES.

FOR THAT IS TAKEN 1 pound of Turpentine and 2 measures of turpentine oil that is well stirred with the yolks of 6 eggs, so that it is well mixed into a yellow salve. With this salve all wounds that are soft and ooze a lot should be bound, just as all wounds that are close to the bone, or sinew or parts that deal with speed,[235] wounds on the withers, crown and other parts of the foot.

---

232 My more poetic attempt to preserve the same rhyme scheme:
"The troll sat in camp
The horse got a cramp,
Spit in the hand, punch in the mouth
Healing is in, and sickness is out!"

233 This appears in another MS though it needs to be found for its Latin name.

234 Not sure about usage, but this sounds more like aphids than lice...

235 *bråskaktig*, jfr 53 with brosk. This is a part of a horse's anatomy that I am unfamiliar with, but is clearly a part of this writer's vocabulary.

N:o 53.
BASILIK SALVE

THIS IS PREPARED from pitch, resin and yellow wax, of each 4 measures, which is melted over a slow fire and into which is stirred one quart of cottonseed oil. This salve can be used for wounds that don't want to produce any puss, but rather are dry and swollen at the edges. It will soften up parts of the wound and produce blisters that are necessary for the healing of the wound. It is also useful to soften up brittleness and dry hoof if you massage it with it. It is on the other hand less useful for wounds on the leg, sinew or the speedy parts.

N:o 54.
CAPPSITISK SALVE

THIS IS PREPARED from 4 measures of verdigris ground finely and boiled to a salve with a third of a Quart vinegar and 12 measures of honey in a clay pot that should be so large that it won't boil over when it froths; this salve is used to dry [*mygg*: a type of red sore in the abdomen on horses] and [*rasp*: a type of rash that affects horses in the joints], when they produce a lot of moisture. It is also useful in all those wounds and sores where the flesh that is growing back is too loose and fungal and that produces a material that is too thin and watery. This salve is drying and works against rot.

N:o 55.

HORN SALVE is prepared from equal amounts of cottonseed oil, yellow wax and pig fat, Venetian turpentine and yellow honey. The oil, fat and wax are melted together on a slow fire, and when it has melted, the turpentine and honey is stirred in, until it becomes cold. This salve is useful to apply to the body on horses that have brittle hooves, but it can be applied to the hoof itself with syrup (molasses?) that one has made black with a little lamp-black.

N:o 56.
CAMPHOR OIL

FOR THIS YOU TAKE a measure of camphor torn apart to a powder and some drops of liquor, and after that is mixed with two thirds of a quart of Linseed oil, and half so much of Turpentine oil. This oil is useful to disperse stiffness in the joints and to massage into the bow or the forelock, or other parts which through exertion have become tender or stiff.

N:o 57.[236]

THIS MEDICINE is a miracle for the well-meaning, wherein the Almighty's grace deigns to appear, this medication taken internally and is united with

---

[236] This text, presumably an assembly of miracle cures one might recite to encourage greater

a chill in the stomach, then like a sweet Mercurius or messenger whose rising vapors are released without with all these allowing moisture to flee into the veins and sinews. Since it doesn't combine with the 'ammunition for the anus' it is communicated strongly and retains its strength when it is driven out through urine and going to the toilet.

Of this medication 15 drops taken internally in the evening after having eaten and before going to bed, will drive slowly the suffering of pain, all types of frustration and heavy labor, and that which is unexplainable, when it melts the stone it makes the flesh grow; yea, it has healed a man's wounds that through continual injury were already 11 years old, and which wounds were sometimes so stinking of pus that maggots crept in and out and floated so nastily that the patient stank where he was, and whatever he wore on his body rotted at that moment. He became completely healed, yea, everything was done completely for 3 cuts during these eleven years' time, where different stones were taken out of the same flowing sore. Which this, my truthful tale of ignorance will criticize, but the love for one so miraculous truth is raised. He asked the patient himself by the name of Aodolph Carolius Jonkhort, farmer at Motesteg in Harlem. Another nasty patient Abreham Manner, dwelling at Sparne had practiced medicine for 5 years previously, and in addition with two times promoted to Oprateuren in Amsterdam, addressed, although as he was completely exhausted.

N:o 58.
THE CORRECT WAY TO SHOOT.

THE SHOTGUN should be prepared in this way: take 2 measures of mercury, 2 measures of saltpeter, 4 measures of *adipis humanis* (human fat), and let it move inside the shotgun, and work it long enough that it comes up out of the muzzle, or take a piece of a board from a coffin in which a mother who died in childbirth has layed, and cut it inside the butt of the shotgun, then whatever you shoot at will be hit.

N:o 59.
ANOTHER.

BE CAREFUL when three hunters stand together at New Years, then take moss from a dead man's skull, grind it and mix it with lead, then cast the bullet or shot from that, between 11 and 12 o'clock at night, without saying a word. When they're ready, drop a little cottonseed oil on them.

---

confidence in the formulas, is obviously partially corrupt, and was probably copied from something like a package of an itinerant pharmacist, with all the copying inaccuracies that inevitably arise. The rather meandering nature of this section indicates to me that it was copied but poorly, perhaps being translated from Dutch. In the manuscript, there is a page and a half after this section (N:o 57) that is left blank.

N:o 60.
ANOTHER.
WHEN A MURDERER is autopsied/dissected by the medics, then his abdomen will be sewn back together, the needle with which this is accomplished, take and put it so that it will go into the butt-screw hole and then is screwed in. Then shoot with the shotgun at an animal, without being careful to aim, but you will surely hit your target even so.

N:o 61.
ANOTHER.
WHEN YOU LOAD, then take the bullet or the shot in your mouth, and put the word "Wårdt. ke." then let them fall through the muzzle and pound it down and shoot.

N:o 62.
ANOTHER.
TAKE a sewing needle with which a corpse has been sewn into its shroud, and break it apart into five pieces. Put four pieces of it underneath the butt, and the fifth with the eye where you usually hold your thumb, then one will hit the target that you're shooting at.

N:o 63.
ANOTHER.
WRITE the following words on paper or parchment, and tie the scrap on the right arm, then you'll always hit your target –
+ Rithas + Tetra + Grammaton + On + Chabriel + Agla +

N:o 64.
SO THAT YOUR SHOTGUN WON'T BE HEXED.
ON GOOD FRIDAY before the sun comes up, shoot a raven or a hen, which is completely black. Take some of its heart, tongue and liver, and put the three types up against the butt screw, then for the entire year it will shoot with luck, and no one can hex it.

N:o 65.
TO BE ABLE TO SHOOT TWICE AS FAR OR THRICE WITH A POOR SHOTGUN OR PISTOL.
WHEN YOU LOAD then take ordinary gun powder and put in it prepared camphor as big as a pea, then it will shoot three times as far.

N:o 66.
TO SHOOT AND HIT YOUR MARK.
TAKE a corpse bone, dried, and grind it to powder, and mix it amongst the

lead when you cast shot, and some amongst the powder, and carry a little with you, then you'll always hit what you shoot at. –

N:o 67.
ANOTHER.
TAKE a garlic clove and stick it into a snake's head, and bury it at a certain place, and when it has grown up, then dry it to a powder and mix it with the gunpowder. It will always hit, and it will make three head-shots.

N:o 68.
TO ALWAYS SHOOT AND HIT THE TARGET.
TAKE a boy's umbilicus, and have it mounted in (plated in?) silver when the Sun is in the sign of Capricorn, and use it to get your aim. What you see through it you'll hit. NB, it is easy to get from a midwife.

N:o 69.
ANOTHER.
HAVE a paper with you on which is written "Apolin, Cegame, Sangta Alfoni Rait. Truit," pound it onto the gunpowder instead of the ammunition.

N:o 70.
TO HEX A SHOTGUN.
TAKE the rags that one has cleaned your shotgun with, bore a hole in an oak, towards the rising sun, and put it into the hole. Seal it with a wedge of Hagton[237] in it, then no one can hit anything with that shotgun until it is taken out.

N:o 71.
IN ANOTHER WAY.
WHEN SOMEONE has shot something, then take a hair or a feather from it, and put it in an ash tree. As long as it sits there, no shot will meet its mark. – NB, Be careful that no one sees it, because then you can have inconvenience from it.

N:o 72
SO THAT A HUNTER CAN'T FIRE A SHOT.
WHEN YOU SEE HIM go out hunting, then say "Mattheus, Lucas and Johannes, the four Evangelists, they must preserve the life of all animals today, and the holy Abraham I give I give to a protector, in the name of the Father and of the Son and of the Holy Ghost, that he will be unable to make a clear shot." As soon as you see him load, then take a piss. –

---

237 [No actual footnote in MS –Eds.].

N:o 73.
SO THAT NO ONE CAN HEX YOUR SHOTGUN.
TAKE a piece of bread that you found by chance, pulverize the same and mix it with the gunpowder.

N:o 74.
ANOTHER.
TAKE peas in your mouth, on Christmas eve chew them apart and blow with them on the shotgun.

N:o 75.
ANOTHER.
CARRY the shotgun three times under the right leg, or turn the flint with the backmost forward.

N:o 76.
TO MAKE SURE BULLETS OR SHOT.
On the night of the Feast of the Ascension day[238] pour bullets or shot and say to each one, "I conjure you this night, when in the morning Jesus was awakened from the dead, that you travel, Travel, through sky, blood and flesh as well as Maria."[239]

N:o 77.
TO HAVE THREE ACCURATE SHOTS EACH DAY.
CUT three chips from a church or chapel threshold on the first Sunday after the new moon before the sun comes up. Load them in the shotgun and shoot them off, so that you can get hold of them again, then bury them under a church threshold on Good Friday. As long as they lie there and don't rot, you will have three good shots.

---

238 Kristi Himmelfärds dag, The Feast of the Ascension of Christ, May 12.

239 A number of factors make this an interesting spell. Firstly, it conjures by the power of the resurrection, which is more correctly placed at Easter rather than at the Ascension. Then the double mention of Mary, at a time when the Reformation had already taken firm hold of southern Sweden, is puzzling. It denotes rather a lack of any liturgical knowledge at all. *Uppväckt* rather than *Vaknade*? Perhaps this is an older piece, only partially remembered, and thus without a liturgical context into which it can be fit. Two Marias may mean a recitation of two "Ave Marias" which may mean this spell is from before the Reformation, prior to 1530s.

N:o 78.
SO ONE CAN'T HEX YOUR SHOTGUN.
TAKE natron, a leaf of marjoram, the gall of a black dog, and lapwing feathers and cense the shotgun with it, then it'll be good again, if it had ever been cursed.

N:o 79.
SO THAT A DOG WON'T LEAVE YOU.
TAKE some of your dog's hair in secrecy, roll it together and put it under your table foot, then he'll not go away.

N:o 80.
SO THAT ANIMALS MUST STAND STILL.
WHEN you see one, then say "Efusagenefra Palastria omaria Plastula" three times.

N:o 81.
SO THAT BIRDS CAN'T FLY OUTSIDE A CERTAIN CIRCLE OR TERRAIN.
TAKE a corpse skull and write upon it the following:
"BIDE ME, bird on the branch, as the dead man in the Grave in the name of the Father and of the Son and of the Holy [Ghost]." Take the skull in your right hand and walk around the place where the bird keeps himself, and say: "Bide me, bird, in the name of the Trinity, God the Father, Son and the Holy [Ghost].", do this three times, then they can't fly away from there –

N:o 82.
SO THAT NO DOG CAN HUNT HARES FOR THAT DAY.
WHEN YOU SEE the hunter tease the dogs, then put both thumbs inwards, and say three times, "Huss Tonis," then it won't work.

N:o 83.
TO ESTABLISH A PLACE WHERE NO ONE CAN SHOOT EXCEPT MYSELF.
TAKE a cat's skull. Put peas in it and bury it where you begin the rounds. Allow the peas to grow up, and when they are somewhat grown up through the earth, then take and move them from that place in a circle, so that there is 3 or 4 yards' distance between each pea, until you come back to where the skull is. Then no one can shoot there other than you yourself.

N:o 84.
SO THAT NO DOG CAN CATCH A HARE.

SAY as soon as you see a hare: "Springa Marie cat preserve you, life's bullets are behind you, in the name of the Father and of the Son and of the Hol. [y Ghost]." Then turn your balls in your pants,[240] then the mouths of the dog will be locked.

N:o 85.
HARES, TO CHARM SO THAT THEY CAN'T GET OUT OF THE PLACE.

ON APRIL FIRST, let a hunter catch a hare. Immediately chop off the right foot and take both eyes out of its head. Let him, that is, let him lie blinded on the ground, the foot and both eyes lie in a clay pot, and put into an anthill until the last of April so that the ants have eaten off all the meat. Take the bone, carry it with you, when you see a hare then quickly stick the bone in the ground, then he can't run away from there, but you can catch him with your hands.

N:o 86.
AN ENEMY, SO THAT HE CAN'T ANSWER YOUR SPEECH.

SAY these words to him: "Aglaria Pidhol garia Ananus Qepta" and blow towards him. Then he'll not know where he should go, and can't answer anything –

N:o 87.
ANOTHER.

WRITE these words on a bayberry leaf, a Tuesday at 7 o'clock: "Gabriel, Raphael, Michael, Uriel" and carry it with you –

N:o 88.
TO MAKE YOURSELF HARD, SO THAT NO BULLET WILL PIERCE YOU –

HANG these words around your throat: "Anna + B Teno[241] + Schatana + ( ) if you don't want to believe, then hang it on a dog or other animal ( ) and say as well "Ariel + Oriel Aclifek + Aptanter in nomine Patri et Filii et Spiritus Sancti Amen."

---

240 Sw. "wänd en lomma uti byxorna" "turn your balls in your pants." *lomma* = pung.
241 *Teno*, could be *Tens*. Unclear.

N:o 89.
TO HEX A SHOTGUN WHEN YOU HEAR THE SHOT GO OFF.

THEN STAND ON your left heel, spin three times counterclockwise, cut with the knife some turf loose under the heel while you are standing on same. Step off. Take up the turf under the heel and turn it upside down, then it is done.

N:o 90.

IF YOU APPLY a shotgun in the muzzle with hen's feces, then it will be thoroughly hexed.

N:o 91.
TO TAKE THE FIRE FROM A HUNTER.

WHEN YOU SEE that he is ready to shoot, then turn around and aim with the muzzle and the hunter towards the ground, then turn the shotgun right, and let him shoot if you want to.

N:o 92.
TO COMPEL THEM TO YOU, WHO HAVE HEXED YOUR SHOTGUN.

THE SHOTGUN is taken apart and cleaned, and the thread you clean it with you take with you, and bore a hole in an oak on the north side and put in the guage with which the barrel is cleaned, and have a plug of hawthorn ready that fits the hole. When the shot is made, then immediately the plug should be put into the hole. And then you knock slowly on the same until the one who has hexed your shotgun comes.

N:o 93.
SO THAT A TREE OR BUSH WILL WITHER AWAY.

TAKE a nail from a coffin that has been in a grave, and hit it into the root of the tree, then it will whither and die out.

N:o 94.
SO THAT A HUNTER WILL NOT SHOOT.

WHEN I SEE HIM go a-hunting, meet him or catch up to him, then I go to the side, so that he won't see it, and I take up three pieces of horse dung or some other garbage of whatever I can find. Spit three times on it, and throw it after the one I don't want to be able to shoot, and I say to myself, "You will not shoot in Hell any life today" even three times, the it is done in the same way with the other two pieces of dung I have left. Then he won't hit anything that day.

N:o 95.
TO CURE TOOTHACHE.
ONE WRITES with ink or pencil on four bites:

    Rågam _____ 1
    Wagam _____ 2
    Omgan _____ 3
    Ingan _____ 4

The patient bites a third of one of the above pieces and gives a dog a whole bite. When it is eaten by the patient and the dog, then the patient eats the second third of his bite, and gives again a whole bite to the dog. When it is consumed it is done in the same way with what is left. Observe though, if it is a woman it should be a bitch and if a man then a male. The same when the above is established, then one wants to write away the tooth ache with good 9 times then it will surely help. If he is not so crazy (with pain?) then also give a cotton ball with some drops of Hops oil in it. NB, Spanish hops oil –

N:o 96.
TO CHARM AWAY TROLLSHOT.
JESUS WENT his way forth, then there was a troll on a high mountain. And he had a bow. "Where will you shoot," he said. It answered "both people and animals, that which flies and walks;" "Now, shoot at a forest where no one dwells, shoot at a lake where no one rows, shoot into Hell and into the Red Sea, that I say to you, and the pain shall immediately go away from you, Swen Persson, in the name of the Trinity, God and Son and the Holy Spirit's Name. Amen –

N:o 97.
TO CURE THE HEAVES IN HORSES.
ONE ALLOWS a hen to starve for three days, and then is given to it ½ Quart grain that it should keep inside for ½ a 24-hour day (12 hours), then the gizzard is cut open, and the grain with the rest is taken out, and immediately is sewn together and is greased with butter so that the hen is whole again. The grain with the rest that was taken out, is mixed with a little water and flour, from which is made three oblong balls, of which one is put down into the horse's throat, when he is fasting and he should fast after that for 2 hours. The same thing is done with the other two. This should be done 8 mornings in a row. It usually helps.

N:o 98.
TO STOP BLEEDING.
JESUS CHRIST carried his own cross, the blood ran in battling torrents. Your blood N. N. shall stop running, with Jesus' own will. I stop your bleeding for

you, Stina Persdotter, i the name of the Trinity, God the Father, the Son and the Holy Spirit's name Amen –

N:o 99.
TO DULL PAIN.

Jesus walked into the church yesterday, soothed and healed all wounds, yours as well as his own, so that it wouldn't either ache or smart. I charm it away for you, Lars Eriksson, in the name of the Trinity, Amen

N:o 100.
TO RECITE AWAY BÄFWERSLAGET.[242]

SAINT PER wend a-wading. Why don't you wade as well, you cramp with tightness? Tighten with your 10 fingers, 12 pure Angels of God with three Maria, the trouble will be beached. Until the one, the one released the second, and water the third. Comfort took, the cramping from the chest and the bar to the back, so I do with you, Stina Pers Dotter, in the Trinity's name 3 times.

N:o 101.
TO BIND THE WOMB OF A WOMAN.

JESUS AND MARIA went over a bridge. Jesus went forth and Maria stood. "What is the cause of it?" said Jesus. "The mother tears me and Björn's Gramma stretches me." "Bandaged and bound," said Jesus. If I knew with 10 of your fingers and 12 of God's angels fall to the back where you are used to lying, I say to you here with Elin Svens Dotter in the name of the Trinity, and tie three knots in a string that is held around the abdomen and tie it then firmly around the abdomen, then she won't get the mother-pains any more.

N:o 102. [Second handwriting][243]
THE ART OF COOKING ... GREASE.

TO A HALF MARK of unsalted butter is added:
camphor like a little pea
the same amount of asafetida
Solanum Dulcamara a spoonful
[unreadable] a little more than a spoonful
Red onion like a nut
Garlic as d:o d:o (two cloves?)

---

242 According to Sahlgren, *bäfver* has more to do with *bifvra* (or cramping) than the mammal, and thus may indicate an intestinal malady that comes upon one suddenly (*slag*), such as colic, peritonitis, appendicitis, or various sorts of intestinal or bowel obstructions.

243 Sahlgren writes that "this last recipe is written with pencil of a younger hand, and is partly unreadable. The overwriting is as good as obliterated."

[ON THE LAST PAGE IS:]

[THIRD HAND]

The veritable pieces of art
of
C
P. Carlström

[FOURTH HAND]

Authored by C. O. Svahn 1st Magic Professor
C. O. Swans

C. O. S.

APPENDIX

Toward a Swedish Botanical Pharmacopœia

COMMONLY OCCURRING FOLK NAMES FOR SUBSTANCES IN BLACK ART BOOKS

1. Alloe Sackotriom: *aloe succotrina* (a lily from the Cape)
2. Bernsten: (*bärnsten*, amber, even now used as a flavoring agent in Aalborg's Akvavit)
3. Bäfvergäll: *Castoreum* (beaver-musk)
4. Dyfvelsträck: Asafetida (*Ferula asafœtida*)
5. Fenum Grekum: fenugreek
6. Flygrönn, flyrön, et al.: (*Sorbus aucuparia*, or mountain ash: Often birds' droppings contain rowan seeds, and if such droppings land in a fork or hole where old leaves have accumulated on a larger tree, such as an oak or a maple, they may result in a rowan growing as an epiphyte on the larger tree. Such a rowan is called a "flying rowan" and was thought of as especially potent against witches and their magic, and as a counter-charm against sorcery. Sir J. G. Frazer, 814, top.)
7. Groblakka/groblad (literally "healing leaf"): *Plantago major* (plantain)
8. Järnört: *Verbena officinalis*
9. Libbesticka/Limmburstuck (German *Liebesstöck*): *Ligusticum levisticum* (lovage)
10. Malört: *Artemisia absinthium* (Wormwood)
11. Mastrix: Gum Mastic
12. Myrkam=myrrh
13. Natron: Sodium Hydroxide
14. Ormhalla/ormgalla: *Anguis fragilis* (Slow worm or Blind worm), or, more likely *Ophioglossum vulgatum* (Adder's tongue)
15. Paradiskorn: *aframomum melegueta*
16. Skt Johannes Bröd:
17. Sassafras: *sassafras officinalis*
18. Spansk Gröna: verdigris (copper carbonate or copper chloride, used in folk medicine as an anti-fungal)
19. Spisglas (spetsglans) antimonglas (*antimony* or *stibnite*, a metalloid commonly metallic silvery white, crystalline, and brittle element that is used especially as a constituent of alloys and in medicine.)

20. Svafvel: Sulfur
21. Säfvenbom: (säv=rush, so perhaps Calamus root, *Acorus calamus*?)
22. Tibast/Tidebast: *Daphne mezereum*
23. Vändelrot: *Valeriana officinalis radix*
24. Väyrot: *Rosmarinus officinalis*
25. Wirack: Olibanum

BIBLIOGRAPHY OF WORKS CITED

Almqvist, Bo. *Norrön niddiktning: traditionshistoriska studier i versmagi, 1. Nid mot furstar*. Nordiska texter och undersökningar 21. Stockholm: Almqvist & Wiksell, 1965.

———. *Norrön niddiktning: traditionshistoriska studier i versmagi, 2. Nid mot missionärer; Senmedeltida nidtraditioner*. Nordiska texter och undersökningar 23. Stockholm: Almqvist & Wiksell, 1974.

Alver, Bente Gullveig, Bengt af Klintberg, Birgitte Rørbye and Anna-Leena Siikala, eds. *Botare: En bok om etnomedicin i Norden*. Stockholm: LTs förlag, 1980.

Ambrosiani, Sune, Sigurd Erixon and Gustaf Hallström, eds. *Etnologiska Studier tillägnade Nils Edvard Hammarstedt 3.3.1921*. Föreningen för svensk kulturhistoria 2. Stockholm: A.-B. Svenska Teknologföreningens förlag, 1921.

Andenaes, Johannes. "Deterrence and Specific Offenses." *The University of Chicago Law Review* 38.3 (Spring, 1971): 537–53.

Ankarloo, Bengt and Gustav Henningsen, eds. *Early Modern European Witchcraft: Centres and Peripheries*. Oxford: Oxford UP, 1990.

Ankarloo, Bengt and Stuart Clark, eds. *Witchcraft and Magic in Europe*. Philadelphia: University of Pennsylvania Press. Series.
  Vol. 1: *Biblical and Pagan Societies*
  Vol. 2: *Ancient Greece and Rome*
  Vol. 3: *The Middle Ages*
  Vol. 4: *The Period of the Witch Trials*
  Vol. 5: *The Eighteenth and Nineteenth Centuries*
  Vol. 6: *The Twentieth Century*

Anonymous, ed. *Svartkonstbok, (Fader Abrahams Svartkonstbok)*. Stockholm: E. Svenssons boktryckeri, 1877.

Astakhova, A. M. "The Poetical Image and Elements of Philosophy in Russian Exorcisms." *VII Mezdunarodnyj kongress antropologiceskix i ètnograficeskix nauk*, Moskva, 3–10 avgusta 1964 g. VII Congres international des Sciences Anthropologiques et Ethnologiques, Moscou, 3 août–10 août 1964 6 (1969): 266–72.

Bailey, Michael D. "The Disenchantment of Magic: Spells, Charms and Superstition in Early European Witchcraft Literature." *American History Review* (April 2006): 383–404.

Baldinger, Max. *Aberglaube und Volksmedizin in der Zahnheilkunde*. Basel: Np., 1936.

Balzer, Marjorie Mandelstam, ed. *Shamanism: Soviet Studies of Traditional Religion in Siberia and Central Asia*. Armonk NY: M. E. Sharpe, 1990.

Bang, A. Chr. *Norske hekseformularer og magiske opskrifter.* Norske Videnskabsselskabets Skrifter, II, (No. 1, 1901) Historisk-filosofisk klasse. Kristiania: A. W. Brøggers Bogtrykkeri, 1901.

Baroja, Julio Caro. *The World of the Witches.* Translated by O. N. V. Glendinning. Chicago: University of Chicago Press, 1965.

Barry, Jonathan, Marianne Hester and Gareth Roberts, eds. *Witchcraft in Early Modern Europe: Studies in Culture and Belief.* Cambridge: Cambridge UP, 1996.

Bartels, Max. "Über Krankheitsbeschwörung." *Zeitschrift des Vereins für Volkskunde* (1895): 1-40.

Basilov, V. N. "Chosen by the Spirits" in Mandelstam Balzer, *Shamanism.*

Bergstrand, Carl-Martin. *Gammalt från Kind: Folkminnen från Kinds härad i Västergötland.* I-III. Göteborg: Gumperts förlag, 1959-1961.

———. *Trolldom och klokskap i Västergötland under 1800 talet.* Distribution, Borås: H. Borgströms bokhandel, 1932. Lund: Aktiebolaget Skånska Centraltryckeriet, 1932.

Betz, Hans Dieter, ed. *The Greek Magical Papyri in Translation including the Demotic Spells. Volume One: Texts.* Chicago: Chicago UP, 1986.

Bianchi, Lorenzo. "Greichische Zaubervorschriften," *Hessische Blätter für Folkskunde* 13 (1914): 103-14.

Biedermann, Hans. *Medicina Magica: Metaphysische Heilmethoden in Spätantiken und mittelalterlichen Handschriften.* Graz: Akademische Druck- und Verlagsanstalt, 1972.

———. *Handlexikon der Magischen Künste von der Spätantike bis zum 19. Jahrhundert,* 2. ed. Graz: Akademische Druck- und Verlagsanstalt, 1973.

Birlinger, Anton. "Besegnungen." *Germania* N. R. 5, 17 (1872): 75-76.

Blécourt, Willem de. "The Witch, Her Victim, The Unwitcher and the Researcher: The Continued Existence of Traditional Witchcraft." in Ankarloo and Clark, *Witchcraft and Magic in Europe: The Twentieth Century,* 141-219.

Blumler, Martin Frederick. *A History of Amulets.* Translated by S. H. (?). Collectanea Adamantæa XVIII. Edinburgh: N.p., 1887.

Bø, Olav. "Rational Folk-Medicine." in Tillhagen, *Papers on Folk-Medicine,* 143-53.

Bringéus, Nils-Arvid. "Västboprästens svartkonstböcker." *Svenska landsmål och svenskt folkliv* (1967): 13-27.

———. ">>Röda boken<< påträffad." *Svenska landsmål och svenskt folkliv* (1991): 89-91.

Brix, Hans. "Nye studier i nordisk runmagie." *Aarbøger for nordisk oldkyndighed og Historie* (1929): 1-188.

Bø, Olav. "Trollformlar." *Kulturhistorisk leksikon for nordisk middelalder fra vikingatid til reformasjonstid* XVIII (1974): 674-78.

Campbell, Åke, Waldemar Liungman, and Sigfrid Svensson, eds. *Nordiskt folkminne: Studier tillägnade C. W. von Sydow, 12/21/1928*. Stockholm: C. E. Fritzes Hovbokhandel, 1928.

Chireau, Yvonne P. *Black Magic: Religion and the African American Conjuring Tradition*. Berkeley: University of California Press, 2003.

Cockayne, Oswald. *Leechdoms, Wortcunning and Starcraft of Early England*. Vols. I & II. London, 1864-66.

Christiansen, Reidar Th. "Die finnischen und nordischen Varianten des zweiten Merseburgerspruches: eine vergleichende Studie." *FF Communications* 18 (1914): 77-218.

———. "En prøve av en ny utgave av norske trollformler." *Festskrift til Hjalmar Falk* (1927): 262-78.

———, ed., Pat Shaw Iversen, trans. *Folktales of Norway*. Chicago: University of Chicago Press, 1964.

Christoffersson, Olof. "Supriania, Fru Alstads Socken, Skytts Härad." *Folkminnen och Folktankar*, 1915.

Cleasby, Richard, Guðbrand Vigfusson and Sir William A. Craigie, eds. *An Icelandic-English Dictionary*. Oxford: The Clarendon Press, 1982. First impression, 1874.

Codrington, R. H. *The Melanesians*. Oxford: The Clarendon Press, 1891.

Crecelius, W. "Alte Segensformeln," *Zeitschrift für deutsche Mythologie und Sittenkunde* 1 (1853): 277-80.

Davidson, Hilda R. Ellis. "Chapter 2. Hostile Magic in the Icelandic Sagas." In *The Witch Figure: Festschrift honouring the 75th birthday of Katharine M. Briggs* (Boston: Routledge and Kegan Paul, 1973), 20-41.

Davíðson, Ó. "Isländische Zauberzeichen und Zauberbücher." *Zeitschrift des Vereins für Volkskunde* 13 (1903): 50-?; 267-?.

———. *Galdur og galdramál á Íslandi*. Reykjavík: N.p., 1940-43.

Davies, Owen. *Cunning Folk: Popular Magic in English History*. London: Hambledon and London, 2003.

———. *Grimoires: A History of Magic Books*. Oxford: Oxford UP, 2009.

De Vries, Jan. *Altgermanische Religionsgeschichte* I & II. Berlin: deGruyter, 1970.

Dickie, Matthew W. *Magic and Magicians in the Greco-Roman World*. London: Routledge, 2001.

Dieck, Alfred. "Magische Krankenbehandlung nach des 'Zweiten Merseburger Zauberspruches' bis ca. 1930." *Heilen und Pflegen* 19, Hessische Blätter für Volks- und Kulturforschung. (1986): 155-65.

Dillner, Elisabet. "Lisa of Finshult and her 'Smöjträ.'" In Tillhagen, *Papers on Folk-Medicine*, 117-31.

Djurklou, Gabriel. *Nerikes folkspråk och folklif. Anteckningar*. Örebro, 1860.

Dobkin, Marlene. "Fortune's Malice: Divination, Psychotherapy and Folk Medicine in Peru." *Journal of American Folklore* 82 (1969): 132-41.

Dömötör, Tekla. "A Type of Hungarian Faith-Healing Charm and its Background." *Arv* 28 (1972): 21–35.

Dolphini, G. "Sulle formule magiche e le benedizione nella traditione germanica." *Reale Istituto Lombardo di Scienze e Lettere – Rendiconti*, Mailand 101 (1967): 23–62.

Dundes, Alan, ed. *International Folkloristics: Classic Contributions by the Founders of Folklore*. Lanham, MD: Rowman & Littlefield, 1999.

Edsman, Carl-Martin. "Folklig sed med rot i heden tid." *Arv* 1&2 (1946): 145–76.

———. "Sjätte och sjunde Mosebok." *Saga och sed* (1962): 63–102.

———. *A Swedish Female Folk-Healer from the beginning of the 18th century*. Skrifter utgivna av Religionshistoriska institutionen i Uppsala IV (Humanistiska facultet). Uppsala: Almqvist & Wiksell, 1967.

———. "Svartkonstböcker i sägen och historia." *Saga och sed* (1959): 160–68.

Eis, Gerhard. *Altdeutsche Zaubersprüche*. Berlin: deGruyter, 1964.

Ek, Sven B. "Tre svartkonstböcker." In *Eslövs museums skriftserie* 2. (Eslöv: Eslövs Nya Boktryckeri, 1964), 7–37.

Eliade, Mircea. Willard Trask, trans. *Shamanism: Archaic Techniques of Ecstasy*. Bollingen Series LXXVI. Princeton: Princeton UP, 1964. French original, 1951.

Elworthy, Frederick Thomas. *The Evil Eye*. 1895. Reprint NY: The Julian Press, 1986.

Ericksson, Jörgen I. *Blodstämmare och handpåläggare: Folklig läkekonst och magi i Tornedalen och Lappland*. Stockholm: Gimle Förlag, 1992.

Ericksson, Manne. *Kommunförteckning till underlagskarta över Sverige i skalan 1:600000* utgiven genom Landsmålsarkivet i Uppsala, Nordiska Muséet, Svenska Ortnamnsarkivet, Landsmålsarkivet i Lund och Folkminnesarkivet i Lund. Stockholm: A.-B. Kartografiska institutet, Esselte AB. 1938.

Evans-Pritchard, E. E. "The Morphology and Function of Magic. A Comparative Study of Trobriand and Zande Rituals and Spells." *American Anthropologist* 31 (1929): 619–41.

———. *Witchcraft, Oracles and Magic among the Azande*. Abridged with an introduction by Eva Gillies. Oxford: Oxford UP, 1976.

Fanger, Claire, et al., ed. *Conjuring Spirits: Texts and Traditions of Medieval Ritual Magic*. University Park, PA: The Pennsylvania State UP, 1998.

Faraone, Christopher A. *Talismans and Trojan Horses: Guardian Statues in Ancient Greek Myth and Ritual*. Oxford: Oxford UP, 1992.

———. and Obbink, Dirk, eds. *Magika Hiera: Ancient Greek Magic and Religion*. Oxford: Oxford UP, 1991.

Favret-Saada, Jeanne. *Deadly Words. Witchcraft in the Bocage*. Translated by Catherine Cullen. Cambridge: Cambridge UP, 1980.

Flint, Valerie I. J. *The Rise of Magic in Early Medieval Europe*. Princeton, NJ: Princeton UP, 1991.

Flowers, Stephen E. *Runes and Magic: Magical Formulaic Elements in the Older Runic Tradition*. American University Studies Series I, Germanic Languages and Literature, vol. 53. New York: Peter Lang, 1986.

Forbes, Thomas R. "Verbal Charms in British Folk Medicine." *Proceedings of the American Philosophical Society* 115.4 (1971): 293–316.

Forsblom, Valter W. *Magisk Folkmedisin. Finlands Svenska Folkdiktning 7, Folktro och Trolldom*, no. 5. Helsingfors: Skrifter utgivna av Svenska Litteratursällskapet i Finland CXLVII (147), 1919–27.

———. "Magiska räkneformler" in Campbell, Liungman, and Svensson, eds. *Nordiskt folkminne*, 126–35.

Frazer, Sir James George, *The Golden Bough: A Study in Magic and Religion*, 1 Volume, Abridged Edition. New York: Macmillan, 1922.

Fåhræus, Robin. "Basic Facts concerning Humoral Pathology and Relics of these in the Language and in Folkmedicine." In Tillhagen, *Papers on Folk-Medicine*, 7–21.

Gamache, Henri, ed. *The Mystery of the Long Lost 8th, 9th, and 10th Books of Moses, together with the legend that was of Moses and 44 keys to universal power.* Bronx, NY: Original Publications, 1983.

Geijer, Herman. "Troll-Marksens Svartkonstbok." *Fornvårdaren* (1923–24), I:1–2, 59–69.

Genzmer, Felix. "Die Götter des zweiten Merseburger Zauberspruchs." *Arkiv för nordisk filologi* 63 (1948): 55–72.

———. "Da signed Krist – thû biuol'en Wuodan." *Arv* 5 (1949).

———. "Germanische Zaubersprüche." *Germanisch-romanische Monatsschrift* (Heidelberg) N. F. 1, 32 (1950): 21–35.

Grambo, Ronald. "Forvisningssteder i norske trollformler." *Maal og minne* (1967): 67–78.

———. "Metodiske betraktninger omkring et fremtidig typeregister for norske trollformler" *Nordnytt* 3/4 (1969): 44–45.

———. "Studiet av nordiske trollformler. Et kort notat om forskningsoppgaver som venter." *RIG* 56.4 (1973): 113–15.

———. "Models of Magic." *Norveg* 18 (1975): 77–109.

———. *Norske trollformler og magiske ritualer*. Oslo-Bergen-Tromsø: Universitetsforlag, 1979.

Granberg, Gunnar. *Skogsrået i yngre nordisk folktradition*. Skrifter utgivna av Gustav Adolfs Akademien för Folklivsforskning 3 (1935).

Granlund, John. "Curing 'Knarren' (Peritendinitis or Tendovaginitis)." In Tillhagen, *Papers on Folk-Medicine*, 29–67.

———. *Trollformler från Värmlands och Dalarnes bergslag*. Västsvenska folkminnen, 1929.

Grendon, Felix. "The Anglo-Saxon Charms." *Journal of American Folklore* 22 (1909): 105–237.

Grimm, Hans. "Heilsegen aus der Batschka." *Südostdeutschen Forschungen* 2 (1937): 418–26.

Grimm, Jakob. *Deutsche Mythologie vols I & II*. Göttingen: Dieterichsche Buchhandlung, 1844. 2nd ed. See especially Volume II: Chapter 38 "Sprüche und Segen," 1173–97.

Grimsson, Atrid. *Svartkonstbok: Om shamanism, folklig läkekonst och magi*. Stockholm: Vattumannenförlag, 1992.

Götlind, Johan. *Saga, Sägen och Folkliv i Västergötland*. Uppsala: A.-B. L. Norblads Bokhandel, 1926.

Hagberg, Louise. "Ordets makt." *Fataburen: Nordiska Muséets och Skansens Årbok* (1932): 75–88.

Hagström, Charlotte and Lena Marander-Eklund, *Frågelistan som källa och metod*. Lund : Studentlitteratur, 2005.

Hall, J. A. "Negro Conjuring and Tricking." *Journal of American Folklore* 10 (1897): 241–43.

Halpern, Barbara Kerewsky and Foley, John Miles. "The Power of the Word: Healing Charms as an Oral Genre." *Journal of American Folklore* 91 (1978): 903–24.

Hampp, Irmgard. *Beschwörung – Segen – Gebet: Untersuchungen zum Zauberspruch aus dem Bereich der Volksheilkunde*. Veröffenlichungen des Staatlichen Amtes für Denkmalpflege Stuttgart, Reihe C: Volkskunde, bd. 1. Stuttgart: Silberburg-verlag, 1961.

Hand, Wayland D. *Magical Medicine: The Folkloric Component of Medicine in the Folk Belief, Custom, and Ritual of the Peoples of Europe and America*. Berkeley: University of California Press, 1980.

Hansen, H. P. "Danske Trolddomsbøger." *Folkeminder udgivet af Foreningen 'Danmarks Folkeminder'* 4 (1958): 145–65.

Harris, Joseph. "Cursing with the Thistle: 'Skírnismál' 31, 6–8, and OE Metrical Charm 9, 16–17." *Neuphilologische Mitteilungen* 76 (1975): 26–33.

Haskins, James. *Voodoo & Hoodoo: The Craft as Revealed by Traditional Practitioners*. London: Scarborough House, 1990.

Hauge, Hans Egil. *Smältgummor, trollgubbar och andra kloka*. Skriften utgiven av Föreningen för folkminnenas bevarande (Gävle) 1 (1964).

Hellquist, Magdalena, ed. *Folklivet i Åkers och Rekarne Härader av Gust: Ericsson, metallarbetare. 3. Tro, vantro, övertro*. Skrifter utgivna genom Dialekt- och folkminnesarkivet i Uppsala, Ser. B:18. Uddevalla: Bohusläningens Boktryckeri, 1992.

Helm, K. "Zur Erklärung des ersten Merseburger Zaubersprüches." *Beiträge zur Geschichte der deutschen Sprache und Literatur*. (Halle/S.) Von Hermann Paul und Wilhelm Braune gegrundet.

Hepding, Hugo. "Beiträge zu magischen Formeln." *Hessische Blätter für Volkskunde* 23 (1924).

Heurgren, Paul. *Salomoniska Magiska Konster: Utdrag ur en Westboprests Svartkonstböcker*. 1918. Reprint G. Wendelholms förlag, 1986.

Hoffmann-Krayer, Eduard, Hanns Bächtold-Stäubli, and Gerhard Lüdtke eds. *Handwörterbuch des deutschen Aberglaubens*. Berlin and Leipzig: deGruyter, 1927–42.

Holm, Gwen de l', trans. *Sjätte och sjunde mosebok samt Moses besvärjelser: Den svarta bibeln*. Stockholm: G. Wendelholm förlag, 1986.

Hästesko, F. A. *Länsisuomalaiset tautienloitsut*. Dissertation: Helsinki: N. D.

———. "Motivverzeichnis westfinnischer Zaubersprüche nebst Aufzählung der bis 1908 gesammelten Varianten." *FF Communications* 19 (1914).

Hødnebø, Finn. "Trolldomsbøker." *Kulturhistorisk leksikon for nordisk middelalder fra vikingtid til reformasjonstid* 18 (1974): 670–73.

Honko, Lauri. *Krankheitsprojektile*. Helsinki: FF Communications 178 (1959).

———. "On the Effectivity of Folk-Medicine." ["*Om folkmedicinens effectivitet*"] In Tillhagen, *Papers on Folk-Medicine*, 132–42.

Hultkrantz, Åke. "The Healing Methods of the Lapps: Some aspects from the point of view of comparative religion." In Tillhagen, *Papers on Folk-Medicine*, 167–93.

Hurston, Zora N. "Hoodoo in America." *Journal of American Folklore* 44 (1931): 317–417.

Jarausch, Konrad. "Der Zauber in den isländersagas." *Zeitschrift des Vereins für Volkskunde*. N. F. 1, (1930): 237–68.

Johanssen, Jens Christian V. "Faith, Superstition and Witchcraft in Reformation Scandinavia." In Ole Peter Grell, ed. *The Scandinavian Reformation: From Evangelical Movement to Institutionalisation of Reform* (Cambridge: Cambridge UP, 1995), 179–211.

Johansson, Egil. "Literacy Campaigns in Sweden." *Interchange* 19.3/4 (Fall-Winter, 1988): 135–62.

Johansson, Swea. *Oklokt men klokt: Kloka gubbar och gummar, del II*. Ljungby: Ljungby Grafiska, 1984.

Johnsson, Pehr, ed. "En skånsk klok och hans svartkonstbok." *RIG: föreningens för svensk kulturhistoria tidskrift* 4 (1918): 208–12.

Jordan, Wilvert C. "Voodoo Medicine." In Williams, Richard A., ed. *Textbook of Black-Related Disease* (NY: McGraw-Hill, 1975), 715–38.

Kahle, B. "Krankheitsbeschwörung des Nordens." *Zeitschrift des Vereins für Volkskunde* (1895): 194–99.

Kallstenius, Gottfrid. "En svartkonstbok." *Arkiv för norrländsk hembygdsforskning* Härnösand: Härnösands-Postens Tryckeri Aktiebolag, 1918. Häft 1&2.

Kaufmann, F. "Der II Merseburger Zauberspruch." *Hermann Pauls und Wilhelm Braunes Beiträge zur Geschichte der deutschen Sprache und Literatur* 15 (1891): 207–10.

Kedem, M. "Russian Incantations: Magic spells of the Atharvaveda." *Slavica Hierosolymitana* 5/6 (1981): 61–68.

Kemp, P. *Healing Ritual: Studies in the Technique and Tradition of the Southern Slavs.* London: Faber and Faber, 1935.

Kieckhefer, Richard. *Forbidden Rites: A Necromancer's Manual of the Fifteenth Century.* University Park, PA: The Pennsylvania State UP, 1997.

———. *Magic in the Middle Ages. Cambridge Medieval Textbooks.* Cambridge: Cambridge UP, 1990.

Kjellström, Rolf. *Nordiska frågelistor.* Nordiska museet. Kulturhistoriska undersökningen. Stockholm : Kulturhistoriska undersökningen, Nordiska museet, 1995.

Klagstad, Harold L., Jr. "Great Russian Charm Structure." *Indiana University Slavic and East European Studies* 13 (1958): 135–44.

Klintberg, Bengt af. "Magisk diktteknik, Tre exempel." In *Harens klagan: Studier i gammal och ny folklore* (Stockholm: P. A. Norstedt & söners förlag, 1978–82), 7–21.

———. *Svenska Folksägner.* Stockholm: Norstedts Faktapocket, 1972, 1986.

———. *Svenska Trollformler.* Stockholm: Wahlström & Widstrand, 1965.

Krohn, Kaarle. "Wo und wann entstanden die finnischen Zauberlieder?" *Finnisch-Ugrische Forschungen* 1 (1901): 52–72; 147–81.

———. "En finsk-svensk trollformel i Sydösterbotten." In Campbell, Liungman and Svensson, eds., *Nordiskt folkminne*, 195–98.

Kuhn, Adelbart. "Indische und germanische Segenssprüche," *Zeitschrift für vergleichende Sprachforschung* 13 (1864): 49–74, 113–57;

Kuna, Ralph R. "Hoodoo: The Indigenous Medicine Psychiatry of the Black American." *Mankind Quarterly* 18.2 (1977): 137–51.

Kvideland, Reimund and Henning Sehmsdorf, eds., *Nordic Folklore: Recent Studies.* Indiana University Press, 1989.

———, eds. *Scandinavian Folk Belief and Legend.* Minneapolis: University of Minnesota Press, 1988.

Leeuw, G. van der. "Die sogenannte epische Einleitung der Zauberformeln." *Zeitschrift für Religionspsychologie* 6 (1933): 161–80.

Leland, Charles Godfrey. *Gypsy Sorcery and Fortune Telling.* 1891. Reprint New Hyde Park: University Books, 1963.

Lengertz, William, ed. *En svartkonstbok från Kristianstads län: En nyfunnen handskrift i Perstorp, med en översikt over Naturläkare, kloka och undergörare i Skåne.* Malmö och Lund: Förlag Lengertz, 1937.

Lid, Nils. *Trolldom: nordiske studiar.* Oslo: Cammermeyers boghandel, 1950.

Lieban, Richard W. *Cebuano Sorcery: Malign Magic in the Philippines.* Berkeley: University of California Press, 1967.

Lindahl, Carl, John McNamara and John Lindow, eds. *Medieval Folklore: A Guide to Myths, Legends, Tales, Beliefs, and Customs.* Oxford: Oxford UP, 2002.

Linderholm, Emanuel. "Signelser och besvärjelser från medeltid och nytid." *Svenska landsmål och svenskt folkliv* 41 (1927, -29, -39): 1–478.

———. "Nordisk magi: studier i nordisk religions- och kyrkohistoria." *Svenska landsmål och svenskt folkliv* 20 (1927, 1929, 1939): 1–479.

Lindow, John. *Scandinavian Mythology: An Annotated Bibliography*. New York: Garland, 1988.

———, trans. and ed. *Swedish Legends and Folktales*. Berkeley: University of California Press, 1978.

Lindqvist, Ivar. *Galdrar*. Göteborg: Elander, 1923.

Lindqvist, N. *En isländsk svartkonstbok från 1500-talet*. Uppsala: Appelbergs Boktryckeri Aktiebolag, 1921. Subsequently reprinted in English translation by Stephen Flowers, trans., *The Galdrabók: An Icelandic Grimoire*. York Beach, ME: Samuel Weiser, 1989.

Lindskoug, Ossian, ed. *Lappmannen Jon Johanssons Signerier och Besvärjelser: Svartkonst från Lappland*. Malmö: Förlag Maiander, 1917.

Little, Lester K. *Benedictine Maledictions: Liturgical Cursing in Romanesque France*. Ithaca: Cornell UP, 1993.

Ljungberg, H. *Den nordiska religionen och kristendomen*. Nordiska texter och undersökningar II, Dissertation, Uppsala, 1938.

Ljunggren, Karl Gustav. "Två magiska formler från 1600-talets Halmstad." *Saga och sed* (1959): 70–74.

Luck, Georg, ed. and trans. *Arcana Mundi: Magic and the Occult in the Greek and Roman Worlds*. Baltimore: The Johns Hopkins University Press, 1985.

Lundberg, Lars, ed. "En svartkonstbok." *Göinge-bladet*. Lund: Grahns tryckeri, 1989(1):11–13; 1989(2):28–31; 1989(3):20–23.

Lykiardopoulos, Amica. "The Evil Eye: Towards an Exhaustive Study." *Folklore* 92.2 (1981): 221–30.

Magnusson, Magnus and Hermann Pálsson, eds. and trans. *The Vinland Sagas: The Norse Discovery of America*. New York: Viking Penguin, 1965.

Mair, Lucy. *Witchcraft*. NY, Toronto: World University Library, McGraw Hill, 1969.

Mannhardt, W. *Antike Wald- und Feltkulte*. 2nd edition by W. Heuschkel. Vol. 1: *Der Baumkultus der Germanen und ihrer Nachbarstämme: Mythologische Untersuchung*. 1875. Reprint Berlin: Borntræger, 1904.

Mansikka, V. J. *Über russische Zauberformeln mit Berücksichtigung der Blut- und Verrenkungssegen*. Annales Academiæ Scientiarum Fennicæ, Series B, vol. 1, no. 3. Helsinki: Finnish Literary Society, 1900.

———. "Litauische Zaubersprüche." *FF Communications* 87 (1929): 1–116.

Marquès-Rivière, Jean. *Amulettes, talismans et Pantacles dans les traditions orientales et occidentales*. Paris: Payot, 1972.

Marstrander, Sverre. "En Sator-formel fra Trøndelag." In *Det kongelige norske vedenskapers Selskab, Museet. Årsberetning* (Trondheim, 1949), 90–104.

Masser, Achim. "Zum zweiten Merseburger Zaubersprüch." *Paul und Braunes Beiträge zur Geschichte der deutschen Sprache und Literature* (Tübingen) 94 (1972): 19–25.

Mauss, Marcel [with Henri Hubert]. "Esquisse d'une théorie générale de la magie." *L'année sociologique* 7 (1904). Later published as Part 1 of the authors' collection *Sociologie et anthropologie*. Here, translated as *A General Theory of Magic*. New York: W. W. Norton, 1972.

Melton, J. Gordon. *Magic, Witchcraft and Paganism in America: A bibliography*. New York: Garland, 1982.

Merrifield, Ralph. *The Archæology of Ritual and Magic*. New York: New Amsterdam Books, 1987.

Meurger, Michel and Claude Gagnon. *Lake Monster Traditions: A CrossCultural Analysis*. London: Fortean Tomes, 1982.

Middleton, John, ed. *Magic, Witchcraft and Curing*. Austin: University of Texas Press, 1967.

Midthaug, Leif. "En sak om signeri på Hedemarken 1666." Med bemerkninger av Reidar Th. Christiansen. *Bygd og bonde* (1922): 157–78.

Miller, V. F. "Assiriiskie zaklinaniia i russkie narodnye zagovory, ["Assyrian Incantations and Russian Popular Charms"], in *Russkaia mysl'* [*Russian thought*] 7 (1896).

Mullen, Patrick B. "The Function of Magic Folk Belief among Texas Coastal Fishermen." *Journal of American Folklore* 82 (1969): 214–25.

Müller-Ebeling, Claudia, Christian Rätsch, and Wolf-Dieter Storl. Annabel Lee, trans. *Witchcraft Medicine: Healing Arts, Shamanic Practices and Forbidden Plants*. Rochester, VT: Inner Traditions, 2003. [English version of *Hexenmedizin*. Aarau, Schweiz: AT Verlag, 1998.]

Neusner, J., E. S. Frerichs and Paul V. McC. Flesher, eds. *Religion, Science and Magic: In Concert and in Conflict*. New York: Oxford UP, 1989.

Nildin-Wall, Bodil and Jan-Inge Wall. *Det ropades i skymningen… Vidskepelse och trolldomstro på Gotland*. Skrifter utgivna av Språk- och folkminnesinstitutet Dialekt-, ortnamns- och folkminnesarkivet i Göteborg 3. Uppsala: Almqvist & Wiksell, 1996.

Nilsson, Bo G., Dan Waldetoft, Christina Westergren, eds. *Frågelista och berättarglädje : om frågelistor som forskningsmetod och folklig genre*. Nordiska museet.Stockholm : Nordiska museets förlag, 2003.

Nordland, Odd. "The Street of 'the Wise Women': A contribution to the sociology of folk-medicine." In Tillhagen, *Papers on Folk-Medicine*, 105–16.

Ohrt, Ferdinand. *Danmarks Trylleformler, I & II*. Copenhagen: Gyldendalske Boghandel. Vol. I, 1917; Vol. II, 1921.

———. *Da signed Krist. Tolkning af det religiøse indhold i Danmarks Signelser og Besværjelser*. Copenhagen: N.p., 1927.

———. *De danske besværjelser mod Vrid og Blod: tolkning og forhistorie*. Det kongelige Danske Videnskabernes Selskab, Historisk-filologiske Meddelelser 6.3 (1922).

———. *Die ältesten Segen über Christi Taufe und Christi Tod in religionsgeschichtlichem Lichte*. Det kongelige Danske Videnskabernes Selskab, Historiskfilosofiske Meddelelser XXV:1, Copenhagen: Levin & Munksgaard, 1938.

———. "Fluchtafel und Wettersegen." *FF Communications* 86 (1929): 1–16.

———. "Om Merseburgformlerne som galder: En efterladt afhandling." *Danske studier* 35 (1938): 125–36.

———. "Segen." *Handwörterbuch des deutschen Aberglaubens* (1935–36). 7:1582–1620.

———. *Trylleord, fremmede og danske*. In *Danmarks folkeminder* 25 (1922).

———. "Über Alter und Ursprung der Begegnungssegen." *Hessische Blätter für Volkskunde* 35 (1936): 49–58.

O'Keefe, Daniel Lawrence. *Stolen Lightning: The Social Theory of Magic*. New York: Continuum Press, 1982.

Olrik, Axel. "Episke love i Gote-ættens oldsagn." *Danske studier* 4 (1907): 193–201.

Pálsson, Hermann, ed. and trans., *Seven Viking Romances*. New York: Viking Penguin, 1985.

Peuckert, Will-Erich. *Pansophie: Ein Versuch zur Geschichte der weißen und schwarzen Magie*. Stuttgart: W. Kohlhammar Verlag, 1936.

———. "Die Ägyptischen Geheimnisse." *Arv* 10 (1954): 40–96.

Pollington, Stephen. *Leechcraft: Early English Charms, Plantlore and Healing*. Trowbridge: Redwood Books, 2000.

Pop, Mihai. "L'incantation: Narration, mythe, rite." *Schweizerisches Archiv für Volkskunde* 68/69 (1972–73): 541–50.

Pleijel, Hilding. *Den svenska folkkulturens religions- och kyrkohistoriska bakgrund*. Lund: Etnologiska institutionen med Folklivsarkivet, 1983.

Qvigstad, J. *Lappische Heilkunde*. Instituttet for sammenlignende kulturforskning, (Oslo) B 20 (1932).

Ramat, P. "Per una tipologia degli incantesimi germanici." *Strumenti critici* 24 (1974): 179–97.

Reichborn-Kjennerud, Ingjald. "Lægeraadene i den eldre Edda." *Maal og minne* (1923): 1–57.

———. "Navnets og ordets makt i norsk folkemedisin." *Maal og minne* (1924): 158–91.

———. *Vor gamle trolldomsmedisin (I–V)* Oslo: N.p., 1928–1947.

Rietz, Johan Ernst. *Svenskt Dialektlexikon: Ordbok öfver svenska allmogespråket I & II*. Lund: C. W. K. Gleerups Förlag, 1962.

Roper, Jonathan, ed., *Charms and Charming in Europe*. New York: Palgrave MacMillan, 2004.

Rudolph, Ebermut. "Zur Psychologie deutschsprachiger Spruchheiler." In *Heilen und Pflegen* 19, Hessische Blätter für Volks- und Kulturforschung, (Marburg: Jonas Verlag, 1986), 147–53.

Ruong, Israel. "Att minnas, känna och jojka." Matts Arnberg, Israel Ruong, Håkan Unsgaard, eds., *Jojk*. Sveriges Radios förlag, 1969.

Russell, Jeffrey Burton. *A History of Witchcraft. Sorcerers, Heretics and Pagans*. London: Thames and Hudson, 1980.

Rustad, Mary S., ed.and trans. *The Black Books of Elverum*. Lakeville, MN: Galde Press, 1999.

Ryan, W. F. *The Bathhouse at Midnight: Magic in Russia*. University Park, PA: The Pennsylvania State UP, 1999.

Rääf, Leonhard Fredrik., K. Robert V. Wikman, ed. *Svenska Skrock och Signerier*. Kungliga Vitterhets Historie och Antikvitets Akademiens Handlingar, Filologisk-filosofiska serien 4. Stockholm: Almqvist & Wiksell, 1957.

Rørbye, Birgitte. *Kloge folk og skidtfolk: kvaksalveriets epoke i Danmark*. København: Politikens Forlag, 1976.

———. "Den illegale sygdomsbehandling som folkloristisk problem: Bidrag til en socio-kulturel oversigt for Danmark." *Fataburen: Nordiska museets och Skansens årsbok*, (1976), 203–20.

Sahlgren, Jöran. "C. O. Svahns svartkonstbok." *Folkminnen och folktankar* 5 (1918): 169–205.

Sandblom, J. A., ed. *Petter Johan Johannesson, 1841, varuti jag skrifver varjehanda*. Malmö: Förlag Maiander, 1917.

Schön, Ebbe. *Häxor och trolldom*. Kristianstad: Kristianstads Boktryckeri, 1991.

Schröder, F. R. "Balder und der zweite Merseburger Zauberspruch," in *GermanischRomanische Monatsschrift* (Heidelberg) 34 (1953): 161–83.

Schwietering, J. "Der erste Merseburger Spruch," in *Zeitschrift für deutsches Altertum und deutsche Literatur* 55 (1914): 148–56.

Sebeok, Thomas. "The Structure and Content of Cheremis Charms, Part I." *Anthropos: Internationale Zeitschrift für Völker- und Sprachenkunde* 48 (1953): 369–88.

———, and Orzack, Louis H. "The Structure and Content of Cheremis Charms, Part II." *Anthropos: Internationale Zeitschrift für Völker- und Sprachenkunde* 48 (1953): 760–72.

Simpson, Jacqueline, trans. *Legends of Icelandic Magicians*. The Folklore Society (Mistletoe Series): D. S. Brewer and Rowman and Littlefield, 1975.

Skinner, Stephen, ed. *The Fourth Book of Occult Philosophy*. Berwick, ME: Ibis, 2005.

Skjelbred, Ann Helene Bolstad. *Bibliografi over alternativ medisin og behandling i Norge til og med 1980*. Universitetsbiblioteket i Oslo, Skrifter 13 (1983): 22–24.

Sjödahl, N., ed. "Jugas Olof Jonssons svartkonstbok med kommentarer." *Meddelanden från Dalarnes Forminnesförening* IX (1924): 35–57.

Snell, John E. "Hypnosis in the Treatment of the 'Hexed' Patient." *American Journal of Psychiatry* 124 (1967): 311–16.

Sokolov, Yuriy M. *Russian Folklore*, Catherine Ruth Smith, trans., [Original: *Ruskii fol'klor*, 1938] Detroit: Folklore Associates, 1971.

Solem, Sverre. "Tru eller overtru?" *Gauldalsminne* (1968): 524–27.

Stattin, Jochum. *Näcken. Spelman eller gränsvakt?* Stockholm: Carlssons bokförlag, 1992.

Staugård, Frants. *Den folkliga medicinen: Svart magi eller sunt förnuft?* Stockholm: LiberFörlag, 1979.

Steiner, Roland. "Observations on the Practice of Conjuring in Georgia." *Journal of American Folklore* 14 (1901): 173–80.

Stokker, Kathleen. "Between Sin and Salvation: The Human Condition in Legends of the Black Book Minister." *Scandinavian Studies* 67 (1995): 91–108.

———. *Remedies and Rituals: Folk Medicine in Norway and the New Land*. St. Paul, MN: Minnesota Historical Society Press, 2007.

———. "'The Would-Be Ghost': Why Be He a Ghost? Lutheran Views of Confession and Salvation in Legends of the Black Book Minister." *ARV: Scandinavian Yearbook of Folklore* 47 (1991): 143–52.

———. "To Catch a Thief: Binding and Loosing and the Black Book Minister," *Scandinavian Studies: Nordic Narrative Folklore* 61 (1989): 353–74.

Storms, G. *Anglo-Saxon Magic*. 1948. Reprint New York: Gordon Press, 1974.

Ström, Folke. *Nordisk hedendom: tro och sed i förkristen tid*. Stockholm: Esselte Studium, 1985.

Strömbäck, Dag. *Sejd: Textstudier i nordisk religionshistoria*. Nordiska texter och undersökningar utgivna i Uppsala av Bengt Hasselman 5. Stockholm: Hugo Gebers Förlag, 1935.

Svenska litteratursällskapet i Finland. *Finlands Svenska Folkdiktning VII. Folktro och Trolldom*. Helsingfors: Tidnings- och tryckeri-aktiebolagets tryckeri, 1919.

Svärdström, Elisabeth. Högstenableckets rungalder. *Fornvännen: Tidskrift för svensk antikvarisk forskning* (1967/1): 12–21.

von Sydow, C. W. "Det ovanligas betydelse i tro och sed," *Folkminnen och folktankar* XIII (1926): 23 ff.

Sørensen, Jørgen Podemann. "The Argument in Ancient Egyptian Magical Formulæ." *Acta Orientalia Danica, Fennica, Norvegica, Svecica* XLV (1984): 5–19.

Sørensen, S. "Recepten som magisk dokument." *Norges Apotekerforenings tidsskrift* 6 (1927): 95–108.

Tambiah, S. J. "The Magical Power of Words." *Man* 3 (1968): 171–208.

———. "Form and Meaning of Magical Acts: A Point of View." Horton, R., ed. *Modes of Thought* (London: Faber and Faber, 1973), 199–229.

Tangherlini, Timothy. *Interpreting Legend. Danish Storytellers and Their Repertoires*, Milman Parry Studies in Oral Tradition. New York: Garland, 1994.

———. "'How do you know she's a witch?': Witches, Cunning Folk, and Competition in Denmark." *Western Folklore* 59 (Summer/Fall 2000): 279–303.

Thomas, Keith. *Religion and the Decline of Magic*. New York: Charles Scribner's Sons, 1971.

Tillhagen, Carl-Herman. "Die Zaubermacht des Ungewöhnlichen." *Schweizerisches Archiv für Volkskunde* 68/69 (1972–73): 666–75.

———. *Folklig Läkekonst*. Stockholm: Nordiska Muséet, 1958.

———. "Jonas Fredric Carlströms samling 1700-talslekar." *Arv* 1/2 (1947): 47–96.

———. "Material and Research Methods within Folkmedicine." In Tillhagen, *Papers on Folk-Medicine*, 194–204.

———, ed. *Papers on Folk-Medicine given at an Inter-Nordic Symposium at Nordiska Museet, Stockholm 8–10 May, 1961*. Stockholm: Almqvist & Wiksell, 1963.

Titiev, M. "A Fresh Approach to the Problem of Magic and Religion." *Southwestern Journal of Anthropology* 13(1960): 292–98.

Tornehed, Stig. *Kungsbacka gumman*. Varberg: Nordhallands hembygdsförening skriftserie III, 1965.

Tylor, Edward. *Primitive Culture*. New York: Appleton, 1871.

Vaughan-Sterling, Judith A. "The Anglo-Saxon Metrical Charms: Poetry as Ritual." *Journal of English and Germanic Philology* 82 (1983): 186–200.

Vetter, George B. "Words and Word Magic. The Psychology of Prayer and Profanity." In *Magic and Religion: Their Psychological Nature, Origin and Function* (New York: Philosophical Library, 1958), 175–88.

Vukanovic, T. P. "Obscene Objects in Balkan Religion and Magic." *Folklore* 92.1 (1981): 43–53.

Wall, Jan-Inge. *Hon var en gång tagen under jorden...: Visionsdikt och sjukdomsbot i Gotländska trolldomsprocesser*. Skrifter utgivna genom Dialekt- och Folkminnesarkivet i Uppsala, Serie B:19, Uppsala: Almqvist & Wiksell, 1989.

———. *Mjölktjuvande väsen i yngre nordisk tradition*, Studia ethnologica Uppsaliensia, 3 and 5. Lund: Carl Bloms boktryckeri, 1977–78.

———. "Resorna till Josefsdal." *Svenska landsmål och svenskt folkliv* (1987): 99–120.

———. *Tjuvmjölkande väsen. I. Äldre nordisk tradition*. Studia Ethnologica Upsaliensia 3. Acta Universitatis Upsaliensis. Uppsala: Carl Bloms Tryckeri, 1977.

———. *Tjuvmjölkande väsen. II. Yngre nordisk tradition*. Studia Ethnologica Upsaliensia 5. Acta Universitatis Upsaliensis. Uppsala: Carl Bloms Tryckeri, 1978.

Webster, Hutton. *Magic: A Sociological Study*. Stanford: Stanford UP, 1948.

Wellman, Alice. *Spirit Magic*. New York: Berkeley Publishing, 1973.

Wessén, Elias and Lars Levander,eds. *Våra ord: deras utal och ursprung*. Nacka: Esselte Studium Herzogs, 1982.

Weston, L. M. C. "The Language of Magic in Two Old English Metrical Charms." *Neuphilologische Mitteilung, Bullitin of the Modern Language Society* 86.2 (1985): 176–86.

Wigström, Eva. *Folkdiktning, visor, sägner, gåtor, ordspråk, ringdansar, lekar och barnvisor, samlad och upptecknad i Skåne av Eva Wigström, I & II.* Köpenhavn: K. Schönberg, 1880–1881.

Wikman, K. Rob. V. "Tecken och orsak." *Arv* 1/2 (1947): 32–46.

———., ed., *Johan J. Törners Samling af Widskeppelser, med inledning och anmärkningar.* Skrifter utgivna av Kungl. Gustav Adolfs Akademien. 15. Uppsala and Stockholm: Almqvist & Wiksell, 1946.

———. "Törners 'Svartkonstbok.'" In *Nordisk Folkminne: Studier tillägnade C. W. von Sydow, 12/21/1928* (Stockholm: C. E. Fritzes Hovbokhandel, 1928), 247–55.

Wilson, Stephen. *The Magical Universe: Everyday Ritual and Magic in Pre-Modern Europe.* London & New York: Hambledon and London, 2000.

Wistrand, Per Gustaf, ed. "En småländsk svartkonstbok." *Fataburen* (1906): 239–44.

———. "Signelser från Småland, antecknade under några på Nordiska museets bekostnad företagna resor 1879 och 1880." In *Meddelanden från Nordiska museet* (Stockholm: P. A. Norstedt, 1898), 15–50.

Wolf-Knuts, Ulrika, ed. *Djävulen: Seminarium den 13 november 1990.* IF rapport nr 13, Folkloristiska institutionen vid Åbo Akademi. Åbo: Åbo Akademis copieringscentral, 1992.

Zacher, J. "Das Hildebrandslied, die Merseburger Zaubersprüche und das fränkische Taufgelöbnis." *Zeitschrift für deutsche Philologie* 4 (1873): 461–72.

Zandee, J. "Das Schöpferwort im alten Ägypten." In *Verbum. Essays on some aspects of the religious function of words, dedicated to Dr. H. W. Obbink.* Studia Theologica Rheno-Traientina 4, (Utrecht: V/H Kemink en zoon, N.p., 1964), 33–66.

INDEX

A

abdomen/-inal, 549, 592, 605, 608, 610, 617
Abraham, 210, 211, 259, 379, 381, 382, 400, 402, 426, 431, 435, 462, 463, 611
Absalom, 435
abscess/-es, 100, 302
abyss, 301, 302, 447, 448, 451, 458, 469
accident/-al, 88, 121, 363, 393, 530, 574
ache/-ing/-s, 130, 138, 240, 273, 287, 288, 302, 305, 311, 312, 313, 314, 316, 327, 339, 344–46, 356, 357, 358, 364, 365, 375, 376, 420–22, 439, 491, 495, 508-10, 516, 542, 543, 570, 585, 589, 590, 616, 617
acid, 357, 495
Acorus calamus, Calamus root, 246, 620
adder, snake, 363, 619
addiction, 170
adipis humanis, human fat, 609
Adonai, various spellings, 262–65, 378–83, 385, 387–88, 468
Aframomum melegueta, (Paradise seed), 239, 250, 619
afterbirth, 499
agat (agate), 458
Agrippa, Henry Cornelius, 121
Ahlström, Bengt, 137–42, 145, 147, 171, 195, 197, 214, 215, 219, 238, 246, 259
ailment/-s, 130, 169, 172, 177, 328, 438, 496, 539
air, 66, 105, 106, 241, 250, 253, 263, 266, 272, 283, 287, 291, 293, 295, 326, 330, 348, 379, 380, 382, 397, 404, 417, 419, 420, 438, 439, 458, 461, 472, 482, 485, 488, 493, 499, 518, 541, 588, 602
alchemy, 146, 189
alcohol/-s, 66, 275, 455, 596
alcoholic/-ism, 82, 130
alder, 362, 367, 483, 484, 497, 511, 531, 585, 601
aldermeadow, 98
Alehagen, Anders i, 61, 66, 72, 74, 80, 82, 91, 97, 98, 113, 114, 122, 123, 214
Algopaticum, 594

allopathic medicine, 210
alloy/-s, 146, 300, 619
almanac/-s, 110, 183, 541
almond oil, 296, 420, 495, 500, 507, 509, 515, 516
almonds, 421
aloe, 239, 250, 251, 269, 596, 619
alon, 512, 513
alphabet/-ic/-s, 32, 36, 158, 172, 213
alruna, see mandrake, 98
altar, 365, 387, 391, 415, 443, 564, 568, 571, 603
altarcloth, 294
alum, 242, 248, 398
amber, 239, 250, 251, 289, 305, 354, 413, 499, 516, 572, 576, 598, 619
ambergris, 269, 558, 598
ammonium, 502
ammunition, 130, 131, 175, 245, 294, 472, 480, 482, 483, 484, 518, 545, 601, 602, 609, 611
amniotic sack, 86
amulet/-s/-ic, 23, 39, 117, 333, 336, 338–39
ancestral spirits, 60
anelisa, black, 252
anesthetize/-d, 302, 474, 589, 593
angelica (root), 396
Angelica, 269, 425
angels/-ic, 81, 109, 115, 150, 201, 208, 241, 346, 361, 373, 376, 379, 382, 388, 409, 426, 449, 520, 534, 560, 581, 617
angry, 71, 328, 333, 355, 364, 397, 505, 523
Anguis fragilis, 293, 294, 351, 525, 619
animal/-s, 43, 46, 69, 83, 86, 117, 128, 130, 131, 136, 138, 147, 153, 154, 172, 188, 199, 218, 237, 243, 245, 249, 250, 253, 258, 269, 275, 278, 286–88, 308, 309, 318–21, 324, 326–28, 345, 348, 355, 360, 362, 365–69, 397, 428, 430–33, 442, 473, 476–86, 488, 517, 519, 520, 522, 530, 537, 542, 547, 548, 549, 551, 553, 554, 558, 568, 575, 576, 579, 580, 584, 585, 586, 592, 595, 599, 602, 603, 607, 610, 611, 613, 614, 616
animism/-tic, 54

anis/-e, 420, 435, 507
ankle, 256
ant stone, 283
ant/-s, 277, 283, 295, 252, 371, 511, 542, 562, 614
anterinum, 598
anthill/-s, 228, 262, 271, 274, 277, 283, 290, 304, 371, 445, 475, 482, 493, 559, 570, 582, 614
antimony/-ium, 269, 285, 396, 583, 619
anus, 441, 500, 510, 513, 609
apertusar, 85
aphids, 607
apiary, 131
apostle/-s/-ic, 94, 100, 166-67, 209, 218, 373, 376, 379-82, 401, 407, 534, 564, 588-89
apothecary, 145, 242, 252, 256, 261, 267, 293, 372, 396, 443, 505, 537, 539, 547, 548, 554
apotropaic/-poeisis, 25, 62
appendicitis, 617
apple/-s, 262, 349, 351, 363, 364, 424, 524, 525, 540, 544, 562, 606
applepowder, yellow, 514
apprenticeship, 72, 78, 86-92, 97, 110, 170, 217
archangel/-s, 379-82, 388, 400, 462, 463
archdemon, 172
Ariel/-l, 379-83, 462-63, 614
ark, Noah's, 312, 414
arm (body part), 90, 223, 226, 227, 229, 230, 244, 245, 254, 276, 297, 329, 337, 340, 349, 351, 352, 356, 358, 360, 362, 363, 367, 376, 429, 440, 475, 481, 482, 498, 499, 516, 518, 521, 524, 525, 555, 556, 562, 564, 574, 575, 583, 610
armpit, 337, 429, 494, 570
arrest, 571
arrows, 224, 244,
arsenic, 227
Artemisia abrotanum, 227
Artemisia absinthium, 445, 492, 507, 619
Artemisia vulgaris, 226, 227, 234, 606
artery/-ies, 308-10, 445, 494, 507, 513, 596
Asafetida, 239, 250, 251, 257, 269, 273, 285, 289, 293, 294, 301, 391, 396, 447, 474, 502, 514, 584, 598, 599, 617, 619
asafœtida, 207, 354, 355, 522, 619
ash/-es, 200, 232, 251, 257, 280, 295, 301, 328, 355, 362, 363, 450, 455, 480, 501, 511, 537, 544, 558, 561, 565, 569, 578, 579, 611, 619
Aspelands (län county), 194, 600
aspen (tree), 234, 244, 247, 258, 371, 556
aspirin, 421
ass, animal, 270, 281
ass, body part, 398
Astaroth, 404
astrological, 165, 189, 267
Atropa belladonna, wolfberry, 226
attack, 130, 178, 206, 215, 298, 299, 317, 516
autopsy, 610

autumn, 328, 332, 341, 342, 344, 398, 478, 485, 545
awl, 291, 348, 517
axe, 293, 310, 316, 321, 481, 482, 504, 525
axe hammer, 486
Azande, 39

B

backbone, 295
bait, 236, 485, 554
bakablad, 494, 495
balsam/-s, 295, 420, 505, 507, 509, 544
balsamic oil, 496, 544
Balthazar, 408, 428
bandage/-s/-ed, 268, 270, 271, 301, 316, 496, 507, 508, 512, 513, 515, 588, 593, 617
banish/-ed/ing, 374, 382, 418
baptism/-al/-ize/-d, 144, 249, 293, 308, 389, 399, 433, 456, 553, 554, 555, 585
bark/-ing, 133, 154, 225, 230, 247, 276, 316, 362, 369, 371, 414, 421, 472, 485, 497, 501, 510, 512, 547, 558, 562, 566, 569, 590
barley, 259, 507, 546, 579
barn, 69, 82, 100, 142, 175, 287, 328, 344, 442, 443, 453, 537, 546, 555, 558
barren women, 509
Bartholomew (various spellings), 227, 234, 401, 489
basil, 232, 288, 353, 524
basilisk, 293, 608
basket/-s, 502, 503, 505
bat/-s, 129, 224, 225, 228, 233, 237, 241, 261, 276, 277, 280, 283, 291, 292, 294, 295, 351, 353, 480, 483, 500, 506, 514, 522, 525, 540, 554, 561, 566, 568, 572, 602
bath/-e/-ed/-es, 289, 346, 446, 494, 569, 607
battle/-s/-ing, 132, 244, 616
bay laurel leaf, 458, 513
bay laurel, 226, 458
bay oil, 496, 513
bayberry/-ies, 249, 282, 289, 504, 614
beach/-ed/-es, 310, 438, 439, 617
beak/-s, 292, 497, 529, 570
beans, 494, 499, 507, 593
bear/-s, 131, 245, 259, 318, 322, 327, 328, 329, 343, 450, 480-81, 557
beard, 63, 148
beast/-s, 109, 112, 152, 199, 323, 362, 500, 531
beaver, 269, 419, 522, 598, 619
Beck oil, 433, 434, 588
bed, 73, 86, 130, 226, 230, 250, 255, 266, 276, 282, 292, 304, 325, 330, 333, 334, 337, 342, 344, 369, 397, 420, 434, 439, 440, 441, 447, 492, 500, 505, 524, 555, 556, 567, 595, 599, 606, 609
bee/-s, 131, 290, 396, 397, 582, 593, 598
beech (tree), 257, 308, 512, 515

Beelzebub (various spellings), 142, 192, 260, 299, 302, 304, 393, 394, 397, 404, 465, 514, 565, 570, 571, 581, 591
beer, 246, 247, 249, 253, 271, 275, 286, 295, 348, 353, 421, 494, 498, 500, 506, 508, 509, 510, 511, 515, 516, 526, 562, 567, 572, 592, 606
beervinegar, 257,
beet, 420
beetwater, 572
Belial, 397, 404, 581
Belladonna, 226, 445
belly, 293, 374, 375, 377, 431, 509, 510, 513, 535, 554, 558, 580
benediction, 271, 309, 310, 312, 317, 318, 324, 326, 327, 339, 342, 343, 344, 378, 429, 434, 503, 589, 590
benevolence/-t, 30, 31, 59, 62, 66, 67, 68, 116, 131, 134, 142, 152, 153, 157, 167, 177, 178, 183, 206, 215
berensten, (various spellings), see amber, 354, 396, 598, 619
Bergamot, 261
berries, 74, 251, 367, 500, 502
betony, 496
bewitch/-ed/-ing/-ment, 98, 147, 162, 275, 276, 280, 282, 376, 378, 475, 476, 518, 599, 600
Bhia-root, (stenört), 455
Bible/-ical, 35, 81, 94, 95, 103, 106, 124, 157, 165, 167, 212, 213, 568
bicarbonate, 539
bind/-s, 144, 158, 167, 201, 241, 264, 268, 286, 301, 302, 305, 306, 307, 310, 312, 318, 319, 323, 353, 358, 359, 360, 361, 362, 363, 364, 371, 374, 377, 392, 394, 395, 397, 398, 412, 413, 426, 428, 429, 435, 446, 450, 463, 466, 468, 470, 472, 488, 489, 491, 505, 510, 515, 518, 520, 521, 522, 523, 535, 557, 560, 563, 568, 581, 586, 588, 589, 595, 617
binding/-s, 45, 47, 58, 99, 133, 136, 138, 140, 141, 143, 149, 152, 158, 159, 160, 164, 166, 168, 169, 171, 174, 178, 184, 226, 290, 302, 314, 318, 319, 360, 374, 377, 385, 392, 412, 413, 467, 535, 567, 588
birch, 70, 278, 287, 336, 349, 369, 485, 497, 502, 504, 527, 531, 558
bird/-s, 86, 87, 97, 184, 185, 225–27, 231, 237, 297, 304, 348, 360, 366, 368, 373, 375, 376, 395, 399, 405, 406, 408, 413, 425, 430, 433, 473, 476–78, 481–86, 488, 494, 497, 498, 499, 505, 517, 520, 529, 531, 532, 535, 560, 563, 565, 573, 578, 584, 588, 601–3, 613, 619
birthday, 435
birthmark, 87
bitch, 616
bite/s, 36, 89, 257, 271, 307, 314, 324, 326, 337, 356, 358, 363, 427, 429, 434, 438, 473, 479, 481, 486, 498, 509, 537, 538, 550, 551, 556, 562,
567, 571, 575, 585, 588, 616
bitten, 232, 508, 536, 550, 556, 588
bitter, 421, 438, 495, 500, 509, 516, 576
blacksmith, see also smith, 146, 147
bladder, 163, 274, 279, 419, 491, 511, 514, 515
blade/-s, 83, 132, 144, 267, 307, 358, 364, 481, 493
bleed/-s, 154, 240, 253, 258, 274, 287, 296, 305, 336, 341, 354, 361, 510, 515, 563, 593
bleeding, 34, 35, 43, 89, 94, 130, 151, 173, 175, 177, 191, 239, 240, 253, 260, 269, 270, 272, 274, 275, 299, 301, 309, 310, 341, 349, 354, 432, 434, 440, 445, 446, 474, 487, 494, 499, 510, 512, 514, 516, 547, 554, 557, 559, 582, 583, 587, 594, 616
blemish/-es, 315, 316, 326, 340, 341, 342, 431, 499
blessing/-s, 215, 253, 378, 389, 448, 450, 453, 467, 468
blight/-ing, 182, 190, 195, 196
blind/-s/-ed/-ness, 93, 133, 151, 360, 449, 458, 460, 479, 614, 619
blister/-s, 247, 249, 257, 288, 293, 294, 346, 431, 438, 441, 511, 513, 516, 536, 556, 608
blood-red, 105
blood-root, 563
blood, 34, 47, 89, 93, 105, 106, 115, 116, 154, 173, 184, 206, 212, 218, 224, 225, 226, 228, 230, 233, 235, 237, 239, 241, 243, 247, 249, 253, 256, 258, 260, 261, 266, 267, 268, 269, 270, 271, 272, 273, 275, 276, 277, 281, 282, 286, 287, 288, 290, 291, 293, 294, 299, 302, 304, 306, 307, 308, 309, 310, 311, 312, 313, 321, 322, 323, 325, 326, 335, 336, 337, 338, 341, 345, 351, 352, 353, 354, 356, 360, 361, 362, 364, 365, 368, 370, 374, 376, 377, 378, 385, 392, 395, 407, 412, 413, 414, 415, 421, 429, 430, 432, 433, 434, 439, 440, 442, 443, 445, 446, 452, 453, 454, 455, 457, 461, 470, 473, 474, 475, 477, 481, 486, 490, 491, 494, 496, 497, 499, 500, 501, 504, 506, 507, 509, 511, 512, 513, 520, 522, 524, 525, 526, 531, 535, 539, 540, 544, 546, 550, 553, 554, 559, 561, 562, 563, 564, 565, 566, 567, 568, 570, 571, 573, 574, 576, 577, 582, 584, 585, 587, 590, 591, 592, 599, 600, 603, 604, 605, 606, 612, 616
bloody, 253, 302, 375, 399, 445, 587, 591
blue, 255, 287, 375, 376, 397, 414, 420, 513, 515, 557, 589, 590
blueberry, 496
bluing (remedy), 542
boar, 488
boat, 269, 326, 505
bobcat/-s, 131, 546
body, 23, 26, 27, 28, 49, 57, 167, 170, 180, 195, 196, 199, 224, 228, 244, 246, 250, 252, 260, 268, 274, 283, 293, 294, 297, 299, 302, 307, 312, 321, 325, 333, 337, 340, 341, 344, 345, 374,

382, 394, 432, 440, 441, 443, 445, 446, 450, 467, 468, 469, 483, 489, 521, 535, 542, 545, 553, 561, 567, 574, 576, 579, 583, 588, 593, 599, 602, 608, 609
bog, 314
boils, 247, 302, 436, 507, 508, 511, 557
bombs, 339
bonds, 244, 286, 306, 470
bone-dust, 150, 307
bone, 34, 61, 83, 121, 130, 138, 154, 157, 240, 247, 248, 252, 255, 268, 270, 281, 289, 290, 291, 294, 307, 311, 312, 314, 317, 319, 326, 329, 333, 337, 346, 359, 360, 365, 369, 374, 375, 376, 377, 396, 399, 415, 425, 430, 431, 432, 439, 440, 441, 450, 475, 478, 501, 502, 511, 515, 520, 523, 526, 530, 531, 535, 540, 548, 550, 557, 570, 583, 584, 585, 590, 592, 604, 607, 610, 614
bonemeal, 547
borax, 275, 563
border/-s, 24, 25, 136, 160, 320, 582,
borderland, 314
boskapspulver, cattle powder, 558
Boswellia serrata, 594
botany/-ical, 26, 207, 208, 619
bottle/-s, 110, 138, 246, 257, 268, 273, 274, 275, 295, 296, 304, 338, 421, 434, 442, 443, 458, 465, 466, 476, 492, 497, 512, 544, 559, 574, 575, 592
bowel, 35, 499, 617
bowl/-s, 84, 85, 250, 297, 298, 329, 351, 410, 446, 455, 476, 528, 585
boy/-s, 45, 90, 112, 234, 249, 279, 341, 343, 457, 494, 501, 540, 545, 611
brain/-s, 269, 419, 494, 511, 512, 562
brandy, 144
brass, 144, 298, 300, 325, 406
bread, 179, 182, 213, 233, 239, 242, 245, 250, 251, 260, 268, 269, 322, 351, 355, 356, 364, 378, 388, 425, 433, 465, 479, 496, 497, 502, 511, 512, 514, 516, 519, 524, 528, 533, 538, 542, 546, 552, 555, 556, 559, 565, 567, 593, 595, 599, 603, 612
breast/-s, 165, 352, 487, 488, 489, 512, 525, 606
breath/-e, 43, 169, 211, 277, 294, 425, 475, 483, 490, 556
brew/-ed/-ing, 130, 253, 326, 378, 396, 592, 596, 597
brick, 247, 344
bride, 250, 318, 505, 579
bridegroom, 250, 497
bridge, 245, 272, 314, 356, 357, 358, 359, 360, 434, 617
bridle, 234, 487, 488, 489, 567
bronchitis, 490
bronze, 458
broom/-s, 275, 296, 298, 486, 525, 555

broth, 73, 74, 88, 486, 513, 569, 596
brother, 79, 240, 260, 291, 292, 402
buck/-shot, 480, 484
buckthorn, 483
buckwood, 496
bug/-s, 254, 422, 451, 481, 567
bull/-s, 376–78, 497, 501, 538
bullet/-s, 131, 224, 225, 294, 324, 333, 339, 348, 432, 479–84, 517, 526, 542, 546, 561, 602, 603, 609, 610, 612, 614
bumps, 316, 337, 344, 494, 499
burial, 122, 231, 399, 409, 429, 473
burn, 47, 229, 232, 238, 242, 255, 259, 267, 273, 279, 280, 286, 295, 301, 312, 319, 320, 336, 346, 362, 363, 364, 398, 419, 424, 425, 428, 445, 455, 482, 490, 496, 511, 514, 521, 525, 537, 542, 548, 557, 558, 565, 569, 594, 607
burns (ailment), 130, 257, 496, 507, 509
bush/-es, 353, 379, 425, 478, 485, 537, 565, 615
butcher, 258
butt, 576, 609, 610
butter, 68, 130, 193, 232, 249, 252, 320, 336, 378, 398, 423, 435, 442, 492, 507, 547, 599, 616, 617
butterwort, 232
button/-s, 253, 266, 271, 300, 444, 446, 447, 455
buttonhole, 556

C

cabbage, 249
cake, 322, 493, 506, 568
calamus, 246, 620
calcium, 495
Calendula officinalis, 232
Calf-head, 239, 598
calf/-ves, 147, 239, 241, 250, 268, 276, 376–78, 445, 497, 498, 500, 501, 538, 567
camphor, 235, 242, 246, 280, 289, 296, 353, 422, 504, 607, 608, 610, 617
cancer (disease), 437, 455, 491
candle/-s, 133, 226, 234, 242, 276, 280, 283, 284, 292, 295, 431, 460, 485, 568, 604
Candlemas, 242
canker sore, 491
Capricorn, 611
cardamom, 491
caries, 492
carnivorous, 232
carrot, 170, 296, 459, 506
Cartinel-seeds, 293
Casper, 408, 428
castor/-eum, 269, 273, 289, 293, 294, 396, 419, 474, 522, 598, 619
castrated, 282, 555
cat/-s, 230, 237, 244, 297, 346, 392, 422, 493, 548,

555, 562, 563, 568, 580, 604, 613, 614
catalyst, 113
cataract/-s, 315, 316, 341, 342, 431, 515
cattle-powder, 269
cattle, 68, 232, 293, 315, 318, 319, 320, 322, 323, 328, 376, 397, 473, 488, 497, 529, 532, 537, 549–53, 555, 556, 558, 559, 580, 584
caul, 86, 97, 312, 494
cauldron, 196, 330
cavity, 559
cellulitis, 288
cemetery/-ies, 60, 61, 157, 311, 327, 332, 345, 346, 465, 466, 520, 523, 597, 603
cense, 232, 242, 250, 252, 253, 281, 287, 288, 289, 293, 396, 473, 485, 499, 504, 506, 511, 513, 514, 516, 530, 597, 598, 599, 600, 606, 613
chains, 226, 290, 385, 427
chalk, 242, 292, 293, 297, 350, 418, 528, 589
charcoal, 596
charlatan/-ry, 85, 211
charm/-s, 23, 24, 27, 31–42, 45, 48–50, 79, 88, 92, 93, 95, 96, 98, 106, 112, 128–34, 136, 137, 139, 140, 145, 147–51, 154, 157, 165, 167, 169, 170, 172, 173, 175–78, 182, 183, 185, 187, 189, 191, 194, 196, 197, 199, 202, 206–10, 216–18, 614, 616, 617, 619
charms, Anglo-Saxon, 197
chaste/-ity, 373, 455, 470, 473, 535
cheap, 428
cheese, 68, 283, 284, 304, 378, 558, 562, 606
chemist/-ry, 146, 207, 218
cherry/-ies, 496, 512
cherub, 379, 380, 381, 382, 383
chervil, 494
chest, 199, 225, 257, 276, 282, 286, 293, 316, 325, 331, 339, 340, 350, 411, 420, 433, 447, 475, 476, 496, 506, 507, 508, 509, 526, 528, 551, 562, 572, 578, 582, 593, 617
chick/-s, 226, 277, 287, 292, 301, 364, 371, 419, 424, 498, 505, 511, 524, 546, 570, 602, 604
chicken/-s, 235, 604
chicory, 296
chief/-s, 462, 463
child/-ren, 24, 46, 73, 82, 87, 116, 133, 177, 234, 247, 248, 256, 258, 298, 309, 316, 317, 319, 357, 397, 426, 427, 428, 431, 454, 457, 494, 495, 498, 499, 507, 508, 514, 530, 543, 550, 560, 569, 576, 582
childbirth, 133, 177, 244, 498, 516, 531, 609
childhood, 64, 163, 330, 549, 582
chill/-s, 239, 271, 419, 529, 609
chimney, 247, 282, 296, 419, 529, 599
chin, 294, 488, 587, 593
chives, 205
chloroform, 259
cholera, 303

chop/-ped, 86, 116, 117, 223, 281, 293, 294, 310, 313, 352, 358, 422, 475, 486, 500, 582, 591, 592, 596, 614
Christmas, 75, 76, 77, 231, 260, 327, 349, 356, 425, 447, 502, 506, 527, 532, 612
church/-es, 75, 77, 83, 92, 98, 104, 109, 111, 113, 115, 116, 123, 125, 157, 158, 166, 180, 181, 198, 214, 249, 262, 283, 294, 302, 325, 329, 338, 349, 351, 365, 391, 399, 402, 415, 436, 440, 442, 455, 457, 458, 467, 487, 493, 498, 499, 502, 503, 506, 525, 544, 548, 563, 571, 572, 573, 603, 606, 612, 617
churchyard, 246, 248, 252, 253, 255, 269, 271, 272, 282, 285, 291, 293, 329, 331, 338, 367, 415, 424, 430, 433, 434, 438, 444, 445, 452, 474, 497, 523, 526, 530, 531, 532, 574, 579, 580, 583, 584, 586, 599
cinnamon, 515
cinquefoil, 505
cipher/-s, 27, 107, 153, 192
circle/-s, 79, 147, 163, 182, 233, 243, 265, 266, 286, 302, 307, 340, 350, 362, 368, 379, 382, 383, 386, 388, 393, 410, 418, 457, 461, 462, 463, 464, 501, 520, 527, 532, 542, 544, 560, 566, 569, 583, 588, 613
circumambulation, 75, 77, 92, 407
circumcision, 399
circumlocution/-s, 36, 62, 207
clairsentient, 59
clairvoyant, 74, 83
Clavicula Salomonis, 159, 160, 166, 182, 417
claw/-s, 256, 282, 318, 346, 352, 354, 522, 529, 553, 568, 570, 571
clay, 252, 256, 277, 278, 364, 421, 472, 505, 536, 590, 599, 608, 614
clean, 176, 215, 228, 232, 236, 280, 281, 282, 288, 291, 295, 296, 300, 349, 367, 397, 415, 431, 466, 472, 477, 484, 486, 489, 506, 533, 541, 593, 597, 615
clergy, 66–67, 111
clock/-s, 77, 82, 228, 249, 289, 319, 320, 332, 336, 338, 342, 344, 345, 436, 452, 465, 522, 553, 560, 569, 586, 603, 609, 614
clockbells, 300
cloth, 80, 81, 82, 143, 223, 228, 229, 236, 242, 256, 273, 277, 279, 280, 282, 287, 289, 293, 296, 297, 298, 305, 346, 347, 351, 391, 392, 399, 415, 420, 421, 423, 481, 486, 491, 501, 506, 508, 525, 537, 538, 539, 540, 547, 561, 564, 567, 569, 577, 583, 584, 592, 593, 596
clothes/ing, 62, 63, 72, 244, 246, 250, 262, 283, 289, 295, 317, 331, 350, 358, 395, 428, 457, 472, 484, 492, 500, 516, 524, 528, 556, 561, 567, 570, 575
clove/-s, 367, 597, 611, 617
clover, 38, 494, 495, 498, 514

coal/-s, 200, 231, 232, 237, 243, 249, 250, 252, 255, 257, 259, 262, 274, 299, 305, 308, 325, 378, 420, 494, 496, 497, 512, 546, 555, 558, 578, 581, 597
coalfire, 599
cock/-s, 240, 477
cockroach, 511
coffee, 90, 170, 288, 312, 317, 324, 325, 330, 335, 347, 460, 475
coffin, 36, 74, 109, 122, 137, 223, 282, 331, 365, 425, 452, 466, 503, 567, 581, 582, 603, 609, 615
coin, 254, 255, 268, 286, 299, 326, 329, 338, 339, 345, 346, 369, 387, 409, 429, 430, 434, 441, 447, 450, 458, 473, 487, 552, 568, 579
colic, 130, 246, 269, 287, 420, 422, 491, 495, 516, 596, 607, 617
collarbone, 339
collusion, 469
colon, 501, 510
color/-s, 43, 63, 228, 234, 235, 277, 299, 370, 397, 472, 576, 586, 589, 606
colorless, 489
comb, 282, 368, 414, 511, 545, 566
communion, 67, 77, 244, 245, 283, 518, 522, 523, 571, 580
condemn/-nation/-ed, 31, 116, 198, 215, 395, 575
confidence, 87, 172, 196, 198, 211, 212, 216, 334, 493, 573, 609
confusion, 263, 312, 321, 324, 326, 327, 340, 342, 343, 344, 443
Conium maculatum, 235
consecrated/-ion, 125, 144, 263, 453, 462, 497, 502, 505, 547, 561
consort/-s, 43, 404
constipated/-ion, 130, 249, 398, 422, 491, 509, 592
contagion/-us, 35, 37, 129, 145, 294, 428
control, 31, 48, 69, 98, 111, 112, 130, 132, 133, 147, 149, 175, 179, 198, 217, 290, 330, 395
Conu Plâster, 422
cook/-ed/-ing, 46, 74, 88, 128, 130, 228, 234, 242, 244, 247, 256, 259, 277, 278, 295, 296, 330, 366, 421, 422, 447, 486, 506, 508, 512, 538, 544, 569, 617
copper chloride, 619
copper, 298, 300, 325, 406, 441, 455, 565, 574, 619
coral, 239, 250, 251, 252, 289, 396, 474, 537, 597598
Coralia rubra (Red Coral Stone), 597
cord/-s, 262, 488, 494
cork/-ed, 261, 262, 274, 295, 304, 348, 421, 465, 476, 517, 577, 592
corn, 591
cornflour, 420
corns, 578, 591
corpse, 74, 231, 233, 243, 248, 255, 271, 273, 278, 285, 289, 292, 293, 327, 329, 338, 339, 428, 450, 452, 484, 501, 504, 505, 511, 522, 541, 542, 543, 570, 586, 597, 606, 610, 613
corrupt/-ion, 378, 381, 387, 570, 609
Cotoneaster vulgaris, 529
cottage, 72, 128, 157, 320
cotton-wood, 422
cotton, 252, 305, 420, 422, 490, 491, 495, 500, 507, 509, 595, 616
cottonseed/-s, 235, 275, 289, 315, 421, 593, 608, 609
cough, 256, 420, 424, 433, 500, 501, 508, 510, 513, 544, 558, 562, 591, 606,
coughing, 576
countryside, 23, 199
courage/-ous, 241, 355, 356, 433, 440, 441, 442, 443, 453, 457
court, 73, 88, 116, 133, 154, 179, 182, 183, 223, 229, 255, 272, 283, 290, 298, 351, 357, 371, 372, 394, 434, 474, 503, 523, 524, 529, 549, 550, 551, 552, 569, 571, 575, 587
cousin, 399
cow/-s, 42, 43, 68, 69, 83, 87, 91, 131, 133, 162, 163, 214, 235, 259, 268, 269, 271, 293, 318, 322, 324, 328, 335, 336, 343, 344, 359, 378, 419, 423, 425, 433, 440, 442, 447, 449, 450, 456, 473, 488, 491, 497, 498, 499, 500, 501, 513, 537, 541, 542, 547, 548, 557, 565, 579, 580, 592, 596
crab/-s, 524, 558, 593
crabapple, 512
craft, 133, 146, 344
cramp/-s/-ing, 297, 347, 590, 607, 617
crane, 558
cranial, 64
cranium, 329
crayfish, 114, 256, 542
cream, 249, 256, 361, 442, 460, 492, 507, 564
creature/-s, 112, 227, 293, 359, 389, 468
crossbones, 189
crossroad/-s, 274, 285, 325, 336, 442, 446, 464, 487, 521, 556, 579, 604
crow/-s, 236, 301, 425, 486
crown/-s, 120, 282, 292, 295, 326, 329, 332, 339, 345, 373, 376, 395, 399, 407, 413, 429, 453, 454, 456, 470, 473, 535, 537, 538, 539, 549, 607
crystal, 83, 493
cuckoo/-s, 223, 237, 425, 498, 508, 515, 522, 562, 584
cucumbers, 254
Culpepper, Nicholas, 349
cumin, 251, 289, 422, 497
cuneiform, 417
cunning, 50, 51, 58, 93, 96, 99, 124, 134, 135, 139, 143, 144, 147, 151, 160, 163, 164, 166, 178, 179, 180, 184, 187, 196, 198, 199, 202, 203, 324, 333, 340, 346, 533
cunningfolk, 163, 164
cup, 247, 288, 317, 325, 335, 414, 542
cure, 47, 48, 61, 93, 108, 129, 138, 203, 247, 248, 252,

253, 254, 256, 258, 260, 269, 271, 279, 282,
286, 287, 288, 342, 343, 344, 346, 368, 420,
421, 432, 434, 438, 443, 445, 446, 498, 499,
500, 505, 507, 556, 576, 579, 580, 581, 585,
591, 592, 616
cures, 47, 76, 89, 105, 150, 170, 175, 188, 190, 197, 247,
317, 446, 454, 507, 508, 595, 608
curse, 45, 58, 69, 82, 144, 190, 196, 299, 306, 336, 345,
361, 362, 364, 365, 366, 368, 450, 508, 543,
548, 601
cursed, 71, 72, 302, 366, 367, 368, 423, 524, 548, 603,
613
cursing, 44, 133, 145, 154, 190, 196, 207
Cyprian, St., 155, 157, 180-81, 190, 201, 373, 399, 534,
536
Cyprianus, 47, 48, 50, 214, 595

D

dance/-s, 96, 166, 275, 345
dandelion, 170, 460
danger/-s, 27, 75, 82, 89, 111, 121, 122, 183, 199, 290,
302, 314, 326, 341, 350, 458, 467, 528, 557
Danish, 47, 136, 142, 214, 373, 481, 536
Daphne mezereum, 251, 259, 354, 447, 502, 522, 593,
598, 620
dark/-ness, 77, 78, 110, 144, 165, 166, 217, 235, 324,
330, 334, 404, 436, 449, 460, 554, 571
daughter, 68, 78, 91, 294, 331
dawn, 478, 555
day, 24, 67, 75, 76, 77, 87, 111, 114, 115, 143, 157, 162,
217, 224, 226, 227, 228, 234, 238, 239, 240,
247, 249, 250, 257, 258, 263, 265, 267, 271,
275, 277, 286, 288, 295, 296, 301, 307, 319,
328, 329, 330, 333, 334, 337-39, 342, 343,
344, 346, 349, 355, 370, 372, 374, 375, 377,
391, 396, 407, 412, 413, 414, 419, 420, 424, 431,
432, 435, 443, 444, 452, 460, 477, 478, 482,
484, 485, 488-90, 491, 494, 497, 501-3, 510,
524, 527, 532, 534, 535, 543, 546, 548, 549,
554, 556, 558, 564, 565, 566, 568, 569, 572,
573, 576, 592, 595, 596, 597, 601, 605, 606,
612, 613, 615, 616
daylight, 537, 540, 541
dead, 61, 77, 93, 116, 122, 130, 133, 151, 152, 154, 184,
191, 232, 235, 236, 243, 244, 246, 258, 291,
292, 293, 295, 320, 330, 332, 333, 338, 339,
341, 357, 361, 364, 367, 377, 379, 380, 392,
395, 397, 399, 411, 413, 426, 431, 438, 443,
446, 453, 458, 466, 481, 485, 494, 502, 505,
518, 520, 521, 539, 549, 561, 568, 571, 574,
588, 593, 609, 612, 613
deaf/-ness, 248, 296, 449, 495
death, 87, 108, 116, 134, 138, 152, 157, 166, 177, 190,
194, 234, 235, 265, 266, 302, 306, 328, 336,
338, 339, 341, 343, 361, 373, 375, 376, 377,
404, 439, 447, 456, 461, 472, 473, 501, 535,
536, 567, 572, 604, 606
deception/-s, 62, 154
decks of cards, 65-66
Dee, John, 159
defense, 83, 244, 359, 581
deformities, 247, 248, 255, 258
della Porta, Giambattista, 104
demons, 86, 112, 115-17, 121, 132, 141, 150, 171, 180, 184,
199, 206, 213, 215, 217, 274
Denderslag, 239, 251, 252
Denmark, 40, 116, 201, 213
dental, 492, 559
depression/-ed, 24, 317, 318, 321, 323, 324, 326, 331,
335, 438, 439, 443
destroy, 68, 260, 327, 328, 333, 353, 376, 377, 412,
430, 450, 451, 603
devil/-s, 48, 66-68, 75, 76, 78, 81, 82, 92, 94, 97, 104,
105, 109, 110, 113-16, 122, 123, 149, 165, 198,
199, 206, 207, 240, 241, 253, 259, 260, 263,
264, 273, 274, 286, 290, 298, 299, 301, 305,
308, 324, 329, 331, 334-36, 337, 338, 351,
354, 355, 362-64, 377, 378, 385, 391, 392,
394, 395, 397, 398, 413, 419, 429, 430, 433,
435, 446, 448, 470, 473, 482, 492, 499, 502,
504, 505, 518, 522, 528, 533, 534, 535, 537,
542, 553-55, 559, 565, 570, 571, 588, 589,
597, 599
devilish/-ness, 330, 332, 373, 377, 399, 400, 506
devilry, 337, 369
dew, 248, 255, 286, 472, 553
diabolism, 97, 215
diarrhea, 35, 133, 153, 156, 422, 423, 425, 476, 495,
514, 525, 526, 539, 558, 592, 600, 601
dice, 229, 285, 411, 568, 604
dill, 491, 506, 516
dirt, 61, 83, 245, 253, 301, 307, 317, 329, 331, 332, 338,
345, 346, 369, 432, 475, 498, 501, 521, 560,
561, 564, 579, 583, 585, 588, 599
disappear/-ed, 79, 91, 95, 232, 243, 246, 248, 250,
258, 272, 302, 313, 314, 316, 329, 336, 346,
353, 391, 411, 427, 438, 439, 440, 441, 443,
444, 451, 502, 542, 544, 556, 578, 580, 581,
589-91, 593, 607
disciple/-s, 93, 151, 240, 263, 307, 374, 377, 392, 412,
437, 535
discomfort, 169, 197, 357
discord, 133, 505, 555, 556
disease/-s/-ed, 60, 62, 92, 129, 188, 214, 294, 428, 455,
512, 596
disguise, 146, 192, 329
distill/-ed/ing, 130, 193, 233, 253, 396, 419, 490, 491,
539, 584, 592, 596
distillation, 596, 597
distillery, 190
Dittany, 278

divination, 75, 117, 152, 153, 154, 156, 160, 172, 178, 182, 187, 191, 195, 199
divinatory, 60, 75, 132
divine/-ing, 44, 60, 65, 76, 80, 81, 83, 85, 117, 132, 158, 172, 184, 218, 349, 350, 372, 378, 380, 382, 405, 407–9, 413, 417, 527
diviner/-s, 65, 158
divorce, 133, 149
Djinn, 379
doctor/-s, 25, 31, 47, 133, 138, 183, 240, 282, 344, 346, 378, 441,
dog/-s, 65, 84, 133, 154, 199, 225, 228, 230, 231, 233, 237, 239, 260, 276, 297, 346, 350, 354, 368, 371, 472, 479, 505, 528, 532, 565, 567, 580, 602, 613, 614, 616
dogwood, 483
Doomsday, 269
door/-s, 86, 118, 138, 227, 243, 253, 285, 287, 291, 293, 297, 304, 313, 319, 368, 391, 415, 424, 426, 427, 428, 429, 435, 440, 442, 457, 458, 475, 476, 537, 544, 551, 572, 584, 597, 606
dose/-s/-ing, 235, 249, 257, 507, 598, 599
dough, 240, 259, 272, 281, 287, 354, 420, 425, 494, 499, 507, 508, 526, 597
dove, 245, 331, 349, 525
dowsing, 353
dragon/-s, 132, 143, 158, 199, 241, 256, 259, 267, 269, 350, 385, 391, 392, 395, 412, 452, 528
dream/-s, 168, 255, 278, 284, 543, 556, 578
drool, 283, 284
dropsy, 530
drowned, 352, 430
drugs, 74
drum-sickness, 87, 549
drums, 65, 96
drunk/-ard, 72, 74, 82, 86, 88, 92, 242, 247, 257, 288, 311, 415, 439, 440, 448, 491, 492, 494, 499, 501, 507, 508, 509, 524, 572
dualism, 97, 98
ducks, 366, 478, 483, 485
dueling, 154,
dung, 207, 236, 273, 354, 356, 476, 522, 565, 615
durklop/-p, 496, 497, 512, 516
dust, 60, 150, 291, 307, 329
dyfvelsträck, see also *Ferula asafoetida* 207, 522, 598, 619
dysentery, 592
dysfunction, sexual, 24

E

eagle/-s, 318, 483
ear/-s, 130, 195, 229, 235, 243, 248, 253, 262, 273, 296, 297, 369, 376, 412, 422, 455, 465, 472, 478, 487, 495, 496, 497, 500, 509, 512, 516, 519, 520, 531, 532, 538, 545, 546, 548, 584, 600, 602, 604
eardrum, 296
earthworms, 295
earwax, 195, 481, 531, 602
Easter, 231, 478, 503, 542, 566, 612
eczema, 94
eel/-s, 233, 236, 273
egg, 225, 228, 230, 235, 241, 244, 248, 257, 279, 280, 286, 352, 371, 420, 421, 497, 505, 506, 511, 516, 529, 530, 543, 546, 548, 555, 557, 570, 605, 607
eggshell, 281
eggwhite, 236, 237, 594
elderberry, 593
elf/-ves, 97, 158, 241, 374, 376, 392, 412, 413, 534, 535, 600
elfberry, 515
elm, 496
Elohim, 263, 379, 380, 381, 382, 383, 384, 385, 387, 388, 389, 400, 468
emerald, 458
enchantment, 318, 321, 333, 344, 501, 505
enemy/-ies, 85, 131, 137, 153, 199, 225, 227, 230, 242, 244, 255, 261, 280, 282, 283, 286, 290, 299, 306, 319, 320, 331, 335, 339, 357, 363, 372, 374, 377, 392, 412, 438, 453, 472, 523, 535, 567, 614
England, 50, 56, 109, 164
English, 24, 26, 31, 33, 41, 50, 51, 52, 58, 96, 98, 110, 112, 124, 127, 138, 143, 159, 181, 207, 216, 224, 271, 286, 298, 379, 404, 490, 542, 576, 596
entrails, 604
entryway, 72, 496
envy/-ious, 130, 131, 134, 286, 318, 321, 322, 323, 324, 329, 330, 331, 429, 439, 442, 472, 554, 557
ephesia grammata, 36, 128, 129, 172, 195, 196
epilepsy, 286, 317, 428, 530
epiphyte, 619
Equifetum arvense, 349
eruptions, skin, 175
erysipelas, 248, 249, 288, 572
escape, 70, 77, 132, 229, 477, 479, 482, 485, 488, 520, 548
eternity, 333, 338, 384, 447, 448, 468
Euphorbia helioscopia, 593
Eustachian tubes, 248
evergreen, 407, 479, 564, 565, 574, 577, 582, 601
evidence, 28, 89, 129, 134, 137, 142, 181, 187, 206, 209, 596
evil eye, 71
evil, 43, 48, 61, 64, 67, 69, 70, 71, 74, 78, 85, 87, 90, 92, 98, 114, 117, 118, 121, 122, 138, 158, 159, 195, 232, 235, 241, 250, 253, 257, 269, 274, 276, 301, 302, 306, 307, 318, 321, 323, 324, 326, 331, 332, 335, 337, 339, 344, 345, 355, 364, 373, 374, 375, 376, 377, 386, 392, 394,

396, 397, 406, 412, 413, 414, 417, 429, 430, 431, 432, 433, 434, 438, 439, 440, 441, 442, 443, 444, 445, 447, 448, 449, 450, 451, 453, 456, 458, 473, 489, 494, 500, 513, 530, 534, 535, 550, 573, 586, 588, 595, 597, 598, 599, 602, 606
evocation/-s, 156, 160, 172, 184, 201, 214, 215, 240
excrement, 454, 506
execution, 128, 144, 145
executor, 137
exhortation/-s, 157, 158, 218, 307, 374, 376, 378, 392, 397, 399, 407, 417, 462–64, 534, 535, 550
exorcism, 34, 36, 130, 156–58, 173, 180, 208, 241, 245, 330, 373, 375, 391–93, 404, 412, 413, 475, 534, 535
exorcist, 157, 179, 418
eye, 43, 62, 70, 71, 91, 142, 149, 156, 226, 231, 261, 266, 279, 299, 302, 308, 315, 316, 321, 335, 342, 360, 396, 420, 425, 431, 439, 442, 449, 500, 533, 538, 545, 563, 565, 570, 571, 574, 582, 601, 610
eyeball, 261
eyelashes, 349, 525
eyes, 108, 130, 170, 175, 225, 230, 237, 261, 269, 277, 290, 295, 297, 306, 313, 317, 330, 331, 336, 341, 342, 364, 370, 376, 391, 412, 420, 424, 425, 450, 452, 457, 460, 469, 476, 490, 493, 495, 511, 513, 515, 518, 523, 524, 538, 570, 573, 604, 614
eyesocket/-s, 62, 279

F

face/-s, 31, 191, 233, 242, 253, 280, 291, 309, 369, 384, 397, 421, 450, 487, 489, 491, 495, 507, 510, 525, 548, 562, 593
fairies, 97
family/ies, 29, 69, 72, 87, 89, 90, 91, 103, 113, 132, 140, 165, 178, 188, 189, 190, 232, 328, 338, 454, 533, 559
fang, 583
farm/-s, 65, 76, 83, 86, 110, 112, 118, 133, 141, 142, 157, 158, 175, 177, 214, 241, 244, 253, 261, 281, 311, 320, 322, 323, 326, 331, 335, 337, 369, 397, 413, 441, 447, 449, 454, 466, 498, 534, 537, 538, 549, 551, 554, 584, 599
farmer/-s, 47, 107, 118, 119, 131, 138, 143, 162, 179, 311, 320, 323, 326, 328, 331, 335, 336, 337, 341, 346, 538, 554, 609
fasting, 246, 257, 262, 287, 397, 398, 616
fat/-ty, 247, 255, 256, 288, 289, 296, 319, 370, 373, 425, 485, 598, 601, 608, 609
fate/-s, 65, 69
fauna, 520
Faust, 47, 48, 141, 171, 240, 272
feast, 77, 101, 224, 227, 228, 234, 329, 477, 612

feather/-s, 223, 234, 236, 237, 276, 291, 304, 348, 352, 354, 362, 366, 368, 415, 419, 424, 472, 476, 482, 483, 504, 517, 520, 531, 537, 542, 545, 564, 568, 578, 604, 611, 613
February, 242, 436, 543
feces, 35, 234, 244, 287, 424, 425, 476, 549, 554, 558, 572, 582, 592, 594, 615
feet, see foot, 166, 229, 255, 262, 263, 266, 275, 287, 290, 292, 317, 327, 353, 356, 360, 373, 376, 385, 395, 413, 420, 431, 450, 461, 464, 470, 477, 482, 486, 491, 508, 530, 535, 537, 546, 572, 592, 603, 605
female, 65, 78, 260, 376, 397, 404, 426, 478, 563, 590
fence, 322, 433, 449, 450, 497, 580, 582, 586, 597
fenkols pith, 501
fenugreek, 269, 285, 289, 558, 619
fermented/-s, 236, 258, 429, 592
fern, 77
fernis/-sa, 300
fertilize/-ation, 209, 236, 541
Ferula asafœtida, 207, 522, 619
fetish/-es, 72, 79, 85, 86, 112, 117
fetus, 242, 494
fever/-s/-ing/-ish, 24, 73, 239, 286, 420, 441, 446, 511, 514, 529, 536, 559
fey, 425
fiancé/-e/-s, 86, 132, 240, 331, 332, 539
fibel, 593
fiber, 564
fiddle (instrument), 133, 152, 154, 165, 167, 173, 345, 476
fiddler/-s, 166, 338, 366, 367
field/-s, 67, 111, 205, 236, 270, 287, 344, 479, 485, 537, 541, 554, 583, 607
fiend/-s, 232, 397, 412
fig, 256, 470
fight/-s/-ing, 273, 294, 473, 474, 481, 570, 575
filth, 324, 422, 597
finger, 115, 227, 239, 240, 241, 244, 256, 257, 270, 271, 279, 297, 307, 310, 311, 316, 332, 333, 336, 338, 339, 340, 346, 348, 356, 358, 368, 369, 391, 398, 399, 412, 413, 429, 434, 475–77, 483, 484, 486, 487, 505, 506, 507, 508, 511, 513, 518, 519, 522, 524, 530–32, 542, 559–61, 565, 566, 570, 571, 576, 577, 579, 583, 589, 599, 603, 604, 605, 617
fingernails, 195
fir/-s, 314, 331, 363, 476, 478, 480–81, 525, 531
fire/-s, 24, 66, 108, 130, 131, 145, 200, 224, 228, 234, 240, 242, 243, 245, 247, 249, 250, 252, 255, 260, 266, 273, 274, 277, 278, 280, 286, 287, 290, 298, 300, 301, 304, 308, 312, 313, 317, 324, 325, 326–28, 330, 336, 348, 360, 361, 363, 366, 367, 368, 369, 373, 376, 379, 380, 382, 398, 399, 404, 413, 420–22, 428, 432, 438, 439, 441, 455, 461, 466, 477, 480, 482,

483, 504, 506, 507, 508, 510, 517, 518, 520, 521, 523, 534, 537, 538, 546, 562, 563, 569, 576, 577, 589, 593, 597, 600, 603, 605, 608, 611, 615
firelight, 391
firestone, 522
firmament/-s, 262, 462, 557
fish, 236, 279, 363, 405, 425, 433, 450, 501–5, 511, 514, 538, 554, 556, 564
fistulas, 247, 508
flame/-s, 328, 414, 459, 460
flax, 354, 431, 510, 513, 515, 525
flea/-s, 348, 526, 567
flesh, 34, 248, 265, 270, 286, 295, 314, 319, 321, 322, 325, 326, 350, 374, 392, 413, 432, 439, 440, 441, 443, 470, 493, 503, 527, 535, 572, 582, 590, 608, 609, 612
flint, 477, 482, 504, 518, 561, 600, 612
flood, 269, 299, 308, 310, 432, 433, 496, 582
flora, 214
flour, 259, 271, 272, 288, 329, 360, 421, 425, 434, 442, 499, 507, 542, 558, 584, 616
flower/-s/-ing, 77, 160, 255, 331, 420, 442, 454, 497, 499, 500, 508, 509, 515, 516, 558, 572, 592
flu, 152
flute, 430
Fly agaric, 576
flygrön/-n, also *flyrön/-n*, = *Sorbus aucuparia*, 239, 251, 259, 280, 289, 293, 294, 347, 413, 414, 501, 513, 597, 599, 619
foal, 68, 391, 550
foam, 339, 530
fog, 450, 553
food-poisoning, 343
food, 73, 196, 198, 215, 229, 232, 234, 236, 247, 254, 257, 297, 313, 319, 325, 353, 424, 440, 496, 509, 511, 540, 543, 586, 604
foot, see feet, 47, 223, 230, 246, 256, 273, 275, 278, 279, 282, 290, 298, 314, 319, 320, 325, 326, 337, 341, 347, 353, 356, 357, 360, 363, 364, 369, 370, 372, 445, 466, 472, 476, 482, 484, 486, 505, 506, 508, 516, 521, 522, 525, 530, 531, 537, 551, 563, 565, 570, 571, 576, 579, 581, 589, 607, 613, 614
footbaths, 296
footprint/-s, 36, 144, 145, 223, 268, 336, 337, 466, 480, 485, 532, 556, 601, 603
footstep/-s, 337, 361, 407
Forbium, 289
forehead, 63, 233, 256, 487, 488, 543
forest/-s, 64, 158, 219, 241, 342, 343, 357, 368, 376, 396, 404, 412, 482, 483, 484, 502, 520, 530, 568, 588, 616
forestfowl, 478
forge, 600
formulæ, 33, 34, 36, 37, 39, 48, 88, 89, 94, 128, 129, 136, 151, 177, 194, 228, 240, 429, 530, 571, 609
fortitude, 75, 239, 268, 321, 322, 323, 327, 332, 335, 339, 343, 344, 412, 433, 442, 582
fortune/-s, 43, 90, 131, 215
fowl, 235, 478
fox/-es, 228, 231, 256, 268, 428, 430, 479, 480, 484, 485, 486, 530, 546, 580, 582
fråssa, 271, 303, 490
freckles, 421
freedom, 132, 393, 502
Friday, 224, 262, 267, 275, 283, 287, 304, 358, 407, 414, 447, 484, 485, 487, 537, 554, 557, 559, 566, 597, 610, 612
friend/-s, 88, 162, 263, 297, 395, 438, 453, 481, 521, 538, 539, 540, 543, 565, 572, 606
friendship, 180
frog/-s, 230, 231, 235, 238, 277, 279, 281, 475, 493, 503, 511, 512, 531, 561, 570
frossa/-n, 24, 239, 286, 490, 507, 509
frost, 355, 356, 529
froth, 538, 608
fruit, 218, 232, 260, 262, 287, 289, 296, 308, 329, 378, 397, 415, 442, 483, 498, 508, 519, 547
fuldelberries, 273
fulslag, 530
fun, 72, 273, 440
fundelrot, 269
funeral, 475
fungal, 608, 619
future/-s, 25, 31, 74, 75, 76, 118, 129, 132, 184, 189, 215, 219, 379, 458, 491

G

Gabriel, 100, 187, 188, 379, 380, 381, 382, 400, 427, 462, 463, 614
gall, 233, 259, 280, 281, 293, 489, 506, 508, 529, 561, 572, 580, 613
gallbladder, 370, 497
gallows, 286, 324, 504, 505, 568, 580
gallstones, 607
gambling, 132, 148, 153, 178, 199, 241, 255, 261, 278, 285, 294, 299, 575, 578
garbage, 291, 615
garden, 34, 55, 66, 138, 270, 290, 310, 319, 374, 377, 392, 395, 407, 412, 413, 438, 439, 441, 535, 586, 589
garlic, 239, 242, 251, 269, 275, 293, 294, 353, 354, 355, 367, 378, 397, 414, 421, 474, 486, 495, 506, 512, 522, 548, 556, 562, 566, 580, 584, 591, 592, 594, 597, 598, 606, 611, 617
gate/-s, 66, 440, 442, 537
gatepost, 313
geese/goose, 236, 286, 354, 398, 483, 485, 489, 530, 582
German, 32, 47, 48, 60, 104, 105, 124, 136, 141, 155,

159, 188, 207, 214, 224, 231, 232, 273, 275, 278, 417, 499, 507, 510, 619
Germany, 28, 41, 47, 85, 119
Gethsemane, 34, 270, 374, 377
ghost/-s, 79, 125, 158, 173, 224, 232, 239, 240, 241, 243, 254, 259, 260, 264, 265, 268, 269, 270, 272, 274, 286, 287, 292, 298, 299, 301, 302, 303, 304, 313–26, 329, 334, 335, 337, 338, 340, 345, 346, 347, 374–78, 382, 383, 389, 391–98, 400, 405, 409, 411–13, 429, 445–54, 456, 459, 465, 468, 469, 473–75, 496, 502, 534, 535, 536, 537, 543, 544, 547, 548, 550, 553, 554, 557, 561, 563, 564, 565, 569, 571, 585, 587–90, 611, 613, 614
gin, 562, 596
ginger, 246, 248, 455, 558, 593
girdle, 563
girl/-s, 87, 150, 234, 241, 244, 249, 261, 277, 278, 279, 290, 291, 304, 306, 307, 328, 331, 332, 341, 342, 349, 355, 363, 364, 434, 457, 475, 493, 494, 495, 505, 506, 524, 525, 527, 540, 543, 547, 549, 553, 554, 577, 605, 606
gizzard, 472, 576, 616
glass, 230, 236, 239, 246, 249, 250, 251, 277, 281, 289, 315, 332, 333, 339, 348, 370, 414, 429, 441, 442, 458, 474, 487, 493, 526, 574, 592, 593
glitter, 421
glove/-s, 479, 540, 561
glue, 153, 236, 281
gnome, 142
goal/-s, 34, 103, 127, 198, 209, 381
goanisse, 132, 141, 142, 214, 261
goat, 35, 288, 328, 343, 427, 442, 476, 507, 508, 511, 515, 538, 572
goats-blood, 513
godfather, 473
Gods, 263, 359, 434, 473
goiter, 316
gold, 143, 297, 298, 300, 311, 333, 349, 350, 351, 353, 356, 379, 399, 406, 408, 414, 448, 518, 527, 528
goldsmith, 226
Golgotha, 407
Goliath, 244
gout, 288, 295, 375, 376, 394, 491
grain/-s, 235, 236, 271, 298, 356, 369, 420, 423, 424, 425, 427, 438, 439, 482, 494, 496, 497, 519, 542, 546, 561, 576, 579, 584, 592, 596, 599, 603, 616
granddaughter, 157, 191
grandfather, 157, 345
grandmother, 157
grapes, 232, 419
grapevines, 232
grass, 251, 271, 277, 360, 364, 365, 421, 473, 487, 498, 505, 506, 507, 508, 513, 532, 541, 553, 563

grasshopper, 521
grave/-s, 61, 122, 150, 184, 240, 248, 273, 293, 307, 329, 338, 345, 346, 365, 367, 399, 413, 424, 445–48, 458, 466, 470, 475, 520, 548, 553, 560, 586, 588, 613, 615
gravesite, 83
gravestone/-s, 246, 346, 449, 452, 582
graveyard/-s, 60, 150, 245, 301, 329, 331, 332, 346
Greek, 27, 45, 52, 58, 158, 171, 180, 201, 374, 379, 411, 461
greensnake, 258
greyhouse (mugwort), 234
grimoire/-s, 27, 45, 47, 48, 50, 121, 160, 164, 182, 214, 219, 230, 417, 418
Grimoireum Verum, 160
grouse, 477
gun, 131, 348, 360, 367, 472, 477, 479, 481, 517, 541, 610
gunpowder, 240, 260, 275, 276, 289, 301, 366, 426, 514, 519, 531, 537, 542, 545, 546, 600, 602, 611, 612
gunshot, 364, 481

H

hail, 366, 531
hair, 63, 130, 177, 232, 244, 258, 270, 275, 289, 290, 321, 325, 339, 348, 353, 397, 425, 430–32, 450, 454, 473, 494, 504, 506, 511, 516, 517, 521, 537, 549, 555, 558, 562, 567, 579, 581, 583, 588, 593, 603, 611, 613
hairs, 277, 325, 452, 473, 511, 514, 516, 543, 547, 561, 567
hallucinations, 133
ham, 249, 275
hammer, 231, 261, 282, 313, 417, 482, 557, 591
hamstrings, 607
hand/-s, 23, 24, 28, 30, 33, 34, 35, 39, 40, 42, 43, 47, 57, 78, 85, 88, 94, 98, 109, 112, 118, 120, 121, 134, 140, 144, 148, 158, 159, 165, 174, 177, 185, 189, 191, 206, 209, 212, 225, 226, 238, 239, 241, 248, 254, 256, 258, 261, 270, 273, 276, 278, 279, 282, 286, 289–91, 295, 299, 302, 307, 318, 325, 326, 328, 329, 330, 332, 333, 337, 340, 342, 349, 351, 352, 354, 355, 356, 358, 359, 368, 369, 373, 374, 376, 377, 381, 385, 388, 391, 392, 395, 397, 399, 407, 409, 412–14, 421, 425, 426, 427, 430, 434, 436, 439, 441, 442, 448, 451, 456, 458, 465, 466, 470, 472, 475, 476, 478, 479, 481, 483, 484, 486, 492, 499, 501, 502, 504, 508, 515, 522, 523, 527, 528, 530, 531, 535, 536, 543, 545, 549, 551, 561, 562, 564, 566, 571, 572, 576, 577, 578, 580, 582, 584, 588, 589, 590, 592, 597, 603, 605, 607, 608, 613, 614, 617, 618
handwriting, 27, 80, 147, 176, 194, 209, 248, 250, 600,

617
hare, 131, 133, 226, 230, 233, 235, 237, 273, 276, 280, 281, 297, 336, 363, 370, 378, 424, 479, 484, 486, 506, 511, 514, 515, 525, 531, 546, 554, 567, 572, 580, 605, 613–14
harehunt, 485
harm, 34, 130, 131, 132, 133, 134, 149, 152, 154, 190, 197, 225, 227, 229, 240, 241, 244, 250, 253, 278, 294, 332, 333, 346, 358, 359, 360, 374, 378, 382, 392, 404, 412, 428, 462, 463, 464, 476, 481, 483, 501, 522, 534, 535, 550, 551, 569, 588, 589, 590, 595, 600
harmful, 58, 61, 165, 182, 197
harmless, 195, 216, 392
harness/-es, 244, 258, 487, 576
harp, 338, 428
Hårpex oil, 284
hårpix oil, 280
hart, 281, 353
hartshorn, 256, 505
harvest/-ing, 46, 130, 132, 328, 340, 341, 440, 537, 541
haunt, 555
hauntings, 376, 377, 395, 473, 534, 600
hawk, 278
hawthorn, 308, 392, 615
häxa/-n, 61, 67, 68, 89, 96, 134
häxor, 67, 83, 99
hay, 230, 251, 291, 292, 296, 328, 341, 369, 556, 580, 584, 590, 592, 597
hazel, 233, 302, 307, 349, 350, 352, 353, 387, 413, 444, 478, 495, 497, 524, 527, 580, 588
hazelnut, 249, 290, 302, 444, 489
hazelwives, 534
head/-s, 46, 67, 70, 86, 116, 117, 122, 147, 195, 213, 231, 232, 234, 247, 248, 250, 251, 253, 255, 261, 265, 270, 271, 276–78, 280, 281, 292, 296, 301, 305, 312, 314, 316, 327, 329, 334, 337, 339, 340, 349, 351, 352, 353, 364, 367, 369, 372, 373, 375, 376, 379, 380, 385, 388, 395, 409, 413, 415, 419, 421, 428, 440, 444, 445, 447, 451, 453, 456, 470, 473, 475, 477, 482–89, 499, 504, 506, 508, 509, 510, 511, 514, 516, 525, 527, 528, 535, 543, 547, 558, 561, 562, 565, 567, 569, 570, 572, 574, 575, 578, 581, 582, 586, 588, 590, 602, 603, 611, 614
headache, 248, 419, 420, 440, 495, 543
headless, 75, 280, 425
headstone, 465, 466
heal, 61, 73, 119, 121, 131, 138, 149, 151, 152, 179, 191, 203, 207, 215, 242, 255, 257, 274, 288, 295, 312, 317, 320, 322, 340, 343, 356, 359, 360, 361, 362, 364, 368, 431, 438, 439, 441, 442, 455, 487, 491, 493, 495, 500, 512, 513, 518, 530, 536, 551, 591, 594, 607
healer/-s, 23, 29, 31, 39, 53, 61, 67, 73, 83, 88, 89, 94, 96, 119, 134, 137, 140, 142, 144, 167–68, 170, 183, 197, 198, 202, 207, 216, 398, 441
healing, 35, 43, 44, 46, 50, 55, 56, 59, 61, 62, 68, 73, 74, 75, 79, 81, 82, 83, 88, 94, 97, 109, 113, 116, 117, 118, 121, 130, 131, 137–40, 142, 144, 145, 146, 147, 149, 151–54, 156, 157, 163, 167–69, 172, 175, 177, 178, 182, 183, 187, 190, 191–93, 195–99, 206, 207, 209, 216, 217, 238, 246, 253, 255, 306, 314, 320, 324, 340, 342, 344, 355, 375, 398, 423, 436, 440, 441, 444, 454, 490, 496, 513, 524, 529, 547, 552, 559, 598, 599, 607, 608, 619
health, 24, 62, 73, 109, 129, 134, 152, 154, 157, 167, 175, 178, 179, 217, 394, 441, 473, 556
healthy, 50, 248, 274, 295, 297, 310, 312, 317, 324, 343, 344, 347, 444, 482, 511, 537, 538
heart, 95, 129, 210, 223, 224, 225, 228, 231, 233, 237, 244, 245, 246, 256, 268, 273, 276, 278, 280, 281, 282, 283, 287, 291, 293, 294, 301, 304, 346, 348, 349, 352, 353, 358, 361, 363, 364, 366, 367, 368, 371, 412, 415, 452, 472, 473, 475, 476, 481, 482, 494, 499, 500, 503, 505, 506, 509, 512, 518, 519, 521, 522, 524, 525, 526, 527, 529, 531, 540, 542, 561, 564, 566, 578, 601, 602, 605, 610
heartburn, 490
hearth, 163, 313
heat, 262, 273, 297, 510, 529, 532, 589, 596, 607
heathen/-s, 37, 358
heaves, 257, 398, 576, 595, 616
Hebrew, 56, 81, 160, 171, 293, 382, 387, 418, 461
hedgehog, 506, 526, 556, 563, 568
heifer/-s, 138, 376–78
heirloom, 349, 527
hell, 34, 48, 92, 145, 157, 183, 192, 200, 201, 239, 240, 265, 266, 268, 269, 270, 272, 273, 286, 290, 293, 294, 299, 310, 311, 319, 323, 324, 334, 336, 337, 346, 362, 369, 373, 375, 379, 380, 382, 383, 387, 388, 389, 392, 395, 397, 404, 412, 413, 417, 428, 429, 432, 433, 434, 443–45, 461, 467–70, 475, 514, 518, 534, 536, 553, 554, 557, 563, 565, 569–71, 581, 615, 616
hellstone, 512
hemlock, 514
hemorrhoids, 441, 510
hemp, 236, 503, 516, 562
hen/-s, 228, 235, 236, 248, 250, 287, 291, 328, 352, 371, 424, 442, 476, 477, 478, 485, 497, 504, 505, 511, 524, 530, 538, 545, 548, 554, 576, 584, 604, 605, 610, 615, 616
henbane, 501, 507, 508, 514, 516
Heptameron, 121
herb/-s, 39, 46, 88, 91, 136, 138, 195, 230, 275–78, 283, 285, 290, 396, 490–500, 506, 508, 509, 515, 569, 605
hernia, 606
heron, 504, 505, 515, 556, 564, 577

herring, 236, 242, 293, 485, 543
hex/-es, 68, 69, 72, 73, 85, 90, 149, 152, 173, 190, 218, 224, 239, 242, 243, 245, 253, 279, 286, 295, 301, 348, 355, 356, 360, 361, 367, 368, 434, 435, 438, 442, 447, 448, 450, 473, 498, 499, 504, 507, 517, 521, 526, 532, 537, 538, 540, 541, 542, 544, 546, 547, 548, 561, 565, 568, 576, 601, 610, 611, 612, 613, 615
hexed, 24, 52, 69, 86, 109, 130, 162, 177, 190, 193, 232, 242, 245, 253, 260, 262, 295, 301, 308, 347, 348, 366, 367, 430, 435, 439, 442, 446, 481, 482, 483, 485, 489, 498, 499, 504, 517, 518, 519, 522, 531, 532, 533, 540, 541, 542, 545, 546, 548, 550, 559, 581, 599, 601, 606, 610, 615
hexing, 89, 133, 154, 167, 169, 173, 177, 179, 182, 195, 207, 347, 348, 438, 452, 497, 517
hidden, 27, 33, 43, 68, 70, 78, 85, 97, 98, 112, 115, 118, 124, 132, 147, 152, 158, 160, 165, 172, 213, 218, 255, 258, 369, 379, 380, 406, 408, 409, 413, 416, 417, 452, 454, 465, 467, 484, 485, 506, 528, 532, 574, 604
Hippocratic oath, 152
hive, 131, 397
hoarse/-ness, 326, 491, 510, 515
hog, 541
home, 52, 60, 62, 65, 71, 72, 75, 81, 85, 90, 105, 107, 117, 118, 133, 143, 157, 162, 179, 194, 196, 201, 207, 241, 243, 251, 254, 255, 262, 286, 297, 298, 305, 319, 320, 325, 330, 333, 334, 339, 341, 342, 344, 345, 363, 375, 423, 424, 428, 434, 442, 447, 456, 475, 486, 499, 502, 518, 537, 538, 539, 568, 569, 573, 576, 580, 586, 596, 602, 603
homelessness, 96
homeopath, 455
homesickness, 433
homogeneous, 215, 218
honey, 232, 257, 322, 353, 359, 485, 492, 500, 501, 504, 506, 507, 508, 510, 512, 563, 594, 605, 608
honeycomb, 593
hooch, 596
hoodoo, 216
hoof/-ves, 137, 287, 319, 369, 537, 567, 579, 608
hoopoe, 225, 227, 231, 237
hops, 289, 616
Horba origanum, 598
horn, 35, 256, 337, 445, 476, 608
hornet, 319
horse/-s, 34, 36, 53, 60, 61, 91, 137, 138, 147, 156, 192, 193, 223, 227-29, 234, 235, 239, 242, 257, 258, 262, 268, 269, 270, 272, 274, 275, 282, 285, 289, 294, 297, 314, 322-24, 328, 335, 347, 355, 356, 359, 360, 369, 374, 391, 398, 421, 428, 442, 446, 476, 486-89, 496, 497, 501, 513, 521, 522, 531, 533, 538, 541, 542, 544-46, 548, 554, 555, 562, 567, 568, 576, 581-83, 588, 592-96, 604, 607, 608, 615, 616
horseshoe-nails, 484
horseshoe, 281, 410, 444, 484, 581, 591, 597
horsetail, 349, 533
hound, 532
house/-s/-ing, 43, 48, 66, 75, 86, 115, 129, 138, 158, 170, 189, 227, 229, 235, 243, 250, 253, 254, 261, 283, 286, 293, 297, 298, 317, 323, 326, 329, 336, 341, 344, 397, 413, 420, 436, 443, 451, 453, 458, 466, 497, 505, 539, 547, 554, 584, 599
household/-s, 46, 47, 48, 75, 106, 113, 203, 213, 425, 551, 603
howl/-ing, 276, 323
human/-s, 31, 60, 68, 73, 78, 109, 125, 130, 147, 152, 154, 157, 163, 172, 175, 177, 178, 183, 187, 188, 190, 191, 193, 195, 198, 206, 217, 233, 240, 249, 256, 258, 262, 265, 276, 281, 285, 287, 291, 294, 321, 327, 329, 345, 350, 360, 369, 375, 396, 415, 422, 424, 431, 433, 455, 457, 462, 463, 477, 495, 501, 502, 504, 511, 523, 526, 528, 545, 548, 549, 563, 571, 574, 580, 584, 592, 594, 601, 609
hunger/-y, 226, 254, 364, 450, 605
hunt/-ing, 130, 131, 133, 147, 154, 175, 177, 195, 196, 198, 199, 213, 224, 225, 294, 308, 476-78, 480, 483-84, 520, 532, 546, 563, 565, 576, 577, 601, 605, 611, 613, 615
hunter/-s, 175, 245, 273, 477, 480, 546, 609, 611, 613, 614, 615
husband, 138, 231, 459
husk, 316
hut/-s, 478, 485
hypnotism, 170, 330
hyssop, 507

I

ice, 322, 592
illiteracy/-ate, 48, 213, 219
illness, 31, 40, 43, 53, 68, 73, 74, 76, 81, 84, 85, 88, 93, 94, 98, 105, 118, 121, 130, 144, 147, 177, 180, 190, 196, 198, 214, 297, 314, 340, 346, 376, 429, 476, 495, 500
imp, 86
imprisonment, 179, 182, 226, 552
impure/-ities/-y, 247, 373, 400, 408, 434, 496, 512, 534, 569, 573, 606, 607
inanimate, 130, 131, 137
incense/s, 23, 128, 136, 147, 176, 178, 193, 197, 218, 239, 250, 251, 253, 259, 284, 396, 418, 445, 474, 513, 595, 596, 598, 599
incontinence, 279
incurable, 72, 346, 429

India ink, 280
indigestion, 357
infant, 177, 247
infanticide, 133, 177
infatuation, 132
infection/-s/-ed, 100, 232, 346, 365, 499, 508, 600
influenza, 490
infusion, 493
ingot, 324, 546
injury/-ies, 34, 130, 132, 153, 154, 180, 198, 243, 248, 255, 314, 315, 342, 350, 357, 378, 451, 467, 469, 473, 482, 483, 493, 524, 528, 543, 546, 548, 578, 591, 592, 594, 598, 599, 609
ink, 29, 105, 106, 159, 165, 173, 188, 189, 191, 194, 241, 279, 280, 415, 475, 616
innocent, 117, 183, 600
inorganic, 238
insane, 63, 64, 130, 273, 325, 374, 430, 438, 450
insects, 508
insomnia, 133
integrity, 192
interrogation, 73, 183
intestine/-s/-al, 269, 283, 360, 420, 509, 617
intimacy/-ate, 74, 113, 123, 217
intoxication, 331
invincibility, 132, 282, 400
invisibility, 132, 152, 153, 178, 182, 187, 195, 329, 349
invisible, 130, 132, 228, 229, 231, 277, 279, 285, 292, 321, 324, 327, 329, 330, 337, 340, 352, 353, 354, 363, 370, 380, 381, 424, 440, 441, 443, 458, 465, 493, 524, 546, 558, 564, 570, 571, 574, 575, 604, 606
invocation, 142, 154, 173, 199, 201, 462, 465
iron, 83, 144, 226, 243, 244, 267, 269, 284, 298, 300, 301, 324, 326, 330, 340, 373, 376, 410, 427, 432, 480, 485, 486, 487, 488, 489, 532, 546, 557, 563, 566, 593
ironwood, 414
ironwort, 234
irritation, 327
itch/-ing, 246, 344, 422
itinerant/-cy, 59, 63, 64, 65, 66, 96, 97, 107, 609
ivy, 234, 499

J

jackknife/-ves, 292, 585
jaundice, 130, 163, 296, 419, 529
jaw, 562
jealous, 318, 324, 532
jewels, 458
Jews, 290, 306, 319, 374, 377, 535, 456, 589
jinx, 293
journey, 179, 330, 339, 374, 537, 538, 573, 576
juice, 108, 170, 235, 279, 421, 425, 459, 490, 491, 500, 508, 509, 514, 515, 572, 593
juniper, 249, 288, 295, 308, 425, 484, 485, 486, 495, 497, 500, 502, 509, 510, 515, 532, 544, 561, 562, 563, 566

K

Kabbala, 416, 417
Kastorium, 598
kettle, 223, 247, 288, 296, 355, 556
key/-s, 80, 92, 124, 132, 158, 159, 160, 166, 272, 277, 317, 318, 416, 417, 426, 466, 479, 495, 506, 508, 561
keyhole, 559
kidney/-s, 170, 247, 279, 301, 412, 445, 459, 460, 486, 491
kill, 69, 83, 154, 245, 255, 292, 338, 358, 361, 365, 376, 377, 412, 445, 472, 479, 481, 493, 531, 539, 574, 579, 583, 592
killer, 83, 268
kiln, 568
king, 116, 240, 299, 306, 373, 379, 380, 381, 382, 383, 400, 404, 417, 426, 432, 448, 451, 453, 455, 468
kiss/-es, 226, 227, 277, 291, 304, 363, 399, 423, 444, 506, 524, 537, 540, 547, 605
kitchen, 69, 128, 207
knee/-s, 118, 335, 361, 386, 388, 415, 448, 449, 458, 478, 483, 519, 522, 554, 555, 576
knife blade, 355
knife measures, 256
knife points, 444
knife/-ves, 44, 69, 79, 83–85, 100, 144, 145, 170, 224, 238, 249, 256, 267, 269, 270, 271, 280, 283, 292–93, 312, 313, 316, 324, 327, 329, 336, 337, 340, 346, 347, 349, 358, 359, 391, 422, 426, 427, 429, 433, 444, 446, 449, 458, 466, 472, 474, 482, 484, 486, 487, 499, 504, 518, 520, 527, 539, 554, 555, 558, 563, 566, 567, 569, 580, 581, 585, 586, 588, 593, 601, 604, 615
knot/-s, 249, 293, 346, 347, 435, 457, 487, 488, 538, 583, 599, 601, 617

L

lady/folk, 69, 226, 254, 258, 351, 477, 478, 525, 543, 547, 606
lake, 34, 91, 114, 116, 214, 236, 268, 269, 283, 311, 323, 326, 335, 342, 346, 359, 365, 404, 430, 431, 500, 501, 502, 503, 530, 550, 564, 567, 576, 584, 588, 616
lamb, 375, 488, 538, 582
lame/-ness, 36, 137, 147, 223, 270, 282, 449, 450, 512, 581
lamp, 280, 295, 567, 608
land/-s, 28, 41, 46, 111, 116, 128, 142, 254, 319, 323, 338,

343, 365, 404, 502, 537, 541, 585, 563, 619
language, 46, 96, 105, 136, 155, 181, 184, 207, 213, 218, 226, 417, 480
lantern, 276, 284
Lapis Infinalis, 261
lapus, 225
lapwing/-s, 234, 352, 358, 370, 486, 524, 601, 602, 606, 613
lard, 236, 242, 273, 275, 312, 314, 342, 441, 504, 505, 515, 542, 551, 563, 564, 568, 570, 577, 580, 591
lark, 570
Lasunabula, 265, 461
latex, 559
Latin, 136, 159, 171, 195, 208, 213, 229, 276, 282, 293, 374, 398, 415, 461, 499, 510, 598, 607
lavender oil, 434
Lazarus, 426
lead (element), 45, 60, 61, 83, 225, 276, 277, 296, 298, 300, 348, 446, 479, 483, 489, 515, 517, 574, 602, 609, 611
leaf/-ves, 136, 138, 140, 152, 155, 156, 158, 159, 160, 164, 166, 168, 169, 171, 173, 174, 175, 185, 191, 194, 196, 226, 232, 234, 236, 288, 290, 329, 339, 349, 421, 422, 458, 483, 491, 492, 493, 497-99, 501, 508, 510, 511, 512, 513, 514, 519, 527, 530, 534, 586, 596, 613, 614, 619
leather, 143, 155, 159, 168, 189, 191, 212, 274, 334, 362, 363, 369, 465, 466, 521, 580
leek, 294, 497, 508, 510
leg, 61, 76, 138, 253, 254, 255, 260, 270, 292, 314, 325, 346, 351, 356, 360, 431-33, 449, 478, 483, 487, 494, 499, 508, 516, 528, 533, 537, 546, 551, 574, 583, 593, 608, 612
Lemmus amphibius, water rat, 564
lemon, 431, 513, 515
lice/louse, 195, 235, 289, 294, 328, 353, 421, 422, 481, 501, 511, 530, 542, 546, 567, 579, 596, 602, 607
licorice, 256, 257, 500, 516, 572
lightning, 404, 457
lily/-ies, 420, 495, 515, 599, 619
limb/-s, 248, 255, 288, 295, 310, 311, 312, 326, 376, 440, 441, 442, 443, 452, 491, 494, 506, 512, 514, 515, 516, 542, 562, 585, 589, 590, 599
limbless, 574
lime, 236, 354, 445, 496, 497, 500, 512, 526, 579, 596
linden, 279, 293, 509, 513, 562, 563
linen, 162, 223, 228, 242, 273, 277, 279, 351, 415, 420, 422, 486, 491, 501, 506, 508, 512, 525, 529, 537, 577, 583, 584
linseeds /oil, 300, 592, 593, 594, 596, 608
lion, 244, 413,
liquor, 82, 144, 162, 233, 242, 246, 247, 248, 249, 253, 268, 269, 271, 273, 280, 288, 295, 311, 312, 313, 314, 315, 317, 318, 320, 321, 323, 324,

325, 326, 330, 332, 333, 334, 335, 339, 340, 343, 344, 347, 354, 396, 422, 429, 435, 438, 441, 445, 446, 448, 453, 455, 474, 491, 497, 498, 499, 501, 505, 508, 516, 521, 539, 540, 543, 556, 572, 584, 592, 596, 597, 607, 608
literacy/-ate, 24, 33, 46, 81, 113, 117, 129, 164, 213, 219
liver, 225, 237, 276, 282, 314, 322, 323, 364, 374, 377, 494, 526, 531, 557, 572, 602, 610
livermoss, 600
livestock, 46, 68, 85, 130, 131, 133, 145, 147, 167, 169, 175, 178, 182, 187, 190, 193, 195, 203, 206, 242, 243, 249, 253, 256, 262, 279, 282, 288, 299, 323, 328, 355, 357, 359, 360, 376, 395, 442, 469, 537, 547, 548, 550, 584, 599, 600
lizard, 255
Ljustorp, 168, 438, 444
lobster, 563
lock/-s, 63, 132, 153, 177, 187, 230, 243, 277, 318, 352, 358, 362, 367, 423, 466, 477, 479, 484, 485, 494, 497, 498, 529, 541, 542, 559, 573, 577
log/-s, 34, 319, 326, 330, 346, 355, 357, 358, 359, 431, 443, 529, 530, 550, 584, 588, 590
lore, 43, 45, 47, 78, 79, 88, 90, 92, 94, 124, 128, 136, 146, 151, 167, 168, 178, 195, 199, 205, 208, 209, 210, 212, 216, 217, 406
lost, 82, 120, 124, 178, 179, 209, 211, 249, 268, 274, 276, 322, 334, 342, 372, 444, 533, 555
lottery/ies, 132, 169, 184, 199, 291, 292, 417, 424, 437, 568, 575, 578
lovage, 207, 293, 294, 474, 498, 565, 584, 619
love, 100, 132, 149, 188, 198, 226, 236, 244, 250, 258, 261, 265, 277, 278, 280, 281, 290, 291, 349, 351, 352, 354, 363, 364, 424, 445, 453, 475, 525, 547, 565, 575, 605, 606, 609
lozenge, 493
Lucifer/-s, 334, 337, 338, 385, 404, 429, 430, 435, 581
luck, 24, 38, 69, 89, 130, 131, 132, 133, 153, 154, 177, 184, 190, 195, 198, 199, 201, 213, 250, 294, 330, 354, 360, 361, 363, 368, 378, 447, 449, 451, 476, 482, 483, 494, 498, 502, 504, 518, 520, 553, 563, 568, 572, 575, 576, 583, 585, 597, 602, 603, 604, 610
lucky, 131, 352, 354, 405, 407, 408, 409, 429, 448, 449, 472, 484, 494, 503, 505, 526
lung, 256, 314, 322, 323, 364, 374, 377, 496, 526, 530, 531, 554, 557, 567, 590
Luther, Martin, 66, 125, 195, 213
lye, 232, 421, 557
lynx, 480, 546

M

machines, 339
mage, 76, 332, 373
maggots, 609
magi, 35, 51, 63, 219

magician/-s, 23, 42, 46, 62, 63, 67, 96, 110, 151, 181, 201
magnet/-ism, 261, 330
magpie, 282, 306, 485, 518, 519, 601
maiden/-s, 116, 175, 195, 280, 281, 284, 315, 321, 369, 421, 484, 572, 573, 575, 585, 601, 605, 606, 607
maidenhood, 540, 606, 607
Makorge, 539
malady/-ies, 83, 192, 257, 311, 324, 491, 499, 549, 576, 617
malaria, 130, 419
male, 78, 81, 233, 258, 260, 305, 351, 376, 396, 397, 404, 423, 424, 445, 514, 515, 528, 543, 590, 606, 616
malefica/-ia/-ium, 62, 69, 96, 198, 206, 215, 327
malevolence/-t, 30, 31, 59, 60, 61, 67, 68, 83, 97, 98, 116, 131, 132, 134, 137, 142, 144, 145, 147, 150, 152, 153, 167, 173, 177, 183, 187, 190, 193, 195, 196, 197, 198, 206, 321, 378, 502
mallards, 478
malört, see *artemisia abstinthium*, 445, 492, 500, 619
malt, 245, 320, 322, 323, 378, 540, 584, 596, 603
Mandragora officinalis, mandrake, 61, 98, 199
mane, 398, 488, 501, 595
manure, 289, 335, 423, 424, 541, 542
maple, 538, 550, 619
marble, 536
Marbuel/is, 132, 141, 142, 171, 172, 201, 214, 262, 263, 264, 265, 266, 461, 462, 463, 464
March, 135, 143, 146, 179, 185, 191, 436, 477, 492, 554, 606
mare, 118, 119, 305, 324, 356, 497, 498, 512, 563
Margareta, 310, 315, 335, 437
marjoram, 237, 613
marksman/-ship, 175, 195, 531, 603
marriage/-s, 187, 215, 250
marrow, 288, 312, 322, 326, 431, 432, 439, 440, 441, 557
marry/-ied, 68, 82, 106, 241, 250, 310, 355, 505, 544, 547
Mars, 267
Martinsmas, 485
martyr/-ed/-s, 181, 361, 373, 376, 402, 403, 520, 534
mason, see stonemason, 344
Mastic, 239, 250, 251, 252, 619
Maundy Thursday, 75, 77, 86, 229, 262, 274, 304, 414, 487, 497, 503, 544, 566, 576, 600
May, 174, 179, 229, 344, 385, 432, 444, 451, 454, 477, 492, 538, 541, 545, 554, 558, 612
meadow, 61, 319, 344, 432, 442, 485, 569, 583
measles, 507
meat, 73, 247, 249, 296, 330, 398, 486, 515, 530, 591, 594, 605, 614
medallions, 446
medicine/-s, 23, 24, 25, 26, 38, 58, 59, 61, 63, 99, 105, 113, 117, 134, 138, 141, 163, 177, 197, 210, 341, 439, 455, 458, 607, 608, 609, 619
Melchior, 408, 428
memory/ies, 128, 132, 157, 163, 165, 177, 180, 231, 232, 289, 421, 436, 451, 495, 499, 561, 562
menses/menstrual, 195, 294, 504
Mentha sativa, Heart's joy, 509
Mercurius, 609
mercury, (as in quicksilver), 197, 236, 240, 276, 280, 292, 293, 294, 354, 367, 435, 449, 453, 465, 476, 493, 496, 497, 499, 504, 514, 544, 546, 548, 561, 562, 563, 566, 567, 568, 604, 609
mergnass (powder), 256
Merien incense, 284
mermaid/-s, 91, 123, 124, 241
metal, 144, 197, 298, 381, 414
metalloid, 619
metallurgist, 75, 153, 173
metallurgy, 133, 146
meteoric iron, 267
Michaelsmas, 521
midnight, 49, 75, 82, 457
midsummer, 76, 77, 255, 349, 414, 478, 491, 522, 527, 533, 541, 566, 569, 572, 592
midwife, 611
migration, 28, 39, 45, 47
milk-defiler, 378
milk-pitcher, 256
milk-stealing, 131,
milk, 42, 43, 68, 69, 83, 116, 131, 133, 152, 156, 162, 182, 214, 233, 235, 247, 249, 259, 269, 280, 293, 294, 319, 320, 322, 332, 335, 336, 378, 431, 439, 442, 455, 491, 501, 507, 508, 511, 513, 543, 544, 546, 548, 555, 557, 562, 563, 564, 568, 576, 593, 596, 599, 606, 607
milkhares, 235, 336
milkmaid, 79
mill, 262, 299, 308, 541, 561, 582
mime, 86
mind, 35, 37, 38, 121, 129, 153, 175, 180, 210, 216, 290, 298, 327, 329, 334, 340, 343, 406, 424, 456, 523, 525, 563
mineral, 396
mining, 429
mint, 236, 496, 506
miracle/-s, 47, 200, 201, 218, 280, 399, 483, 608
mirror, 228, 229, 329, 417, 487, 571
miscarriage, 579
misfires, 131, 518,
missing, 107, 140, 156, 174, 201, 273, 306, 334, 423, 439
mist, 524, 563
mistletoe, 507
modern, 28, 49, 51, 63, 65, 93, 94, 96, 131, 145, 151, 152, 166, 168, 180, 197, 216, 542, 573
modernization, 192

molasses, 494, 608
mole/-s, 255, 256, 283, 352, 368, 369, 445, 472, 501, 539, 578, 583
Monday, 228, 407, 579
money, 50, 177, 187, 190, 198, 228, 278, 280, 283, 299, 336, 339, 352, 354, 387, 391, 441, 465, 468, 473, 526, 529, 555, 556, 557, 568, 569, 571, 573, 574, 575
monk, 29, 515
monster, 432
moon, 82, 240, 242, 247, 248, 255, 265, 292, 297, 339, 346, 352, 354, 358, 359, 361, 373, 375, 376, 379, 380, 395, 404, 413, 426, 435, 485, 486, 499, 503, 520, 522, 580, 599, 612
moons, 247, 248, 250, 255, 459
moonshine, 596
moose, 241, 331, 480
mortal/-s, 184, 375
mortar, 232, 299, 421, 455, 591
Moses, 47, 48, 104, 105, 124, 313, 416, 417, 440
mosquito, 434
moss, 276, 314, 458, 518, 521, 559, 583, 609
mother, 24, 68, 76, 78, 79, 87, 91, 107, 133, 177, 224, 248, 258, 259, 271, 293, 313, 315, 324, 342, 355, 371, 403, 444, 447–56, 458, 478, 494, 499, 513, 516, 529, 582, 604, 609, 617
motherhood, 509
motherless, 177
moths, 434
Mount Ararat, 312
mountain, 68, 251, 268, 269, 271, 280, 318, 323, 326, 343, 346, 365, 376, 395, 404, 405, 412, 413, 429, 431, 438, 481, 485, 501, 529, 530, 534, 544, 556, 616, 619
mouse/mice, 240, 241, 248, 261, 307, 374, 378, 391, 392, 397, 412, 433, 479, 492, 512, 535, 558, 567, 586, 588, 589
mouth, 132, 150, 226, 227, 233, 242, 248, 249, 258, 273, 274, 277, 280, 283, 284, 290, 291, 292, 294, 304, 307, 313, 323, 324, 326, 329, 339, 351, 355, 357, 362, 366, 376, 377, 420, 423, 424, 444, 458, 488, 490, 498, 506, 512, 518, 523, 524, 525, 528, 529, 538, 542, 543, 546, 547, 554, 559, 560, 571, 575, 584, 585, 593, 599, 602, 605, 607, 610, 612, 614
mule, 374
mum oil, 495
mumia, 455
muscle/-s, 337, 429, 607
musgot, 499, 516
mushroom/-s, 248, 279, 479, 481, 497, 511, 512, 576
musk, 239, 250–52, 269, 273, 414, 419, 505, 511, 516, 522, 566, 584, 598, 619
musket, 572
mustard, 249, 259, 288, 308, 353, 507, 510, 579, 595
mute, 505

muzzle, 234, 243, 245, 295, 353, 479, 480, 481, 482, 483, 484, 487, 531, 532, 576, 609, 610, 615
myrrh, 239, 250, 251, 396, 619

N

nail, 36, 137, 150, 223, 231, 232, 253, 281, 282, 307, 313, 325, 331, 376, 410, 425, 427, 449, 484, 485, 514, 532, 537, 565, 568, 574, 580, 581, 583, 585, 586, 591, 603, 615
nails, 144, 192, 261, 271, 282, 325, 352, 373, 376, 395, 413, 430, 444, 448, 459, 470, 473, 522, 535, 554, 581, 591, 597, 599, 602
naked, 74, 115, 262, 317, 387, 450, 599
Natron, see Sodium hydroxide, 445, 510, 613, 619
naturopaths, 110
navel, 420, 495, 496, 509, 513, 514, 516, 578
neck, 63, 227, 228, 231, 242, 245, 275, 276, 286, 316, 317, 420, 446, 487, 488, 572, 579
necromancy, 133, 172, 191
needle/-s, 231, 240, 243, 244, 250, 266, 268, 271, 273, 278, 287, 298, 305, 315, 349, 414, 425, 428, 465, 479, 484, 503, 506, 527, 535, 543, 557, 563, 566, 574, 579, 584, 586, 610
neglect/-s/-ed, 45, 47, 80, 163, 462, 463, 467
neighbor/-s, 28, 45, 68, 69, 88, 111, 113, 134, 162, 210, 217, 258, 330, 333, 440
nephew, 116
nerve/-s, 131, 340, 342
nest, 225, 226, 227, 244, 277, 292, 319, 352, 353, 364, 370, 371, 397, 423, 424, 479, 498, 505, 524, 529, 530, 546, 558, 559, 560, 569, 572, 602, 605
nettle/-s, 344, 505
newborn, 86, 256, 391, 59, 600
nicotine, 445
niece, 88
nightmare, 475
nigromancy, 417
nipple, 558, 578
nit/-s, 353, 421, 586
nitrialmoniæ, 296
nixie, 166, 446, 562
noaijde, 38, 39
nobility, 373
noise, 263, 463, 478
noon, 251, 407, 592
north, 82, 133, 194, 214, 250, 262, 274, 290, 299, 310, 313, 325, 329, 359, 361, 365, 367, 410, 436, 439, 457, 482, 502, 526, 531, 568, 570, 578, 580, 585, 599, 602, 615
northeast, 157
northern, 28, 40, 46, 49, 94, 121, 136, 156, 193, 194, 225, 268, 272, 273, 357, 404 450, 457
Norway/-gian, 28, 40, 50, 66, 125, 191, 214, 218, 437
nose, 248, 288, 309, 488, 493, 513, 544, 563, 574, 587,

591, 607
nosebleed/-s, 192, 261, 496, 513, 546, 563, 592
nostril/-s, 294, 507, 544, 548, 559, 584, 595
November, 267, 552
nut, 276, 444, 506, 576, 578, 617
nutmeg, 491, 562
nutshell, 351, 525
nymph, 214

O

oak-alden, 496
oak, 261, 304, 308, 364, 366, 387, 397, 496, 497, 501, 507, 510, 543, 544, 565, 590, 611, 615, 619
oars, 326
oat, 69, 247, 285, 296, 398, 433, 487, 582
oatmeal, 489
obey, 201, 333, 451, 460, 573, 577, 597
ocean, 310, 321, 323, 427, 439, 563
October, 143, 157, 166, 435, 436, 541
ocular, 62
odor, 294, 559
oil/-s, 70, 235, 246, 247, 249, 259, 268, 275, 280, 283, 284, 288, 289, 295, 296, 305, 354, 396, 419, 420, 421, 422, 433, 434, 491, 493, 495, 496, 499, 500, 504, 506, 507, 508, 509, 510, 511, 512, 513, 514, 515, 516, 522, 526, 544, 546, 549, 592, 593, 594, 595, 607, 608, 609, 616
ointments, 110, 128
olibanum, 223, 239, 250, 251, 289, 598, 620
olive, 259, 505
onion/-s, 293, 422, 494, 496, 497, 499, 505, 510, 515, 600, 617
onthiemonium, 396
onyx, 354
opal, 458
Ophioglossum vulgatum (Adder's tongue), 619
opium, 242, 514
opponent, 357, 523
oral, 30, 32, 33, 34, 35, 38, 39, 45, 46, 47, 50, 55, 57, 89, 94, 136, 137, 139, 147, 148, 151, 153, 154, 155, 165, 167, 169, 172, 173, 174, 175, 176, 178, 187, 191, 192, 197, 202, 206, 207, 217, 218, 556, 558
orally, 33, 129, 172, 186, 217, 406, 465, 574
orange, 577
Orchis maculata, 597, 606
ore, 234, 284, 298, 300, 338, 351, 451
oregano, 226
organ/-s, 46, 130, 177, 233
Origanum vulgare, 226
orison, 172, 180, 181
otter/-s, 223, 227, 237, 485
outhouse, 272, 378
oven, 247, 251, 347, 358, 360, 424, 517, 536, 538, 548, 558, 599, 601

owl, 211, 278, 352, 478, 570
ox/-en, 488, 537, 538, 541
oxmeat, 228

P

pacify, 302, 418
pact/-s, 62, 105, 106, 113, 115, 116, 123, 165, 201, 212, 215
pagan, 45, 49, 96, 142
pain/-s, 34, 86, 90, 100, 138, 145, 170, 173, 243, 246-49, 253, 254, 258, 269, 272, 273, 274, 287, 288, 295, 297, 305, 310-12, 314, 315, 317, 318, 324, 327, 336, 337, 342-47, 356, 357, 358, 364, 365, 376, 394, 422, 432, 433, 434, 435, 438, 439, 441, 469, 474, 480, 489, 495, 499, 500, 506, 507, 508, 509, 515, 529, 530, 542, 543, 550, 551, 559, 572, 585, 588, 589, 590, 593, 595, 609, 616, 617
paint, 231, 235, 565
panaritium, 530
pants, 63, 333, 378, 497, 614
Paracelsus, 454
Paradise, 239, 250, 251, 271, 302, 431, 524
paraffin, 549
paraphernalia, 44, 48, 131, 144, 193, 362, 518, 522
parasites, 130, 422
parchment, 136, 191, 218, 228, 278, 280, 468, 610
parent/-s, 52, 87, 91, 247, 248, 319, 329, 330, 331, 438
parsley, 499, 509
party-goers, 166, 505
party, 166, 505, 572
pea/-s, 231, 240, 258, 275, 279, 285, 289, 329, 422, 424, 447, 493, 520, 545, 548, 571, 591, 607, 610, 612, 613, 617
peace, 231, 240, 241, 259, 261, 264, 278, 286, 290, 291, 298, 299, 302, 305, 307, 309, 325, 329, 332, 346, 361, 369, 370, 374, 375, 377, 392, 400, 412, 413, 430, 431, 432, 433, 435, 440, 443, 444, 449, 452, 453, 455, 456, 457, 458, 459, 463, 470, 502, 522, 535, 548, 564, 569, 571
peacock, 276
pear/-s, 308, 540
peat, 348, 517, 518, 521
pee/-ing, 256, 258, 281, 291, 296, 307, 348, 410, 498, 526, 529, 532
pentagram/-s, 242, 254, 280, 418
Pentecost, 327, 603
pepper/-s, 246, 269, 420, 494, 495, 507, 510, 516
peppermint, 434
pergament, 228
peritonitis, 617
pestilence, 232, 371
petals, 237
pheasant, 512
pig/-s, 117, 138, 234, 242, 247, 258, 273, 297, 441, 442,

445, 497, 508, 532, 548, 564, 572, 582, 583, 600, 608
pigeon, 236
pike, 279
pills, 434, 501
pimple/-s, 315, 316, 365, 421, 424, 425, 530
pin/-s, 238, 258, 259, 325, 362, 531, 541, 542, 543, 547, 598, 599
pincushion, 484
pine, 271, 281, 331, 479, 482, 594
pineapple, 508
Pinguicula vulgaris, butterwort, 232, 439
piss/-ing, 237, 256, 276, 296, 477, 485, 497, 499, 538, 539, 583, 611
pistol, 610
pitch, 287, 293, 434, 538, 591, 594, 608
pitchfork, 291
pith, 501
plague/-d, 324, 366, 423, 432, 539, 585
planets, 240, 262, 359, 373, 376, 382, 406, 413, 462, 520, 522
plant/-s, 77, 136, 160, 169, 199, 207, 208, 226, 231, 232, 288, 300, 446, 447, 454, 490, 493, 498, 525, 545, 567, 591, 592, 594
Plantago lanceolata, 237
plantain (*Plantago major*), 224, 251, 273, 490, 496, 512, 619
plaster/-s, 23, 128, 129, 138, 149, 192, 215, 218, 242, 257, 373, 510, 513
Platanthera bifolia, 605
plum tree, 407
Pluto, 570
poison/-s, 61, 130, 154, 234, 239, 243, 297, 314, 346, 371, 432, 556
poisoning, 434
poisonous, 158, 227, 241, 255, 278, 279, 346, 351, 358, 376, 377, 392, 395, 412, 413, 419, 528, 539, 540, 553
poop, 489
Pope, 104, 455
poppy, 491, 507, 562
porcupine, 293, 563
pork, 425, 594
porridge, 249, 259, 546
portal/-s, 253, 460, 554
potash, 285, 526
potato/-es, 434, 540, 541, 543, 596
powder/-s/-ed, 224, 225, 227, 229, 240, 245, 249, 250, 255, 256, 257, 259, 260, 269, 275, 279, 280, 281, 285, 286, 287, 296, 301, 316, 341, 342, 347, 348, 349, 355, 366, 396, 419, 444, 447, 481, 482, 483, 488, 490, 496, 500, 501, 502, 504, 508, 509, 511, 512, 513, 514, 515, 516, 517, 518, 521, 525, 531, 532, 542, 545, 548, 558, 566, 567, 576, 577, 579, 596, 598, 601, 602, 603, 608, 610, 611

powerlessness, 31
prank/-s, 70, 492
pray, 47, 283, 313, 317, 364, 375, 376, 386, 388, 389, 406, 438, 439, 440, 441, 442, 443, 448, 449, 450, 451, 452, 453, 454, 456, 458, 467, 512, 580
prayer/-s, 48, 53, 81, 93, 118, 119, 144, 167, 179, 180, 197, 299, 302, 306, 309, 313, 324, 339, 356, 360, 373, 375, 389, 391, 395, 415–17, 435, 459, 470, 497, 502, 516, 535, 536, 548, 550
predator/-s, 131, 318, 343, 396, 429, 512, 553
pregnancy/-t, 117, 130, 177, 246, 279, 368, 493, 498, 508, 566, 567, 579, 582
Prekebo, Kristina i, 60, 61, 69, 84, 89, 90, 120, 121
Prekeborskan, 60, 121
priest/-s, 43, 66, 67, 104, 111, 112, 113, 122, 123, 144, 338, 389, 400, 401, 475, 502, 503, 506, 521, 561, 569, 572
prison, 331
prophecy/-ies, 44, 65, 116
prosperity, 406, 448, 450
protect, 130, 131, 154, 190, 215, 256, 318, 321, 332, 333, 348, 367, 398, 443, 449–51, 452, 453, 502, 514, 517, 521, 522, 530, 544, 546, 583, 598
protection, 44, 130, 131, 132, 153, 154, 167, 169, 172, 173, 178, 193, 196, 198, 224, 253, 333, 414, 435, 436, 449, 453, 455, 458, 546
psalm, 165, 243, 265, 299, 339, 579
psoriasis, 94
psychic, 23, 30, 39, 59, 129, 130, 133, 156, 163, 167, 169, 170, 172, 173, 178, 198
pub, 133
puella, 493,
puke, see milkhare, 131, 133, 336
Pulfris fumalis, 598
pulse, 280, 310, 420, 495
pulver/-ize, 273, 275, 316, 342, 496, 514, 547, 548, 593, 594, 598, 612
punish, 261, 448, 456, 531
punishment, 31, 389, 451, 522
pus/-s, 249, 436, 556, 608, 609
pustules, 346

Q

quackery, 24
quarrel/-s, 371, 555
queen, 245, 516, 582
quickroot, 229
quicksilver, 351, 354, 367, 465, 489, 528
quill, 236, 489, 568
quinine oil, 509
quintin oil, 419, 495

R

rabbit, 230
rabies, 295, 530
rag/-s, 66, 176, 185, 325, 521, 529, 611
rage/-ing, 302, 304, 354, 355
rain, 339, 404, 427, 539, 541, 547
rainbow, 404
ram/-s, 538, 555, 563
rancid, 281, 296, 542, 591
rash/-es, 317, 608
raspberry/-ies, 514, 563
rats, 261, 330, 348, 433, 526, 539, 542, 564, 571, 584, 586
raven, 47, 132, 154, 200, 201, 225, 227, 229, 233, 237, 282, 283, 287, 292, 301, 323, 338, 352, 353, 354, 362, 368, 371, 397, 415, 424, 448, 472, 473, 476, 489, 504, 506, 525, 529, 546, 578, 610
raw, 31, 32, 199, 205, 209, 226, 279, 300, 371, 398, 486, 497, 515
recipe/-s, 23, 31-33, 44, 46, 47, 49, 50, 89, 106, 117, 128, 129, 136, 140, 142, 145-47, 149, 151, 154, 155, 163, 169, 170, 174, 176, 177, 178, 182, 187, 190, 192, 193, 195, 196, 197, 207, 208, 210, 215, 216, 218, 246, 289, 312, 313, 474, 490, 505, 598, 617
reindeer, 310, 330
remuneration, 50, 133, 209, 328
rensel, 311, 312, 327, 337, 339, 344, 345
resin, 223, 512, 559, 594, 608
revenant/-s, 443, 455, 473, 534
revenge, 216, 331, 429
rheumatic, 438
rhinoceros, 256
rhizome, 522
rhubarb, 249, 500
rib/-s, 260, 496, 497, 504, 512
ribbon, 555
rice, 552
rich/-ness, 23, 28, 29, 205, 213, 291, 328, 330, 335, 379, 453, 468
riches, 97, 290, 371, 456, 458
rickets, 130, 316, 317, 342, 431
rifle, 24, 52, 489, 518
ring/-s, 80, 226, 244, 270, 271, 276, 281, 285, 296, 297, 317, 328, 329, 336, 338, 339, 350, 358, 405, 409, 415, 423, 441, 444, 446, 455, 497, 503, 504, 505, 518, 520, 521, 524, 528, 532, 537, 559, 561, 566, 567, 568, 573, 604
ringflower, 232
ringworm, 420
ripe/-n, 236, 296, 424, 500, 545, 571
rival, 546
river/-s, 35, 97, 239, 244, 248, 250, 260, 299, 306, 308, 309, 319, 324, 354, 355, 368, 369, 430, 440, 443, 476, 529, 554, 587, 589
road/-s, 36, 112, 116, 223, 228, 241, 262, 268, 270, 272, 287, 311, 314, 321, 322, 323, 324, 325, 326, 335, 343, 346, 356, 358, 376, 427, 431, 440, 442, 451, 458, 475, 503, 537, 554, 590, 604
robbery/-ing, 104, 123, 132, 133, 241, 426, 430, 448, 564
rock/-s, 34, 93, 166, 267, 311, 319, 337, 351, 356, 360, 364, 428, 429, 494, 496, 497, 512, 528, 530, 534, 564
rod/-s, 132, 156, 158, 349, 350, 353, 378, 379-82, 387, 405, 407, 408, 409, 417, 527
roof, 294, 442, 453, 455, 498, 548, 555, 580, 582, 597
roomroot, 286
rooster/-s, 236, 267, 282, 283, 285, 287, 291, 352, 414, 425, 476, 511, 545, 561, 562, 566, 570
root/-s, 25, 31, 133, 170, 214, 223, 226, 227, 232, 234, 246, 249, 256, 258, 259, 269, 282, 289, 290, 296, 310, 312, 314, 322, 359, 362, 371, 373, 396, 397, 419, 423, 431, 445-48, 455, 460, 469, 484-86, 489-502, 506-10, 512-15, 534, 541, 544, 556, 557, 561, 564, 583, 591, 592, 596, 597, 598, 599, 604, 606, 607, 615, 620
rootstalk, 522
rope/-s, 329, 350, 399, 504, 505, 528
rose, 237, 273, 276, 288, 394, 419, 421, 494, 495-97, 509, 510, 513, 590, 591, 593, 598
rosewater, 233, 496, 509
Rosmarinus officinalis, rosemary, 223, 290, 620
rotten, 237, 503, 581, 604
rowan, 280, 308, 367, 482, 501, 544, 566, 576, 580, 604, 619
rump, 291, 318, 398, 547, 555, 559
rune/-s/-ic, 96, 172, 369, 470, 574
rural, 23, 128, 165, 198, 210, 213, 218, 219, 398
rute/ruta, 230, 277, 513
Rutewater, 289
rye, 236, 378, 413, 478, 479, 537, 541, 579, 580, 590

S

sabbath/-s, 68, 77, 299
saffron, 227, 242, 506, 562
Sagittarius, 603
Saint Anthony's Fire, 507, 508, 510
salalmoniac, 275
saliva, 79, 287, 298, 593
Salmeack/salmiak, 257, 502
salt, 138, 234, 242, 245, 252, 271, 287, 293, 298, 320, 322, 323, 324, 356, 378, 422, 424, 439, 440, 441, 442, 451, 453, 454, 458, 494, 496, 497, 499, 506, 510, 511, 515, 519, 538, 543, 548, 554, 558, 593, 603
saltkernel, 479
saltpeter, 567, 609
salve/-s, 62, 110, 247, 248, 249, 275, 288, 312, 341, 361,

396, 421, 495, 505, 506, 507, 508, 513, 515, 516, 588, 594, 607, 608
Salvia, 275, 421
Sámi, 28, 38, 39, 61, 79, 94, 150, 152, 310
sand, 195, 271, 316, 321, 427, 431, 438, 439, 485, 592
sandalwood, 261, 296
Sanskrit, 37
sapling/-s, 233, 387, 413, 532, 544, 556
Sasafas (sassafras?) wood, 396
Sassafras officinalis, sassafras, 239, 251, 420, 598, 619
Satan, 108, 142, 213, 244, 261, 274, 310, 319, 323, 324, 334, 388, 427, 430, 431, 432, 433, 435, 448, 459, 466, 513, 514, 536, 590
Sator square, 283, 284
Saturday, 272, 309, 407, 414, 432, 465, 557, 599
Satyr's herb, 515
scabies, 246, 285, 289, 361, 421, 510, 596, 600
scabs, 507
scalp, 419
scar, 63, 64
scavenge, 485
scimitar, 410
Scirpus cæspitosis, 597
scissors, 254, 451
Scorpio, 267
scorpion/-s, 130, 234, 267, 296, 515
scrofula, 257, 258
scrotum, 555
scry/-ing, 83-85, 144, 441
scurvy, 138, 364, 457, 509, 582
scythe, 340
sea/-s, 59, 94, 95, 97, 107, 144, 182, 192, 202, 209, 246, 302, 308, 313, 323, 365, 426, 432, 433, 440, 443, 478, 613, 616
seafowl, 478
secret/-s, 23, 27, 36, 43, 45, 46, 56, 73, 92, 93, 94, 95, 113, 119, 122, 145, 158, 159, 165, 172, 187, 192, 202, 203, 227, 248, 282, 349, 352, 360, 362, 370, 416, 417, 421, 433, 506, 510, 525, 529, 545, 549, 573, 580
secretions, 156
secure/-ity, 125, 196, 198, 217, 329, 448
seed/-s, 236, 239, 241, 250, 251, 265, 271, 287, 290, 293, 294, 296, 349, 353, 354, 391, 413, 414, 422, 431, 491, 496, 500, 501, 502, 505, 507, 508, 510, 519, 512, 513, 515, 516, 525, 533, 542, 562, 569, 579, 583, 599, 600, 619
seizures, 286
September, 156, 174, 436
serpent, 158, 265, 379, 380, 385, 388, 413, 431, 470, 514, 605
shame, 292, 299
shark, 65
shave/-ing, 281, 282, 287, 298, 304, 369, 370, 415, 482, 522, 531, 538, 545, 555, 563, 564, 566, 574, 583, 597
sheath, 224, 569
shed, 160, 243, 293, 353, 376, 385, 397, 485, 497, 537, 580, 584, 602
sheep, 242, 288, 289, 296, 328, 353, 376, 377, 378, 442, 474, 485, 486, 497, 498, 500, 511, 514, 515, 538, 541, 542, 546, 547, 549, 582, 594, 596, 602
shin, 547
shirt, 255, 261, 334, 339, 357, 369, 378, 458, 521, 541, 558, 569, 599
shit, 378, 541, 558
shoe/-s, 36, 71, 72, 106, 107, 223, 229, 231, 234, 250, 255, 268, 272, 275, 278, 282, 297, 310, 317, 356, 363, 369, 428, 434, 486, 489, 521, 524, 525, 545, 571, 575, 581, 583, 597, 603
shoemaker, 551
shoestring, 419
shoot/-ing, 130, 131, 147, 201, 224, 225, 229, 243, 245, 260, 262, 275, 276, 287, 294, 295, 301, 333, 347, 352, 353, 355, 359, 361-68, 373, 425, 430, 472, 473, 475-85, 488, 500, 517-22, 529, 542, 545, 546, 550, 556, 558, 561, 563, 565, 567, 568, 575, 576, 577, 601-3, 605, 609-13, 615, 616
shore/-s, 116, 323, 430, 563
shot/-s, 85, 129, 130, 131, 190, 224, 225, 240, 243, 246, 276, 279, 280, 295, 324, 330, 339, 348, 352, 355, 359, 362, 363, 365, 366, 367, 368, 378, 393, 428, 438, 439, 446, 450, 472, 477, 479-84, 488, 489, 499, 501, 514, 517, 518, 519, 522, 529, 530, 531, 532, 542, 545, 546, 550, 551, 559, 568, 572, 577, 583, 601, 603, 609, 610, 611, 612, 615
shotgun/-s, 85, 89, 109, 130, 131, 133, 137, 142, 147, 149, 154, , 172, 175, 177-79, 182, 190, 193, 195, 196, 223, 224, 225, 240, 243-45, 260, 262, 275, 276, 279, 280, 294, 295, 301, 308, 347, 348, 353, 361, 362, 363, 364, 365, 366, 367, 368, 369, 430, 472, 476, 477, 478, 480, 481, 482, 483, 484, 488, 489, 499, 517-22, 531, 532, 539, 541, 542, 545, 546, 561, 563, 565, 567, 568, 575-79, 583, 601-3, 609, 610, 611, 612, 613, 615
shoulder/-s, 225, 298, 314, 325, 326, 339, 430, 434, 444, 473, 476, 477, 481, 482, 493, 558, 580
siblings, 438
sick/-ness, 24, 83, 90, 108, 118, 138, 144, 151, 157, 162, 179, 203, 233, 246, 247, 249, 256, 257, 260, 275, 279, 286, 288, 293, 296, 297, 298, 303, 312, 313, 317, 322, 324, 325, 330, 335, 340, 343, 346, 347, 353, 364, 375, 376, 377, 397-99, 414, 419, 420, 431, 432, 438, 443-47, 450, 459, 482, 495, 496, 497, 500, 506, 507, 509, 511-14, 556, 565, 566, 579, 582, 584, 585, 593, 601, 607

sickle, 327
sieve, 281, 579
sigil/-s, 36, 96, 121, 160, 201, 281, 329, 380-81, 417
silence, 74, 77, 165, 260, 301, 345, 470, 480, 526, 537, 540
silent, 76, 92, 93, 94, 189, 192, 193, 196, 235, 243, 251, 280, 286, 290, 292, 293, 297, 317, 349, 371, 398, 457, 466, 472, 493, 527, 581, 597
silently, 250, 255, 258, 260, 261, 262, 281, 286, 291, 296, 298, 308, 317, 334, 375, 466, 472, 478, 569, 580, 586, 599
silk, 143, 226, 268, 276, 339, 362, 363, 368, 444, 506, 531, 555, 574, 578
silver, 182, 249, 254, 268, 286, 298, 299, 300, 311, 325, 349, 351, 379, 387, 406, 408, 409, 414, 421, 429, 430, 441, 444, 447, 473, 502, 518, 527, 528, 531, 543, 546, 552, 566, 579, 597, 600, 611
simulacrum, 199, 350, 528
sinew/-s, 34, 270, 314, 329, 346, 374, 431, 432, 440, 441, 511, 514, 515, 535, 590, 607-9
skeleton, 305, 332, 495
skin/-s, 34, 89, 130, 149, 175, 177, 191, 228, 229, 242, 270, 288, 292, 293, 307, 314, 318, 322, 327, 328, 330, 357, 363, 365, 422, 432, 440, 481, 482, 491, 500, 503, 512, 513, 523, 542, 545, 558, 562
skull/-s, 64, 189, 256, 258, 276, 285, 286, 291, 292, 329, 396, 424, 466, 502, 514, 518, 520, 521, 545, 548, 563, 566, 570, 571, 580, 601, 609, 613
sky/ies, 267, 291, 333, 404, 612
slaughter/-ed, 144, 258, 267, 330, 538, 549
sleep, 114, 133, 179, 226, 232, 233, 249, 261, 273, 276, 277, 278, 280, 281, 282, 284, 328, 344, 349, 369, 372, 415, 434, 439, 440, 442, 443, 449, 451, 452, 458, 460, 491, 494, 499, 505, 508, 515, 525, 527, 555, 562, 578
sleeping, 133, 278, 282, 352, 369, 370, 475, 564, 569, 571
slime, 73, 172, 248, 296
smell, 366, 479, 490
smith/-y, 119, 133, 146, 231, 300, 484, 551, 581, 604
smoke, 252, 255, 282, 293, 296, 348, 419, 445, 482, 483, 489, 517, 530, 537, 539, 545
snake/-s, 36, 73, 74, 88, 89, 117, 130, 132, 172, 229, 233, 234, 235, 243, 259, 268, 270-72, 280, 291-97, 302, 304, 307, 314, 319, 348, 351, 355, 358, 360, 414, 425, 427, 428, 444, 445, 472, 473, 476, 483, 497, 503, 504, 506, 517, 525, 528, 536, 537, 539, 547, 550, 551, 553-58, 561, 563, 564, 566, 569, 571, 572, 578, 588, 601, 606, 611
snakebite, 53, 79, 270, 272, 314, 427, 536, 550, 553
snakegrass, 505
snakeskin, 521, 565, 571

snakestone, 578
snare, 366, 486
sneeze/-s, 494, 496, 497, 606
sniff, 584
snort/-ed, 248, 496, 513
snout, 318, 377, 433, 489, 537, 548
snow, 290, 370, 373, 404, 479, 485, 486, 532, 578
snuff, 61, 89, 351, 352, 429, 525
soap, 232, 288, 295, 421, 422, 507, 508, 538, 567, 593, 607
Sodium hydroxide, 445, 619
Sodomites, 550
soil, 115, 253, 404
Solanum dulcamara, 617
Solomon, 160, 166, 400, 417
Sorbus aucuparia, 619
sore/-s, 47, 108, 130, 144, 355, 365, 489, 491, 500, 507-10, 512, 513, 536, 542, 572, 608, 609
sorrow/-ful, 345, 376, 436, 572, 574
Spanish, 239, 250, 251, 296, 559, 598, 616
spanskgröna, 492, 594
sparrow, 505, 520
spear, 373, 395, 399, 413, 470, 500, 506, 535
spertus, 86, 132
sphere, 60, 134, 147, 175, 218
spice/-s, 226, 495, 545
spider, 370, 592, 593
spike/-s, 261, 410, 432, 482, 484
spine, 70, 143
spirit/-s, 44, 48, 53, 54, 59, 60, 63-65, 73, 85, 86, 91, 94, 96, 97, 113, 115, 116, 118, 121, 124, 130, 132, 133, 141, 142, 152, 158, 159, 169, 170, 172, 184, 193, 201, 208, 214, 215, 224, 228, 230, 241, 246, 262-65, 269, 275, 298, 301, 302, 306, 307-12, 324, 326, 329, 330, 332, 333, 334, 338, 343, 350, 354-57, 359-61, 363-65, 372-79, 381, 382, 385-89, 392, 394, 395, 412, 413, 416-18, 430, 431, 435, 441, 447, 448, 449, 451, 452, 454, 456-59, 462-70, 472, 473, 475, 484, 501, 502, 518-23, 526, 528, 532, 534, 535, 547, 557, 563, 569, 573, 574, 576, 588, 596, 602, 616, 617
spiritual/-ity, 66, 103, 109, 112, 144, 157, 199, 209, 217
Spisglas (antimony), 250, 619
spit/-s/-ting, 238, 248, 262, 274, 295, 297, 311, 313, 316, 319, 335-36, 338, 340, 346, 347, 359, 362, 378, 435, 438, 448, 454, 456, 479, 482, 484, 486, 504, 507, 512, 518, 529, 536, 537, 538, 539, 540, 542, 543, 544, 547, 586, 599, 601, 607, 615
splinter/-s, 274, 391, 421, 498, 603
spoon/-s, 249, 287, 289, 298, 313, 316, 325, 501, 510
spoonful, 256, 277, 279, 287, 288, 421, 422, 491, 500, 595, 598, 617
spouse, 133
sprain/-s, 53, 130, 270, 272, 312, 314, 342, 347, 432,

550, 551, 590
springwort, 498
sprite, 91, 104, 114, 158, 166, 217, 219, 298, 395
spruce, 465, 485, 594
squirrel, 195, 482, 570, 602
stab/-ed/-ing/-s, 79, 83, 144, 145, 226, 291, 302, 336, 337, 359, 364, 391, 470, 484, 487, 499, 504, 567, 604
stag, 445
stake, 371, 518, 565
stallion, 281, 291, 297, 305, 356
star/-s, 147, 230, 240, 275, 280, 310, 319, 320, 357, 359, 361, 373, 376, 382, 395, 404, 408, 413, 418, 427, 457, 497, 520, 522, 534, 561
starling, 278, 352, 423, 601
staunch (blood), 93, 272, 308, 310, 317, 341, 345, 361
steal/-s, 68, 133, 182, 285, 328, 335, 427, 457, 486, 498, 501, 504, 546, 564, 573, 603
stealing, 42, 43, 69, 152, 332, 335
steam, 83
Stearine, 431
steel, 83, 144, 226, 267, 298, 300, 315, 324, 340, 356, 391, 428, 432, 444, 446, 450, 472, 479, 507, 531, 532, 557, 566
stibnite, 619
stillborn, 560
sting/-s, 36, 233, 246, 265, 290, 315, 319, 351, 355, 358, 363, 432, 476, 509, 525, 557, 562, 567, 605
stinger/-s, 36, 258, 291, 294, 295, 319, 444, 539, 547, 561, 563, 571, 572
stink/ing, 272, 378, 490, 609
stitch/-es, 491, 506, 541, 542, 584
stole/-n, 62, 84, 85, 104, 123, 138, 231, 238, 246, 254, 259, 260, 261, 268, 271, 274, 281, 284, 299, 304, 305, 323, 332, 333, 334, 349, 359, 361, 365, 366, 369, 370, 378, 398, 415, 429, 440, 442, 443, 466, 485, 487, 502, 522, 527, 555, 564, 569, 570, 571, 574, 579, 581, 582, 583
stomach, 74, 77, 230, 247, 249, 252, 256, 258, 260, 261, 279, 297, 299, 312, 317, 319, 347, 353, 357, 358, 375, 397, 419, 420, 425, 431, 432, 456, 491, 495, 500, 501, 502, 504, 506, 508, 509, 514, 530, 539, 541, 549, 591, 609
stone/-s, 54, 80, 96, 101, 132, 145, 154, 225, 226, 228, 230, 240, 241, 242, 244, 247, 251, 252, 256, 260, 262, 268, 269, 271, 277, 279, 282, 283, 285, 286, 292, 297, 301, 307, 308, 313, 320, 321, 323, 324, 326, 336, 338, 346, 351–59, 363–65, 370, 371, 374, 378, 379, 388, 391, 392, 396, 397, 404, 406, 409, 412, 423, 424, 431, 432, 443, 446, 448, 457, 465, 478, 491, 504, 506, 507, 509, 515, 522–24, 526, 528, 529–32, 535, 536, 537, 544, 546, 550, 554, 556–58, 563, 564, 572, 574, 575, 576, 578, 584, 585, 588, 589, 590, 593, 597, 598, 604,

605, 606, 609
stonechat, 225
stonemason, 106
stonesparrow, 477
stool, 249, 275, 546
storax, 261, 281
strain, 295, 296, 422
strangle/-s, 294, 541, 595
straw/-s, 275, 292, 315, 326, 327, 340, 369, 466, 556, 557, 559, 589, 590
strawberry, 108, 343
strength, 132, 133, 137, 153, 187, 190, 199, 227, 228, 231, 239, 241, 262, 265, 268, 273, 274, 275, 285, 290, 294, 334, 335, 374, 388, 389, 392, 395, 404, 412, 436, 441, 442, 443, 457, 501, 554, 568, 592, 609
strike/-s, 261, 272, 293, 313, 388, 392, 443, 477, 497, 519, 531, 557, 565, 591
string/-s, 133, 152, 154, 167, 173, 195, 338, 345, 366, 367, 428, 474, 476, 502, 578, 617
stroke, 256, 258, 347
strong, 49, 62, 64, 72, 97, 109, 144, 193, 217, 240, 246, 248, 269, 289, 292, 294, 295, 304, 307, 348, 352, 353, 374, 388, 392, 407, 412, 458, 479, 487, 488, 492, 498, 515, 526, 531, 535, 559, 562, 582, 599, 607
stronger, 128, 294, 324, 337, 546
strongest, 388, 448, 451, 452, 456
suburban, 210
suck, 235, 323, 495, 554, 557, 585
suffer/-ed, 92, 97, 233, 262, 274, 302, 309, 328, 335, 361, 377, 448, 449, 453, 466, 522, 542, 543, 547
suffering, 67, 68, 246, 248, 262, 266, 306, 325, 327, 336, 337, 339, 343, 344, 359, 374, 375, 376, 378, 394, 398, 399, 406, 439, 443, 444, 451, 455, 461, 473, 535, 549, 550, 554, 565, 585, 589, 590, 598, 609
sugar, 242, 279, 296, 315, 316, 340, 342, 420, 455, 475, 492, 500, 540
suicide, 313, 329, 339
sulfur (various spellings), 79, 197, 239, 250, 251, 276, 280, 287, 289, 293, 294, 298, 378, 391, 414, 502, 504, 505, 506, 507, 511, 514, 516, 532, 537, 539, 566, 567, 584, 594, 596, 597, 598, 599, 620
summer, 99, 186, 245, 248, 292, 295, 318, 319, 320, 328, 331, 341, 343, 344, 405, 479, 503, 539, 545
sun, 224, 229, 238, 240, 245, 250, 251, 255, 261, 262, 263, 265, 275, 277, 278, 280, 290, 295, 297, 299, 301, 308, 312, 313, 316, 325, 355, 359, 361, 362, 363, 369, 371, 373, 375, 376, 379, 380, 387, 392, 395, 398, 404, 407, 413, 426, 431, 458, 461, 464, 465, 479, 485, 518, 519, 520, 522, 525, 532, 536, 540, 543, 544, 553,

556, 561, 564, 565, 566, 567, 570, 572, 578,
581, 586, 588, 589, 600, 603, 605, 610, 611,
612
sunburn, 252, 421
Sunday/-s, 77, 123, 250, 260–62, 268, 278, 280, 294,
306, 307, 308, 311, 349, 351, 363, 368, 373,
375, 376, 387, 392, 398, 399, 407, 414, 415,
436, 465, 466, 484, 502, 503, 520, 525, 534,
535, 543, 564, 565, 566, 567, 568, 571, 599,
603, 612
sunlight/-ny, 240, 244, 447, 505
sunrise, 77, 284, 407, 414, 519, 538, 600
sunset, 245, 257, 258, 322, 325, 326, 335, 339, 341,
407, 531, 555, 597
sunwise, 518, 521
superstition/-s, 40, 64, 88, 94, 179, 182, 186, 206, 210,
528, 532, 549, 552
surgery, 63, 64
swallow (bird), 226, 227, 232, 244, 256, 259, 277, 304,
353, 357, 359, 363, 364, 370, 371, 419, 423,
424, 511, 524, 525, 557, 558, 565, 572, 604,
605
swan/-s, 194, 478, 483, 485, 561, 618
swear/-ing/-s, 76, 115, 224, 240, 349, 474, 527
sweat/-ing, 297, 327, 328, 349, 351, 375, 391, 399, 413,
419, 481, 500, 509, 514, 525, 592
swelling/-s, 249, 346, 357, 360, 365, 441, 491, 495,
508, 515, 530, 536, 589, 591–93, 607
swine, 430, 431, 583
swollen, 441, 495, 509, 510, 512, 516, 608
sword/-s, 132, 116, 154, 155, 358, 388, 393, 410, 411,
561, 566, 569
swordfights, 154

T

taboos, 73, 144
tail, 296, 356, 392, 398, 484, 488, 520, 531, 539, 545,
547, 600, 601
tallow, 281, 283, 295, 425, 485, 486, 536, 538, 558,
594, 604
talons, 318
tanning, 579, 580
target, 35, 85, 131, 145, 177, 245, 326, 338, 366, 512,
520, 531, 532, 568, 610, 611
Tartar, 249, 305
Taurus, 229
tea, 170, 247, 288, 316, 491, 493
tears, 116, 438
teaspoon/-s, 252, 288, 420, 425
teeth, see tooth/-ache.
tejte (magic), 61
temperament, 215, 239
temple/-s, 376, 389, 431, 491, 507, 515
temptation/-s, 536, 569
tentrafflus, 251

terpentine, 607
terrain, 613
testicle/-s, 282, 515
tete (magic), 61
Tetragrammaton, various spellings, 230, 265, 378,
379, 380, 381, 382, 383, 387, 388, 389, 468,
610
Tetragrammator, 378-79
Teufelsdreck, 207
thatching, 597
thaumaturgy, 167
thaw, 485
theft, see thievery
theology/-ians, 195
therapy, 94
thief, 83, 84, 99, 104, 125, 142, 149, 156, 163, 238, 246,
252, 254, 259, 261, 271, 281, 282, 284, 285,
292, 299, 332, 333, 334, 339, 366, 369, 370,
378, 406, 415, 426, 435, 466, 498, 502, 504,
564, 565, 568, 570, 571, 574, 580, 581, 582,
583
thievery, 172, 308, 398, 466
thieves, 132, 133, 145, 149, 271, 273, 285, 299, 332,
339, 361, 415, 427, 429, 435, 568, 580
thigh/-s, 260, 365, 483, 487, 489, 494, 499, 504, 516,
574, 577
thimble, 288
thirst/-y, 226, 282, 573, 605
thorn/-s/-y, 351, 373, 376, 395, 399, 407, 453, 454,
456, 465, 470, 473, 528, 535, 550, 553, 599
Thornberry tree, 407
thread/-s, 159, 226, 244, 251, 259, 268, 271, 273, 274,
276, 292, 293, 300, 305, 329, 336, 339, 348,
368, 395, 423, 425, 502, 504, 506, 513, 517,
525, 531, 538, 539, 574, 578, 583, 586, 615
threat/-s, 107, 121, 122, 130, 132, 213, 328, 584
threaten/-ed, 108, 144, 341, 343, 450
threshold/-s, 243, 253, 274, 285, 287, 291, 293, 298,
364, 368, 435, 476, 489, 537, 539, 573, 584,
591, 599, 602, 612
thrive/-ing, 68, 69, 247, 287, 376, 432, 451, 511, 567,
568, 583, 600
throat, 66, 225, 226, 229, 305, 340, 385, 420, 441,
494, 500, 506, 510, 512, 523, 543, 592, 593,
614, 616
throatbone, 504
thrush (bird), 231, 278
thumb/-s, 310, 327, 379, 446, 531, 532, 568, 599, 610,
613
thunder, 404
Thursday, 75, 77, 82, 86, 115, 229, 238, 245, 246, 251,
254, 262, 271, 274, 278, 287, 299, 304, 316,
317, 327, 329, 332, 335, 336, 338, 339, 345,
346, 358, 359, 362, 363, 365, 369, 371, 398,
399, 407, 414, 415, 424, 444, 464, 465, 475,
487, 493, 497, 503, 518, 519, 520, 522, 525,

526, 531, 537, 543, 544, 564, 566, 567, 568, 570, 571, 573, 574, 576, 581, 586, 597, 599, 600, 604
Tiberg_874413, Tiberg, Emil, 113–16
Tidebast, (various spellings), 242, 251, 354, 447, 489, 502, 522, 598, 620
tin, 234, 249, 295, 298, 300, 349, 396, 413, 422, 533, 579, 580
tincture/-s, 215, 218, 493, 495, 516
toad, 132, 292, 297, 299, 351, 414, 528, 566
toadstone, 297
tobacco, 422, 596
toe/-s, 229, 273, 325, 354, 434, 440, 518
toilet, 609,
Tolfmannakraft, 285
tomb, 602
tomfoolery, 293
tomte, 132, 142, 214, 343
tomtegubbe, 215, 436
tongue/-s, 43, 150, 223, 225, 227, 229, 231, 235, 236, 237, 277, 279, 281, 282, 290, 298, 304, 307, 314, 322, 323, 352, 357, 359, 363, 364, 371, 374, 376, 377, 412, 423, 424, 438, 439, 441, 442, 446, 450, 523, 524, 539, 546, 547, 553, 556, 557, 565, 573, 575, 592, 605, 610, 619
tonify, 170
tonsils, 593
tooth/teeth, 36, 92, 100, 116, 130, 150, 175, 193, 232, 239, 240, 242, 249, 253, 258, 274–76, 287, 296, 305, 307, 310, 311, 313, 318, 322, 323, 374, 376, 377, 412, 420, 421, 422, 434, 438, 486, 492, 495, 501, 505, 507, 508, 509, 556, 559, 570, 590, 593, 595, 606, 616
toothache/-s, 92, 141, 191, 192, 238, 242, 253, 258, 259, 260, 274, 287, 296, 302, 313, 345, 420, 422, 434, 438, 490, 508, 559, 563, 590, 591, 593, 595, 616
traitor, 299
transfix/-ed/-ing, 130, 131, 133, 142, 145, 156, 163, 207, 252, 268, 271, 273, 285, 286, 318, 319, 343, 361, 388, 426, 428, 435, 475, 504, 554, 557, 560, 571, 580, 583
trap/-s, 131, 175, 235, 360, 361, 366, 373, 485, 486, 502, 503, 505
trash, 480
treasure/-s, 46, 115, 132, 153, 156, 158, 160, 172, 178, 199, 213, 240, 286, 349, 350, 351, 379, 380, 383, 387, 391, 392, 406, 407–9, 411, 412, 416, 417, 467, 468, 473, 527, 528, 568
treatment/-s, 25, 64, 74, 80, 88, 89, 110, 177, 192, 214, 216, 296, 314, 315, 317, 318, 325, 326, 327, 339, 344, 416, 422, 596
tree/-s, 79, 223, 243–45, 251, 256, 258, 260, 262, 267, 279–81, 287, 289, 292, 293, 296, 305, 308, 310, 313, 314, 323, 324, 329, 331, 348, 349, 362–63, 366, 367, 368, 370, 387, 397, 405,
407, 421, 423, 424, 430, 435, 436, 454, 477, 479, 481–86, 497–501, 508, 512, 517, 519, 521, 524, 527, 529, 530, 544, 546, 547, 553, 556, 559, 560, 561, 578, 581, 582, 585, 586, 590, 598, 604, 611, 615, 619
trial/-s, 45, 67, 97, 122, 179, 180, 182, 183, 202, 225, 339, 372, 441
triangle/-ular, 292, 465, 555
troll/-s, 51, 60, 68, 95, 96, 129, 130, 133, 158, 165, 191, 194, 195, 241, 312, 324, 332, 355, 359, 363, 365, 370, 374, 376, 392, 395, 412, 413, 415, 438, 439, 446, 450, 534, 535, 546, 558, 559, 591, 607, 616
Trolldom, 56, 67, 99, 100, 122, 161, 201, 552
trollhare, 182, 546
trollman, 60, 546
trollshot, 324, 529, 592, 616
trollwives, 534
tuberculosis, 434, 455, 509, 563, 584
Tuesday, 407, 614
turkey, 568, 578
turnips, 279
turpentine, 246, 247, 360, 507, 607, 608
turtle, 371
turtledove, 525
twig/-s, 70, 260, 336, 363, 397, 413, 414, 436, 485, 585, 586, 590, 597, 601
twine, 158, 296
twins, 561

U

udder, 557
ulcer, 606
umbilical/-us, 494, 611
uncle, 88, 330
unclean/-ness, 394, 489, 563
unclear, 96, 148, 154, 162, 164, 474, 477, 605, 614
undergarments, 506
underslip, 276
underwear, 579
undress, 344, 567
unhex/-ed, 260, 368, 481
unlucky, 112, 450, 504
Upupa epos, 225
urban, 167, 169
Uriel/-l, 379, 380, 381, 382, 400, 462, 463, 614
urinate/-s/-ing, 279, 419, 491, 511, 514, 515
urine, 79, 163, 279, 367, 419, 434, 454, 455, 490, 496, 497, 500, 507, 508, 509, 511, 530, 549, 562, 582, 592, 609

V

Valeriana officianalis, valerian, 269, 273, 322, 419, 447, 501, 502, 507, 522, 620
Vändelrot, see also valerian, 419, 447, 620
vapor/-s, 457, 524, 609
vein/-s, 78, 256, 269, 314, 321, 351, 473, 587, 593, 594, 609
venereal disease, 455
vengeance, 87, 132, 133, 134, 147, 149, 152, 154, 190, 196, 332, 337, 429
venom, 233, 556, 588
Venus, 159
Verbena officinalis, verbena, 228, 234, 511, 514, 619
verdigris, 289, 434, 492, 513, 594, 608, 619
vermin, 130, 190, 328, 330, 433
vervain, 496
vespers, 77, 502
Vespertilio murinus, see bat, 566
vetiver, 543
vice, 79, 288, 389
victim, 24, 58, 82, 84, 132, 354, 556
victory, 262, 264, 265, 461
vine, 279
vinegar, 233, 237, 256, 273, 280, 288, 419, 421, 494, 495, 500, 506, 507, 508, 510, 511, 512, 513, 543, 562, 576, 594, 595, 608
viola, 112, 118
violate/-ors, 62, 122
violence/-t, 83, 334
violin, 338, 345
viper/-s, 229, 298, 301, 368, 392, 395
virak, 223, 242
Virgin Mary, 150, 170, 228, 224, 241, 243, 259, 260, 265, 268, 269, 270, 271, 272, 290, 302, 311, 314, 319, 320, 322, 324, 335, 345, 356, 359, 360, 373, 377, 380, 381, 413, 415, 417, 426, 427, 428, 432, 433, 442, 447, 449, 450, 451, 452, 453, 454, 455, 456, 461, 474, 508, 535, 547, 553, 557, 580, 588, 590, 612
virgin/-s, 46, 226, 227, 228, 230, 235, 260, 269, 276, 278, 280, 281, 291, 305, 306, 348, 364, 368, 372, 403, 424, 468, 492, 494, 506, 526, 543, 565, 566, 567, 572
virginity, 243, 492
Viridarium norvegicum, 227
virility, 276
virtue/-s, 25, 103, 225, 229, 306, 499, 507, 569
visible, 329, 333, 363, 406, 440, 441, 443, 462, 573
viskärring, 60
vismän, 42
vitriol, 287, 502
vodka, 596
voice, 128, 132, 190, 378, 415, 460, 477, 492, 526, 532, 562
void, 494

vomited/-ing, 297, 506, 539
vows, 144
vulnerability, 85

W

wagon-grease, 235
wagon, 300, 345, 420, 574
walnut, 495, 499, 514, 516, 569, 593
Walpurgismas, 521
waning, 82, 95, 104, 170, 242, 247, 248, 250, 255, 292, 297, 339, 346, 354, 358, 485, 580
warn/-ed, 73, 75, 243, 467
warning/-s, 109, 247, 378, 598
wart/-s, 130, 234, 499, 510, 515, 544, 578
wasp/-s, 319, 432, 434
water, 35, 60, 83, 84, 85, 91, 104, 108, 114, 133, 138, 157, 158, 166, 179, 182, 228, 230, 233, 236, 239, 240, 241, 243, 244, 247, 248, 249, 250, 251, 252, 255, 256, 257, 261, 266, 269, 272, 273, 274, 275, 277, 279, 280, 281, 283, 285, 286, 287, 288, 289, 290, 292, 293, 294, 296, 297, 298, 299, 302, 306, 307, 308, 309, 310, 311, 312, 313, 314, 315, 316, 317, 318, 325, 326, 327, 339, 340, 341, 343, 344, 345, 346, 347, 351, 353, 354, 360, 369, 374, 377, 379, 380, 382, 391, 395, 397, 399, 404, 405, 406, 413, 415, 419, 420, 421, 422, 424, 429, 434, 435, 438, 439, 442, 446, 454, 455, 461, 467, 470, 476, 485, 486, 489-97, 499-503, 506, 508-17, 526, 528, 530, 531, 534, 542, 543, 544, 552, 554, 555, 556, 559, 563, 564, 567, 568, 569, 570, 576, 578, 582, 585, 586, 588, 590, 592, 596, 597, 599, 600, 606, 616, 617
waterhorses, 392, 534, 535
waterlevel, 478
watersprites, 412, 413
waterway, 579
waves, 358, 440, 443
wax, 83, 234, 235, 242, 243, 276, 280, 283, 284, 370, 483, 489, 508, 512, 519, 531, 538, 568, 608
waxing moon, 247
waybread, 224
weak/-ness, 248, 255, 271, 297, 300, 407, 420, 422, 441, 494, 495, 516, 559
wealth/-y, 60, 103, 115, 116, 132, 156, 169, 175, 197, 214, 216, 217
weapon/-s, 244, 254, 283
weather, 114, 280, 348, 485, 505, 518, 547
weave/ing, 464, 503, 543, 547, 579
wedding, 96, 101, 250, 276, 317, 333, 423, 446, 518, 521, 532, 548, 566
Wednesday, 251, 407, 531, 539, 543, 597, 599
Weihrauch, 223
werewolf, 60
west/-ern, 28, 49, 50, 99, 104, 137, 185, 218, 274, 359,

379, 404, 410, 488, 553, 602
whale, 295, 554
wheat, 235, 482, 499, 500, 579,
wheatear, 225, 237
whet/-ting, 283, 449
whetstone, 504
whinchat (bird), 225
whip, 279, 324, 336, 363, 373, 472, 488, 519, 532
whirlwind, 83
whore/-s, 540, 568, 573
wick, 280, 283, 284, 295
wicked/-ness, 427, 438, 586
wife, 71, 106, 116, 143, 231, 232, 234, 255, 278, 279, 297, 550, 551, 552, 561, 566, 573, 579, 582, 599
wight/-s, 95, 97, 142, 214, 215, 261, 324, 326, 327, 338, 412, 413, 438, 534, 586
wightbite, 441
wilderness, 388, 469
wildfire, 131, 196, 252, 287, 298, 523
willow, 421
wind/-s, 70, 179, 241, 287, 316, 319, 325, 336, 369, 397, 406, 410, 420, 438, 439, 476, 478, 480, 486, 488, 499, 503, 588
wine, 233, 235, 242, 245, 256, 262, 273, 274, 275, 280, 283, 289, 304, 419, 421, 490, 492, 494, 499, 507, 509, 510, 515, 516, 521, 559, 576, 592, 593
winner, 58, 262, 461
winning/-s, 132, 169, 178, 184, 261, 302, 547
winrutta, 419
winter, 117, 182, 292, 333, 334, 342, 355, 398, 479, 538, 541, 549
winterflower, 289
wish/-es, 62, 67, 152, 233, 240, 241, 244, 261, 262, 264, 267, 278, 282, 294, 307, 320, 327, 332, 336–39, 346, 374, 377, 380, 381, 389, 392, 397, 407, 412, 428, 434, 446, 448, 452, 463, 475, 476, 535, 545, 547, 548, 553, 555, 568, 569, 573, 574, 575, 576, 577
witch/-es, 31, 44, 59, 60, 61, 67–69, 77, 83, 96–100, 116, 134, 190, 200, 206, 306, 321, 327, 331, 332, 378, 395, 502, 572, 597, 598, 606, 619
witchcraft, 49, 62, 68, 85, 89, 131, 134, 147, 182, 183, 196, 197, 198, 307, 358, 359, 363, 371, 502, 505, 514, 522
witchery, 152
wizard, 43, 48, 66, 72, 191
wolf-berry, 226
wolf-print, 395
wolf-skin, 330
wolf/ves, 131, 193, 225, 228, 231, 237, 245, 275, 283, 318, 327, 328, 329, 330, 343, 349, 355, 395, 373, 450, 480, 481, 485, 501, 525, 527, 530, 546, 580, 593, 595
womb, 290, 415, 510, 617

wonder/-s, 46, 93, 94, 110, 133, 144, 145, 147, 151, 172, 180, 187, 198, 415, 436
wood, 34, 82, 144, 155, 174, 237, 245, 251, 255, 271, 328, 330, 336, 358, 359, 363, 365, 396, 415, 477, 482, 496, 511, 512, 547, 548, 550, 563, 579, 584
woodcarver, 137
wooden-shoes, 377
woodland, 173
woodpecker, 498, 559
woods, 281, 308, 318, 319, 320, 326, 328, 334, 342, 343, 357, 362, 370, 430, 433, 479, 483, 485, 486, 518, 520, 521, 531, 532, 554, 556, 564, 567, 568, 577
woodwives, 376, 395, 412, 413, 534
wool/-en, 62, 255, 268, 273, 289, 296, 336, 395, 555, 579
worm, 235, 247, 289, 331, 356, 358, 450, 492, 504, 508, 550, 551, 557, 564, 580, 581, 585, 586, 588, 594, 619
wormwood, 619
wound/-s, 144, 232, 246, 255, 257, 269, 270, 272, 288, 301, 302, 306, 309, 314, 316, 356, 360, 365, 373, 376, 399, 421, 427, 434, 446, 487, 493, 495, 506, 514, 529, 535–38, 550, 559, 561, 562, 572, 583, 587, 588, 591, 594, 607–9, 617
wrath/-ful, 158, 211, 245, 290, 302, 468, 523

Y

yarn, 62, 273, 336, 370
yarrow, 497
yeast, 247, 366, 476, 541, 549, 601
yolk/-s, 279, 280, 607
youth/-s, 76, 88, 209, 238, 345

Z

Zebaoth (various spellings), 254, 380, 383, 384, 388, 468
Zion, 384, 468
zodiac, 267

ABOUT FOLK NECROMANCY IN TRANSMISSION

The Folk Necromancy in Transmission series at Revelore Press examines the folk magical expressions and interrelations of the histories, philosophies, and practices of spirit conjuration, ghost-lore, eschatology, charm-craft, demonology, and the mass of rituals, protocols, and beliefs signalled by the terms "nigromancy," "necromancy" and their various equivalents in traditions across the world.

Here we take the canonical and reveal the folkloric expression; here the historical text inspires new practice and discourse. This series will not simply chart the print history of grimoires, or their socio-political context, but explore their actual magical usage. Within this exploration comes discourse on and with those traditions, extant or extinct, deemed "necromantic" that are passed through oral transmission.

With these goals in mind, we are proud to be working towards future publications, such as an anthology on women's necromancy and female exorcists, further work on the Good Saint Cyprian of Antioch, and yet the work is only beginning…

Raising the dead, we acknowledge the raising of necromancy itself, for it is still the breath of the reader that gives new life to the Dead from the bones of old Books. This is a folk necromancy that is at once extant and revived, inspired and yet-to-be. Here we walk hand-in-hand with the patrons of this particular Art.

COLOPHON

Svartkonstböcker: A Compendium of the Swedish Black Art Book Tradition was typeset by Joseph Uccello using Damien (Revolver Type Foundry), made by Lukas Schneider, Shaker (Jeremy Tankard Typography), Eskapade Fraktur (TypeTogether), made by Alisa Nowak, and Miniscule (256tm), made by Thomas Huot-Marchand.

www.ingramcontent.com/pod-product-compliance
Lightning Source LLC
Chambersburg PA
CBHW081737100526
44591CB00016B/2651